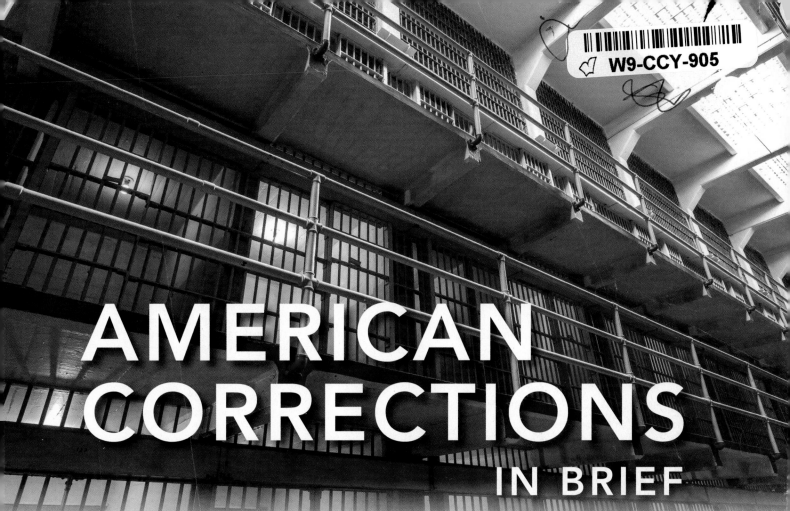

AMERICAN CORRECTIONS
IN BRIEF

THIRD EDITION

TODD R. CLEAR
Rutgers University

MICHAEL D. REISIG
Arizona State University

CAROLYN PETROSINO
Bridgewater State University

GEORGE F. COLE
University of Connecticut

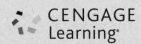
CENGAGE
Learning®

Australia • Brazil • Mexico • Singapore • United Kingdom • United States

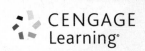

CENGAGE Learning

American Corrections in Brief, **Third Edition**
Todd R. Clear, Michael D. Reisig,
Carolyn Petrosino, George F. Cole

Product Director: Marta Lee-Perriard

Senior Product Manager: Carolyn Henderson Meier

Associate Content Developer: Jessica Alderman

Product Assistant: Valerie Kraus

Senior Marketing Manager: Kara Kindstrom

Senior Content Project Manager: Christy Frame

Managing Art Director: Andrei Pasternak

Senior Manufacturing Planner: Judy Inouye

Photo Researcher: Manoj Kiran Chander,
Lumina Datamatics

Text Researcher: Lakshminarasimhan Venkatraman,
Lumina Datamatics

Production Service: Greg Hubit Bookworks

Photo Development: Sarah Evertson

Copy Editor: Donald Pharr

Proofreader: Carrie Crompton

Illustrator: Lotus Art

Text and Cover Designer: Lisa Delgado

Cover Image: Jorg Greuel/Getty Images

Compositor: MPS Limited

For product information and technology assistance, contact us at **Cengage Learning Customer & Sales Support, 1-800-354-9706**.

For permission to use material from this text or product, submit all requests online at **www.cengage.com/permissions**. Further permissions questions can be e-mailed to **permissionrequest@cengage.com**.

Library of Congress Control Number: 2015946270

Student Edition:
ISBN: 978-1-305-63373-5

Cengage Learning
20 Channel Center Street
Boston, MA 02210
USA

Cengage Learning is a leading provider of customized learning solutions with employees residing in nearly 40 different countries and sales in more than 125 countries around the world. Find your local representative at **www.cengage.com**.

Cengage Learning products are represented in Canada by Nelson Education, Ltd.

To learn more about Cengage Learning Solutions, visit **www.cengage.com**.

Purchase any of our products at your local college store or at our preferred online store **www.cengagebrain.com**.

Unless otherwise noted, all content is © Cengage Learning 2017

Printed in the United States of America
Print Number: 01   Print Year: 2015

BRIEF CONTENTS

CONTENTS

P A R T

2

CORRECTIONS IN THE COMMUNITY 57

Chapter 5   PROBATION SUPERVISION 112

PART

3

INSTITUTIONAL CORRECTIONS 139

PART 4

CORRECTIONAL ISSUES 245

PREFACE

This is the third edition of *American Corrections in Brief*. We wrote this text in order to offer faculty who have used *American Corrections*, now in its eleventh edition, a briefer, more applied corrections text that lives up to the authors' rigorous standards for scholarship and state-of-the-art coverage. This text is designed to thoroughly introduce students to the dynamics of the corrections system without overwhelming them, in a format that students will find exciting and that will encourage them to achieve at a higher level.

We developed *American Corrections in Brief* to be not simply an abridged version of *American Corrections* but to be a whole new book. This third edition strengthens what teachers found most useful in the first two editions and reworks some of the material to provide more complete topical coverage of the field of corrections. The result is, we think, an *American Corrections in Brief* that offers exceptional coverage of the field in a format that is accessible, applied, and richly informed by scholars, reviewers, and adopters like yourself.

AN OVERVIEW OF THE TEXT

American Corrections in Brief introduces students to the subject of corrections in just thirteen chapters—fewer than any other textbook available for the course—and features a special emphasis on applying theory and research to the real world of correctional practice. To enhance student orientation to this real-world focus, we have developed special elements that "tell it like it is." These elements will assist students as they become informed citizens and especially if they consider corrections as a career. Students will also find the Careers in Corrections boxes informative, because these features describe such essentials as the nature of the job, requirements for entry, earnings, and future outlook.

Throughout the book, examples from today's headlines are used to link the concepts and information to actual correctional situations relevant to today's students and tomorrow's practitioners. What's more, we have labored to produce a text that is truly reflective of today's correctional environment. As most of us are aware, the corrections system is changing more rapidly today than perhaps at any other time in the last 40 years. Today, the political left and right have aligned for the first time in decades, and there is a broad national call for downsizing the corrections system. How will this play out in the realm of policy and practice? Critical-thinking exercises and discussion questions found throughout the book raise the types of dilemmas that future correctional leaders will face.

In today's world, correctional professionals are increasingly focusing their attention on research by scholars who have demonstrated the shortcomings of correctional practices and have urged alternatives. In this book, we thus not only examine the history of corrections and the exciting changes that have occurred to make the field what it is today but also look to the future of corrections by appraising research-based solutions to current issues.

In *American Corrections in Brief* we offer a provocative analysis of contemporary corrections that is based on up-to-date research and reflects current weaknesses in the system. By acknowledging the system's problems, we hope that our account will inspire suggestions for change. We believe that when human freedom is at stake, policies must reflect research and be formulated only after their potential effects have been carefully considered. In other words, we hope that any changes we inspire will be good ones. We also hope that a new generation of students will gain a solid understanding of all the aspects of their complex field.

In learning about corrections, students gain a unique understanding of how social and political forces affect the way that organizations and institutions respond to a particular segment of the community. They learn that social values come to the fore in the correctional arena because the criminal sanction reflects those values. They also learn that in a democracy, corrections must operate not only within the framework of law but also within the boundaries set by public opinion. Thus, as a public activity, corrections is accountable to elected representatives, but it must also compete politically with other agencies for resources and "turf."

Two key assumptions run throughout the book. One is about the nature of corrections as a discipline; the other concerns the best way to analyze correctional practices:

- **Corrections is interdisciplinary.** The academic fields of criminal justice, sociology, psychology, history, law, and political science contribute to our understanding of corrections. This cross-fertilization is enriching, yet it requires familiarity with a vast literature. We have structured our text with a strong focus on coherence to make this interdisciplinary approach comprehensive yet accessible.

- **Corrections is a system.** In our book the system concept serves as a framework for analyzing the relationships among the various parts of corrections and the interactions between correctional professionals and offenders. The main advantage of this perspective is that it allows for dispassionate analysis of correctional practices. It also makes students aware that corrections is a dynamic, changing system where discretion by administrators and officers influences the lives of those under supervision.

ORGANIZATION OF THE TEXT

Correctional officials and political leaders are continually asking, "Where is corrections headed?" Does the future hold that American corrections will continue to lead the developed world in numbers incarcerated? Might there be a return to the rehabilitation emphasis of the past? Will there be further calls to privatize corrections? In *American Corrections in Brief* we explore these and other issues in four major sections: the correctional context, corrections in the community, institutional corrections, and correctional issues.

In Part One, "The Correctional Context," we describe societal issues that frame our contemporary experience of corrections. We examine the general social context of the corrections system and the history of American corrections (Chapter 1). The purpose of punishment, forms of the criminal sanction, and the sentencing process are examined in Chapter 2. Part One thus presents the foundations of American corrections—context, history, goals, organizations, and offenders—and does so in vastly fewer pages than most texts, which leaves us with more time to spend on institutional and community corrections as well as the complex emerging issues and challenges that characterize the corrections system in the twenty-first century.

In Part Two, "Corrections in the Community," we look at the current state of correctional practices at the local level. It is in the community where most offenders are supervised. Jails and other short-term facilities are scrutinized in Chapter 3; probation and intermediate sanctions, by which most offenders are handled, in Chapter 4; and community supervision practices in Chapter 5.

Because imprisonment remains the core symbolic and punitive mechanism of institutional corrections, Part Three, "Institutional Corrections," examines it in detail. We discuss prisons at the state and federal level (Chapter 6), the prison experience (Chapter 7), and prison management (Chapter 8). Chapter 9 is devoted to the developing recognition of the unique correctional needs of the various groups of people managed within the correctional context, indicating a greater willingness of correctional officials to address new realities Taken together, Parts Two and Three offer a succinct yet comprehensive introduction to the development, structure, and methods of each area of the existing corrections system, portraying them in light of the continuing issues described in Part One of the text.

Part Four, "Correctional Issues," is unique to this text in that we examine a number of cutting-edge issues and trends that are at the forefront of correctional discussions. These issues have been chosen because of their currency and focus. They present dilemmas for correctional researchers and administrators who are trying to deal with problems that are new to the system. Chapter 10 describes the great expansion of the number of incarcerated offenders reentering the community and the current efforts to more effectively manage those offenders who struggle with adjustment, short of reincarceration. Chapter 11 deals with legal issues surrounding prisoners' rights as well as the law with regard to the death penalty. This chapter, perhaps more than any other, illustrates the dynamic nature of the law. Prisoners' rights is far from being a settled area, as new and interesting questions are periodically taken up by the courts. For example, although the use of lethal injections is lawful, certain chemicals used in the process may not be. This question is now on the calendar of the U.S. Supreme Court. Chapter 12 offers an expanded treatment of juveniles, drawing lessons from long-standing reform movements that have been taking place in that arena. In Chapter 13, "The Future of Corrections," we take both a retrospective view of American corrections and a view toward its future. These chapters are designed to raise questions in the minds of readers so that they can begin to grapple with important issues.

WHAT'S NEW IN THE THIRD EDITION

We have made a number of changes and improvements in this edition. Throughout the book, we have updated all tables, figures, and text with the most recent data available, which means that you will gain an understanding of the most current trends in corrections. For example, we give extended discussion to today's decline in the number of people in the correctional system, describing the implications for correctional policy and practice.

In order to provide additional currency, we have reworked many of the chapter-opening vignettes and boxed features. In addition, we have expanded coverage of timely, pressing topics such as private prisons, women in prison, and developments in community corrections. Following is a list of chapter-by-chapter changes to this new edition.

Chapter 1—What Is Corrections? starts with a new chapter introduction updated with current statistics and correctional trends. One emerging trend, private prisons, is introduced here. This chapter also discusses evidence-based corrections and justice reinvestment as two movements that may indicate a new era in correctional policy. Lastly, we have updated the Focus on Correctional Practice box ("Two States Struggle with Mass Incarceration: Texas and California") with more recent data.

Chapter 2—The Punishment of Offenders presents more thorough coverage of "three strikes" laws and restoration. We have also included a new chapter-opening vignette about Bob Bashara, who was convicted of hiring a man to murder his wife. Much of the boxed feature content has been reworked, including a new Focus on Correctional Practice box ("Early Methods of Execution"), a revised Focus on Correctional Policy box ("Politics and Sentencing: The Case of Crack Cocaine"), and a new Myths in Corrections box regarding California's Proposition 36 and recidivism rates ("Three Strikes and You're Out").

Chapter 3—Jails: Corrections at the Local Level includes several new topics, such as the debate over private jails and the declining populations and changing gender mix in jails. There are two new boxes: the Focus on Correctional Policy box ("California Turns to Its Jails to Deal with Crowding") and a Do the Right Thing box, which takes a look at "pay to stay" programs in jails. The Careers in Corrections box ("Correctional Officer—Local Jails") has been updated to include the most current earnings information.

Chapter 4—Community Corrections: Probation and Intermediate Sanctions contains two new boxes: the Focus on Correctional Policy box ("How Much Are the Various Alternative Sanctions Used?") and the Focus on Correctional Practice box ("Rethinking Revocation of Community Supervision"). We have also updated the Focus on Correctional Technology box ("Objective Risk-Assessment Systems").

Chapter 5—Probation Supervision takes an expanded look at the contents of a presentence investigation and has new coverage regarding the use of power by probation officers, including the issue of probation officers carrying firearms.

Chapter 6—Prisons picks up the discussion of private prisons from Chapter 1 and explains more about this controversial trend.

Chapter 7—The Prison Experience has a new Focus on Correctional Practice box ("Prison Commissary Items") and an updated "The Prison Economy" section.

Chapter 8—Prison Management starts with a new chapter-opening vignette detailing a prison attack on two correctional officers. This chapter also expands upon the connection between prison architecture and violence, detailing a new study (2014) that shows differing levels of violent activity in prisons with varying layouts. Both the Myths in Corrections box ("Sexual Victimization in State Prisons") and Careers in Corrections box ("Correctional Officer") have been updated.

Chapter 9—Special Populations contains a more detailed section on elderly offenders, as well as an extended dialogue regarding how the policy of deinstitutionalization has facilitated the development of the mentally ill in prisons. We have also included a new section on the military veteran prisoner and the challenges of this group as a special correctional population.

Chapter 10—Reentry into the Community begins with a new chapter-opening vignette concerning the former governor of Virginia, Robert McDonnell, who was found guilty of public corruption. We elaborate more on release mechanisms, including the trend of prisoners maxing out, and have a fuller discussion of revocation.

Chapter 11—Legal Issues and the Death Penalty more thoroughly examines the issues experienced by women in prisons, specifically the controversy concerning the shackling of female prisoners while they are in active labor and/or during delivery; this practice has Eighth Amendment challenges. There is a new section titled Lethal Injections—Are They Painless? This section addresses the most recent debate about the effectiveness of particular drugs used in lethal injection executions.

Chapter 12—Corrections for Juveniles incorporates a new chapter-opening vignette about Adolpho Davis, who was sentenced to life in prison without parole for murders he committed as a juvenile, and introduces the implications of *Miller v. Alabama* for previously sentenced minors. We have also written a new Do the Right Thing box that outlines the ethical implications in the case of Carlton Franklin, a middle-aged man tried in juvenile court for a murder he committed at age 15.

Chapter 13—The Future of Corrections contains an expanded section on correctional leadership as well as a new discussion about the current prison reform climate and the need to restructure prisons and the correctional system in general.

SPECIAL FEATURES

Several features make this book an especially interesting introduction to corrections:

- **Opening vignettes:** Each chapter opens with a description of a high-profile correctional case. Taken from today's headlines, each vignette dramatizes a real-life situation that draws the student into the chapter's topic. Instructors will find these "lecture launchers" an important pedagogical tool to stimulate interest. For example, Chapter 10, "Reentry into the Community," describes the rise and fall of convicted felon and ex-governor of Virginia, Robert Francis McDonnell. Students will consider the importance of resources and social capital implied in this vignette when it comes to community supervision in contrast to that of most offenders returning to society.

- **Focus On:** In this feature, the real-world relevance of the issues discussed in the text is made clear by vivid, in-depth accounts by correctional workers, journalists, prisoners, parolees, and the relatives of those who are in the system. *American Corrections in Brief* includes three types of Focus boxes: Correctional Technology, Correctional Policy, and Correctional Practice. Each box provides an example of the focus and presents critical-thinking questions for analysis and discussion. Focus on Correctional Technology presents examples of the use of contemporary technologies such as the use of "telemedicine" in prisons found in Chapter 7. Focus on Correctional Policy in Chapter 5 examines policies to meet current challenges such as dealing with people convicted of drug offenses. Focus on Correctional Practice describes contemporary practices such as the experience of a young offender's experience in jail (Chapter 3). We believe that students will find that the material in each Focus box enhances their understanding of the chapter topic. Instructors will find that the Focus boxes will provoke class discussion that will enhance the text.

- **Myths in Corrections:** This feature contrasts popular beliefs about corrections with the reality as presented by research findings. One of the big challenges for people who teach about corrections is that students come in with preconceptions that are often inaccurate. By showing that "the facts" can counter commonly held perceptions, we make it possible for teachers to point out other areas where commonly held opinion is not necessarily completely correct.

- **Careers in Corrections:** In appropriate chapters, students will find one or more boxes in which a particular occupation is described. The material includes the nature of the work, required qualifications, earnings, and job outlook, plus a source for further information.

- **Do the Right Thing:** Correctional workers are often confronted with ethical dilemmas. In these boxes we present a scenario in which an ethical question arises. We then ask students to examine the issues and consider how they would act in such a situation. The scenarios have been developed to encourage students to grapple with the "right thing" and to provide the basis of a writing assignment.

- **Glossary:** One goal of an introductory course is to familiarize students with the terminology of the field. We have avoided jargon in the text but include terms that are commonly used in the field. Such indispensable words and phrases are set in bold type, and the term and its definition have been placed in the margin. A full glossary with definitions of all terms is located at the back of the book.

- **Graphics:** We have created tables and figures that clarify and enliven information so that it can be perceived easily and grasped accurately.

- **Photographs:** *American Corrections in Brief* contains a complete program of dynamic photographs spread throughout the book. These reveal many aspects of corrections ordinarily concealed from the public eye. The photographs provide students with a real-world view of correctional policies and practices.

- **Integrated Learning Objectives and Other Student Aids:** At the beginning of each chapter is an outline of the topics to be covered, followed by the learning objectives mentioned above. These tools are designed to guide students as they progress through the chapter. At the end of each chapter, students will find a summary (again, keyed to the learning objectives) as well as discussion questions and a list of key terms.

CORRECTIONS: A DYNAMIC FIELD

As textbook authors, we have a responsibility to present current data, provide coverage of new issues, and describe innovative policies and programs. As noted above, we have been assisted by the comments of an exceptionally knowledgeable team of reviewers who suggested current issues that they wanted to discuss in their classrooms. Among these topics are the following:

- **The death penalty:** The introduction in the 1970s of lethal injection as an execution method has resulted in a flurry of court cases challenging this approach as a violation of the cruel and unusual punishment clause of the Eighth Amendment to the Constitution. In 2008 this claim was examined by the U.S. Supreme Court, which ruled in *Baze v. Rees* that attorneys for the death row inmates had not proven that lethal injection was in conflict with the amendment. However, the last word on this issue seems not to have been spoken, as botched executions continue to command headlines and new cases enter the judicial system. Because an ever-increasing number of death row inmates are being released when new evidence shows that they were erroneously convicted, the use of the death penalty will continue to be a major source of debate among legislators, scholars, and correctional officials.

- **Incarceration trends:** Although rates of violent crime have dropped to 1970 levels, the incarceration rate remains high. Today, however, there is an emerging consensus that incarceration rates are too high and policy makers should find ways to reduce the number of people behind bars. Advocates on both the left and the right are now urging states to find ways to begin to cut down on the number of prisoners. As almost half the states now experience small reductions in prison populations, there will be ripple effects throughout the corrections system. These issues are discussed in Chapter 1 and elsewhere throughout the book.

- **Reentry:** Each year approximately 700,000 offenders are released from prison and returned to their communities. Disturbingly, in some states recidivists make up the largest group of new admissions to prison. In response, assisting felons in the reentry process has become a major focus of correctional policy. The problems encountered by parolees as they adjust to the community are dealt with extensively in Chapter 10.

- **Management of prison staff:** The introduction of women as correctional officers in prisons for males and the increased staffing of males in prisons for women have created problems in the workplace. Initially, questions were raised about the effectiveness of women as correctional officers, but in recent years charges of sexual abuse by male officers have also created problems for prison administrators.

- **Evidence-based practice:** There has been a growing movement for "evidence-based" practice in dealing with those under community supervision—probation or parole.

Public statements by former U.S. Attorney General Eric Holder and the development of programs within the U.S. Justice Department's Office of Justice Programs have spurred this thrust. Probation and parole officers are encouraged to make decisions based on methods that have been shown to be effective by well-designed research methods.

■ **Correctional law:** Beginning in the 1970s, the U.S. Supreme Court started developing an extensive case law designed to uphold the rights of probationers, prisoners, and parolees. Many of these decisions were in response to the prisoners' rights movement, which directed attention to the conditions of confinement in many penal institutions. Although the Court has not been as active in developing new laws during the past decade, prisoners continue to bring cases that challenge aspects of their incarceration.

■ **Incarceration of women:** As the number of female prisoners has increased, so too has research on the impact of maternal incarceration on children. Administrators in a number of states have devised programs to provide opportunities for women to maintain contact with their children.

■ **Private prisons:** Since the advent of private prisons in the 1970s, questions have been raised about whether they are more cost-effective than public prisons. Until recently, research on this question has been lacking. As states deal with severe budgetary problems, the future of private prisons is uncertain.

■ **The prison experience:** Prison gangs have been a major problem in some corrections systems for some time. Different strategies have been developed to deal with these gangs. Prison rape is also an issue that has brought a national spotlight on inmate safety. New evidence provides national estimates on the prevalence of sexual violence in prisons and how correctional officials handle victimization reports.

■ **Technology in corrections:** The introduction of the newest technological devices and systems is having a major impact on corrections. For example, from the 1980s, when the first tracking devices were attached to probationers, to today's use of global positioning systems, to telemedicine in prisons, corrections has been at the forefront in the use of technology. The impact of technology on corrections is only now being measured, as seen by the results of research in many states. As "evidenced-based decision making" becomes a high priority of correctional administrators, the use of the latest technology is bound to greatly influence future policies and practices.

ANCILLARY MATERIALS

Cengage Learning provides a number of supplements to help instructors use *American Corrections in Brief* in their courses and to aid students in preparing for exams. Supplements are available to qualified adopters. Please consult your local Cengage Learning sales representative for details.

To access additional course materials, please visit **www.cengagebrain.com**. At the CengageBrain.com home page, search for the ISBN of your title (from the back cover of your book) using the search box at the top of the page. This will take you to the product page where these resources can be found.

For the Instructor

ONLINE INSTRUCTOR'S MANUAL The manual includes learning objectives, key terms, a detailed chapter outline, a chapter summary, lesson plans, discussion topics, student activities, "what if" scenarios, media tools, and a sample syllabus. The learning objectives are correlated with the discussion topics, student activities, and media tools. The manual is available for download on the password-protected website and can also be obtained by e-mailing your local Cengage Learning representative.

ONLINE TEST BANK Each chapter of the test bank contains questions in multiple-choice, true/false, completion, essay, and critical-thinking formats, with a full answer key. The test bank is coded to the learning objectives that appear in the main text, references to the section in the main text where the answers can be found, and Bloom's taxonomy. Finally, each question in the test bank has been carefully reviewed by experienced criminal justice instructors for quality, accuracy, and content coverage. The Test Bank is available for download on the password-protected website and can also be obtained by e-mailing your local Cengage Learning representative.

CENGAGE LEARNING TESTING, POWERED BY COGNERO This assessment software is a flexible, online system that allows you to import, edit, and manipulate test bank content from the *American Corrections in Brief* test bank or elsewhere, including your own favorite test questions; create multiple test versions in an instant; and deliver tests from your LMS, your classroom, or wherever you want.

ONLINE POWERPOINT® LECTURES Helping you make your lectures more engaging while effectively reaching your visually oriented students, these handy Microsoft PowerPoint slides outline the chapters of the main text in a classroom-ready presentation. The PowerPoint slides are updated to reflect the content and organization of the new edition of the text and feature some additional examples and real-world cases for application and discussion. Available for download on the password-protected instructor companion website, the presentations can also be obtained by e-mailing your local Cengage Learning representative.

For the Student

MINDTAP FOR AMERICAN CORRECTIONS IN BRIEF With MindTap™ Criminal Justice for *American Corrections in Brief*, you have the tools you need to better manage your limited time, with the ability to complete assignments whenever and wherever you are ready to learn. Course material that is specially customized for you by your instructor in a proven, easy-to-use interface keeps you engaged and active in the course. MindTap helps you achieve better grades today by cultivating a true understanding of course concepts, with a mobile app to keep you on track. With a wide array of course-specific tools and apps—from note taking to flashcards—you can feel confident that MindTap is a worthwhile and valuable investment in your education.

You will stay engaged with MindTap's video cases and career scenarios and remain motivated by information that shows where you stand at all times—both individually and compared to the highest performers in class. MindTap eliminates the guesswork, focusing on what's most important, with a learning path designed specifically by your instructor and for your corrections course. Master the most important information with built-in study tools such as visual chapter summaries and integrated learning objectives that will help you stay organized and use your time efficiently.

ACKNOWLEDGMENTS

Ours has been a collective effort in which drafts of each chapter were reviewed by at least one other author, revised, and then set out to review by a group of criminal justice faculty who teach at a range of colleges and universities. These reviewers were enthusiastic about the project and gave us helpful advice on the text's organization and content. We hope that this book reflects our enthusiasm for our field and the satisfaction we have found in it.

In writing *American Corrections in Brief* we were greatly assisted by people who merit special recognition. Criminal justice instructors who reviewed the second edition of the text were most helpful in pointing out its strengths and weaknesses; we took their comments seriously and hope that readers will find their educational needs met more fully. We gratefully acknowledge the valuable contributions of the following reviewers:

Steven Block, Central Connecticut State University
Jonathan E. Cella, Central Texas College
Natasha A. Frost, Northeastern University
Kay King, Johnson County Community College
Leslie K. Palmer, Inver Hills Community College

We have also been assisted in writing this edition by a diverse group of associates. Chief among them is Carolyn Henderson Meier, Senior Product Manager, who supported our efforts and kept us on course. Jessica Alderman, our Associate Content Developer, reviewed our efforts and made important suggestions in keeping with the goals of the book. Kara Kindstrom, the Marketing Manager for Criminal Justice, has skillfully guided the presentation of *American Corrections in Brief* to faculty and students. The project has also benefited much from the attention of Christy Frame, Content Project Manager, as well as production manager Greg Hubit, copyeditor Donald Pharr, and proofreader Carrie Crompton. The talented Lisa Delgado designed the interior and cover of the book. Ultimately, however, the full responsibility for the book is ours alone.

Todd R. Clear
tclear@rutgers.edu

Michael D. Reisig
reisig@asu.edu

Carolyn Petrosino
cpetrosino@bridgew.edu

George F. Cole
University of Connecticut

THE CORRECTIONAL CONTEXT

Part One examines the social context of the corrections system. Chapter 1 asks the question "What is corrections?" and examines the purposes of corrections within the criminal justice system. The systems framework of analysis is introduced because it provides a means of understanding the interconnections of corrections with other criminal justice units. To further the understanding of corrections, a brief history of American corrections from the Revolutionary War to the present shows the development of ways that society has dealt with problems of social control. Chapter 2 looks at punishment, with an examination of the history of penology from the Middle Ages to the American Revolution. Next, the theoretical basis for the objectives of punishment is discussed, followed by the forms of the criminal sanction as implemented through the sentencing process. The issue of unjust punishment completes the chapter. ■

CHAPTER

1

What Is Corrections?

Something remarkable is happening in American corrections. For over 40 years—longer than most readers of this book have been alive—the corrections system has been growing. Between 1973 and 2010, the corrections system grew more than six-fold, a faster rate of growth than any other social statistic applying to the United States. In other words, nothing else in contemporary U.S. history has grown the way corrections has grown.

The expansion of imprisonment illustrates these changes. In 1973, when the current increase in the number of people in

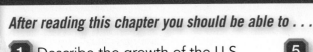

Learning Objectives

After reading this chapter you should be able to . . .

1 Describe the growth of the U.S. corrections system in the last 40 years and discuss at least three issues raised by that growth.

2 Define the systems framework and explain why it is useful.

3 Name the various components of the corrections system today and describe their functions.

4 Discuss what we can learn from the "great experiment of social control."

5 Distinguish the basic assumptions of the penitentiary systems of Pennsylvania and New York.

6 Discuss the elements of the Cincinnati Declaration.

7 Understand the reforms advocated by the Progressives.

8 Discuss the forces and events that led to the present crime control model.

9 Describe the changes that are going on today and why they are important.

For most of the last 40 years, the American correctional system has been on a steady path of growth, with ever-increasing numbers of people on probation, on parole, in jail, and in prisons.

prison first started, the prison incarceration rate was 96 per 100,000 Americans. For the next 37 years, the number of prisoners increased—during periods when crime went up, but also during periods when crime declined; during good economic times and bad; during times of war and times of peace.

At first, for most of the 1970s, this growth was caused by rising rates of crime. But the prison population growth continued during the 1980s, when crime rates stabilized, and continued to grow throughout the 1990s, even though crime rates fell between 1993 and 2008 by more than

(continued from previous page)

50 percent.[1] Since 1990, the swelling prison population seems to be entirely the result of tougher criminal justice policies rather than changes in crime rates.[2] (See "Myths in Corrections: High U.S. Crime Rates.")

In 2008 the U.S. imprisonment rate reached 506 per 100,000. Correctional budgets had grown by over 600 percent during that 35-year period. Today, almost 3,000 people are on death row,[3] and another 140,000 are serving life sentences.[4] Counting prisons and jails, more than 2.2 million Americans are incarcerated, making the total incarceration almost 700 per 100,000 residents, a stunning 1 percent of all adults. ■

AMERICAN CORRECTIONS TODAY

Although most Americans think of prisons when they think of corrections, about 70 percent of persons under supervision are not in prisons or jails but live in the community on probation or parole. The story of a generation-long period of growth occurred for these noninstitutional forms of corrections as well. (The pattern of growth for American corrections since 1980 is shown in **Figure 1.1**.) This means that Americans have experienced one of the greatest policy experiments in modern history. Never before has the United States seen such growth in its corrections system—an expansion that has lasted for a full generation.

There are signs that this long-term pattern may be beginning to change. Between 2009 and 2012, state prison populations dropped over 2 percent, led by a nearly 20-percent drop in California's prison population.[5] The nation's imprisonment rate dipped below 500 per 100,000 for the first time since 2006, and in 2010 half the states had net reductions in the number of prisoners.

One result has been that correctional costs are also declining for the first time. From 1982 to 2001, total state expenditures on corrections more than tripled. But faced with growing fiscal pressures, states have begun to try to control their correctional costs, and since 2002 those expenditures have decreased almost 10 percent.[6] Today, 16 states are planning to *close* at least one prison, and six of those have actually closed prisons.[7] And prisons are not the only part of the corrections system that is declining. For the fifth consecutive year, probation caseloads have dropped, and the number of people in jail has declined for the fourth consecutive year.[8]

This pattern is remarkable, given U.S. history during the past 40 years, but it is too early to know whether this is the start of a new trend. Indeed, the prison population once

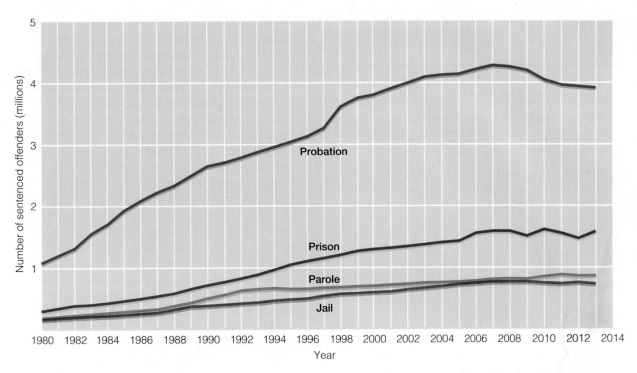

FIGURE 1.1

Correctional Populations in the United States, 1980–2013

Although the increase in prison population receives the most publicity, a similar level of correctional growth has occurred in probation and parole.

Sources: Latest data available from the Bureau of Justice Statistics correctional surveys, www.ojp.usdoj.gov: *Annual Survey of Jails, Annual Parole Survey, Annual Probation Survey, National Prisoner Statistics Population Midyear Counts, Correctional Populations in the United States, 2013.*

since the 1970s. And even though many states had reductions in the number of prisoners, the overall prison population grew in half the states.

So, while something remarkable is going on in the American corrections system, whether we are seeing a brand-new trend or just a slowing down of the old one is yet to be determined. Either way, by any measure, the U.S. corrections system has seen a sustained period of extraordinary, steady growth for more than a generation. This is something that has never happened before in the United States or anywhere else (see "Focus on Correctional Policy: The Great Experiment in Social Control"). Unless something changes, it has been estimated that almost 7 percent of people born in 2001—teenagers today—will go to prison at some time during their lives.[9]

Today, a chorus of voices debates the wisdom of the large corrections system. Both liberals and conservatives rightfully worry that the expansion of corrections has affected some groups more than others. Nearly one-third of all African American men in their twenties are under some form of correctional control, and one in six African American males has been in prison.[10] Americans of all political stripes also share a concern that the costs of corrections, more than $70 billion per year, are out of line. Prison budgets—by far the most expensive portion of the overall penal system—grow even when money for education and others services lag. Probation caseloads and daily jail populations have also grown, and they obviously cost money, as well. With growing public concern about the quality of schools and health care, people of all political persuasions are tempted to ask if so much money is needed for corrections. This is especially true during a period when budget deficits loom large in most states. Political leaders are particularly leery about continuing to invest in what many, especially conservatives, see as a system that is not as effective as it ought to be.[11] As crime continues to go down, more and more people wonder if we need so many fellow citizens under correctional control.

MYTHS in Corrections

High U.S. Crime Rates

THE MYTH: The United States has such a huge prison system, compared with other countries, because it has much more crime.

THE REALITY: Compared with the burglary rates of Australia and England, America's is the lowest, and its assault and robbery rates fall in between those of the other two countries. The U.S. incarceration rate is four times higher than that of either country.

Source: The Sentencing Project, *New Incarceration Figures: Growth in Population Continues* (Washington, DC: Author, 2006).

Corrections, then, is a topic for public debate as never before. A generation ago, most people knew very little about corrections. Prisons were alien "big houses," infused with mystery and located in remote places. The average American had no direct knowledge of "the joint" and no way of learning what it was like. Most people did not even know what probation and parole were, much less have an opinion about their worth. About 6.9 million Americans are now in the corrections system. Of today's men in their thirties, almost 1 in 28 has been in prison; if current patterns continue, 11 percent of male children born this year (a third of male African Americans) and 2 percent of female children will go to prison.[12] Add to these numbers the impact on fathers and mothers, brothers and sisters, aunts and uncles, and husbands, wives, and children, and you have an idea of how pervasive corrections is today—especially for poor Americans and people of color.

People who study corrections want to learn more about the problems that rivet our attention. They want to see beyond the three-minute news story, to understand what is happening to people caught in the system. And they suspect that what seems so simple from the viewpoint of a politician arguing for a new law or of news reporters sharing the latest crime story may in fact be far more complex for the people involved.

Some of those who study corrections will choose the field as a professional career. They will become a part of the ever-changing landscape of a field that is as fascinating as it is immensely rewarding. Among them will be the field's future leaders, people who will be a part of the next generation of corrections, as the field continues to grow. In the chapters that follow, we describe an array of professional positions that people might choose as they begin their correctional career. We have written this book to provide the kind of foundation a person will need to be effective as a correctional professional in the complex environment in which corrections operates.

One theme in this book is that things are not as simple as they look. New laws and policies seldom achieve exactly what they were intended to do, and they often have unintended consequences. In this text we explore the most important issues in penology, from the effectiveness of rehabilitation to the impact of the death penalty, with the knowledge that each issue has more than one side.

More than two out of every five Americans are under some form of correctional supervision. Most of them live among us in the community.

focus on correctional policy

The Great Experiment in Social Control

Most of you reading this were born after 1972. Indeed, nearly half of the U.S. population was born after 1972. For members of this group, it is entirely "normal" to see the populations of Americans in prison, in jail, and under correctional supervision increase every year. For their entire lives, they have seen corrections grow in good economic times and bad, during periods of rising crime and of dropping crime, while the "baby boom" generation (Americans born between 1946 and 1964) hit their twenties and thirties—the peak crime-prone age—and clogged the criminal justice system.

The large and growing correctional populations that seem so normal have not always been so. From 1900 until about 1970, U.S. prison populations were quite stable, hovering between 90 and 120 inmates per 100,000 citizens. After nearly 40 years of steady growth, the rate of incarceration is now five times as high as where it started. By 2010, the number of prisoners reached the highest point in U.S. history—and the highest in the world. Further, at no other time in history, here or elsewhere, has a 35-year growth in prisoners occurred.

We might call this phenomenon the "great experiment in social control," for it has defined a generation of Americans who have witnessed the greatest expansion in government control ever undertaken by a democratic state.[13] Researchers have tried to explain the sources of this growth in the U.S. corrections system. Some of it is caused by increases in crime, just as some is caused by the increased effectiveness of criminal justice at apprehending, arresting, and convicting criminals. But mostly this experiment has to do with changes in punishment policy. In the United States the chances of a felon getting a prison sentence instead of probation have increased steadily for several decades, to the point where the chance of getting a probation sentence is now a fraction of what it used to be. Not only are more felons being sent to prison rather than receiving probation; the amount of time they face in prison has increased as well.

Some scholars have tried to explain the unprecedented punitiveness of the late-twentieth-century U.S. policy. They discuss the importance of American politics and culture, and they expressly point to the effects of two decades of the "war on drugs." Simply put, the policy experiment in social control came about as people grew ever more exasperated with crime and disorder, and a multitude of changes in sentencing and correctional practices came together to make correctional populations grow, whether crime rates rose or not.

Yet why this punitiveness occurred is far less interesting than what its results have been. Over the coming years, researchers, scholars, and intellectuals will begin to try to understand what we have learned from this great experiment.

The effects of the great experiment in social control fall into three broad areas. First and foremost, there is the question of crime: How has the growth in the corrections system affected rates of crime? Because so many factors affect crime, it is not easy to isolate the effects of a growing corrections system from other factors, such as the economy or times of war. Researchers who have tried to do so reach divergent conclusions, but even the most conservative scholars of the penal system now seem to agree that further growth will have little impact on crime.[14] Others note that because the crime rate today is about the same as it was in the early 1970s, when the penal system began to grow, it is not likely that the effects of the corrections system on crime have been large.[15]

A second category of effects is social. Here, there is a growing worry that a large corrections system—especially a large prison system—damages families and communities and increases racial inequality.[16] For example, it is estimated that more than 1.5 million children have parents in prison. How does that experience affect their life chances? And what does it mean to have more than one in four African American males end up in prison?

Critical Thinking

1. How does a large penal system affect the pursuit of justice?
2. Is it right to have people who break the law end up being sanctioned in the way that America punishes them?
3. Have we become a more just society as a result of this great experiment in social control?

We begin with a seemingly simple question: What is the purpose of corrections? In answering this question, we shall engage a pattern that recurs throughout the book. Any important correctional issue is complicated and controversial. The more you learn about a given issue, the more you will see layers of truth; your first findings will be bolstered by evidence and then challenged by further investigation and deeper knowledge.

In the end we think you will acknowledge that there are few easy answers but plenty of intense questions. Near the beginning of each chapter we present areas of inquiry that each chapter will explore.

THE PURPOSE OF CORRECTIONS

It is 11:00 A.M. in New York City. For several hours, a five-man crew has been picking up trash in a park in the Bronx. Across town on Rikers Island, the view down a corridor of jail cells shows the prisoners' hands gesturing through the bars as the prisoners converse, play cards, share cigarettes—the hands of people doing time. About a thousand miles to the south, almost 400 inmates sit in isolated cells on Florida's death row. In the same state, a woman on probation reports to a community control officer. On her ankle she wears an electronic monitoring device that tells the officer if she leaves her home at night. On the other side of the Gulf of Mexico, sunburned Texas inmates in stained work clothes tend crops. Almost due north in Kansas, an inmate-grievance committee in a maximum-security prison reviews complaints of guard harassment. Out on the West Coast, in San Francisco, a young man on his way to work checks in with his parole officer and drops off a urine sample at the parole office. All these activities are part of **corrections**. And all the central actors are offenders.

Punishing people who break society's rules is an unfortunate but necessary part of social life. From the earliest accounts of humankind, punishment has been used as one means of **social control**, of compelling people to behave according to the norms and rules of society. Parents chastise their children when they disobey family rules, groups ostracize individuals who deviate from expected group norms, colleges and universities expel students who cheat, and governments impose sanctions on those who break the criminal laws. Of the various ways that societies and their members try to control behavior, criminal punishment is the most formal, for crime is perhaps the most serious type of behavior over which a society must gain control.

In addition to protecting society, corrections helps define the limits of behavior so that everyone in the community understands what is permissible. The nineteenth-century sociologist Emile Durkheim argued that crime is normal and that punishment performs the important function of spotlighting societal rules and values. When a law is broken, citizens express outrage. The deviant thus focuses group feeling. As people unite against the offender, they feel a sense of mutuality or community. Punishing those who violate the law makes people more alert to shared interests and values.

Three basic concepts of Western criminal law—offense, guilt, and punishment—define the purpose and procedures of criminal justice. In the United States, Congress and state legislatures define what conduct is considered criminal.

The police, prosecutors, and courts determine the guilt of a person charged with a criminal offense. The postconviction process then focuses on what should be done with the guilty person. The central purpose of corrections is to carry out the criminal sentence. The term *corrections* usually refers to any action applied to offenders after they have been convicted and implies that the action is "corrective," or meant to change offenders according to society's needs. Corrections also includes actions applied to people who have been accused—but not yet convicted—of criminal offenses. Such people are often under supervision, waiting for action on their cases—sitting in jail, undergoing drug or alcohol treatment, or living in the community on bail.

When most Americans think of corrections, they think of prisons and jails. This belief is strengthened by legislators and the media, which focus much attention on

corrections
The variety of programs, services, facilities, and organizations responsible for the management of individuals who have been accused or convicted of criminal offenses.

social control
Actions and practices, of individuals and institutions, designed to induce conformity with the norms and rules of society.

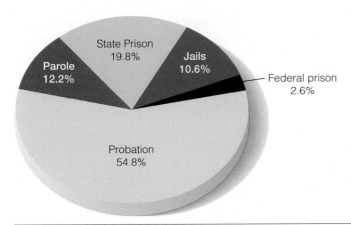

FIGURE 1.2
Percentage of People in Each Category of Correctional Supervision
Although most people think of corrections as prisons and jails, about two-thirds of offenders are in fact supervised within the community.

Source: Bureau of Justice Statistics, www.ojp.usdoj.gov/bjs, December 2014.

incarceration and little on community corrections. As **Figure 1.2** shows, however, almost two-thirds of all people under correctional supervision are living in the community on probation or parole.

Corrections thus encompasses all the legal responses of society to some prohibited behavior: the variety of programs, services, facilities, and organizations responsible for managing people accused or convicted of criminal offenses. When criminal justice researchers, officials, and practitioners speak of corrections, they may be referring to any number of programs, processes, and agencies. Correctional activities are performed by public and private organizations; involve federal, state, and local governments; and occur in a variety of community and closed settings. We can speak of corrections as a department of the government, a subfield of the academic discipline of criminal justice, an approach to the treatment of offenders, and a part of the criminal justice system.

Corrections is all these things and more.

A SYSTEMS FRAMEWORK FOR STUDYING CORRECTIONS

Corrections is every bit as complex and challenging as the society in which we live. Having a framework will help you sort out the complex, multidimensional nature of corrections. In this book we use the concept of the corrections system as a framework for study. A **system** is a complex whole consisting of interdependent parts whose operations are directed toward common goals and are influenced by the environment in which they function. For example, interstate highways make up a transportation system.

Students of criminal justice are used to thinking of it as a system that deals with crime. The various components of criminal justice—police, prosecutors, courts, corrections— are seen as integral parts of that system. Corrections functions within that system as a set of operations that processes people who have been accused of or convicted of crimes. But what does this term really mean? Can the systems concept also be used as a framework for the study of corrections? To answer this question, we outline some of the important elements of the system and apply them to corrections.

system
A complex whole consisting of interdependent parts whose operations are directed toward common goals and are influenced by the environment in which they function.

Goals

Corrections is certainly a complicated web of processes that, ideally, serve the goals of fair punishment and community protection. These twin goals—punishment and protection— not only define the purpose of corrections but also serve as a criterion by which we evaluate correctional work. Correctional activities make sense when they seem to punish offenders fairly and offer some community protection.

When these two functions of punishment and protection do not correspond, corrections faces goal conflict. For example, people may believe that it is fair to release offenders on parole once they have served their sentences, but they may also fear possible threats that parolees pose to the community.

Interconnectedness

Corrections can be viewed as a series of processes: sentencing, classification, supervision, programming, and revocation, to name but a few. Processes in one part of the corrections system affect, in both large and small ways, processes in other parts of the system.

For example, when a local jail changes its policies on eligibility for work release, this change will affect the probation caseload. When a parole agency implements new drug-screening practices, the increased number of violators uncovered by the new policy will affect the size of jail and prison populations. When probation officers fail to check their facts for a presentence investigation report, poorly reasoned sentences and correctional assignments may result.

These processes all affect one another because offenders pass through corrections in a kind of assembly line with return loops. After criminals are convicted, a selection process determines which offender goes where, and why. This sifting process is itself uncertain and often hard to understand. Most, but not all, violent offenders are sent to prison. Most, but not all, violators of probation or parole rules receive a second chance. Most, but not all, offenders caught committing crimes while supervised by correctional authorities will receive a greater punishment than offenders not under supervision.

Figure 1.3 shows examples of interconnections among correctional agencies as they deal with offenders who have been given different sentences. Note that in Case 1, the offender is sentenced, presumably for a misdemeanor, to probation, drug treatment, and community service. This offender was detained in jail prior to sentencing. An officer of the Department of Probation has prepared a presentence investigation report that recommends the sentence to be imposed by the judge. The Department of Probation then provides supervision of the offender, and through a contract with a nongovernmental agency, Community Corrections, Inc., the drug treatment and community service requirements of the sentence are carried out. Because the offender presumably fulfilled the terms of the sentence, no feedback loops are indicated where the offender's probation has been revoked with resentencing. Even with this somewhat "routine" case, note the interconnectedness of the criminal justice agencies involved.

Case 2 is more complex in that it involves incarceration followed by community supervision by a parole officer. Here, a different set of correctional agencies must deal with the offender, in part because the person experienced a period of incarceration. After prison, the person in Case 2 did not fulfill the conditions of his release on parole; the figure indicates that at some point it was revoked, and he was resentenced, presumably to further incarceration. There was a close interdependence between the way parole operated and the eventual actions of the prison system, with several points of feedback between the community-based correctional staff and those who work in the prison.

These are only two examples of the wide variety of ways a person can be processed through the corrections system. A large number of possible combinations of actors and decisions can occur in corrections, although the cases in Figure 1.3 are among the most common ways that the system operates. To get its work right, the system adapts and innovates, and new ways of processing people who have been convicted of crime emerge.

Case 1: Two years of probation, drug treatment, and 50 hours of community service.

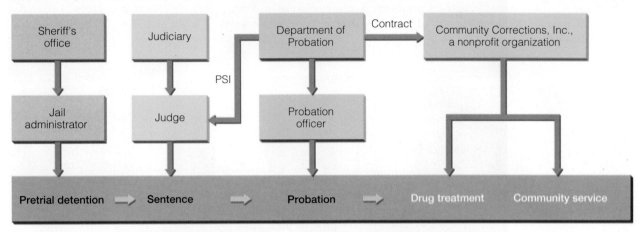

Case 2: Two years of incarceration to be followed by community supervision on parole.

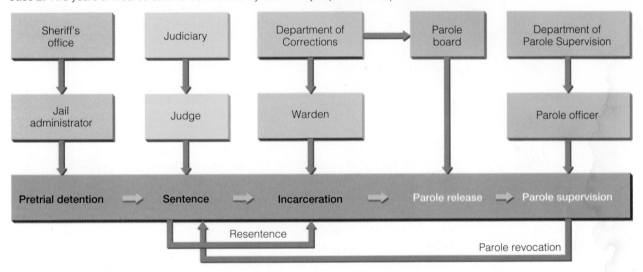

FIGURE 1.3
Interconnectedness of Correctional Agencies in Implementing Sentences
Note the number and variety of agencies that deal with these two offenders. Would you expect these agencies to cooperate effectively with one another? Why or why not?

Environment

As they process offenders, correctional agencies must deal with outside forces such as public opinion, fiscal constraints, and the law. Thus, a given correctional agency will sometimes take actions that do not seem best suited to achieving fairness or public protection. At times, correctional agencies may seem to work at odds with one another or with other aspects of the criminal justice process.

Corrections has a reciprocal relationship with its environment. That is, correctional practices affect the community, and community values and expectations in turn affect corrections. For example, if the prison system provides inadequate drug treatment, offenders return to the community with the same drug problems that they had when

Corrections has links to other criminal justice agencies. The police, sheriff, prosecutors, and judiciary all play important roles. What are some of the problems that develop out of these necessary links?

they were locked up. When citizens then lose confidence in a corrections system, they tend not to spend tax dollars on its programs.

Feedback

Systems learn, grow, and improve according to the feedback they receive about their effectiveness. When a system's work is well received by its environment, the system organizes itself to continue functioning this way. When feedback is less positive, the system adapts to improve its processes.

Although feedback is crucial for corrections, this system has trouble obtaining useful feedback. When things go well, the result is the absence of something—no new crimes or no prison riots—those are things that *might* have occurred but did not. Figuring out such things is difficult at best. In contrast, when corrections fails, everybody knows: The media report new crimes or expose scandals in administration. As a result, corrections systems and their environments tend to overrespond to correctional failure but remain less aware of success.

Complexity

As systems grow and mature, they tend to become more complex. Twenty-five years ago, the "three P's"—probation, prisons, and parole—dominated correctional practice. Today, all kinds of activities come under the heading of corrections, from pretrial drug treatment to electronically monitored home confinement, from work centers, where offenders earn money for restitution, to private, nonprofit residential treatment programs.

The complexity of the corrections system is illustrated by the variety of public and private agencies that compose the corrections system of Philadelphia County, Pennsylvania, as shown in **Table 1.1**. Note that offenders are supervised by various service agencies operating at different levels of government (state, county, municipal) and in different branches of government (executive and judicial).

Table 1.1 The Distribution of Correctional Responsibilities in Philadelphia County, Pennsylvania

Note the various correctional functions performed at different levels of government by different agencies. What correctional agencies does your community have?

Correctional Function	Level and Branch of Government	Responsible Agency
Adult Corrections		
Pretrial detention	Municipal/executive	Department of Human Services
Probation supervision	County/courts	Court of Common Pleas
Halfway houses	Municipal/executive	Department of Human Services
Houses of corrections	Municipal/executive	Department of Human Services
County prisons	Municipal/executive	Department of Human Services
State prisons	State/executive	Department of Corrections
County parole	County/executive	Court of Common Pleas
State parole	State/executive	Board of Probation and Parole
Juvenile Corrections		
Detention	Municipal/executive	Department of Public Welfare
Probation supervision	County/courts	Court of Common Pleas
Dependent/neglect	State/executive	Department of Human Services
Training schools	State/executive	Department of Public Welfare
Private placements	Private	Many
Juvenile aftercare	State/executive	Department of Public Welfare
Federal Corrections		
Probation/parole	Federal/courts	U.S. courts
Incarceration	Federal/executive	Bureau of Prisons

Sources: Taken from the annual reports of the responsible agencies.

THE CORRECTIONS SYSTEM TODAY

The American corrections system today employs more than 700,000 administrators, psychologists, officers, counselors, social workers, and others. The federal government, the 50 states, more than 3,000 counties, and uncounted municipalities and public and private organizations administer corrections at an average annual cost of over $50 billion.[17]

Corrections consists of many subunits, each with its own functions and responsibilities. These subunits—probation offices, halfway houses, prisons, and others—vary in size, goals, clientele, and organizational structure. Some are government agencies; others are private organizations contracted by government to provide specific services to correctional clients. A probation office is organized differently from a halfway house or a prison, yet all three are part of the corrections system and pursue the goals of corrections.

However, there are important differences among subunits of the same general type. For example, the organization of a five-person probation office working closely with

"People work" is central to the mission of corrections. Correctional professionals must learn how to master uncertain technologies and employ uncertain strategies in their everyday work.

Wendy Maeda/Boston Globe/Getty Images

federalism
A system of government in which power and responsibilities are divided between a national government and state governments.

prison
An institution for the incarceration of people convicted of serious crimes, usually felonies.

jail
A facility authorized to hold pretrial detainees and sentenced misdemeanants for periods longer than 48 hours. Most jails are administered by county governments; sometimes they are part of the state government.

probation
An agency that supervises the community adjustment of people who are convicted of crimes but are not sentenced to confinement in prison or jail.

intermediate sanctions
A variety of punishments that are more restrictive than traditional probation but less severe and costly than incarceration.

one judge in a rural setting differs from that of a more bureaucratized 100-person probation office in a large metropolitan system. Such organizational variety may help or hinder the system of justice.

Federalism, a system of government in which power and responsibility are divided between a national government and state governments, operates in the United States. All levels of government—national, state, county, and municipal—are involved in one or more aspects of the corrections system. The national government operates a full range of correctional organizations to deal with the people convicted of breaking federal laws; likewise, state and local governments provide corrections for people who have broken their laws. However, most criminal justice and correctional activity takes place at the state level. Only about 1 percent of individuals on probation, 10 percent of those on parole, and 11 percent of those in prison are under federal correctional supervision.

Despite the similarity, from state to state, of behaviors that are labeled criminal, important differences appear among specific definitions of offenses, types and severity of sanctions, and procedures governing the establishment of guilt and treatment of offenders. In addition, many variations in how corrections is formally organized appear at the state and local levels. For example, four state corrections systems—California, Florida, New York, and Texas—handle more than one-third of all state prisoners and about two-fifths of all offenders under correctional control in the United States; each of these four states has developed different organizational configurations to provide corrections.

The extent to which the different levels of government are involved in corrections varies. The scope of the states' criminal laws is much broader than that of federal criminal laws. As a result, just over 400,000 adults are under federal correctional supervision. At last count, there were 102 federal **prisons** and 1,719 state prisons. **Jails** are operated mainly by county governments, but in six states they are integrated with the state prison system.

As noted in **Figure 1.4**, criminal justice costs are borne by each level of government, with well over 90 percent of correctional costs falling on state and local governments. In most states the agencies of community corrections—**probation** and **intermediate sanctions**—are run by the county government and are usually part of the judicial branch. However, in some jurisdictions the executive branch runs them, and in several

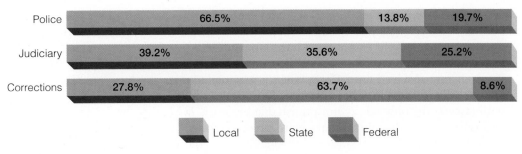

Police	66.5%	13.8%	19.7%
Judiciary	39.2%	35.6%	25.2%
Corrections	27.8%	63.7%	8.6%

Local   State   Federal

FIGURE 1.4
Distribution of Justice System Expenditures by Level of Government

Over the past 40 years the American corrections system has seen a sustained period of remarkable growth, with the costs of corrections mostly borne by state governments.

Source: BJS *Bulletin*, May 2004.

states this part of corrections is run by statewide organizations. In all states, **parole** is a function of the executive branch of state government.

In the last 25 years, there has been a substantial growth in the use of **private prisons**—prisons that are operated by private companies under contract with the government, generally turning a profit for the company and its investors. Private prisons operate at all levels of the corrections system—county jails, as well as state and local facilities, both for adults and for juveniles. It has been estimated that 8 percent of all those who are incarcerated are held in one of the more than 100 private facilities.[18] Private prisons are controversial, for reasons we explore in Chapter 6.

That the United States is a representative democracy complicates corrections. Officials are elected, legislatures determine the objectives of the criminal law system and appropriate the resources to carry out those objectives, and political parties channel public opinion to officeholders on such issues as law and order. Over time the goals of correctional policies have shifted. For example, between 1940 and 1970, corrections was oriented toward liberal rehabilitative policies; since about 1970, however, conservative, get-tough crime control policies have influenced corrections. Questions of crime and justice are thus inescapably public questions, subject to all the pressures and vagaries of the political process.

Clearly, corrections encompasses a major commitment on the part of American society to deal with people convicted of criminal law violations. The increase in the number of offenders under supervision in the past decade has caused a major expansion of correctional facilities, staff, and budgets; some might say that corrections is now a big business.

How did we get here? What happened to create the corrections system we know today—this big, complex, and multifaceted system? To answer these questions requires a review of the history of corrections. We begin our review of contemporary corrections in the United States by looking back to the colonial period.

parole
A system of supervision of those who have been released from confinement, sometimes including the option of early release from confinement before the expiration of the sentence.

private prison
The operation of a prison by a private company under contract with a local, state, or the federal government, often as a for-profit business.

THE HISTORY OF CORRECTIONS IN AMERICA

The Colonial Period

During the colonial period (1620–1776), Americans lived under laws and practices transferred from England and adapted to local conditions. As in England, banishment, corporal punishment, the pillory, and death were the common penalties. But unlike the mother country, with its crowded jails and houses of corrections, the colonies seldom used institutions for confinement.

In 1682, with the arrival of William Penn, the founder and proprietor of what became Pennsylvania, that colony adopted "The Great Law." This was based on humane Quaker principles and emphasized hard labor in a house of correction as punishment for most crimes. Death was reserved for premeditated murder. The Quaker Code in Pennsylvania survived until 1718, when it was replaced by the Anglican Code, which was already in force in other colonies. The latter code listed thirteen capital offenses, with larceny the only felony not punishable by death. Whipping, branding, mutilation, and other corporal punishments were prescribed for other offenses, as were fines. Enforcement of this code continued throughout the colonies until the Revolution.

During the colonial period, jails were used mainly to hold people awaiting court action or those unable to pay their debts. Only rarely were convicted offenders jailed for their whole sentences; the stocks, whipping post, and gallows were the places for punishment. Little thought was given to reforming offenders; such people were considered naturally depraved.

The Arrival of the Penitentiary

From 1776 to around 1830, a revolution occurred in the American idea of criminal punishment. The new correctional philosophy reflected many ideas of the Declaration of Independence, including an optimistic view of human nature and of individual perfectibility. Emphasis shifted from the assumption that criminal behavior was part of human nature to a belief that offenders could be reformed.

penitentiary
An institution intended to isolate prisoners from society and from one another so that they could reflect on their past misdeeds, repent, and thus undergo reformation.

In the first decades of the nineteenth century, the creation of **penitentiaries** in Pennsylvania and New York attracted the attention of legislators in other states, as well as investigators from Europe. American reformers were influenced by the Englishman John Howard, whose book *The State of Prisons in England and Wales* (1777) described the horrible conditions and lack of discipline in those institutions. English reaction to Howard's book resulted in Parliament passing the Penitentiary Act of 1779, which called for a house of hard labor based on four principles:

1. A secure and sanitary building
2. Inspection to ensure that offenders followed the rules
3. Abolition of fees charged offenders for their food
4. A reformatory regime

At night, prisoners were to be confined to their cells. During the day, they were to work silently in common rooms. Prison life was to be strict and ordered. The new institution should be a place of industry. More importantly, it should be a place that offered criminals opportunities for penitence (sorrow and shame for their wrongs) and repentance (willingness to change their ways). In short, the penitentiary served to punish and to reform.

Howard's idea of the penitentiary was not implemented in England until 1842, 50 years after his death, but in the United States his ideas were applied much more quickly.

THE PENNSYLVANIA SYSTEM   In 1790 the Pennsylvania legislature authorized construction of institutions for the solitary confinement of "hardened and atrocious offenders." The first of these was created out of a portion of Philadelphia's Walnut Street Jail. This three-story building had eight dark cells on each floor. A yard was attached to the building. Only one inmate occupied each cell, and no communication of any kind was allowed. From a small grated window high on the outside wall, inmates "could perceive neither heaven nor earth."

separate confinement
A penitentiary system developed in Pennsylvania in which each inmate was held in isolation from other inmates, with all activities, including craft work, carried on in the cells.

When the Walnut Street Jail soon became overcrowded, the legislature approved construction of additional institutions for the state: Western State Penitentiary, on the outskirts of Pittsburgh, and Eastern State Penitentiary, in Cherry Hill, near Philadelphia. The opening of Eastern in 1829 marked the full development of the penitentiary system based on **separate confinement**.

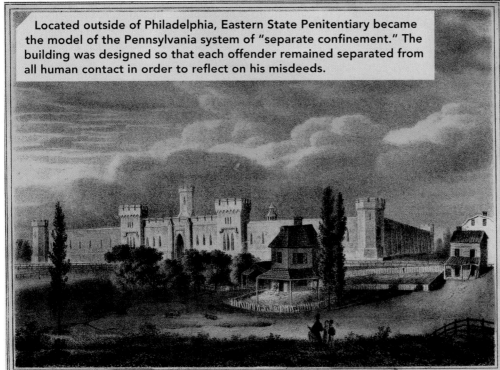

Located outside of Philadelphia, Eastern State Penitentiary became the model of the Pennsylvania system of "separate confinement." The building was designed so that each offender remained separated from all human contact in order to reflect on his misdeeds.

The Eastern Penitentiary, Philadelphia, printed by Wild & Chevalier, c.1838 (litho), Wild, John Caspar (c.1804-46)/ Library Company of Philadelphia, PA, USA/Library Company of Philadelphia/The Bridgeman Art Library

Eastern State Penitentiary was designed with cell blocks extended from a central hub like the spokes of a wheel. Each prisoner ate, slept, worked, and received religious instruction in his own cell. The inmates did not see other offenders. In fact, their only human contact was the occasional visit of a clergyman or prison official.[19]

The Pennsylvania system was based on five principles:

1. Prisoners would not be treated vengefully but should be convinced that through hard and selective forms of suffering they could change their lives.

2. Solitary confinement would prevent further corruption inside prison.

3. In isolation, offenders would reflect on their transgressions and repent.

4. Solitary confinement would be punishment because humans are by nature social beings.

5. Solitary confinement would be economical because prisoners would not need long periods of time to repent, fewer keepers would be needed, and the costs of clothing would be lower.

Within five years after its opening, Eastern endured the first of several investigations. The reports detailed the extent to which the goal of separate confinement was not fully observed, physical punishments were used to maintain discipline, and prisoners suffered mental breakdowns because of the isolation. Separate confinement had declined at Eastern by the 1860s, when crowding required doubling up in each cell, but Pennsylvania did not abolish it until 1913.[20]

THE NEW YORK (AUBURN) SYSTEM In 1819 New York opened a penitentiary in Auburn that became a rival to Pennsylvania's concept of separate confinement. In 1821 Elam Lynds became the warden at Auburn. Instead of duplicating the complete isolation practiced in Pennsylvania, Lynds worked out a new **congregate system** of prison discipline. Inmates were held in isolation at night but congregated in workshops during the day. They were forbidden to talk or even to exchange glances while on the job or at meals. Lynds believed that industrial efficiency should be the main purpose of the prison. He instituted a reign of discipline and obedience that included the lockstep and

congregate system
A penitentiary system developed in Auburn, New York, in which inmates were held in isolation at night but worked with other prisoners during the day under a rule of silence.

Early prisons emphasized a congregate system of discipline, obedience, and work. The aim was to teach the prisoners to submit to authority.

Museum of the City of New York/The Art Archive at Art Resource, NY

the wearing of prison stripes. Furthermore, he considered it "impossible to govern a large prison without a whip."[21]

Whereas inmates of the Pennsylvania penitentiaries worked in their cells, those in New York were employed in workshops both as therapy and as a way to finance the institution. Convict labor for profit became a major part of Auburn and other northeastern penitentiaries. Through this system the state negotiated contracts with manufacturers, which then delivered raw materials to the prison for conversion by the inmates into finished goods. By the 1840s, Auburn was producing footwear, barrels, carpets, carpentry tools, harnesses, furniture, and clothing. Wardens who adopted the New York system seemed to be more concerned with instilling good work habits than with rehabilitating prisoners' character.

DEBATING THE SYSTEMS   During this era, advocates of both the Pennsylvania and the New York plans debated on public platforms and in the nation's periodicals over the best methods of punishment (see **Table 1.2**). Proponents of the New York system maintained that inmates first had to be "broken" and then socialized by means of a rigid discipline of congregate but silent labor. Advocates of Pennsylvania's separate system rejected such harshness, renouncing physical punishments. The New Yorkers countered that their system cost less, efficiently tapped convict labor, and developed individuals who eventually would be able to return to the community with the discipline necessary for the industrial age. The Pennsylvanians responded that New York had sacrificed the principal goal of the penitentiary (reformation) to the goal of cost-effectiveness. They contended that exploiting inmates through large-scale industry failed to promote the work ethic and only embittered them.

PRISONS IN THE SOUTH AND WEST   Scholars tend to emphasize the nineteenth-century reforms in the populous Northeast and neglect penal developments in the

Table 1.2 Comparison of the Pennsylvania and New York (Auburn) Penitentiary Systems

	Goal	Implementation	Method	Activity
Pennsylvania (Separate System)	Redemption of the offender through the well-ordered routine of the prison	Isolation, penance, contemplation, labor, silence	Inmates are kept in their cells for eating, sleeping, and working	Bible reading, work on crafts in cell
New York (Auburn) (Congregate System)	Redemption of the offender through the well-ordered routine of the prison	Strict discipline: obedience, labor, silence	Inmates sleep in their cells but come together to eat and work	Work together in shops making goods to be sold by the state

South and the West. Early in the nineteenth century, prisons, some on the penitentiary model, were built in Georgia, Kentucky, Maryland, and Virginia. Later prisons, such as in Jackson, Mississippi (1842), and Huntsville, Texas (1848), were built on the Auburn model. But further expansion ended with the Civil War. After the Civil War, southerners began the task of rebuilding their communities and primarily agricultural economy. They lacked funds to build prisons but faced an increasing (especially African American) population of offenders. Given these challenges, southern states developed the **lease system**, whereby, for a fee, the state provided inmate labor to private contractors engaged in agriculture, logging, mining, and construction.

With the exception of San Quentin (1852), the sparse population of the West did not lend itself to the construction of many prisons until the latter part of the nineteenth century. Prior to statehood, western prisoners were held in territorial facilities or federal military posts or prisons. Until Congress passed the Anticontract Law of 1887, restricting the employment of federal prisoners, leasing programs existed in many western states.

lease system
A system under which inmates were leased to contractors who provided prisoners with food and clothing in exchange for their labor.

The Reformatory Movement

By the mid-1800s, reformers were disillusioned with the penitentiary. Within 40 years of being built, penitentiaries had become overcrowded, understaffed, and minimally financed. Discipline was lax, brutality was common, and administrators were viewed as corrupt.

Across the Atlantic, Alexander Maconochie urged England to use the **mark system** of graduated terms of confinement. Penalties would be graded according to the severity of the crime, and offenders would be released from incarceration according to their performance. A certain number of marks would be given at sentencing, and prisoners could reduce the number by voluntary labor, participating in educational and religious programs, and good behavior. Maconochie thus argued for sentences of indeterminate length and a system of rewards. Through these incentives, offenders would be reformed so that they could return to society. Although Maconochie's ideas were not implemented in England, they did cross the Atlantic and influenced penologists in America.

mark system
A system in which offenders are assessed a certain number of points at the time of sentencing, based on the severity of their crime. Prisoners could reduce their term and gain release by earning marks through labor, good behavior, and educational achievement.

CINCINNATI, 1870 The National Prison Association (predecessor of the American Correctional Association) and its 1870 meeting in Cincinnati embodied a new spirit of reform. In its famous Declaration of Principles, the association advocated a new design for penology: Prisons should be operated on a philosophy of inmate change, with reformation rewarded by release. Sentences of indeterminate length would replace fixed sentences, and proof of reformation would be a requirement for release. Classification of prisoners on the basis of character and improvement would encourage the reformation program. However, like the reformers before them, the 1870 advocates looked to

The reformatory movement emphasized education and training. On the basis of their conduct and achievement, inmates moved toward their release.

institutional life and programs to effect rehabilitation. Inmates would be made well-adjusted citizens, but the process would take place behind walls.

reformatory
An institution for young offenders that emphasized training, a mark system of classification, indeterminate sentences, and parole.

THE ELMIRA REFORMATORY   The first **reformatory** took shape in 1876 at Elmira, New York, when Zebulon Brockway was appointed superintendent. Brockway believed that diagnosis and treatment were the keys to reform and rehabilitation. He questioned each new inmate to explore the social, biological, psychological, and "root cause(s)" of the offender's deviance. An individualized work and education treatment program was then prescribed. Inmates followed a rigid schedule of work during the day, followed by courses in academic, vocational, and moral subjects during the evening. Inmates who did well achieved early release.[22]

Designed for young, first-time felons, the approach at Elmira incorporated a mark system of classification, indeterminate sentences, and parole. Once the courts had committed an offender to Elmira, the administrators could determine the release date; the only restriction was that the time served could not exceed the maximum prescribed by law for the particular offense.

A three-grade system of classification was linked to the indeterminate sentence. Each offender entered the institution at grade 2, and if the inmate earned nine marks a month for six months by working hard, completing school assignments, and causing no problems, he could be moved up to grade 1—necessary for release. If he failed to cooperate and violated rules of conduct, thus showing indifference to progress and lack of self-control, he would be demoted to grade 3. Only after three months of satisfactory behavior could he reembark on the path toward eventual release.[23] In sum, this system placed "the prisoner's fate, as far as possible, in his own hands."[24]

Elmira's proclaimed success at reforming young felons was widely heralded, and by 1900 the reformatory movement had spread throughout much of the nation. Yet by the outbreak of World War I, in 1914, it was already declining. In most institutions the architecture, the attitudes of the guards, and the emphasis on discipline differed little from past orientations. Too often, the educational and rehabilitative efforts took a back seat to the traditional emphasis on punishment. Yet the reformatory movement contributed such practices as the indeterminate sentence, inmate classification, rehabilitative programs, and parole, all of which inspired prison reformers well into the twentieth century.

Corrections in the Twentieth Century

In the first two decades of the 1900s, reformers known as the Progressives attacked the excesses of big business and urban society. They advocated government actions against the problems of slums, vice, and crime. As members of the **positivist school** of criminology, the Progressives looked to social, economic, biological, and psychological factors rather than religious or moral explanations for the causes of crime, and they applied modern scientific methods to determine the best treatment therapies. The positivist school shifted the focus from the criminal act to the offender. By the 1920s, probation, indeterminate sentences, presentence reports, treatment programs, and parole were being promoted as a more scientific approach to criminality. These elements had been proposed at the 1870 Cincinnati meeting, but the Progressives and their allies in corrections were now instrumental in implementing them throughout the country.

Although the Progressives' focus on rehabilitation has been much criticized, probation, indeterminate sentences, and parole remain dominant elements of corrections to this day. Perhaps this is because they provide authority to criminal justice officials and affirm the vitality of the rehabilitative idea. However, these three crucial reforms provided the structure for yet another change in corrections.

THE RISE OF THE MEDICAL MODEL   Much Progressive reform was based on the idea that criminals could be rehabilitated through treatment, but not until the 1930s were serious attempts made to implement what became known as the **medical model** of corrections. Under the banner of the newly prestigious social and behavioral sciences, the emphasis of corrections shifted to treating criminals as people whose social, psychological, or biological deficiencies had caused them to engage in illegal activity.

The concept of rehabilitation as the primary purpose of incarceration took on national legitimacy in 1929, when Congress authorized the new Federal Bureau of Prisons to develop institutions that would ensure the proper classification, care, and treatment of offenders. By the 1950s, many states, particularly California, Illinois, New Jersey, and New York, developed programs designed to reform prisoners. Most other states adopted at least the rhetoric of rehabilitation, changing statutes to specify that treatment was the goal of their corrections system and that punishment was an outdated concept. Prisons were thus to become something like hospitals and would rehabilitate and test the inmate for readiness to reenter society. In many states, however, the medical model was adopted in name only: Departments of prisons became departments of corrections, but the budgets for treatment programs remained about the same.

Because the essential structural elements of parole, probation, and indeterminate sentences existed in most states, incorporating the medical model required only adding classification systems to diagnose offenders and treatment programs to cure them.

Initially, the number of treatment programs was limited, but it increased sharply after World War II. Group therapy, behavior modification, shock therapy, individual counseling, psychotherapy, guided group interaction, and many other approaches all became part of the "new penology." However, the administrative needs of the institution often superseded the treatment needs of the inmate. For example, prisoners tended to be assigned to the facilities, jobs, and programs that had openings rather than to those that would provide the prescribed treatment.

Critics of prison treatment programs pointed out that even during the 1950s, when the medical model was at its height, only 5 percent of state correctional budgets was allocated for rehabilitation. Although states adopted the rhetoric of the medical model, custody remained the overriding goal of institutions.

FROM MEDICAL MODEL TO COMMUNITY MODEL   As we have seen, social and political values in the broader society greatly influence correctional thought and practices. During the 1960s and 1970s, the United States experienced the civil rights movement, the war on poverty, and resistance to the Vietnam War. Americans also challenged governmental institutions dealing with education, mental health, juvenile delinquency, and

positivist school
An approach to criminology and other social sciences based on the assumption that human behavior is a product of social, economic, biological, and psychological factors and that the scientific method can be applied to ascertain the causes of individual behavior.

medical model
A model of corrections based on the assumption that criminal behavior is caused by social, psychological, or biological deficiencies that require treatment.

corrections. In 1967 the President's Commission on Law Enforcement and Administration of Justice reported the following:

Crime and delinquency are symptoms of failures and disorganization of the community. . . . The task of corrections, therefore, includes building or rebuilding social ties, obtaining employment and education, securing in the larger senses a place for the offender in the routine functioning of society.[25]

community corrections
A model of corrections based on the assumption that reintegrating the offender into the community should be the goal of the criminal justice system.

This analysis was consistent with the views of **community corrections** advocates, who felt that the goal of the criminal justice system should be the reintegration of offenders into the community.

The 1971 inmate riot and hostage taking at New York State's Attica Correctional Facility aided the move toward community corrections. After four days of negotiations, a helicopter began dropping CS gas (an incapacitating agent) on the inmates milling around in the prison yard. After the gas came a rain of bullets from state police guns that hit 128 men and killed 29 inmates and 10 hostages.

For many, the hostilities at Attica showed prisons to be counterproductive and unjust. They urged officials to make decarceration through community corrections the goal and pressed for greater use of alternatives to incarceration such as probation, halfway houses, and community service.

Community corrections called for a radical departure from the medical model's emphasis on treatment in prison. Instead, prisons were to be avoided because they were artificial institutions that interfered with the offender's ability to develop a crime-free lifestyle.

Proponents argued that corrections should turn away from psychological treatment in favor of programs that would increase offenders' opportunities to become successful citizens. Probation would be the sentence of choice for nonviolent offenders so that they could engage in vocational and educational programs that increased their chances of adjusting to society. For the small portion of offenders who had to be incarcerated, the amount of time in prison would be only a short interval until release on parole. To further the goal of reintegration, correctional workers would serve as advocates for offenders as they dealt with governmental agencies providing employment counseling, medical treatment, and financial assistance.

The reintegration idea was dominant in corrections for about a decade, until the late 1970s, when it gave way to a new punitiveness in conjunction with a rise in crime. Advocates of reintegration claim, as did advocates of previous reforms, that the idea was never adequately tested. Nevertheless, community corrections remains one of the significant ideas and practices in the recent history of corrections.

THE DECLINE OF REHABILITATION   Beginning in the late 1960s, the public became concerned about rising crime rates. At the same time, studies of treatment programs

The attack by the New York National Guard to quell the inmate riot at Attica State Prison in 1971 took the lives of 39 people. The public's reaction aided the move to community corrections.

AP Images

challenged their worth and the Progressive assumption that state officials would exercise discretion in a positive manner. Critics of rehabilitation attacked the concepts of indeterminate sentence and parole, urging that treatment be available on a voluntary basis but that it not be tied to release. In addition, proponents of increased crime control called for longer sentences, especially for career criminals and violent offenders.

According to critics of rehabilitation, its reportedly high rates of recidivism (offenders committing new crimes after release) proved its ineffectiveness. Probably the most thorough analysis of research data from treatment programs was undertaken by Robert Martinson. Using rigorous standards, he surveyed 231 reports of rehabilitation programs in corrections systems. They included such standard rehabilitative programs as educational and vocational training, individual counseling, group counseling, milieu therapy, medical treatment, parole, and supervision. Martinson summarized his findings by saying, "With few and isolated exceptions, the rehabilitative efforts that have been reported so far have had no appreciable effect on recidivism."[26]

Critics of the rehabilitation model also challenged as unwarranted the amount of discretion given to correctional decision makers to tailor the criminal sanction to the needs of each offender. In particular, they argued that the discretion given to parole boards to release offenders is misplaced because decisions are more often based on the whims of individual members than on the scientific criteria espoused by the medical model.

THE EMERGENCE OF CRIME CONTROL   As the political climate changed in the 1970s and 1980s, and with the crime rate at historic levels, legislators, judges, and officials responded with a renewed emphasis on a **crime control model**. By 1980, the problem of crime and punishment had become an intense subject for ideological conflict, partisan politics, and legislative action.[27]

The critique of the rehabilitation model led to changes in the sentencing structures of more than half of the states and to the abolition of parole release in many. The new determinate sentencing laws were designed to incarcerate offenders for longer periods of time. In conjunction with other forms of punishment, the thrust of the 1980s was toward crime control through incarceration and risk containment.

The punitive emphasis of the 1980s and 1990s appeared in the importance placed on dealing more strictly with violent offenders, drug dealers, and career criminals.[28] It was also reflected in the trend toward intensive supervision of probationers, the detention without

crime control model
A model of corrections based on the assumption that criminal behavior can be controlled by increased use of incarceration and other forms of strict supervision.

The crime control model was based on the idea that tough penalties imposed severely would deter people from committing crimes and prevent recidivism. It has not worked out that way.

Bettmann/Corbis

bail of accused persons thought to present a danger to the community, reinstitution of the death penalty in 37 states, and the requirement that judges impose mandatory penalties for persons convicted of certain offenses or having extensive criminal records.

A NEW ERA OF RATIONAL STRATEGIES?   By the beginning of the twenty-first century, the effect of these "get-tough" policies was evidenced by the record numbers of prisoners, the longer sentences being served, and the size of the probation population. Some observers point to these policies as the reason why the crime rate has begun to fall. Others ask whether the crime control policies have really made a difference given demographic and other changes in the United States.

As the national economy soured in 2007, states began to rethink the costs associated with the crime control model. Actions have been taken in a number of states to reduce correctional budgets, especially the high cost of incarceration. At the same time, an "**evidence-based corrections**" movement has emerged. Policy makers and legislators are increasingly expecting correctional leaders to justify their programs by pointing to a body of research that supports their effectiveness. To support this movement, for example, the federal government has established a new center that promotes evidence-based practices in the correctional system.[29] This development emphasizes the role of research and careful planning in the design and implementation of correctional programs (see "Do the Right Thing").

> **evidence-based corrections**
> A movement to ensure that correctional programs and policies are based on research evidence about "what works."

There are now signs that the change is becoming more than a blip on the correctional radar. Conservatives and liberals alike are developing a new consensus that prison is not the answer to crime and that strategic thinking is needed to contain costs and protect the public, but also to reduce the overuse of imprisonment as a correctional tool. These ideas call for a renewed focus on effective prisoner reentry, which will reduce recidivism rates. They also support "**justice reinvestment**" strategies that save money by reducing the number of prisoners and then use some of those funds to invest in crime prevention in the community. The National Research Council of the National Academies of Science recently published a report that signals the weaknesses of a prison-based correctional policy and the need for a reduction in its use.[30] This emerging consensus, not unlike the one that led to the get-tough movement in the 1970s, may herald a new era in the correctional history of the United States. Only time will tell.

> **justice reinvestment**
> A movement in which money saved by reducing prison populations is used to build up crime-prevention programs in the community.

Table 1.3, which traces the history of correctional thought and practices in the United States, highlights the continual shifts in focus.

Where Are We Today?

In this first quarter of the twenty-first century, the time may be ripe for another look at correctional policy. The language now used in journals of corrections differs markedly from that found in their pages 40 years ago. The optimism that once dominated

---

DO the Right Thing

You are the assistant to the chief of probation in a medium-sized jurisdiction. The judge in your court is running for reelection. You just returned from a conference in Washington, DC, where a new program designed to provide housing and good jobs for people on probation was described and the evaluations showing its effectiveness were presented. You have informed your boss and the judge about the new program, and you tell them that you think your probation department should implement it. But the judge has her doubts because she is afraid it will be used against her during the election as being "soft on crime." Your boss says the new program does not sound "new" at all, but instead is something that has been tried before—and it failed. But they both say it is up to you.

Critical Thinking

Write a short essay saying how you would approach this problem. What would you do, and why?

Table 1.3 History of Corrections in America

Note the extent to which correctional policies have shifted from one era to the next and how they have been influenced by various societal factors.

CORRECTIONAL MODEL							
Colonial (1600s–1790s)	Penitentiary (1790s–1860s)	Reformatory (1860s–1890s)	Progressive (1890s–1930s)	Medical (1930s–1960s)	Community (1960s–1970s)	Crime Control (1970s–2010s)	Rational Strategy?
Features							
Anglican Code Capital and corporal punishment, fines	Separate confinement Reform of individual Power of isolation and labor Penance Disciplined routine Punishment according to severity of crime	Indeterminate sentences Parole Classification by degree of individual reform Rehabilitative programs Separate treatment for juveniles	Individual case approach Administrative discretion Broader probation and parole Juvenile courts	Rehabilitation as primary focus of incarceration Psychological testing and classification Various types of treatment programs and institutions	Reintegration into community Avoidance of incarceration Vocational and educational programs	Determinate sentences Mandatory sentences Sentencing guidelines Risk management	Focus on reentry Evidence-based programs Justice reinvestment
Philosophical Basis							
Religious law Doctrine of predestination	Enlightenment Declaration of Independence Human perfectability and powers of reason Religious penitence Power of reformation Focus on the act Healing power of suffering	NPA Declaration of Principles Crime as moral disease Criminals as "victims of social disorder"	The Age of Reform Positivist school Punishment according to needs of offender Focus on the offender Crime as an urban, immigrant, ghetto problem	Biomedical science Psychiatry and psychology Social work practice Crime as signal of personal "distress" or "failure"	Civil rights movement Critique of prisons Small is better	Crime control Rising crime rates Political shift to the right New punitive agenda	Need to do "what works" Need to reduce "mass incarceration" Crime best handled by prevention, not punishment

corrections has waned. For the first time in four decades the financial and human costs of the retributive crime control policies of the 1990s are now being scrutinized (see "Focus on Correctional Practice"). With budget deficits in the billions, states are facing the fact that incarceration is very expensive. Are the costs of incarceration and surveillance justified? Has crime been reduced because of correctional policies? Are we safer today?

People worry that the answer to these questions is "no." Indeed, compared to the mid-1970s, today we have six times the number of people under correctional authority, and we spend much more than six times the amount on the corrections system. But crime rates, after having fluctuated wildly for 30 years, are today about what they were back then. Anyone who stands back and looks at this history and today's world has to ask, "How might we better organize and carry out the corrections system so that we might preserve what is best about it, while jettisoning some of the least effective, most undesirable aspects of corrections today?"

focus on correctional practice

Two States Struggle with Mass Incarceration: Texas and California

The two largest state prison systems in the nation are operated by California and Texas. At the end of the first decade of the 2000s, both systems faced a crisis. They approached the crisis in quite different ways, but their story illustrates the new conversation about incarceration in America.

California houses one in seven of all state prisoners, and its taxpayers cough up more than $9 billion annually to do so, a whopping $43,000 per locked-up person per year. Its facilities are so overcrowded and their management so strained that a series of court cases declared various aspects of California prison conditions faulty, and in 2005 the state prisons were placed under court supervision, including medical and dental care, mental health care, juvenile incarceration, and due process for parolees. Court-ordered fixes for these and other deficits cost California more than $8 billion.

Ironically, California's incarceration rate is not far above the national average, and it sends felons to prison at about the same rate as the nation as a whole. But it has for years had the highest recidivism rates of any state in the country, returning two-thirds of its parolees to prison within three years of release. This return rate helped sustain a high prison population through repeated

recycling of people through the prison system. California also has a very influential prison officers' union, the California Correctional Peace Officers Association, which has grown so large that its members constitute 16 percent of California's state employee pool, spending $8 million each year lobbying for higher pay and tougher correctional policies.

Few experts expected California to be able to deal with the crisis. Facing a projected revenue deficit of $42 billion, the state could not afford an aggressive program of prison expansion. Finally, in 2011 the U.S. Supreme Court stepped in to order California to reduce its prison population, and the crisis peaked. Governor Edmund G. Brown announced a new policy of "public safety realignment" that called for local governments to take responsibility for many of the nonviolent people in the state prison system.

In the first year, public safety realignment transferred more than 20,000 people from the prison system to local correctional programs, saving the state about $1.5 billion and helping California reduce its prison population by almost 10 percent, the largest drop in the nation. Then, California voters approved two propositions, Proposition 36 (in 2012), which rolled back some of California's most-severe repeat

THE CORRECTIONAL CHALLENGE

As we have described the history of corrections, a pattern emerges. Much of the correctional story is about *ideas* that often run in cycles. There have been periods of time when dominant correctional thought emphasized the inherent redeemability of people who break the law, and correctional authorities sought to organize their efforts in ways that encouraged redemption. At other times, a belief in strictness and authority has prevailed, and authorities have emphasized the need for rules that are closely monitored and strictly enforced. Sometimes the field has experimented with a strong commitment to institutionally based strategies; other times the creative center of corrections has been in community-based approaches. Almost any "new" idea can be traced back to an earlier idea.

The challenge for the field of corrections is to learn from this history effectively. The question is not so much how to avoid repeating history—correctional history seems ever to be repeated. The question is how to advance correctional success even as old ideas return to the fore.

The problems we have described are what combine to make the field of corrections controversial and therefore engrossing for those who study it. Yet as compelling as these problems may be, they are only a sidelight to the central appeal of the field of corrections. The questions that corrections raises concerning social control are fundamental to defining society and its values. Seemingly, every aspect of the field raises questions that concern deeply held values about social relations. For example, what kinds of services and treatment facilities should inmates infected with HIV/AIDS receive? Should corrections be more concerned with punishing offenders for crimes or with providing programs to help them overcome the problems in their lives that contribute to crime?

offender sentencing reforms of the 1990s, and Proposition 47 (in 2014), which reduced nonserious and nonviolent property and drug crimes from felonies to misdemeanors, eliminating prison as a sentencing option.

Still, California has not met the prison population goals set by the federal court. Instead of reducing the population to no more than 37 percent above designed capacity by 2014, the state's numbers fell short. The court has extended its deadline for meeting the population requirement to 2016. However, it is clear that California will struggle to do so: In 2104 the total prison population grew by 1,400.

Fiscal realities led the **Texas** legislature to change directions with its prison policy, as well. After California, Texas has the largest prison population in the United States, putting people behind bars at a rate of 160 percent of the national average. In 2005 the state's experts said the prison system would be facing a shortfall of 17,000 beds over the next five years, and the Texas Department of Criminal Justice proposed spending $400 million to build 4,000 new beds. A strapped state legislature did the math and figured that even if it ponied up the one-time funds to build these cells, running them would add more than $100 million to every year's correctional operating budget. Leaders sought another way.

Instead, a nonpartisan state commission recommended that Texas try to reduce the demand for prison space by reducing recidivism rates. The state's conservatives and liberals agreed that simply expanding prisons made little sense. Texas undertook a new strategy involving a $200-million investment in treatment programs that divert

people from prison, a reduction in the length of the supervision term for probationers and parolees, and an enhancement of the capacity of probation to provide supervision early in the sentence. The package, which was passed with strong legislative support, was expected to save up to $250 million in its first two years. And for the first time in its history, Texas will be closing a prison—a century-old prison in Sugar Land.

The early results seemed to justify this new approach, with judges sentencing more people to probation with drug treatment, and the parole board is releasing people from Texas prisons at twice the historical rate. But more recent data are troubling. After a decline of almost 1 percent in the state's prison population just after these reforms, prison numbers started creeping back up. With a combination of increased prison admissions and a decrease in parole releases, the state added almost 2,000 prisoners in 2013.

Critical Thinking

1. Why are states working so hard to control their prison populations?
2. What are the social and political implications of the Texas strategy, compared to California's?
3. Which correctional system would you rather live under, and why?

Sources: Joan Petersilia, "California Prison Downsizing and Its Impact on Local Criminal Justice Systems" *Harvard Law & Policy Review*, May 2014; E. Ann Carson, "Prisoners in 2013," BJS *Bulletin*, September 2014.

Is placing surveillance devices in people's homes a good idea or an invasion of privacy? Questions of interest to researchers, students, and citizens hardly end here. Crucial public and private controversies lurk at every turn. In your own studies and throughout your life, you will find you cannot answer the questions inherent in these controversies without referring to your own values and those of society.

People who undertake careers in corrections often do so because they find the field an excellent place to express their most cherished values. Probation and parole officers frequently report that their original decision to work in these jobs stemmed from their desire to help people. Correctional officers often report that the aspect of their work they like best is working with people who are in trouble and who want to improve their lives. Administrators report that they value the challenge of building effective policies and helping staff perform their jobs better. The field of corrections, then, helps all these individuals to be fully involved with public service and social life. Corrections is interesting to them in part because it deals with a core conflict of values in our society—freedom versus social control—and it does so in ways that require people to work together.

Summary

 Describe the growth of the U.S. corrections system in the last 40 years and identify at least three issues raised by that growth.

The U.S. prison system has grown for almost 40 years, and today it supervises six times more people than it did in 1972, when the prison system started to grow. In 2010 jails, probation, and prisons declined. The correctional growth situation raises issues of costs, effectiveness, and fairness.

2 Define the systems framework and explain why it is useful.

A system is a complex whole consisting of interdependent parts whose operations are directed toward common goals and influenced by the environment in which they function. It is a useful concept because it helps us understand how the various aspects of corrections can affect one another.

3 Name the various components of the corrections system today and describe their functions.

Corrections consists of many subunits. Institutional corrections includes prisons and jails, and it confines people who have been sentenced by the courts (or, in the case of jails, people who are awaiting trial). Community corrections supervises people who are either awaiting trial or have been sentenced by the court but are still living in the community. There are also private organizations that provide various services to people under correctional authority.

4 Discuss what we can learn from the "great experiment of social control."

The growth in the corrections system has been more a result of deliberate policies that increase the severity of sentences, and has not had as much to do with changes in crime rates.

5 Distinguish the basic assumptions of the penitentiary systems of Pennsylvania and New York.

The penitentiary ideal, first incorporated in Pennsylvania, emphasized the concept of separate confinement. Inmates were held in isolation, spending their time in craft work and considering their transgressions. In the New York (Auburn) congregate system, inmates were held in isolation but worked together during the day under a rule of silence.

6 Discuss the elements of the Cincinnati Declaration.

A Declaration of Principles was adopted at the 1870 Cincinnati meeting of the National Prison Association. The declaration stated that prisons should be organized to encourage reformation, rewarding it with release. It advocated indeterminate sentences and the classification of prisoners based on character and improvement. The reformers viewed the penitentiary practices of the nineteenth century as debasing, humiliating, and destructive of inmates' initiative.

7 Understand the reforms advocated by the Progressives.

The Progressives looked to social, economic, biological, and psychological factors rather than religious or moral explanations for the causes of crime. They advocated the development of probation, indeterminate sentences, treatment programs, and parole.

8 Discuss the forces and events that led to the present crime control model.

The rise of crime in the late 1960s and questions about the effectiveness of rehabilitative programs brought pressure to shift to a crime control model of corrections, with greater use of incarceration and other forms of strict supervision.

9 Describe the changes that are going on today and why they are important.

A combination of concerns about the huge costs of the prison system and the belief that more-effective strategies exist for dealing with people who are convicted of crimes has led to an emerging conservative and liberal consensus to deemphasize prisons and increase the importance of "strategies that work."

Key Terms

community corrections 22
congregate system 17
corrections 8
crime control model 23
evidence-based corrections 24
federalism 14
intermediate sanctions 14
jail 14

justice reinvestment 24
lease system 19
mark system 19
medical model 21
parole 15
penitentiary 16
positivist school 21
prison 14

private prison 15
probation 14
reformatory 20
separate confinement 16
social control 8
system 9

For Discussion

1. Contrast the role of crime with the role of politics in the growth of corrections. Why is this contrast important?
2. What do you see as some of the advantages and disadvantages of the systems concept of corrections?
3. Feedback is an important aspect of a system. How does the corrections system get feedback? In what ways does feedback affect corrections?

4. Assume that the legislature has stipulated that rehabilitation should be the goal of corrections in your state. How might people working in the system displace this goal?
5. Suppose that you are the commissioner of corrections for your state. Which correctional activities might come within your domain? Which most likely would not?

Notes

1 Michael R. Rand, "Criminal Victimization, 2008," BJS *Bulletin,* September 2009.

2 Jennifer C. Karberg and Allen J. Beck, "Trends in U.S. Correctional Populations: Findings from the Bureau of Justice Statistics" (paper presented at the National Committee on Community Corrections, Washington, DC, April 16, 2004).

3 Tracey L. Snell, *Capital Punishment—2013: Statistical Tables* (Washington, DC: Bureau of Justice Statistics, 2014).

4 Asley Nellis, "Throwing Away the Key: The Expansion of Life Without Parole Sentences in the United States," *Federal Sentencing Reporter* 23 (no. 1, October 2010): 27–32.

5 E. Ann Carson, "Prisoners in 2013," BJS *Bulletin,* September, 2014, p. 12.

6 Tracey Kyckelhahn, "State Corrections Expenditures, FY 1982–2010," BJS *Bulletin,* December 2012.

7 Nicole Porter, *On the Chopping Block: State Prison Closings—2012* (Washington, DC: Sentencing Project, 2012).

8 Lauren E. Glaze and Danielle Kaeble , *Correctional Populations in the United States—2013* (Washington, DC: Bureau of Justice Statistics, 2014).

9 Thomas P. Bonczar, "Prevalence of Imprisonment in the U.S. Population, 1974–2001," BJS *Special Report,* August 2003.

10 Bruce Western, *Punishment and Inequality in America* (New York: Russell Sage, 2006).

11 David Dugan and Steven M. Teles, "The Conservative War on Prisons," *Washington Monthly,* November–December 2012, pp. 25–31.

12 Bonczar, "Prevalence of Imprisonment."

13 Todd R. Clear and Natasha Frost, *The Punishment Imperative, The Rise and Failure of the Great Punishment Experiment* (New York: NYU Press, 2013).

14 Raymond V. Liedka, Anne Morrison Piehl, and Bert Useem, "The Crime Control Effects of Incarceration: Does Scale Matter?" *Criminology and Public Policy* 5 (no. 2, 2006): 245–76.

15 Todd R. Clear, *Imprisoning Communities: How Mass Incarceration Makes Impoverished Communities Worse* (New York: Oxford University Press, 2008).

16 Western, *Punishment and Inequality.*

17 Pew Charitable Trusts, *The High Cost of Corrections in America* (Washington, DC: Author, 2012).

18 James J. Stephan, *Census of State and Federal Correctional Facilities, 2005* (Washington, DC: Bureau of Justice Statistics, 2008); and Carson, "Prisoners in 2013."

19 Norman Johnston, *Eastern State Penitentiary: Crucible of Good Intentions* (Philadelphia: Philadelphia Museum of Art, 1994).

20 Negley K. Teeters and John D. Shearer, *The Prison at Philadelphia's Cherry Hill* (New York: Columbia University Press, 1957), 63.

21 Gustave de Beaumont and Alexis de Tocqueville, *On the Penitentiary System in the United States and Its Application to France* (Carbondale: Southern Illinois University [1833] 1964), 201.

22 Edgardo Rotman, "The Failure of Reform: United States, 1865–1965," in *The Oxford History of the Prison,* edited by Norval Morris and Michael Tonry (New York: Oxford University Press, 1995), 174.

23 Alexander W. Pisciotta, *Benevolent Repression: Social Control and the American Reformatory-Prison Movement* (New York: New York University Press, 1994), 20.

24 Pisciotta, *Benevolent Repression,* p. 41.

25 U.S. President's Commission on Law Enforcement and Administration of Justice, *The Challenge of Crime in a Free Society* (Washington, DC: U.S. Government Printing Office, 1967), 7.

26 Robert Martinson, "What Works? Questions and Answers About Prison Reform," *Public Interest* 35 (Spring 1974): 22.

27 Michael Tonry, *Sentencing Matters* (New York: Oxford University Press, 1996), 3.

28 Michael Tonry and Joan Petersilia, "American Prisons at the Beginning of the Twenty-first Century," in *Prisons,* edited by Michael Tonry and Joan Petersilia, vol. 26 of *Crime and Justice: A Review of Research,* edited by Michael Tonry (Chicago: University of Chicago Press, 1999), 3.

29 See Bureau of Justice Assistance, Center for Program Evaluation and Performance Measurement, www.ojp.usdoj.gov/BJA /evaluation/evidence-based.htm, accessed June 22, 2010.

30 National Research Council, *The Growth of Incarceration in the United States: Causes and Consequences* (Washington, DC: National Academies Press, 2014).

CHAPTER 2

The Punishment of Offenders

"All rise!"

The people in the Wayne County courtroom stood as Judge Vonda Evans mounted the dais. On that fifteenth day of January 2015, the courtroom was filled with attorneys, reporters, and onlookers. Judge Evans was about to sentence the wealthy Grosse Pointe Park businessman Bob Bashara, who was convicted of hiring a man to murder his wife of twenty-six years, Jane Bashara.

The Bashara trial rocked the small city of Grosse Point Park, Michigan, which borders the east side of Detroit. This reaction was to be expected. After all, prior to the Bashara incident, Grosse Point Park had not had a homicide in years. And according to

After reading this chapter you should be able to . . .

1 Know about the "Age of Reason" and its effect on corrections.

2 Understand the major goals of punishment.

3 Be familiar with the different criminal sanctions that are used.

4 Explain the types of sentences that judges hand down.

5 Discuss the problem of unjust punishment.

Bob Bashara's attorney, Lillian Diallo, argues for leniency at his sentencing hearing after his conviction for his wife's murder. Bashara paid a local handyman $2,000 to kill his wife. He was eventually sentenced to life without parole.

AP Images/Detroit News/David Coates

ecutors, the murder of Jane Bashara rred in her home, before her body was ed to an alley in Detroit.

uring the trial, prosecutors argued Bob Bashara's motivation for hiring his yman, Joe Gentz, to kill his wife was

Bashara stood to inherit his wife's assets, which included a sizable retirement fund. Prosecutors also argued that, with his wife out of his life, Bob Bashara would be free to immerse himself in the BDSM (bondage, discipline, sadomasochism) activities that he

(continued from previous page)

Before sentencing, family members of Jane Bashara were allowed to speak about how her murder had changed their lives. Jane's sister, Julie, said, "You killed my amazing sister. How could you? She had so much left to do, she had so many plans. You stole her life, betrayed her in the most evil way possible and watched as she died in horror and pain." Jane's mother, Lorraine, said, "I miss Jane terribly every day. There will never, ever be closure for what he did to my daughter."

Speaking in court, Judge Evans said before handing down her sentence, "You once said you were 'living the dream.' Now you're experiencing a nightmare you created. You destroyed your life, and the lives you touched were damaged by your touch. I have no mercy for you." Bob Bashara was sentenced to life in prison.[2]

Was the outcome of the Bashara trial just? Should the judge have sentenced Bashara to a shorter term of imprisonment? Does this sort of crime warrant the death penalty? Did the sentence given to Bashara fulfill society's responsibility to punish illegal behavior? What rationale governed the punishment?

These questions are important when considering the purpose of corrections. In this chapter we discuss the goals of corrections, review different criminal sanctions, and talk about the sentencing process. As we explore these topics, we will discuss their links to one another and to historical and philosophical issues. ■

PUNISHMENT FROM THE MIDDLE AGES TO THE AMERICAN REVOLUTION

Since ancient times, societies have had to deal with the question of what to do with those who break community rules. Over time, the ways in which offenders have been dealt with have changed considerably. Indeed, many of the ancient forms of punishment would shock the conscience of most American citizens and would never be considered appropriate for dealing with criminals today. (See "Focus on Correctional Practice" to review a variety of methods once used to execute the condemned.) Nevertheless, much of what is currently done is influenced by earlier punishments, philosophies, and practices, especially those from England.

The earliest-known comprehensive statements of prohibited behavior appear in the Sumerian Law of Mesopotamia (3100 B.C.E.) and the Code of Hammurabi, developed by the king of Babylon in 1750 B.C.E. These written codes were divided into sections to classify different types of offenses and contained descriptions of the punishments to be imposed on offenders. Another important ancestor of Western law is the Draconian Code of ancient Greece in the seventh century B.C.E. This code was the first to erase the distinction between citizens and slaves before the law. The Draconian code described the legal procedures and also the forms of punishment that could be inflicted: "stoning to death; throwing the offender from a cliff; binding him to a stake so that he suffered a slow death and public abuse before dying; or the formal dedication of the offender to the gods."[3] Lesser punishments might be prohibiting the burial of offenders and the destruction of their houses.

In Rome the law of the Twelve Tables (450 B.C.E.) and the code compiled by Emperor Justinian in 534 B.C.E. helped lay the groundwork of European law. As in Greece and other ancient societies such as Egypt and Israel, Roman lawbreakers were made into slaves, exiled, killed, imprisoned, and physically brutalized.[4] In most of Europe, forms of legal sanctions that are familiar to us today did not appear until the beginning of the Middle Ages, in the 1200s. Before this time, Europeans viewed responses to crime as a private affair, with vengeance a duty to be carried out by the person wronged or by a family member. Wrongs were avenged in accordance with the **lex talionis**, or law of retaliation ("an eye for an eye, a tooth for a tooth"). During the Middle Ages the custom of treating offenses as personal matters to be settled by individuals gradually gave way to the view that the peace of society required the public to participate in determining guilt or innocence and in exacting a penalty.

In the later Middle Ages, especially during the 1400s and 1500s, the authority of government grew, and the criminal law system became more fully developed. With the breakdown of the feudal order and the emergence of a middle class, other forms of punishment were applied. In addition to fines, five punishments were common in Europe and America before the 1800s. These included galley slavery—the practice of forcing men to row ships; imprisonment—primarily for those awaiting trial; transportation—moving

lex talionis
Law of retaliation; the principle that punishment should correspond in degree and kind to the offense ("an eye for an eye, a tooth for a tooth").

During the Middle Ages, various punishments were imposed on the body of the offender. This engraving by Ulrich Tengler, published in 1509, shows some of the punishments used in Germany in that era.

Die verschiedenen im Mittelalter üblichen Strafen und Hinrichtungsarten
Ulrich Tenglers Laienspiegel, Augsburg 1509

The Usual Punishments in Germany during the Middle Ages, illustration from 'Laienspiegel' by Ulrich Tengler, published Augsburg 1509 (engraving) (photo), German School, (16th century)/Bibliotheque Nationale, Paris, France/Archives Charmet/Bridgeman Images

focus on correctional practice

Early Methods of Execution

Over the course of human history, a variety of methods have been used to execute the condemned. In *Discipline and Punish*, Michel Foucault provides an excellent example of medieval punishment by recounting the sentence handed down to Robert-François Damiens, who was convicted of trying to assassinate King Louis XV:

> He is to be taken and conveyed in a cart, wearing nothing but a shift, holding a torch of burning wax weighing two pounds; in the said cart to the Place de Greve, where on a scaffold that will be erected there, the flesh will be torn from his breasts, arms, thighs and calves with red-hot pinchers, his right hand, holding the knife with which he committed the said parricide, burnt with sulphur, and, on those places where the flesh will be torn away, poured molten lead, boiling oil, burning resin, wax and sulphur melted together and then his body drawn and quartered by four horses and his limbs and body consumed by fire, reduced to ashes and his ashes thrown to the winds.

Newspapers reported that Damiens's death was even more horrible than the sentence required. Because the horses were not able to pull him "limb from limb," the executioners resorted to hacking off his arms and legs while he was still alive.

Although the most severe forms of executions were usually reserved for offenders convicted of treason, many medieval punishments appear unnecessarily barbaric and violate the laws of humanity by today's standards. Provided here are descriptions of seven methods of execution used during centuries past. Unlike in the United States today, prisoners who were subjected to the methods discussed here were executed in public, often in front of large crowds.

Boiled Alive

This form of execution involved immersing the condemned in a boiling liquid, such as water, oil, or pitch. The process through which the criminal was killed varied. In some countries the condemned was tied up and immersed up to the neck in liquid that was slowly brought to a boil. In other places the knees of criminals were tied to their chests, after which they were tossed headfirst into the boiling liquid. Boiling was used throughout the Far East and Europe for hundreds of years. In the 1300s, executions by boiling in Germany drew considerable crowds of onlookers. In England, boiling was used for the crime of poisoning in the first half of the sixteenth century.

Broken on the Wheel

Many variations of this method were practiced over the centuries. One approach involved stretching the condemned over a table or bench, tying him or her down, and placing a large, spiked wheel on top of the body. It was not uncommon for executioners to begin by severing one of the criminal's hands with an axe. After doing so, the executioner used a large iron bar or hammer to drive the wheel into the person's body, pulverizing bones and ultimately causing death. This method of execution dates back to the second century in the Roman Empire. Such methods were used well into the eighteenth century throughout Western Europe.

Burned Internally

This form of punishment entailed pouring some form of liquid, such as boiling pitch or molten lead, down the condemned

---

offenders from the community to another region or country; corporal punishment—inflicting pain on the offender's body; and death.

Because officials prior to the 1800s considered public punishment to be a useful deterrent, sanctions were usually carried out in the market square for all to see. The punishments themselves were harsh: Whipping, mutilation, and branding were used extensively, and death was a common penalty for many felonies.

The Age of Reason and Correctional Reform

Enlightenment (Age of Reason)
The 1700s in Europe, when concepts of liberalism, rationality, equality, and individualism dominated social and political thinking.

The late 1700s stand out as a remarkable period. At that time scholars and social reformers in Europe and America were rethinking the nature of society and the place of the individual in it. In this period, known as the **Enlightenment**, or **Age of Reason**, traditional assumptions were challenged and replaced by new ideas based on rationalism, the importance of the individual, and the limitations of government. The Enlightenment affected views on person's throat. Another approach to internal burning entailed inserting a red-hot iron rod in the prisoner's anus. Although there are recorded instances of burning to death internally in England, this method was rarely used because it was far less fantastic a spectacle relative to hangings and beheadings.

Flayed Alive

This bloody method of execution dates back to at least 200 B.C.E. It was used mostly in China and Turkey, but recorded instances of the practice in Europe also exist. This method entailed taking a sharp, scalpel-like object and methodically stripping the skin of the condemned while the victim was still alive. In time, death came upon the skinned prisoner. Castration was also known to be included in this form of execution.

Hanged, Drawn, and Quartered

This form of execution, called the "three-in-one death penalty," was largely reserved for offenders who had committed the worst crime, treason. The process began by hanging the condemned for a short period of time. After being let down and while still choking and unable to speak, the traitor was stretched out on a table. The executioner, wielding a bladed instrument, would then slit open the stomach and begin removing the intestines with his hands. Sometimes this step was preceded by castration. If the traitor survived the disembowelment, the executioner would extract the heart from the chest. Bodily remnants were burned to ashes in a nearby fire. Finally, the bloody corpse was beheaded and the torso quartered. These five sections of the body were scattered about the locale to remind residents and visitors that the cost of crime was high. This form of execution was used in England from approximately the 1500s to the early 1800s. Versions of this method were also employed in France and in colonial America.

Iron Maiden

This coffin-like device was typically made of wood, with a full-length portrait of a woman painted on the doors. Numerous spikes were fastened along the inside of the doors, designed to penetrate the body of the person who was placed in the contraption. Two daggers affixed to the back of the maiden's head were intended to pierce the eyeballs. After the screaming had subsided, which could take hours, the bottom of the iron maiden would swing open so the bloody and ravaged cadaver could be removed. This method was used in Germany and Spain in the 1500s.

Rack

This tool of execution consisted of two large axles, each arranged some distance apart. The condemned would be placed in between the axles with his wrists attached by rope to the axle above his head. The ankles would be tied with rope to the axle near his feet. When the executioners began to turn the axles, the ropes tightened, and the condemned person's body would stretch. The device could be locked to hold the body at a particular point. Ultimately, the stretching continued to a point where the prisoner's knees, elbows, and shoulders dislocated. The rack and similar execution devices were used throughout Europe for centuries. The rack was used not only to kill but also as a means of extracting information from those who were unwilling to divulge it.

Critical Thinking

1. How do the methods described here compare to current methods of execution, such as the electric chair, hanging, and lethal injection?

2. Would the execution methods used centuries ago better deter crime?

3. Why do you suppose that these early practices were abandoned?

4. Should the public be allowed to witness executions in the United States? Why? Why not?

Sources: Geoffrey Abbott, *Executions: A Guide to the Ultimate Penalty* (West Sussex, UK: Summersdale, 2005); Phil Clarke, Liz Hardy, and Anne Williams, *Executioners: Men and Women Who Kill for the People* (London: Futura, 2008); Michel Foucault, *Discipline and Punish* (New York: Pantheon, 1977), 4.

---

law and criminal justice. Reformers began to raise questions about the nature of criminal behavior and the best methods of punishment.

The result was a major shift in penal thought and practice. Correctional practices moved away from inflicting pain on the body of the offender toward methods that would set the individual on a path of honesty and right living. Of the many people who promoted correctional reform, two stand out: Cesare Beccaria (1738–1794), the Italian founder of what is now called the classical school of criminology, and Jeremy Bentham (1748–1832), an English reformer who developed a utilitarian approach to crime and punishment.

Cesare Beccaria and the Classical School

The rationalist philosophy of the Enlightenment, with its emphasis on individual rights, was applied to criminal justice by Cesare Beccaria, who argued that the only justification for punishment is utility: the safety it affords society by preventing crime.[5] Beccaria focused on the lack of a rational link between the gravity of given crimes and the severity of punishments. Six principles underlie the reforms Beccaria advocated, principles from which the classical school of criminology emerged:

1. The basis of all social action must be the utilitarian concept of the greatest good for the greatest number of people.

2. Crime must be considered an injury to society, and the only rational measure of crime is the extent of injury.

3. Prevention of crime is more important than punishment for crimes.

4. The accused have a right to speedy trials and to humane treatment before trial, as well as every right to bring forward evidence on their behalf.

5. The purpose of punishment is deterrence, not revenge. Certainty and swiftness of punishment, rather than severity, best secure this goal.

6. Imprisonment should be more widely employed, with better quarters and with prisoners classified by age, sex, and degree of criminality.

Beccaria summarized the thinking of those who wanted to rationalize the law: "In order for punishment not to be, in every instance, an act of violence of one or many against a private citizen, it must be essentially public, prompt, necessary, the least possible in the given circumstances, proportionate to the crime, dictated by laws."[6]

Jeremy Bentham and the "Hedonic Calculus"

utilitarianism
The doctrine that the aim of all action should be the greatest possible balance of pleasure over pain, hence the belief that a punishment inflicted on an offender must achieve enough good to outweigh the pain inflicted.

One of the most provocative thinkers of English criminal law, Jeremy Bentham is best known for his utilitarian theories, often called his "hedonic calculus." He claimed that one could categorize all human actions and could, either through pleasurable (hedonic) incentives or through punishment, direct individuals to desirable activities. Undergirding this idea was his concept of **utilitarianism**, the doctrine that rational people behave in ways that achieve the greatest pleasure while bringing the least pain; they are constantly calculating the pluses and minuses of potential actions.[7]

In Bentham's view, criminals were somewhat childlike or unbalanced, lacking the self-discipline to control their passions by reason. Accordingly, the law should be organized so that the offender would derive more pain than pleasure for a wrongful act. Potential offenders would recognize that legal sanctions were organized according to this scheme, and they would be better deterred from committing crimes.

Bentham sought to reform the criminal law so that it emphasized deterrence and prevention. The goal was not to avenge an illegal act but to prevent commission of such an act in the first place. Because excessive punishment was unjustified, the punishment would be no more severe than necessary to deter crime: not "an act of wrath or vengeance," but one of calculation tempered by considerations of the social good and the offender's needs.[8]

European Influences on Punishment in America

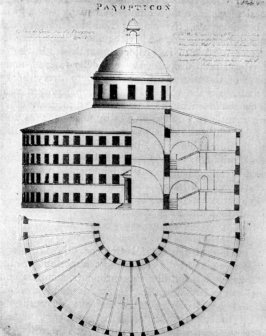

In 1796 Jeremy Bentham designed the "panopticon" so that each prisoner was kept in a cell set in such a way as to prevent him from being aware of whether or not he was under observation by the staff.

PANOPTICON

Mansell/Time & Life Pictures/Getty Images

European (especially English) trends and practices influenced the punishment of offenders in America, especially during the early years of the new republic (see Chapter 1). Although the work of Cesare Beccaria affected penal policies throughout much of the Western world, corrections in colonial America followed English ideas and practices. Further, although transatlantic ties have continued over the years, punishment and sentencing practices have developed in decidedly American ways in responding to social and political policies in the United States.

THE PURPOSE OF CORRECTIONS

Rationales for punishment are influenced by a number of factors. These factors may be philosophical, political, or social, and they often change from one historical era to the next. Popular ideas about the causes of crime also affect the rationales used for specific sanctions. The ideas of the classical school of criminology resulted in doing away with brutal punishments for minor offenses and moving toward the ideal of "making the punishment fit the crime." Later, the emergence of the positivist school and the development of the social and behavioral sciences contributed to the belief that punishments should be designed on a case-by-case basis to meet the needs of individual offenders.

What do we mean by the term *punishment*? Professor Herbert Packer wrote that punishment is marked by three elements:

1. An offense.
2. The infliction of pain because of the commission of the offense.
3. A dominant purpose that is neither to compensate someone injured by the offense nor to better the offender's condition but to prevent further offenses or to inflict what is thought to be deserved pain on the offender.[9]

Packer's description emphasizes two major goals of punishing criminals: inflicting deserved suffering on offenders and preventing crime in the future.

In the United States, criminal sanctions are used to accomplish four goals: retribution, deterrence, incapacitation, and rehabilitation. This chapter reviews each of these traditional justifications of punishment. Keep in mind that while judges may say their sentences are intended to accomplish a particular goal, the conditions in correctional facilities and the actions of probation officers may be inconsistent with that goal. Therefore, it is not uncommon for sentencing and correctional policies to be carried out in such a way that no one goal dominates.

Retribution (Deserved Punishment)

Retribution is punishment inflicted on a person who has broken the law and so deserves to be punished. The biblical saying "an eye for an eye, a tooth for a tooth" sums up the idea of retribution. Retribution means that people who commit crimes that are similar in terms of the seriousness or the amount of suffering they cause their victims should receive punishments that are alike. Retribution is deserved punishment; offenders must "pay their debts to society." This idea does not focus on future criminal acts, nor does it concern the personal deficiencies of the offender. Instead, retribution focuses only on the offense. Offenders are penalized for the illegal acts because fairness and justice require that they be punished.

retribution
Punishment inflicted on a person who has infringed the rights of others and so deserves to be penalized. The severity of the sanction should fit the seriousness of the crime.

Although the idea of retribution lost much of its appeal during the Age of Reason and the growing popularity of utilitarian approaches to punishment, some people argue that retribution is a basic human emotion. They believe that if the government fails to take action and provide retributive sanctions to express community disapproval for criminal acts, then citizens will take the law into their own hands and punish offenders. According to this view, otherwise law-abiding citizens may behave inappropriately if the government fails to satisfy society's desire for retribution. Retribution helps society emphasize the standards that it expects all members to uphold.

Does this argument apply for all crimes? If a rapist is not adequately punished, then the friends and family of the victim may be tempted to exact their own retribution. What about a young adult who smokes marijuana? Would the community care if the government failed to impose a retributive sanction? What about other offenders who commit relatively minor, nonviolent crimes? Even when handling less serious crimes, it may be useful to use retributive punishments to remind the general public of the law and the important values that it protects.

In recent decades the idea of retribution has regained some popularity. The renewed interest is largely a result of growing dissatisfaction with rehabilitation. Using the concept of "just deserts" (or deserved punishment) to define retribution, some people argue that a person who infringes on other people's rights deserves to be punished. This approach is based on the philosophical view that punishment is a moral response to the harm caused to society. Accordingly, punishment should be used only to exact retribution for the wrong inflicted and not to achieve other goals, such as deterrence, incapacitation, and rehabilitation.[10]

Deterrence

Many people think of criminal punishment as a way to keep people from committing crime. Politicians talk about being "tough on crime," and in some states television commercials tell viewers about the penalties for certain crimes. Both are efforts to send a message to would-be criminals that crime does not pay. This approach dates back to Jeremy Bentham's theory of utilitarianism. Bentham and other eighteenth-century reformers believed that human behavior was governed by an individual's calculation of the costs and benefits of one's action. For example, before stealing a car, a potential offender considers the punishment that others have received and weighs it against the enjoyment of temporarily possessing an automobile.

general deterrence
Punishment of criminals that is intended to be an example to the general public and to discourage crime by others.

Modern-day criminologists talk about two types of deterrence. **General deterrence** presumes that citizens will choose not to commit a crime because they have observed the punishments that criminals have received, and they will conclude that the costs of crime outweigh any benefits. For general deterrence to be effective, members of the general public must believe that if they commit a crime, there is a very good chance that they will be caught by the police, prosecuted in a court of law, and punished severely.

specific deterrence
Punishment inflicted on criminals to discourage them from committing future crimes.

A second type of deterrence, termed **specific deterrence**, targets the decisions and behavior of offenders who have already been convicted. Under this approach, the amount and kind of punishment are calibrated to discourage a criminal from deciding to commit a crime in the future. If the punishment is severe enough, then the convicted offender may conclude, "The price I paid for my crime was too painful, so I will not commit crime in the future because I do not want to be punished again."

Deterrence assumes that people think rationally before they act (they weigh the costs against the benefits of their actions). Some people are skeptical of this assumption. What about people who commit crimes under the influence of drugs or alcohol? What about offenders who suffer from mental illness or experience psychological problems that cloud their decision making? What about individuals who are unable to control their impulses? Critics question whether these offenders are capable of making rational decisions. Still others point out that for most crimes, the likelihood that an offender will be apprehended by the police is very low, which greatly limits the deterrent effect of a punishment. To be an effective deterrent, punishment must be perceived as fast, certain, and severe.

Incapacitation

incapacitation
Depriving an offender of the ability to commit crimes, usually by detaining the offender in prison.

Incapacitation assumes that society can eliminate an offender's ability to commit further crimes by placing him or her in a correctional facility or by execution. This idea is expressed in the saying "Lock 'em up and throw away the key!" The practice of incapacitating offenders is not a new idea. Banishment from the community was a method of incapacitation used by primitive societies centuries ago. Today, imprisonment is the usual method of incapacitation. Convicted criminals can be confined in prisons and prevented from harming society for the length of their sentence. The death penalty is the ultimate method of incapacitation.

Any punishment that physically restricts an offender can have an incapacitating effect, even when the original purpose of the sentence is retribution, deterrence, or rehabilitation. Sentences based on incapacitation are future oriented. If the judge believes that an offender is likely to commit future crimes, then a severe sentence may be imposed—even for a relatively minor crime. Under the theory of incapacitation, for example, a person who shoplifts and has been convicted of the offense on ten previous occasions may receive a severe sentence. His or her criminal record suggests that the most recent conviction was not a unique event and that he or she will commit additional crimes if released from jail. In this way incapacitation focuses on the characteristics of the offender rather than on the characteristics of the offense.

Critics of incapacitation ask whether it is fair for a chronic shoplifter to receive a stiffer sentence than a one-time offender who assaulted another person in the heat of passion. Questions are also raised about how to determine sentence length. Presumably, offenders will not be released until the government is reasonably sure they will not commit additional crimes. But can a person's future behavior be predicted accurately? This raises another interesting question: Should people be punished for crimes that the government believes they might commit if they are released from prison?

The concept of **selective incapacitation** has received greater attention in recent years. This approach focuses on sentencing to long prison terms offenders who repeat certain types of crimes. More specifically, the criminal justice system selectively uses incapacitation when "career criminals" are apprehended and convicted. This practice is consistent with research which shows that a relatively small number of offenders commit a large number of violent and property crimes. Although selective incapacitation is appealing to many people, it is very expensive to incarcerate repeat offenders for long periods of time.

selective incapacitation
Making the best use of expensive and limited prison space by targeting for incarceration those offenders whose incapacity will do the most to reduce crime in society.

Rehabilitation

Rehabilitation refers to the goal of restoring the convicted offender to a constructive place in society through vocational or educational training or therapy. Many Americans find rehabilitation appealing because they want offenders to lead crime-free, productive lives after leaving prison. For nearly a century, supporters of rehabilitation have argued that correctional professionals can use a variety of techniques to identify and treat the causes of criminal behavior. Because rehabilitation focuses on the offender, the relationship between the length of a sentence and the seriousness of the crime is inconsistent.

rehabilitation
The goal of restoring the convicted offender to a constructive place in society through vocational training, educational services, and/or therapy.

Compare this correctional education program in Kuna, Idaho, to the Elmira Reformatory in Chapter 1. When it comes to rehabilitation in correctional facilities, what has changed, and what has not?

AP Images/Newspaper Member/Idaho Press-Tribune, Adam Eschbach

Offenders will return to society once they are "cured." Therefore, people who commit less serious offenses may spend considerable time in prison if experts believe they need a longer period of time to be rehabilitated. By contrast, a person who committed murder may be granted early release by showing signs that the psychological or emotional problems that led to the crime have been corrected.

In theory, judges who view rehabilitation as the primary goal should not set a fixed sentence. Rather, they should sentence offenders to a minimum and maximum period of time so that parole boards may release inmates when offenders have been rehabilitated. Such sentences are called indeterminate sentences. This sentencing strategy is justified by the belief that prisoners will not participate in treatment programs that can aid in their rehabilitation if they know when they are going to be released back into the community. Rather, prisoners will be more likely to cooperate with counselors, psychologists, and other professionals who can help them with their rehabilitation when their release from prison depends on them doing so.

From the 1940s through the 1970s, rehabilitation was widely believed to be an important correctional goal. During the past four decades, however, influential studies of rehabilitation programs have challenged the idea that we can cure criminal offenders.[11] Today, many lawmakers, prosecutors, and judges have abandoned the goal of rehabilitation in favor of retribution, deterrence, and incapacitation.

New Approaches to Punishment

During the past decade, many people have called for shifts away from punishment goals that focus either on the offender (rehabilitation, specific deterrence) or the crime (retribution, general deterrence, and incapacitation). Some have argued that the current goals of the criminal sanction leave out the needs of the crime victim and the community. Crime has traditionally been viewed as violating the state, but people now recognize that a criminal act also violates the victim and the community. In keeping with the focus of police, courts, and corrections on community justice, advocates are calling for **restoration** to be added to the goals of the criminal sanction.

restoration
Punishment designed to repair the damage done to the victim and community by an offender's criminal act.

The restorative perspective views crime as more than a violation of penal law. The criminal act practically and symbolically denies community. It breaks trust among citizens and requires that the community determine how best to communicate that the offender is not above the law and the victim is not beneath its reach. Crime victims suffer losses involving damage to property and self. The primary aim of criminal justice should be to repair these losses. Crime also challenges the essence of community, to the extent that community life depends on a shared sense of trust, fairness, and interdependence.

Critics say that the retributive focus of today's criminal justice system denies the victim's need to be acknowledged and isolates community members from the conflict between offender and victim. By shifting the focus to restorative justice, sanctions can provide ways for the offender to repair harm. However, others warn that society should approach restorative justice with caution because many procedural safeguards are impaired.[12]

Restoration-oriented programs take many forms; most involve the participation of the offender, the victim, and the community. The offender must take responsibility for the offense, agree to "undo" the harm through restitution, and affirm a willingness to live according to the law. The victim must specify the harm of the offense and the resources necessary to restore the losses suffered; the victim must also lay out the conditions necessary to diminish any fear or resentment toward the offender. The community helps with the restorative process, emphasizing to the offender the norms of acceptable behavior, providing support to restore the victim, and offering opportunities for the offender to perform reparative tasks for the victim and the community. Finally, it provides ways for the offender to get the help needed to live in the community crime free.[13]

Research suggests that restoration-oriented programs can be effective. For example, Heather Strang and her colleagues' comprehensive review of the research literature on one

Table 2.1 Hypothetical Punishments for Bob Bashara

At sentencing, the judge usually gives reasons for the punishment imposed. Here are some statements Judge Vonda Evans *might* have made, depending on the correctional goal she wanted to promote.

Goal	Judge's Statement
Retribution	I am imposing this sentence because you deserve to be punished for the crimes committed against a woman who trusted you. Your criminal behavior in this case is the basis for your punishment. Justice requires me to impose a sanction that reflects the value the community places on right conduct.
Deterrence	I am imposing this sentence so that your punishment will serve as an example and deter others who may contemplate similar actions. In addition, I hope that the sentence will deter you from ever again committing such an act.
Incapacitation	I am imposing this sentence so that you will be unable to violate the law while imprisoned. Because you have not been convicted of prior offenses, selective incapacitation is not warranted.
Rehabilitation	The trial testimony of your psychiatrists and the information contained in the presentence report make me believe that aspects of your personality led you to violate the law. I am therefore imposing this sentence so that you can be treated in ways that will rectify your behavior so you will not break the law again.

type of restoration program—face-to-face meetings with victims and offenders—found that these programs reduce future involvement in prosecutable crimes. Strang and associates also found evidence that such programs benefit crime victims. In particular, victims who willingly meet with offenders experience fewer post-traumatic stress symptoms.[14]

Criminal Sanctions: A Mixed Bag?

How should society justify criminal sanctions? Should the purpose be deterrence or incapacitation? What about retribution or rehabilitation? Often, justifications for specific sanctions overlap. A term of imprisonment may by justified by the goal of retribution, but the prison term may also deter the offender from committing future crimes. Does rehabilitation conflict with other goals? For example, will a prison sentence still deter would-be criminals if inmates are given educational and vocational opportunities? By the same token, can inmates be rehabilitated if forced to live in unpleasant prison conditions?

Trial judges carry out the difficult task of crafting sentences that accommodate these different goals in each case. A judge may sentence an identity thief to a long prison term to set an example for others, even though the offender poses little physical threat to the community. The same judge may sentence a violent youthful offender to a shorter period of incarceration because the youth is believed to be a good candidate for rehabilitation.

To see how these goals might be enacted in real life, consider again the sentencing of Bob Bashara. Table 2.1 shows various hypothetical sentencing statements that Judge Evans *might* have given, depending on prevailing correctional goals.

We next consider the ways that goals are applied through the use of various forms of punishment. Keep in mind the underlying goal or mixture of goals that can be used to justify each sanction.

FORMS OF THE CRIMINAL SANCTION

When most people think about punishment, incarceration immediately comes to mind. However, community supervision such as probation and intermediate sanctions is used far more often than sending offenders to prison. As **Figure 2.1** shows, criminal

Of all correctional measures, incarceration represents the greatest restriction on freedom. These inmates are part of America's huge incarcerated population. Since 1980 the number of Americans in prisons and jails has quadrupled.

AP Images/Rich Pedroncelli

sanctions in the United States range from probation to prison. In rare situations the death penalty is imposed. Intermediate sanctions, such as community service and day reporting, are located toward the center of the continuum.

Experts argue that the greater number of sentencing options gives judges more ability to exercise their professional judgment to fashion punishments that are appropriate for both the crime and the offender. By using alternatives to incarceration, such as intermediate sanctions, trial judges can reserve expensive prison space for violent offenders. In contrast, nonviolent offenders can serve their sentences under supervision in the community. But there is no standard approach to sentencing offenders. Many states use sentencing guidelines to direct judicial decisions regarding punishment. Other states have adopted determinate sentences, and some continue to use indeterminate sentences. Mandatory sentences, such as three-strikes laws, are also used in many jurisdictions. As we examine the various forms of criminal sanctions, keep in mind that judges have discretion in determining the appropriate sentence.

PROBATION

Offender reports to probation officer periodically, depending on the offense, sometimes as frequently as several times a month or as infrequently as once a year.

INTENSIVE SUPERVISION PROBATION

Offender sees probation officer three to five times a week. Probation officer also makes unscheduled visits to offender's home or workplace.

RESTITUTION AND FINES

Used alone or in conjunction with probation or intensive supervision and requires regular payments to crime victims or to the courts.

COMMUNITY SERVICE

Used alone or in conjunction with probation or intensive supervision and requires completion of set number of hours of work in and for the community.

SUBSTANCE ABUSE TREATMENT

Evaluation and referral services provided by private outside agencies and used alone or in conjunction with either simple probation or intensive supervision.

FIGURE 2.1

Escalating Punishments to Fit the Crime

This list includes generalized descriptions of many sentencing options used in jurisdictions across the country.

Source: *Seeking Justice: Crime and Punishment in America* (New York: Edna McConnell Clark Foundation, 1997), 32–33.

Incarceration

Nearly 6.9 million men and women are under correctional supervision in the United States. Approximately 2.2 million of these individuals (or 32.2 percent) are incarcerated in prisons or jails. Incarceration remains the standard punishment for people who commit serious crimes.[15] Individuals who support the use of incarceration usually believe that imprisonment deters potential offenders. But it is also a very expensive form of punishment. For example, it is estimated that the average cost of incarcerating someone in a state prison for one year is $31,286. The costs ranges from $14,603 in Kentucky to $60,076 in New York.[16] Moreover, inmates who serve prison terms often experience problems reentering society when they are released.

In penal codes, legislatures stipulate the type of sentence and the length of time in prison imposed for different crimes. Three basic sentencing structures are used: (1) indeterminate sentences, (2) determinate sentences, and (3) mandatory sentences. Each type of sentence provides judges varying levels of discretion and also reflects different goals of criminal sanction.

INDETERMINATE SENTENCES   Penal codes with **indeterminate sentencing** require a minimum and maximum amount of times for offenders to serve in prison (for example, 1 to 5 years, 2 to 10 years, 10 to 20 years, and so on). The judge informs the offender of the sentence range at the time of sentencing. Indeterminate sentences are used when the dominant

indeterminate sentence
A period of incarceration with minimum and maximum terms stipulated so that parole eligibility depends on the time necessary for treatment; indeterminate sentences are closely associated with the concept of rehabilitation.

DAY REPORTING

Clients report to a central location every day where they file a daily schedule with their supervision officer showing how each hour will be spent — at work, in class, at support group meetings, etc.

HOUSE ARREST AND ELECTRONIC MONITORING

Used in conjunction with intensive supervision; restricts offender to home except when at work, school, or treatment.

HALFWAY HOUSE

Residential settings for selected inmates as a supplement to probation for those completing prison programs and for some probation or parole violators. Usually coupled with community service work and/or substance abuse treatment.

BOOT CAMP

Rigorous military-style regimen for younger offenders, designed to accelerate punishment while instilling discipline, often with an educational component.

PRISONS AND JAILS

More-serious offenders serve their terms at state or federal prisons, while county jails are usually designed to hold inmates for shorter periods.

goal is rehabilitation because they give correctional officials and parole boards control over how much time a prisoner serves. At sentencing, the offender also learns when he or she will be eligible for parole, which is usually at some point after the minimum term has been served. However, the parole board will ultimately decide when the prisoner is released.

determinate sentence
A fixed period of incarceration imposed by a court; determinate sentences are associated with the concept of retribution.

DETERMINATE SENTENCES   States that use **determinate sentences** require a specific period of time (for example, 2 years, 5 years, 10 years) that an offender is imprisoned. At the end of the term, after subtracting time off for good behavior, the prisoner is automatically released from prison. The judgment of a parole board as to whether an inmate has been rehabilitated does not affect when an inmate will be released. Determinate sentences became more common when the general public and politicians grew dissatisfied with the goal of rehabilitation in the 1970s. Determinate sentences are used when the goal is retribution (deserved punishment).

Some states that use determinate sentencing allow the judge to choose a specific time that an inmate is to serve in prison from a range (for example, 14–20 months) into which most cases should fall. This sentence structure is called a determinate **presumptive sentence**. Judges can deviate from the penal code when sentencing an offender, but only when special circumstances exist. Whichever form of determinate sentencing is used, offenders know how long they will serve in prison at the time of sentencing. The use of determinate sentencing limits judicial discretion, which helps limit disparity in sentencing for offenders who are found guilty of similar crimes.

presumptive sentence
A sentence for which the legislature or a commission sets a minimum and maximum range of months or years. Judges are to fix the length of the sentence within that range, allowing for special circumstances.

mandatory sentence
A sentence stipulating that some minimum period of incarceration must be served by people convicted of selected crimes, regardless of background or circumstances.

MANDATORY SENTENCES   **Mandatory sentences** (often called "mandatory-minimum sentences") require that inmates convicted of selected crimes serve a minimum amount of time. The sentencing judge's discretion is very limited. Under this sentencing structure the judge is not allowed to consider the circumstances surrounding the crime or the background of the offender, nor may she or he impose a sentence that does not involve incarceration. Mandatory sentences are usually reserved for certain types of violent crimes, drug crimes, habitual offenders, and crimes involving the use of a firearm.

The "three strikes and you're out" laws, which have been adopted in several states and by the federal government, provide one example of mandatory sentencing. These laws require that judges sentence offenders who have three felony convictions to long prison terms, including life without the possibility of parole. Three-strikes laws increase

Seated, former New England Patriots football star Aaron Hernandez learns he has been found guilty of first-degree murder in the shooting death of Odin Lloyd in June 2013. He was sentenced to life imprisonment without the possibility of parole.

AP Images/Pool Photo/Dominick Reuter

the size of prison populations and also help create large, aging prison populations. Research shows that three-strikes sentences have little impact on reducing rates of serious crime.[17] Some states are rethinking whether their three-strikes laws are working as intended. For example, California approved Proposition 36 in late 2012, changing the provisions of the state's three-strikes law in two important ways. The new law requires that third-strike offenders most recently convicted of a serious or violent felony be eligible for a 25-years-to-life sentence. It also allows certain inmates serving life sentences under the old law to petition the court to request resentencing. Inmates are eligible for resentencing if the court finds that they do not pose an unreasonable risk of harm to society. Thus far, supporters of the new law argue that the results are encouraging. For example, approximately 1,000 inmates were released in the ten months after Californians voted for Proposition 36. Because of these individuals' prior criminal behavior and because of their long stays in prison, many people might expect that these offenders would return to prison at very high rates. This has not happened. (See Myths in Corrections: "Three Strikes and You're Out.")

MYTHS in Corrections

Three Strikes and You're Out

THE MYTH: If released, nonviolent inmates convicted under "three-strikes" laws will return to prison at high rates.

THE REALITY: According to data from the California Department of Corrections and Rehabilitation, the reincarceration rate for prisoners released under Proposition 36 is 1.3 percent. For all other inmates released from California state prisons during the same time period, the reincarceration rate is 30 percent.

Source: Stanford Law School Three Strikes Project and NAACP Legal Defense and Education Fund, *Proposition 36 Progress Report: Over 1,500 Prisoners Released, Historically Low Recidivism Rate* (Stanford, CA: Stanford Law School, 2014).

THE SENTENCE VERSUS ACTUAL TIME SERVED   Regardless of how much discretion that judges have to fine-tune the sentences they give, the prison sentences that are imposed may bear little resemblance to the amount of time actually served. In reality, parole boards in indeterminate-sentencing states have broad discretion in release decisions once the offender has served the minimum portion of the sentence. In addition, offenders can have their prison sentence reduced by earning **good-time** credits for good behavior, at the discretion of the prison administrator.

Most states have good-time policies. Days are subtracted from a prisoner's minimum or maximum term for good behavior or for participation in vocational, educational, or treatment programs. Correctional officials consider these policies necessary for maintaining institutional order and reducing crowding. Good-time credit provides an incentive for prisoners to follow institutional rules.

The amount of good time one can earn varies among the states, usually from five to ten days per month. In some states, once 90 days of good time are earned, the credits cannot be taken away as a punishment for misbehavior.

good time
A reduction of an inmate's prison sentence, at the discretion of the prison administrator, for good behavior or for participation in vocational, educational, and treatment programs.

Intermediate Sanctions

Because of prison crowding and the lack of probation supervision, policy makers have become more and more interested in the development and use of **intermediate sanctions.** These punishments are less severe and costly than prison but are more restrictive than traditional probation. Intermediate sanctions include monetary sanctions, such as fines, restitution, and forfeiture of illegally gained assets. Such sanctions may also restrict freedom. These punishments include home confinement and intensive probation supervision. Judges using an intermediate sanctions approach may also require the offender to perform community service.

Intermediate sanctions are often most effective when used in combination. These bundles of sanctions should reflect the severity of the offense, the characteristics of the offender, and the needs of the community. In addition, mechanisms must be put in place to deal with offenders who fail to meet the conditions of their sentence. If criminal justice officials fail to adequately monitor offenders who receive intermediate sanctions,

intermediate sanctions
Punishments that are more restrictive than traditional probation but less severe and costly than incarceration.

then citizens may begin to question the legitimacy of such programs. (See Chapter 4 for a full discussion of intermediate sanctions.)

Probation

The most frequently applied criminal sanction in the United States is **probation**, a sentence that an offender serves in the community under supervision. Nearly 57 percent of adults under correctional supervision are on probation (approximately 3.9 million adults in 2013).[18] Probation is designed to supervise offenders while they try to straighten out their lives. Probation is not a right; it is a judicial act that is granted by the grace of the state. Conditions are imposed specifying how the offender is to behave during the length of supervision. Probationers may be required to take drug tests, obey curfews, keep a job, go to school, and stay out of certain parts of town or away from specific people. People on probation may also be required to meet regularly with a probation officer. If such conditions are not met, the supervising officer may recommend to the court that the probation be revoked and that the offender serve the rest of the sentence in jail or prison. Probation may also be revoked if the offender commits a new crime.

Sometimes probation is tied to incarceration. In some jurisdictions, the court can modify an offender's prison sentence. After he or she has served a short period of time in prison, the court may resentence the offender to probation. This is often referred to as **shock probation**. An offender on probation may also be required to spend intermittent periods, such as weekends or nights, in jail.

Probation is generally advocated as a way of rehabilitating offenders who have committed less serious crimes and who have modest criminal records. It is viewed as a less expensive and more effective way of supervising offenders than prison. Incarceration may embitter youthful or first-time offenders and put them in the company of more-hardened criminals, who may teach them more-sophisticated ways of committing crime. (See Chapters 4 and 5 for a full discussion of probation.)

Death

The United States is one of only a few Western democracies that use the death penalty. Of all the criminal sanctions, the death penalty remains controversial for a variety of reasons. The issue has been addressed several times in the courts. In fact, the U.S. Supreme Court suspended use of the death penalty from 1968 to 1976. The Court eventually decided that capital punishment does not violate the Eighth Amendment's prohibition of cruel and unusual punishments. Executions started again in 1977.

The number of people sentenced to death increased dramatically after 1980, as shown in **Figure 2.2**. Only during the past several years has this increase leveled off and declined slightly. On October 1, 2014, 3,035 people awaited execution in the United States.[19] California has the largest death row population of any state.

As of January 22, 2015, 1,398 people have been executed in the United States since 1976. More than one-third (or 518) of these executions took place in Texas. Although a majority of states and the federal government have the death penalty available as a criminal sanction, 1,138 (or 81.4 percent) of the executions since 1976 were conducted in the South.[20]

The methods of execution used in the United States include hanging, firing squad, gas chamber, electric chair, and lethal injection. The vast majority of inmates executed in the United States since 1976 were put to death by lethal injection. Although it is rarely used, several states still maintain an operational electric chair. For example, condemned prisoners in Alabama can request electrocution instead of lethal injection. In South Carolina, inmates are asked to choose either electrocution or lethal injection. Until ruled unconstitutional by the Nebraska Supreme Court in 2008, electrocution was the only method of execution for condemned inmates in that state. Hanging is also still

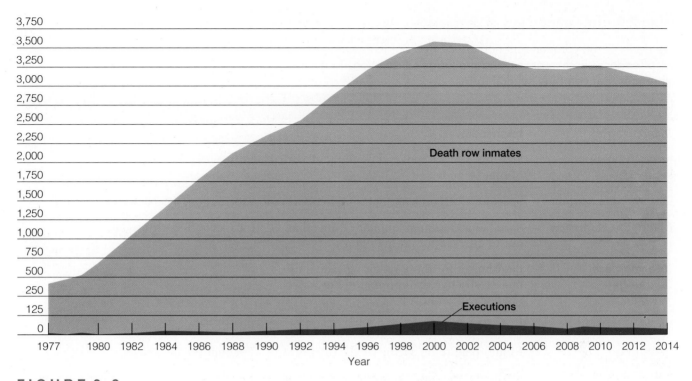

FIGURE 2.2

People Under Sentence of Death and People Executed, 1977–2014

Since 1976, hundreds of new offenders have been added to death row each year, yet the number of executions has never been greater than 98. What explains this situation?

Source: Death Penalty Information Center, www.deathpenaltyinfo.org, January 22, 2015.

used, but in only two states. In the state of Washington, inmates can request hanging instead of lethal injection. Condemned prisoners in New Hampshire may be executed by hanging if lethal injection is not possible. While executions may be carried out using the gas chamber and the firing squad in a handful of states, these states also use lethal injection.[21]

What will the future hold for capital punishment in the United States? Will the pace of executions increase? Will the number of offenders on death row continue to grow? Will alternatives such as life imprisonment for convicted murderers be used instead? Might the United States abolish the death penalty? These questions remain to be answered. (See Chapter 11 for a full discussion of the death penalty.)

Forms and Goals of Sanctions

The criminal sanction takes many forms. The ways that offenders are punished serve different purposes. Table 2.2 summarizes how different sanctions work and how they reflect different punishment philosophies. Many of these sanctions are used to achieve one or more punishment goals. As we consider the sentencing process, keep in mind that judges use their discretion to set the punishment according to the provisions of the law and the characteristics of the offender.

Not all punishments are as visible to the general public as prisons, jails, and community corrections. A number of laws and regulations diminish the rights and privileges of ex-offenders. These "invisible punishments" include (1) denying felons the right to vote, (2) allowing termination of parental rights, (3) establishing felony conviction as grounds for divorce, (4) restricting access to certain occupations, and (5) barring felons from public welfare programs and benefits.[22] Many reformers believe that abolishing these invisible punishments will help ex-prisoners successfully reenter society.

Table 2.2 The Punishment of Offenders

The goals of the criminal sanction are carried out in a variety of ways, depending on the provisions of the law, the offender's characteristics, and the judge's discretion. To achieve punishment objectives, judges may impose sentences that combine several forms.

Form of Sanction	Description	Purpose
Incarceration	Imprisonment	
Indeterminate sentence	Specifies a maximum and minimum length of time to be served	Incapacitation, deterrence, rehabilitation
Determinate sentence	Specifies a certain length of time to be served	Retribution, incapacitation, deterrence
Mandatory sentence	Specifies a minimum amount of time that must be served for given crimes	Incapacitation, deterrence
Intermediate Sanctions	Punishment for those requiring sanctions more restrictive than probation but less restrictive than prison	
Fine	Money paid to the state by the offender	Retribution, deterrence
Restitution	Money paid to the victim by the offender	Retribution, incapacitation, deterrence
Forfeiture	Seizure by the state of property either illegally obtained or acquired with resources illegally obtained	Retribution, incapacitation, deterrence
Community service	Requires the offender to perform work for the community	Retribution, deterrence
Home confinement	Requires the offender to stay in home during certain times	Retribution, incapacitation, deterrence
Intensive probation	Requires strict and frequent reporting to the probation officer	Retribution, incapacitation, deterrence
Boot camp/Shock probation	Short-term institutional sentence emphasizing physical development and discipline, followed by probation	Retribution, incapacitation, deterrence
Probation	Allows the offender to serve a sentence in the community under supervision	Retribution, incapacitation, rehabilitation
Death	Execution	Retribution, incapacitation, deterrence

THE SENTENCING PROCESS

Judges are responsible for sentencing convicted offenders. Although legislatures establish penal codes that specify the sentences that judges can impose, such laws usually allow judges to exercise their discretion. Judges may combine various forms of punishment to tailor the sanction to the offender. For example, a judge may rule that two sentences run concurrently (at the same time) or consecutively (one after the other). The judge may even decide that part of the period of imprisonment will be suspended. In other situations, the offender may receive a combination of intermediate sanctions, such as probation, restitution, community service, and a fine. A judge may also delay imposing a sentence but reserve the power to set penalties at a later date if the offender misbehaves.

When a judge looks into the offender's eyes and pronounces sentence, what thinking has gone into the sentence? A number of factors influence judicial discretion during sentencing. Social science research shows that several factors influence the sentencing process: (1) the attitudes of the judge, (2) the administrative context, and (3) the presentence report.

The Attitudes of the Judge

Lawyers know that judges differ in their sentencing decisions. The differences can be explained partly by administrative pressures, conflicting goals of the criminal justice system, and the influence of community values. Sentencing decisions also depend on judges' attitudes about offenders' **blameworthiness**, protecting the community, and the practical implications of the sentence.

When judges think about the blameworthiness of an offender, they typically consider the seriousness of the offense, the offender's criminal history, and the role that the offender played in committing the crime. For example, a judge may impose a harsh sentence on a repeat offender who personally planned and committed a terrible act of violence. Judges also differ in their attitudes toward the need to protect the community. If a judge views a particular offender as dangerous, he or she may decide to incapacitate the offender so that he or she cannot hurt anyone else in the future. Finally, in each case judges also take practical matters into consideration. For example, a judge who is sentencing a mother with children may opt for a different sentence compared to a single woman without children who committed a similar crime. Judges also need to consider the size of probation caseloads and prison crowding when considering which sentence to impose.

The Administrative Context

The administrative context influences judges' sentencing decisions. This point is easy to see when comparing assembly-line-style misdemeanor courts to the more-formal proceedings of felony courts. Misdemeanor courts have limited jurisdiction and can impose sentences of only up to one year in jail. Very few of the cases actually result in

blameworthiness
The amount of blame that the offender deserves for the crime.

Marissa Alexander is released from custody after having been convicted of firing a gun at her estranged husband. She claimed self-defense. Judges must consider blameworthiness in deciding how much punishment is deserved for a crime.

AP Images/Newspaper Member/The Florida Times-Union/Bob Mack

incarceration. Most cases result in less restrictive sanctions, such as fines, restitution, community service, probation, or a combination of punishments. These courts hear about 90 percent of all criminal cases.

Misdemeanor courts are busy places and can spend only a short amount of time on each case. Because weak cases have been filtered out, it is commonly assumed that people appearing in court are either guilty or will plead guilty. Sentencing decisions are mass-produced. The clerk reads the citation, a guilty plea is entered by the defendant, and the judge pronounces the sentence. The court then moves on to the next case. This process is repeated continuously throughout the session.

Felony courts deal with offenders who allegedly committed more-serious crimes. When compared to misdemeanor courts, the atmosphere in felony courts is less chaotic and more formal. Exchange relationships among courtroom actors, such as the judge, prosecutor, and defense attorney, can help bring about plea bargains, which can reduce caseload burdens. Sentencing decisions are shaped, at least in part, by the relationships, negotiations, and agreements among the members of the courtroom work group.

The Presentence Report

presentence report
A report prepared by a probation officer, who investigates a convicted offender's background to help the judge select an appropriate sentence.

When making sentencing decisions, judges use **presentence reports** to help them select an appropriate sentence. These reports are usually written by probation officers, who investigate the convicted person's background, criminal record, job status, and mental health. Based on their findings, probation officers in many states will make a sentence recommendation to the court. These reports are also used to help classify probationers, prisoners, and parolees for treatment and risk assessment. (Presentence reports are fully discussed in Chapter 5.)

The presentence report eases the strain that judges may feel when making a sentencing decision because some of the responsibility is shifted to the probation department. Given the number of available punishment alternatives, presentence reports are helpful to judges because they provide guidance. When thinking about presentence reports, it is important to ask two questions:

1.   Should judges rely so much on the presentence report?
2.   Does the time spent preparing it represent the best use of probation officers' time?

"Do the Right Thing" shows some of the difficulties a judge might face when imposing a sentence with little more than a presentence report to consider.

Sentencing Guidelines

sentencing guidelines
An instrument developed for judges indicating the usual sanctions given previously to particular offenses.

Since the late 1980s, **sentencing guidelines** have been used by several states and the federal government to shape sentencing decisions. States that adopted guidelines did so in hopes of accomplishing various goals; these may include reducing disparity in sentencing for similar offenses, increasing or decreasing punishments for certain types of offenders and offenses, establishing truth-in-sentencing, reducing prison crowding, and making the sentencing process more rational. Although statutes provide a variety of sentencing options for particular crimes, guidelines point the judge to more-specific actions that have been used previously in similar cases.

Legislatures and (in some states and the federal government) commissions construct sentencing guidelines as a grid of two scores. As shown in Table 2.3, one dimension relates to the seriousness of the offense, the other to the offender's criminal history. The offender score is obtained by totaling the points allocated to such factors as the number of juvenile, adult misdemeanor, and adult felony convictions; the number of times incarcerated; the status of the accused at the time of the last offense, whether on probation or parole or escaped from confinement; and employment status or educational achievement. Judges look at the grid to see what sentence should be imposed on a particular offender who has committed a specific offense. Judges may also go outside

Table 2.3 Minnesota Sentencing Guidelines Grid (Presumptive Sentence Length in Months)

The italicized numbers within the grid denote the range within which a judge may sentence without the sentence being deemed a departure. Offenders with no imprisonment felony sentences are subject to jail time according to law.

	LESS SERIOUS ◄────────► MORE SERIOUS						
	CRIMINAL HISTORY SCORE						
	0	**1**	**2**	**3**	**4**	**5**	**6 or more**
Murder, second degree (intentional murder; drive-by shootings)	306 *261–367*	326 *278–391*	346 *295–415*	366 *312–439*	386 *329–363*	406 *346–480[a]*	426 *363–480[a]*
Murder, third degree Murder, second degree (unintentional murder)	150 *128–180*	165 *141–198*	180 *153–216*	195 *166–234*	210 *179–252*	225 *192–270*	240 *204–288*
Assault, first degree Controlled substance crime, first degree	86 *74–103*	98 *84–117*	110 *94–132*	122 *104–146*	134 *114–160*	146 *125–175*	158 *135–189*
Aggravated robbery, first degree Controlled substance crime, second degree	48 *41–57*	58 *50–69*	68 *58–81*	78 *67–93*	88 *75–105*	98 *84–117*	108 *92–129*
Felony DWI	36	42	48	54 *46–64*	60 *51–72*	66 *57–79*	72 *62–86*
Assault, second degree Felon in possession of a firearm	21	27	33	39 *34–46*	45 *39–54*	51 *44–61*	57 *49–68*
Residential burglary Simple robbery	18	23	28	33 *29–39*	38 *33–45*	43 *37–51*	48 *41–57*
Nonresidential burglary	12[b]	15	18	21	24 *21–28*	27 *23–32*	30 *26–36*
Theft crimes (over $2,500)	12[b]	13	15	17	19 *17–22*	21 *18–25*	23 *20–27*
Theft crimes ($2,500 or less) Check forgery ($200–$2,500)	12[b]	12[a]	13	15	17	19	21 *18–25*
Sale of simulated controlled substance	12[b]	12[a]	12[a]	13	15	17	19 *17–22*

☐ Presumptive commitment to state imprisonment. First-degree murder is excluded from the guidelines by law and continues to be a mandatory life sentence.

☐ Presumptive stayed sentence; at the discretion of the judge, up to a year in jail and/or other nonjail sanctions can be imposed as conditions of probation. However, certain offenses in this section of the grid always carry a presumptive commitment to state prison.

[a] M.S. § 244.09 requires the Sentencing Guidelines to provide a range of 15% downward and 20% upward from the presumptive sentence. However, because the statutory maximum sentence for these offenses is no more than 40 years, the range is capped at that number.

[b] One year and one day.

the guidelines if aggravating or mitigating circumstances exist; however, they must provide a written explanation of their reasons for doing so.

Although sentencing guidelines may make sentences more uniform, and thus reduce disparity, many judges object to having their discretion limited in this manner. Discretion still exists in the process, even when sentencing guidelines are used. However, sentencing discretion has shifted from the judge to the prosecutor.[23] The ability of prosecutors to choose the charge and to plea bargain has affected the accused: They now realize that they must plead guilty and cooperate in order to avoid the harsh sentences specified for some crimes.

DO the Right Thing

Seated in her chambers, Judge Carla Tolle read the presentence report of the two young women she would sentence when court resumed. She had not heard these cases. As often happened in this overworked courthouse, the cases had been given to her only for sentencing. Judge Jeremy Johnson had handled the arraignment, plea, and trial.

The codefendants had run a check-fraud scheme and had stolen nearly $6,000 from four local banks. As she read the reports, Judge Tolle noticed that the convicted women looked pretty similar. Each offender had dropped out of high school, had held a series of low-paying jobs, and had one prior conviction for which probation had been imposed.

Then she noticed the difference. Kelby Murphy had pleaded guilty to the charge in exchange for a promise of leniency. Dawn Amaral had been convicted on the same charge after a one-week trial. Judge Tolle pondered the decisions that she would soon have to make. Should Amaral receive a stiffer sentence because she had taken the court's time and resources? Did she have an obligation to impose the light sentence recommended for Murphy by the prosecutor and the defender?

There was a knock on the door. The bailiff stuck his head in. "We're ready, Your Honor."

"Okay, let's go."

Critical Thinking

How would you decide? What factors would weigh in your decision? How would you explain your decision?

UNJUST PUNISHMENT

Unjust punishment can occur because of sentencing disparities and wrongful convictions. The prison population in most states contains a higher proportion of African American and Hispanic men than appears in the general population. Are these sentencing disparities caused by racial prejudice and discrimination, or are other factors at work? Wrongful convictions occur when an innocent person is nonetheless found guilty by plea or verdict. They also include those cases in which the conviction of a truly guilty person is overturned on appeal because of due process errors.

Sentencing Disparity

sentencing disparity
Divergence in the length and types of sentences imposed for the same crime or for crimes of comparable seriousness when no reasonable justification can be discerned.

Sentencing disparities occur when no justification is given for imposing very different penalties on offenders with similar criminal histories who committed the same offense. Disparities can arise because members of certain social groups may commit more crimes than do members of other groups. However, when judges single out offenders because of their race, ethnicity, class, and/or gender, and treat them more harshly during sentencing, these judges are guilty of discrimination.

The current research on sentencing is inconclusive. Nevertheless, studies do show that young black males and Hispanics receive longer prison sentences than do white offenders.[24] Do these disparities stem from the prejudicial attitudes of judges, police, and prosecutors?

Researchers have shown that the relationship between race and sentencing is complex and that judges consider many defendant and case characteristics. Critics argue that judges not only assess legally relevant factors, such as offender blameworthiness, dangerousness, and recidivism risk, but also extralegal factors such as race, gender, and age. The interaction among these many different factors can result in disproportionately severe sentences given to members of certain social groups, such as young African American men.[25] In recent decades, critics have pointed to the laws dealing with the possession and sale of crack cocaine that they believe have resulted in racially based disparity in criminal sentences (see "Focus on Correctional Policy" regarding this issue).

focus on correctional policy

Politics and Sentencing: The Case of Crack Cocaine

The American public first heard about crack cocaine in the mid-1980s. The media reported that it was extremely addictive and cheaper than the powdered form of cocaine. Fear soon spread that crack not only was the drug of choice in the ghetto but was also being used by middle-class, suburban Americans. To address the problem, Congress passed the Anti-Drug Abuse Act in the fall of 1986. The law specified that conviction for possession or distribution of 5 grams of crack cocaine (the weight of about two pennies) would mean a mandatory five-year sentence with no parole. Possession of greater amounts could lead to a life sentence with no chance of parole. At that time people did not seem to notice that the crack penalty equaled a 100:1 ratio, compared with conviction for possession or distribution of the more-expensive powdered cocaine. In other words, before a powdered cocaine user or seller received a five-year sentence, he or she would have to possess 500 grams of the powdered substance.

The impact of the 1986 law was immediate. From 1988 to 1989, the number of drug offenders incarcerated shot up by more than 5,500, at the time the largest one-year increase ever recorded by the Federal Bureau of Prisons. By 2008, nearly 20,000 federal prisoners were serving sentences for crack cocaine offenses. Approximately 82 percent of defendants sentenced in federal court for dealing crack were African American. The disparity between punishments for crack- and powdered-cocaine offenders soon became a major issue for African Americans.

In 2007 the Supreme Court ruled that federal judges could use discretion to shorten prison terms for crack-cocaine offenders (*Kimbrough v. United States*). The ruling was intended to reduce the disparity between crimes involving crack and powdered cocaine. More recently, Congress passed the Fair Sentencing Act of 2010. This new law greatly reduces the powder-to-crack sentencing ratio (from 100:1 to 18:1). The law also eliminates the five-year mandatory minimum sentences for possession of 28 grams or less of crack cocaine with the intent to distribute. While the law should reduce sentencing disparity in future cases, it is not retroactive. This means that approximately 9,000 federal inmates convicted of crack offenses (a large portion of whom are African American) will remain in prison for the time being.

The failure to make the law retroactive has been challenged in court (*United States v. Blewett*). So far, the law has been upheld, and many observers do not expect the Supreme Court to intervene. The Obama administration recognizes that the old law and its 100:1 ratio was unjust, and favors legislative remedies, such as passing a law that would make the Fair Sentencing Act retroactive for some crack offenders. Who would be eligible? That would be determined on a case-by-case basis.

Critical Thinking

1. Does the Fair Sentencing Act adequately address the disparity between the sentences given in crack-cocaine cases and those given in cases involving the powdered form of cocaine?

2. Why did it take lawmakers so long to address this perceived injustice?

3. Should elected officials further reduce the crack-to-powder sentencing ratio? If so, what should the ratio be?

Sources: *Kimbrough v. United States*, 522 U.S. 85 (2007); *United States v. Blewett*, 719 F.3d 482 (2013); Linda Greenhouse, "Crack Cocaine Limbo," *New York Times*, www.nytimes.com/2014/01/06/opinion/greenhouse-crack-cocaine-limbo.html, January 5, 2014; Jay Weaver, "Florida Man Among 8 Whose Harsh Crack Cocaine Sentences Commuted by Obama," *Miami Herald*, www.miamiherald.com/2014/01/04/3852566/florida-man-among-8-whose-harsh.html, January 4, 2014; Charlie Savage, "Obama Commutes Sentences for 8 in Crack Cocaine Cases," *New York Times*, www.nytimes.com/2013/12/20/us/obama-commuting-sentences-in-crack-cocaine-cases.html, December 19, 2013.

Wrongful Conviction

A serious dilemma for the criminal justice system concerns people who endure **wrongful conviction.** Whereas the public expresses much concern over those who "beat the system" and go free, people pay comparatively little attention to those who are innocent yet convicted. Such cases can be corrected by decisions of the courts or through pardon or clemency decisions by governors (state cases) or the president (federal cases). But achieving correction through either method can be very difficult.

The development of DNA technology has increased the number of people who have been convicted by juries and later exonerated by science (see "Focus on Correctional

wrongful conviction
A conviction that occurs when an innocent person is found guilty by either plea or verdict.

Wiley Bridgeman, left, embraces his brother, Kwame Ajamu, as they walk from a Cleveland, Ohio, courthouse, free men. After spending 39 years in prison, the two brothers were exonerated of their 1975 murder conviction. Eddie Vernon, who swore at the original trial that the brothers committed the crime, had just recanted his testimony and admitted that the prosecutors told him what to say on the stand.

AP Images/Phil Long, File

Technology"). However, because the great majority of cases do not produce biological material to be tested, one can only speculate about the error rate in these cases. As of January 2015, 325 innocent people had been released from prison after DNA testing excluded them as perpetrators of the rapes and murders for which they had been convicted and imprisoned.[26] Twenty of the exonerated had served time on death row. In addition to DNA testing, many of the exonerations have resulted from the discovery that police and prosecutors had ignored or hidden evidence or that the conviction was based on testimony from an untruthful informant.

focus on correctional technology

DNA Testing of Evidence

The use of DNA (deoxyribonucleic acid) testing of evidence presented to juries has greatly increased during recent decades. First used in 1989, this technology identifies people through their distinctive gene patterns (also called genotypic features). DNA is the basic component of all chromosomes; all the cells in an individual's body, including those in skin, blood, organs, and semen, contain the same unique DNA. The characteristics of certain segments of DNA vary from person to person and thus form a genetic "fingerprint." For example, forensic labs can analyze samples of hair and then compare them with those of suspects.

Critical Thinking

1. Do issues of rights and privacy arise when DNA testing is used to identify perpetrators of criminal acts?

2. Alternatively, do convicted felons have a right to have their DNA tested and compared to the evidence presented by prosecutors?

Sixty-five percent of the people exonerated by DNA testing have been financially compensated. Laws to compensate people who were wrongly incarcerated have been passed by 29 states, the federal government, and the District of Columbia. The amounts of these awards differ from state to state.

Why do wrongful convictions occur? According to the Innocence Project, a non-profit organization that is dedicated to exonerating wrongfully convicted individuals, a number of factors lead to wrongful convictions, including eyewitness error, unvalidated or improper forensic science, false confessions, and informant testimony. Beyond the fact that the real criminal is still free in such cases, the standards of our society are damaged when an innocent person has been wrongly convicted.

Whether unjust punishments result from racial discrimination or wrongful convictions, they do not serve the ideals of justice. Unjust punishments raise fundamental questions about the criminal justice system and the society that it serves.

Summary

1 Know about the "Age of Reason" and its effect on corrections.

In the latter part of the eighteenth century, the Enlightenment (Age of Reason) brought changes in penal policy. Rather than stressing physical punishment of the offender, influential thinkers sought methods for the reforming of offenders.

2 Understand the major goals of punishment.

The four major goals of punishment are retribution (or deserved punishment), deterrence (both general and specific), incapacitation, and rehabilitation. These goals differ in focus. Rehabilitation and specific deterrence focus on the offender. Retribution, general deterrence, and incapacitation focus on the crime. An emerging goal of punishment, restoration, focuses on the needs of the crime victim and the community.

3 Be familiar with the different criminal sanctions that are used.

Criminal sanctions can be placed along a continuum, ranging from probation to incarceration. Although far less common, the death penalty is also used in the United States. *Intermediate sanctions* is a term used to describe penalties, such as fines and community service, that are more severe than probation but less punitive than incarceration.

4 Explain the types of sentences that judges hand down.

Judges generally hand down three types of sentences. Indeterminate sentences stipulate a minimum and maximum term that convicted offenders will serve in prison. For example, a prisoner may receive a sentence ranging from 2 to 10 years. The prisoner's release is usually determined by a parole board. Determinate sentences result in a fixed period of incarceration, such as 5 years. Once the specified amount of time has been served, the inmate is automatically released. Mandatory sentences (or "mandatory-minimum sentences") require that an inmate serve a minimum amount of time. "Three strikes and you're out" laws are one example of a mandatory sentence.

5 Discuss the problem of unjust punishment.

Unjust punishments can occur because of sentencing disparities and wrongful convictions. Sentencing disparities occur when offenders with similar criminal histories who commit the same offense receive different penalties without explanation. Disparities are considered discriminatory when judges base their decisions to hand down different sentences on the race, ethnicity, class, and/or gender of the offender. Wrongful convictions occur when an innocent person is found guilty by either plea or verdict. DNA evidence has helped exonerate innocent people who have been wrongly convicted. To create a system that is more just, reformers want to reduce sentencing disparities and wrongful convictions.

Key Terms

blameworthiness 49

determinate sentence 44

Enlightenment (Age of Reason) 34

general deterrence 38

good time 45

incapacitation 38

indeterminate sentence 43

intermediate sanctions 45

lex talionis 33

mandatory sentence 44

presentence report 50

presumptive sentence 44

probation 46

rehabilitation 39

restoration 40

retribution 37

selective incapacitation 39

sentencing disparity 52

sentencing guidelines 50

shock probation 46

specific deterrence 38

utilitarianism 36

wrongful conviction 53

For Discussion

1. What should be the dominant goal of the criminal sanction? Why?

2. What are the prospects for rehabilitating offenders? Should we assume that all offenders can be rehabilitated?

3. How much discretion should judges have when imposing sentences? What justifies the latitude given to judges?

4. Suppose that you are a state lawmaker. What considerations will influence your vote on the process by which criminal sanctions are set?

Notes

[1] Robert Allen, "Jury Finds Bob Bashara Guilty of First-Degree Murder," *Detroit Free Press*, www.freep.com/story/news/local/michigan /wayne/2014/12/18/bob-bashara-jane-bashara-murder-trial /20584559, December 18, 2014.

[2] Gina Damron and Elisha Anderson, "Memorable Quotes from Bob Bashara's Sentencing," *Detroit Free Press*, www.freep.com/story/news /local/michigan/detroit/2015/01/15/bashara-sentencing-quotes /21835503, January 15, 2015.

[3] Edward M. Peters, "Prisons Before the Prison: The Ancient and Medieval Worlds," in *The Oxford History of the Prison*, edited by Norval Morris and Michael Tonry (New York: Oxford University Press, 1995), 5.

[4] Peters, "Prisons Before the Prison," pp. 3–47.

[5] Mark M. Lanier and Stuart Henry, *Essential Criminology* (Boulder, CO: Westview, 1998), 67.

[6] Harry E. Barnes and Negley K. Teeters, *New Horizons in Criminology* (New York: Prentice-Hall, 1944), 461.

[7] Gilbert Geis, "Jeremy Bentham," in *Pioneers in Criminology*, edited by Herman Mannheim (Montclair, NJ: Patterson Smith, 1973), 54.

[8] Michael Ignatieff, *A Just Measure of Pain* (New York: Pantheon, 1978), 27.

[9] Herbert L. Packer, *The Limits of Criminal Sanction* (Stanford, CA: Stanford University Press, 1968), 33–34.

[10] Andrew von Hirsch, *Doing Justice* (New York: Hill & Wang, 1976), 49.

[11] Robert Martinson, "What Works? Questions and Answers About Prison Reform," *Public Interest* 35 (Spring 1974): 22–54.

[12] Leena Kurki, "Restorative and Community Justice in the United States," in *Crime and Justice: A Review of Research,* vol. 27, edited by Michael Tonry (Chicago: University of Chicago Press, 2000), 235–303.

[13] Kathleen Daly and Gitana Proietti-Scifoni, "Reparation and Restoration," in *The Oxford Handbook of Crime and Criminology*, edited by Michael Tonry (New York and Oxford: Oxford University Press, 2011).

[14] Heather Strang, Lawrence W. Sherman, Evan Mayo-Wilson, Daniel Woods, and Barak Ariel, *Restorative Justice Conferencing (RJC) Using Face-to-Face Meetings of Offenders and Victims: Effects of Offender Recidivism and Victim Satisfaction. A Systematic Review* (Oslo: Campbell Systematic Reviews, 2013).

[15] Lauren E. Glaze and Danielle Kaeble, *Correctional Populations in the United States, 2013* (Washington, DC: U.S. Government Printing Office, 2014), 2.

[16] Christian Henrichson and Ruth Delaney, *The Price of Prisons: What Incarceration Costs Taxpayers* (New York: Vera Institute of Justice, 2012), 9.

[17] John L. Worrall, "The Effect of Three-Strikes Legislation on Serious Crime in California," *Journal of Criminal Justice* 32 (July–August 2004): 283–96.

[18] Glaze and Kaeble, *Correctional Populations in the United States, 2013*, p. 2.

[19] Death Penalty Information Center, *The Death Penalty in 2014: Year End Report* (Washington, DC: Author, 2014), 3.

[20] See www.deathpenaltyinfo.org, January 22, 2015.

[21] Ibid.

[22] Jeremy Travis, "Invisible Punishment: An Instrument of Social Exclusion," in *Invisible Punishment: The Collateral Consequences of Mass Imprisonment*, edited by Marc Mauer and Meda Chesney-Lind (New York: New Press, 2002), 17–18.

[23] John Wooldredge and Timothy Griffin, "Displaced Discretion Under Ohio Sentencing Guidelines," *Journal of Criminal Justice* 33 (2005): 301.

[24] Darrell Steffensmeier, Jeffrey Ulmer, and John Kramer, "The Interaction of Race, Gender, and Age in Criminal Sentencing: The Punishment Cost of Being Young, Black, and Male," *Criminology* 36 (November 1998): 763–97.

[25] Samuel Walker, Cassia Spohn, and Miriam DeLone, *The Color of Justice* (Belmont, CA: Wadsworth, 1996), 154.

[26] See www.innocenceproject.org, January 22, 2015.

CORRECTIONS IN THE COMMUNITY

Part Two Although Americans tend to think of prisons when they hear the word *corrections*, most people under correctional supervision live among us in the community on probation or parole. Therefore, it is at the local community level that we begin our examination of policies and practices in jails and other short-term facilities (Chapter 3), probation and intermediate sanctions (Chapter 4), and the supervision by probation officers of offenders in the community (Chapter 5). ■

Jails: Corrections at the Local Level

The largest jail in the world occupies 1.5 million square feet, as large as Pittsburgh's new convention center. Called the "Twin Towers Correctional Facility," because of its two large towers, the facility is run by the Los Angeles County Sheriff's Department. Built in 1997 to hold about 4,000 people, it may be the largest jail in the world, but it is only one of nine correctional facilities under the authority of the sheriff of Los Angeles County, and it handles only a small part of the county's jail workload. The population of people under the sheriff's correctional authority numbers nearly 22,000, and the jail system processes about 400,000 people through its doors every year—the

After reading this chapter you should be able to . . .

1 Describe the history of the jail and its current function in the criminal justice system.

2 Describe who is in jail and why they are there.

3 Discuss the kinds of jails in the United States.

4 List the main issues facing jails today.

5 Outline the problem of bail and list the main alternatives to bail.

6 Outline the problems of jail administration.

7 Describe new developments in jails and jail programs.

8 Critically assess the future of the jail.

The Los Angeles County Men's Central Jail is the largest in the world. American jails are typically overcrowded, frequently brutalizing, and often neglected.

David Bro/ZUMA Press/Corbis Wire/Corbis

...ulation of Omaha, Nebraska. Until ...ntly, the Los Angeles jail population was ...ning, down one-fifth from two decades ...¹ But today this jail is growing again, ...alifornia has moved 12,000 people from ...risons to its jails in order to comply with ...urt order to reduce prison crowding.²

(See Focus on Correctional Policy.) So California's most important local jail just got more important, not just for Los Angeles but for the whole state.

Jails are a strange correctional hybrid: part detention center for people awaiting trial, part penal institution for sentenced...

(continued from previous page)

misdemeanants, part refuge for social misfits taken off the streets. Jails hold men, women, and juveniles of all colors who have been accused of violating the law. Jails are the traditional dumping ground not only for criminals but also for petty hustlers, derelicts, junkies, prostitutes, the mentally ill, and disturbers of the peace, mainly from the poorer sections of cities. Thus, jails' functions include those of the workhouse of the past.

Students interested in improving corrections during their future careers could find no area in more obvious need of reform than U.S. jails. Among the institutions and programs of the corrections system, jails are the one most neglected by scholars and officials and least known to the public. Uniformly jam-packed and frequently brutalizing, jails almost never enhance life. Many criminal justice researchers agree that of all correctional agencies, jails are the oldest, most numerous, most criticized, and most stubbornly resistant to reform.

With an estimated 11.7 million jail admissions per year, more people directly experience jails than experience prisons, mental hospitals, and halfway houses combined.[3] Even if we consider that some of these individuals are admitted more than once, probably at least 7–8 million different people are detained in a jail at some time during the year.

In this chapter we examine problems of operating jails and how some people avoid pretrial detention. We also raise questions about the role of corrections in this type of facility, where prisoners generally sit idle without access to treatment and rehabilitative programs. ■

THE CONTEMPORARY JAIL: ENTRANCE TO THE SYSTEM

Jails are the entryway to corrections. They house both accused individuals awaiting trial and sentenced offenders, usually serving one-year terms or less. People appealing sentences are often held in jail as well, as are those awaiting transfer to other jurisdictions. Nationally, about 731,208 people are under jail authority in the nation's 2,830 jails on any one day; more than 92 percent of them are behind bars, with the remainder under some form of community release.[4]

Jail populations have actually been in decline for the last few years, just as other correctional populations have declined. Today's jail population is down almost 8 percent from its peak in 2008, and nationally, jails are filled at only 84 percent capacity. This is good news for most jail systems because for almost three decades, jails have been the target of repeated criticism for overcrowding and brutal conditions.

Jails are perhaps the most frustrating component of corrections for people who want to apply treatment efforts to help offenders. Of the enormous numbers of people in jail, many need a helping hand. But the unceasing human flow usually does not allow time for such help—nor are the resources available in most instances.

Origins and Evolution

Jails in the United States descend directly from feudal practices in twelfth-century England. At that time, an officer of the crown, the *reeve,* was appointed in each *shire* (what we call a county) to collect taxes, keep the peace, and operate the *gaol* (jail). The *shire reeve* (from which the word *sheriff* evolved), among other duties, caught and held in custody, until a formal court hearing determined guilt or innocence, people accused of breaking the king's law. With the development of the workhouse in the sixteenth century, the sheriff took on added responsibilities for vagrants and the unemployed who were sent there. The sheriff made a living by collecting fees from inmates and by hiring out prison labor.

English settlers brought these traditions and institutions with them to the American colonies. After the American Revolution, the local community elected law enforcement officials—particularly sheriffs and constables—but the functions of the jail remained unchanged. Jails were used to detain accused persons awaiting trial, as well as to shelter misfits who could not be taken care of by their families, churches, or other groups.

The jails were often in the sheriffs' homes and run like the sheriffs' households. Detainees were free to dress as they wished and to contribute their own food and necessities: "So long as they did not cost the town money, inmates could make living arrangements as pleasant and homelike as they wished."[5] Local revenues paid room and board for detainees who could not make independent contributions.

In the 1800s the jail began to change in response to the penitentiary movement. Jails retained their pretrial detention function but also became facilities for offenders serving short terms, as well as housing vagrants, debtors, beggars, prostitutes, and the mentally ill. Although the fee system survived, other changes took place. The juvenile reformatory movement and the creation of hospitals for the criminally insane during the latter part of the nineteenth century siphoned off some former jail inhabitants. The development of probation also removed some offenders, as did adult reformatories and state farms, and inmates were now segregated by sex. However, even with these innovations, the overwhelming majority of accused and convicted misdemeanants were held in jail. This pattern has continued into modern times.

Population Characteristics

Not until 1978 did the Bureau of the Census, for the Bureau of Justice Statistics, conduct a complete nationwide census of jails. Repeated every five years by local officials, the census collects information on inmates in jails that hold people beyond arraignment (that is, usually more than 48 hours). Excluded from the count are people in federal and state facilities. An annual survey of the top one-third largest jails, which hold about 75 percent of the inmate population, supplements these five-year nationwide counts.

The most recent National Jail Census shows that about 86 percent of inmates are men, nearly two-thirds are under 35 years old, almost half are white, and most have little education and a very low income.[6] The demographic characteristics of the jail population differ from those of the national population in many ways: People

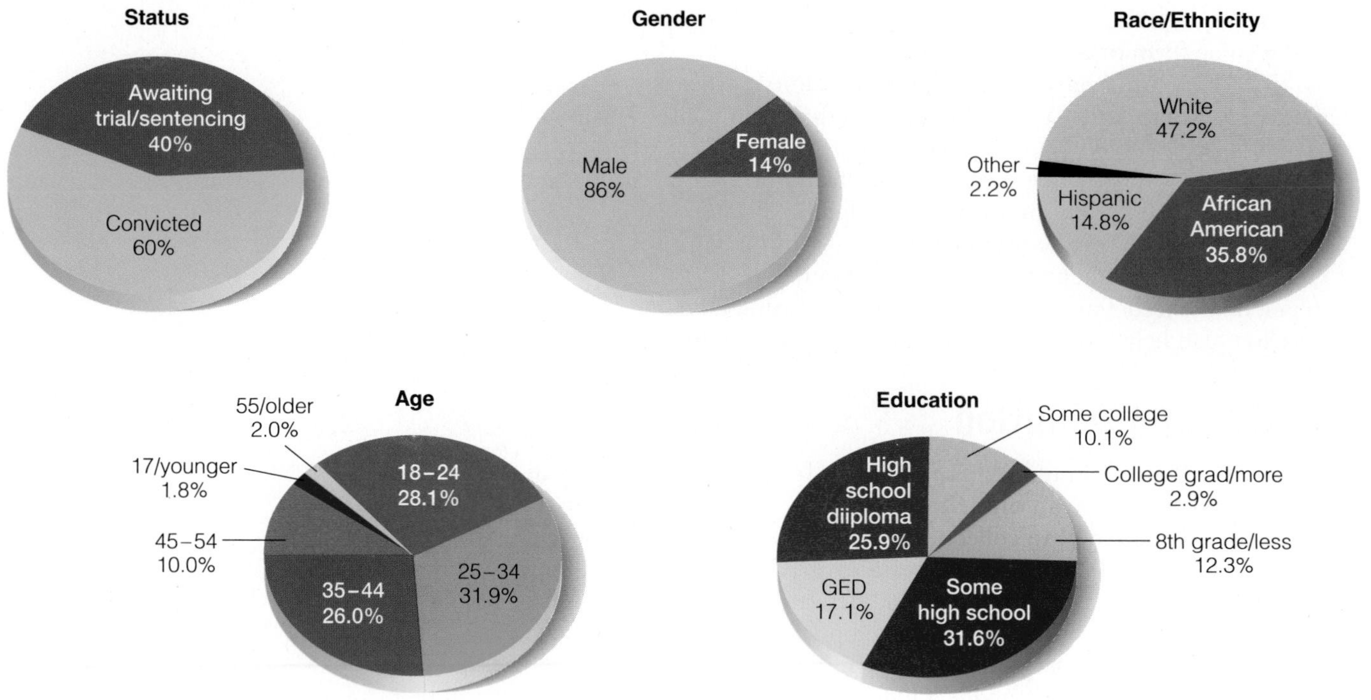

FIGURE 3.1

Characteristics of Adult Jail Inmates in U.S. Jails

Compared with the American population as a whole, jails are disproportionately inhabited by men, minorities, the poorly educated, and those with low incomes.

Source: Todd D. Minton and Daniela Golinelli, *Jail Inmates at Midyear 2013—Statistical Tables* (Washington, DC: Bureau of Justice Statistics, 2014); BJS *Bulletin*, May 2013.

in jail are younger and disproportionately people of color, and most are unmarried (see **Figure 3.1**). It is notable that the gender mix in jails has been changing. Since 2010, the number of men in jails has declined by 4.2 percent while the number of women has *increased* by almost 11 percent.[7]

As with prisons, jail populations vary from region to region and from state to state. The proportion of a state's population in jail, known as the *jail rate*, is high in the West and South (see **Figure 3.2**). In many states where prisons are filled to capacity, sentenced felons awaiting transfer sit in jails.

One of the most troubling trends in jails is the increasing rate of incarceration for African Americans. In 1990 the jail incarceration rate for African Americans was 560 per 100,000. Since then the rate has increased by about 50 percent, to 831 per 100,000. The incarceration rate for white Americans has gone from 89 per 100,000 to 167 per 100,000, more than an 80-percent increase. Most of the increase in jail population is because of the great increase in the number of African Americans incarcerated. What might explain this situation?

Administration

lockup
A facility authorized to hold people before court appearance for up to 48 hours. Most lockups (also called drunk tanks or holding tanks) are administered by local police agencies.

Of the 2,830 jails in the United States, 80 percent have a county-level jurisdiction, and most are administered by an elected sheriff. An additional 600 or so municipal jails are in operation. Only in six states—Alaska, Connecticut, Delaware, Hawaii, Rhode Island, and Vermont—are jails for adults administered by the state government. There are also an estimated 13,500 police **lockups** (or drunk tanks) and similar holding facilities authorized to detain people for up to 48 hours. The Federal Bureau of Prisons operates 11 jails for detained prisoners only, holding 11,000 inmates. There are 37 privately

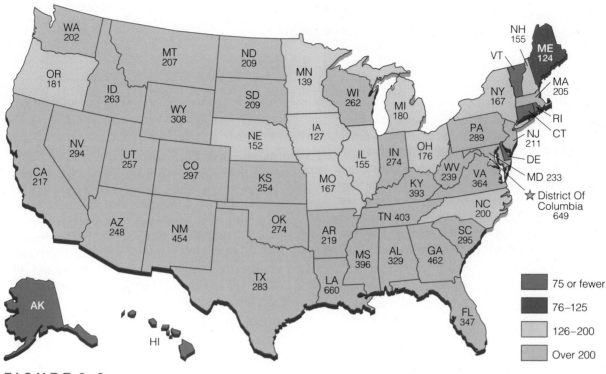

FIGURE 3.2
People Incarcerated in Local Jails per 100,000 Population, by State
What accounts for the fact that incarceration rates in jails differ from state to state?

Note: Six states—Alaska, Connecticut, Delaware, Hawaii, Rhode Island, and Vermont—have integrated jail–prison systems; therefore, information for these states is not given.

Source: Todd D. Minton, *Jail Inmates at Midyear 2012: Statistical Tables* (Washington, DC: Bureau of Justice Statistics, May 2013).

operated jails, under contract to state or local governments, and they house 1 percent of the total jail population.[8]

The capacity of jails varies greatly. The 50 largest jurisdictions hold almost one-third of the nation's jailed inmates. The two jurisdictions with the most inmates, Los Angeles County and New York City, together hold approximately 36,000 inmates in multiple jails, or 5 percent of the national total. For example, Rikers Island, the New York City Correctional Facility, holds more than 14,000 people, but most jails are much smaller, with two-fifths holding fewer than 50 people. However, these small facilities are dwindling in number because of new jail construction and the creation of regional, multicounty facilities.

As facilities to detain accused people awaiting trial, jails customarily have been run by law enforcement agencies. We might reasonably expect that the agency that arrests and transports defendants to court should also administer the facility that holds them. Typically, however, neither sheriffs nor deputies have much interest in corrections. They often think of themselves as police officers and of the jail as merely an extension of their law enforcement activities. In some major cities, municipal departments of correction, rather than the police, manage the jails.

Jail administrators face problems that good management practices cannot always overcome. One problem is that jails hold people for a variety of reasons. About 17,000 of those confined in jails are being held on immigration and customs violations. Another 66,000 are under jail supervision while living in the community.[9] These people count in the jail population, even though they are under electronic monitoring or some other sort of noncustodial program. Such special populations have further complicated the problem of jail management.

Another problem is that many jails still receive funds through a **fee system**, whereby the costs of housing, food, and services are averaged and a standard amount

fee system
A system by which jail operations are funded by a set amount paid per day for each prisoner held.

careers in Corrections

CORRECTIONAL OFFICER—LOCAL JAILS

Nature of the Work

Most jails are operated by county governments, and three-quarters of jails are under the jurisdiction of an elected sheriff. The approximately 470,000 correctional officers in the jail system admit and process more than 11 million people a year in either pretrial or sentenced categories. Officers must supervise individuals during the most dangerous, postarrest phase, when arrestees may be both stressed and violent. The constant turnover of the jail population is an additional problem in terms of maintaining security and stability.

Required Qualifications

A candidate for employment must be at least 18 to 21 years of age, be a U.S. citizen, have a high school education, have no felony convictions, and have some work experience. Candidates must be in good health and meet formal physical fitness, eyesight, and hearing standards. Some local departments provide training for officers according to criteria set by the American Jail Association. In some states,

regional training academies are available to local correctional agencies. On-the-job training is a major resource for officer candidates.

Earnings and Job Outlook

Employment of correctional officers is projected to grow 5 percent from 2012 to 2022, slower than the average for all occupations. Although budget constraints and a falling crime rate will require fewer workers, job openings will continue to become available because the dangers associated with the job cause many to leave the occupation each year. The median annual wage for correctional officers and jailers is $39,040. The lowest 10 percent earn less than $26,040, and the top 10 percent earn more than $67,250.

More Information

For more information, see the *Occupational Outlook Handbook*, "Correctional Officers—Local Jails."

Source: Bureau of Labor Statistics: *Occupational Outlook Handbook.*

(say, $10 per day per prisoner) is remitted to the sheriff's department. This creates an incentive for poor jails to skimp on food, services, and prisoner support. Often, the sheriff uses money saved on housing prisoners to augment the kinds of law enforcement services that attract public support and are therefore helpful at the polls. See "Careers in Corrections" for more information about working in a local jail.

The American jail is often called the ultimate ghetto because most of the more than 700,000 people in jail are poor. They are held in jail awaiting disposition of their cases, serving sentences under one year, or awaiting transfer to state prison.

Jails have "holding cells" where last night's arrestees are kept as they await their first appearance before a judge. The holding cell in Muskegon County (Portland) Oregon is typical for its bareness and sense of desperation.

Ken Stevens/Mlive.Com/Landov

Regional Jails

Most local jails are located away from major population centers, and many hold as few as 30 people. Although the state may provide a portion of their operating funds, the smallest jails lack essential services, such as medical care, that must be provided no matter how few people may need them.

One recent trend designed to remedy these problems is regionalization: the creation of combined municipal–county or multicounty jails. This multijurisdictional or **regional jail**, fiscally sound though it may be, has been slow to catch on because it negatively affects several interest groups. Local political and correctional leaders do not want to give up their autonomy and/or their control over patronage jobs, and reformers often object to moving inmates away from their communities. Citizens who oppose having regional jails "in their backyard" make finding locations to build regional jails difficult. Nevertheless, the number of jails in the United States actually dropped in the mid-1990s, as outmoded facilities were closed in favor of building new, always larger— and often regional—replacement facilities. Today, the 200 largest jails house more than more than half of all those in jail.

A new trend is for regional jails to be privately run, under a contract with the local government. Advocates for private jails point out that local governments, strapped for cash, can operate their jails at less cost if they contract with a private company to build and run the jail. Private companies like to build their jails in depressed rural areas where construction costs and labor are both cheaper. Hard-hit rural economies are tempted by the promise of the boost to the local economy that private jails seem to offer.

But the experience of privatization has not been uniformly positive. Critics say that private companies make their money by paying staff less to work there and by skimping on services. Moreover, the private contract creates a perverse incentive to keep the jail full, no matter what. Many local rural areas have found that that their economies do better with other kinds of economic development strategies.

regional jail
Facility operated under a joint agreement between two or more government units, with a jail board drawn from representatives of the participating jurisdictions, and having varying authority over policy, budget, operations, and personnel.

PRETRIAL DETENTION

Imagine that you have been arrested by the police and accused of a crime. They have handcuffed you, read you your rights, and taken you to the station for booking. Frightened, you have a hundred questions, but the police treat you as if your fears were

focus on correctional policy

California Turns to Jails to Deal with Crowding

In 2011 the U.S. Supreme Court ordered the California Department of Corrections to reduce its overcrowding by cutting the prison population by more than 10,000 within six months, and eventually releasing as many as 33,000 people from its prison system over the next two years. California Governor Jerry Brown responded by promoting a new policy called "Public Safety Realignment." Under the policy, thousands of nonserious felons are sentenced to county-level penalties, operated by a community corrections partnership (probation, jails, and community services).

Many of these felons will be supervised by probation, but if the sentence calls for confinement, the person is sent to the local jail. When people under local supervision violate the terms of their sentences, they must be sentenced to local jail instead of state prison. Thus, the Realignment Act forces local authorities to deal with most of the people convicted of crimes locally, and to handle supervision and misconduct locally as well. In the first eight months of the act, the state's prison population came down by more than 28,000, but California's jail population has gone up by more than 10,000.

The policy is called realignment because it attempts to put the incentives for costs savings where they really count. In California, county-level judicial and probation systems play a major role in the size of the prison system by sentencing people to prison and revoking them from probation. Because the state pays for the costs of the prison system, these county officials have no incentive to restrict the number of people they send to state prison. Realignment keeps offenders in the community and provides additional funding to help counties accommodate the influx of people. In the first year of realignment, $400 million was provided to the counties, growing annually to more than $1 billion by 2013–2014. These funds can be used to expand staff and build new programs, with the aim of reducing recidivism.

Realignment makes sense to a lot of people. By requiring the counties to handle the bulk of the correctional population, there will be a pressure to innovate, reduce recidivism, and engage in better programming. Sheriffs have been generally supportive of the change, but many of them worry about deteriorating conditions in the local jails. These facilities had already been crowded, and many of them are old. Sheriffs believe that the additional money for programs is a good thing, but to be fully effective, additional jail capacity may need to be built.

Critical Thinking

1. How does it affect the traditional mission of jails to have so many state prisoners housed there?
2. What are the ripple effects for the local criminal justice system under realignment?
3. What new policies are needed to support the changes in California's jail system?

Source: Joan Petersilia, *Voices from the Field: How California Stakeholders View Public Safety Realignment* (Palo Alto: Stanford Law School, 2013).

---

irrelevant to their work. You may be angry with yourself for what you have done. You may be frustrated that you cannot seem to control the flow of procedure: fingerprints, mug shots, long waits while detectives and prosecutors discuss you without acknowledging your presence. Slowly you begin to understand that you have acquired a new status: accused offender.

Then you are taken to the detention section of the jail. If it is an advanced facility, you are placed in a holding room for an intake interview. There your situation is explained to you, you are asked questions about your background that will help determine how best to manage you while you are in jail, and you are told what you can expect next. If, however, you are in one of many jails with no formal intake procedure, you are simply put in the holding tank. If you are a man, several strangers will likely be in the cell with you, men whose stories you do not know and whose behavior you cannot predict. If you are a woman, you probably will be by yourself. In either case, once the guard leaves, you are on your own behind bars, and the full extent of your situation begins to sink in. This can be an especially trying period for those detainees who are thrust into a hostile and threatening environment, as discussed in "Do the Right Thing."

DO the Right Thing

Some jails are strapped for cash. With the economy struggling and lots of fiscal pressure on local government, jail administrators are being asked to cut costs. Already, there are laws that require people who are sentenced to jail to pay the daily costs of their stay in jail—as much as $80 per day. One California sheriff had a great idea: Why not charge some people (who can afford it) a premium to be incarcerated—and then make sure their incarceration is as soft and problem-free as possible? This idea is called "pay to stay," and it allows people to cover the costs of their incarceration and receive better treatment (better cells and food)—and it also adds money to the jail coffers.

Critics say this is unfair—well-to-do people should not be able to buy their way out of jail conditions, the equivalent of flying first-class. Proponents say that it imposes an extra fine on people who can afford it, which then goes to reduce the costs of jail for all the taxpayers.

You are a jail administrator, running a jail that is in financial trouble. Some members of the local city council have asked you whether they should implement a "pay-to-stay" program in the jail, providing an upgraded jail experience for $100 per day. The council is split; they want to know your advice.

Critical Thinking

1. Should local jails provide better incarceration conditions for people who can afford to pay for them?
2. What are the ethics of this policy?

Source: Robert Weisberg, "Pay-to-Stay in California Jails and the Value of Systematic Self-Embarrassment," *Michigan Law Review First Impressions* 106 (no. 55, 2007).

In such circumstances, many people panic. Consider the experience of Jimmy James, described in "Focus on Correctional Practice." He had never been jailed before, and his "legs shook as he walked into the jail's administrative area." In fact, the hours immediately following arrest are often a time of crisis, stemming from the arrested person's sense of vulnerability and hopelessness, fear of lost freedom, and sheer terror. One-third of the deaths that occur in jails are suicides.[10] Not surprisingly, most of these suicides happen within the first 6–10 hours after lockup, and most psychotic episodes occur during or just after jail intake.

Other factors can exacerbate the crisis brought on by arrest and detention. Often the arrestee is intoxicated or on drugs, a state that may have contributed to the crime for which the person is being held. Sometimes the criminal behavior stems from an emotional instability that may worsen in detention. Especially for young offenders, the oppressive reality can trigger debilitating depression. Unquestionably one of the most crucial times for arrestees is the period immediately following arrest.

Special Problems of Detainees

Beyond the initial crisis of being arrested and jailed, people who are detained for an extended period often face serious problems. The most significant are mental health problems, substance dependency, medical needs, and legal problems. Because so many jail inmates have these problems, jails have often been referred to as the social agency of last resort.

MENTAL HEALTH PROBLEMS Growing attention is being paid to the mental health of arrestees whose behavior,

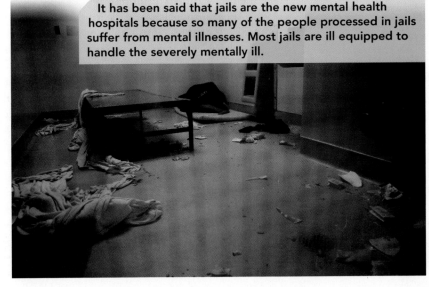

It has been said that jails are the new mental health hospitals because so many of the people processed in jails suffer from mental illnesses. Most jails are ill equipped to handle the severely mentally ill.

Patrick T. Fallon/Bloomberg/Getty Images

focus on correctional practice

Jimmy's First Day in Jail

Jimmy James sat in the back of the Mountain View police car, his hands cuffed behind his back. He had never been arrested before, and thoughts about jail tormented his mind. When Jimmy saw news reports depicting the crowded conditions and violence, he didn't pay much attention. The trauma of confinement was the furthest thing from his mind. Yet he found trouble by downloading nude pictures from the Internet. Facts later revealed that the girls in the pictures were underage, and Jimmy now faced felony charges for child pornography.

The police officers drove in to a basement garage and parked their vehicle. After one of the officers opened the car's rear door, Jimmy stepped out, his heart pounding. The officer gripped Jimmy by the handcuff, making him feel as if he were a dog on a leash. The officer guided Jimmy into an elevator. When the door opened again, Jimmy saw the madness of the large King County Jail.

Jimmy's legs shook as he walked into the jail's administrative area. His first stop was booking. To his right were prisoners packed in a series of open holding cages. The cages resembled the dog pound, he thought, though instead of yelping and barking dogs, Jimmy heard the blustering cacophony that came from scores of young, seemingly angry men. He hoped the officers would not lock him inside with the other prisoners.

As the jail staff took Jimmy into custody, the officers lost interest in him. He was fingerprinted, positioned for his mug shot, and then led toward the bullpens.

"Can I go into that one?" Jimmy gestured toward the bullpen that held only three prisoners seated on a bench, each of whom looked contrite.

"No can do," the jailer said. "That's the misdemeanor tank. You're in with the felons, Class A."

The jailer unlocked the gate to the most crowded cage. "Step inside," the jailer ordered.

Jimmy hesitated, and the prisoners taunted him. "Step inside, bitch," he heard one prisoner yell. "Don't get scared now. What is it, homey, you too good to be in here with us?"

"Get in," the jailer ordered.

Jimmy walked into the cage. Once the jailer locked the gate behind him, Jimmy passed his cuffs through the bars and the jailer freed his wrists. Then the jailer walked away, leaving the prisoners to themselves.

The crowd of strangers frightened Jimmy. He was 21, shorter than average height and with a slender build. His sand-colored hair was thinning prematurely. He didn't have anywhere to sit, so he walked toward the back of the cell and leaned against the wall.

A larger prisoner stepped toward Jimmy. "What up, big dog?"

Jimmy didn't know how to respond. He nodded his head.

"Where you from?"

Jimmy didn't want to talk to anyone. He stood silent against the wall, with hunched shoulders, and bowed his head toward the floor.

---

while not seriously criminal, is socially bizarre—those who are only partially clothed, who speak gibberish or talk loudly to themselves, who make hostile gestures, and so on. These people, whose behavior is unpredictable and to some extent uncontrollable, formerly were transported to mental institutions, where they could be treated. But with the nationwide deinstitutionalization movement, they have become outpatients of society, and they often spend time in jail instead of receiving the psychiatric treatment they once might have received. Estimates are that almost two-thirds of jail prisoners have a history of mental problems; for one-fifth of people in jails, there is a very recent history of mental disorder.[11] Nevertheless, fewer than half of jails offer any form of psychological care at all, and less than 10 percent of jail inmates receive any form of mental health treatment.[12]

Observers say the number of inmates considered mentally ill is increasing. However, police have few alternatives to confinement for people who behave oddly or self-destructively, even if they are more nuisances than criminals. Furthermore, unstable people often respond to the stress of jail with emotional outbursts and irrational behavior. Jails not only draw from but also add to the ranks of the mentally disturbed.

Most jails lack the resources to provide care for mentally ill offenders. Three-fourths of all jails have no rehabilitative staff, and among the remainder the vast majority of

"I'm sayin'," the aggressive prisoner persisted, "you ain't tryin' to talk?"

Jimmy kept silent.

"Okay, okay," the prisoner said. "I feel ya. But check dis out. Wussup wit dat watch?"

Jimmy looked up, realizing his efforts at disappearing were not working. "What do you mean?"

"I'm sayin', wassup wit dat watch? You know some'nes gonna take it up off you once you get to the block."

"Why?"

"You's in jail, fool. Straight gangstas up in here. Best let me hold it for you. I'm a take care it, make sure you get it back when your daddy post bail."

Jimmy thought for a split second. He didn't want any problems. The watch wasn't fancy, just a simple digital model with an alarm. Knowing he probably wouldn't see it again, he unfastened the Velcro band and handed it over.

"Dat's wassup, homey." The prisoner strapped the prize on his wrist. "I'm a take good care you up in here. What dey got you up in here for, youngun?"

"Internet porn."

"Internet porn. Wus dat?"

"Internet porn, you know, downloading nude pictures from the Web."

"They be lockin' mothafuckas up for dat?"

"Well, the models were underage."

The prisoner smiled. "Oh, you be likin' dem kids."

"I didn't know the models were underage."

"Uh-huh. Was dey little girls or little boys?"

"They were young women. I'm not gay, you know."

"Ain't no one sayin' you was gay. I's just axin', dat's all. But check dis out, youngun. When we gets up on da block, don't be talkin' 'bout your case. Just stay close to me. I'ma look out for ya."

The jailer returned to the bullpen. He unlocked the gate and called names to step out. Jimmy made his way through the crowd, as did his unnamed protector. The jailer handed the men a roll of dingy sheets, a threadbare blanket, and a brown sack that held two pieces of white bread with bologna. The prisoners marched through the jail's corridor, passing through various sliding gates until they reached a housing unit. "Grab a mat," the jailer ordered, "and find yourself a home on the floor."

Jimmy couldn't believe he would have to live in such conditions. Sleeping mats were everywhere. A list on the wall posted 30 names waiting for cell space. The bathrooms were open, lacking a modicum of privacy. A stench of dried urine permeated the air. Noise from table games, aggressive voices, and a television blasting rap songs contributed to the frenetic energy in the housing unit. He would go crazy if he had to stay in jail long, Jimmy thought.

"Don't even sweat it," the larger prisoner said. "We goin' crash right here. I'm a look out for ya, youngun."

Jimmy quivered. He sat on the mat that he had dropped, held his knees, and waited, afraid for what might happen next.

Critical Thinking

1. Is Jimmy's experience typical of first-time offenders detained in jail?

2. What would most concern you if you were detained?

3. Do jail personnel have a responsibility to ensure that detainees are treated properly by fellow prisoners?

Source: Written by Michael Santos.

---

rehabilitative personnel lack training to deal with severe cases of mental and emotional stress, particularly when threats of self-injury are involved. Consequently, mentally disturbed inmates often languish in jails, where they are abused by other inmates, misunderstood by correctional workers, and left untreated by professional personnel.

However, the news is not all bad; some positive steps have been taken to divert the mentally ill from jail. Many jails now screen new arrivals for mental health problems, with specially trained counselors interviewing and evaluating pretrial detainees. Inmates with mental health problems are usually referred to local social service agencies for treatment and may be diverted from criminal prosecution in order for treatment to proceed.

SUBSTANCE DEPENDENCY Nationally, half of all people placed in jail are under the influence of alcohol or an illegal drug at the time of arrest, and over two-thirds, more than 400,000 jail inmates, have a history of substance abuse. More than half of those entering jail have a history of failed drug treatment, often during previous jail or probation terms.[13] In a study of 10 large cities, between 56 percent and 82 percent of all arrestees tested positive for illicit substances at the time of arrest.[14]

The most dramatic problems posed by offenders' drug abuse occur during withdrawal, when the addict's body reacts to the loss of the substance on which it has grown dependent. Both alcoholics and drug addicts suffer withdrawal, but it is especially painful for the latter group and may last as long as a week. Addicts may attempt suicide to escape the pains of withdrawal, and a higher percentage of drug addicts than nonaddicts succeed in the attempt. Early identification of the drug addict is therefore a high priority in urban jails, for withdrawal symptoms can be assuaged by methadone maintenance or a prisoner can be released to an addiction treatment facility. Despite the short stays of inmates in jails, specialized treatment programs designed especially for jails have shown some success. However, although there is a great need for substance abuse treatment in jails, only 16 percent of those in jail receive it while there.[15]

Every jail regularly houses alcoholic offenders, many of whom, during the initial hours of confinement, are physically sick, hallucinating, and paranoid. These symptoms tend to be viewed as inconveniences rather than as conditions requiring treatment. Few jails provide any real form of treatment, and treatment by outside agencies is often just as rare because these agencies prefer voluntary clients to offenders.

MEDICAL NEEDS Detainees have many medical needs, ranging from minor scrapes and bruises sustained during arrest and booking to major injuries sustained during the crime and its aftermath. To these injuries can be added the routine health deficiencies of any lower-class citizen: infections, poor nutrition, lack of dental care, and so forth. Taken together, more than one-third of those in jail report a physical ailment of some sort.[16] Even so, many of the nation's jails do not routinely screen for infectious diseases, such as tuberculosis.

For the most part, citizens who end up in jail, on charges or through sentences, lack medical insurance, so whatever medical care they receive is provided by the jail itself. Almost 60 percent of America's jails make prisoners pay for at least some of the medical care they receive; two-thirds of those jails require payment for all services. Forty percent provide the health care through on-site staff or other government employees. Even in the jails that seek to address inmate health problems, services are problematic, and many inmates have complained about the quality of care that they are offered.

A good picture of the most pressing medical needs that people have when they enter jail is provided by statistics about deaths of those in jail custody. Such cases are rare: Less than one-tenth of 1 percent of all people in jails die while in custody. Just over half die as a result of an illness they had when they entered the jail. It used to be that HIV/AIDS was a major cause of jail death, but progress in detection and treatment has drastically reduced the number of people who die from that disease. By contrast, one-quarter of all jail deaths result from heart disease.[17] **Figure 3.3** shows the causes of death in jails.

LEGAL NEEDS Pretrial detainees need access to legal assistance to cope with their situation. In the emotionally stressful postarrest period, suspects need information about what will happen prior to their trial. They also need legal help in securing release through bail or diversion. If release is not possible, they must have help in preparing their case, negotiating with the prosecutor about charges, or directing the attorney to people who may provide an alibi or exonerating evidence. Not surprisingly, research consistently shows that people locked up in jail until trial suffer a disadvantage in preparing their defense. People in jail are likely to need a public defender, an appointed counsel, or an attorney provided by contract. Unfortunately, because they must process large numbers of cases for relatively small fees, criminal defense attorneys cannot spend much time locating witnesses, conducting investigative interviews, and preparing testimony. Therefore, for many detainees these essential defense plans are only partially pursued.

Detainees can expect to spend long periods without seeing an attorney. In fact, most have only one or two hurried conversations with their attorneys before they appear in court. To add insult to injury, detainees are brought to court in shackles and jail-issue clothing, in dramatic contrast to well-groomed defendants who have been able to remain free. Detainees once employed have long since been fired. In short, detainees have relatively dim prospects.

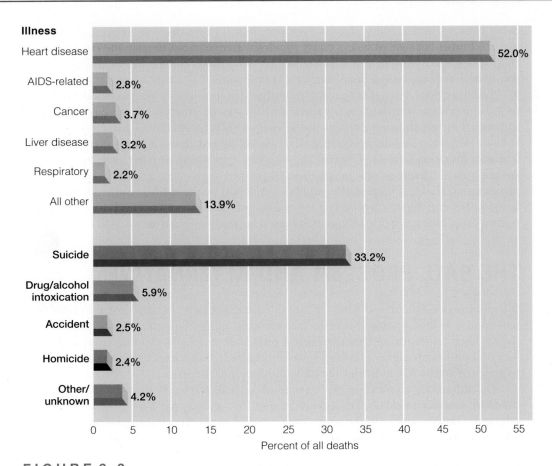

Illness

- Heart disease — 52.0%
- AIDS-related — 2.8%
- Cancer — 3.7%
- Liver disease — 3.2%
- Respiratory — 2.2%
- All other — 13.9%

- Suicide — 33.2%
- Drug/alcohol intoxication — 5.9%
- Accident — 2.5%
- Homicide — 2.4%
- Other/ unknown — 4.2%

Percent of all deaths

FIGURE 3.3
Causes of Death for People in Jail Custody
Most people who die in jail do so because of physical illness they had when they entered, but one-third commit suicide, which is a sign of a mental illness.

Source: Margaret E. Noonan, *Mortality in Local Jails and State Prisons, 2000–2010—Statistical Tables* (Washington, DC: Bureau of Justice Statistics, 2012), 5.

PRETRIAL DETAINEES' RIGHTS   Unlike prisoners, pretrial detainees have not been convicted of the crimes for which they are being held. Technically, they are innocent, yet they are detained under some of the worst conditions of incarceration. In the 1970s, several courts reasoned that such people should suffer no more restrictions than are necessary to ensure their presence at trial and that legal protections for detainees should exceed those for sentenced prisoners.

However, in 1979 the U.S. Supreme Court overruled the lower courts by limiting pretrial detainees' rights. As will be discussed in Chapter 11, the Court in *Bell v. Wolfish* ruled that conditions can be created to make certain that detainees are available for trial and that administrative practices designed to manage jails and to maintain security and order are constitutional.[18] The Justices said that restrictions other than those that ensure court appearance may legitimately be imposed on detainees and that when jail security, discipline, and order are at stake, detainees may be treated like other prisoners. The Supreme Court has also ruled that people who are in jail, incarcerated on other charges, may be questioned without having a full *Miranda* warning regarding their rights to counsel and to avoid self-incrimination.[19]

Release from Detention

One of the most startling facts about U.S. jails is that more than half of their occupants are awaiting trial. For many, this pretrial detention will last a long time: The average delay between arrest and sentencing is more than six months.[20] In urban jails the wait is often longer because of heavy court backlogs. Remarkably, despite the constitutional right to a speedy trial, in some court systems defendants can expect to languish in jail for up to a year or more before their cases come to trial.

Small wonder, then, that recent years have seen a major emphasis on programs to aid the release of offenders awaiting trial. Rates of pretrial release have gradually grown, from less than 50 percent in the early 1960s to nearly 90 percent in some of today's largest urban areas. Nationally, it is estimated that 58 percent of felony defendants awaiting trial are released prior to the disposition of their case, half of them within a day.[21] Even so, the proportion of people in jail who are there because they are awaiting trial has increased from about one-half to three-fifths in the last 10 years. Some jails continue to have severe crowding problems, but the emphasis on pretrial release programs has helped most jails keep their daily populations down.

THE BAIL PROBLEM AND ALTERNATIVES

When someone is arrested for a crime, the court seeks to ensure that the defendant will appear at the appointed time to face charges. Judges have traditionally responded to this need by requiring that the person post **bail**, normally ranging from $1,000 to $25,000 (although higher amounts may be required), to be forfeited if the accused fails to appear. **Figure 3.4** indicates the bail amounts that judges set.

Defendants have two principal ways to make bail. They may post the full amount to the court, where it is held until the case is decided. Or they may pay a set fee to a **bondsman**, who posts the amount with the court; the fee varies depending on the jurisdiction.

Dissatisfaction with the bail process stems from several factors. First, many defendants—perhaps 90 percent of pretrial detainees—are effectively indigent and cannot afford bail. Second, money is a weak incentive for appearance in court in many cases because the people who can afford bail are the ones most likely to appear at trial without the threat of its forfeiture. To many, the most disquieting factor is that human freedom can be had for a price. Imprisoning people merely because they are too poor to pay for their release seems in opposition to our cultural ideals and our concept of justice.

To avoid the problems of bail, some jurisdictions have increased the use of citations and summonses. For nonserious offenses, police can give the accused a "ticket" specifying a court appearance date and thus avoid having to take the accused into custody. Experiments with this approach indicate that it effectively reduces demands for short-term detention space. **Figure 3.5** shows the various ways that detainees may be released prior to the disposition of their case.

Release on Recognizance

By far the most successful alternative approach allows defendants to be released solely on their promise to appear at trial, a practice known as **release on recognizance (ROR)**.

bail
An amount of money, specified by a judge, to be posted as a condition for pretrial release to ensure the appearance of the accused in court.

bondsman
An independent businessperson who provides bail money for a fee, usually 5–10 percent of the total.

release on recognizance (ROR)
Pretrial release because the judge believes that the defendant's ties in the community are sufficient to guarantee the defendant's appearance in court.

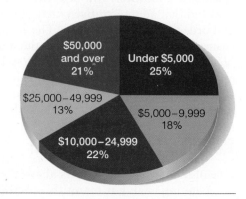

FIGURE 3.4
Amount of Bail Set by the Judge
Most judges set low bail amounts for defendants, yet even these amounts are hard for some indigent people to raise.

Source: Bureau of Justice Statistics, *Felony Defendants in Large Urban Counties, 2004* (Washington, DC: U.S. Department of Justice, 2006), 16.

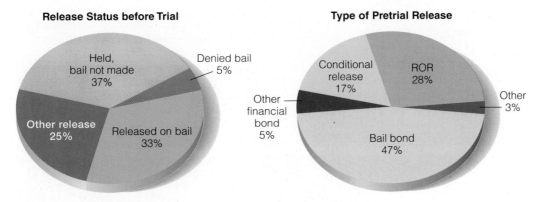

FIGURE 3.5
Types of Pretrial Release
A variety of mechanisms are used to ensure that most people are released from jail pending trial.

Source: Thomas H. Cohen and Tracey Kyckelhahn, *Felony Defendants in Large Urban Counties, 2006* (Washington, DC: Bureau of Justice Statistics, 2010), 6.

ROR programs assume that ties to the community (residence, family, employment) give people an incentive to keep their promise to appear and to retain their status in the community.

ROR defendants frequently have higher appearance rates than do defendants freed through various bail programs; they also have lower rearrest rates and higher rates of sentences to probation rather than prison. ROR programs have demonstrated clearly that the vast majority of accused people can be safely released into the community on their promise to return for trial. Loss of bail is an unnecessary threat. The rate of willful failure to appear in most jurisdictions is normally less than 5 percent.

Despite the benefits of ROR, questions arise. Because ROR requires that defendants have ties to the community, only a small number of defendants can usually participate. One national analysis of ROR found that women are more likely than men to be released, and African Americans less likely than whites. Moreover, these effects vary from one region of the country to another, with African Americans least likely to be released on recognizance in the West and South, even when controlling for other factors related to the release decision (offense, age, and previous record).[22]

Some jurisdictions have begun to experiment with pretrial release under some form of supervision. Nationally, about 63,000 jail inmates are under some form of supervised release. Forty percent of these are supervised by probation officers or other counselors, or are under pretrial supervision; 9 percent attend **day reporting centers**; 18 percent perform community service; and another 19 percent are under **electronic monitoring**.[23]

Pretrial Diversion

As an alternative to adjudication, **pretrial diversion** began with the belief that formally processing people through the criminal justice system is not always beneficial. Each of the three main reasons advanced in support of pretrial diversion has provoked controversy:

1. Many offenders' crimes are caused by special problems—vagrancy, alcoholism, emotional distress—that cannot be managed effectively through the criminal justice system.

2. The stigma attached to formal criminal labeling often works against rehabilitation and promotes an unnecessarily harsh penalty for a relatively minor offense.

3. Diversion is cheaper than criminal justice processing.

day reporting center
Facility where offenders such as pretrial releasees and probation violators attend daylong intervention and treatment sessions.

electronic monitoring
Community supervision technique, ordinarily combined with home confinement, that uses electronic devices to maintain surveillance on offenders.

pretrial diversion
An alternative to adjudication in which the defendant agrees to conditions set by the prosecutor (for example, counseling or drug rehabilitation) in exchange for withdrawal of charges.

Bail-bond providers proliferate near local courthouses, such as on this street across from the main courthouse in New Orleans.

Ann Hermes/Christian Science Monitor/Getty Images

For the most part, correctional leaders agree that jails can do little for inmates who have mental, emotional, or alcohol-related problems. For such people, social programs are more suitable than jails. There is less agreement about appropriate treatment for those whose problems are less clearly beyond their own control—unemployed and un-skilled youths, multiple drug users, and episodic offenders, to name a few. Their marginal criminality may stem primarily from their disadvantaged status, and their status can be seen as at least partly their own fault. Diversion from the criminal justice system is controversial because to some critics it allows some people to "get off easy." Yet the rationale for diverting them is attractive. The jail sanction does little to alter their disadvantaged status; indeed, the stigma of a conviction often decreases their chances of becoming productive citizens. A more enlightened policy would deflect them from criminal justice processes and instead put them into reparations programs. That is, in fact, the precise aim of most pretrial diversion.

Conduct During Pretrial Release

People who are awaiting trial would seem to have a special incentive to behave well. If they show up for court with a job and prospects for a good future, it will be harder for a judge to impose a sentence of confinement. If they show they can adjust well to the community during the period between the arrest and the trial, then the judge will likely take that into account when it comes time to impose a sentence. **Figure 3.6** shows that people who are released pending trial have much better trial outcomes than those who are not released.

It may be surprising, then, that many defendants do not behave well during their period of release before trial. While the vast majority—78 percent—of defendants on some form of pretrial release show up for every court hearing, more than one in five do not. These are called **absconders,** and unless there is some good reason they missed the court date, a warrant is sent out for their arrest. They are considered fugitives. Nationally, one-fourth of these fugitives (6 percent of all defendants) remain at large at least one year after they were supposed to have had their trial.[24]

The failure to appear for trial is not the only form of misbehavior that happens when people are released before trial. Almost one in five (18 percent) of all people

absconders
People who fail to appear for a court date and have no legitimate reason for doing so.

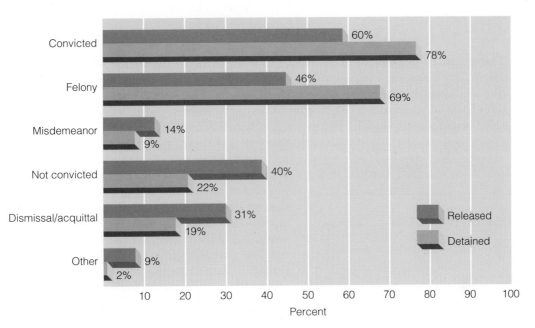

FIGURE 3.6
Pretrial Release and Adjudication Outcome
Most who are released pending trial receive more-lenient sentences than those who are not.

Source: Bureau of Justice Statistics, *Pretrial Release of Felony Defendants in State Courts*, November 2007, Table 5.

released while awaiting trial are rearrested before their trial date arrives, two-thirds of them for a felony.[25] The high arrest rate of those granted pretrial release has been a significant concern to people interested in jail reform. They wonder if some sort of supervision or treatment program would help keep these numbers down. They also see that high rates of arrests for this population lead to questions about the effectiveness of the pretrial system.

Preventive Detention

Even as ROR and other pretrial-release programs have moved forward, the heightened public concern about misconduct by people who are released while awaiting trial has led to a political movement to prevent pretrial release, especially release on bail. With **preventive detention**, defendants who are regarded as dangerous or likely to commit crimes while awaiting trial are kept in jail for society's protection. In 1984 the Comprehensive Crime Control Act authorized the holding of an allegedly dangerous defendant without bail if the judge finds that no conditions of release would ensure the defendant's appearance at trial and at the same time ensure the safety of the community.

The notion of the need for protection from accused criminals has been subjected to sustained analysis. Many scholars believe that holding in custody a person who has not been convicted of committing a crime but who someone thinks might commit a crime violates the due process provisions of the Constitution. Others argue that the practice is impractical and potentially nefarious. In reality, only a small proportion—fewer than one in five—of all defendants who are released pending trial are arrested for another crime before trial, and many of those are not convicted of the new crime.

Political pressure to incorporate the public's safety concerns into release decisions has become so strong that well over half of the states have laws allowing preventive detention. The U.S. Supreme Court, in *Schall v. Martin* (1984) and *United States v. Salerno* (1987), approved preventive detention practices.[26]

preventive detention
Detention of an accused person in jail, to protect the community from crimes that the accused is considered likely to commit if set free pending trial.

THE SENTENCED JAIL INMATE

The sentenced jail inmate presents special difficulties for the correctional administrator, mainly because of the short duration of the term and the limitations of the jail's physical plant. By definition, jail terms are shorter than prison terms—typically 30–90 days for a misdemeanor. Felons commonly serve from six months to a year, and on some occasions serious felons (convicted of sexual assault or robbery, for example) will serve two years or more.[27] (See "Myths in Corrections.") In many cases the sentence ultimately imposed is "time served" because the judge believes that the time already spent in pretrial detention—when by law the person was presumed innocent—is sufficient, or more than sufficient, punishment for the offense committed. The real punishment is not the sentence but rather the impact on the offender of the unpleasant, costly, and harmful conditions of life behind bars from arrest up to case disposition. In short, the process is the punishment.

Of those sentenced to additional jail time, misdemeanants constitute the forgotten component of local criminal justice operations. Over half were under criminal justice system supervision at the time of their arrest—probation, parole, or pretrial release—and these people are well-known to the justice system. Nearly three-quarters have previously been sentenced to probation or confinement. They also have a range of treatment needs. More than four-fifths have a history of illegal drug use; 29 percent are unemployed; and, of the employed, 40 percent earn less than $1,000 per month. More than one-third have experienced a serious physical injury, and almost one-fifth have been abused.[28]

Their short terms make treatment difficult. Most have not graduated from high school, and many are illiterate, yet educational programming is unlikely to yield results

MYTHS in Corrections

Jails Are for Misdemeanants

THE MYTH: Jail sentences are more for misdemeanants than they are for felons.

THE REALITY: Nearly 40 percent of felony defendants are eventually sentenced to jail, a rate that is almost the same as prison sentences for felonies.

Source: Bureau of Justice Statistics, *Felony Defendants in Large Urban Counties* (Washington, DC: U.S. Department of Justice, 2006), iii.

The lack of rehabilitative programs in most jails means that inmates have little to keep them occupied.

John Moore/Getty Images News/Getty Images

in such a short time, especially with adults. For example, offenders can rarely earn a high school equivalency diploma in one or two months, and prospects for continued education after release are dim. Similar impracticalities are inherent in job training programs, which may require 25–30 weeks to complete. In addition, job placement prospects are spotty for the former inmate, who may not even have the help of a parole or probation officer in looking for work. Treatment programs for the mentally ill, the emotionally disturbed, and alcoholics and drug addicts suffer from the same time constraints.

In sum, with isolated exceptions, jail time is the worst kind of time to serve as a correctional client. For corrections, jail is an expensive and largely ineffective proposition—a revolving door that leads nowhere.

To deal with these problems, reformers have begun to emphasize the importance of carefully planned and supported reentry programs. Jail administrators are to begin preparing for the sentenced jail inmate's release from the first day of confinement,[29] and partnerships with community supervision agencies are encouraged to provide more support for the person who is returning to the community from the jail.[30]

ISSUES IN JAIL MANAGEMENT

American jails are faced with numerous problems, many of them age-old: lack of programs, poor financial resources, antiquated facilities, and so on. Here we discuss five of the most important issues related to jail: legal liability, jail standards, personnel matters, community programs for jails, and the jail facility itself.

Legal Liability

Jail employees may be legally liable for their actions. When a government official (such as a correctional officer) uses his or her authority to deprive a citizen of civil rights, the victim can sue the official to halt the violation and to collect damages (both actual and punitive) and recoup legal costs (42 U.S.C. 1984). Supervisors, including wardens, can

Numerous legal suits for jail overcrowding have resulted in many newly contructed jails all around the country, like this one in New Orleans.

Michael DeMocker, NOLA.com/The Times-Picayune/Landov

also be liable for the actions of staff members—even if the supervisors were not aware of those actions—if it can be shown that they should have been aware. A lack of funds does not excuse an administrator from liability for failing to train staff sufficiently or to provide basic, constitutionally required custodial arrangements. Local governments that administer the jails are also liable for injurious conduct.

Many people believe that court decisions awarding civil judgments under Section 1983 of the United States Code are an open invitation for prisoners to sue, and sue they do. Prisoners have litigated just about every conceivable aspect of the conditions of incarceration, from hours of recreation to quality of food. The most successful suits have been those showing that an employee's action has contributed to a situation that harmed a prisoner.

The threat of litigation has forced jails to develop basic humane practices for managing offenders. Civil damages and legal fees of more than $1 million have been awarded often enough to draw the attention of sheriffs, jail managers, and local government officials. Budgets for jails have been increased to reflect the additional costs of developing training programs, classification procedures, and managerial policies to prevent actions leading to liability suits.

Jail Standards

One of the best ways to reduce litigation is to develop specific standards for routine jail operating practices and procedures. Standards are important for at least three reasons. First, they indicate proactive criteria for jail management, which helps eliminate the "Monday morning quarterback" (rehashed in hindsight) aspect of much litigation. If jails are following standard procedures, they cannot be held as accountable as they otherwise would for problems that inmates experience during incarceration. Second, standards provide a basis by which administrators can evaluate staff performance: They need merely determine whether staff are complying with operational standards. Third, standards aid the planning and evaluation of jail programs by giving program managers a target to consider in their work.

Even so, authorities are uncertain about the best way to design and implement jail standards. Some experts argue that standards should be binding. Generally, this means that an oversight agency visits each jail in the state and determines whether its programs are consistent with the standards. Jails that fail to comply with standards are given a deadline by which to meet them. If they do not, they may be fined—or even closed down.

Other experts argue that because jails differ so much in size and needs and because so many of them suffer from underfunding and inadequate facilities, holding all jails accountable for meeting the same inflexible set of standards is unreasonable. These experts push for voluntary guidelines by which program goals for jail operations would be set by groups such as the American Correctional Association and monitored by teams of professionals.

The bottom line is that if jail administrators do not implement standard practices, the courts will intervene. Even new jails are not immune to this problem: In the late 1980s, jails commonly came under court orders soon after opening, and sometimes even before opening.

Personnel Matters

Local correctional workers are among the most poorly trained, least-educated, and worst-paid employees in the criminal justice system. Many take custodial positions on a temporary basis while awaiting an opening in the ranks of the sheriff's law enforcement officers. Of the approximately 234,000 jail employees noted in the last census, about 72 percent performed direct custody functions, 13 percent were clerical and maintenance workers, 7 percent were professionals, and 1 percent were in education.[31]

Personnel problems facing jail administrators stem from several factors, but the primary one is probably a combination of low pay and poor working conditions. Local correctional workers earn substantially less than firefighters and police officers in the same jurisdiction. And whenever these correctional workers can, they leave for better-paying jobs with less stressful working conditions. However, many correctional employees have only limited education and do not fare well in competition for better positions, so they must stay where they are.

Understaffing further worsens these poor working conditions. Jails are 24-hour operations. Assuming that the typical jurisdiction has a 40-hour workweek with normal holidays and leave time, nearly five full-time employees are required to fill one position around the clock. The national ratio of inmates to custodial employees in jails is about 4.3 to 1, which translates to about 25 to 1 for each staff workday. In essence, each jail employee must be able to control 25 inmates or more, which helps account for the common practice of simply locking the doors and leaving inmates in their cells all day.

Community Programs for Jails

The number of people confined in jails reached near-crisis proportions in the early 1990s. The jail population, which had remained fairly stable during the 1970s, more than doubled between 1983 and 1993, and then again between 1993 and 2008. During this period of time, many—perhaps most—of America's jails started to house more people than the facility was designed to keep: Overcrowding resulted. Hundreds of jails were forced to close, and at one time more than one in seven jails were put under some form of court order.[32] Today, only about 7 percent of jails face such orders.[33]

Jail administrators know that overcrowding produces problems in jail management. Cells intended to hold one or two people were sometimes holding three, four, even five inmates. It was not uncommon for prisoners to sleep in hallways, with or without mattresses. Direct and immediate consequences of overcrowding were violence, rape, and a variety of health problems. Certainly, tempers flare in close quarters, and the vulnerable inmate becomes a likely victim. And remember this: Many of the people subjected to these conditions have not yet been tried and must be presumed to be innocent.

Leading jail administrators began to develop solutions to jail overcrowding. Two centered on people detained before trial: (1) increasing the availability of release options, such as ROR and supervised release, and (2) speeding up trials. Work release was directed toward people serving time. Today, these programs have become common, and about 8 percent of people sentenced to jails serve much of their time in the community. **Table 3.1** shows the kinds of programs that enable jailed inmates to be placed in the community.

Oddly, building new jails—or increasing the capacity of existing facilities—apparently has little effect on the problem of overcrowding. Instead, policies regarding the use of jails, combined with crime rates in the jurisdiction served by the jails, seem to determine the amount of crowding. Wide variations exist among jurisdictions in patterns of jail use, controlling for population served. Some jails are heavily used, others less so. The most-crowded jails tend to be those housing "pass-through" populations—arrestees and detainees—and these tend to be larger facilities as well. This may explain the common phenomenon of new jails with expanded capacities opening, only to suffer renewed conditions of crowding. The solution to crowding is not as much jail capacity as it is jail policy.

The Jail Facility

According to a survey of sheriffs, almost 30 percent of all jail cells are at least 50 years old, despite an unprecedented construction boom to replace old facilities. Jails are expensive structures, costing as much as $100,000 per cell to build—and perhaps

Table 3.1 Jail Inmates in the Community

To reduce crowding, many jails have developed programs that enable some inmates to remain in the community instead of being confined.

Type of Program	Number of Inmates
Weekender programs	11,369
Electronic monitoring (EM)	11,950
Home detention (no EM)	809
Day reporting	5,200
Community service	11,680
Other pretrial supervision	10,464
Other work programs	7,165
Treatment programs	2,449
Other outside programs	4,180
Total	65,266

Source: Scott D. Minton, *Jail Inmates at Midyear 2011—Statistical Tables* (Washington, DC: Bureau of Justice Statistics, 2012), 8.

New-generation jails employ "podular" unit designs, with cells located around a common perimeter allowing direct supervision of the jail's residents.

AP Images/Newspaper Member/The Bulletin/Joe Kline

$200,000 per cell when financing is taken into consideration. Running a physically out-moded jail can be more expensive still.

As recently as 1983, even such basic items as radios and television sets were lacking in over half of all jails. With idle time, poor physical security, and little or no chance to participate in programs, prisoners are often cheek by jowl, day in and day out. Crowded cells make for threatening environments that may translate into potentially

focus on correctional technology

Eye Scanning in Jails

The federal government is spending $500,000 to help the National Sheriffs' Association perfect a way to reduce the number of jail escapes. The new system uses eye scanners to establish the identity of anyone leaving the jail. In a series of $10,000 grants made to about 45 sheriffs' agencies across the country, the U.S. Justice Department hopes to create a national database that better identifies, registers, and tracks inmates. The hope is to build a nearly foolproof identification system to put a stop to all escapes. Most of the $10,000 grants paid for the equipment to be installed and also offered a small portion toward training.

Eye scanners have been used for years by a few jails, the U.S. military, some European airports, and private companies, but they remain rare, primarily because of the cost. But this is the first attempt at a nationwide effort to employ the technology on a systematic basis. "While this technology has been around generally for 10 to 15 years, it just hasn't gotten into the mainstream yet," said Fred Wilson, the director of the project. "You have to remember that the average law enforcement agency is very small and they can't afford this stuff."

The sheriffs and Biometric Intelligence and Identification Technologies teamed to select the demonstration sites from more than 400 that were interested in installing scanners. The agencies chosen ranged from big operations like the Los Angeles County Sheriff's Department and the Las Vegas Metro Police to small departments such as in Story County, Iowa.

Scanning inmates is quicker and far better than the old technology of fingerprinting. Sheriffs complain that a fingerprint search can take hours or even days, but results are nearly instant with an iris scan. A person simply looks into a camera, which uses infrared light to illuminate and map the iris. Each iris is unique and contains about six times more features than a fingerprint. "Within 15 seconds you can get an identification back on who this is," Story County Sheriff Paul Fitzgerald said. "If we can get every state involved in this, that would be tremendous. Just like the fingerprint databases."

Critical Thinking

1. Are there civil liberties issues in requiring those arrested and detained to provide a sheriff with this type of "fingerprint"?
2. Could a national database be developed using this technology?

Source: Associated Press, "Iris Scans May Prevent Mistaken Release of Inmates," reprinted by National Public Radio, readingeagle.com/article.aspx?id=200250.

---

costly lawsuits. Often, the only way to counteract poor security in older jails is to hire extra staff. For these reasons and others, many jurisdictions have turned toward what is called the **new-generation jail.** This jail, through its unique design and set of programs, attempts to use the physical plant to improve the staff's ability to manage and interact with the inmate population and to provide services. Three general concepts are employed: podular design, interaction space, and personal space.[34] (For a look at another new idea, see "Focus on Correctional Technology.")

The **podular unit** (derived from *pod* and *modular*) is a living area for a group of inmates that defines a post or a watch. The podular unit replaces the old cell blocks. Twelve to 25 individual cells are organized into a unit (the pod), which serves as a self-contained minijail. Typically, the cell doors open into a common living area where the inmates of the pod can congregate.

The new-generation jail tends to reinforce interaction of various sorts. For example, inmates have greater freedom to interact socially and recreationally, and correctional staff are in direct physical contact with them throughout the day, in what is called the **direct supervision** approach. In older jails, bars and doors separate correctional officers from inmates; the new-generation jail places them in the same rooms with inmates. The inmates are also given personal space and may stay in their individual cells to pursue their own interests when they wish. They may even have keys to their own quarters within the pod.

new-generation jail
A facility with a podular architectural design and management policies that emphasize interaction of inmates and staff and provision of services.

podular unit
Self-contained living areas, for 12–25 inmates, composed of individual cells for privacy and open areas for social interaction. New-generation jails are made up of two or more pods.

direct supervision
A method of correctional supervision in which staff members have direct physical interaction with inmates throughout the day.

The new structure offers several advantages over older jails. First, its economics are flexible. When jail populations are low, whole pods can be temporarily shut down, saving personnel and operational costs. Second, minimum standards for recreation time and nonlockup time can be met routinely without costly construction or renovation. Third, supervising staff is less demanding, for staff have greater autonomy to manage their pods. Fourth, policy makers have learned that new-generation jails are as much as 20 percent cheaper to construct, and they provide more-effective inmate security and supervision. Finally, the new-generation concept results in less violence and fewer inmate infractions, leaving staff feeling more secure in their work.

However, the greatest advantages are programmatic. In larger jails, pods can serve specialized offender groups who share a need, such as for remedial educational services, or who for any reason (for example, AIDS, gang affiliation, or offense type) need to be segregated from the rest of the jail population. Thus, the needs of the inmate can become a more significant factor in the nature of the confinement.

Placing correctional staff in closer contact with inmates also has benefits. Prisoners often show symptoms of depression or behave disruptively because of stress or the emotional strain of confinement; this can become more troublesome without appropriate staff response. When correctional officers are physically closer to inmates, they can more readily become aware of feelings or behavior that may require attention. Further, the physical structure can potentially moderate staff–inmate conflict. By getting to know one another better, staff and inmates can learn to live together on easier terms. Thus, in the long run the new-generation jail can help overcome the correctional officer's traditional alienation from inmates and break down the false stereotypes it fosters. The officer in proximity to inmates learns to rely on communication skills and judgment rather than depending on force in controlling the inmate population.

Despite its advantages, all is not well with the new-generation jail. For one thing, it is hard to sell the concept to a public who underestimates the painfulness of the jail experience and sees the new system as a means of coddling offenders. That more than half of jail inmates typically have *not* yet been convicted of a crime does not dampen the public's desire for harsh punishment of offenders. Jail administrators need to inform political decision makers about the fiscal and programmatic advantages of the new jail.

A second problem is more troubling: Many new jails become outmoded between the planning stage and completion of construction. Legal standards may change, creating new requirements for cell space, recreation space, visitation areas, and the like. Inadequate attention may have been given to possible programmatic needs. Often, the very existence of a new jail leads to such an enthusiastic response by judges and other criminal justice officials that the new facility quickly becomes crowded.

THE FUTURE OF THE JAIL

Few government functions in the United States are under assault from as many camps as the jail is. Reform groups call for more-humane jail conditions; the media expose jails as cruel, crowded, and counterproductive; inmates sue their keepers for mistreatment, often successfully; and experts describe jails as failures.

In some respects the jail's importance to the criminal justice system has seldom been greater than it is today. With many prisons more crowded than they are legally permitted to be, jails have become a backup resource for managing the many offenders for whom the state lacks space. As local governments experiment with ways to improve the credibility of the criminal justice system, solutions seem inevitably to involve the jail—for work release, for enforcing court orders for probationers, for new laws against drunkenness, and for other initiatives. Local decision makers have more control over jails and jail policy than over facilities operated by state correctional agencies.

Moreover, the jail is an expensive item in county and municipal budgets. The average cost of a day in jail varies greatly, but for a large urban jail it can be quite high. A day in New York City's Rikers Island—the nation's most expensive stay—costs $228, and the next-most expensive, the Multnomah County (Portland, Oregon) jail, is no bargain at $103 per day. Even in the "cheap" jails in Houston ($27 per day) and Phoenix ($25 per day), the price adds up, as one bed for a year can cost $10,000 to maintain. One-fourth of the Harris County (Houston) annual budget goes to law enforcement, with more than three-quarters of a million dollars spent daily on sentenced and unsentenced detainees.[35]

Perhaps because of the jail's budgetary costs and system centrality, three general trends—if they continue—bode well for its future. First, many jurisdictions have renovated or replaced jail facilities since the early 1970s. The overwhelming difficulties associated with decrepit physical plants are at least partially overcome by this new construction. Second, many jurisdictions are joining together to build and maintain a single jail to serve their collective needs. Although political problems abound in such an arrangement—politicians resist giving up authority over jail budgets—this movement seems to be gaining adherents. Perhaps most important is the growing emphasis on strengthening alternatives to jail. Experts have pointed out that pretrial alternatives, such as supervised release, and sentencing alternatives, such as drug treatment or specialized probation, are both less costly and more effective than traditional jail.[36]

Summary

1 Describe the history of the jail and its current function in the criminal justice system.

Jails in the United States descend from feudal practices in twelfth-century England, in which the *shire reeve* (from which the word *sheriff* evolved) caught and held in custody people accused of breaking the king's law. English settlers brought these traditions and institutions with them to the American colonies. Today, jails are the entryway into the criminal justice system and a place of confinement for less serious law violators.

2 Describe who is in jail and why they are there.

Two kinds of people are in jail: those who are awaiting trial and people who are sentenced to terms of confinement that are less than a year in duration. Jails house mostly young men, particularly young men of color. The majority of those in jail are serving sentences for crimes, and the remainder are awaiting adjudication of charges (including probation and parole revocation).

3 Discuss the kinds of jails in the United States.

The smallest jails are police lockups. Most other jails are run by county government, although there are also municipal jails under the authority of larger cities' governments. In some areas, regional jails serve multiple city and county governments.

4 List the main issues facing jails today.

Jails struggle with the need to provide services to people who are awaiting trial, in part because their stay may be short and they are also not yet convicted of any crimes. Jails also face the need to deal with problems among detainees, especially mental health, substance abuse, medical problems, and legal needs.

5 Outline the problem of bail and list the main alternatives to bail.

Being held in bail is damaging to a defendant's life circumstances, as well as being detrimental to his or her chances at trial and sentence. Financial bail systems discriminate against the poor, who constitute the vast majority of jail detainees. Bail alternatives, such as release on recognizance and pretrial diversion, apply to only a portion of those awaiting trial.

6 **Outline the problems of jail administration.**

Jail administrators are legally liable for their treatment of people who are incarcerated there. This liability is made problematic by the fact that there are some written standards for jails to meet, but many jails lack sufficient funds to meet them. Because jails often pay less than other aspects of the justice system, it can be difficult to recruit and retain high-quality personnel. Finally, outmoded jail facilities make it extremely difficult to maintain good programs.

7 **Describe new developments in jails and jail programs.**

In order to deal with the problems of jails, there has been a recent movement to increase the use of the "new-generation jail" concept, in which jail detainees are kept in podular units instead of cells and security is maintained by direct supervision methods.

8 **Critically assess the future of the jail.**

Jails are an expensive part of local government budgets, yet they are often a neglected aspect of local public safety services. The prospects of jails are looking up, though, because of extensive efforts to renovate old jails and build new ones, and to design these replacements in ways that offer better services and improved security.

Key Terms

absconders 74
bail 72
bondsman 72
day reporting center 73
direct supervision 81

electronic monitoring 73
fee system 63
lockup 62
new-generation jail 81
podular unit 81

pretrial diversion 73
preventive detention 75
regional jail 65
release on recognizance (ROR) 72

For Discussion

1. What special problems and needs do jail detainees have? Why? What problems do these needs pose for jail administrators?

2. What are the pros and cons of preventive detention? How might this tactic affect crime control? Due process?

3. How would you balance tensions between jail management and public safety?

4. What are some problems that you would expect to encounter if you were in charge of providing rehabilitative programs in a jail?

Notes

[1] James Austin, Wendy Naro-Ware, Roger Ocker, Robert Harris, and Robin Allen, *Evaluation of the Current and Future Los Angeles County Jail Population* (Malibu, CA: JFA Institute, 2012); see also www.lasd.org/divisions/correctional.

[2] Todd D. Minton and Daniela Golinelli, *Jail Inmates at Mid-Year, 2013—Statistical Tables* (Washington, DC: Bureau of Justice Statistics, 2014).

[3] Ibid, p. 3.

[4] Ibid, p. 2.

[5] David Rothman, *Discovery of the Asylum* (Boston: Little, Brown, 1971), 56.

[6] Minton and Golinelli, *Jail Inmates*, p. 4.

[7] Ibid, p. 2.

[8] James Stephan and Georgette Walsh, *Census of Jail Facilities, 2006* (Washington, DC: Bureau of Justice Statistics, 2011).

[9] Minton and Golinelli, *Jail Inmates*, p. 9.

[10] Margaret E. Noonan, *Mortality in Local Jails and State Prisons, 2000–2010—Statistical Tables* (Washington, DC: Bureau of Justice Statistics, 2012), 5.

[11] BJS *Special Report*, September 2006, p. 2.

[12] Bureau of Justice Statistics, *Census of Jails, 1999* (Washington, DC: U.S. Government Printing Office, 2002), 40.

[13] BJS *Special Report*, July 2005.

[14] Office of National Drug Control Policy, *ADAM II: 2010 Annual Report* (Washington, DC: Executive Office of the President, 2011).

[15] BJS *Special Report*, July 2004.

[16] BJS *Special Report,* November 2006.

[17] Noonan, *Mortality in Local Jails,* p. 5.

[18] *Bell v. Wolfish,* 441 U.S. 520 (1979).

[19] *Howes v. Fields,* 617 F.3d 813 (2011).

[20] BJS *Bulletin,* December 2004, p. 9; BJS *Bulletin,* October 2001, p. 9.

[21] Thomas H. Cohen and Tracey Kyckelhahn, *Felony Defendants in Large Urban Counties, 2006* (Washington, DC: Bureau of Justice Statistics, 2010), 6; Bureau of Justice Statistics, *Pretrial Release of Felony Defendants in State Courts* (Washington, DC: U.S. Government Printing Office, 2007), 7.

[22] Sheila Royo Maxwell and Jessica Davis, "The Salience of Race and Gender in Pretrial Release Decisions: A Comparison Across Multiple Jurisdictions," *Criminal Justice Policy Review* 10 (no. 4, 2000): 491–502.

[23] Minton and Golinelli, *Jail Inmates,* p. 8.

[24] Bureau of Justice Statistics, *Felony Defendants in Large Urban Counties, 2004* (Washington, DC: U.S. Government Printing Office, 2008), 21.

[25] Ibid.; Cohen and Kyckelhahn, *Felony Defendants.*

[26] *Schall v. Martin,* 467 U.S. 253 (1984); *United States v. Salerno,* 481 U.S. 739 (1987).

[27] BJS *Special Report,* July 2004, p. 5.

[28] Ibid, pp. 8–10.

[29] Jeff Mellow, Debbie Mukamal, Stefan LoBuglio, Amy Solomon, and Jenny W. L. Osborne, *The Jail Administrator's Toolkit for Reentry* (Washington, DC: Urban Institute, 2008).

[30] Amy Solomon, Jenny W. L. Osborne, Stefan LoBuglio, Jeff Mellow, and Debbie Mukamal, *Life After Lock-up: Improving Reentry from Jail to the Community* (Washington, DC: Urban Institute, 2008).

[31] Stephan and Walsh, *Census of Jail Facilities*; see also Bureau of Justice Statistics, *Census of Jails, 1999,* p. 25.

[32] Bureau of Justice Statistics, *Census of Jails, 1999,* p. 16.

[33] Stephan and Walsh, *Census of Jail Facilities.*

[34] Brandon K. Applegate, "Jails and Pretrial Release," in *The Oxford Handbook of Crime and Criminal Justice,* edited by Michael Tonry (New York: Oxford University Press, 2011), 795–824.

[35] Jessie Bogan, "America's Jail Crisis," *Forbes,* www.forbes.com/2009/07/10/jails-houston-recession-business-beltway-jails.html, July 13, 2009.

[36] Amanda Petteruti and Nastassia Walsh, *Jailing Communities: The Impact of Jail Expansion and Effective Public Safety Strategies* (Washington, DC: Justice Policy Institute, 2008).

CHAPTER 4

Community Corrections: Probation and Intermediate Sanctions

When Jerry Brown took office as governor of California in 2010, one of his top priorities for immediate action was to fix a corrections system in crisis. The federal courts had declared the California prison system to be overcrowded, and California was facing a court order to reduce its prison population count by more than 40,000—a number larger than the *entire* prison population of all but eight states. The answer was "California Public Safety Realignment," a plan designed to shift the correctional function for people convicted of nonviolent crimes away from costly state prisons toward the

After reading this chapter you should be able to . . .

1 Describe the history and development of probation, including how it is organized today.

2 Describe the rationale for intermediate sanctions.

3 Illustrate the continuum-of-sanctions concept.

4 List the various types of intermediate sanctions and who administers them.

5 Explain some of the problems associated with intermediate sanctions.

6 Describe what it takes to make intermediate sanctions work.

7 Explain how community corrections legislation works and describe its effectiveness.

8 Assess the role of the "new correctional professional."

9 Critically assess the future of probation, intermediate sanctions, and community corrections.

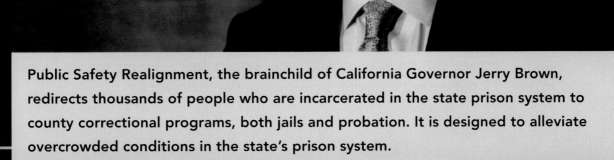

AP Images/Rich Pedroncelli

Public Safety Realignment, the brainchild of California Governor Jerry Brown, redirects thousands of people who are incarcerated in the state prison system to county correctional programs, both jails and probation. It is designed to alleviate overcrowded conditions in the state's prison system.

more-efficient local corrections systems, especially probation and community corrections.[1] By the beginning or 2015, California had reduced its prison population by almost 50,000, from its all-time high in 2006, to just

Brown's advisors worried that the prospect of moving large numbers of people out of prison and into other settings would make him politically vulnerable to accusations of being "soft on crime." But that has not

(continued from previous page)

November 2014 with an even larger majority vote, and California voters overwhelmingly passed Proposition 47, which downgraded some felonies to misdemeanors so that people convicted of these crimes would not go to prison. Proposition 47 also allowed about 10,000 people in prison to apply to be resentenced and released, depending on their criminal history and risk to the community.[3]

These changes are going on in other places as well. The Texas legislature, dominated by fiscal and political conservatives, decided to strengthen alternatives to incarceration. Rather than spend nearly $2 billion on new prison construction and operations to accommodate the growth, policy makers reinvested a fraction of this amount ($241 million) in a network of residential and community-based treatment and diversion programs. Within a year, the Texas prison population began to fall.[4]

California and Texas have the two largest prison systems in the United States. Their experiences illustrate a trend in state governments wanting to control the costs of their prison system by investing in nonprison alternatives.

Prison is *expensive*, no doubt about it. Nearly $50 billion is spent each year to imprison people who have been convicted of serious crimes. Even with a budget of this size, prison handles only a portion of criminal offenders. Two-thirds of people under correctional authority are not behind bars but instead are being supervised in the community.

It is inconceivable that the United States would ever be able to handle its huge correctional load without having most people under some form of community supervision. Putting a person behind bars costs 25 to 50 times as much per year as it does to put a person on probation for a year. If we were to eliminate community penalties from the arsenal of correctional methods, the incarceration rate would explode to nearly five times more than it is today, and correctional costs would experience a monumental increase. To the contrary, in these days of economic strain, policy makers are reviewing prison budgets to see if they can find a less expensive way to carry out punishments.

But what is the alternative?

Clearly, society needs a strong system whereby offenders may be punished outside of prison walls. For the past century, probation has been the primary alternativ..o incarceration. However, it is also true that corrections nee.ls .d.litio..al sanctions that are tougher and more exacting than probation but less costly and damaging than prison. In this chapter we describe programs designed to keep offenders in local community corrections instead of prisons. We begin by discussing the assumptions that underlie community corrections. We then examine the most common community penalty: a sentence to probation. (How probation supervision works is covered in Chapter 5.) Next, we offer a more detailed description of the contemporary idea of intermediate sanctions. ■

COMMUNITY CORRECTIONS: ASSUMPTIONS

Community corrections is the primary punishment alternative to incarceration in contemporary society. It seeks to keep offenders in the community by building ties to family, employment, and other normal sources of stability and success. This model of corrections assumes that the offender must change, but it also recognizes that factors within the community which might encourage criminal behavior (unemployment, for example) must also change. Four factors are usually cited in support of community corrections:

1. Many offenders' criminal records and current offenses are not serious enough to warrant incarceration.
2. Community supervision is cheaper than incarceration.
3. Rates of recidivism, or returning to crime, for those under community supervision are no higher than for those who go to prison.
4. Ex-inmates require both support and supervision as they try to remake their lives in the community.

Community corrections is based on the goal of finding the least-restrictive alternative—punishing the offender only as severely as needed to protect the community and to satisfy the public. Advocates call for programs to assist offenders in the community so they will have opportunities to succeed in law-abiding activities and to reduce their contact with the criminal world. It is through probation and intermediate sanctions that community corrections is incorporated in the U.S. corrections system.

PROBATION

Over half of all adults under correctional authority are serving probation sentences. In 2013 this meant more than 3.9 million people, or more than two-and-one-half times the number of adults in prisons, with about 2 million people being placed on parole each year.[5] Despite the wide use of probation, its critics tend to give it short shrift, often portraying it as "a slap on the wrist." They are uneasy with the idea that probation is the only alternative to incarceration.

Probation is based on the idea that in lieu of imprisonment, the offender is allowed to live in the community under supervision and demonstrate a willingness to abide by its laws. There are lots of doubts about probation. Many people think that probation needs to change. This notion is so widespread that a well-known scholarly work on correctional policy once referred to probation as "a kind of standing joke."[6] These views sharply contrast with official policies. For example, during the past decade alone, the federal government devoted more than a quarter of a billion dollars to improve and expand probation, and more effective correctional supervision in the community is one of the most important aims of contemporary corrections. Further, advocates of intermediate sanctions point to probation as the basis of our whole system of penalties.

What is really true about probation? How effective is it? How important is it today? In this chapter we describe the function of probation in corrections and review numerous studies of probation supervision and court services. Although in today's correctional environment, probation is increasingly coupled with a variety of intermediate sanctions, in this chapter we consider traditional probation services. Our review demonstrates that, as in most other areas of corrections, probation agencies work amid social and political ambivalence about punishment. This ambivalence, together with uncertainty about treatment methods, leaves probation in a quandary: We ordinarily rely heavily on it to deal with people who have broken the law, but we also show limited confidence in its corrective capacities.

The History and Development of Probation

In the United States, probation began with the innovative work of John Augustus, who was the first to provide bail for defendants, under authority of the Boston Police Court in 1841. However, the roots of probation lie in earlier attempts, primarily in England, to mitigate the harshness of the criminal law.

BENEFIT OF CLERGY   From the 1200s until the practice was abolished in 1827, people accused of serious offenses in England could appeal to the judge for leniency by reading in court the text of Psalm 51. The original purpose of this benefit of clergy was to protect people under church authority, such as monks and nuns, from the power of the king's law. Because this benefit was gradually extended to protect ordinary citizens from capital punishment, Psalm 51 came to be known as the "neck verse." The requirement that the person be able to read favored the upper social classes. Eventually, common thugs memorized the verse so they could pretend to read it before the court and thus avail themselves of its protection; judges then became more arbitrary in granting the benefit. In the United States, people criticized benefit of clergy because of its unequal application and baffling legal character—charges that are often directed at probation today.

judicial reprieve
A practice under English common law whereby a judge could suspend the imposition or execution of a sentence on condition of good behavior on the part of the offender.

JUDICIAL REPRIEVE   Judges have long understood the need to grant leniency to some offenders, and they regularly seek ways to deflect the full punitive force of the law. In nineteenth-century England, **judicial reprieve** became widespread. If an offender requested it, the judge could suspend either the imposition or execution of a sentence for a specified length of time, on condition of good behavior by the offender. At the end of that time, the offender could apply to the Crown for a pardon.

In the United States, judicial reprieve took a different form and led to a series of legal controversies. Rather than limiting the duration of the reprieve, many judges suspended imposition of punishment as long as the offender's behavior remained satisfactory. The idea was that the reprieved offender who remained crime-free need not fear the power of the court; however, the offender who committed another crime was subject to punishment for both crimes.

In 1916 the U.S. Supreme Court declared the discretionary use of such indefinite reprieves unconstitutional.[7] The Court recognized the occasional need to suspend a sentence temporarily because of appeals and other circumstances, but it found that indefinite suspension impinged on the powers of the legislative and executive branches to write and enforce laws. With this decision, probation became subject to the provisions of the states' penal codes.

RECOGNIZANCE   In a search for alternative means to exercise leniency in sentencing, nineteenth-century judges began to experiment with extralegal forms of release. Much

In this austere building in the 1830s, Judge Peter Oxenbridge Thatcher of the Boston Municipal Court originated the practice of recognizance, which led to the development of probation.

Library of Congress Prints and Photographs Division [LC-US262-73134]

of this innovation occurred among the Massachusetts judiciary, whose influence on modern probation was enormous.

One of the trailblazers was Boston Municipal Court Judge Peter Oxenbridge Thatcher, the originator of the practice of **recognizance**. In 1830 Thatcher sentenced Jerusha Chase "upon her own recognizance for her appearance in this court whenever she was called for."[8] In 1837 Massachusetts made recognizance with monetary sureties into law. What made this important was the implied supervision of the court—the fact that the whereabouts and actions of the offender were subject to court involvement.

Both reprieve and recognizance were aimed at humanizing the criminal law and mitigating its harshness. The practices foreshadowed the move toward individualized punishment that would dominate corrections a century later. The major justifications for probation—flexibility in sentencing and individualized punishment—already had strong support. Yet the justice system still needed an institutionalized way of performing recognizance functions.

As the first probation officer, John Augustus was the first to formalize court leniency. Because his philanthropic activities made Augustus a frequent observer in the Boston Police Court, the judge deferred sentencing a man charged with being a common drunkard and released him into Augustus's custody. At the end of a three-week probationary period, the man convinced the judge that he had reformed and therefore received a nominal fine.

Besides being the first to use the term *probation*, Augustus developed the ideas of the presentence investigation, supervision conditions, social casework, reports to the court, and revocation of probation. He screened his cases "to ascertain whether the prisoners were promising subjects for probation, and to this end it was necessary to take into consideration the previous character of the person, his age, and the influences by which he would in future be likely to be surrounded."[9] His methods were analogous to casework strategies: He gained offenders' confidence and friendship, and by helping them get a job or aiding their families in various ways, he helped them reform.

recognizance
A formally recorded obligation to perform some act (such as keep the peace, pay a debt, or appear in court when called) entered by a judge to permit an offender to live in the community, often after posting a sum of money as surety, which would be forfeited by nonappearance.

THE MODERNIZATION OF PROBATION   From its origins in Boston, probation eventually extended to every state and federal jurisdiction. As it developed, the field underwent a curious split. Augustus and his followers had contributed a humanitarian orientation that focused on reformation. In contrast, the new probation officers came largely from the law enforcement community—retired sheriffs and policemen—who had their own orientation.

The strain between the so-called law enforcement role of probation, which emphasizes surveillance of the offender and close controls on behavior, and the social worker role, which emphasizes provision of supportive services to meet offenders' needs, continues today—with no resolution in sight. Advocates of the law enforcement model argue that conditions for community control must be realistic, individualized, and enforceable. Proponents of the social work model believe that supervision must include treatment to help the offender become a worthwhile citizen. Each view has dominated at one time or another in the past half-century.

In the 1940s leaders in probation and other correctional branches began to embrace ideas from psychology about personality and human development. Probation began to emphasize a medical model, with rehabilitation as its overriding goal. This new focus moved probation work—or at least its rhetoric—into the realm of the professions. Although not even a small number of probation departments fully implemented this approach, the ideas underlying it dominated the professional literature.

reintegration model
The belief that crime is caused by poverty, inequality, and lack of opportunity; dealing with crime requires that the effect of these problems be reduced.

The medical model remained influential through the 1960s, when the **reintegration model** came to the fore. This model assumed that crime is a product of poverty, racism, unemployment, unequal opportunities, and other social factors. Probation was seen as central because it was the primary existing means of working with the offender in the problem's context—the offender's community. Methods of probation began to change from direct service (by psychological counseling) to service brokerage: After being assessed, clients were put in touch with appropriate community service agencies. Government studies heralded the need to deal effectively with correctional clients in community contexts, and federal funds were shifted to community-based correctional agencies, including probation agencies. (For a look at a current, innovative approach to probation services delivery, see "Focus on Correctional Practice: New York City Probation Goes Nontraditional.")

In the latter part of the 1970s, thinking about probation changed again in a manner that continues to this day. The goals of rehabilitation and reintegration have given way to an orientation widely referred to as *risk management*. The goal here is to minimize the probability that an offender will commit a new offense, especially by applying tight controls over the probationer's activities and maintaining careful surveillance (see "Myths in Corrections"). Today, offenders are placed on probation in one of four ways. Most commonly, judges impose a sentence of probation directly (60 percent). Sometimes, the judge imposes a sentence of prison that is suspended pending good behavior (22 percent). For still other offenders who are already on probation, an additional sentence is imposed, but its activation is suspended (9 percent). Finally, the court may require that some period of incarceration be served prior to probation; this is called a *split sentence* (9 percent). This last option was quite popular in the 1990s, but its use has waned in the last few years. This may be because many probationers face jail while awaiting trial or because prison space is limited. (We discuss the effectiveness of probation supervision in Chapter 5.)

Who gets probation? In the past it was thought that probation should be reserved for first-time offenders who have committed lesser

MYTHS in Corrections

Who Is on Probation?

THE MYTH: Probation is for nonserious crimes.

THE REALITY: One of every four people convicted of a violent crime receives a probation sentence, and 27 percent of weapons offenders receive a probation sentence.

Source: "Felony Sentences in State Courts, 2006," BJS *Bulletin*, July 2009.

focus on correctional practice

New York City Probation Goes Nontraditional: NeOns for Probation Reporting

The New York City Department of Probation is one of the largest probation departments in the nation, supervising more than 30,000 adults and 15,000 juveniles each year. Each of these probationers is required to report to a probation officer as a condition of the court's sentence. For most of recent history, this could be quite an arduous task—probation offices were located in centralized courthouses that often required long commutes followed by long waiting times to see the probation officer. This was ironic because the office report was usually fairly innocuous: a few questions, a drug test, and an admonition to stay out of trouble—certainly not worth the heavy investment of time.

NYC Probation Commissioner Vincent Schiraldi has begun to change all that. He has instituted a new plan designed to "do less harm, do more good, and do it in the community."

The core for this new strategy is the NeOn: Neighborhood Opportunity Network. These are community centers located where the probationers live (and not in the courts), run by probation but co-located with a wide array of community-based organizations that provide services. The idea is not just to "take office reports," as was traditionally true in the old model, but instead to link probation to job training, educational support services, and other means that enable the person on probation to be better integrated into the range of NYC services that help people succeed in life, rather than just stay crime-free.

NeOns are built to be probationer-friendly. Rather than big waiting rooms and long wait times, NeOns have been architecturally designed to minimize wait time and maximize contact with direct-service providers. Probationers are treated as "clients" rather than "offenders." The goal is to provide the kind of support needed for people on probation to succeed in life, rather than merely "stay out of trouble."

The new approach has been a sea change in New York City probation, requiring the retraining of probation officers and the recalibration of the entire probation system, too. Although it is too early to know if it is working, it is certainly already well known to have generated new excitement on the part of probation staff and new, positive responses by the clients who used to be mere "probationers."

Critical Thinking

1. Would the NeOn approach be successful in your community?
2. What political factors are necessary for NeOns to succeed?

Source: Urban Omnibus, "From Waiting Rooms to Resource Hubs: Designing Change at the Department of Probation," http://urbanomnibus.net/2012/10 /from-waiting-rooms-to-resource-hubs-designing-change-at-the-department -of-probation.

---

crimes. This idea has changed over time: Today, 50 percent of probationers have been convicted of a felony, and about one-fifth have been convicted of a violent crime. The ethnic/race and gender characteristics of probationers compared to those incarcerated are shown in **Table 4.1**.

Table 4.1 Ethnicity and Gender of Probationers and Prisoners by Percentage

Probationers are more likely to be white and female than are offenders who are confined in prison or jail.

	Race				Sex	
	White	African American	Hispanic	Other	Male	Female
Probation	55	30	13	2	76	24
Jail	43	39	16	1	88	12
Prison	38	38	21	3	92	8

Sources: Most-recent reports of the Bureau of Justice Statistics.

INTERMEDIATE SANCTIONS

intermediate sanctions
A variety of punishments that are more restrictive than traditional probation but less severe and costly than incarceration.

People who think probation is "too lenient," but who recognize the costliness of prison, argue that we need a range of sanctions falling between prison and probation: **intermediate sanctions**. These are sanctions that restrict the offender more than does simple probation and that constitute actual punishment for more-serious offenders. The use of probation is more than a century old, but intermediate sanctions are a more recent aspect of correctional policy.

In fact, while the case for intermediate sanctions instead of probation seems strong, the argument for intermediate sanctions *instead of prison* is just as solid. Indeed, to treat prison as the primary means of punishment is wrong on two grounds. First, most sanctions in Western democracies do not involve imprisonment. In the United States, as we have seen, probation is the most common sanction: For every offender in prison or jail, three are on probation or parole. In Europe, this is even more evident. For example, Germany imposes fines as a sole sanction on two-thirds of its property offenders; in England, the figure approaches half. Community service is the preferred sanction for most property offenders in England. Sweden, the Netherlands, France, Austria, and virtually all other European Union countries use such sanctions far more than incarceration. Because nonprison sanctions occur worldwide, it makes little sense to think of them as nonpunishment.

The second reason to question prison as the primary punishment is that it is simply not effective in most cases. We expect prison to teach the offender something and divert him or her from a life of crime, but evidence speaks to the contrary. Studies now show that people who go to prison do worse after their release than they would have done under a sentence to a community penalty.[10]

Finally, intermediate sanctions allow a closer tailoring of the punishment to the offender's situation. For many offenders, a fine is adequate punishment. Others may be required to complete a drug treatment program. Still others can be confined to home for a while. In sum, intermediate sanctions, tailored to fit the offender's circumstances, may provide the greatest justice for many. This may be one reason that public opinion surveys so consistently find support for intermediate sanctions as alternatives to prison and traditional probation.

continuum of sanctions
A range of correctional management strategies based on the degree of intrusiveness and control over the offender, along which an offender is moved based on his or her response to correctional programs.

To achieve their objectives, corrections systems have developed a **continuum of sanctions**—a range of punishments that vary in intrusiveness and control, as shown in Figure 4.1. Probation plus a fine or community service may be appropriate for minor offenses, whereas six weeks of boot camp followed by intensive probation supervision may be right for serious crimes.

After his DWI conviction, Olympic champion swimmer Michael Phelps was placed on probation for 18 months and ordered to continue receiving treatment for alcoholism. This kind of intermediate sanction is commonly used to avoid incarceration in cases of drunk driving.

Landov/Paul J. Richards/AFP/Getty Images

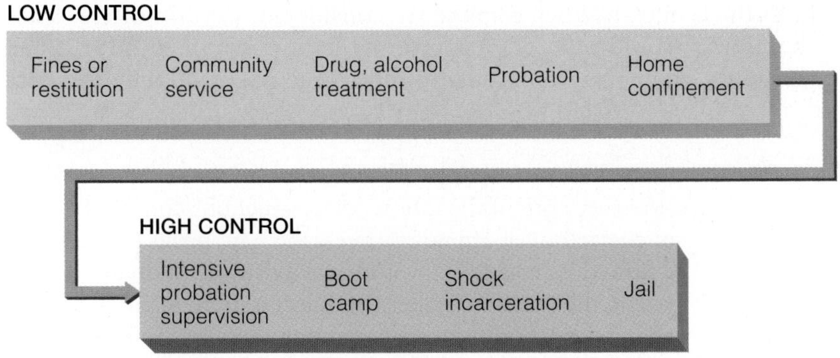

LOW CONTROL

| Fines or restitution | Community service | Drug, alcohol treatment | Probation | Home confinement |

HIGH CONTROL

| Intensive probation supervision | Boot camp | Shock incarceration | Jail |

FIGURE 4.1
Continuum of Sanctions
Judges may use a range of intermediate sanctions, from those exerting a low level of control to those exerting a high level.

Problems with Intermediate Sanctions

Despite the growing range of alternatives to incarceration, all is not well with the intermediate sanctions movement. Problems arise in selecting which agencies will operate the process and which offenders will receive the sanction. A greater problem is the question of net widening.

SELECTING AGENCIES   Administrators of such traditional agencies as jails, prisons, probation, and parole often argue that they should also administer intermediate sanctions. They claim they have the staff and experience to design new programs. They suggest that to maintain program coherence, they should be the ones who ought to operate all correctional processes. Critics counter that because traditional correctional organizations must give highest priority to their own operations, they cannot give adequate attention or support to midrange alternatives.

SELECTING OFFENDERS   A second issue has to do with selecting the "right" offenders for alternative programs (see "Do the Right Thing"). Many argue that violent or drug-marketing offenses are so abhorrent that a nonincarcerative program is not appropriate. Others contend that these offenders are best able to adjust to these programs.

DO the Right Thing

You are a judge who is about to sentence James Walters, a nineteen-year-old who has pled guilty to breaking and entering. It is the second time he has been convicted of this crime; the first time was three years ago, when he was only sixteen, and he was processed as a juvenile delinquent.

As the probation report reads, "Mr. Walters has already received a chance to succeed on probation, and he was largely uncooperative. While he did not have any additional arrests during his two-year probation term, he was often late for appointments with his probation officer and showed little motivation for treatment. A brief period of incarceration is called for."

The victim of the crime says, "He broke a window and stole my new computer. The whole thing cost me

$950 to make right. I'd like to get my money back, and then some."

Walters is completely broke and has no job, and you know that to order restitution would be fruitless.

The prosecutor has asked for a six-month county jail sentence, but the defense attorney argues that Walters is a perfect candidate for the new probation restitution center, in which he would earn the money to pay the victim back for the damages.

Critical Thinking

What would you do? Send Walters to jail or give him a chance to make restitution? If restitution, how would it be enforced?

In practice, both the crime and the criminal are considered. Certain offenses are so serious that the public would not tolerate intermediate punishments for them. At the same time, judges want programs to respond to the needs of the offenders they sentence.

NET WIDENING   Critics of intermediate sanctions say that they *widen the net* of social control. This accusation strikes at the very core of the intermediate sanctions concept because instead of reducing the control exerted over offenders' lives, the new programs actually increase it. You can readily see how this might occur. With the existence of an alternative at each possible point in the system, the decision maker can select a more intrusive option than ordinarily would have been imposed. For instance, community service can be added to probation; shock incarceration can be added to a straight probation term.

Available evidence reveals that implementing intermediate sanctions has had three consequences:

1. *Wider nets:* The reforms increase the proportion of people in society whose behavior is regulated or controlled by the state.

2. *Stronger nets:* By intensifying the state's intervention powers, the reforms augment the state's capacity to control people.

3. *Different nets:* The reforms create new jurisdictional authority or transfer it from one agency or control system to another.

Varieties of Intermediate Sanctions

In the United States, the desire to strengthen alternatives to incarceration is a relatively recent phenomenon, stemming in large part from concerns about the long-standing rise in imprisonment beginning in the 1970s and continuing until very recently. People saw this pattern of growth and tried to develop ways of slowing it down. Building stronger alternatives to incarceration seemed a logical idea.

Some alternatives have been around for a long time. Probation as a sentence has been available to judges for more than a century, and this is true for fines, as well. The main issue that reformers have faced with these long-standing sanctions is how to make them more attractive to judges so that they might use them more readily. In the case of probation, this has generally meant making it "tougher," with more intensive supervision, more intrusive court-ordered conditions, and stricter enforcement. Regarding fines, the challenge has been to make them variable enough that a range of crimes, from less to more serious, can be appropriately sanctioned that way.

Other alternatives are much more recent. The advent of geo-spatial software made electronic monitoring possible—it was only an idea in people's forward-thinking imaginations as recently as 40 years ago. Other kinds of sanctions that use drugs to control behavior are also quite recent.

In the latest round of new alternatives, reformers have begun to create specialized courts that provide distinctive kinds of support for subpopulations. For example, drug courts deal with people having trouble staying clean of substance abuse, reentry courts handle people who are returning to the community from prison, and community courts handle problems that may not seem like serious issues but that create particular difficulties for communities—such as street prostitution and public nuisance violations.

How the various sanctions programs relate to one another depends on the jurisdiction using them. For example, one county may use intensive supervision in lieu of a jail sentence; another may use intensive supervision for probation violators. We have organized our description of the main types of intermediate sanctions according to which agencies administer them—the judiciary, probation departments, or correctional departments.

SANCTIONS ADMINISTERED PRIMARILY BY THE JUDICIARY   The demand for intermediate sanctions often comes from judges dissatisfied with their sentencing options. In courts that have managerial authority over probation, this discontent has translated into new probation programs. Other courts have sought to expand their sentencing options by relying more on programs within their control, such as pretrial diversion, fines, forfeiture, community service, and restitution. These programs aim primarily at reducing trial caseloads, especially focusing on less serious offenders who ought not to tie up the court system. The programs also seek to impose meaningful sanctions without incarceration.

The effectiveness of these programs is mixed. Studies have found that, without such programs, many—perhaps most—of the offenders who were ordered to provide community service and restitution would have been punished with a traditional probation sentence. This does not speak strongly to community service being a real solution for correctional crowding. The most comprehensive study of community service versus imprisonment finds persuasive evidence that community service results in *lower* recidivism rates than prison for offenders with similar backgrounds.[11] Moreover, offenders subjected to restitution experience it as both punitive and rehabilitative. And community service cases may end up having lower rearrest rates than would be expected if they had been sentenced differently.

Pretrial Diversion Pretrial-diversion programs typically target petty drug offenders. A strategy in Wayne County (Detroit), Michigan, exemplifies this practice. First-time arrestees for drug possession are "fast-tracked" into drug treatment programs within hours of arrest. They are promised that if they successfully complete the drug treatment program, the charges against them will be dropped.

Fines More than $3 billion in fines is collected annually in the United States. Yet, compared with other Western democracies, the United States makes little use of fines as the sole punishment for crimes more serious than motor vehicle violations; nationally, about 1 percent of felons receive fines as the sole penalty.[11] Instead, judges typically use fines with other sanctions, such as probation and incarceration. Judges cite the difficulty of enforcing and collecting fines from impoverished defendants as the reason they do not make greater use of them. They fear that fines would be paid from the proceeds of additional illegal acts and that fines let affluent offenders "buy" their way out of jail while forcing the poor to serve time.

In Europe, fines are used extensively, are enforced, and are normally the sole sanction for a wide range of crimes. The amounts are geared to both the severity of the

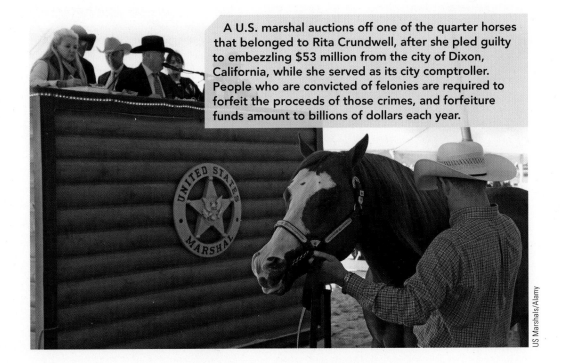

A U.S. marshal auctions off one of the quarter horses that belonged to Rita Crundwell, after she pled guilty to embezzling $53 million from the city of Dixon, California, while she served as its city comptroller. People who are convicted of felonies are required to forfeit the proceeds of those crimes, and forfeiture funds amount to billions of dollars each year.

US Marshals/Alamy

day fine
A criminal penalty based on the amount of income that an offender earns in a day's work.

forfeiture
Government seizure of property and other assets derived from or used in criminal activity.

offense and the resources of the offender. To deal with the concern that fines exact a heavier toll on the poor than on the wealthy, Sweden and Germany have developed the **day fine**, which bases the penalty on the offender's income. For example, a person making $36,500 a year and sentenced to 10 units of punishment would pay $3,650; a person making $3,650 and receiving the same penalty would pay $365.

Forfeiture   **Forfeiture**, in which the government seizes property derived from or used in criminal activity, can take both civil and criminal forms. Under civil law, property used in criminal activity (for example, automobiles, boats, or equipment used to manufacture illegal drugs) can be seized without a finding of guilt. Under criminal law, forfeiture is imposed as a consequence of conviction and requires that the offender relinquish various assets related to the crime. These assets can be considerable. For example, in 2010 state and federal officials confiscated $1.8 billion worth of assets from drug dealers.[12]

However, forfeiture is controversial. Critics argue that confiscating property without a court hearing violates citizens' constitutional rights. In 1993 the U.S. Supreme Court restricted the use of summary forfeiture.[13] Today the use of this form of sanction is less common.

Community Service and Restitution   Although for years judges have imposed community service and restitution, few judges have used them as exclusive sanctions. Recently, with prisons overcrowded and judges searching for efficient sentencing options, interest in these sanctions has increased.

Community service requires the offender to provide a specified number of hours of free labor in some public service, such as street cleaning, repair of run-down housing, or hospital volunteer work. **Restitution** is a sum of money that the offender must pay either to the victim or to a public fund for crime victims.

Both alternatives rest on the assumption that the offender can atone for his or her offense with a personal or financial contribution to the victim or to society. These approaches have been called *reparative alternatives* because they seek to repair some of the harm done. Such approaches have become popular because they force the offender to make a positive contribution to offset the damage, thus satisfying a common public desire that offenders not "get away" with their crimes.

community service
Compensation for injury to society by the performance of service in the community.

restitution
Compensation for financial, physical, or emotional loss caused by an offender, in the form of either payment of money to the victim or to a public fund for crime victims, as stipulated by the court.

In Austin, Texas, the community court requires people who are convicted of low-level crimes to clean the streets of rubbish. Advocates of the community court say that people who commit crimes ought to "pay back" to the public through community service.

Marjorie Kamys Cotera/Bob Daemmrich Photography/Alamy

The effectiveness of these programs is mixed. Studies have found that without such programs, many—perhaps most—of the offenders who were ordered to provide community service and restitution would have been punished with a traditional probation sentence. This bodes poorly for community service as a real solution for correctional crowding. Nor have community service and restitution programs proved especially effective at reducing the criminal behavior of their participants; in fact, they may even have somewhat higher failure rates than do the regular supervision cases.

Drug courts are a way to enable judges to provide close oversight of people who are on probation after being convicted of crimes involving drug abuse. The drug court model creates a specialized court devoted to a subset of offenders who exhibit drug-related criminality. Probation supervision is tailored to provide treatment for drug abuse, and the drug court judge is directly involved in the progress of treatment, meeting face-to-face with the probationer on a regular basis. Judicial involvement is meant to establish an incentive for the offender to follow the probation treatment plan by giving positive reinforcement when it is followed and imposing sanctions when it is not. Well-designed studies have shown that the drug court model has reduced recidivism, sometimes by a large margin.[14] However, because people who fail in the drug court model receive much longer sentences than they might have if they had not faced the drug court, cost savings through drug courts are much less than might be anticipated.[15]

drug court
A specialized way of handling drug-involved offenders in which the court takes a more active role in the probationer's progress while the probationer is under supervision.

SANCTIONS ADMINISTERED IN THE COMMUNITY Probation leaders have developed new intermediate sanctions programs that increase the level of surveillance and control. They have revamped older programs to make them more efficient and able to fit more probationers.

Day Reporting (Treatment) Centers In Chapter 5 we describe the problem of probation failure. Recently, as prisons have become more and more crowded, and prison budgets more strained, judges have become reluctant to incarcerate people who were failing on probation, except for serious crimes. Instead, they have developed probation-run enforcement programs: **probation centers**, where persistent probation violators reside for short periods; *day reporting centers,* where violators attend daylong intervention and treatment sessions; and **restitution centers**, where those who fall behind in restitution are sent to earn money to make payments on their debt.

All three types of centers are usually referred to as day reporting centers, and they are modeled after an innovation developed in Great Britain in the 1970s. In the United States, these facilities vary widely, but all provide a credible option for probation agencies to enforce conditions when prisons are overcrowded. Most day reporting centers use a mix of common correctional methods. For example, some provide a treatment regime comparable to that of a halfway house—but without the problems of running a residential facility. Others provide contact levels equal to or greater than intensive supervision programs, in effect creating a community equivalent to confinement. However, studies of day reporting centers have found disappointing results, suggesting that the model neither saves money nor reduces recidivism.[16]

probation center
Residential facility where persistent probation violators are sent for short periods of time.

restitution center
Facility where probationers who fall behind in restitution are sent to make payments on their debt.

Intensive Supervision **Intensive supervision probation (ISP)** targets offenders who are subject to incarceration, providing strict supervision and control. Even the most-ambitious programs require only daily meetings between probation officers and offenders. Such meetings, which might last ten minutes or less, can never occupy more than a small portion of the offender's waking hours, so ISP programs assume that the burden for "making it" falls on the probationer.

Evaluations of ISP programs have found that they can reduce rearrest rates but that doing so always comes at a cost. Because of the closer contact between probation officers and their clients, many more rules violations are uncovered. Therefore, ISP programs often have higher technical failure rates than regular probation does. Indeed, the most rigorous study of ISP in California found that ISP clients did much worse under the stricter rules, without a reduction in rearrests.[17] When all is said and done, ISPs in

intensive supervision probation (ISP)
Probation granted with conditions of strict reporting to a probation officer with a limited caseload.

Urine testing has become a standard part of most community corrections and probation supervision programs. One reason that some people fail programs is that their urines turn out to be "dirty," showing evidence of continued use of banned substances.

California not only failed to reduce crime but actually cost the public more than if the programs had not been started in the first place.

home confinement
Sentence whereby offenders serve terms of incarceration in their own homes.

Home Confinement   Under **home confinement**, offenders are sentenced to incarceration but serve their term in their own homes. Variations are possible. For instance, after a time some offenders might be allowed to go to work or simply leave home for restricted periods of the day; others might be allowed to maintain employment for their entire sentence.

Home confinement is appealing. It costs the state nothing to house the offender; the offender pays for lodging, subsistence, and often even the cost of an electronic monitor. More importantly, significant community ties can be maintained—to family, friends (restricted visitation is ordinarily allowed), employers, and community groups. The punishment is more visible to the community than if the offender were sent to prison. The goals of reintegration, deterrence, and financial responsibility are served simultaneously. When people know a little bit about home confinement, they tend to favor it for many kinds of crimes.

Electronic Monitoring   One of the most popular new approaches to probation supervision is surveillance by electronic monitors. Electronic monitoring is ordinarily combined with and used to enforce home confinement. The number of offenders currently being monitored is difficult to estimate because the equipment manufacturers consider this to be privileged information. However, the best estimates are that about 20 different companies provide electronic monitoring for more than 200,000 offenders—a total that has doubled in a decade.[18] But only a handful of these offenders were diverted from a prison or jail sentence to the monitoring. For the rest, electronic monitoring is a condition of a probation sentence.

Two basic types of electronic monitoring devices exist. Passive monitors respond only to inquiries; most commonly, the offender receives an automated telephone call from the probation office and is told to place the monitor on a receiver attached to the phone. Active devices that use satellite tracking to provide 24-hour verification of an offender's exact location have recently become more feasible.

Advocates for these systems point out that monitoring devices are more humane than prison or jail because offenders keep their jobs and stay with their families. In addition, probation officers are free to spend more time addressing the offenders' needs rather than just providing surveillance. A study of electronic monitoring for people convicted of sex crimes in California found being monitored electronically increased the rates of compliance with California law and decreased rates of absconding.[19] In Denmark the use of electronic monitoring for younger offenders has been associated with improvements in social adjustment.[20] The companies that provide electronic monitoring claim that a "new generation" of devices and programs will more closely integrate monitoring into treatment aspects of programs, rather than just providing surveillance.

SANCTIONS ADMINISTERED IN INSTITUTIONS AND THE COMMUNITY Correctional agencies have had to develop intermediate sanctions to manage the burgeoning load of offenders. Some correctional agencies rely on electronic monitoring to support an early-release program, but shock incarceration and boot camps are the two most common responses to overcrowding.

Shock Incarceration The fact that the deterrent effect of incarceration wears off after a very short term of imprisonment has led to experimentation with **shock incarceration**. The offender is sentenced to a jail or prison term; then, after the offender has served 30 to 90 days, the judge reduces the sentence. The assumption is that the offender will find the jail experience so distasteful that he or she will be motivated to "stay clean."

Shock incarceration is controversial. Its critics argue that it combines the undesirable aspects of both probation and imprisonment. Offenders who are incarcerated lose their jobs, have their community relationships disrupted, acquire the label of convict, and are exposed to the brutalizing experiences of the institution. Further, the release to probation reinforces the idea that the system is arbitrary in decision making and that probation is a "break" rather than a truly individualized supervision program. It is hard to see how such treatment will not demean and embitter offenders. Further, many studies of shock incarceration show no reduction in recidivism rates. But interest has remained high, leading to a new form of the shock technique called boot camp.

shock incarceration
A short period of incarceration (the "shock"), followed by a sentence reduction.

Correctional boot camps attempt to recreate the harsh discipline of military boot camps, hoping that the discipline will pay off in lower recidivism rates. Evaluation studies have not shown this approach to be very successful.

focus on correctional policy

How Much Are the Various Alternative Sanctions Used?

There are numerous alternatives to prison—in this book, we list well more than a dozen. In practice, though, how much are they used?

Like so much in the American corrections system, the answer varies from place to place. For example, the rate of people under community supervision averages about 2,000 per 100,000 adults (about 2 percent), but ranges from a high of over 7,000 (Georgia) to a low of under 600 (New Hampshire). So the answer to the question really is "It depends."

That said, some forms of criminal sanctions are used extensively. More than a third of all those convicted of a felony are fined, one in five are ordered to do community service, and one-tenth must pay restitution. For most of these people, the financial penalty is not the only requirement—they are also placed under community supervision and required to obey its conditions.

Some forms of alternative penalties are waning in use. Boot camps have recently become less popular, as research has failed to show their effectiveness. Intensive supervision programs and shock incarceration programs, very popular in the 1980s, have declined in recent years—for some of the same reasons of lack of supporting evidence. The use of electronic monitoring systems, having grown rapidly in the 1990s, seems now to be stabilizing.

On the other hand, the number of drug courts has increased dramatically—there are at least 2,800 of these courts at last count. Other reentry programs have also blossomed as policy makers try to find ways to reduce recidivism rates for people under supervision in the community.

Thus, it can be fairly said that the number of alternative correctional strategies is always changing, as new ideas come along and old ones prove problematic.

---

boot camp
A physically rigorous, disciplined, and demanding regimen emphasizing conditioning, education, and job training that is designed for young offenders.

Boot Camp   One variation of shock incarceration is the **boot camp**, in which offenders serve a short institutional sentence and then go through a rigorous, paramilitary regimen designed to develop discipline and respect for authority. The daily routine includes strenuous workouts, marches, drills, and hard physical labor.

Proponents of boot camps argue that many young offenders get involved in crime because they lack self-respect and cannot order their lives. Consequently, the boot camp model targets young first offenders who seem to be embarking on a path of sustained criminality. Rigorous evaluations show that this sanction does not reduce rates of recidivism,[21] although there may be savings in correctional costs if boot camp failures spend less time in prison after their failures.[22] As a result, critics argue that military-style physical training and the harshness of the experience do little to overcome problems that get inner-city youths in trouble with the law. In fact, follow-ups of boot camp graduates show that they do no better than other offenders after release. This ineffectiveness has led several authorities to close down their boot camps. But even more troubling are the charges of fatal physical abuse that led the state of Florida to close all of its boot camps.

Alternative sanctions are not employed uniformly across the United States. See "Focus on Correctional Policy: How Much Are the Various Alternative Sanctions Used?" for examples.

Making Intermediate Sanctions Work

Intermediate sanctions profess lofty goals such as improving justice, saving money, and preventing crime. Yet the limited record on intermediate sanctions suggests that these goals are not always accomplished. If intermediate sanctions are to work, they must be carefully planned and implemented. Even then, they must overcome obstacles and resolve such issues as sentencing philosophies and practices, offender-selection criteria, and surveillance and control methods.

SENTENCING ISSUES   The most important issue concerning the use of intermediate sanctions has to do with sentencing philosophy and practice. In recent years, greater

focus on correctional practice

Rethinking Revocation of Community Supervision

When someone is placed under some form of community supervision, the sentencing authority usually sets a series of "conditions of supervision": rules that the person will have to obey. These rules are quite varied, ranging from fairly straightforward financial penalties such as restitution, fines, or fees to quite idiosyncratic requirements such as driving restrictions or limitations on places a person can visit. When someone fails to follow a sentencing condition, the sentencing authority can revoke community supervision status and send the person to prison. This can add up to a lot of prison time—often a third or more of the people going into prison are sent there after having their community supervision status revoked because they have violated the conditions of supervision. Critics say we need a whole new approach to such conditions.

For one thing, the logic underlying the imposition of certain conditions is not always apparent. Sentencing authorities often impose multiple financial penalties, even when the person's ability to pay is questionable—fines, restitution, and court fees will often amount to several thousand dollars, for example. Some conditions seem unrealistic—people are often told not to associate with others who have criminal records, even when this means staying away from many family members and neighbors. Other conditions seem downright odd. One probationer was required "never to sit in the front seat of a car," while another was instructed "not to get pregnant." Sometimes, a condition can be meaninglessly vague: "Be of good behavior."

Too often, so many conditions are stacked onto a person that it seems unlikely that anyone would be able to successfully follow all of them. This may be one of the reasons that enforcement of conditions suffers from so much disparity. Misbehavior that will get one person back in court facing prison for a year or two will result in a simple chewing out for another.

Reformers argue that our system of supervision conditions needs to be changed in four main ways:

1. Rather than community supervision, most people should be punished with fines or short jail terms. If a person is fined or ordered to pay restitution, this should be the entire penalty, and no additional supervision should be required.

2. Community supervision conditions should be limited only to requirements that are directly related to risk of new criminality so that the purpose of community penalties is to aid in successful reintegration into the community.

3. The length of time that a person should serve under community supervision should be short—only long enough for a person to demonstrate successful reintegration into the community.

4. To reduce disparity in the enforcement of conditions, a guidelines system should be used that matches the seriousness of the infraction to the severity of the enforcement.

Critics of community supervision say that this kind of reform would not only make the rules more logical and meaningful but that it would also reduce the number of people who end up back in prison because of revocation.

Critical Thinking

1. What would happen if there were more use of fines and other penalties and less use of probation and other forms of community supervision?

2. Is it reasonable to focus community supervision on "risk management" and leave other functions to other aspects of the corrections system? Why or why not?

Source: Cecelia Klingele, "Rethinking the Use of Community Supervision," *Journal of Criminal Law and Criminology* 103 (no. 4, 2013): 1015–69.

emphasis has been placed on deserved punishment: the idea that similar offenses deserve penalties of similar severity. Intermediate sanctions could potentially increase the number of midrange severe punishments and thereby improve justice.

Yet advocates of deserved punishment argue that it is not automatically evident how intermediate sanctions compare with either prison or probation in terms of severity, nor is it clear how different intermediate sanctions compare with one another. When intermediate sanctions are used to reduce prison crowding, the issue becomes even murkier. For example, is it fair for some offenders to receive prison terms while others who have similar offenses receive the intermediate sanction alternative?

principle of interchangeability
The idea that different forms of intermediate sanctions can be calibrated to make them equivalent as punishments despite their differences in approach.

For intermediate sanctions to be effective, exchange rates consistent with the **principle of interchangeability** must be developed so that one form can be substituted for or added to another form. In other words, different forms of intermediate sanctions must be calibrated to make them equivalent as punishments despite their differences in approach. For example, 2 weeks of jail might be considered equal to 30 days of intermittent confinement, 2 months of home confinement, 100 hours of community service, or a month's salary.

In practice, some observers have tried to structure this principle of interchangeability by describing punishment in terms of units: A month in prison might count as 30 units; a month on intensive supervision might count as 10. Thus, a year on ISP would be about the same as a four-month prison stay. To date, no one has designed a full-blown system of interchangeability, although both the federal sentencing guidelines and those in Oregon embrace the concept of punishment units. The future will likely bring attempts to create interchangeability based on equivalence in punishments.

SELECTION OF OFFENDERS   If intermediate sanctions are to work, they must be reserved for appropriate offenders; which offenders are chosen, in turn, depends on a program's goals. No matter what the program's goals are, however, intermediate sanctions must be made available regardless of race, sex, or age.

The Target Group   Intermediate sanctions have two general goals: (1) to serve as a less costly alternative to prison and (2) to provide a more effective alternative to probation. To meet these goals, intermediate sanctions managers search for appropriate offenders to include in their program—often a difficult task.

Prison alternatives are designed for offenders who would otherwise be incarcerated. But how can we be certain that an offender given an alternative sanction would have otherwise been sentenced to prison? In most jurisdictions a person who is sentenced to probation is legally eligible for a prison sentence. Research shows that even though many offenders who are sentenced to intermediate sanctions are eligible for prison, most—if not all—actually would have been placed on probation instead. Yet there are plenty of prison-bound offenders who seem to be appropriate candidates for intermediate sanctions: One study of offenders entering California prisons found that as many as one-fourth would have been suitable for this alternative.[23]

Because of judges' reluctance to divert offenders from prison, many intermediate sanctions programs billed as prison alternatives actually serve as probation alternatives. As an example, consider boot camp programs, which are usually restricted to first-time property offenders ages 16 to 25. Boot camp, then, cannot be considered an effective prison alternative because young, first-time property offenders seldom go to prison.

Clearly, when intermediate sanctions are applied to the wrong target group, they cannot achieve their goals. When prison alternatives are applied to nonprison cases, they cannot save money. When probation-enhancement programs are provided to low-risk clients, they cannot reduce much crime.

Problems of Bias   Race, sex, and age bias are of particular concern for intermediate sanctions. Because getting sentenced to an intermediate sanction involves official (usually judicial) discretion, the concern is that white, middle-class offenders will receive less-harsh treatment than will other groups. In fact, unless program administrators work hard to widen their program's applicability, nonwhites will most likely remain incarcerated rather than receive alternative sanctions, and minorities will most likely be subjected to tougher supervision instead of regular probation.

Alternative sanctions also tend to be designed for men, not women. One could argue that this is reasonable because men make up over 80 percent of the correctional population, but the patently unfair result may be that special programs are available *only* for men. Moreover, some experts on female offenders challenge the design of intermediate sanctions, which is often based on tough supervision. They argue that measures for many women offenders should instead emphasize social services.

The solution to the problem of bias is neither obvious nor uncontroversial. Most observers recognize that some discretion is necessary in placing offenders in specialized programs. They believe that without the confidence of program officials, offenders are likely to fail. This means that automatic eligibility for these programs may not be a good idea. It may be necessary to recognize the potential for bias and to control it by designing programs especially for certain populations, such as women, making certain that cultural factors are taken into account in selecting offenders for these programs.

SURVEILLANCE AND CONTROL   Intermediate sanctions have, for the most part, been developed during a period in which correctional policy has been enmeshed in the politics of "getting tough on crime." Not surprisingly, most of these alternatives tend to emphasize their toughness. Boot camps are described as providing no-nonsense discipline; intensive supervision expressly incorporates surveillance and control as primary strategies. Certainly, this rhetoric is useful in obtaining public support for the programs. But do the programs themselves benefit from being so unabashedly tough?

Growing evidence indicates that the tough aspects of intermediate sanctions may not be totally positive (see "Focus on Correctional Practice: Rethinking Revocation of Community Supervision"). As we have seen, when both the requirements of supervision and the surveillance of offenders increase, more violations are detected and more probationers face revocation of probation. However, if "being tough"—upgrading standards and their enforcement—has no impact on crime but instead merely costs more money (through the need to process more violators), where is the benefit? Some people wonder whether the costs of stricter measures outweigh the benefits.

For those who favor "tough" probation, there is a new project that offers a glimmer of hope. It is called Project HOPE.[24] The project started when a Hawaii judge, Steven Alm, became frustrated with the long line of probation revocations he kept confronting in his courtroom. Many of the probationers came to him after their ninth or tenth violation, long after they had settled into a pattern of violations. Instead, together with probation administrators, he developed a new approach that would use short sanctions, swiftly implemented, imposed after the first violation. Dubbed Hawaii's Opportunity Probation with Enforcement (HOPE), the project begins with a stern warning offered by the court: "The first dirty urine or missed appointment and you will be back in jail, only to come out back on probation and start over again." The program works that way; probationers who violate their probation are taken before the judge the day of the violation and go right to jail for about a week. Then they come back out on probation. The idea is to make sanctions credible but not draconian, and to force probationers to choose whether they go to jail or not by their behavior.

Results of Project HOPE have been impressive. Compared to a control group, HOPE probationers have fewer dirty urines, have fewer missed appointments, have fewer arrests, and spend much less time behind bars.[25] The results have been so impressive that the U.S. Department of Justice is promoting widespread dissemination of the model. But some criminologists think the enthusiasm for HOPE is premature. They say that the original program applied to only a subset of people in jail, and knowing that correctional panaceas rarely live up to their claims, they call for more studies of HOPE-style efforts.[26] (For a new development in recidivism management, see "Focus on Correctional Technology"; compare this to "Focus on Correctional Practice: New York City Probation Goes Nontraditional," found earlier in this chapter.)

THE NEW CORRECTIONAL PROFESSIONAL

Without a doubt, the advent of intermediate sanctions has changed the work world of the professional in corrections. The long-standing choice between prison and probation now includes community and residential options that run the gamut from tough, surveillance-oriented operations to supportive, treatment-based programs. The

focus on correctional technology

Objective Risk Assessment Systems

Community corrections managers need a way to determine which cases present the most risk to the community. But predicting a person's likelihood of recidivism is a tricky business. Often, people with serious previous crimes will do well on probation, but sometimes people with no prior record will perform quite badly in the community. Obviously, being wrong about a prediction of future criminality poses real problems for community corrections sentencing.

One of the ways to improve predictions is to use "objective risk assessment instruments." These instruments look at past cases to determine which factors seem to be most predictive of new arrests and which seem to suggest successful completion of the probation term. Once these factors are known, a probationer is assessed to determine which of these factors apply to his or her case. The factors are "added up" into a total score—the total number of positive factors minus the number of negative factors. The result is a "risk score." The risk score does not say whether a person will or will not be rearrested, but it does represent *how much of a risk* a person represents of rearrest, compared to people with higher or lower scores. With most systems, the higher the score, the greater the risk.

There are several objective risk assessment systems in use today. One of the most popular is the Level of Service Inventory–Revised™ (LSI-R™), developed from 157,947 North American youth and adult offenders from 10 jurisdictions. The LSI-R combines 54 different factors taken from 10 areas of functioning:

- criminal history
- education/employment
- financial
- family/marital
- accommodation
- leisure/recreation
- companions
- alcohol/drug use
- emotional/personal
- attitudes/orientation

The use of risk assessment is well established in community corrections. Scholars say that the next important challenge is to use these assessments to improve supervision outcomes. Many of the factors that go into the risk assessment are *static*, meaning they do not change (e.g., criminal history). But other factors, such as "employment status" and "alcohol/drug use," are considered *dynamic* because they can change over time. Community supervision strategies can be expressly designed to change these dynamic risk factors so that the person comes to represent less of an overall risk to the community.

Critical Thinking

1. What problems do you see with implementation of an objective risk assessment system?

2. Should a risk assessment system be the only tool for decision makers?

3. What would happen if risk assessment became the first step in the design of the community treatment process?

Sources: Faye S. Taxman and Michael S. Caudy, "Risk Tells Us Who, But Not What or How: Empirical Assessment of the Complexity of Criminogenic Needs to Inform Correctional Programming," *Criminology & Public Policy* 14 (no. 1, 2015): 71–103; for LSI-R, see www.mhs.com/product .aspx?gr=saf&id=overview&prod=lsi-r.

---

kinds of professionals needed to staff these programs vary from recent college graduates to experienced and well-trained mental health clinicians. However, central to this growth are three major shifts in the working environment of the new correctional professional.

First, nongovernment organizations have emerged to administer community corrections programs. Hundreds of nonprofit agencies now dot the correctional landscape. These organizations contract with probation and parole agencies to provide services to clients in the community.

Second, an increased emphasis on accountability has reduced individual discretion. Professionals currently work within boundaries, often defined as guidelines, that specify policy options for different case types. For instance, a staff member may be told that each offender must be seen twice a month in the office and once a month in the community and that each time a urine sample must be taken. Rules such as these not only constrain discretion but also provide a basis for holding staff accountable.

Third, the relationship between the professional and the client has become less important than the principles of criminal justice that underlie that relationship. Instead of training in psychology and counseling, for instance, the new correctional professional receives training in law and criminal justice decision making. This means that the sources of job satisfaction have shifted from helping offenders with their problems toward simply shepherding offenders through the system.

Thus, the new correctional professional is more accountable for decision making and is more oriented toward the system in carrying out agency policy. This shift has significant implications for the motivation and training of staff, but it also means that in the traditional three-way balance among offender, staff, and bureaucracy, the last has grown in importance.

COMMUNITY CORRECTIONS LEGISLATION

The differences in the style and philosophy of correctional programs in different localities reflect a basic truth about law and order: Beliefs about right and wrong, as well as values about how to deal with wrongdoers, differ from one locality to the next. Over the years the concept of community corrections has revolved around many themes, but one core idea has endured—that local governments know best how to deal with their own crime problems. As such, local and state laws reflect unique ways of implementing community corrections, even though they share similar goals. As we will see in the following discussions, the implementation and evaluation of community corrections are designed to take these local differences into account.

Reducing the Reliance on Prison

Community corrections legislation is best understood in terms of its goal to reduce reliance on prisons. In pursuit of this goal, it embraces a wide spectrum of alternatives to incarceration among which judges and other criminal justice system officials can choose.

In the late 1960s and early 1970s, several states considered legislation that would establish financial and programmatic incentives for community corrections. For example, in 1965 California passed the Probation Subsidy Act, which sought to reimburse counties for maintaining offenders in the local corrections system instead of sending them to state facilities. Lawmakers developed a formula to determine the number of offenders who ordinarily would be sent to state institutions and to pay the counties a specified sum for each offender not sent to prison. The counties could then use the money to strengthen probation and other local correctional services in order to handle the additional offenders.

In 1973 Minnesota passed the first Comprehensive Community Corrections Act, which funded local corrections systems with money saved by state corrections when individuals were not sentenced to state facilities. The Minnesota model proved very popular, and by 1995 more than half of U.S. states had passed community corrections legislation.

Community corrections legislation is based on the idea that local justice systems have little incentive to keep their own offenders in local corrections. Tax revenues fund state-administered institutions, so communities spend little to send large numbers of offenders there. In contrast, keeping offenders in jail or on local probation costs citizens much more because their local taxes pay for those services.

Evaluation of Community Corrections Legislation

The main thrust of community corrections legislation—to limit dependence on prison—can be broken down into three aims:

1. To reduce the rate and number of people sentenced to state correctional facilities.
2. To reduce tax revenues spent on corrections by transferring both the costs and the funding to less-expensive local correctional facilities.
3. To reduce prison populations.

Have these aims been achieved? The answer is complicated.

Several evaluations of California's Probation Subsidy Act have been made.[27] All agree on one point: The availability of probation subsidies resulted in several local policy shifts and local compensatory decisions. Adult and juvenile commitments to state facilities decreased immediately following the enactment of the probation subsidy, but many of these people went to local jails instead of prison. Thus, the subsidy served primarily to transfer the incarceration of offenders from state-funded prisons to state-subsidized local corrections—hardly a resounding victory for community corrections. Other studies show that community corrections acts have had limited impact on prison populations in most states that have enacted such legislation.

Has community corrections legislation failed? The results are not entirely conclusive. All studies have found that some offenders were shifted to local corrections, and this news is encouraging. The problem is to control local correctional programs to ensure that the prison commitments are actually reduced under the new policies, as the legislation intended. The community corrections acts that allow local government to contract with private, nonprofit businesses that provide services to offenders claim that they create private jobs while reducing commitments to prison, and this aspect may benefit all concerned.

Certainly, community corrections is no panacea. The desire to reduce the number of offenders in prison must be supported by procedures to control the manner in which local programs handle offenders.

THE FUTURE OF COMMUNITY CORRECTIONS

What does the future hold for intermediate sanctions and community corrections? Certainly, those who support these programs must address three recurring problems.

First, some way must be found to overcome the seemingly inevitable tendency of the criminal justice system to resist placing offenders in less restrictive options and to keep increasing the level of corrections. As we have seen, studies of nonprison alternatives find that even the most successful programs enroll only a minority of offenders who would otherwise have been incarcerated. The usual pattern is first to place offenders in prison and then to release them to the community. New, alternative programs are filled with people who formerly would have been placed on regular probation. Nonprison programs, whether intermediate sanctions or community corrections programs, must improve their ability to attract the kinds of offenders for which they are intended.

Second, community support for these programs must increase. Too often, citizens fear the offenders in their midst. Active measures must be taken to allay those fears, to help citizens become comfortable with a correctional mission that recognizes a wide array of programs rather than favoring incarceration.

Third, the purposes of these sanctions must be clarified. No program can operate successfully for long without clearly defined goals. The goals of most programs today state vague and often competing generalizations: rehabilitation, protection of the community, reintegration, cost-effectiveness, reduction of overcrowding, and so on. Although no legitimate government operation can reject any of these considerations, some ordering of priorities and clarification of objectives must occur before these new forms of correctional functions can take their rightful place as core operations in the overall system.

justice reinvestment
Savings from community corrections used to help build up the crime-prevention programs in communities that have the most people under community supervision.

The lessons of community corrections have been developed into a new model of community-based correctional incentives called **justice reinvestment**. It is well-known that a high proportion of people who end up in prison come from a small number of very poor communities, where jobs are scarce and conditions are bleak. Justice reinvestment is the idea that the money saved when people are diverted from prison back to those communities ought to be used to make those communities better places for the people who live there—including people who might otherwise be in prison (see "Focus on Correctional Policy: Community Corrections Today").

focus on correctional policy

Community Corrections Today

The Pew Charitable Trusts has been trying to help states deal with their problems of burgeoning prison populations. To do this, Pew advocates a series of measures that create fiscal and programmatic incentives for decision makers to keep people convicted of crimes in local corrections systems rather than sending them to state prisons. Pew stresses a five-point agenda:

1. Evidence-based practices—develop supervision and services based on studies of "what works" to reduce recidivism.

2. Earned compliance credits—provide incentives for people under community corrections to reduce the length of their sentences when they successfully complete programs.

3. Administrative sanctions—when correctional clients struggle under community-based alternatives, develop administrative sanctions (such as house arrest) for dealing with them rather than returning them to prison.

4. Performance incentive funding—when community programs reduce recidivism, give them an increase in funding.

5. Performance measurement—make sure that programs are having their intended effects.

The key idea underlying the Pew model is an aspect of "justice reinvestment." What this means is the program intends to divert a large number of people from prison, thus saving money. But some of those savings are designed to be spent in communities that suffer from high rates of crime and are the homes to large numbers of people who have been involved in the criminal justice system. In this way, programs that work can be strengthened, and communities that face substantial problems with crime and disadvantage can start to improve.

Critical Thinking

1. Saving money through incentives for administrators to keep offenders in the community and out of prison is only one part of the justice reinvestment approach. What do you think about implementing the second aspect of the approach, using the savings to deal with crime and the problems of the disadvantaged affected neighborhoods?

2. What stakeholders would have to give their support to make the justice reinvestment approach successful?

Source: Pew Charitable Trusts, "Strengthen Community Corrections," www.pewcenteronthestates.org/report_detail.aspx?id=47134.

Summary

1 **Describe the history and development of probation, including how it is organized today.**

Probation has its heritage in European practices that attempted to alleviate the harshness of the criminal law. In the United States, probation goes back to the 1830s, when John Augustus volunteered to "stand bail" for people in the Boston Police Court. Today, probation exists as a sentencing option in every state of the United States, sometimes operated by the courts and sometimes by the correctional department.

2 **Describe the rationale for intermediate sanctions.**

Intermediate sanctions are used because many people believe that a sentence to probation is not strict enough but that prison is too extreme. To implement intermediate sanctions, many jurisdictions have developed the continuum-of-sanctions concept, which offers a range of correctional options between prison and probation. Courts offer pretrial diversion, fines, forfeiture, community service, and restitution; probation departments offer day reporting centers, intensive supervision, home confinement, and electronic monitoring; correctional departments offer shock incarceration and boot camps. Intermediate sanctions struggle with the problem of widening the net of social control. To be effective, they have to target the right group of offenders and place less emphasis on surveillance and control, and more emphasis on services.

3 **Illustrate the continuum-of-sanctions concept.**

Corrections systems have developed a range of punishments that vary in intrusiveness and control, so there are many types of punishments other than simply probation or prison. Probation plus a fine or community service may be appropriate for minor offenses, whereas six weeks of boot camp followed by intensive probation supervision may be right for serious crimes.

4 **List the various types of intermediate sanctions and who administers them.**

Sanctions administered primarily by the judiciary include pretrial diversion, fines, forfeiture, community services, and restitution. Sanctions administered by community corrections include day reporting and probation treatment centers, intensive supervision probation, home confinement, and electronic monitoring. Sanctions administered by institutional corrections include shock incarceration and boot camps.

5 **Explain some of the problems associated with intermediate sanctions.**

Problems with intermediate sanctions include the selection of the appropriate agencies to run them, selecting the right offenders to place in them, and avoiding widening the net.

6 **Describe what it takes to make intermediate sanctions work.**

To make intermediate sanctions work, there must be interchangeability of sanctions so that penalties in the community can be compared to penalties in confinement. The right offenders need to be selected for the right programs, and problems of bias must be avoided. Surveillance and control must be carefully used so that sanctions do not backfire.

7 **Explain how community corrections legislation works and describe its effectiveness.**

Community corrections legislation encourages communities to keep offenders locally instead of sending them to prison. The communities can then use some of the correctional costs that were saved as funds for local programs that manage those offenders. These strategies work when the cost incentives are large enough to reward communities for keeping offenders locally and when jail is not used as a replacement for prison.

8 **Assess the role of the "new correctional professional."**

"New correctional professionals" can work within a context of strong bureaucratic guidelines and high expectations of accountability. They are at ease dealing with nongovernmental agencies, and they possess a range of skills in motivating offenders to use an array of correctional services.

9 **Critically assess the future of probation, intermediate sanctions, and community corrections.**

Community-based correctional approaches face challenges of getting public support for keeping offenders in community programs instead of sending them to incarceration. They must clarify their mission and become more-crucial components of the correctional array of programs. Justice reinvestment strategies offer one viable way of doing this. Community corrections legislation attempts to change the incentives facing local court systems so that it pays off to retain people convicted of crimes in the community rather than to send them to the state's prison system. It works by giving local areas some of the costs of incarceration, as long as the local area does not send the offender to prison. The rise of intermediate sanctions and community corrections has given birth to a new kind of correctional professional, one who is more accountable for decision making about correctional issues. The future of community-based correctional methods will depend upon the development of proven options for dealing with offenders in community contexts and the development of community support for placing people in those options.

Key Terms

For Discussion

1. Is probation a "strong and effective" aspect of corrections? What are the main points in support of each side of the argument?

2. How do intermediate sanctions work better—as a way of improving on probation or as a way of avoiding the negatives of imprisonment? Why?

3. Should intermediate sanctions be run by traditional probation and prison systems or by new agencies seeking to serve as alternatives to them?

4. What does the California probation subsidy program tell us about the interdependence of various elements of corrections?

5. Why do states with similar crime rates sometimes have different incarceration rates?

6. Do you think that intermediate sanctions are acceptable to the general public? Why or why not?

Notes

1 "Public Safety Realignment," www.cdcr.ca.gov/realignment.

2 Sam Stanton, "Prisons Reach Court-Ordered Inmate Levels a Year Ahead of Schedule," *Sacramento Bee,* January 29, 2015.

3 See http://ballotpedia.org/California_Proposition_47,_Reduced _Penalties_for_Some_Crimes_Initiative_(2014).

4 Reid Wilson, "Tough Texas Gets Results by Going Softer on Crime," *Washington Post,* November 17, 2014.

5 Erinn J. Herberman and Thomas P. Bonczar, *Probation and Parole in the United States, 2013* (Washington, DC: U.S. Bureau of Justice Statistics, 2015).

6 Robert Martinson, "California Research at the Crossroads," *Crime & Delinquency* 22 (April 1976): 191.

7 *Ex Parte United States,* 242 U.S. 27 (1916). Often referred to as *Killits.*

8 *John Augustus, First Probation Officer* (New York: Probation Association, 1939), 30. First published as *John Augustus, a Report of the Labors of John Augustus, for the Last Ten Years, in Aid of the Unfortunate* (Boston: Wright & Hasty, 1852).

9 Ibid, p. 34.

10 William D. Bales and Alex R. Piquero, "Assessing the Impact of Imprisonment on Recidivism," *Journal of Experimental Criminology* 8 (2012): 71–101; see also Daniel S. Nagin, Francis T. Cullen, and Cheryl Lero Jonson, "Imprisonment and Reoffending," *Crime and Justice* 38 (no. 1, 2009): 115–200; Amy Elizabeth Lerman, "The People Prisons Make: Effects of Incarceration on Criminal Psychology," in *Do Prisons Make Us Safer? The Benefits and Costs of the Prison Boom,* edited by Steven Raphael and Michael Stoll (New York: Russell Sage Foundation, 2009); and Francis T. Cullen, Cheryl Lero Jonson, and Daniel S. Nagin, "Prisons Do Not Reduce Recidivism: The High Cost of Ignoring Science," *Prison Journal* 91 (no. 3, 2011): 48–65.

11 U.S. Department of Justice, *Felony Defendants in Large Urban Courts* (Washington, DC: U.S. Government Printing Office, 2008), 32.

12 Kathleen Maquire, ed., *Sourcebook of Criminal Justice Statistics,* U.S. Department of Justice, Bureau of Justice Statistics (Albany, NY: University of Albany, School of Criminal Justice, Hindelang Criminal Justice Research Center, 2009), Table 4.45.2010.

13 *Austin v. United States,* 61 Lw. 4811 (1993).

14 John Roman, "Cost–Benefit Analysis of Criminal Justice Reforms," *National Institute of Justice Journal* 272 (2013): 31–38.

15 Michael Rempel, Mia Green, and Dana Kralstein, "The Impact of Adult Drug Courts on Crime and Incarceration: Findings from a Multi-Site Quasi-experimental Design," *Journal of Experimental Criminology* 8 (no. 2, 2012): 165–92.

16 Douglas J. Boyle, Laura M. Ragusa-Salerno, Jennifer L. Lanterman, and Andrea Fleisch Marcus, "An Evaluation of Day Reporting Centers for Parolees," *Criminology & Public Policy* 12 (no. 1, 2013): 117–44.

17 Joan Petersilia and Susan Turner, *Intensive Supervision for High-Risk Offenders: Three California Experiments* (Santa Monica, CA: Rand, 1990).

18 James Kilgore, "The Rise of Electronic Monitoring in Criminal Justice," *Counterpunch,* April 30, 2012, www.prisonlegalnews.org /(S(s0v5rm45wi1lyx45tpoien55))/displayArticle.aspx?articleid =24254&AspxAutoDetectCookieSupport=1.

19 Susan Turner, Alyssa W. Chamberlain, Jesse Jannetta, and James Hess, "Does GPS Improve Recidivism Among High Risk Sex Offenders?" *Victims & Offenders* 10 (no. 1, 2015): 1–18.

20 Lars H. Andersen and Signe H. Andersen, "Effects of Electronic Monitoring on Social Welfare Dependence," *Criminology & Public Policy* 13 (no. 3, 2014): 349–80.

21 Jean Bottcher and Michael E. Ezell, "Examining the Effectiveness of Boot Camps: A Randomized Experiment with a Long-Term Follow Up," *Journal of Research in Crime and Delinquency* 42 (no. 3, 2005): 309–32.

22 Grant Duwe and Deborah Kerschner, "Removing a Nail from the Boot Camp Coffin: An Outcome Evaluation of Minnesota's Challenge Incarceration Program," *Crime & Delinquency* 54 (no. 4, 2008): 614–43.

23 Joan Petersilia, "California's Correctional Paradox of Excess and Deprivation," *Crime and Justice: A Review of Research* 37 (2008): 207–78.

24 Mark A. Kleiman, *When Brute Force Fails: How to Have Less Crime and Less Punishment* (Princeton, NJ: Princeton University Press, 2009).

25 Angela Hawken and Mark Kleiman, *Managing Drug Involved Probationers with Swift and Certain Sanctions: Evaluating Hawaii's Project HOPE,* document no. 229023, report to the National Institute of Justice, December 2009.

26 Stephanie A. Duriez, Francis T. Cullen, and Sarah M. Manchak, "Is Project HOPE Creating a False Sense of Hope? A Case Study in Correctional Popularity," *Federal Probation* 78 (no. 2, 2014): 57–70.

27 Paul Lerman and Lloyd Ohlin, *Community Treatment and Social Control* (Chicago: University of Chicago Press, 1977).

CHAPTER 5

Probation Supervision

During the early morning hours of February 8, 2009, Robyn Fenty was brutally attacked and beaten in a Los Angeles neighborhood. Her face was badly bruised and swollen from the pummeling she received during the battery. More popularly known as Rihanna, the Grammy-nominated singer named her boyfriend, Chris Brown, as her attacker.

Brown, a popular R&B singer, was arrested and subsequently pled guilty to felony assault. Los Angeles Superior Court Judge Patricia Schnegg sentenced Brown on August 26, 2009. Not unlike many offenders, Brown was sentenced to probation and not to a term of incarceration. But despite Chris Brown's celebrity and affluence, Judge Schnegg attached a number of conditions along with the five-year probation term. Brown is required to satisfy six months of physical labor as community service, to stay at least 100 yards away from Rihanna unless they're both attending music industry events (in which case he

Learning Objectives

After reading this chapter you should be able to . . .

1. Describe the two functions of probation.

2. Discuss the purpose and content of the presentence investigation report.

3. Describe the major issues involved in the presentence investigation.

4. Describe the dynamics that occur among the probation officer, the probationer, and the probation bureaucracy.

5. Discuss the different kinds of probation conditions and why they are important.

6. Define *recidivism* and describe its importance to probation.

7. Define *evidence-based practice* and discuss its importance.

8. Describe what is known about the effectiveness of probation supervision.

9. Discuss the revocation of probation, including "technical" revocation.

R&B singer Chris Brown was already on probation for assaulting his then-girlfriend, Rihanna, when he was charged with assaulting a stranger who wanted a photo with him. His original probation was revoked, and he went to jail for 108 days.

AP Images/Mario Anzuoni; Pool

be no closer than 10 yards from her) he next five years, and to undergo one of domestic violence counseling.

presentence investigation (PSI) report ided the judge with background infor-on on Chris Brown, including any prior

history of arrests or other criminal involvements, reports of any substance abuse problems, as well as positive accomplishments and favorable social habits. Toward that end, the PSI described two previous violent incidents. The first happened about

(continued from previous page)

three months before the February beating while the couple was traveling in Europe; Rihanna slapped Brown during an argument, and he shoved her into a wall. In the second, Brown allegedly broke the front and passenger side windows on a Range Rover they were driving while visiting Barbados. Neither attack was reported to the police. Other portions of the PSI included letters of support from those in the music industry and a pastor. Brown's sentence was in line with recommendations agreed to by prosecutors as part of a plea bargain. Nevertheless, the sentence was criticized by many as too lenient.[1]

How does a probation officer supervise a celebrity like Chris Brown? Is his supervision similar to other probationers who have been sentenced for felony assault? Are high-profile probationers managed in the same manner as ordinary probationers? Is it likely that Chris Brown will successfully complete his probation term because, as an entertainer, he knows that he will constantly be in the public eye? But what factors usually determine how a probationer is supervised? Should the crime be the primary aspect, or should the probationer's individual history take precedence? What is the nature of the policies that govern supervision? These and other related issues concerning probation supervision are the focus of this chapter. ■

THE DUAL FUNCTIONS OF PROBATION: INVESTIGATION AND SUPERVISION

Probation officers have traditionally performed two major functions: investigation and supervision. Regardless of the specifics of a given probation agency's structure or practices, certain aspects of investigation and supervision are uniform.

Investigation involves the preparation of a **presentence investigation (PSI)**, which the judge uses, as in the case of Chris Brown, in sentencing an offender. Typically, the court orders the PSI after the offender's conviction (often on a guilty plea). Before the sentencing date, the probation officer conducts the investigation and prepares the PSI.

The PSI process typically begins with an interview of the offender to obtain basic background information. The probation officer then seeks to verify, clarify, and explore the information derived (or omitted) from the initial interview. The final PSI document summarizes the officer's findings, evaluates the offender, and often recommends a sentence.

presentence investigation (PSI)
An investigation and summary report of a convicted offender's background, which helps the judge decide on an appropriate sentence. Also known as a presentence report.

Probation supervision begins once an offender is sentenced. Supervision policies and practices vary greatly among agencies but usually involve three steps:

1. The probation officer establishes a relationship with the offender and defines the roles of officer and offender.

2. The officer and offender establish supervision goals to help the offender comply with conditions established by the court (often directed at helping the offender confront significant needs or problems in his or her life).

3. On the basis of the offender's response to supervision, the officer decides how to terminate probation. Options include early termination because of satisfactory adjustment, termination because the sentence has expired, or revocation because of a new conviction or violation of probation conditions set by the judge or probation officer.

Investigation and supervision are different. In investigating clients and preparing PSIs, probation officers work primarily with other human service professionals—teachers, officials, psychologists, and so forth. They also work with the judge to provide the kind of information that will enable the judge to impose the best sentence based on the facts of the case. In contrast, supervision is filled with uncertainty and the possibility of error. With no standard solutions to the complex problems that most probationers face, probation officers may experience little sense of accomplishment. Their supervisory work consists of a series of tasks loosely connected to possible rehabilitation. Often, the rewards for this work are inconsistent and intangible.

This difference between the two functions often puts informal pressure on probation officers to give investigation a higher priority than supervision. Investigations produce substantive reports that are ultimately used by a judge. Superiors can see the excellence of an investigation more readily than that of supervision; in effect, then, producing a sound, professionally appealing PSI can seem more important than serving the offender described in that report.

To circumvent this problem, large probation departments "specialize" their staff—they assign some officers exclusively to supervision and others to investigation. However, this produces some inefficiency. For example, the supervising officer must learn much of the information that the presentence officer already knows. Similarly, when probationers are convicted of new offenses, the supervising officer is often the best person to write a PSI, given his or her familiarity with the case. Ironically, specialization does not necessarily change the supervision function. Frequently, the best staff members are assigned to the PSI units, and top priority goes to maintaining an adequate PSI workforce, even in the face of unwieldy supervision caseloads.

In any case, it is much easier to manage a probation system whose workers are specialized. Such a system enhances accountability for the timeliness and accuracy of PSIs and more easily ensures the operation of supervision routines according to agency policies. Therefore, the trend is toward specialization of these functions, treating them as two different jobs.

THE INVESTIGATIVE FUNCTION

As noted above, the presentence investigation serves mainly to help the judge select an appropriate sentence. It also helps with the eventual classification of the offender regarding probation supervision, treatment planning, possible incarceration, and parole.

Purpose

Apart from its many other uses, the PSI plays its most important role in the sentencing process. This is especially true because of judicial discretion. Individual judges, even in the same court system, may weigh factors in a case differently. Therefore, the PSI must be comprehensive enough to provide necessary information to judges with varying sentencing perspectives. For example, the rehabilitative goal requires assessment of the offender's treatment needs: Does the offender have special problems, circumstances, or needs that led to the criminal behavior? Can these problems be overcome by community services combined with careful supervision to prevent further criminal involvement? But the goal of community protection leads to a different concern: Will the offender continue criminal behavior if allowed to remain in the community? How might that potential risk be minimized?

In practice, most judges seek some balance between rehabilitation and risk management. Rather than pursuing a single value in sentencing, judges ordinarily ask a more complicated question: If this offender is not a risk to the community, is there some rehabilitative reason to keep him or her in the community—a reason strong enough to overcome the objection that probation tends to depreciate the seriousness of the offense?

There is also the issue of plea bargaining. When the sentence has already been proposed in the process of negotiation between the prosecutor and the defense attorney, the role of the PSI is altered. Instead of helping the judge decide the case, the PSI helps determine whether the negotiated agreement is appropriate.

According to some, such continued constraints mean that the PSI's importance is vastly overestimated. Often, they say, the sentence is determined by facts about the case, the crime, and the plea agreement, more so than anything the PSI can uncover. Others argue that the traditional PSI is a relic of the medical model of corrections, when judges relied on clinical assessments of defendants awaiting sentencing.[2] Small wonder, then, that some studies have shown that rather than read it in its entirety, most judges scan a PSI for a few relevant facts so they can make sure that their intended decision makes sense.[3]

Contents

For many years, the ideal PSI was thought to be a lengthy narrative description of the offense and offender, culminating in a recommendation for sentencing and a justification for that recommendation (see "Focus on Correctional Practice: Sample Presentence Report"). Early PSI-writing manuals stressed length and breadth of coverage. Now, however, people are questioning the assumption that more information is always better. Information theory suggests that PSIs that are short and to the point are not necessarily less useful than long ones.

A shortened, directed, and standardized PSI format is becoming more common. This approach may seem less professional, but in practice it places even greater responsibility on the probation officer. It requires the officer to know the case and the penal code well enough to know precisely what information the judge will require to evaluate the sentencing options.

The content of the PSI does not differ greatly whether completed by a federal, state, or county probation officer. Many individuals and agencies are contacted by probation officers to contribute information such as that found in the sample PSI mentioned earlier. However, there are some differences in federal PSIs, including the requirement of the defendant to make a detailed and full accounting of his or her financial

The presentence investigation (PSI) plays an important role in sentencing. The PSI often contains information about special problems that influenced the commission of the criminal act. Probation officers must gather information about offenders from teachers, family members, and employers to complete this report.

Joel Gordon

focus on correctional practice

Sample Presentence Report

State of New Mexico
Corrections Department
Field Service Division
Santa Fe, New Mexico 87501
Date: January 4, 2013
To: The Honorable Manuel Baca
From: Presentence Unit, Officer Brian Gaines
Re: Richard Knight

Appearing before Your Honor for sentencing is 20-year-old Richard Knight who, on November 10, 2012, pursuant to a Plea and Disposition Agreement, entered a plea of guilty to Aggravated Assault Upon a Peace Officer (Deadly Weapon) (Firearm Enhancement), as charged in Information Number 10-5736900. The terms of the agreement stipulate that the maximum period of incarceration be limited to one year, that restitution be made on all counts and charges whether dismissed or not, and that all remaining charges in the Indictment and DA Files 39780 be dismissed.

Prior Record
The defendant has no previous convictions. An arrest at age 15 for disorderly conduct was dismissed after six months of "informal probation."

Evaluation
The defendant is an only child, born and raised in Albuquerque. He attended West Mesa High School until the 11th grade, at which time he dropped out. Richard declared that he felt school was "too difficult" and that he decided that it would be more beneficial for him to obtain steady employment rather than to complete his education. The defendant further stated that he felt it was "too late for vocational training" because of the impending one-year prison sentence he faces, due to the Firearm Enhancement penalty for his offense.

The longest period of time the defendant has held a job has been for six months, with Frank's Concrete Company. He has been employed with the Madrid Construction Company since August 2008 (verified). Richard lives with his parents,

who provide most of his financial support. Conflicts between his mother and himself, the defendant claimed, precipitated his recent lawless actions by causing him to "not care about anything." He stressed the fact that he is now once again "getting along" with his mother. Although the defendant contended that he doesn't abuse drugs, he later contradicted himself by declaring that he "gets drunk every weekend." He noted that he was inebriated when he committed the present offense.

In regard to the present offense, the defendant recalled that other individuals at the party attempted to stab his friend and that he and his companion left and returned with a gun in order to settle the score. Richard claimed remorse for his offense and stated that his past family problems led him to spend most of his time on the streets, where he became more prone to violent conduct. The defendant admitted being a member of the 18th Street Gang.

Recommendation
It is respectfully recommended that the defendant be sentenced to three years incarceration and that the sentence be suspended. It is further recommended that the defendant be incarcerated for one year as to the mandatory Firearm Enhancement and then placed on three years probation under the following special conditions:

1. That restitution be made to Juan Lopez in the amount of $662.40
2. That the defendant either maintains full-time employment or obtains his GED [general equivalency diploma]
3. That the defendant discontinues fraternizing with the 18th Street Gang members and terminates his own membership in the gang

---

Critical Thinking

1. Do you agree with the recommendations for Richard Knight's sentence?
2. Is there additional information that you would like to have if you were the sentencing judge?

---

status, assets, and liabilities. The economic status of defendants may be more heavily emphasized in federal PSIs for at least two reasons: White-collar and corporate crimes are more often chargeable under federal law, and the option of restitution or heavy fines for these offenses may be effective aspects of punishment. In addition, federal regulations require that an inmate incarcerated in a federal prison pay a cost-of-incarceration fee, unless exempted. Finally, federal probation officers must also reference federal sentencing guidelines in the PSI.

To be useful, PSIs must offer valid and reliable information. Two techniques improve validity and reliability: verification and objectivity. *Verification* occurs when PSI information is cross-checked with some other source for accuracy. If the offender states during the PSI interview that he or she has no drinking problem, for example, the investigator questions the offender's family, friends, and employer before writing "No apparent problem" in the PSI.

Objectivity is aided by avoiding vague conclusions about the case. For instance, rather than describe the offender as *immature* (a term subject to various interpretations), the PSI writer might describe the offender's observed behaviors that suggest immaturity: poor work attendance, lack of understanding of the seriousness of the offense, and so forth.

victim impact statement
Description in a PSI of the costs of the crime for the victim, including emotional and financial losses.

The victims' rights movement of the 1970s included a drive to have the PSI reflect not just the offender's circumstances but also the impact of the crime on the victim. Called a **victim impact statement,** this new section of the standard PSI requires the probation officer to interview the victim and then present, in the victim's own words, the damage caused by the crime. Victims' advocates claimed that adding these statements to the PSI would let the judge better appraise the seriousness of the crime and choose a sentence that best served both offender and victim. Critics worried that the judge would be unfairly prejudiced by articulate victims and those who overestimated their true losses. However, studies have shown that the addition of victim impact statements to PSIs has little effect on sentencing.

Recommendations

Sentencing recommendations in PSIs are controversial because a person without authority to sentence is nevertheless suggesting what the sentence should be. For this reason, not all probation systems include sentencing recommendations in the PSI. Yet there is a well-established tradition of recommendations by nonjudicial court actors because the judge normally solicits recommendations from the defense and prosecution, as well as the probation officer. But what the probation officer says may carry extra weight because presumably it is an unbiased evaluation of the offender based on thorough research by someone who understands the usefulness of probation and is familiar with community resources. These considerations may explain why judges so often follow the recommendations in the PSI.

Agreement between PSI recommendations and the sentences subsequently imposed by judges range from 70 percent to over 90 percent. Of course, it is hard to know whether judges are following the officers' recommendations or whether the officers' experience has given them the ability to come up with recommendations that they believe the judges will select. If the reason for the congruence between a probation officer's recommendations and the sentences imposed is the judge's confidence in the officer's analysis, that confidence may be misplaced. Just how accurate is the probation officer in assessing whether an offender is suitable for community supervision (probation) or incarceration? One evaluation found that "in only a few instances did the offenders recommended for probation behave significantly better than those recommended for prison."[4] The study speculated that perhaps the better outcome for probationers is a result of differences in the level of caseload difficulty, suggesting that prognostic inaccuracy arose because officers did not have time to verify information reported in the PSI because of their heavy caseloads.

The recommendation may be most useful when a plea-bargaining agreement includes a sentence. In such cases, the PSI is a critical check on the appropriateness of the negotiated settlement, permitting the judge to determine whether any factors in the offense or in the offender's background might indicate that the agreement should be modified or rejected.

Disclosure

In view of the importance of the PSI to the sentencing decision, one would think that the defendant would have a right to see it. After all, it may contain irrelevant or inaccurate information that the defense would want to dispute at the sentencing hearing.

Nevertheless, in many states the defense does not receive a copy of the report. The case most often cited in this regard is *Williams v. New York* (1949), in which the judge imposed a death sentence on the basis of evidence in the confidential PSI despite the jury's recommendation of a life sentence.[5] The U.S. Supreme Court upheld the judge's decision to deny the defense access to the report. Without this access, the defense was incapable of challenging the PSI's contents at the sentencing hearing. (For a glimpse of other potential problems with PSIs, see "Do the Right Thing.")

Cases and state law since 1949 have reduced the original restrictive impact of *Williams.* At least one U.S. Circuit Court of Appeals has held that the PSI cannot refer to illegally seized evidence excluded from a trial.[6] And 16 states require full disclosure of the PSI. In the other states, the practice is generally to "cleanse" the report and then

DO the Right Thing

People v. Freeman—2009 NY Slip Op 08520

After defendant pleaded guilty to rape in the third degree, County Court imposed the agreed-upon sentence of 1 to 3 years in prison. Defendant does not challenge the judgment of conviction. Rather, his appeal focuses on the court's determination not to redact certain information from the presentence investigation report (hereinafter PSI).

The information should have been redacted because the PSI contained clearly erroneous information and was inconsistent with statutory procedures. The probation officer who authored the PSI completed and attached a risk assessment instrument on the form contemplated under the Sex Offender Registration Act (see Correction Law art 6-C [hereinafter SORA]). This presented several problems. The risk assessment instrument is not legislatively intended to be considered at sentencing where incarceration will be imposed, rendering presentation of the form premature. . . . Second, under SORA the Probation Department is not the proper agency to complete a risk assessment instrument . . . [requiring recommendation from Board of Examiners of Sex Offenders], . . . (and) [requiring district attorney to file written statement of determinations sought]. Third, County Court noted that the form contained serious errors. The court pointed out each error and recited the correct information under each such category for the record, but declined defense counsel's request to redact the entire form from the PSI.

Failing to redact erroneous information from the PSI created an unjustifiable risk of future adverse effects to defendant in other contexts, including appearances before the Board of Parole or other agencies. If the sentencing minutes are inadvertently separated from the PSI or an agency relies on the unedited original version at the Probation Department . . . defendant will have to not only refute the information in the PSI but also explain why the sentencing court apparently did not correct the PSI. An inaccurate PSI could keep a defendant incarcerated for a longer duration of time, affect future determinations of his or her legal status in court, as well as affect other rights regulated by the state. These risks are enough to justify redaction. Accordingly, we now order that the risk assessment instrument be redacted from all copies of defendant's PSI.

ORDERED that the judgment is affirmed, and the County Court of Columbia County is directed to redact the risk assessment instrument from all copies of defendant's presentence investigation report.

Critical Thinking

People v. Freeman reminds us that the PSI affects decisions beyond those that occur at the judicial bench in the criminal justice system. In light of this fact, to what extent should investigative probation officers seek to corroborate information they receive from others concerning the offender's life?

Source: Adapted from *People v. Freeman*—2009 NY Slip Op 08520.

disclose it. *Cleansing* involves deleting two kinds of statements: (1) confidential comments from a private citizen that, if known to the offender, might endanger the citizen and (2) clinical statements or evaluations that might be damaging to the offender if disclosed. Moreover, many judges allow the defense to present a written challenge of any disclosed contents of the PSI.

Private PSIs

client-specific planning
Process by which private investigative firms contract with convicted offenders to conduct comprehensive background checks and suggest to judges creative sentencing options as alternatives to incarceration.

Private investigative firms have recently begun to provide judges with PSIs. These firms work in one of two ways. Some contract with defendants to conduct comprehensive background checks and provide judges with creative sentencing options as alternatives to incarceration. In this approach, often called **client-specific planning**, the firm serves as an advocate for the defendant at the sentencing stage. In the second approach, the court hires a private investigator to provide a neutral PSI.

Privately conducted PSIs have sparked controversy. Because the defendant pays for client-specific planning, many people view it as an unfair advantage for upper-class and middle-class offenders, who can afford the special consideration that the advocacy report provides. These concerns are well taken; as advocates of private PSIs point out, their reports often result in less severe sentences for their clients.

The neutral private PSI also raises serious issues. Proponents say that private investigators do what the probation department does—only better. Yet critics question whether private firms ought to be involved in the quasi-judicial function of recommending sentences. Moreover, the liability of private investigators for the accuracy and relevance of the information that they provide to courts is unclear. Also, private PSIs, when purchased by the court, probably cost taxpayers more than do the traditional alternatives.

THE SUPERVISORY FUNCTION

Offenders placed on probation supervision come from a mix of backgrounds, and their conviction charges range in seriousness. Compared with inmates in prison and jail, probationers are more likely to be white and slightly more likely to be female

Gloucester County probation officer Ronald Moore tickles eight-month-old Giovanna Mahon as her dad, Charles, holds her after graduating from drug court.

Calista Condo/South Jersey Times/Landov

(see Table 4.1 in Chapter 4). Of the 4.3 million offenders on probation, about one in six was convicted of a violent offense, and another two in six of a property offense. Half had at least one conviction before they were arrested on the charge leading to probation. The variety of offenders requires a range of supervision strategies.

As in the case of PSIs, probation supervision follows universally accepted standards. The supervising probation officer frequently has the responsibility to develop a case plan for the probationer that observes such standards. The purpose of the case plan is to prescribe a combination of activities and reporting features that are based on the needs of the probationer. A well-crafted case plan could help the probationer better avoid counterproductive behaviors that eventually lead to crime. (A sample case plan for probationer Richard Knight, from our sample PSI, is in the Focus on Correctional Practice, "Sample Supervision Plan.") As indicated, the case plan describes a set of goals and objectives for the probationer to work toward and simultaneously signals what could send him or her to prison should he or she fail in any one of these areas.

Both probation officers and even clients, to some degree, generally enjoy wide latitude in carrying out their respective duties. To show how this latitude is exercised in practice, we describe the three major elements of supervision: the officer, the offender, and the bureaucracy.

The Officer

The probation officer faces role conflict in virtually every aspect of the job. Most of this conflict originates in the uneasy combination of two responsibilities: (1) enforcing the law and (2) helping the offender. Although the responsibilities may be compatible, they often are not. See "Careers in Corrections" for more information on the work, entry requirements, and earnings and job outlook of state and county probation officers.

focus on correctional practice

Sample Supervision Plan

Client	Richard Knight	Signed: _____
Probation Officer	James Wilson	Probation Officer: _____
Supervision Level	_____ High	Client: _____
	__X__ Regular	Date: _____
	_____ Minimum	

Richard Knight will:

1. Provide check stubs showing monthly restitution payment of $50.
2. Obtain GED assessment from Nuestra Familia Educational Center.
3. Complete job training course at New Mexico Technical High School.
4. Keep curfew of 8 P.M. on weekdays and 10 P.M. on weekends.

Critical Thinking

1. The case plan requires probationer Knight to complete a job training course at New Mexico Technical High School. Although the probationer is accountable to the probation officer, to what are the community service agencies accountable if they are unable to provide the contracted services?

2. How might delays in such services affect Mr. Knight's probation experience?

careers in Corrections

PROBATION OFFICERS: STATE AND COUNTY

Nature of the Work
State and county probation officers have two main functions. First, they conduct investigations and write reports about and recommendations on offenders for the courts, keeping the judge up-to-date on offenders' compliance with the conditions of their probation terms. Second, they supervise probationers' adjustment to the community, maintaining contact with them and providing guidance based on their risk levels and specific needs. Officers are usually required to spend more time with offenders who need more rehabilitation and counseling, or with those who pose a higher risk than others. Agencies and jurisdictions can also determine the maximum number of cases an officer is allowed to manage. Officers may handle anywhere from 20 to 100 cases at any given time.

Required Qualifications
Prospective probation officers are expected to have a four-year degree in criminal justice, social work, or some other related field, although specific requirements vary among states. A master's degree or related work experience is recommended and even required by some employers. Written, psychological, physical, and oral testing is ordinarily part of the application process, and good mental and physical health is a prerequisite to working as a probation officer.

Convicted felons may be disqualified from this field of employment. Computer-related knowledge and skills are helpful, and strong interpersonal abilities are needed as well, because probation officers interact with a wide range of people in the pursuit of their duties. Because of the large number of reports that a correctional treatment specialist or probation officer will produce over his or her career, candidates should possess strong writing skills. Newly hired officers and specialists receive additional on-the-job training for up to one year after being hired.

Earnings and Job Outlook
Probation officers earned a median of $47,840 in 2011. The two middle quartiles earned from $36,920 to $64,810. The top 10 percent earned greater than $82,000, while the lowest 10 percent brought in less than $31,500. Local government officers and specialists earned a mean wage of $52,750, compared with the state mean wage of $52,860 in May 2011. The employment growth rate for probation officers is expected to be average from 2010 through 2020.

More Information
Information about state and county employment opportunities can be found at various state and local probation websites, including the website for Probation Officer Careers, Jobs, and Training Information.

---

power
The ability to force a person to do something that he or she does not want to do.

authority
The ability to influence a person's actions in a desired direction without resorting to force.

The chief conflict between the officer's two roles arises from the use of power and authority. In human relations, these terms have specific meanings. **Power** is the ability to force a person to do something that he or she does not want to do. **Authority** is the ability to influence a person's actions in a desired direction without resorting to force. Thus, a person who chooses to exercise power in a relationship can almost always be shown to lack authority.

The problem of power and authority is a thorny one for probation officers. Officers are expected to exercise the power of law in controlling offenders under their supervision. This is one reason that in many jurisdictions, probation officers are legally classified as "peace officers," with the power of arrest. Yet the actual power of the role is less than it seems in some jurisdictions: Short of exercising their formal power to arrest or detain probationers, probation officers can normally do little to force compliance with the law. And the powers of arrest and revocation are themselves carefully constrained by case law and statutes. But there has been a gradual shift in policy toward affording probation officers greater capacity to wield power. In more jurisdictions than ever before, probation officers have the option of carrying firearms while on duty. The justification for this change is twofold: self-protection and to increase cooperation and diffuse potentially volatile situations when in the neighborhoods or homes of resistant probationers. According to a national survey conducted in 2013 by New Jersey's Administrative Office of the Courts, the majority of states have provided authorization for firearms, but probation officers must undergo psychological testing and gun safety training.

Probation officers prefer to rely more heavily on their authority rather than on power: It is a more efficient and ultimately more effective tool. The techniques of authority in probation are like those in social casework, but many people question their applicability in a role permeated by the power of law. They point out that the principles of social work have long been based on self-determination, which lets clients decide the nature, goals, and duration of the intervention—a condition not always feasible in the probation setting.

In response to the complicated nature of their authority, probation officers often define their role in very simple terms, as if choosing between two incompatible sets of values: protecting the public versus helping offenders, enforcing the law versus doing social work, and so on. But such simple classification does not resolve the ambiguities of the probation officer's job. The officer frequently receives only vague guidelines for supervision, resulting in wide disparities at times. Recently, probation specialists have argued that officers' roles can best be melded through a new technique referred to as motivational interviewing. This is "an approach that was first developed and applied in the field of addictions but has broadened and become a favored approach for use with numerous populations . . . [of] 'involuntary clients,'" such as probationers.[7]

Motivational interviewing involves a variety of interpersonal techniques that increase the effectiveness of correctional treatment by interacting with the client in ways that promote the client's stake in the change process. The strategy promises to do the following:

■ Help the officer get "back into the game" of behavior change.

■ Identify effective tools for handling resistance and keeping difficult situations from getting worse.

■ Keep the probation officer from doing all the work.

■ Place the responsibility for behavior change on the probationer.[8]

motivational interviewing
A method for increasing the effectiveness of correctional treatment, in which workers interact with clients in ways that promote the clients' stake in the change process.

Even for the most effective probation officers, however, role conflict makes the job difficult. Probation officers are now held accountable for any abridgment of the community's safety resulting from acts of commission or omission in performing their duties. In practice, this means that they must make reasonable efforts to monitor the behavior of clients and to exercise caution with those whose backgrounds make them potential risks to the community. The most famous case that established this principle involved a probationer convicted of sexual assault. His probation officer helped him get a job as a maintenance worker in an apartment complex, which gave him access to keys to various apartments. In obtaining the position for the probationer, the officer withheld his client's past record from the employer. The probationer sexually assaulted several apartment residents, who later sued the probation officer for covering up the probationer's record. The court decided in favor of the victims, ruling that probation officers are indeed liable for their conduct as government employees.[9]

The liability of probation officers (and parole officers as well) is an area of law not yet well formulated. And this issue has certainly made operational procedures in probation more important than ever. To defend against possible allegations of misconduct, probation officers need to document their actions so that they can meet any potential challenge.

The Offender

The offender's response to supervision strongly influences the overall effectiveness of probation. Some offenders respond favorably to probation and get along well with their probation officers; others are resentful or resistant.

The offender's response to probation depends in part on his or her perception of the officer's power. Most probationers believe that they have little effect on the supervision process. Although probation officers' real power is limited by law and bureaucracy, offenders may see the officer as occupying a commanding role. Officers decide on the style of supervision—whether supportive or controlling—and offenders have little direct influence on even this decision. Therefore, probationers often perceive themselves as relatively powerless in the face of potentially arbitrary decisions by the officers.

Probationers thus commonly resent their status, even when most people think they should be grateful for "another chance." In response, many probation officers try to involve the client in determining goals and strategies and in actively solving problems, rather than simply requiring the offender to seek assistance. Such strategies are aimed at reducing the perceived discrepancy between the power of the officer and the powerlessness of the client.

The Bureaucracy

All supervision activities take place in the context of a bureaucratic organization, which imposes both formal and informal constraints. *Formal constraints* are the legal conditions of probation, whether standard, punitive, or treatment; these are set by the court or written into law. **Standard conditions**, imposed on all probationers, include reporting to the probation office, notifying the agency of any change of address, remaining gainfully employed, and not leaving the jurisdiction without permission. **Punitive conditions**, including fines, community service, and some forms of restitution, are designed to increase the restrictiveness or painfulness of probation. A punitive condition usually reflects the seriousness of the offense. **Treatment conditions** force the probationer to deal with a significant problem or need, such as substance/alcohol abuse or anger management. An offender who fails to comply with a condition is usually subject to incarceration; thus, one main purpose of the officer's supervision is to enforce compliance with the conditions.

In spite of conceptual distinctions, in practice the rationale for different conditions can become blurred. Standard conditions regarding drug treatment may be imposed because they are thought to increase the impact of drug treatment; restitution may be seen as an important part of an offender's change in attitude. Yet with numerous conditions, some quite meaningful to the offender and others not, all the conditions can lose credibility. If the offender disobeys a trivial condition, the probation officer may well choose to look the other way, leading the probationer to wonder if *any* conditions will be enforced. Moreover, scattershot conditions cloud the officer's authority and overall plan to assist the client.

In sum, the informal world of supervision is best understood as a complex interaction between officers (who vary in style, knowledge, and philosophy) and offenders (who vary in responsiveness and need for supervision) in a bureaucratic organization that imposes significant formal and informal constraints on the work.

THE EFFECTIVENESS OF SUPERVISION

In light of such complexity, the effectiveness of probation supervision is difficult to assess. It depends on several factors: the skills of the officer, the availability of services such as employment counseling or drug treatment, and the needs and motives of the probationer. For many years, experts believed that reducing probation officers' caseloads could make supervision more effective. They reasoned that smaller caseloads would let officers devote more attention to each case, thereby improving services. Frequently cited standards called for caseloads of 35 to 50, although empirical study had never justified such figures. During the 1960s and 1970s, dozens of experiments were conducted to find the optimal caseload. Yet subsequent reviews of those studies showed that caseload reduction alone did not significantly reduce **recidivism**—the return of a former correctional client to criminal behavior, as measured by new arrests or other problems with the law—among adult probationers. Even the field's most effective advocate for probation and parole supervision, the American Probation and Parole Association, has been unable to uncover a link between the size of a caseload and the effectiveness of supervision.[10]

standard conditions
Constraints imposed on all probationers, including reporting to the probation office, reporting any change of address, remaining employed, and not leaving the jurisdiction without permission.

punitive conditions
Constraints imposed on some probationers to increase the restrictiveness or painfulness of probation, including fines, community service, and restitution.

treatment conditions
Constraints imposed on some probationers to force them to deal with a significant problem or need, such as substance abuse.

recidivism
The return of a former correctional client to criminal behavior, as measured by new arrests or other problems with the law.

Why don't smaller caseloads improve supervision effectiveness? Perhaps the assumption that "more supervision is better supervision" is too simplistic. Many factors—including the overall supervision experience, classification of offenders, officers' competence, treatment types, and policies of the probation agency—contribute to effectiveness more than does caseload.

Case Management Systems

Case management systems help focus the supervision effort of probation officers on client problems, which are identified using a standardized assessment of probationer risks and needs. In 1980 the National Institute of Corrections developed what it calls a "model system" of case management. This model has five principal components, each designed to increase the effectiveness of probation supervision:

1. *Statistical risk assessment.* Because fully accurate predictions are impossible, there is pressure to assess risk conservatively—to consider the client a risk even when the evidence is ambiguous. This tendency toward overprediction (estimating that a person's chance of being arrested is greater than it actually is) means officers will spend time with probationers who actually need less supervision. The use of statistically developed risk assessment instruments reduces overprediction and improves the accuracy of risk classifications.

2. *Systematic needs assessment.* Subjective assessments of clients' needs often suffer from probation officers' biases and lack of information. With systematic needs assessment, officers can more consistently and comprehensively address probationers' problems by evaluating them according to a list of potential needs.

3. *Contact supervision standards.* Probation officers understandably tend to avoid "problem" clients and spend more time with cooperative ones. However, those who pose the greatest risk and have the greatest needs require the most time. Based on the needs assessments, offenders are classified into supervision levels. Each level has a minimum supervision contact requirement, with the highest-risk or highest-need offenders receiving the most supervision.

4. *Case planning.* The broad discretion given probation officers to supervise their clients can lead to idiosyncratic approaches. When a probation officer must put the supervision plan in writing, the result is likely to be a better fit between the client's problems and the officer's supervision strategy. In addition, the officer's work is more easily evaluated.

5. *Workload accounting.* Because different cases have varying supervision needs, simply counting cases can misrepresent the overall workload of an agency. A better system for staffing the agency involves time studies that estimate the number of staff needed to carry out supervision.

This five-part model has enjoyed widespread support from probation and parole administrators, and studies show that it reduces recidivism.[11] It has come to be considered standard practice in virtually every large probation agency in the United States, and several other countries have adopted it.

Structured case management systems help probation staff decide which approach to supervision that clients most need: intensive supervision, special services, or traditional probation monitoring. When clients are placed in the most appropriate supervision approach, probation effectiveness increases. Despite strong support for the use of case management systems, recent studies have found that most probation officers do not use case management principles when supervising their probationers.[12]

Evidence-Based Supervision

Researchers have begun to systematically investigate the differences between programs that work—that is, programs that reduce recidivism—and those that do not. This

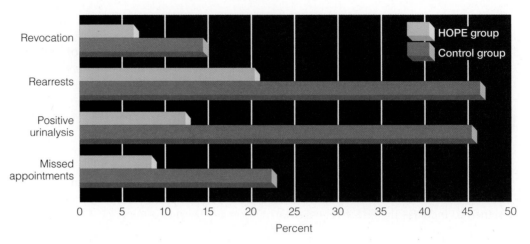

FIGURE 5.1

The Effectiveness of Evidence-Based Programming in Community Supervision Programs

Community-based programs that follow the four principles of effective programs reduce recidivism rates, whereas programs that fail to do so see higher recidivism rates.

Sources: A. Hawken and M. Kleiman, *Managing Drug Involved Probations with Swift and Certain Sanctions: Evaluating Hawaii's HOPE* (Washington, DC: U.S. Department of Justice, National Institute of Justice, 2009); Vermont Center for Justice Research, *Evidence-Based Initiatives to Reduce Recidivism: A Study Commissioned by Act No. 41 2011–2012 Legislative Session* (State of Vermont, Norwich Studies and Analysis Institute, 2011).

---

evidence-based practice
Using correctional methods that have been shown to be effective by well-designed research studies.

endeavor is called **evidence-based practice**. Studies suggest that among the most important characteristics of programs for probationers, four stand out:

- Focus the program on high-risk probationers (risk principle).
- Provide greater levels of supervision to higher-risk clients (supervision principle).
- Provide treatment programs designed to deal with the problems that produce a higher risk level (treatment principle).
- Make referrals to treatment programs (referral principle).[13]

These "effectiveness" principles matter greatly in the design of probation supervision programs. Viewed by some as a promising program, the Hawaii Opportunity Probation with Enforcement (HOPE) program was developed according to evidence-based principles of risk, need, appropriate treatment, and supervision. It targets high-risk probationers who are substance abusers. Meeting these principles was found to play an important role in the program's overall effectiveness. A recent evaluation of the HOPE program reported favorable outcomes that were influenced by evidence-based practices.[14] (See **Figure 5.1**.) One of the key findings of this line of research is that programs that primarily focus on surveillance-oriented supervision do not seem to work very well.[15] Overall, the evidence-based movement in community supervision has tended to support the value of programs when they are applied to high-risk probationers and use methods that are designed to reduce the risk. Some people suggest that this line of research supports a range of specialized services for probationers with special types of problems.

Specialized Supervision Programs

The needs of probationers vary dramatically. Sex offenders require different supervision strategies than do cocaine addicts; mentally ill offenders must be handled differently than embezzlers. However, because caseloads often exceed

To be effective, probation supervision requires that probation officers be able to meet with their clients in their homes. Field supervision enables probation officers to see a side of their clients' lives that does not come through as clearly in office visits.

Travis Dove/The New York Times/Redux

100 probationers per officer, officers have begun to group probationers with similar problems into a single caseload. This specialization allows the probation officer to develop more expertise in handling each problem, and it promotes a concentrated supervision effort.

Studies show that this approach has promise. For example, employment counseling programs and support services improve employment possibilities, and specialized treatment for sex offenders on probation has shown promise. Specialized services have been found to be more effective than traditional services for otherwise very difficult subgroups of probationers, including domestic violence cases[16] and probationers with mental illness.[17]

Recent interest in the problem of substance abuse has increased the attention given to probationers affected by drugs and alcohol. Several specialized programs designed to combat probationers' drug use typically take advantage of new techniques for drug surveillance and treatment. **Urinalysis** determines if an offender is using drugs. **Antabuse**, a drug that stimulates nausea when combined with alcohol, inhibits drinking. **Methadone**, a drug that reduces craving for heroin, spares addicts from painful withdrawal symptoms. These approaches are often combined with close surveillance in order to reinforce abstinence during probation (see "Focus on Correctional Policy: Dealing with the Drug Offender").

Another specialized program pairs the probation officer more closely with street police. Officers who work in tandem with the police often receive caseloads of especially tough probationers. The police liaison allows for more-effective searches and arrests and gives probation officers access to police information about probationers.

Specialization of supervision will likely continue to grow in popularity. One reason has to do with an increasing recognition of the seriousness of the problems faced by probationers and parolees. In one sample of probationers, 40 percent were under the influence of alcohol at the time of their offense, and 14 percent had been using illegal drugs.[18] Statistics such as these point to the importance of providing specialized programs for probationers whose problems with drugs or alcohol lead to repeat criminality and revocation.

urinalysis
A technique used to determine whether someone is using drugs.

Antabuse
A drug that, when combined with alcohol, causes violent nausea; it is used to control a person's drinking.

methadone
A drug that reduces the craving for heroin; it is used to spare addicts from painful withdrawal symptoms.

focus on correctional policy

Dealing with the Drug Offender

The Nebraska Community Corrections Center's Specialized Substance Abuse Supervision (SSAS)[19] program targets high-risk felony drug offenders on probation. It is based on evidence-based principles and has the aim of reducing recidivism and meeting treatment and other needs of the offender. As with any effective treatment program, offender assessment is critical. SSAS provides substance abuse treatment in addition to cognitive behavioral therapy and other program elements to deter relapse and further successful community adjustment.

Still, the challenges in dealing with the drug offender are daunting. It is estimated that 70 percent to 85 percent of offenders were involved with drugs or alcohol during past or current offenses.[20] Most probationers found to have a substance abuse history are required to complete a treatment program as part of the conditions of their probation. Therefore, most probationers are subject to mandated treatment. But some researchers ask how the mandated aspect of treatment might affect program effectiveness.

A recent study (2012) provides some insight into this question. Kimberly Kras interviewed offenders who were required to undergo substance abuse treatment to satisfy probation or parole conditions. Her findings indicated that although some offenders do resent the mandate for treatment, they also understand that treatment increases the possibility of sobriety and a successful community adjustment.[21] Offenders also admitted that the possibility of being caught for a probation violation served as a strong motivator for adhering to the treatment mandate. An interesting observation made by some offenders is that they saw the probation (or parole) officer as only an "enforcer" of their participation in mandated treatment, with little to no other connection. Therefore, the offender's participation became more about avoiding sanctions than making progress in understanding the dynamics of his or her substance abuse.

Critical Thinking

Evidence-based principles are designed to help probation officers better manage drug-addicted offenders under supervision in the community. Although these options are informative and beneficial, they should not overshadow the importance of the human aspect of supervision, treatment, and the officer–offender relationship. How might a probation officer establish a balanced approach between the use of evidence-based practices and maintaining a responsive officer–offender working relationship?

Source: Todd R. Clear, Val B. Clear, and Anthony Braga, "Intermediate Sanctions for Drug Offenders," *Prison Journal* 73 (Summer 1993): 178–98.

Performance-Based Supervision

performance-based supervision
An approach to probation that establishes goals for supervision and evaluates the effectiveness of meeting those goals.

Questions about the effectiveness of community supervision have spawned **performance-based supervision**, an approach that emphasizes "results" in setting priorities and selecting activities. The focus on results affects both the strategies and the agencies of client supervision.

The performance-based movement has called for a new emphasis on public safety in probation.[22] Rather than promoting a shapeless belief in offender rehabilitation, this new philosophy of probation squarely accepts responsibility for adopting approaches that help enhance the safety of the public. One of the most relevant expressions of this new philosophy is called "broken windows probation"[23] because it adopts the view that probation should be responsible for doing everything it can—even in dealing with problems of public disorder—to improve public safety. By accepting public safety as a primary aim, probation leaders recognize the critical role that probation can play not just in reducing crime but also in enriching community life by contributing to a sense of personal security and quality of life. The "broken windows" idea enables probation to embrace new problem-solving and partnership strategies that have proved successful for law enforcement.

Probation organizations that adopt a performance-based orientation express the focus on public safety in two ways. First, they choose supervision strategies that reflect what is known about the effectiveness of supervision. In most cases this means providing the most attention to the highest-risk cases, emphasizing the reduction of the kinds of problems that most contribute to crime and consistently reinforcing crime-free behaviors. Second, they set goals for improved supervision outcomes with their clients. Measuring whether these goals are accomplished gives the probation administrator the ability to know whether the supervision methods are "performing correctly" or need to be changed.

The announcement of the broken windows model has received a great deal of fanfare in the profession—not to mention some criticism. But the ideas promoted by the model are already gaining ground in probation departments around the country, and it appears that what the model proposes is increasing in popularity.

In short, the performance movement shifts the focus of supervision plans from activities to results—from what probation officers do to what they accomplish. The test of probation, in this circumstance, is how well the sentence turns out in the end.

Is Probation Effective Regardless?

Almost all studies of the effectiveness of probation supervision compare different strategies. They often find no difference in outcomes, and even when there is a difference, it is typically modest. The frequency of such weak results for probation studies leads some scholars to conclude that probation "doesn't work" or that its effects are minimal at best. This often makes prison seem to be a more powerful option by comparison, even though it costs much more than probation.

Again, these studies almost always compare one kind of probation to another. They do not compare probation with "doing nothing" because doing nothing is not a reasonable option. Yet what if probation is considerably better than "doing nothing"? What if the various *methods* of probation supervision vary little in their impact but probation itself works?

We have no completely convincing studies of this question. (What judge would want to engage in an experiment where a sentence of "nothing" was routinely given to a random sample of convicted felons?) But a recent study suggests that probation works perhaps far better than most people might suspect. Designed to find out whether the personal relationships of probationers affected their likelihood of being arrested, the study followed a sample of probationers for the first eight months of their probation term. What the study found was that a few case factors predicted the likelihood of new criminal behavior (carrying guns or using drugs or alcohol) but that, overall, the entire sample exhibited a large and abrupt reduction in criminal activity immediately following being placed on probation, and the initial reduction lasted the duration of the study. This reduction in criminality had little to do with life circumstances but instead appeared to be a general effect of probation sentences.[24] Although a few studies do not prove anything certain, the fact that being on probation itself may matter more than the kind of probation that one experiences is good news.

REVOCATION AND TERMINATION OF PROBATION

technical violation
The probationer's failure to abide by the rules and conditions of probation (specified by the judge), resulting in revocation of probation.

Probation status ends in one of two ways: (1) the person successfully completes the period of probation, or (2) the person's probationary status is revoked because of misbehavior. Revocation can result from a new arrest or conviction or from a **technical violation**.

focus on correctional practice

Sample Revocation Form

ORDER OF REVOCATION, STATE OF NEW MEXICO
In the 1st District Court of New Mexico, Santa Fe

Defendant: <u>Richard Knight</u>
Case Number: 2010-00235
Matter: *State of New Mexico v. Richard Knight*
Date: April 15, 2013

The above named defendant has been charged with the violation of probation, as follows:

1. Failure to make restitution as ordered by the court

2. Association with the 18th Street Gang in violation of the order of the court

On <u>January 4, 2013</u> the defendant was convicted of the crime of <u>Aggravated Assault Upon a Peace Officer (Deadly Weapon) (Firearm Enhancement), as charged in Information Number 10-5736900</u> and was notified of his rights, and given a copy of the probation order of the court.

On March 23, 2013, Probation Officer <u>Brian Gaines</u> informed the court of probable cause that the probationer was in violation of the following probation conditions:

1. That restitution be made to Juan Lopez in the amount of $662.40

2. That the defendant discontinues fraternizing with the 18th Street Gang members and terminates his own membership in the gang

Defendant was (1) provided with a copy of the alleged violations, (2) informed that any statement s/he made could be used against him/her, (3) informed of the right to obtain assistance of counsel and to have one provided if indigent, and (4) informed of the date of the probation revocation hearing.

Pursuant to this allegation, the defendant:
__X__ admitted the violations
_____ asked for a hearing on the charges
__X__ waived counsel
_____ sought the assignment of counsel due to indigency status

The court finds that
__X__ sufficient evidence exists to support the allegation of a violation of probation
_____ the evidence of a violation of probation is insufficient

In finding that a violation of probation has occurred, the court relied on the following evidence: <u>testimony by the probation officer that restitution had not been paid; testimony by the probation officer that he observed the defendant in the company of gang members; admission under oath by the defendant that these allegations were true.</u>

Based on the court's finding of a violation of probation, the following sentence is ordered:

1. A jail term of 30 days

2. Attendance in the Gang Violence Reduction Program of the probation department

3. Intensive probation supervision following release from jail.

Signed: *Judge Manuel Baca*

Critical Thinking

1. Considering the content of the Knight PSI, do you think additional information could have better predicted his problem areas?

2. Do you think Knight's failure could have been prevented by his probation officer? If so, in what way?

Revocations for technical violations are somewhat controversial because behaviors that are not ordinarily illegal—changing one's residence without permission, failing to attend a therapy program, neglecting to report to the probation office, and so forth—can result in incarceration. Some years ago, technical violations were common whenever probationers were uncooperative. Today, probation is revoked when the rules violation persists or poses a threat to the community. There are many developments that could trigger revocation, but the process itself must observe a number of due process requirements. The Focus on Correctional Practice illustrates a "Sample Revocation Form" for our probationer Richard Knight.

Probation officers often make their own arrests when their clients violate the terms of their probation. How does this law enforcement responsibility affect the role of the probation officer?

John Patriquin/Portland Press Herald/Getty Images

Probation officers have broad discretion to investigate potential rules violations and even new crimes. The U.S. Supreme Court has ruled that people on probation may be searched when the probation officer has a "reasonable suspicion" that a crime or rules violation may have been committed.[25] This means that probation officers need neither search warrants nor "probable cause"—the higher standard for searches that applies to citizens who are not under correctional supervision—to believe that a crime has occurred. See **Figure 5.2** for more on revocation.

According to most studies of probation revocation, from one-fifth to one-third of probationers fail to abide by the terms of their probation. However, a widely

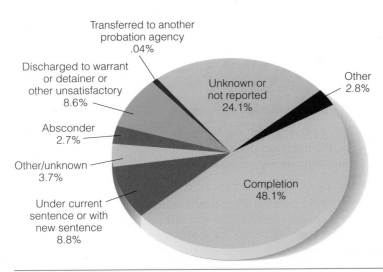

Transferred to another
probation agency
.04%

Discharged to warrant
or detainer or
other unsatisfactory
8.6%

Absconder
2.7%

Other/unknown
3.7%

Under current
sentence or with
new sentence
8.8%

Unknown or
not reported
24.1%

Other
2.8%

Completion
48.1%

FIGURE 5.2

Type of Termination from Probation

The most likely outcome of probation is that people complete their probation terms, but there are many kinds of probation failure.

Source: Bureau of Justice Statistics, *Probation and Parole in the United States, 2008, Statistical Tables,* December 2009. Appendix Table 4—Adults Exiting Probation, by Type of Exit.

MYTHS in Corrections

What Region in the United States Has More Probationers Convicted of Felony Offenses?

THE MYTH: The Northeast, with its older metropolitan centers and high crime rates, has the largest number of offenders on probation for felony convictions.

THE REALITY: The South is the only region in the United States that has more offenders on probation for felony rather than misdemeanor convictions.

Source: Bureau of Justice Statistics, *Annual Probation Survey, 2007*, February 2009, Appendix Table 6—Adults on Probation, by Type of Offense, http://bjs.ojp.usdoj.gov/index.cfm?ty=pbdetail&iid=1631.

publicized Rand Corporation study found much higher rates of violation, raising the concern of probation administrators. For 40 months, the Rand researchers followed a sample of probationers from two urban California counties who had been placed on probation for serious felonies. A majority had technical violations, and more than one-third were reincarcerated for them. Overall, 65 percent were arrested for a felony or misdemeanor, but only 51 percent were actually convicted of the crime. Although many of those who had technical violations went back to prison, some of those with new convictions did not. In other words, some probation "failures"—people who get arrested for a new crime—remain on probation even after their convictions, sometimes when the crimes are serious. This study found that once a person is placed on probation, serious misbehavior does not necessarily result in removal from the community.[26]

Yet the kind of person placed on probation varies dramatically from place to place (see "Myths in Corrections"), so failure rates also vary. Probation agencies that supervise more-serious offenders can be expected to have higher rates of revocation. When people on probation live in impoverished neighborhoods, they are rearrested at much higher rates than those who live in less disadvantaged neighborhoods—regardless of their background characteristics.[27] In locations where probationers have serious criminal histories, some probation departments have begun to collaborate with police departments to improve the capacity of both agencies to guard public safety.

As mentioned earlier, because revocation of probation is a serious change in the offender's status, the courts have determined that the offender has several due process rights in the revocation procedure. The U.S. Supreme Court ruled that a probationer has the right to counsel at a revocation and sentencing hearing.[28] In a later decision the Supreme Court further clarified revocation procedures.[29] The approved practice is to handle the revocation in three stages:

1. *Preliminary hearing (sometimes waived).* The facts of the arrest are reviewed to determine if there is probable cause that a violation has occurred.

2. *Hearing.* The facts of the allegation are heard and decided. The probation department presents the evidence to support the allegation, and the probationer has an opportunity to refute the evidence. Specifically, the probationer has the right to see written notice of the charges and the disclosure of evidence of the violation, to testify and to present witnesses and evidence to contradict the allegations, to cross-examine adversarial witnesses, to be heard by a neutral and detached officer, and to review a written statement of findings. Unless unusual grounds exist to deny counsel, the probationer also has the right to an attorney.

3. *Sentencing.* With an attorney present, the judge decides whether to impose a term of incarceration and, if so, the duration of the term. This stage is more than a technicality because after a minor violation, probation is often reinstated with greater restrictions.

For those who successfully complete probation, the sentence is terminated. Ordinarily, the probationer is then a completely free citizen again, without obligation to the court or to the probation department.

PROBATION IN THE COMING DECADE

In the second decade of the new century, probation faces many significant challenges. These challenges present different demands as well as opportunities. After a sustained growth in the U.S. probation population since 1980, numbers have recently decreased. For the fourth consecutive year, the number of offenders placed on probation has dropped. While it may be too soon to call these decreasing numbers a trend, they represent a distinct change from the last several decades. How should probation agencies that are most affected by fewer offenders respond to this development? California and Texas account for a significant number of the reported decreases. Caseloads that typically include 200 and even 300 persons could lessen in those jurisdictions, perhaps providing opportunities to pilot new strategies. This shift in the probation population invites a time of reconceptualization, innovation, and initiation.

Still, the importance of probation for public safety has never been greater; for example, up to 17 percent of felony arrests in one sample of large urban counties were of people who were on probation at the time of their alleged offense.[30] As a result of the renewed emphasis on public safety, many agencies have experienced a resurgence of intensive and structured supervision for selected offenders that reemphasizes the importance of risk and needs assessment. Assessment continues to be a necessary tool for probation because it links two important service areas: public safety and offender needs. Determining the type of supervision as well as the treatment needs of offenders fosters probation effectiveness. Larger probation departments, particularly in metropolitan centers, understand the utility of using a valid standardized instrument to assess offender risk. But all probation departments will need to carefully consider the use of appropriate and effective assessment instruments for the population they serve.

Changing demographics in the United States will also present challenges to probation. America is becoming an increasingly multiethnic and multicultural nation. The most obvious implication of this fact is that both offenders and probation officers will reflect these changes. Therefore, it will be ever more important for probation-officer training to include cultural literacy, recognizing that neighborhoods, civic groups, and other service providers will be more diverse and pluralistic. Probation will need to prepare for these important social changes. Today, the majority of probationers are white. By the year 2050, this will likely change as ethnic and racial minorities collectively will become the new majority in the United States.

As with many governmental agencies, the ability to recognize a changing landscape is important for organizational planning, relevance, and effectiveness. Probation is no exception, and it continues to strive to improve its basic mandate to investigate and supervise. Toward this end, there are two increasingly divergent types of probation in the future. One provides offender services through brokerage: The probation officer serves as a referral agent, involving the probationer in single-focus community service agencies (such as drug treatment programs) that work with a variety of community clients, not just with offenders. In the United Kingdom, probation officers are now referred to as "offender managers." The remaining probationers—a minority of all offenders, to be sure—will receive first-rate supervision and control from highly trained professionals working with reasonable levels of funding and programmatic support. (See "Focus on Correctional Technology.")

Noting the brokerage model of service delivery, probation administrators are also changing the way that they want to be evaluated. Most of the time—and in most of the studies cited in this chapter—probation's effectiveness is determined by rearrest rates: High rates are seen as a sign of ineffective supervision. Yet administrators know that high rearrest rates can also mean that staff is watching high-risk clients vigilantly, something that most citizens would applaud.

Instead, some believe that probation should also be evaluated by a series of "performance indicators" that better reveal whether probation is doing its job. These

focus on correctional technology

Monitoring Tools: GPS, Alcohol Monitoring Bracelets, Automated Fingerprinting Systems, Videoconferencing, and Voice Recognition Programs

Probation officers are responsible for supervising individuals who have received probation instead of a jail term. Their jobs require them to remain in . . . contact with offenders so they can monitor activities and behavior to ensure that probation terms are being met. In the past, this meant a great deal of personal interaction. . . . Innovations in technology have helped make more efficient use of probation officers' time and provided more-accurate monitoring as well.

Today's probation officer may have a number of monitoring tools available to help monitor and supervise probationers:

1. Many probation sentences require offenders to wear an ankle bracelet or carry a monitoring device that transmits coordinates to a global positioning system (GPS). When offenders on probation wear a GPS monitor, probation officers are able to determine the exact geographic location of the offender. The ankle monitor can also send alerts if it is tampered with or the offender ventures beyond the locations that he or she is permitted.

2. In cases of drunk driving violations or other alcohol-related crimes, probation officers may use technology to monitor alcohol consumption. Offenders are required to wear alcohol monitoring bracelets that alert probation officers if the wearer has consumed alcohol. An individual's body temperature rises when alcohol is in the system, and the bracelets are able to detect increased perspiration. Data from the bracelet are downloaded several times a week, and the probation officer can then review the information to determine if the individual has been drinking.

3. Probation officers are also able to use mobile automated fingerprinting systems to help monitor offenders. This technology allows officers to identify individuals and match fingerprints taken anywhere in the field with mug shots that are already on file. A digital image of the fingerprints can also be sent to computers, cell phones, and PDAs, and state and national databases can then be searched. This fingerprinting system allows probation officers to identify offenders and possibly link them to other unsolved crimes.

4. Some probation officers use videoconferencing to interview inmates so they do not have to spend time driving to prisons. Videoconferencing is also used to allow offenders to testify without leaving their jail cells. Voice recognition programs can also be helpful to probation officers because they allow for verification over the phone that offenders are at home or work. Probation officers also use digital-imaging technology to send mug shots to colleagues out in the field so that identification of offenders can be made.

Critical Thinking

Do you think that the dynamics of probation supervision, including the nature of the relationship between probation officers and probationers, will change significantly as a result of the increased use of technology tools in probation?

Source: Adapted from Jennifer Blair, "Probation Technology," www.ehow.com/about_6513464_probation-technology.html.

indicators include the numbers of community service projects performed by probationers, the amount of probation fees and restitution collected, days free of drug use, employment rates, and the number of successful referrals made to service providers. However, detractors claim that even if these performance indicators are high, the public is interested in crime as a bottom line—and that means recidivism rates matter most.

In many respects, probation finds itself at a crossroads. Although probation's credibility is probably as low as it has ever been, the importance of probation as a reliable and cost-effective way to manage the offender is growing dramatically, particularly in view of the prohibitive costs of incarceration in a shrinking economy. Under the strain of this expectation and on-again, off-again public support, probation faces a serious challenge: Can its methods of supervision and service be adapted successfully to high-risk offenders? Many innovations are being attempted, but whether such new programs actually improve probation or detract from it remains unclear. Certainly, these innovations expand the variety of probation sanctions, making them more applicable to more offenders. But do they strengthen the mainstream functions of probation—investigation and supervision? These functions must be improved for probation to succeed in its current and future challenge.

Summary

1 Describe the two functions of probation.

Probation officers have traditionally performed two major functions: investigation and supervision. Investigation involves the preparation of a presentence investigation (PSI), which the judge uses in sentencing an offender. Supervision begins once an offender is sentenced to probation, and it involves three steps: (1) establishing a relationship with the offender, (2) setting supervision goals to help the offender comply with conditions established by the court, and (3) deciding how to terminate probation on the basis of the offender's response to supervision.

2 Discuss the purpose and content of the presentence investigation report.

The PSI plays its most important role in the sentencing process. This is especially true because of judicial discretion. Individual judges, even in the same court system, may weigh factors in a case differently. Therefore, the PSI must be comprehensive enough to provide necessary information to judges with varying sentencing perspectives. A shortened, directed, and standardized PSI format is becoming more common. This approach may seem less professional, but in practice it places even greater responsibility on the probation officer. It requires the officer to know the case and the penal code well enough to know precisely what information the judge will require to evaluate the sentencing options.

3 Describe the major issues involved in the presentence investigation.

The three major issues in PSIs are, first, whether to make sentencing recommendations. They are controversial because a person without authority to sentence is nevertheless suggesting what the sentence should be. For this reason, not all probation systems include it in the PSI. Second is whether to disclose the contents of the PSI to the defendant. In many states the defense does not receive a copy of the report. In the other states the practice is generally to "cleanse" the report of confidential comments and clinical statements, then disclose it. Third is whether private investigative firms ought to be allowed to provide judges with PSIs paid for by the defendant. In this approach the firm serves as an advocate for the defendant at the sentencing stage.

4 Describe the dynamics that occur among the probation officer, the probationer, and the probation bureaucracy.

The probation officer faces role conflict in virtually every aspect of the job. Most of this conflict originates in the uneasy combination of two responsibilities: (1) enforcing the law and (2) helping the offender. Although the responsibilities may be compatible, they often are not. The offender's response to supervision depends in part on his or her perception of the officer's power. Most probationers believe they have little effect on the supervision process. Although probation officers' real power is limited by law and bureaucracy, offenders may see the officer as occupying a commanding role. All supervision activities take place in the context of a bureaucratic organization, which imposes both formal and informal constraints. *Formal constraints* are the legal conditions of probation, whether standard, punitive, or treatment; these are set by the court or written into law.

5 Discuss the different kinds of probation conditions and why they are important.

Standard conditions, imposed on all probationers, include reporting to the probation office, notifying the agency of any change of address, remaining gainfully employed, and not leaving the jurisdiction without permission. Punitive conditions, including fines, community service, and some forms of restitution, are designed to increase the restrictiveness or painfulness of probation. A punitive condition usually reflects the seriousness of the offense. Treatment conditions force the probationer to deal with a significant problem or need, such as substance abuse.

6 Define *recidivism* and describe its importance to probation.

Recidivism is the return of a former correctional client to criminal behavior, as measured by new arrests or other problems with the law. It is the basis on which analysts decide if a probation strategy is working.

7 Define *evidence-based practice* and discuss its importance.

Evidence-based practice is based on an understanding of the differences between programs that work—that is, programs that reduce recidivism—and those that do not. Studies suggest that among the most important characteristics of programs for probationers, four stand out: (1) focus the program on high-risk probationers (risk principle), (2) provide greater levels of supervision to higher-risk clients (supervision principle), (3) provide treatment programs designed to deal with the problems that produce the higher risk level (treatment principle), and (4) make referrals to treatment programs (referral principle).

8 Describe what is known about the effectiveness of probation supervision.

Most studies of the effectiveness of probation supervision find no difference in outcomes for different probation strategies, and even when there is a difference, it is typically modest. This often makes prison seem a more powerful option by comparison, even though it costs much more than probation. But some recent studies suggest that probation works perhaps far better than most people might suspect. When it comes to preventing new arrests, probation may be as effective as highly praised "alternative" sanctions and more effective than jail or prison.

9 Discuss the revocation of probation, including "technical" revocation.

Probation status ends in one of two ways: (1) the person successfully completes the period of probation, or (2) the person's probationary status is revoked because of misbehavior. Revocation can result from a new arrest or conviction or from a *rules violation,* a failure to comply with a condition of probation. Rules violations that result in revocations are referred to as *technical violations.* Revocations for technical violations are somewhat controversial because behaviors that are not ordinarily illegal—changing one's residence without permission, failing to attend a therapy program, neglecting to report to the probation office, and so forth—can result in incarceration.

Key Terms

For Discussion

1. How does the use of probation affect the corrections system? Why is it used so extensively?
2. How does the presentence investigation report contribute to the dispersion of accountability for the sentence that is imposed?
3. How do you think the investigative and supervisory functions of probation can be most effectively organized? What might the judges in your area say about your proposal? What might the department of corrections say?
4. Given the two major tasks of probation, how should officers spend their time? How do they actually spend their time?
5. Why might some probationers be kept in the community after a technical violation, rather than having their probation revoked?

Notes

1 "Chris Brown Gets Five Years Probation for Assault," *MSNBC.com*, http://today.msnbc.msn.com/id/32556521/ns /entertainment-celebrities.

2 Jeanne B. Stinchcombe and Darryl Hippensteel, "Presentence Investigation Reports: A Relevant Justice Model Tool or a Medical Model Relic," *Criminal Justice Policy Review* 12 (no. 2, June 2001): 164–77.

3 Michael D. Norman and Robert C. Waldman, "Utah Presentence Investigation Reports: User Group Perceptions of Quality and Effectiveness," *Federal Probation* 64 (no. 2, 2000): 7–12.

4 Joan Petersilia, Susan Turner, James Kahan, and Joyce Peterson, *Granting Felons Probation: Public Risks and Alternatives* (Santa Monica, CA: Rand, 1985), 39, 41.

5 *Williams v. New York*, 337 U.S. 241 (1949).

6 *Verdugo v. United States*, 402 F.Supp. 599 (1968).

7 Michael D. Clark, "Motivational Interviewing for Probation Staff: Increasing the Readiness to Change," *Federal Probation* 69 (no. 2, December 2005), www.uscourts.gov/fedprob/December _2005/interviewing.html.

8 List adapted from Michael D. Clark, Scott Walters, Ray Gingerich, and Melissa Meltzer, "Motivational Interviewing for Probation Officers: Tipping the Balance Toward Change," *Federal Probation* 70 (no. 1, June 2006): 38–44.

9 *Rieser v. District of Columbia*, 21 Cr.L. 2503 (1977).

10 American Probation and Parole Association, *Probation and Parole's Growing Caseloads and Workload Allocation: Strategies for Managerial Decision Making*, www.appa-net.org/eweb/docs/appa /pubs/SMDM.pdf.

11 P. Gendreau, S. French, and A. Taylor, "What Works (What Doesn't) Revised 2002: The Principles of Effective Correctional Treatment" (unpublished manuscript, University of New Brunswick, St. John, New Brunswick, Canada, 2002).

12 James Bonta, Tanya Rugge, Terri-Lynne Scott, Guy Bourgon, and Annie K. Yessine, "Exploring the Black Box of Community Supervision," *Journal of Offender Rehabilitation* 47 (no. 3, 2008): 248–70.

13 Gendreau, French, and Taylor, "What Works (What Doesn't) Revised 2002."

14 A. Hawken and M. Kleiman, *Managing Drug Involved Probations with Swift and Certain Sanctions: Evaluating Hawaii's HOPE* (Washington, DC: U.S. Department of Justice, National Institute of Justice, 2009); Vermont Center for Justice Research, *Evidence-Based Initiatives to Reduce Recidivism: A Study Commissioned by Act No. 41 2011–2012 Legislative Session* (State of Vermont, Norwich Studies and Analysis Institute, 2011).

15 S. Aos, M. Miller, and E. Drake, *Evidence-Based Adult Corrections Programs: What Works and What Does Not* (Olympia: Washington State Institute for Public Policy, 2006).

16 Matthew T. DeMichele, Ann Crowe, Andrew Klein, and Doug Wilson, "'What Works' in the Supervision of Domestic Violence Offenders: Promising Results from a Study in Rhode Island," *Perspectives* 30 (no. 1, Summer 2006): 46–57.

17 Jennifer L. Skeem and Paula Emke-Francis, "Probation and Mental Health: Responding to the Challenges," *Perspectives* 28 (no. 3, Summer 2004): 22–27.

18 Nebraska Community Corrections Council, http://ccc.nebraska .gov/ssas.html.

19 National Center on Addiction and Substance Abuse at Columbia University, *Behind Bars II: Substance Abuse and America's Prison Population*, www.casacolumbia.org/articlefiles/575-report2010be hindbars2.pdf, 2010.

20 K. R. Kras, "Offender Perceptions of Mandated Substance Abuse Treatment: An Exploratory Analysis of Offender Experiences in a Community-Based Treatment Program," *Journal of Drug Issues* 43 (2013): 124.

21 BJS *Special Report*, March 1998, p. 1.

22 Caliber Associates, "From Theory to Practice: The Lifecycle Document for the Results-Based Management Framework for the Federal Probation and Pretrial Services System," *Federal Probation* 70 (no. 2, September 2006), www.uscourts.gov/fedprob/September _2006/lifecycle.html.

23 Faye Taxman and James Byrne, "Fixing Broken Windows Probation," *Perspectives* 25 (no. 2, 2001): 22–29; Reinventing Probation Council, *Transforming Probation Through Leadership: The "Broken Windows" Model* (New York: Center for Civic Innovation at the Manhattan Institute, 2000).

24 Doris Layton-MacKenzie and Spencer De Li, "The Impact of Formal and Informal Social Controls on the Criminal Activities of Probationers," *Journal of Research in Crime and Delinquency* 39 (no. 3, 2002): 243–76.

25 *United States v. Knights*, 534 U.S. 112 (2001).

26 Petersilia et al., *Granting Felons Probation*, p. 39.

27 Charles E. Kubrin and Eric E. Stewart, "Predicting Who Reoffends: The Neglected Role of Neighborhood Context in Recidivism Research," *Criminology* 44 (no. 2, 2006): 165–97.

28 *Mempa v. Rhay*, 389 U.S. 128 (1967).

29 *Gagnon v. Scarpelli*, 411 U.S. 778 (1973).

30 Brian A. Reaves and Pheny Z. Smith, *Felony Defendants in Large Urban Counties, 1992* (Washington, DC: U.S. Government Printing Office, 1995).

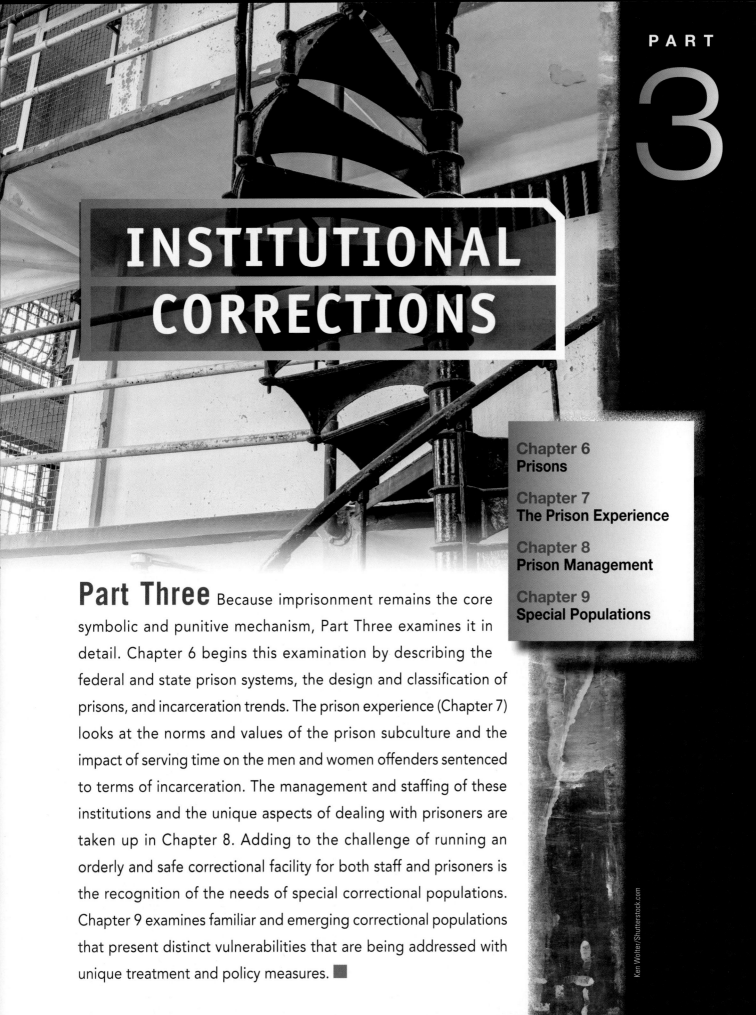

INSTITUTIONAL CORRECTIONS

Part Three Because imprisonment remains the core symbolic and punitive mechanism, Part Three examines it in detail. Chapter 6 begins this examination by describing the federal and state prison systems, the design and classification of prisons, and incarceration trends. The prison experience (Chapter 7) looks at the norms and values of the prison subculture and the impact of serving time on the men and women offenders sentenced to terms of incarceration. The management and staffing of these institutions and the unique aspects of dealing with prisoners are taken up in Chapter 8. Adding to the challenge of running an orderly and safe correctional facility for both staff and prisoners is the recognition of the needs of special correctional populations. Chapter 9 examines familiar and emerging correctional populations that present distinct vulnerabilities that are being addressed with unique treatment and policy measures. ◼

Ken Wolter/Shutterstock.com

CHAPTER 6

Prisons

In September 2014 the Bureau of Justice Statistics reported that 478 people per 100,000 U.S. residents were held in state or federal prisons.[1] When compared to other developed countries, America's incarceration rate is extremely high. For example, consider the incarceration rates (per 100,000 residents) in the following countries: Australia (130), England and Wales (148), France (98), Germany (79), Ireland (88), and the Netherlands (82). Only a handful of counties have an incarceration rate similar to that of the United States. Among these countries are Rwanda (492), Cuba (510), and Russia (475).[2]

A study by the Pew Charitable Trusts notes that "after a 700 percent increase in the U.S. prison population between 1970 and 2005, you'd think the nation would finally have run out of lawbreakers to put behind bars."[3] Why is the incarceration rate so high? Some observers believe that since the mid-1970s the United States has tried to see whether the crime rate can be reduced if greater numbers of offenders are imprisoned.[4] Over the past quarter-century,

After reading this chapter you should be able to . . .

1 Discuss the goals of incarceration.

2 Understand how incarceration is organized.

3 Explain who is in prison.

4 Discuss the explanations for the increase in the incarceration rate.

5 Be familiar with the problem of prison crowding.

Thomson Correctional Center in Thomson, Illinois, completed in 2006 at the cost of $170 million, sat mostly empty as the Illinois prison population stabilized. Finally, in 2012 the federal government bought it, and its first cohort of federal prisoners arrived in 2015.

AP Images/Charles Rex Arbogast

ncarceration rate has more than qua-
led, even though the crime rate in the
ed States has been declining for over
decades. Along with the steady growth
merica's prison population, the amount

operating prisons has also substantially increased. The expansion of the prison population is difficult to understand in light of
lower crime rates, state budgetary problems, and the easing of tough sentencing

(continued from previous page)

Although more than 2.2 million people are incarcerated in U.S. prisons and jails, this population makes up fewer than one-third of people under correctional supervision. Approximately 4.75 million individuals are under correctional supervision in the community (probation and parole).[5] Yet when the subject of the criminal sanction arises, the general public usually thinks first of incarceration. And it is prison that politicians have in mind when they consider changes in the penal code or annual appropriations for corrections.

In this chapter we focus primarily on the incarceration of adult male prisoners, who make up approximately 93 percent of America's prison population.[6] Our discussion will cover the different goals of incarceration, the organization of prisons in the United States, and the different ways that prisoners are incarcerated. We will also look at incarceration trends, consider different explanations for the rise in incarceration, and discuss the problem of prison crowding. In subsequent chapters we will examine the prison experience from the standpoint of both male and female inmates, examine the management of correctional institutions, and examine the staffing of prisons. ■

LINKS TO THE PAST

Prisons are built to last. The oldest prison still operating in America—New Jersey's State Prison in Trenton—opened in 1798 and was rebuilt in 1836. Because institutions built of stone and concrete are not easily redesigned as correctional goals change, prior reform movements can be seen in the architecture and location of many older prisons. For example, the Quakers believed that offenders could be redeemed if removed from the distractions of the city. In line with this view, many correctional facilities were built in rural areas. Doing so removed prisoners from the bad influences found in urban areas, but it also took them away from their families and friends, who could help them reform themselves and become law-abiding citizens. In recent years, however, prisons have been built in rural, economically depressed areas for a different reason: as a means of providing employment for local residents.

Life inside prison differs by the type and location of the institution and the characteristics of the inmates. The image of the "big house" remains imprinted on the minds of most Americans because it has been portrayed in countless movies and television shows. The typical big-house prison of the 1940s and 1950s was a walled prison with large, tiered cell blocks; a yard; shops; and industries. The average inmate population was around 2,500 per institution. These prisoners came from urban and rural areas and, outside the South, were mostly white. Prisoners were isolated from the world outside the walls, and prison life was very structured. There were very few treatment programs, and custody was the primary goal. In fictional depictions of these prisons, the inmates are tough, and the guards are even tougher.

But American correctional institutions have always been more diverse than the movies portray them. For example, during the first half of the twentieth century, prisons located in the South were racially segregated, and prisoners were used as farm labor. Prisoners were not contained inside massive stone and concrete walls, as was common in northern states.

During the 1960s and 1970s, many states built prisons and converted others into "correctional institutions." In these facilities the rehabilitation model was dominant, and treatment programs were administered by counselors and teachers. Even in these facilities, however, security, discipline, and order were high priorities. Inmates during this era enjoyed more constitutional rights as citizens than prisoners during the big-house era. As inmates gained more legal services, the traditional judicial hands-off policy deteriorated, and administrators were forced to be more responsive to judicial rulings and directives to run their institutions according to constitutional mandates.

During the past 40 years, the prison population has changed. The number of African American and Hispanic inmates has greatly increased. More inmates now come from urban areas; more of them have been convicted of drug-related and violent crimes. Incarcerated members of street gangs, which are usually organized along racial or ethnic lines, frequently regroup inside prison and contribute to elevated levels of violence. Another major change has been the rising number of correctional officers who are members of public employee unions, which use collective bargaining to improve working conditions, safety procedures, and training.

Because some politicians have successfully argued that inmates have been treated too softly, many states have reinstated strict regimes in their prisons and have removed educational and recreational programs. Now the focus of corrections is crime control, and the primary emphasis is incarceration. Because the number of people in U.S. prisons has grown steadily during the crime control era, prison crowding has become a problem. Although today's correctional administrators seek to provide humane incarceration, they often struggle with limited resources and must deal with a number of issues that make their jobs more difficult, such as racial strife, legal issues, deteriorating facilities, antiquated architectural designs, and inmate contraband (see the Focus on Correctional Technology, "Combating Inmate Cell Phone Use").

The Stateville Correctional Center in Illinois is an example of the "big house," typical of prisons that predominated during the first half of the twentieth century. These large, multitiered cell blocks are now viewed as not in keeping with today's penology.

AP Images/Chicago Sun-Times, Richard A. Chapman

focus on correctional technology

Combating Inmate Cell Phone Use

Prison officials are always concerned with eliminating contraband. Indeed, officers on the cell blocks, walking the yard, working the shops, and monitoring visiting areas spend a lot of time watching out for drugs and weapons. In today's correctional facility, however, there is a new and growing problem—the cell phone. How widespread is the problem? In one year more than 15,000 cell phones were confiscated from inmates in the California corrections system, nearly one cell phone per 11 prisoners. The federal system, where nearly 2,000 cell phones were confiscated over a four-month period, is also experiencing problems, though to a lesser degree. Although national estimates are not available, it is widely believed that inmate cell phone use is a problem of epidemic proportions in a large number of state and federal prisons. Many of these cell phones are sold illegally to inmates by correctional officers.

Unlike the calls made from prison pay phones, cell phone calls are not systematically monitored. Although many inmates use smuggled cell phones to stay in touch with friends and family, some have used them to harass lawmakers, threaten victims, orchestrate crimes, order hits on rivals, and plan escapes.

To deal with the problem, some states have increased the penalties for inmates who are found to possess cell phones. Other prison systems now use specially trained dogs to find phones stashed in cells and around prison complexes. Many states are interested in using technology that can jam cell phone signals, thus rendering them useless. However, prison officials must make certain that such equipment does not interfere with emergency-response signals outside the walls of the prison.

Critical Thinking

1. How should we deal with correctional officers who provide inmates with cell phones?

2. What else can prison officials do to ensure that inmates do not get cell phones?

3. Do you think that the battle to rid prisons of cell phones can be won? Or is it only the beginning of a battle that will continue as more-advanced remote communication devices are developed?

Sources: Tod W. Burke and Stephen S. Owen, "Cell Phones as Prison Contraband," *FBI Law Enforcement Bulletin* 79 (July 2010): 10–15; Kim Severson and Robbie Brown, "Outlawed, Cellphones Are Thriving in Prisons," *New York Times*, www.nytimes.com/2011/01/03/us/03prisoners .html?pagewanted=all&_r=0; Jack Dolan, "Prisons to Block Use of Smuggled Phones," *Los Angeles Times*, http://articles.latimes.com/2012/apr/17/local /la-me-0417-prison-cellphones-20120417.

THE GOALS OF INCARCERATION

Most people consider security the dominant purpose of a prison. High walls, razor wire, searches, checkpoints, and regular counts of inmates serve the security function: Few inmates escape. More important, such features set the tone for the daily operations. Prisons are expected to be impersonal, quasi-military organizations where strict discipline, minimal amenities, and restrictions on freedom carry out the punishment of criminals.

Three models of incarceration have predominated since the early 1940s: custodial, rehabilitation, and reintegration. Each reflects one style of institutional organization.

custodial model
A model of correctional institutions that emphasizes security, discipline, and order.

1. The **custodial model** assumes that prisoners have been incarcerated for the purpose of incapacitation, deterrence, or retribution. It emphasizes security, discipline, and order, which subordinate the prisoner to the authority of the warden. Discipline is strict, and most aspects of behavior are regulated. This model prevailed in corrections before World War II, and it continues to dominate most maximum-security institutions.

rehabilitation model
A model of correctional institutions that emphasizes the provision of treatment programs designed to reform the offender.

2. The **rehabilitation model**, developed during the 1950s, emphasizes treatment programs designed to reform the offender. According to this model, security and housekeeping activities are preconditions for rehabilitative efforts. As all aspects of

the organization should be directed toward rehabilitation, professional treatment specialists enjoy a higher status than do other employees. Treatment programs exist in most contemporary institutions. But since the rethinking of the rehabilitation goal in the 1970s, very few prisons continue to conform to this model.

3. The **reintegration model** is linked to the structures and goals of community corrections. Recognizing that prisoners will be returning to society, this model emphasizes maintaining offenders' ties to family and community as a method of reform. Prisons following this model gradually give inmates greater freedom and responsibility during their confinement, moving them to halfway houses or work release programs before releasing them under some form of community supervision.

> **reintegration model**
> A model of correctional institutions that emphasizes maintenance of the offender's ties to family and the community as a method of reform, in recognition of the fact that the offender will be returning to the community.

Although one can find correctional institutions that conform to each of these models, most prisons today are mainly custodial. Nevertheless, treatment programs do exist, and even some of the most-custodial institutions attempt to prepare inmates for reentry into free society. Because prisons are expected to pursue many different and often incompatible goals, it would seem that they are almost doomed to fail. Charles Logan believes that the mission of prisons is confinement and that the basic purpose of imprisonment is to punish offenders fairly through terms of confinement proportionate to the seriousness of the crimes. He summarizes the mission of the prison as follows: "to keep prisoners—to keep them in, keep them safe, keep them in line, keep them healthy, and keep them busy—and to do it with fairness, without undue suffering, and as efficiently as possible."[7]

PRISON SYSTEMS

All 50 states and the federal government operate prisons. Offenders are held in 1,292 confinement facilities, nearly 92 percent of which are operated under state authority. Private companies that contract with state authorities run 283 of these facilities. The largest percentage of state confinement facilities are located in the South (47 percent), 20 percent are located in the Midwest, 18.5 percent are in the West, and 14.5 percent are in the Northeast.[8] For the most part, prisons house convicted offenders who have been sentenced to terms of more than one year. Various state governments and the federal government differ in terms of how they organize incarceration, number and types of facilities, staffing, and size of offender populations.

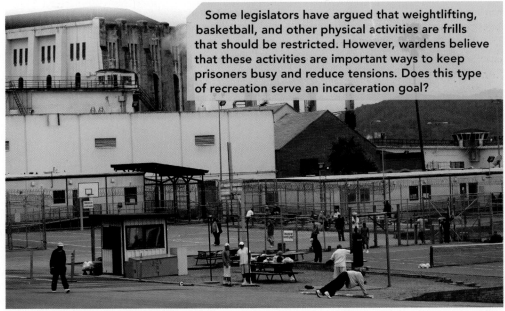

Some legislators have argued that weightlifting, basketball, and other physical activities are frills that should be restricted. However, wardens believe that these activities are important ways to keep prisoners busy and reduce tensions. Does this type of recreation serve an incarceration goal?

Robert Galbraith/Reuters/Landov

The Federal Prison System

Created by Congress in 1930, the Federal Bureau of Prisons is responsible for "the safekeeping, care, protection, instruction, and discipline of all persons charged or convicted of offenses against the United States." Today's bureau is highly centralized, with a director who is appointed by the president; six regional directors, who head up offices to support the operations of federal facilities in their respective regions; and a staff of approximately 40,000, who supervise approximately 210,340 prisoners. The bureau operates a network of 121 institutions.[9]

The Bureau of Prisons is responsible for individuals charged with and convicted of federal crimes. Historically, federal prisons have housed bank robbers, extortionists, people who commit mail fraud, and arsonists. But since the war on drugs started in the 1980s, the number of drug offenders in federal prisons has increased. Prisoners convicted of drug offenses now make up over half of the federal inmate population. There are fewer violent offenders in federal prisons than in many state institutions. Federal prisoners are widely believed to often be a more sophisticated type of criminal, from a higher socioeconomic class, than typical state prisoners. Interestingly, 26 percent of federal inmates are citizens of other countries.[10] **Figure 6.1** presents some key characteristics of federal prisoners.

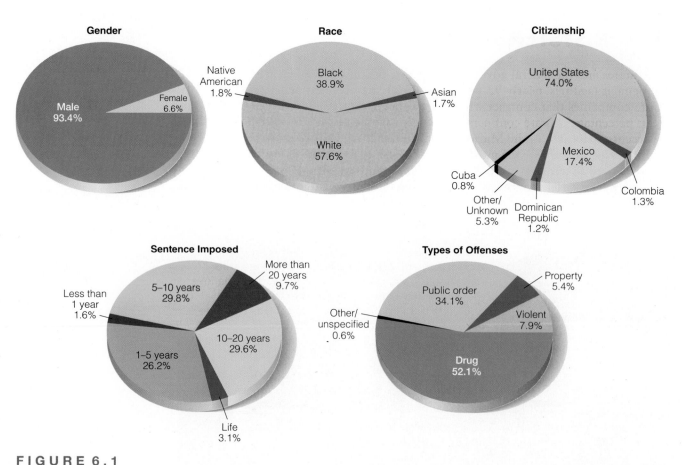

FIGURE 6.1

Characteristics of Federal Prison Inmates

Federal prisoners tend to be male, white, and convicted of drug offenses. A sizable portion of federal inmates are not U.S. citizens, and over half of them received sentences ranging from 5 to 20 years.

Source: Federal Bureau of Prisons, State of the *Bureau, 2010* (Washington, DC: U.S. Government Printing Office, 2010), 3.

The Bureau of Prisons confinement facilities are classified using four security levels, ranging from "minimum" to "high" security. Security classification is based on several features, including the presence of external patrols, security barriers, type of housing, and staff-to-inmate ratio. Facilities designated "administrative" have special missions, such as pretrial detention, treating inmates with serious or chronic medical problems, and containing the most-dangerous inmates in the federal prison population. The bureau is organized so that wardens report to one of the six regional offices. Staff in the regional office perform a variety of functions, such as providing management and technical assistance, conducting training programs, and contracting with community agencies when placing offenders in residential reentry centers.

Historically, the Bureau of Prisons has enjoyed a good reputation and has been viewed as an innovator in the field of corrections.

State Prison Systems

States differ in how they organize their prisons. Nevertheless, in every state the executive branch of government administers prisons. This is an important point because probation is often part of the judiciary, and parole may be separate from corrections. In most states, jails are run by county governments.

Commissioners of corrections, normally appointed by state governors, are responsible for the operation of prisons. Each prison facility is administered by a *warden* (often called a *superintendent*), who reports directly to the commissioner or a deputy commissioner for institutions. The number of employees in state correctional agencies has risen dramatically during the past decade. Nearly 390,000 people—administrators, officers, and program specialists—work in state correctional institutions. Approximately 68 percent of these employees are correctional officers.[11]

States also differ in the number, size, type, and location of correctional facilities. For example, Louisiana's state prison at Angola has an inmate population of about 5,200 that is organized into five different custody levels.[12] In contrast, Vermont's largest prison, the Southern State Correctional Facility in Springfield, is designed to house 370 inmates.[13] Some states, such as California, New York, and Texas, have a wide mix of institutions that differ in size and style. For example, Florida has 142 prison facilities

People who are housed in "secure housing units," or SHUs, get one hour of outdoor recreation time each day—in "outdoor cages" like this one at Corcoran State Prison in California. The rest of the time, they are confined to their cells.

Robert Galbraith/Reuters/Landov

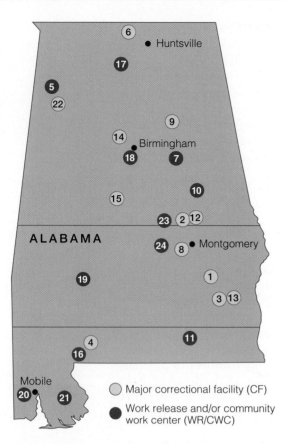

1. Bullock CF
2. Draper CF,
   Elmore CF,
   Thomas F. Staton CF
3. Easterling CF
4. J. O. Davis CF,
   G. K. Fountain CF,
   Holman CF
5. Hamilton WR/CWC
6. Limestone CF
7. Childersburg WR/CWC
8. Kilby CF
9. St. Clair CF
10. Alex City WR/CWC
11. Elba WR/CWC

12. Julia Tutwiler CF
13. Ventress CF
14. Donaldson CF
15. Bibb County CF
16. Atmore WR/CWC
17. Decatur WR/CWC
18. Birmingham WR/CWC
19. Camden WR/CWC
20. Mobile WR/CWC
21. Loxley WR/CWC
22. Hamilton CF
23. Frank Lee WR/CWC
24. Red Eagle WR/CWC

Major correctional facility (CF)

Work release and/or community
work center (WR/CWC)

FIGURE 6.2
The Alabama Prison System
The number and variety of institutions for felons in Alabama is typical of most medium-sized states. What factors might influence the locale of penal institutions?

Source: Alabama Department of Corrections, www.doc.state.al.us/default.aspx, February 17, 2015.

that include correctional institutions, work camps, work release centers, and road prisons.[14] Alabama has 29 facilities, which include maximum- and medium-security facilities, an institution for the aged and infirm, a women's prison, an honor farm, and work release and community work centers (see **Figure 6.2**).

The age, education, and criminal history of the inmate population influence how correctional institutions function. What are the characteristics of inmates in U.S. state prisons? The Bureau of Justice Statistics reports that a majority of prisoners are men, members of minority groups, and convicted of violent crimes (see **Figure 6.3**).[15]

THE DESIGN AND CLASSIFICATION OF PRISONS

In all eras, attempts have been made to design institutions that advance the prevailing goal of corrections.[16] In this section we discuss some of the changes and ideas in prison design. During the 1800s some English and American architects designed prisons to accommodate contemplation, industry, and isolation. These factors were believed to be necessary for inmates to reform. After the Civil War, prison industry became the main focus of corrections. A different prison design emerged during this period, one that made inmate labor more efficient. Later, when custody became the primary goal of corrections, massive, fortress-like institutions were built to ensure security. And during the rehabilitation era of the 1950s and 1960s, new prisons were designed and built in ways

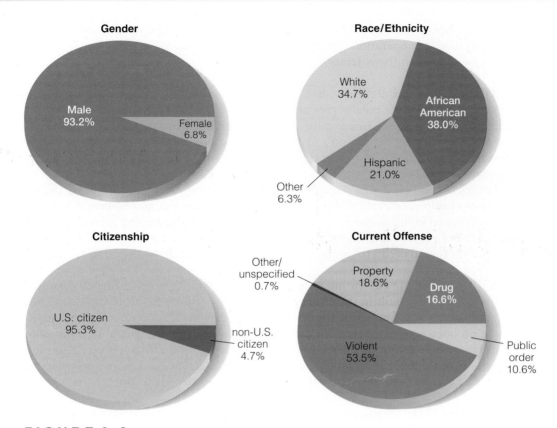

FIGURE 6.3
Characteristics of State Prison Inmates
State prisoners tend to be male and of a racial or ethnic minority, have at least a high school education, and have been convicted of violent offenses.

Source: E. Ann Carson and Daniela Golinelli, *Prisoners in 2012: Trends in Admissions and Releases, 1991–2012* (Washington, DC: U.S. Government Printing Office, December 2013).

thought to promote treatment. At all times, however, the plans of prison architects had to be "realistic" regarding cost.

Today's prisons differ greatly in terms of design and operation. Some states and the federal government have built smaller facilities. But despite the boom in prison construction that took place in the 1990s, many of America's old and large prisons are still in operation. Just like any old and heavily used building, these aging megaprisons are costly to maintain and at times difficult to operate.

Today's Designs

Perhaps more so than in the past, today's prison designs are greatly influenced by the cost of construction and maintenance. Joseph T. Hallinan described the modern prison facility as a "concrete econo-box." From a distance, these institutions may resemble a hospital or suburban high school. Guard towers are no longer used because they are expensive to operate. Today's prisons do not have large concrete and stone walls; razor-wire fences are much cheaper.[17] Although a number of concrete econo-box prisons were built in the 1990s, four basic models of prison design are used in the United States.

THE RADIAL DESIGN Prisons in the early 1800s usually followed the **radial design** of Pennsylvania's Eastern Penitentiary (see **Figure 6.4a**). The control center is located in the center, making it possible to monitor inmate movement. From the center, one or more "spokes" can be isolated from the rest of the institution. This feature is helpful

radial design
An architectural plan by which a prison is constructed in the form of a wheel, with "spokes" radiating from a central core.

if trouble erupts. Although very few newer prisons reflect the radial design, several older prisons still in operation were built to such specifications, including Leavenworth (Kansas) and Trenton (New Jersey).

THE TELEPHONE-POLE DESIGN   In a prison based on the **telephone-pole design**, a long central corridor (or pole) serves as the means for prisoners to go from one part of the institution to another (see **Figure 6.4b**). Jutting out from the corridor are cross-arms, each containing the prison's functional areas: housing, shops, classrooms, recreation area, and so on. The central pole allows continuous surveillance, as well as independently controlled access to each functional area.

> **telephone-pole design**
> A prison architectural plan calling for a long central corridor crossed at regular intervals by structures containing the prisoners' functional areas.

The telephone-pole design is mainly used for maximum-security prisons in the United States. For example, Graterford (Pennsylvania), Marion (Illinois), and Somers (Connecticut) are designed in this fashion. These prisons are built for maintaining custody and can house inmates according to classification levels. Certain housing areas can be used for inmates with special needs, for inmates who have earned special privileges, and so on.

THE COURTYARD STYLE   Some new correctional facilities, including maximum-security prisons, are built in the **courtyard style** (see **Figure 6.4c**). In these facilities the functional units of a prison are housed in separate buildings constructed on four sides of an open square. Movement along the endless corridors, which is common in the telephone-pole design, is replaced by movement across the courtyard to the housing units and other functional areas. In some facilities of this type, such functional units as the dining hall, gym, and school are located in the entry-yard area.

> **courtyard style**
> An architectural design by which the functional units of a prison are housed in separate buildings constructed on four sides of an open square.

THE CAMPUS STYLE   A design long used for juvenile and women's correctional facilities, the **campus style** has been used for some new institutions for men (see **Figure 6.4d**). Relatively small housing units are scattered among the shops, school, dining hall, and other units of the facility. This style is thought to be an important development not only because of the humane features of the design but also because individual buildings can be used more flexibly. As in courtyard-style prisons, inmates and staff must go outdoors to get from one part of the facility to another. The modern prison fences keep inmate escapes to a minimum. Most facilities of this type serve medium- and minimum-security populations.

> **campus style**
> An architectural design by which the functional units of a prison are individually housed in a complex of buildings surrounded by a fence.

The Location of Prisons

Most prisons for adults are located in rural areas. The early prisons were built outside city centers because it was believed that offenders needed to be isolated from urban

a. Radial design

b. Telephone-pole design

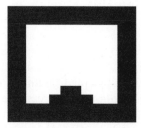

c. Courtyard style

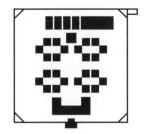

d. Campus style

FIGURE 6.4

Prison Designs Used in the United States

These four basic designs are used throughout the country for most prisons housing adult felons. Each style has certain features related to the goals of "keeping and serving" the prisoners. How does architecture influence the management of these institutions?

distractions and criminal peers. Later in the 1800s, more prisons were built in rural areas because these institutions maintained farms that helped them to be self-sufficient. Even now, new institutions are being built in the countryside. Many people view this as counterproductive. A large number of prison inmates come from cities, and their families often have difficulty visiting them. In addition, prison administrators must rely on the local labor pool to recruit employees. This often means that rural whites are hired to guard urban African American inmates.

A number of factors influence where prisons are constructed. For example, the land needed to construct a correctional facility is usually cheaper in rural areas. Political factors also figure in the decision. Many citizens believe that serious offenders should be incarcerated, but not in their community. This attitude is often referred to as the NIMBY syndrome (Not In My Back Yard!). Some people fear that building a prison in their community will lower property values and that people who come to visit prison inmates will cause problems in the community.[18] These concerns often prevent criminal justice planners from locating facilities in certain areas.

Some poor communities have welcomed prison construction. They believe that prisons will bring jobs that will help improve the local economy. However, research shows that new prisons do not always have the desired impact on economic conditions. New prison employees may live in neighboring counties and commute to work, local residents may lack the qualifications necessary for prison work, and local business may not be awarded contracts to supply new prisons with goods and services.[19]

The Classification of Prisons

State prisons for men are classified according to the level of security deemed necessary. Three security levels are typically used: maximum, medium, and minimum. Forty states and the federal government operate prisons that exceed maximum security, called "super-max" prisons.[20] These facilities are designed to hold the most-disruptive, violent, and incorrigible offenders. California's Pelican Bay Institution and Virginia's Red Onion Institution are examples of prisons designed to hold the "worst of the worst."

Most states have so few female prisoners that they are all housed in one institution; those who require higher levels of security are separated from the general population. In contrast, male inmates are assigned to a specific type of facility. Their placement is determined by several factors, including the seriousness of the offense, the possibility of an escape attempt, and the potential for violent behavior. Because some states do not have a facility for each level of security, a prison may be divided into different security levels. These are called "multilevel" facilities. There are no national design or classification standards. A maximum-security prison in one state may be run similarly to a medium-security facility in another. Nevertheless, some generalizations can be made.

THE MAXIMUM-SECURITY PRISON   Usually an imposing structure surrounded by a high stone or concrete wall with guard towers, the **maximum-security prison** (sometimes called a *closed security prison*) is designed to prevent escapes and to deter prisoners from harming one another. The United States has 355 such facilities housing about 38 percent of all state prisoners.[21]

Inmates live in cells, each with its own toilet and sink. The barred or steel doors may operate electronically so that an officer can confine all prisoners to their cells with a flip of a switch. Because the purpose of this type of facility is custody and discipline, it embraces a military-style approach to order. Prisoners follow strict routines. Head counts are frequent, and inmates are closely monitored—often through closed-circuit television.

These structures are built to last. Many that were built in the late 1800s and early 1900s are still in operation. The design of these old prisons makes it difficult to adapt to newer correctional goals, such as rehabilitation and reintegration. Some of the best-known prisons, such as Attica (New York), Stateville (Illinois), and Yuma (Arizona), are maximum-security facilities.

maximum-security prison
A prison designed and organized to minimize the possibility of escapes and violence; to that end, it imposes strict limitations on the freedom of inmates and visitors.

medium-security prison
A prison designed and organized to prevent escapes and violence, but in which restrictions on inmates and visitors are less rigid than in maximum-security facilities.

THE MEDIUM-SECURITY PRISON There are 438 **medium-security prisons** holding 43 percent of state inmates.[22] From the outside, this type of facility may resemble a maximum-security prison, but it is organized differently, and its atmosphere is less rigid. Prisoners usually have more privileges and contact with the outside world through visitors, mail, and access to radio and television. Medium-security prisons usually place greater emphasis on work and rehabilitation programs. Although the inmates may have committed serious crimes, they are not perceived as hardened criminals. Some of the newer medium-security facilities have a campus or courtyard style, although the razor-wire fences, guard towers, and other security devices remain. In some states, a medium-security prison seems much closer to maximum than to minimum security.

minimum-security prison
A prison designed and organized to permit inmates and visitors as much freedom as is consistent with the concept of incarceration.

THE MINIMUM-SECURITY PRISON The **minimum-security prison** houses the least-violent offenders, long-term felons with clean disciplinary records, and inmates who have nearly completed their term. There are 926 such facilities in the United States that house 19 percent of state inmates.[23] Minimum-security prisons do not have guard towers or walls. Often, chain-link fencing surrounds dormitory-style buildings where inmates live in private rooms rather than cells. There is more personal freedom: Inmates have television sets, choose their own clothes, and move about casually within and between buildings. The system relies on rehabilitation programs and offers opportunities for education and work release. It also offers reintegration programs and support to inmates preparing for release. Some states and the Federal Bureau of Prisons operate minimum-security prison camps where inmates work on forest conservation and fight wildfires. To the outsider, minimum-security prisons may seem to enforce little punishment, but the inmates remain separated from society, and their freedoms are restricted.

Private Prisons

U.S. taxpayers spend billions of dollars each year on prisons.[24] Expenditures include things such as construction, renovations and repairs, equipment purchases, employee compensation, inmate medical care, feeding prisoners, and utilities (electricity, heating oil, water, and trash removal). Many states contract with private companies to furnish food, provide medical care, and provide other services. Although private enterprise has long played a role in American corrections, the scope of services purchased from

The Idaho Correctional Center, near Boise, Idaho, was a private prison run by the Corrections Corporation of America until the FBI launched a criminal investigation into its management. The Idaho Department of Corrections took back responsibility for the facility in July 2014.

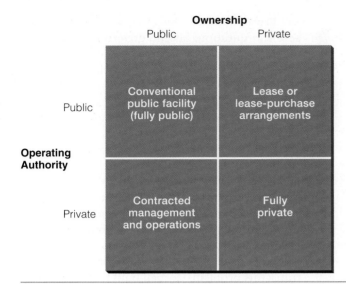

Ownership

Public / Private

Operating Authority — Public / Private

| | Conventional public facility (fully public) | Lease or lease-purchase arrangements |
| | Contracted management and operations | Fully private |

FIGURE 6.5

Four Basic Forms of Public and Private Involvement in Correctional Administration

Ownership and operating authority are the key variables that help us differentiate forms of correctional administration.

Source: Douglas McDonald, "Private Penal Institutions," in *Crime and Justice: A Review of Research*, vol. 16, edited by Michael Tonry (Chicago: University of Chicago Press, 1992), 365.

profit-seeking organizations has expanded greatly in recent decades. In fact, governments now contract with corporations to house prisoners in privately owned and operated facilities.

There are four basic forms of public and private involvement in corrections, as shown in **Figure 6.5**. This model distinguishes between ownership and operating authority. Some institutions are both owned and operated by either government or private enterprise. However, others may be owned by government and operated under contract by a private entity, or owned by a private company and operated by government on a lease or lease-purchase arrangement.

Over the past 30 years, the construction and operation of private prisons have become big business. Private entrepreneurs argue that they can build and run prisons as effectively, safely, and humanely as any level of government. They propose also that they can do so more efficiently, which saves taxpayers money. Pressured by prison and jail crowding, rising staff costs, and growing public sentiment regarding inefficient government, politicians in the early 1980s found such proposals appealing. At year-end 2013, 133,044 state and federal inmates were housed in private facilities. Over half of these prisoners were in the federal system and four states (Texas, Oklahoma, Georgia, and Florida).[25]

Private prisons remain controversial, and several issues continue to be debated. For example, supporters of prison privatization claim that they can run prisons more cheaply than do the states (see Myths in Corrections, "Private Versus Public Prisons"). One study of 48 private and public juvenile correctional facilities concluded that public and private facilities are very similar in terms of environmental quality.[26] The evidence regarding prison programming shows that differences exist between state and private adult institutions: Compared with private prisons, a greater proportion of state and federal correctional facilities provide access to work programs (96.7 versus 55.9 percent), education programs (92.7 versus 59.5 percent), and counseling programs (97.3 versus 74.2 percent).[27] But the percentage of privately owned facilities providing prisoners with basic adult education, secondary education, and vocational training programming has increased substantially since 1995.[28]

Questions about accountability of service providers to public correctional officials are also raised. Critics charge that the profit incentive may result in poor services. In 2010, state officials in Idaho fined Corrections Corporation of America (CCA) more than $40,000 for hiring unqualified alcohol counselors and for troubles associated with medical care at the Idaho Correctional Center. Specifically, the state's audit revealed that CCA delayed providing medications, administering immunizations, and providing mental health care services.[29] Many states have enacted new laws to ensure that the private-prison industry lives up to its contractual obligations.

MYTHS in Corrections

Private Versus Public Prisons

THE MYTH: Private prisons are more effective than public prisons in preparing inmates for life after incarceration.

THE REALITY: A study conducted in Oklahoma that followed 22,359 inmates over a four-year period found that prisoners who served more time and/or a greater proportion of their sentence in a private facility were at greater risk of recidivating when compared to inmates in public prisons.

Source: Andrew L. Spivak and Susan F. Sharp, "Inmate Recidivism as a Measure of Private Prison Performance," *Crime & Delinquency* 54 (July 2008): 482–508.

Private prisons also raise an important philosophical question: Should governments transfer their authority to deprive citizens of the freedoms and liberty to private, profit-seeking corporations? Some argue that prison administration is a basic government function that should not be delegated to private entities.[30] Another concern is whether private companies will always act in ways consistent with the public interest. Unlike the government, private-prison corporations need to fill their cells to be profitable. Some fear that correctional policy may become skewed because contractors will use political influence to build more facilities and to continue programs not in the public interest.

The experience of Cornell Corrections illustrates this problem. Cornell built a 300-bed facility in Rhode Island only to find that the federal prisoners slated to be housed there at $83 per day did not materialize. Rhode Island's political leaders pressed the U.S. Justice Department to fill the facility, but to no avail. Facing angry bondholders and investors, Cornell hired an attorney to scour the country for states seeking beds for their prisoners. Only after North Carolina agreed to send 232 prisoners (including 18 murderers) to Rhode Island was Cornell's fiscal crisis averted, at least temporarily.[31]

The idea of privately run correctional facilities has stimulated much interest among the general public and within the criminal justice community. Privatization itself has a long history in criminal justice, dating as far back as the English practice of transporting convicts to North America and Australia. Jeremy Bentham, well-known for his panopticon prison design, was himself an entrepreneur who unsuccessfully pursued a contract to construct and operate a prison.[32] Regardless of the future of prison privatization, the controversy has forced correctional officials to rethink some strongly held beliefs. In this regard, the possibility of competition from the private sector may have a positive impact.

INCARCERATION TRENDS

From 1930 through 1980, the incarceration rate in the United States remained fairly stable. During this period the rate of prisoners sentenced to federal and state facilities fluctuated from a low of 93 per 100,000 population in 1972 to a high of 139 in 1980. However, the average rate of incarceration increased dramatically in the 1980s (200 per 100,000) and 1990s (389 per 100,000) (see **Figure 6.6**). This growth trend has continued into the twenty-first century. The average incarceration rate from 2000 to 2010 was 490 per 100,000.[33]

This tremendous growth has dramatically changed both the demographics and the offense composition of the prison population. African Americans and Hispanics now make up a large percentage of inmates in U.S. correctional facilities. Prisoners are more likely to be middle-aged, and more women are being incarcerated.

The size and growth of the prison population differ among states. As **Figure 6.7** shows, the five states with the highest incarceration rates (Louisiana, Mississippi, Texas, Oklahoma, and Alabama) are in the South. Many argue that southern attitudes toward crime and punishment account for that region's high prison population. The penal codes in many southern states provide for long sentences, and inmates there spend extended periods in institutions. It is also the region with the highest African

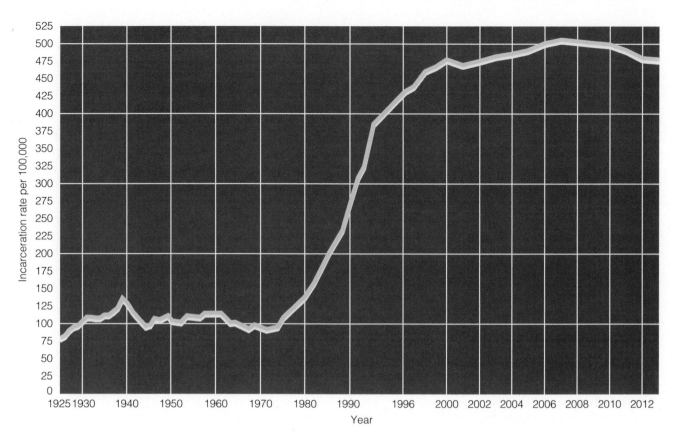

FIGURE 6.6

Incarceration Rate (per 100,000 Population) of Sentenced State and Federal Prisoners

Between 1940 and 1974, the incarceration rate held steady. From 1975 to 2000, there was a continuing increase. The rate today is nearly double what it was in 1988.

Source: E. Ann Carson, *Prisoners in 2013* (Washington, DC: U.S. Government Printing Office, September 2014), 6.

American population, which is incarcerated in numbers far greater than its proportion to the overall population.

Why has the prison population increased so dramatically? Because the violent and property crime rates have been declining as incarceration rates increase, it seems there is little relationship between crime and incarceration. If this is the case, what factors explain the growth?

Explaining Prison Population Trends

Five reasons have been advanced to help explain the increased rate of incarceration in the United States. None of these reasons should be viewed as a single explanation. Rather, each contributes to the equation, with some having a greater impact than others:

1. *Increased arrests and more likely incarceration.* Some observers believe that the billions spent by federal, state, and local governments on the crime problem may be paying off. Although rates of serious crime have declined since the 1970s, arrest rates have increased. Today, offenders who are arrested are more likely to receive a prison sentence. Also, the number of prisoners returning to prison for new crimes or parole violations has increased. About three-quarters of released prisoners are arrested for a new crime within five years of their release.[34]

2. *Tougher sentencing.* Many people think that hardening of public attitudes toward criminals resulted in longer prison sentences, relatively less frequent use

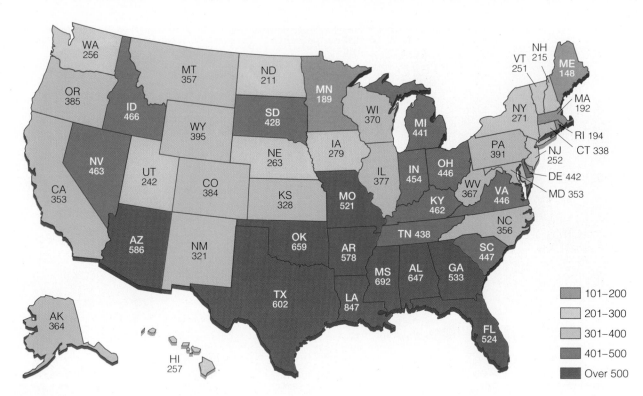

FIGURE 6.7

Sentenced Prisoners in State Institutions per 100,000 Population

What can be said about the differences in incarceration rates among the states? There are not only regional differences but also differences among neighboring states that seem to have similar demographics and crime characteristics.

Source: E. Ann Carson, *Prisoners in 2013* (Washington, DC: U.S. Government Printing Office, September 2014), 7.

of probation, and fewer inmates being released at the time of their first parole hearing. In the past three decades the states and federal government have passed laws that increase sentences for many crimes. In addition, mandatory-sentencing laws greatly limit the discretion of judges with regard to the length of sentences for certain offenders.

3. *Prison construction.* The increased rate of incarceration may be related to the creation of additional space in the nation's prisons. Between 1990 and 2005, more than 500 prisons were built across the country, increasing the number of facilities nationwide by 42 percent.[35] Public resources are typically used to their fullest capacities. Prisons are no exception. When prison space is limited, judges usually reserve incarceration for only the most-violent offenders. However, additional prisons may present a variation of the "Field of Dreams" scenario—build them, and they will come. Creation of additional prison space may thus increase the incarceration rate.

4. *The war on drugs.* Crusades against the use of drugs have happened repeatedly since the 1800s. The most recent war, declared by President Ronald Reagan in 1982, resulted in money for drug enforcement personnel and prison space. The war on drugs has certainly succeeded in packing the nation's prisons with drug-law offenders. In 1980 only 19,000, or 6 percent, of state prisoners had been convicted of a drug offense; by 2013 this figure had risen to 210,200, or nearly 15.9 percent, of inmates in state prisons.[36]

5. *State and local politics.* Can state and local political factors influence correctional policies? Probably the most extensive research on the link between politics and incarceration was conducted by David F. Greenberg and Valerie West. After analyzing the level of incarceration among the 50 states over a 20-year period,

Table 6.1 Incarceration Rates and Violent Crime Rates in Selected Neighboring States

Politics and community values seem to vary in the amount of emphasis that they place on imprisonment as a solution to crime.

	Incarceration Rate	Violent Crime Rate
Pennsylvania	391	355
New York	271	398
Idaho	466	201
Utah	242	195
Wisconsin	370	237
Minnesota	189	221

Sources: E. Ann Carson, *Prisoners in 2013* (Washington, DC: U.S. Government Printing Office, 2014), 7; Federal Bureau of Investigation, *Crime in the United States, 2011,* www.fbi.gov/about-us/cjis/ucr/crime-in-the-u.s/2011/crime-in-the-u.s.-2011/tables/table-4, April 27, 2014.

Greenberg and West found that states with the highest violent crime rates also have higher levels of imprisonment. Greenberg and West also found that states with higher revenues have higher prison populations, that states with more-generous welfare benefits have lower prison populations, that states with more political conservatives have higher prison populations, and that expansive prison policy transcends Democratic and Republican affiliations.[37] One might think that there would be an association among the states between variation in crime rates and variation in incarceration rates—the more crime, the more prisoners. However, some states with high crime rates do not have correspondingly high incarceration rates (see **Table 6.1**).

Public Policy Trends

It is difficult to point to one factor as the main cause of the rapid increase in the incarceration rate during the past several decades. As we have seen, several plausible hypotheses exist. But researchers now recognize that the size of the prison population is not driven by the amount of crime; it is driven by public policy. Public policies are forged in the political arena. Politicians are aware that the public is concerned about crime; the public also has little sympathy for offenders. In this political environment, correctional policies have emerged based on the assumption that crime can be controlled through greater use of incarceration.

Government leaders have enacted policies designed to incarcerate a greater number of offenders for longer periods. This objective has been implemented through increased law enforcement and prosecution spending, mandatory-sentencing laws, truth-in-sentencing requirements, enhanced drug-law enforcement, and tough parole policies. But it is not clear that these policies have reduced crime. Supporters of the policies argue that the decline in crime has come about because large numbers of criminals are in prison. However, some critics argue that incarcerating large numbers of offenders has had little impact on the crime rate.

After 30 years of policies to incarcerate more offenders for longer periods, several states have quietly started to ease their sentencing and parole laws. Some states have granted judges and parole boards wider latitude in sentencing and release decisions. Greater use of intermediate sanctions and nonprison alternatives has helped to lower the prison population in several states as well. Many states have made other changes,

focus on correctional policy

Economic Crisis and Correctional Reform

For decades now, politicians, both Republicans and Democrats, have beat the "get-tough-on-crime" drum during their campaigns and continue to do so once they take office. The results of the movement to get tougher on crime include increasingly punitive correctional policies, such as "three-strikes" laws and mandatory sentences, and an exploding correctional population. Although scholars and policy makers debate whether this shift in correctional philosophy has affected the crime rate, one thing is certain: The amount of taxpayer money allocated to correctional budgets has increased substantially. State correctional budgets have more than quadrupled in the past two decades. In 2010 state governments spent a combined $48.5 billion on corrections.

As the United States works its way through the most recent economic downturn, many politicians are now considering less punitive alternatives to the costly practice of incarcerating more offenders and building more prisons. In Mississippi the governor proposed reinstating early release for good behavior. The governor of Alabama proposed releasing 3,000 nonviolent inmates. Other states, such as Virginia, have considered closing several state correctional facilities.

Such a shift in policy would have been considered political suicide just a few years ago. What is surprising to many onlookers is that many of the supporters touting correctional reform formerly advocated "get-tough" policies.

For example, Kansas state representative Mike O'Neal, a Republican who previously pushed for longer sentences for sex offenders and drug dealers, helped develop a measure to reduce by 20 percent the number of former inmates sent to prison for violating the conditions of their release, such as failing drug tests and not reporting to their parole officer, to save the state money. The budgetary crisis facing many states has brought about a serious discussion about whether states can continue to fund their "get-tough-on-crime" policies.

Critical Thinking

1. What, if anything, does the amount of money we spend on prisons say about our goals as a society?

2. What other policy options should politicians consider to reduce spending on corrections?

3. Do you believe that the general public will support cuts to correctional budgets?

4. Should states consider reducing sentences for certain types of crimes? If so, which crimes?

Sources: National Conference of State Legislatures, "Actions and Proposals to Balance FY 2011 Budgets: Criminal Justice Cuts," www.ncsl.org/?tabid=19645, May 19, 2011; Tracey Kyckelhahn, *State Corrections Expenditures, FY 1982–2010* (Washington, DC: U.S. Government Printing Office, 2012).

such as repealing or reducing mandatory-minimum sentences for drug offenses, expanding treatment-centered alternatives to incarceration, and expanding emergency and early-release mechanisms. These appear to be more than fiscal belt-tightening efforts, instead reflecting shifts in correctional policies that could reduce the ever-spiraling rise of the incarceration rate. (See Focus on Correctional Policy: "Economic Crisis and Correctional Reform" for information on how the economic crisis has forced some states to reform their correctional policies.)

Although the falling crime rate, state budget deficits, and a weakened economy may have contributed to a reduction in the annual increase in the prison population nationwide, and even reductions in prison populations in some states, the U.S. incarceration rate is still among the highest in the world (see "Do the Right Thing"). Further, not all state corrections systems are taking measures to lower incarceration, so growth still continues in many states. Most state and federal correctional administrators and policy makers must as yet deal with the problem of crowded prisons.

Dealing with Crowded Prisons

The skyrocketing prison population has resulted in prison crowding. At the end of 2013, 19 states and the federal government operated at 100 percent or more of

DO the Right Thing

While sitting at his desk, Representative Leon Donohue taps his fountain pen on a stack of papers. Staring out the window, he contemplates an upcoming vote on House Bill 65. If enacted into law, the bill would require adults who possessed 50 grams of cocaine to serve at least 10 years in prison. The most recent opinion poll showed that 52 percent of the public supports the bill.

Rep. Donohue has remained undecided and has said very little in the press about the matter. The congressman believes that cocaine is a threat to public health and is associated with many social problems, such as gun violence, family disruption, and addiction. But he is also concerned whether the state can afford to implement a new mandatory-minimum sentencing law. The Department of Corrections has already sustained a substantial budget reduction during the last legislative session, and more cuts are expected in the near future. This new law will likely contribute to an already large prison population that is unaffordable.

Rep. Donohue considered voting in support of the bill if it lacked the governor's support. However, the governor has yet to indicate whether she would sign the bill into law or veto it.

There is a quick succession of knocks at the door as it opens and the congressman's chief of staff enters. "Okay, Congressman, we need to get you to the floor. Voting on Bill 65 has started."

"I'm ready, Sam. Let's do it."

Critical Thinking

If you were in Donohue's position, how you would vote on House Bill 65? Should the congressman let the results from the recent public opinion poll influence his decision? Should concerns about the state's budget take precedence over "tough-on-crime" laws? If the bill becomes law, where should the state look for additional money to fund its prisons?

capacity.[38] When prisons become too crowded, correctional officials are forced to make room for newly admitted inmates. Sometimes this means placing bunks in corridors and basements. Judges in several states have ordered prisons to address crowding. For example, in 2011 the U.S. Supreme Court upheld a lower court ruling that California reduce its prison population by about 110,000 prisoners over a two-year period to ease overcrowding. In response, state lawmakers passed bills to begin reducing the inmate population starting October 1, 2011.[39] Despite the best efforts to improve

Prison overcrowding is a major challenge in many prison systems today. People are housed in crowded conditions, and with idleness and limited supervision, conflict and other types of disruption can become a problem.

AP Images/Kiichiro Sato

prison conditions, crowding remains an important policy issue because of constitutional concerns, because of the belief that crowding increases inmate violence, and because crowding makes the operation of inmate programs and services more challenging.

Departments of corrections are usually unable to control the flow of offenders sent to them by the courts. To deal with crowded prisons, states are adopting a variety of strategies. Alfred Blumstein identified four approaches that states take to address overcrowding. First, the **null strategy** entails simply doing nothing to reduce crowding. This strategy may be the most politically acceptable strategy because taxpayers will not be asked to pay for new prison construction. However, the courts may ultimately declare that the conditions in crowded facilities are unconstitutional, which would force correctional officials responsible for crowded facilities to adopt a different strategy. An alternative approach, termed the **construction strategy**, entails building more prisons to meet the rising demand for prison space. The increased number of new correctional facilities since 1990 suggests that many states have adopted this strategy.

Some observers argue that rather than merely building more institutions, corrections should reserve prison space for those violent offenders who have not been deterred by prior punishments. Supporters of intermediate sanctions have argued that offenders can be punished in the community after a short period of incarceration. Judges can fashion sentences using a combination of sanctions (fines, restitution, home confinement, community service, and intensive probation supervision) that fit the needs of the offender and the severity of the offense. Increasing the use of intermediate sanctions could reduce the prison population. The final approach entails the use of "backdoor strategies," such as parole, work release, and good time, to get offenders out of prison before the end of their term and free up space for newcomers. More recently, as state governments face economic conditions that force them to reduce their budgets, many politicians are looking for ways to reduce spending on corrections.

DOES INCARCERATION PAY?

Opponents of current penal policies argue that offenders whose crimes do not warrant the severe deprivation of imprisonment are still being sent to prison. They also say that the policy debate does not consider many of the unintended consequences of

null strategy
The strategy of doing nothing to relieve crowding in prisons, under the assumption that the problem is temporary and will disappear in time.

construction strategy
A strategy of building new facilities to meet the demand for prison space.

Family visits are important. They help people who are incarcerated maintain their relationships with loved ones, especially children. They help family members prepare for eventually being reunited after release. Here Isis, age two, gets lots of loving attention from her father, Pharaoh, and her mother, Loretta.

Elijah Nouvelage/Reuters/Landov

imprisonment, such as family and community disruption. Supporters of incarceration believe that recent policies have succeeded in lowering the crime rate. They say that most inmates have committed serious crimes, often with violence, and that they are repeat offenders. Not to incarcerate repeat offenders, they claim, is costly to society.

Have recent incarceration policies been effective? As a Pew Charitable Trusts study notes, "Increasing the proportion of convicted criminals sent to prison, like lengthening time served beyond some point, has produced diminishing marginal returns in crime reduction." This does not mean that incarceration will have no impact—"just that the benefits to public safety of each additional prisoner consistently decrease."[40]

Many people point to the decline in the crime rate over the past decade as an indication that mass incarceration has worked. Is this true? As with other social policy questions, we have no clear-cut answer. Researchers point to many social and economic factors as contributing to the drop in crime, such as shifts in law enforcement, economic expansion, decline in the use of crack cocaine, and demographic changes, in addition to expanded use of incarceration. Bruce Western's analysis of the effects of imprisonment on crime rates from 1971 to 2001 shows that incarceration helped reduce crime and violence but that the contribution was not large. He estimates that the increase in state prison populations from 725,000 to 1.2 million inmates reduced the rate of serious crime 2 to 5 percent—one-tenth of the decline in crime between 1993 and 2001. This decline was purchased for $53 billion in incarceration costs.[41]

Another question comes out of this debate: Should incarceration policies be judged solely by comparing prison costs to crime reduction? Critics point to the hidden costs to society that incarceration brings. These include the offenders' families being left without a wage earner and caretaker, the loss of young men to their communities, the redirection of government resources from societal needs such as health care and education, and the damage done to children by the absence of a parent.

Does incarceration pay? Until a host of crucial methodological problems are solved, no definitive answer can be expected. In particular, we need a more accurate estimate of the number of crimes that each felon commits, a better method of calculating the social costs of crime and incarceration, and a way of determining costs that includes correctional capital, operating costs, and indirect costs. Even if we were to refine the method and obtain a more accurate view of the cost–benefit differential, certain political and moral issues would have to be addressed before a rational incarceration policy could be designed.

Summary

1 Discuss the goals of incarceration.

Three models of incarceration have been used since the 1940s, each of which reflects different goals and styles of institutional organization. The custodial model emphasizes security, discipline, and order for the purposes of incapacitation, deterrence, or retribution. This model prevailed prior to World War II. The rehabilitation model, which developed during the 1950s, views every aspect of organization as directed toward reforming the offender. Toward this end, a variety of treatment programs are used. The reintegration model emphasizes the maintenance of the offender's ties to family and the community. Prisons that employ this model recognize that most inmates will one day return to the community. Accordingly, inmates are gradually given greater freedom and responsibility as they approach release.

2 Understand how incarceration is organized.

American prisons are operated at the federal and state levels. Many of these prisons are very old and located in rural areas. State and federal facilities for men operate at different security levels, such as maximum and minimum security, which restrict inmate movement to a greater or lesser degree. Because so few women are imprisoned, most states house female offenders in a single facility. Most prison facilities are owned and operated by governments; however, many states and the federal government contract with private corporations that provide prison services, including housing inmates in privately owned facilities.

3 Explain who is in prison.

The overwhelming majority of inmates in both federal and state prisons are male. A majority of federal inmates are drug offenders, and fewer federal prisoners are serving sentences for violent offenses when compared to inmates in state institutions. Federal prisoners are widely believed to often be a more sophisticated type of criminal, from a higher socioeconomic class, than typical state prisoners. The majority of federal inmates are white. In state prisons a large number of inmates are members of racial and ethnic minority groups.

4 Discuss the explanations for the increase in the incarceration rate.

Five factors have been put forward to explain the growing incarceration rate. First, there has been a nationwide trend for the police to make more arrests and for the courts to impose incarceration for those convicted of committing crimes. This has not only led to higher numbers of new prison admissions but also to a high number of former inmates returning to prison. Second, tougher sentencing laws have resulted in inmates spending more time, on average, in prison. Third, a large number of new prisons have been built in recent decades, greatly expanding society's ability to incarcerate offenders. Fourth, the "war on drugs" has resulted in the imprisonment of large numbers of drug offenders. Finally, state and local political factors, such as the proportion of the population who are political conservatives, are also related to higher state incarceration rates.

5 Be familiar with the problem of prison crowding.

The problem of prison crowding has become more pressing as greater numbers of offenders are sentenced to prison. Correctional officials are responsible for providing humane treatment and living conditions for the offenders who are sent to their facilities. The federal courts sometimes intervene when correctional officials fail to meet their responsibilities. Several strategies have been identified for dealing with prison crowding, including the null strategy (do nothing) and the prison-construction strategy (build more facilities to meet rising demand).

Key Terms

campus style 150
construction strategy 160
courtyard style 150
custodial model 144

maximum-security prison 151
medium-security prison 152
minimum-security prison 152
null strategy 160

radial design 149
rehabilitation model 144
reintegration model 145
telephone-pole design 150

For Discussion

1. Is the custodial model most appropriate for organizing prisons that operate at different security levels? What model should be used to organize a minimum-security facility?
2. What are some of the strengths and weaknesses of the various prison designs? Are some designs better than others?
3. What questions emerge regarding the practice of contracting with private, for-profit organizations to operate correctional facilities?
4. What explanation of prison population growth seems most accurate to you? What other explanations should be considered?
5. Which of the strategies to deal with prison crowding seems most viable to you? Should officials consider multiple strategies to reduce crowding?

Notes

1 E. Ann Carson, *Prisoners in 2013* (Washington, DC: U.S. Government Printing Office, 2014), 6.

2 Roy Walmsley, *World Prison Population List,* 10th ed. (London: University of Essex, International Centre for Prison Studies, 2013).

3 Pew Charitable Trusts, *Public Safety, Public Spending: Forecasting America's Prison Population 2007–2011* (Washington, DC: Author, 2007), ii.

4 John Irwin and James Austin, *It's About Time: America's Imprisonment Binge* (Belmont, CA: Wadsworth, 2001).

5 Lauren E. Glaze and Danielle Kaeble, *Correctional Populations in the United States, 2013* (Washington, DC: U.S. Government Printing Office, 2014), 2.

6 Carson, *Prisoners in 2013,* p. 2.

7 Charles H. Logan, "Criminal Justice Performance Measures in Prisons," in *Performance Measures for the Criminal Justice System* (Washington, DC: U.S. Government Printing Office, 1993), 13.

8 James J. Stephan, *Census of State and Federal Correctional Facilities, 2005* (Washington, DC: U.S. Government Printing Office, 2008).

9 "About the Bureau of Prisons," www.bop.gov/about, February 17, 2015.

10 Federal Bureau of Prisons, *State of the Bureau, 2010* (Washington, DC: U.S. Government Printing Office, 2010), 3.

11 Stephan, *Census of State and Federal Correctional Facilities, 2005,* Appendix Table 12.

12 Louisiana State Penitentiary, *Annual C-05-001 Report, FY 2009/2010* (Angola, LA: Author).

13 Vermont Department of Corrections, *Facts and Information About the Southern State Correctional Facility,* www.doc.state.vt.us /custody-supervision/facilities/sscfs-folder/facts-and-information -about-the-southern-state-correctional-facility, February 17, 2015.

14 Florida Department of Corrections, *Florida Department of Corrections Fiscal Year 2012–2013 Annual Report,* www.dc.state .fl.us/pub/annual/1213/facil.html.

15 E. Ann Carson and Daniela Golinelli, *Prisoners in 2012: Trends in Admissions and Releases, 1991–2012* (Washington, DC: U.S. Government Printing Office, 2013).

16 Norman Johnston, *Forms of Constraint: A History of Prison Architecture* (Urbana, IL: University of Illinois Press, 2000).

17 Joseph T. Hallinan, *Going up the River: Travels in a Prison Nation* (New York: Random House, 2001), xvi.

18 Randy Martin and David L. Myers, "Public Response to Prison Setting: Perceptions of Impact on Crime and Safety," *Criminal Justice and Behavior* 32 (April 2005): 143–71.

19 Ryan Scott King, Marc Mauer, and Tracy Huling, "An Analysis of the Economics of Prison Siting in Rural Communities," *Criminology & Public Policy* 3 (July 2004): 453–80.

20 Daniel P. Mears, "A Critical Look at Supermax Prisons," *Corrections Compendium* 30 (September–October 2005): 6–7, 45–49.

21 Stephan, *Census of State and Federal Correctional Facilities, 2005,* Appendix tables 5 and 11.

22 Ibid.

23 Ibid.

24 Tracey Kyckelhahn, *State Corrections Expenditures, FY 1982–2010* (Washington, DC: U.S. Government Printing Office, 2012), 2.

25 Carson, *Prisoners in 2013,* p. 14.

26 Gaylene Styve Armstrong and Doris Layton MacKenzie, "Private Versus Public Juvenile Facilities: Do Differences in Environmental Quality Exist?" *Crime & Delinquency* 49 (October 2003): 542–63.

27 Stephan, *Census of State and Federal Correctional Facilities, 2005,* Appendix tables 16, 18, and 19.

28 Caroline Wolf Harlow, *Education and Correctional Populations* (Washington, DC: U.S. Government Printing Office, 2003), 4.

29 Rebecca Boone, "Idaho Fines Private Prison for Contract Violations," *Seattle Times,* http://seattletimes.nwsource.com/html /businesstechnology/2012003529_apidprivateprisonmedicalwoes .html, June 1, 2010.

30 Michael D. Reisig and Travis C. Pratt, "The Ethics of Correctional Privatization," *Prison Journal* 80 (June 2000): 210–22.

31 *New York Times,* November 24, 2005, p. 1.

32 Malcolm M. Feeley, "Entrepreneurs of Punishment: The Legacy of Privatization," *Punishment & Society* 4 (July 2002): 327–33.

33 Kathleen Maguire, ed., *Sourcebook of Criminal Justice Statistics Online,* Table 6.29.2010, www.albany.edu/sourcebook, January 18, 2013.

34 Matthew R. Durose, Alexia D. Cooper, and Howard N. Snyder, *Recidivism of Prisoners Released in 30 States in 2005: Patterns from 2005 to 2010* (Washington, DC: U.S. Government Printing Office, 2014), 1.

35 James J. Stephan, *Census of State and Federal Correctional Facilities, 1995* (Washington, DC: U.S. Government Printing Office, 1997), iv; Stephan, *Census of State and Federal Correctional Facilities,* 2005, p. 1.

36 Carson, *Prisoners in 2013,* pp. 15–16.

37 David F. Greenberg and Valerie West, "State Prison Populations and Their Growth, 1971–1991," *Criminology* 39 (August 2001): 615–54.

38 Carson, *Prisoners in 2013,* p. 31.

39 Ibid., p. 3.

40 Pew Charitable Trusts, *Public Safety,* p. 24.

41 Bruce Western, *Punishment and Inequality in America* (New York: Russell Sage Foundation, 2006), 187.

CHAPTER 7

The Prison Experience

The gray bus with heavy wire mesh over the windows passes through the countryside. Inside, twelve passengers, the driver, and two uniformed guards sit quietly, each looking forward. The miles roll by. The riders do not seem to notice the stares of the curious in passing cars. There is tension in the air.

The twelve passengers are chained, one to another. More than anything else, the chain differentiates this bus and its are captives, being moved from jail to the reception center of the state prison. The chain is for security, to prevent the prisoners from taking over the bus or escaping. But the links also symbolize to the bound people that they are powerless and that the state will determine most aspects of the experience awaiting them in prison. The symbolism of the chain is so great that in the language of the captives, the bus in which they are

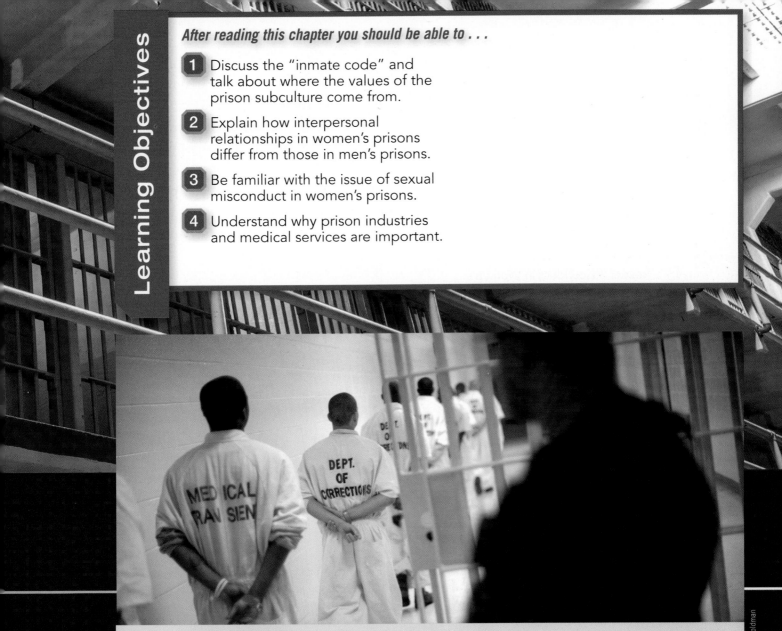

Learning Objectives

After reading this chapter you should be able to . . .

1. Discuss the "inmate code" and talk about where the values of the prison subculture come from.

2. Explain how interpersonal relationships in women's prisons differ from those in men's prisons.

3. Be familiar with the issue of sexual misconduct in women's prisons.

4. Understand why prison industries and medical services are important.

Much of prison time is spent waiting in lines, being counted, and passing through security checkpoints.

AP Images/David Goldman

Even the most hardened criminal must be tense and nervous on entering (or reentering) prison. For the "fish," the newcomer, the first few hours and days are a time of tremendous worry and anxiety: "What will it be like? Is it as bad as the stories I heard in the jail? How should I act? Will I be able to protect myself?" The new prisoner is apprehensive, like an immigrant starting out in a country where the language is incomprehensible, the customs are strange, and the rules are unfamiliar. But unlike the immigrant, the

(continued from previous page)

prisoner has no freedom to choose where and with whom to live.

As we examine the social and personal dimensions of prison life, imagine that you are visiting a foreign land and trying to learn about its culture and daily activities. The prison may be located in the United States, but the traditions, language, and relationships are unlike anything you are used to. ■

PRISON SOCIETY

Since the 1930s, social scientists have studied the maximum-security prison as a functioning community. After all, inmates housed in maximum-security prisons do not serve their time alone. They are part of a prison society that has its own values, roles, language, and leadership structure. These aspects of the prisoner subculture influence how inmates behave. For example, some prisoners choose to withdraw and keep to themselves; others organize themselves along racial or "professional" lines. Still others become influential players in the convict society; they represent prisoner interests and distribute valued goods in return for the support of their fellow inmates.

The concept of the prisoner subculture helps us understand inmate society. Just like members of other groups who are physically separated from society (groups such as soldiers, medical patients, and monks), inmates develop their own myths, slang, customs, rewards, and sanctions. But the idea that the prisoner subculture is completely isolated from the dominant culture in free society is misleading. Contemporary prisons are less isolated than the big-house prisons of the 1940s. Although prisons do create special conditions that force inmates to adapt to their environment, the culture of the outside world penetrates prison walls through television, magazines, newspapers, and inmate contact with friends and family.

Norms and Values

As in any society, the convict world has distinctive norms and values. Often described as the **inmate code**, these norms and values develop within the prison

inmate code
A set of rules of conduct that reflect the values and norms of the prison social system and help define for inmates the image of the model prisoner.

166

social system and help define the inmate's image of the model prisoner. Inmate norms shape how prisoners behave "on the yard" and in other areas such as the mess hall, gym, and work assignments. The culture of the maximum-security prison for men is very masculine. It emphasizes toughness and insensitivity, frowns on softness, and allows the use of hostility and manipulation in one's relations with other inmates and prison staff. Inmates must never show emotion about pain; such feeling is seen as weakness.[1]

The inmate code also emphasizes solidarity of all inmates against the prison staff. The two most important rules of the inmate code are "do your own time" and "don't inform on another prisoner." In his classic study of the New Jersey State Prison at Trenton, Gresham Sykes identified the following rules embodied in the inmate code:

1. *Don't interfere with inmate interests.* Never snitch on another inmate, don't interfere with other prisoners' dealings, don't gossip or talk about other inmates, and don't put a guy on the spot.

2. *Don't quarrel with fellow inmates.* Be cool, and do your own time.

3. *Don't exploit inmates.* Don't go back on your word, don't steal from other inmates, don't sell favors, and repay your debts.

4. *Maintain yourself.* Don't be weak, don't whine, and don't complain. Be a man.

5. *Don't trust the guards or the things they stand for.* Don't be a sucker; members of the prison staff are always wrong, and the prisoners are right.[2]

How does a new inmate (or "fish") learn the inmate code? While in jail awaiting transfer to prison, the convict hears exaggerated stories about prison life. The bus ride to prison, the processing at the prison reception center, and the belittling shouts from the inmates as the newcomers enter the cell blocks all serve as elements of a degradation ceremony that begins the **prisonization** process. But not all prisoners complete this process. In his pioneering work, Donald Clemmer found that shorter sentences, continued contact with the outside world, a stable personality, and refusal to become part of the group weaken the prisonization process.[3]

The prisoner subculture organizes inmates according to the roles that they play and the extent to which they conform to the code. Among the roles described by prison sociologists are the "right guy" or "real man" (an upholder of prisoner values and interests), "square John" (an inmate with a noncriminal self-identity), "punk" (a passive homosexual), "rat" (an inmate who snitches to authorities), and "gorilla" or "wolf" (an aggressive inmate who pursues his own self-interest at the expense of other prisoners).[4] New inmates must quickly decide how they will abide by the inmate code.

A single, overriding inmate code probably does not exist in present-day prisons to the extent that it did during the big-house era. Instead, contemporary inmate society is organized along racial, ethnic, and age lines. The extent to which the inmate code is obeyed also differs from prison to prison. Still, the core commandments that were described by Sykes more than 60 years ago can be found in today's maximum-security prisons for men.

Do all prisoners reject the views of conventional society? Research shows that most inmates hold views on law and justice similar to those held by the general public. But as individuals they also view themselves as exceptions; it is the "other inmates" whose norms are contrary to society.[5] But even inmates who have values that run contrary to the inmate code eventually conform. One reason is survival. The presence of gangs, changes in the type of offender now incarcerated, and changes in prison policy have all contributed to making prison life highly unpredictable.

When compared to the big-house era, it is clear that prison society has changed and that a single code of behavior accepted by the entire population no longer exists. Prison officials face a difficult range of tasks. They must be aware of the different groups, recognize the norms and rules that members hold, and deal with the leaders of many groups rather than with a few inmates who have risen to the top positions in the inmate society.

prisonization
The process by which a new inmate absorbs the customs of prison society and learns to adapt to the environment.

Contemporary prison society is divided into racial, ethnic, and gang subgroups—there is no inmate code to which all prisoners subscribe.

Lucy Nicholson/Reuters

Prison Subculture: Deprivation or Importation?

Where does the prison subculture come from? Gresham Sykes argues that it arises in response to the pains of imprisonment.[6] These pains include features of prison life that inmates find frustrating, such as the deprivation of liberty, autonomy, security, goods and services, and heterosexual relationships. As inmates integrate into prison society, they are better able to adapt, compensate, and cope with the pains of imprisonment.

An alternative explanation holds that the values and norms found in inmate society are imported into prison from the outside world. John Irwin and Donald R. Cressey suggest that the prison subculture is actually three subcultures: convict, thief, and "straight."[7] The convict subculture is found mostly among "state-raised" youths who have been in and out of foster homes, detention centers, reform schools, and correctional institutions since puberty. They are used to living in single-sex society, know the ways of institutional life, and in a sense make prison their home. Prisoners who belong to the thief subculture consider crime a career and are always preparing for the "big score." Irwin and Cressey note that thieves must convey a sense of "rightness" and "solidness" to be considered a "right guy" by their peers. Finally, the "straights," or "square Johns," bring the culture of conventional society with them to prison. They are often one-time offenders who identify more with the staff than with the other inmates. They want to avoid trouble and get through their terms as quietly as possible. In sum, the convict culture results from the deprivations associated with long-term imprisonment; the thief and straight subcultures are imported into prison.

Unconvinced by these perspectives, Edward Zamble and Frank J. Porporino believe that inmate behavior results from how prisoners cope with and adapt to prison life. They note that convicted offenders enter prison with their own set of preincarceration experiences and values. Entering prison is stressful for the repeat offender and the first-timer alike. Each prisoner will adapt the best that he or she knows how. Suppose that two individuals are facing long sentences. Both will experience the same environment, restrictions, and other deprivations of prison. Events in prison are often beyond their control. However, because of their backgrounds and personal attributes, one prisoner may interpret the deprivations of prison life as a result of his own inadequacies, and

Where do the values of the prison subculture come from? Do they stem from the deprivation felt by inmates as they serve their terms, or do the inmates bring the values with them from the outside?

Lucy Nicholson/Reuters/Landov

the other inmate may interpret conditions as unfair and abusive. These perceptions will affect the extent to which the two inmates immerse themselves in inmate society and how they are seen by other inmates and prison staff.[8] So whether the inmate subculture develops because of the pains of imprisonment or is imported by the offender from the world outside the prison walls, each inmate adapts to prison in his or her own way.

Adaptive Roles

Upon entering prison, every new inmate has to answer the question "How am I going to do my time?" Some decide to withdraw and isolate themselves. Others choose to become active members of the inmate social system. The decision on how to do their time will help determine strategies for survival and success.

Most male inmates use one of four basic role orientations to adapt to prison: "doing time," "gleaning," "jailing," and functioning as a "disorganized criminal." John Irwin believes that we can classify most imprisoned felons according to these orientations.[9]

DOING TIME Men "doing time" view their prison term as a brief, inevitable break in their criminal careers, a cost of doing business. They try to serve their terms with the least amount of suffering and the greatest amount of comfort. They live by the inmate code in order to avoid trouble, find activities to fill their days, form friendships with a few other convicts, and generally do what they think is necessary to survive and get out as soon as possible.

GLEANING Inmates who are "gleaning" try to take advantage of prison programs to better themselves and improve their prospects for success after release. They use the resources at hand: libraries, correspondence courses, vocational training, and schools. Some make a radical conversion away from a life of crime.

JAILING "Jailing" is the choice of those who cut themselves off from the outside and try to construct a life within the prison. These are often "state-raised" youths who have spent much of their lives in institutional settings and who identify little with the values of free society. These inmates seek positions of power and influence in the prison society, often becoming key figures in its politics and economy.

On entering prison, each person faces the question "How am I going to do my time?" Gleaners, such as this one taking an entrepreneurship class, take advantage of prison programs to try to learn skills and prepare themselves for release.

AP Images/Gerald Herbert

DISORGANIZED CRIMINAL   The "disorganized criminal" describes inmates who cannot develop any of the other three role orientations. They may be of low intelligence or afflicted with mental or physical disabilities and have difficulty functioning within prison society. They are frequently manipulated by others. These are also the inmates who adjust poorly to prison life, develop emotional disorders, attempt suicide, and violate prison rules.

Prisoners are not members of a loose grouping of individuals, but rather play specific roles in the prison society. The roles they choose reflect the physical and social environment and contribute to their relationships and interactions in prison. How do most prisoners serve their time? Although the media generally portray prisons as violent and chaotic places, most inmates want to get through their sentences without trouble.

The Prison Economy

Just like consumers outside the prison walls, inmates also desire goods and services. The state feeds, clothes, and houses all prisoners, but amenities are usually in short supply. A life of extreme simplicity is part of the punishment. Correctional administrators believe that to maintain discipline and security, rules must be enforced equally. All prisoners must be treated alike. If not, then some prisoners may gain higher position, status, or comfort levels because of their access to goods and services. Prisoners are deprived of nearly everything but bare necessities. Their diets are bland, their routines are monotonous, and their recreational opportunities are limited.

The number of items that a prisoner can buy or receive through legitimate channels differs from state to state and from facility to facility. For example, inmates in some prisons are allowed to have television sets, wear their own clothes, and have hot plates in the cells so they can cook food. Not all prisoners enjoy these luxuries, nor do these luxuries satisfy inmates' desire for other goods. For a list of items available to inmates, see "Prison Commissary Items."

Prisoners can meet some of their needs by purchasing goods at the prison commissary or "store." In many states, inmates are periodically allowed to buy a limited number of items, such as toiletries, snack foods, and other items. Money is withdrawn from inmates' personal accounts to pay for these items. The size of these accounts depend on the amount of money deposited when inmates enter prison, money sent by relatives, and money earned by working low-paying prison jobs. The items sold in the

focus on correctional practice

Prison Commissary Items

Here is a list of items that the Mississippi Department of Corrections makes available to prison inmates in minimum- and medium-security facilities.

Item	Price	Item	Price
Columbian Blend Coffee—3 oz.	$4.00	Deodorant—2.5 oz.	$2.75
Dry Milk—3 quart box	$4.50	Petroleum Jelly—3.75 oz.	$1.90
Soda—20 oz.	$1.69	Comb—5 inches	$0.45
Diet Soda—20 oz.	$1.69	Clear Toothpaste—4 oz.	$2.10
Water—16.9 oz.	$1.20	Security Toothbrush	$0.75
Men's T-Shirt—Small	$3.50	Denture Adhesive—2.4 oz.	$4.50
Men's T-Shirt—Medium	$3.50	Hair Grease—4 oz.	$3.00
Men's T-Shirt—Large	$3.50	Acrylic Mirror 6 x 4.5 in.	$2.30
Men's T-Shirt—XL	$3.50	Insulated Mug with Lid—16 oz.	$2.75
Bleached Tube Socks—Pair	$1.50	Cereal Bowl with Lid—24 oz.	$1.20
Shower Shoes —XL	$2.00	Playing Cards	$2.50
MDOC Tennis Shoes	$34.00	Writing Tablet	$1.45
Security Razor	$0.65	Ink Pen—Black	$0.65
Soap	$2.00	Greeting Card	$1.75
Hand & Body Lotion	$1.20	Postage Stamps—10 @ .46	$4.60
Shampoo—4 oz.	$1.50	Single Postcard	$0.40
Dandruff Shampoo—4 oz.	$1.40	Stamped Envelope	$0.55

Source: www.mdoc.state.ms.us/PDF%20Files/price%20list%202013_1.pdf.

typical prison store in no way satisfy the needs and desires of most prisoners. To meet consumer demand, an informal underground economy exists in many prisons.

As an important feature of prison culture, the informal economy reinforces the norms and roles of the social system and influences how inmates interact with one another. The extent of the economy and its ability to provide desired goods and services (food, drugs, alcohol, and sex) vary according to the extent of official surveillance, the demands of consumers, and the opportunities for entrepreneurship. Inmates' success as "hustlers" determines the luxuries and power they can enjoy.

Real money is not allowed in prison, and the practice of trading goods and services is somewhat limited. The standard currency in the prison economy for many years was cigarettes. They were not contraband, are easily transferable, have a stable and well-known standard of value, and come in "denominations" of singles, packs, and cartons. They are also in demand by smokers. Even those who do not smoke often kept cigarettes for prison currency. However, many prisons around the country have adopted nonsmoking policies, which has largely brought about an end to the use of cigarettes as prison currency. Today, nonperishable food items, like tuna fish and dried noodles, and postage stamps have emerged as the standard form of currency.[10]

Certain prison jobs enhance opportunities for entrepreneurs. For example, inmates who work in the kitchen, warehouse, and administrative office may steal food, clothing,

Spare time in prison is an issue. Games can be a way to pass the time, but they can also be a part of the prison economy, with gambling, debts, and cliques.

Lucy Nicholson/Reuters/Landov

building materials, and even information to sell or trade to other prisoners. The goods may then become part of other market transactions. Thus, exchanging a dozen eggs for two packs of postage stamps may result in reselling the eggs as egg sandwiches, made on a hot plate, for five stamps each. Meanwhile, the kitchen worker who stole the eggs may use the income to get a laundry worker to starch his shirts or a hospital orderly to supply drugs or a "punk" to provide sexual services. Although transactions usually take place between two inmates, they are part of a larger underground market economy.

Transactions in the prison economy may lead to violence when goods are stolen, debts remain unpaid, or agreements are violated. The economy may be temporarily disrupted when officials conduct periodic "lockdowns" and inspections. Confiscation of contraband may result in temporary shortages and inflated prices, but gradually business returns to normal. The prison economy, like that in the outside world, allocates goods and services, provides rewards and sanctions, and is closely linked to the society it serves.

WOMEN IN PRISON

Often referred to as the "forgotten offenders," women prisoners have received little attention from criminal justice scholars. However, the number of incarcerated women has increased over the past 15 years. In 1998 the rate of imprisonment for women was 55 per 100,000 population (a total of 82,716 female prisoners).[11] The rate jumped to 65 per 100,000 residents in 2013, and the female inmate population in state and federal facilities increased to 111,287.[12] **Figure 7.1** shows the incarceration rate for women in each state. States seem to believe that they should run women's prisons as they do prisons for men, with the same policies and procedures. But life in women's prisons differs in many ways when compared to institutions for men. For example, women's facilities are smaller and have looser security and less formal inmate–staff relationships, the underground economy is not as well developed, and female prisoners seem less committed to the inmate code. Women also serve shorter sentences than do men, so the inmate society in women's prisons is more fluid as new members join and other leave.

Most correctional facilities for women look more like a college campus than a maximum-security prison. Usually, a cluster of "cottages" are arranged around a central

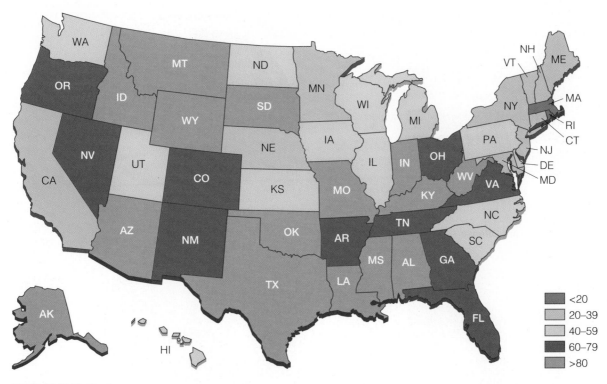

FIGURE 7.1
Rate of Female Imprisonment per 100,000 Populations
What accounts for the varying rates of female incarceration in different regions of the country?

Source: E. Ann Carson, *Prisoners in 2013* (Washington, DC: U.S. Government Printing Office, September 2014), 7.

building that houses central administration, the dining hall, and prison programs. To prevent escapes, these facilities are surrounded by cyclone fences, razor wire, and other devices. Few states operate more than one women's prison, so inmates usually live far from children, families, friends, and attorneys.

Characteristics of Women in Prison

What are the characteristics of women in America's prisons? The Bureau of Justice Statistics reports that the majority of these women are between the ages of 20 and 39, about half are racial or ethnic minorities, and over a third are serving time for a violent offense.[13] About 62 percent of women prisoners are parents of minor children (see **Figure 7.2**).[14]

The main factors distinguishing incarcerated women from men are the nature of offenses, sentence lengths, patterns of drug use, and correctional history.

OFFENSE Although the public commonly believes that most female prisoners are incarcerated for minor offenses such as prostitution, sentences for such crimes are usually served in jails; prisons hold the more-serious offenders, both male and female. In 2013, according to the Bureau of Justice Statistics, 37.1 percent of female state prisoners were serving sentences for violent offenses (compared with 55 percent of male prisoners), 28.2 percent for property offenses (versus 18.1 percent of men), 24.6 percent for drug-related offenses (versus 15.4 percent of men), and 8.9 percent for public-order offenses (versus 10.8 percent of men).[15] The most significant difference between the sexes concerns violent offenses.

SENTENCE For all types of crimes, women prisoners receive shorter maximum sentences than do men. For example, the average prison sentence for murder is 212 months for women and 256 months for men. Differences between men and women are also

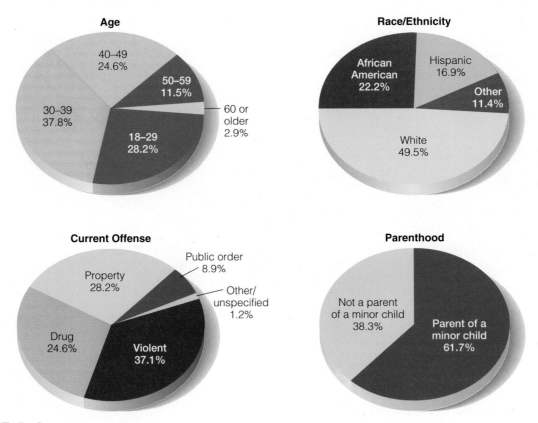

FIGURE 7.2

Characteristics of Women Prisoners

Women prisoners tend to be racial or ethnic minorities, under the age of 40, and convicted of a nonviolent offense.

Sources: E. Ann Carson, *Prisoners in 2013* (Washington, DC: U.S. Government Printing Office, September 2014); Lauren E. Glaze and Laura M. Maruschak, *Parents in Prison and Their Minor Children* (Washington, DC: U.S. Government Printing Office, August 2008).

present for property offenses (48 months for men, 40 months for women), drug offenses (51 months for men, 41 months for women), and weapons offenses (48 months for men, 41 months for women).[16] Shorter sentences are quite frequently a result of women's less serious criminal background, especially regarding the use of violence, when compared with their male counterparts.

DRUG USE Drug use in the month before their most recent offense is slightly greater among female (59.3 percent) than among male (55.7 percent) state prisoners. For federal prisoners, however, this type of drug involvement is higher for men (50.4 percent) than women (47.6 percent), but this gender gap was even wider in the mid-1990s. Methamphetamine use prior to incarceration is higher among female than among male state and federal prisoners. A higher percentage of female state prisoners (60.2 percent) had symptoms consistent with drug dependence or abuse during the 12 months prior to entering prison than did male state prisoners (53.0 percent). Among federal inmates, gender differences for drug dependence and abuse are modest (45.7 percent for men, 42.8 percent for women).[17] The extent of drug use has policy implications because it indicates that a large percentage of female offenders need treatment programs while incarcerated.

CORRECTIONAL HISTORY About 65 percent of the female prisoners (compared with 77 percent of male prisoners) had a history of prior convictions before their current sentence. Differences between men and women on this variable seem related primarily to experiences as juveniles: More men than women reported having been on probation and incarcerated as youths. About 33 percent of women prisoners were on probation at the time of their incarcerating arrest, compared with 20 percent of male inmates.[18]

The Subculture of Women's Prisons

Much of the early research on women's prisons focused on types of relationships among female offenders. As in all types of prisons, same-sex relationships were observed, but unlike those in male prisons, where such relationships are often co-erced, sexual relationships between women prisoners appeared more voluntary. Interestingly, researchers reported that female inmates tended to form "pseudofamilies" in which they adopted various roles—father, mother, daughter, sister—and interacted as a unit rather than identifying with the larger prison subculture.[19] Such cooperative relationships help relieve the tensions of prison life, assist in the socialization of new inmates, and permit individuals to act according to clearly defined roles and rules.

When David Ward and Gene G. Kassebaum studied sexual and family bonding at the California Institute for Women in Frontera in the early 1960s, they found homosexual roles but not familial roles. The women at Frontera seemed to adapt less well to prison, and they did not develop the solidarity with one another that Donald Clemmer and Gresham Sykes found in male institutions. Yet societal expectations for gender and social roles of women were important in the prison subculture.[20]

We need to consider recent shifts in prison life when considering the existing research on women in prison. Just as the subculture of male prisons has changed since the pioneering research of Clemmer and Sykes, the climate of prisons for women has undoubtedly changed. Through interviews with a small group of women prisoners, Kimberly Greer found support for the idea that prisons for women are less violent, involve less gang activity, and do not have the racial tensions found in men's prisons. However, Greer also observed that women's interpersonal relationships were less stable and less familial than in the past. The inmates reported higher levels of mistrust and greater economic manipulation.[21] Thus, we must approach past research with caution.

Researchers do not agree on the extent and nature of same-sex relationships in women's prisons. For example, Imogene L. Moyer points out that the evidence must be analyzed within a framework that recognizes factors in each institutional setting. Before generalizations about social relationships can be made with any confidence, research must assess policies designed to keep prisoners separate, average length of time served, distance from relatives, and level of regimentation.[22] Robert G. Leger found that the lesbians he surveyed had longer sentences, were arrested at a younger age, were more likely to have been previously confined, and had served more time, compared with the heterosexual women with whom they were imprisoned.[23]

A more explicit attempt to compare the subculture of women's prisons with that of men's was made by Rose Giallombardo. Like John Irwin and Donald Cressey, Giallombardo hypothesized that many subcultural features of the institution are imported from the larger society. For example, she found that female inmates express and fulfill social needs through prison homosexual marriage and kinship. Giallombardo suggests that in many ways, the prison subcultures of men and women are similar, with one major exception: The informal social structure of the female prison is somewhat collectivist. It is characterized by warmth and mutual aid extended to family and kinship members; male prisoners adapt by self-sufficiency, a convict code, and solidarity with other inmates.[24] The debate over whether the subculture of prisoners is caused by deprivation or importation has led to some interesting findings in women's institutions. When Heffernan began her study in a women's institution, she expected to find a unitary inmate social structure arising from within the institution, as Clemmer and Sykes had. But Heffernan found no "clear-cut pattern of acceptance or rejection of the inmate social system, nor any relatively uniform perception of deprivations." Unlike male maximum-security prisons, the prison Heffernan studied—like most other women's prisons—had a diverse population with the whole spectrum of offenses. Heffernan shows what Irwin and Cressey only suggest: Prisoners with similar orientations developed "distinctive norms and values, a pattern of interrelationships and certain roles that served their own prison needs."[25] The typical offender brings these orientations with her to the prison.

In a more contemporary study of prison culture, Barbara Owen found that the inmates in the Central California Women's Facility have developed various styles of doing time.[26] Based on the in-prison experience, these styles correspond to the day-to-day business of developing a program of activities and settling into a routine. Owen discovered that one's style of doing time stems from one's commitment to a deviant identity and the stage of one's criminal and prison career. These elements influence the extent to which an inmate is committed to the "convict code" and participating in "the mix."

The vast majority of inmates, according to Owen, want to avoid "the mix"—"behavior that can bring trouble and conflict with staff and other prisoners." A primary feature of "the mix" is behavior for which one can lose good time or be sent to administrative segregation. Being in "the mix" involves "homo-secting," fighting, using drugs, and being involved in conflict and trouble. Owen found that most women want to do their time and go home, but some "are more at home in prison and do not seem to care if they 'lose time.'"[27] The culture of being "in the mix" is not imported from the outside but is internal to the prison, as some inmates prefer the pursuit of drugs, girlfriends, and fighting.

Male versus Female Subcultures

Comparisons of male and female prisons are difficult because most studies have been conducted in single-sex institutions, and most follow theories and concepts first developed in male prisons. However, the following helps clarify subcultural differences:

- Over half of male inmates, but only a third of female prisoners, are serving time for violent offenses.
- Women's prisons are less violent than prisons for men.
- Women are more responsive than men to prison programs.
- Men's prison populations are divided by security levels, but most women serve time in facilities where the entire population is mixed.
- Men tend to segregate themselves by race; this is less true for women.
- Men rarely form intimate relationships with prison staff, but many women share personal information with their keepers.

In contrast to convict society in men's prisons, many women prisons are characterized by a society with strong bonds of support.

AP Images/Newspaper Member/Chugiak Eagle River Star/Cinthia Ritchie

Some critics say that, despite these differences, the current practice of imprisoning women is based on assumptions about violent males.

A major difference between male prisons and female prisons relates to interpersonal relationships. In male prisons, individuals act for themselves and are evaluated by others according to how they adhere to the inmate code. As James G. Fox notes in his comparative study of one women's prison and four men's prisons, men believe that they must demonstrate physical strength and avoid mannerisms that may imply homosexuality. To gain recognition and status within the convict community, the male prisoner must strictly adhere to these values. Men form cliques, but not the family networks found in prisons for women. Male norms emphasize autonomy, self-sufficiency, and the ability to cope with one's own problems, and men are expected to "do their own time." Fox also found little sharing in the men's prisons.[28]

Women place less emphasis on achieving status or recognition within the prisoner community. Fox also observed that women place fewer restrictions on sexual and emotional conduct. As noted previously, in women's prisons close ties seem to exist among small groups that are similar to families. These groups provide emotional support and share resources.[29]

The differences between male and female prison subcultures have been attributed to the nurturing, maternal qualities of women. Some critics argue that such a conclusion stereotypes female behavior and assigns a biological basis to personality where no such basis exists. Of importance as well is the issue of inmate–inmate violence in male and female prisons. The little research that has been conducted indicates that women are less likely to engage in violent acts against their fellow inmates when compared to men.

Sexual Misconduct in Women's Prisons

An issue of great important in women's prisons is sexual misconduct by male correctional officers. Staff sexual misconduct includes any behavior that is sexual in nature (either consensual or nonconsensual) that is directed toward an inmate by an employee, official visitor, or agency representative. Such acts include (1) the touching of genitalia, breasts, or buttocks that is intended to arouse, abuse, or gratify sexual desire; (2) using threats or making requests for sexual acts; and (3) indecent exposure and staff voyeurism for sexual gratification.[30] Sexual misconduct is harmful in that it jeopardizes facility security, creates stress and trauma for those involved, exposes the agency and staff to potential lawsuits, creates a hostile work environment, and victimizes the vulnerable.

Monetary civil judgments awarded to women for mistreatment while in prison can be costly. For example, officials in Oregon reportedly paid a $1.2 million out-of-court settlement to 17 women who were current and former prisoners at Coffee Creek Correctional Facility and who said they were sexually abused by correctional workers.[31]

To deal with the problem of sexual abuse in prison, states have enacted statutes prohibiting sexual relations with correctional clients. Despite these laws, corrections still has a great need for effective sexual harassment policies, training of officers, and better screening of recruits. Some correctional administrators say that part of the problem is the large number of men guarding women.

Incarcerated Mothers and Their Children

Another issue of great concern to many incarcerated women is the fate of their children. Over 60 percent of female inmates in state prisons are mothers of minor children. On any given day, the mothers of an estimated 131,000 minor children are incarcerated in state prisons. Nearly 58 percent of imprisoned mothers do not see their children during their prison sentence. Many of these women were single caregivers. Because of this, many children of incarcerated mothers are cared for by friends and relatives, while 10.9 percent are in state-funded foster care.[32]

Anxiety about children bothers all imprisoned mothers, especially if strangers are caring for their children. Research shows that maternal incarceration adversely affects the life chances of imprisoned women's children. Specifically, children of incarcerated

Many believe that taking babies away from their incarcerated parents too soon disrupts the mother–infant bonding process. Are prison nursery programs a good idea? What else can be done to foster strong mother–infant bonds?

Scott Olson/Getty Images

women are nearly three times more likely to be convicted of a crime as an adult when compared to individuals whose mother was not incarcerated.[33] Enforced separation of children from their mothers can be devastating for both. Many women fear that neither they nor the children will be able to adjust to each other when they are reunited after their long separation.

In most states, babies born in prison must be placed with a family member or a social agency within three weeks of birth. Critics have expressed great concern about such early termination of mother–infant bonding, so some innovative programs now let them stay together longer. Other prisons have developed prison nurseries. Advocates argue that these programs prevent placing the children of incarcerated women in foster care and also allow mothers and children to bond during an important stage in the child development process.[34] Although prison nursery programs are now more common than a decade ago, over 80 percent of state departments of corrections do not have such programs in place. Lorie Smith Goshin and Mary Woods Byrne note that the number of infants involved in prison nursery programs is only a small fraction of the number of children whose mothers are incarcerated. Goshin and Byrne also point out that nursery programs do not address the large number of older children who are left behind when their mothers are sent to prison.[35]

Programs to address the needs of imprisoned mothers and their children are being designed and implemented. In some states, children may meet their mothers at almost any time, for extended periods, in playrooms or nurseries where physical contact is possible. Some states transport children to visit their mothers; some institutions even let children stay overnight with their mothers. But few programs, according to Merry Morash and Pamela J. Schram, "get beyond the assumption that all that is needed is retraining in parental skills, or women's needs are limited to the parenting area."[36]

PRISON PROGRAMS

The thread that links all prisoners, male and female, is time: "time in the joint," "doing time," "good time," "straight time." "How much time did you get?" "When do you come up for parole?" Calendars are prominently displayed in the cells, and some inmates carefully mark the passing of each day.

Prison programs help inmates cope with prison life and also provide them opportunities to improve their lives. Such programs may involve counseling, education, or merely recreation. When rehabilitation is a dominant correctional goal, the parole board sees participation in a treatment program as an indicator that the inmate is ready for community supervision. Perhaps the best justification for prison programs is that they simply keep inmates busy. Work assignments occupy the middle hours of the day, treatment and recreational periods take place before and after work assignments, and special programs (Bible study and Alcoholics Anonymous) take up the remaining hours. Experienced administrators know that the more programs they offer, the less time inmates will have to cause trouble. Administrators also use prison programs as incentives for good behavior. Inmates know that when they break the rules, they will be denied access to programs.

There are a variety of prison programs. The most controversial is the rehabilitative program. Many such programs use psychological treatment to try to alter the propensity for criminal behavior. Some programs attempt to improve job skills and education, while others provide medical services to inmates. Another type is industrial, which involves prisoners making various products. No matter how beneficial a program, it must not conflict with security.

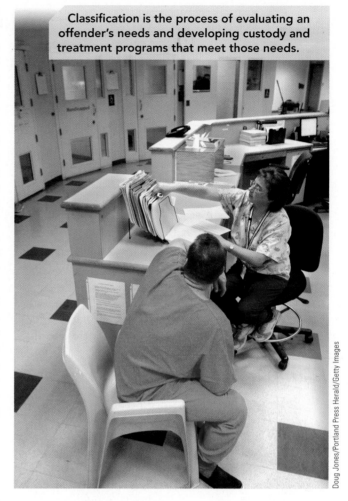

Classification is the process of evaluating an offender's needs and developing custody and treatment programs that meet those needs.

Doug Jones/Portland Press Herald/Getty Images

Classification of Prisoners

Prison procedures are used to classify inmates with respect to security and programs. During the rehabilitation era, **classification** was important because treatment was based on a clinical assessment of the inmate's needs. Although rehabilitation is less emphasized today, prison management still relies on classification, which now focuses on the offender's potential for escape, violence, or victimization by other inmates. Prisoners may be reclassified if they finish treatment programs, if they get into trouble, if they are transferred to another facility, or if they are approaching release to the community.

In most corrections systems, all prison-bound inmates pass through a reception and orientation center where, over three to six weeks, they are evaluated and classified. In some states the center is a separate facility, but generally each institution has its own reception center. Newcomers are stripped of personal belongings and given a uniform, rulebook, medical examination, and shower. This process is done, in part, to underscore the fact that the inmates are no longer free citizens.

In some states, classification consists merely of sorting prisoners on the basis of age, severity of offense, record of prior incarceration, and institutional conduct. Such approaches serve mainly as a management tool to ensure that inmates are assigned to housing units appropriate for their custody level, separated from those who are likely to victimize them, and grouped with members of their work assignment. However, rehabilitation institutions administer batteries of tests, psychiatric evaluations, and counseling so that each prisoner can be assessed for treatment as well as custody. These diagnostic procedures help identify inmates who will benefit the most from specific treatment programs.

Classification decisions are frequently made by committees usually composed of the deputy warden and the heads of departments for custody, treatment, education, industry, and the like. At the hearing, caseworkers and counselors present

prison programs
Any formal, structured activity that takes prisoners out of their cells and lets them perform personal tasks.

classification
A process by which prisoners are assigned to different types of custody and treatment.

DO the Right Thing

Members of the classification committee examined the case folders of the inmates who would appear before them. This morning, 10 newly admitted prisoners were to be classified as to housing and program. Each folder contained basic information about the inmate's education, prior employment, offense, sentence, and counselor's evaluation.

In the small talk before the first inmate arrived, Ralph Arnett, the chief of the classification unit, told the other members that the computer-programming class was filled and that the waiting list was long. However, there was a great need for workers to make mattresses for state institutions.

"But Ralph, some of the guys trying to learn computer programming just can't hack it," said counselor David Baumberger. "I've got a man coming before us who was a math major in college and has already had some computer experience. He would greatly benefit from the extra training."

"That's fine, Dave, but we can't let someone jump ahead, especially when the mattress factory needs workers. I promised Jim Buchanan we'd get him some help."

"But shouldn't we put people into programs that would help them when they get out?" responded Dave.

Critical Thinking

If you were on the classification committee, what would you do? Would you consider moving some of the inmates who were having trouble with the computer-programming class to the mattress shop? What problems might such a decision cause?

information from presentence reports, police records, and the reception process. The inmate appears before the committee, personal needs and assignments are discussed, and decisions are made. The committee makes assignments according to procedures prescribed by the department of corrections and the institution's needs (see "Do the Right Thing").

New predictive and equity-based systems seek to classify inmates more objectively. *Predictive models* are designed to distinguish inmates with respect to risk of escape, potential misconduct in the institution, and future criminal behavior. Clinical, socio-economic, and criminal factors are also given point values, and the total point score determines the security level. *Equity-based models* use only a few explicitly defined legal variables reflecting current and previous criminal characteristics. Such variables as race, employment, and education are not used because they are seen as unfair. Objective systems such as these are more efficient and cheaper than other classification procedures because line staff can be trained to administer and score the instrument without help from clinicians and senior administrators.

Educational and Vocational Programs

One of the oldest ideas in prison programming is to teach prisoners a skill that can help them get a job upon release. Offenders make up one of the most undereducated and underemployed groups in the U.S. population. Ex-prisoners have limited capability to succeed as wage earners in modern society. Many people believe that criminal behavior stems from this kind of economic incapacity, and they urge the use of education and vocational programs to counter it.

EDUCATIONAL PROGRAMS   A significant number of inmates in state prisons failed to graduate from high school.[37] So it is not surprising that programs offering academic courses are among the most popular in today's corrections system. Waiting lists for inmates who want classes are increasing.

In many states, all inmates who have not completed eighth grade are assigned full time to the prison school. Many programs provide basic reading, English, and math skills.

focus on correctional policy

Education in Prison

Most prisoners ended up at Eastern Correctional Facility by committing violent crimes. It's not the type of place you'd expect to walk into and find the inmates studying eighteenth-century European history. Bard College, an elite private college, is offering true liberal arts degrees to some inmates in New York State.

The program, which is privately funded, has been in this prison for six years, and the academics are tough. One inmate says he and other inmates study five or six hours a day outside of class to make the grade. The classes they take change each semester, but what they have in common is that they're not "practical" courses—they're true liberal arts courses, such as English, sociology, philosophy, and German.

Not every Eastern prisoner gets the opportunity; only about 10 percent of the inmates who apply to the college program are accepted. Prison life can be so routine and depressing that it's no wonder these men jump at the chance to escape with their minds, if not with their bodies.

Listening to them talk, one could easily have been in a college quad rather than a prison yard. They spend their free time like so many undergraduates—exercising their intellectual muscles, debating centuries-old notions of ethics, morality, and philosophy. Wes Caines, like most of these men, has children. He says his daughters were his inspiration to go to college: "I really wanted them to have a father figure who, when they looked at their father, he's more than prison, he's more than a prisoner. So everything I've done has been in an effort to be someone that they can be proud of."

The Bard prison program isn't just at Eastern Correctional Facility—it operates in four prisons in New York State and has about 120 students overall. Higher education in penitentiaries used to be common, but in 1994 Congress eliminated federal funding for prisoners to go to college, and many programs folded. The issue was this: Why give a free college education to convicts when so many students who haven't committed crimes can't afford one?

"It's a fair argument, but we treat inmates for medical reasons, we treat inmates for drug addiction—why aren't we treating inmates for educational needs?" says Commissioner Brian Fisher, the head of corrections for New York State.

Fisher says every study he's read shows that inmates given a college education are less likely to commit crimes once they are released. "Education changes people. And I think that's what prisons should do. Change somebody from one way of thinking to a different way of thinking," he says. Is this a liberal penology? Not according to Fisher, who says, "Going to prison is the punishment. Once in prison, it's our obligation to make them better than they were."

Critical Thinking

1. Should prisoners receive a college education at taxpayers' expense?
2. Does it make a difference if the college education is privately funded like the program at Bard?
3. What do you see as problems with such a program?

Source: Adapted from "Maximum Security Education: How Some Inmates Are Getting a Top-Notch Education Behind Bars," *60 Minutes*, CBS News, April 15, 2007.

They also permit prisoners to earn a GED. Although some prisons offer courses in cooperation with a college or university, funding for such programs has come under attack. For example, the Comprehensive Crime Control Act of 1994 bans federal funding to prisoners for postsecondary education. Some states have passed similar laws because of pressure from people who argue that tax dollars should not be spent on the college tuition of prisoners when law-abiding students must pay for their own education. (For more on prison-based college programs, see Focus on Correctional Policy, "Education in Prison.")

Prison education programs face several practical problems. The ability of prisoners to learn is often hampered by a lack of basic reading and computational skills. Moreover, research has increasingly shown a link between learning disabilities and delinquency; many offenders have experienced disciplinary as well as academic failure in school. Thus, prison education must cope with inmates who have neither academic skills nor attitudes conducive to learning.

VOCATIONAL PROGRAMS   These programs are designed to teach inmates job skills necessary for finding employment upon release. However, such programs have been criticized for training inmates for work in less-desirable jobs in industries that already have large labor pools—barbering, printing, welding, and the like. Other problems also plague prison vocational programs. Often, participants are trained on obsolete or inadequate equipment because prisons generally lack the resources to upgrade. Vocational programs rarely teach up-to-date skills. Such programs in women's prisons have been criticized on the grounds that they tend to conform to stereotypes of "feminine" occupations—cosmetology, food service, housekeeping, and sewing. Such training does not correspond to the wider opportunities available to women in today's world.

Offenders also often lack the attitudes and habits necessary to obtain and keep a job—being on time, respect for supervisors, and friendliness to coworkers. Further, many lack the ability to locate a job opening and survive an interview. Therefore, most prisoners need not only to learn a skill but also how to act in the workplace. In prison, inmates are told what to do and where to be each moment from morning to night, which does little to help prisoners develop the attitudes and habits necessary to be successful outside the walls.

Yet another problem is that ex-prisoners are prohibited from working certain jobs because they have been convicted of a felony. Such occupational restrictions force offenders into low-paying, menial jobs, which may lead them back to crime. In some states, barred occupations include nurse, beautician, barber, real estate salesperson, chauffeur, worker where alcoholic beverages are sold, cashier, and insurance salesperson. Ironically, some prison vocational programs actually train inmates for jobs they can never have. Further, ex-inmates may find the stigma of being a convicted felon difficult or impossible to overcome.

Prison Industries

Making prisoners work has always been seen as a way to accomplish many correctional objectives. Historically, hard labor played a central role in punishment. In recent

Prison industry programs not only keep inmates busy but may also help them find a job following release. What factors hurt the chances of ex-prisoners from finding a job?

AP Images/Mike Groll

decades, this idea has gained new popularity with the reemergence of chain gangs in a few southern states. It was even a popular belief at one time that prisoners' labor was legally forfeited as a result of their criminality and that the state could expect to profit from their incarceration.

The theme of labor for profit is accompanied by a concern about inmate idleness. Much of the history of prison industry revolves around the search for suitable ways to occupy inmates' time while also serving the financial interests of forces outside the walls. Four approaches have been used to organize inmate labor.

PIECE PRICE SYSTEM   This system involved the contractor establishing a purchase price for goods that inmates produced with raw materials provided by the contractor. These arrangements were extremely exploitative. Inmates worked in sweatshops, and the fees for their labor were paid to the prisons. The prisoners worked on location during the day and returned to the prison at night. In the *lease system,* a variation of the piece price system, the contractor maintained the prisoners, working them for 12–16 hours at a stretch. These systems provided funds to help prisons operate. However, they also led to corruption. With sizable contracts at stake, kickbacks and bribes were common. Wardens took advantage of easy opportunities to line their pockets with cash. Organized labor and humanitarian reformers opposed these arrangements and successfully lobbied for laws prohibiting contract inmate labor.

PUBLIC ACCOUNT SYSTEM   This system involved the prison purchasing machinery and raw materials with which inmates manufactured salable products. At first, this system was very successful. Profits were made because prisons were able to make products that were cheaper for consumers, and the money that was made was used to subsidize the cost of prison operations. This system proved unsustainable when private industry and labor stopped cooperating after prisons began to turn profits.

STATE-USE SYSTEM   This system involves prison inmates making goods that are purchased by state institutions and agencies exclusively. Prison-made products never enter the free market. Many experts consider this arrangement reasonable and beneficial, and many states mandate that their government agencies purchase goods produced by inmate labor when they are available. Today, the state-use system is the most common form of prison industry. The advantages of this system include the following: Prison labor does not compete with labor pools in the free market, and it provides cheap goods to the state. There are some drawbacks, however. Even when prison products are used only by government, the system preempts the free-labor market. It is also the case that many of the production methods are so outmoded that prisoners often must shed what they have learned before they can succeed in private industry.

PUBLIC WORKS AND WAYS SYSTEM   In this version of the state-use system, inmates work on public construction and maintenance projects: filling potholes, constructing or repairing bridges and buildings, clearing brush from the side of roads, and so on. Advocates praise the tremendous economic benefits of this system. However, prisoners typically do the more-arduous jobs on a project, and then outside craftspeople are hired for the skilled work.

Until very recently, the trend has been away from free-market use of prison labor and toward state monopolies. After 1940 the private use of inmate labor, once the most popular form of prison industry, vanished. One reason was that the public had become increasingly aware of the exploitative character of prison industry. Southern prison systems expanded dramatically after the Civil War, and former slaves accounted for much of this growth. The labor of most of these prisoners was contracted out in one way or another, leading some critics to argue that industrial capitalists had replaced plantation owners as exploiters of the former slaves.

With the rise of the labor movement, state legislatures passed laws restricting the sale of prisoner-made goods so as not to compete with free workers. In 1929 Congress passed the Hawes–Cooper Act, followed by additional legislation in 1935 and 1940, which banned prison-made goods from interstate commerce. By 1940, every state had passed laws banning imports of prison-made goods from other states. These restrictions crippled production and ended the open-market system of employing prisoners. With the outbreak of World War II, however, President Franklin Roosevelt ordered the government to procure goods for the military effort from state and federal prisons. Later, under pressure from organized labor, President Harry Truman revoked the wartime order, and prisoners returned to idleness. By 1973, President Nixon's National Advisory Commission on Criminal Justice Standards and Goals found that few inmates throughout the corrections system had productive work.

The past decade has seen a renewed interest in channeling prison labor into industrial programs that would relieve idleness, allow inmates to earn wages that they could save until release, and reduce the costs of incarceration. In 1979 Congress lifted restrictions on the interstate sale of products made in state prisons and urged correctional administrators to explore private-sector ways to improve prison industry. In the same year, the Free Venture program of the Law Enforcement Assistance Administration made funds available to seven states to develop industries. Once again, inmate labor would compete with free labor. By 1994, 16 states were engaged in Free Venture prison industries, and 5 states—Nevada, New Hampshire, South Carolina, Tennessee, and Washington—allowed inmates to earn wages approaching the federal minimum.

At this time, the supposed efficiencies of private industry in corrections are less dramatic than expected. Inmate labor is cheap, but recent reforms include higher wages for prisoners than those formerly paid by private contractors, and security requirements drive up costs. Regardless of the merits and limitations of private industry in corrections, it makes sense to have inmates work.

Rehabilitative Programs

Rehabilitative programs aim to reform offenders' behavior. Some people argue that imprisonment is so painful that it is itself reformative: Offenders change their ways to avoid repeating the experience. Others argue that convicted criminals should be sent to prison to receive treatment. (See Myths in Corrections, "Prison and Rehabilitation.") But many scholars contend that imprisonment by itself is not reformative enough, that the inmate's prison activities must also be reformative.

In prison, psychological programs seek to treat the underlying emotional or mental problems that led to criminality. Of course, this assumes that such problems are indeed the primary cause of most offenders' criminality—or even that the concept of mental illness makes sense. These assumptions underlie the medical model. However, some critics argue that mental illness is an inadequate explanation of criminal behavior. Many additional factors enter an offender's decision to behave criminally: opportunity, rational motivation, skill, acquaintances, and anger. No one can demonstrate convincingly that some mental problem underlies all or even most of such decisions. (See Chapter 9 for a full discussion of programs designed for inmates with emotional or mental problems.)

MYTHS in Corrections

Prison and Rehabilitation

THE MYTH: Judges should send people to prison to get rehabilitation programs.

THE REALITY: Rehabilitation programs offered in the community are twice as effective at reducing recidivism as are those same programs offered in prison.

Source: Paul Gendreau, Sheila A. French, and Angela Taylor, *What Works (What Doesn't Work)*, rev. ed., Monograph Series Project (Ottawa, Canada: International Community Corrections Association, 2002).

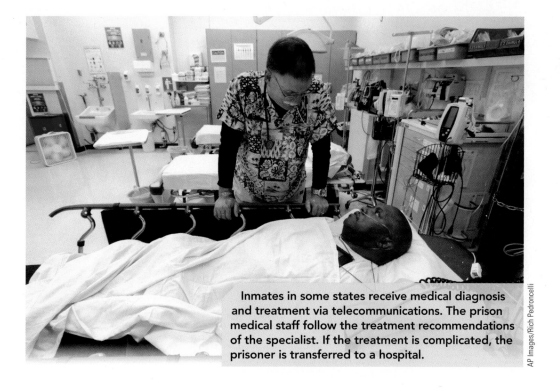

Inmates in some states receive medical diagnosis and treatment via telecommunications. The prison medical staff follow the treatment recommendations of the specialist. If the treatment is complicated, the prisoner is transferred to a hospital.

AP Images/Rich Pedroncelli

Medical Services

Inmates have a well-established right to medical treatment while incarcerated, most effectively defined by the Supreme Court in *Estelle v. Gamble*.[38] The argument for the right to medical treatment is straightforward: Citizens who are confined do not have the capacity to obtain health insurance or sufficient funds to pay for their own health care, and to deny necessary treatments would be cruel.

This is potentially a very expensive right because inmates as a group bring significant health problems with them to prison. Some of these problems stem from the high-risk behavior that many inmates engage in prior to incarceration. For example, needle use during drug abuse is the most frequent cause of HIV transmission and is also the leading cause of **hepatitis C**, an incurable disease of the liver that kills 5 percent of those infected. Unprotected sex also accounts for high rates of sexually transmitted diseases among prisoners. Treatment for most forms of these "lifestyle" diseases (so called because they are typically acquired as a consequence of a high-risk lifestyle) can be complicated and expensive. Today, however, the chances of dying from heart disease or cancer are much greater for inmates than the chances of dying from HIV-related illnesses (see **Figure 7.3**).

The treatment regimen for these diseases involves drugs that reduce the negative effects of the diseases and slow bodily deterioration from the infection. But the most important treatment is prevention through a change in lifestyle. Prison programs that seek to halt the spread of disease within the population are educational, showing prisoners how the diseases are spread and stressing the value of abstinence from drugs and unsafe sexual contact. To date, needle-exchange programs, which have successfully reduced transmission rates on the streets, have not been tried in U.S. prisons because critics say that they would indirectly support illicit drug use inside the walls.

Most prisons offer medical services through a full-time staff of nurses, augmented by part-time physicians under contract to the corrections system. Nurses can take care of routine health care needs and dispense medicines from a secure, in-prison pharmacy;

hepatitis C
A disease of the liver that reduces the effectiveness of the body's system of removing toxins.

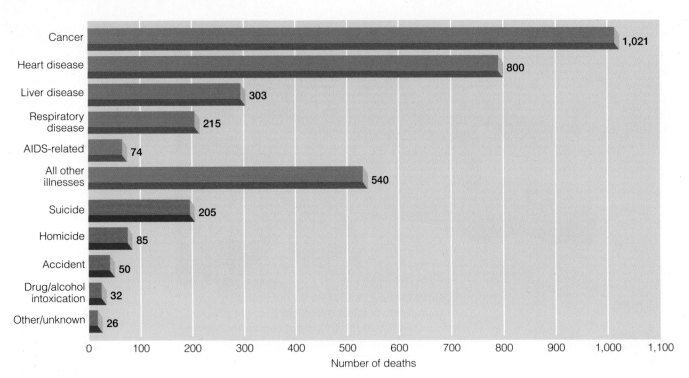

FIGURE 7.3

Leading Causes of State Prisoner Death

Illness-related deaths account for nearly 90 percent of all deaths reported in state prisons

Source: Margaret E. Noonan and E. Ann Carson, *Mortality in Local Jails and State Prisons, 2000-2012 – Statistical Tables* (Washington, DC: Government Printing Office, October 2014), 19.

regularly scheduled visits to the prison by doctors can enable prisoners to obtain check-ups and diagnoses. For cases needing a specialist, surgery, or emergency medical care, prisoners must be transported to local hospitals under close supervision by correctional staff. The aim is for the prison system to provide a range of medical assistance to meet the various needs of the population as a whole. However, because medical care is so expensive, many prison administrators resist providing help until it is absolutely neces-sary. Complaints among prisoners and observers that prison medical care is "second class" are common, and one study has accused prison authorities of purposefully abu-sive health care practices.[39] As shown in **Figure 7.4**, states vary in their per-prisoner spending for health care.

While inmates' needs for health care echo those of the general population, prison-ers pose two special needs, one caused by poverty and the other by aging. Prisoners as a group are very poor, so they often bring to the prison years of neglect of their general health. For example, it is surprising how many prisoners have neglected their teeth so severely that the resulting unsightly smile makes it hard to get any job requiring contact with customers. A round of dental repairs can do wonders to alleviate this practical and personal problem, but outsiders might look at such free dental care as a luxury. Other consequences of being poor, such as an inadequate diet and poor hygiene, also affect the general health of the prison population.

Compared with men, women prisoners usually have more-serious health problems because of their socioeconomic status and limited access to preventive medical care. They also have a higher incidence of mental health problems.[40] Many women have gy-necological problems as well. A higher percentage of female than male prison inmates reported a medical problem since admission.[41]

Pregnant women also need special medical and nutritional resources. Pregnancies raise numerous issues for correctional policy, including special diets, abortion rights,

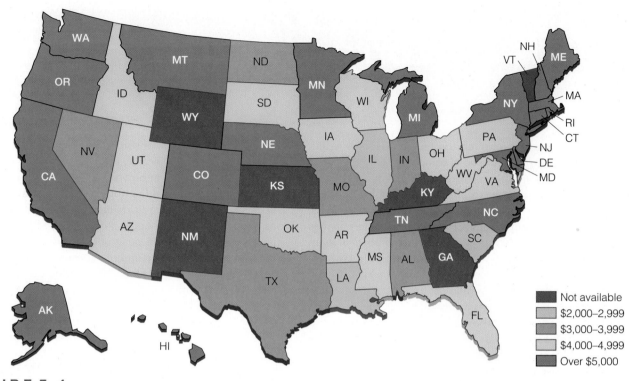

FIGURE 7.4
Yearly Per-Prisoner Spending on Inmate Health Care
Most states spend about $5,800 a year per inmate on health care, but some spend much more and many spend less.

Source: Tracey Kyckelhahan, *State Corrections Expenditures, FY 1982–2010* (Washington, DC: U.S. Government Printing Office, December 2012), 7.

access to delivery room and medical personnel, and length of time that newborns can remain with incarcerated mothers. Most pregnant inmates are older than 35, have histories of drug abuse, have had prior multiple abortions, and carry sexually transmitted diseases. All of these factors indicate the potential for a high-risk pregnancy requiring special medical care.

By far, the most extraordinary health problem in contemporary corrections is the growing number of elderly prisoners. Penal policies of the 1980s and 1990s have resulted in a dramatic increase in the number of offenders serving long sentences, and many of these inmates are now beginning to grow old in prison. Elderly inmates generally have more-complicated and more-numerous health problems, and they eventually reach an age where they cannot work productively in prison assignments. As the length of time away from free society increases, the ability for an inmate to adjust to release decreases to the point that setting some elderly prisoners free, without family or friends, seems a difficult choice. But staying inside has its costs, too. Prisons are difficult places in which to grow old and, finally, die. The large number of geriatric inmates on the path to dying has led some prison systems to form hospice facilities, where younger inmates can care for the elderly as they spend their last days on Earth behind bars.

The rapidly expanding cost of prison health care has led prison officials to look for ways to provide adequate health care less expensively (see Focus on Correctional Technology, "Can Telemedicine Improve Prison Health Care?"). The managed-care strategies that are used to contain health care costs in the free world are now being used in prisons as corrections systems seek to purchase health care on the open market rather than provide it themselves. Many prison officials are beginning to impose restrictions on health care procedures and to find ways of reducing demand among prisoners for health services. Ironically, today imprisoned offenders are the only people living in the United States who enjoy a constitutional right to adequate health care.

focus on correctional technology

Can Telemedicine Improve Prison Health Care?

Although the state is required to provide prisoners health care, the practice of doing so is complicated by a number of factors. For example, crowded prison intake centers make it difficult for staff to effectively establish medical and mental health histories and diagnose existing ailments. Medical record-keeping problems increase the chances that inmates' medical records will be misplaced or even lost when they are transferred to another facility. Low pay and less-than-desirable working conditions make it difficult to hire and retain a staff of medical professionals capable of diagnosing and treating a broad assortment of health problems. These and other factors have contributed to prison health care services that in some states fail to meet constitutional standards.

To improve prison health care, reformers have pushed for technological improvements, such as computerized prisoner medical records that can be accessed by physicians at different institutions. Another reform initiative that has been tested around the United States and appears promising is "telemedicine," which involves the delivery of health care services from remote locations via interactive audiovisual media. The use of telemedicine has several potential advantages. For example, its use provides inmates with access to medical specialists that they might not otherwise have and reduces delays that can happen when seeking attention from specialists. Also, because consultations can take place remotely, security risks associated with transporting inmates to locations outside the prison walls for medical assessment and treatment are significantly reduced.

Can telemedicine improve prison health care? A study funded by the National Institute of Justice evaluated the effectiveness of a telemedicine network in four federal prisons. The study showed that the program was adopted quickly and used frequently. The prison physicians involved in the program reported that the remote consultations were effective, especially with psychiatric and dermatological cases. Prison medical staff were less optimistic about the effectiveness of telemedical consultations involving cardiac matters. The evaluation also revealed that the number of inmate medical transfers was reduced, that the time between an inmate's referral to a medical specialist and the actual consultation declined, and that the cost savings can quickly offset the cost of the required telecommunications equipment.

Critical Thinking

1. Does the practice of telemedicine eliminate the need for highly qualified health care professionals in America's prisons?
2. What are some of the limitations of telemedicine?
3. What other reforms might be implemented to improve prison medical services?

Source: National Institute of Justice, *Telemedicine Can Reduce Correction Health Care Costs* (Washington, DC: U.S. Government Printing Office, 1999).

Summary

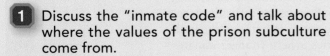

1 **Discuss the "inmate code" and talk about where the values of the prison subculture come from.**

The inmate code is a set of norms and values that develops in the prison social system. It defines the model prisoner in the eyes of inmates and provides a code of conduct that directs inmates on how they should behave in prison. An inmate who projects toughness, keeps his distance from the staff, and does his "own time" is held in high regard. A prisoner who is emotionally weak, snitches on fellow inmates to the staff, and gets involved in other people's business does not enjoy high status. Scholars debate the source of the prison subculture. Some people, such as Clemmer and Sykes, argue that it develops as a response to the prison environment. The different adaptive roles reflect different ways that inmates find to relieve the pains of imprisonment. Other scholars, such as Irwin and Cressey, argue that the prison subculture is primarily imported from the world outside the prison walls.

2 Explain how interpersonal relationships in women's prisons differ from those in men's prisons.

Men form cliques, and norms in male prisons emphasize autonomy, self-sufficiency, and the ability to cope with one's own problems. Men are expected to "do their own time," and they share very little with one another. Women develop close ties and form small groups that are similar to families and provide emotional support and share resources. Women place fewer restrictions on sexual and emotional conduct.

3 Be familiar with the issue of sexual misconduct in women's prisons.

Staff sexual misconduct (instances in which prison officials sexually exploit female inmates) threatens facility security, creates stress and trauma for those involved, exposes the agency and staff to potential lawsuits, creates a hostile work environment, and victimizes people who are vulnerable. Monetary civil judgments awarded to women for mistreatment while in prison can be costly. To deal with the problem of sexual abuse in prison, states have enacted statutes prohibiting sexual relations with correctional clients.

4 Understand why prison industries and medical services are important.

Prison industries are one way to combat idleness and to generate income that the prison can use to offset the costs of operating the prison. Prison industries can also benefit inmates by teaching them marketable skills and work habits that will help them live law-abiding lives when they are released. However, critics argue that most prison-industry programs fail to provide inmates with job skills that will help them find meaningful employment on the outside. Providing medical care to prison inmates is not simply a choice that administrators make; it is required by law. Failing to do so is viewed as "cruel" by the courts. Blood-borne diseases, such as hepatitis C, and the aging prison population are two factors that make providing adequate medical services to prisoners challenging.

Key Terms

classification 179
hepatitis C 185

inmate code 166
prison programs 179

prisonization 167

For Discussion

1. Imagine that you are a new prisoner. What are your immediate concerns? How will you deal with them? What problems do you expect to face?

2. Do the values of the prison culture result from the deprivations of prison, or do inmates bring them from the outside? What was the case 60 years ago?

3. Imagine you are the administrator of a women's prison. What problems would you expect to encounter? How would you handle these problems?

4. What parental rights should prisoners have? Should children be allowed to live in correctional facilities with their mothers? What problems would this practice create?

Notes

[1] Don Sabo, Terry A. Kupers, and Willie London, "Gender and the Politics of Punishment," in *Prison Masculinities*, edited by Don Sabo, Terry A. Kupers, and Willie London (Philadelphia: Temple University Press, 2001).

[2] Gresham M. Sykes, *The Society of Captives* (Princeton, NJ: Princeton University Press, 1958), 63–108.

[3] Donald Clemmer, *The Prison Community* (New York: Holt, Rinehart & Winston, 1940), 299–304.

[4] Sykes, *Society of Captives*, pp. 84–108.

[5] Lucia Benaquisto and Peter J. Freed, "The Myth of Inmate Lawlessness: The Perceived Contradiction Between Self and Other

in Inmates' Support for Criminal Justice Sanctioning Norms," *Law and Society Review* 30 (1996): 508.

[6] Sykes, *Society of Captives,* p. 107.

[7] John Irwin and Donald R. Cressey, "Thieves, Convicts, and the Inmate Culture," *Social Problems* 10 (1962): 142–56.

[8] Edward Zamble and Frank J. Porporino, *Coping, Behavior, and Adaptation in Prison Inmates* (New York: Springer-Verlag, 1988).

[9] John Irwin, *Prisons in Turmoil* (Boston: Little, Brown, 1980), 67.

[10] Seth Ferranti, "With Cigarettes Banned in Most Prisons, Gangs Shift from Drugs to Smokes," *Daily Beast,* www.thedailybeast .com/articles/2013/06/02/with-cigarettes-banned-in-most-prisons -gangs-shift-from-drugs-to-smokes.html, June 2, 2013.

[11] Darrell K. Gilliard, *Prison and Jail Inmates at Midyear 1998* (Washington, DC: U.S. Government Printing Office, 1999), 4.

[12] E. Ann Carson, *Prisoners in 2013* (Washington, DC: U.S. Government Printing Office, 2014).

[13] Carson, *Prisoners in 2013.*

[14] Lauren E. Glaze and Laura M. Maruschak, *Parents in Prison and Their Minor Children* (Washington, DC: U.S. Government Printing Office, 2008).

[15] Carson, *Prisoners in 2013.*

[16] Sean Rosenmerkel, Matthew Durose, and Donald Farole, Jr., *Felony Sentences in State Courts, 2006—Statistical Tables,* Table 3.5, December 2009, http://bjs.ojp.usdoj.gov/content/pub/pdf /fssc06st.pdf.

[17] Christopher J. Mumola and Jennifer C. Karberg, *Drug Use and Dependence, State and Federal Prisoners, 2004* (Washington, DC: U.S. Government Printing Office, 2006).

[18] Lawrence A. Greenfeld and Tracy L. Snell, *Women Offenders* (Washington, DC: U.S. Government Printing Office, 1999), 9.

[19] Esther Heffernan, *Making It in Prison* (New York: Wiley, 1972).

[20] David Ward and Gene G. Kassebaum, *Women's Prisons: Sex and Social Structure* (Hawthorne, NY: Aldine, 1965), 140.

[21] Kimberly R. Greer, "The Changing Nature of Interpersonal Relationships in a Women's Prison," *Prison Journal* 80 (2000): 442–68.

[22] Imogene L. Moyer, "Differential Social Structures and Homosexuality Among Women in Prisons," *Virginia Social Science Journal* (1978): 13–14, 17–19.

[23] Robert G. Leger, "Lesbianism Among Women Prisoners: Participants and Nonparticipants," *Criminal Justice and Behavior* 14 (1987): 463.

[24] Rose Giallombardo, *Society of Women: A Study of Women's Prison* (New York: Wiley, 1966).

[25] Heffernan, *Making It in Prison,* pp. 16–17.

[26] Barbara Owen, *"In The Mix": Struggle and Survival in a Women's Prison* (Albany: State University of New York Press, 1998).

[27] Ibid., p. 179.

[28] James G. Fox, *Organizational and Racial Conflict in Maximum-Security Prisons* (Lexington, MA: Lexington, 1982), 100–102.

[29] Ibid., pp. 100–101.

[30] Paul Guerino and Allen J. Beck, *Sexual Victimization Reported by Adult Correctional Authorities, 2007–2008* (Washington, DC: U.S. Government Printing Office, 2011), 2.

[31] Les Zaitz, "Abuse of Women Inmates at Oregon's Coffee Creek Prison Goes on for Years," *Oregonian,* www.oregonlive.com /politics/index.ssf/2012/04/abuse_of_women_inmates_at_oreg .html, April 29, 2012.

[32] Glaze and Maruschak, *Parents in Prison and Their Minor Children.*

[33] Beth M. Huebner and Regan Gustafson, "The Effect of Maternal Incarceration on Adult Offspring Involvement in the Criminal Justice System," *Journal of Criminal Justice* 35 (2007): 283–96.

[34] Women's Prison Association, *Mothers, Infants and Imprisonment: A National Look at Prison Nurseries and Community-Based Alternatives* (New York: Author, 2009), 5.

[35] Lorie Smith Goshin and Mary Woods Byrne, "Converging Streams of Opportunity for Prison Nursery Programs in the United States," *Journal of Offender Rehabilitation* 48 (2009): 271–95.

[36] Merry Morash and Pamela J. Schram, *The Prison Experience: Special Issues of Women in Prison* (Prospect Heights, IL: Waveland, 2009), 99.

[37] Caroline Wolf Harlow, *Education and Correctional Populations* (Washington, DC: U.S. Government Printing Office, 2003), 2.

[38] *Estelle v. Gamble,* 95 S.Ct. 285 (1976).

[39] John Kleinig and Margaret Leland Smith, *Discretion, Community, and Correctional Ethics* (Lanham, MD: Rowman and Littlefield, 2001).

[40] Doris J. James and Lauren E. Glaze, *Mental Health Problems of Prison and Jail Inmates* (Washington, DC: U.S. Government Printing Office, 2006), 4.

[41] Laura M. Maruschak, *Medical Problems of State and Federal Prisoners and Jail Inmates, 2011–12* (Washington, DC: U.S. Government Printing Office, 2015).

CHAPTER 8

Prison Management

Shortly after 6:00 P.M. in the mess hall at Auburn Correctional Facility, a correctional officer ordered a young inmate to return to his cell. The inmate refused, shoving the correctional officer in the chest. Prison staff quickly restrained the inmate assailant, handcuffing the man before escorting him off to administrative segregation. Shortly after the first combatant was controlled, a second inmate walked into the mess hall and struck another officer in the face, causing cuts and swelling to the nose and forehead.

Officers quickly subdued the second attacker, restraining him and placing him in the disciplinary unit. A medical inspection revealed that the prisoner had bruised knuckles, a swollen eye, and also pain in his leg following the attack.

Commenting on the attack, union spokesman Jim Miller noted that inmate assaults on prison officers had been up over the past year. "It's a situation where people need to recognize the jobs of corrections officers are inherently dangerous and they

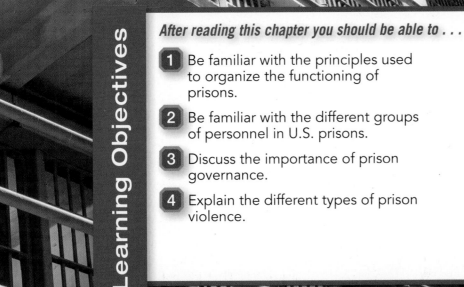

Learning Objectives

After reading this chapter you should be able to . . .

1 Be familiar with the principles used to organize the functioning of prisons.

2 Be familiar with the different groups of personnel in U.S. prisons.

3 Discuss the importance of prison governance.

4 Explain the different types of prison violence.

Managing prisons involves skill, insight into human behavior, and good judgment. Even routine moments can become volatile situations if they are not handled well.

continue to get worse," Miller said. "More resources—technology, staffing—need to be given to staff to reduce the violence inside the facilities."[1] The attacks did trigger a one-week lockdown. During cell searches, officers confiscated five homemade weapons.

It is no secret that prisons can be violent offenders under crowded conditions. Should we assume that violence is this rampant throughout the corrections system? If you were entering prison for the first time, what should you expect? How do prisons function? Are the officers really in charge, or do the inmates "run the

(continued from previous page)

The prison differs from almost every other institution or organization in modern society. It has unique physical features, and it is the only place where a group of employees manage a group of captives. Prisoners must live according to the rules of their keepers and with restricted movements. When reading this chapter, keep in mind that prison managers

1. Cannot select their clients.

2. Have little or no control over the release of their clients.

3. Must deal with clients who are there against their will.

4. Must rely on clients to do most of the work in the daily operation of the institution—work that they are forced to do and for which they are not paid.

5. Must depend on the maintenance of satisfactory relationships between clients and staff.

Given these unique characteristics, how should prisons be run? Further, wardens and other key personnel are asked to perform a difficult job, one that requires skilled and dedicated managers. What rules should guide them?

In this chapter we look at how institutional resources are organized to achieve certain goals. At a minimum, prisoners must be clothed, fed, kept healthy, provided with recreation, protected from one another, and maintained in custody. In addition, administrators may be required to offer vocational and educational programs and use inmate labor in agriculture or industry. Prison staff are charged with a long list of complicated and challenging tasks. To accomplish all this in a population consisting of some of the most antisocial people in the society is surely a Herculean undertaking, one that depends on organization. ■

FORMAL ORGANIZATIONS

The University of Washington, Ford Motor Company, and the California State Prison at Folsom are very different organizations, each created to achieve certain goals. Differing organizational structures let managers coordinate the various parts of the university, auto manufacturer, and prison in the interests of scholarship, production, and corrections, respectively.

A **formal organization** is deliberately established for particular ends. If accomplishing an objective requires collective effort, people set up an organization to help coordinate activities and to provide incentives for others to join. Thus, in a university, a business, and a correctional institution, the goals, rules, and roles that define the relations among the organization's members (the organizational chart) have been formally established.

Amitai Etzioni, an organization theorist, uses the concept of compliance as the basis for comparing types of organizations. **Compliance** is the way that someone behaves in accordance with an order or directive given by another person. In compliance relationships, an order is backed up by one's ability to induce or influence another person to carry out one's directives.[2] People do what others ask because those others have the means—remunerative, normative, or coercive—to get the subjects to comply. **Remunerative power** is based on material resources, such as wages, fringe benefits, or goods, that people exchange for compliance. **Normative power** rests on symbolic rewards that leaders manipulate through ritual, allocation of honors, and social esteem. **Coercive power** depends on applying or threatening physical force to inflict pain, restrict movement, or control other aspects of a person's life.

Etzioni argues that all formal organizations employ all three types of power but that the degree to which they rely on any one of them varies with the desired goal. Thus, although the University of Washington probably relies mainly on normative power in its relationships with students and the public, it relies on remunerative power in relationships with faculty and staff. Although Ford Motors is organized primarily for manufacturing, it may appeal to "team spirit" or "safety employee of the month" campaigns to meet its goals. And although the warden at Folsom may rely on remunerative and normative powers to manage staff to make it the best correctional facility in the United States, in working with prisoners he relies primarily on coercive power. The presence in high-custody institutions of "highly alienated lower participants" (prisoners), Etzioni says, makes the application or threat of force necessary to ensure compliance.[3]

Coercive power undergirds all prison relationships, but correctional institutions vary in their use of physical force and in the degree to which the inmates are alienated. Correctional institutions can be placed on a continuum of custody or treatment goals. At one extreme is the highly authoritarian prison, where the movement of inmates is greatly restricted, staff–inmate relationships are formally structured, and the prime emphasis is on custody. In such an institution, treatment goals take a back seat. At the other extreme is the institution that emphasizes the therapeutic aspect of the physical and social environment. Here, the staff collaborates with inmates to overcome their problems. Between these ideal types lie the great majority of correctional institutions.

However, this custody–treatment continuum may neglect other aspects of imprisonment. Charles Logan points out that we expect a lot of prisons "to correct the incorrigible, rehabilitate the wretched, deter the determined, restrain the dangerous, and punish the wicked." He proposes that the purpose of imprisonment is to "punish offenders—fairly and justly—through lengths of confinement proportionate to the gravity of the offense."[4] Thus, the mission with respect to prisoners has five features:

1. *Keep them in.* The facility must be secure, such that inmates cannot escape and contraband cannot be smuggled in.

2. *Keep them safe.* Inmates and staff need to be kept safe, not only from one another but from various environmental hazards as well.

3. *Keep them in line.* Prisons run on rules, and the ability of prison administrators to enforce compliance is central to the quality of confinement.

4. *Keep them healthy.* Inmates are entitled to have care for their medical needs.

5. *Keep them busy.* Constructive activities, such as work, recreation, education, and treatment programs, are antidotes to idleness.[5]

formal organization
A structure established for influencing behavior to achieve particular ends.

compliance
Obedience to an order or request.

remunerative power
The ability to obtain compliance in exchange for material resources.

normative power
The ability to obtain compliance by manipulating symbolic rewards.

coercive power
The ability to obtain compliance by the application or threat of physical force.

Prison management requires countless moments of interaction between staff and those who are incarcerated. Security dominates the interactions, as do policy and procedure. But the moments of interaction between staff and prisoners are also opportunities for training, personal skill, and human concern to come to the fore.

Prison work entails accomplishing this mission in a fair and efficient manner, without causing undue suffering. The state may have other goals as well, but these are the main objectives.

The Organizational Structure

For any organization to be effective, its leaders and staff must know the rules and procedures, the lines of authority, and the channels of communication. Organizations differ in their organizational hierarchy, in their allocation of discretion, in the effort expended on administrative problems, and in the nature of the top leadership.

CONCEPTS OF ORGANIZATION The formal administrative structure of a prison is a hierarchy of staff positions, each with its own duties and responsibilities, each linked to the others in a logical chain of command. As **Figure 8.1** shows, the warden is ultimately responsible for the operation of the institution. Deputy wardens oversee the functional divisions of the prison: management, custody, programs, and industry and agriculture. Under each deputy are middle managers and line staff who operate the departments. Functions are subdivided according to prison size and population.

Three principles are commonly used to organize the functioning of hierarchically structured prisons: unity of command, chain of command, and span of control. **Unity of command** is the idea that it is most efficient for a subordinate to report to only one superior. If a worker must respond to orders from two or more bosses, things can get chaotic. Unity of command is related to the second concept, **chain of command**. Because the

unity of command
A management principle holding that a subordinate should report to only one supervisor.

chain of command
A series of organizational positions in order of authority, with each person receiving orders from the one immediately above and issuing orders to the one immediately below.

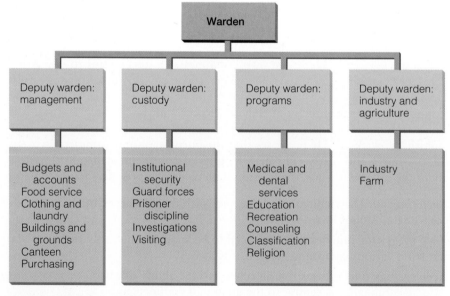

FIGURE 8.1
Formal Organization of a Prison for Adult Felons
The formal organization of an institution may say little about those political and informal relationships among staff members that really govern how the prison operates.

Line personnel, such as correctional officers who supervise work in the fields, have direct contact with inmates and are primarily concerned with security.

AP Images/Gerald Herbert

person at the top of the organization cannot oversee everything, he or she must rely on lower-ranking staff to pass directives down. For example, the warden asks the deputy warden to have custody conduct a shakedown; the deputy warden passes the directive to the captain of the guard, who then has the lieutenant in charge of a particular shift carry out the search. The term **span of control** refers to the extent of supervision by one person. If, for example, a correctional institution offers many educational and treatment programs, the deputy warden for programs may not be able to oversee them all effectively. This deputy warden's span of control is stretched so far that a reorganization and further division of responsibilities may be required.

Two other concepts characterize the organization of correctional institutions: line personnel and staff personnel. **Line personnel** are directly concerned with furthering the institution's goals. They have direct contact with the prisoners. These personnel include the custody force, industry and agricultural supervisors, counselors, and medical technicians. **Staff personnel** support line personnel. They usually work under the deputy warden for management, handling accounting, training, purchasing, and so on.

The custodial employees make up the majority of an institution's personnel. They are normally organized along military lines, from deputy warden to captain to correctional officer. The professional staff, such as teachers and industry supervisors, are separate from the custodial staff and have little in common with them. All employees answer to the warden, but the treatment personnel and the civilian supervisors of the workshops have their own titles and pay scales. Their responsibilities do not extend to providing special services to the custodial employees. The top medical and educational personnel may formally report to the warden but in fact look to the central office of the department of corrections for leadership.

The Impact of the Structure

The organizational structure of correctional institutions has changed over time. In the traditional custodial prison, the warden dominated the guard force and often disciplined employees as strictly as inmates. When rehabilitation became a goal and treatment and educational programs were incorporated, a separate structure for programs, often headed by a deputy warden, was added. Its employees were professionals, such as teachers, social workers, and counselors.

span of control
A management principle holding that a supervisor can effectively oversee only a limited number of subordinates.

line personnel
Employees who are directly concerned with furthering the institution's goals— workers in direct contact with clients.

staff personnel
Employees who provide services in support of line personnel (for example, accountants and training officers).

As some institutions began to focus on rehabilitation, correctional planners and scholars frequently contrasted the traditional prison organization with a collaborative model. For example, most of the 1967 President's Commission on Law Enforcement and Administration of Justice report referred optimistically to the future correctional institution in which a dedicated and professionally trained staff would work with other administrators and with prisoners to identify inmates' problems and to strive for rehabilitation.[6] Such a prison would require several changes that would place less emphasis on controlling inmates, expand the influence of treatment personnel in decision making, and allow prisoners a say in how the facility operates. However, by the 1980s it was hard to find either prisons being run this way or correctional leaders saying that prisons should be run this way.

Correctional institutions are administered more humanely today than they were in the past. This change is in part a response to the presence of rehabilitative personnel and programs, the increased training and professionalism of correctional personnel, the intrusion of the courts, and the growth of citizen groups that monitor prison operations. Protecting society by preventing escapes, keeping inmates safe and healthy, and preparing prisoners for release back into free society are all tasks pursued by various prison staff members.

PRISON STAFF

The multiple goals and separate employee lines of command often cause ambiguity and conflict in the administration of prisons. For example, prison goals can be contradictory or unclear. Conflict between different groups of personnel (custodial staff versus treatment staff) and between staff and inmates presents significant challenges to prison administrators.

Institutional Managers

The warden (or superintendent) is ultimately responsible for prison operations. Not long ago, the prison warden ran the institution without direction from departments of corrections or the intrusion of courts, labor unions, or prisoner support groups. Things are much different today.

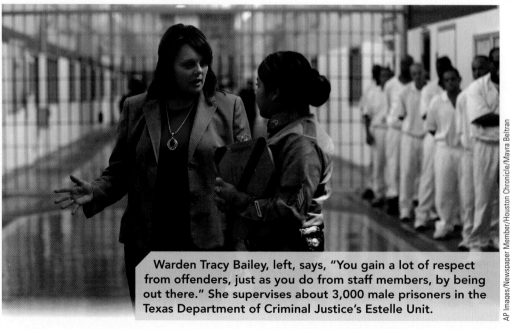

Warden Tracy Bailey, left, says, "You gain a lot of respect from offenders, just as you do from staff members, by being out there." She supervises about 3,000 male prisoners in the Texas Department of Criminal Justice's Estelle Unit.

AP Images/Newspaper Member/Houston Chronicle/Mayra Beltran

The contemporary warden is the prison's main contact with the outside world. Responsible for operating the prison, he or she normally reports to the deputy commissioner for institutions in the central office of the department of corrections. When the warden directs attention and energy outward (to the central office, parole board, or legislature), he or she delegates the daily operation of the prison to a deputy, usually the person in charge of custody. Today, managers in the central office handle such matters as budgets, research and program development, public information, and legislative relations. However, the warden's job security still rests on his or her ability to run the institution effectively and efficiently. At the first sign of trouble, the warden may be forced to look for a new job. The primary duties and tasks of prison wardens are summarized in **Table 8.1**.

Bureaucratic functions often fall to a deputy warden for management, who is responsible for housekeeping tasks: buying supplies, keeping up the buildings and grounds, providing food, maintaining financial records, and the like. However, some states centralize many of these tasks in the office of the commissioner to promote accountability and coordination among constituent institutions. For example, buying supplies from one warehouse that serves all state agencies has decreased the discretion of prison management to contract locally for provisions.

Most personnel assigned to manage services for correctional institutions have little contact with prisoners; in some facilities they work in buildings separate from where inmates live and work. Only personnel directly providing services, such as the head of food services, have direct contact with prisoners.

Table 8.1 Primary Duties and Tasks of Prison Wardens

Contemporary prison wardens place great emphasis on maintaining safety and security. They are also responsible for mundane but important duties such as managing the budget and presiding over the physical plant.

Duties		Tasks		
Administer safety and security operations	Approve security and safety policies and procedures	Ensure facility compliance	Assess safety and security systems	Manage intelligence operations
Manage human resources	Promote equal employment opportunities	Manage staff recruitment process	Authorize/recommend hiring staff	Ensure staff development
Manage critical incidents	Review and approve emergency plans	Monitor emergency scenarios	Ensure readiness of emergency response team	Command intelligence team
Manage the budget	Compile budget requests	Establish budget priorities	Submit and justify budget requests	Monitor and control overtime
Foster a healthy institutional environment	Maintain frequent and direct contact with inmates	Provide meaningful inmate programs	Provide quality inmate-support services	Provide fair inmate-grievance system
Preside over the physical plant	Administer physical plant maintenance plan	Ensure facility safety, security, and sanitation inspections	Monitor allocation of space	Monitor and allocate resources

Source: Rick Ruddell and Tommy Norris, "The Changing Role of Wardens: A Focus on Safety and Security," *Corrections Today* 70 (October 2008): 39.

Correctional Officers—Custody

In most institutions the custodial force has graded ranks (captain, lieutenant, officer), with pay differentials and job titles following the chain of command, as in the military. Unlike the military, which has separate groups of officers and enlisted personnel, the prison requires its lowest-status employee, the correctional officer, to be both a supervisor (of inmates) and a worker (for the warden). This causes role conflict and makes officers vulnerable to corruption by the inmates. Officers know that the warden is judging their performance by the way they manage the prisoners, and they can seldom manage without at least some cooperation from the prisoners. Officers ease up on some rules so prisoners will more willingly comply with other rules and requests. "Careers in Corrections" offers a view of work as a correctional officer.

Over the past three decades, the correctional officer's role has changed greatly. No longer responsible merely for "guarding," the correctional officer is now considered a crucial professional who has the closest contact with the prisoners and performs a variety of tasks. ("Focus on Correctional Technology" discusses one way that technology is being used to narrow the role of correctional officers.) Officers are expected to counsel, supervise, protect, and process the inmates under their care. Correctional officers, then, are human service providers expected to engage in "people work" within an organizational setting. Human service activities undertaken by officers include (1) providing goods and services, (2) acting as referral agents or advocates, and (3) helping with institutional adjustment problems.[7]

Today, because of the demand for well-qualified correctional officers, most states have given priority to recruiting quality personnel. Salaries differ from state to state. In addition to their salaries, most officers can work overtime to supplement their base pay.

careers in Corrections

CORRECTIONAL OFFICER

Nature of the Work

There are 469,500 correctional officers who work in the great array of reformatories, prisons, prison camps, and penitentiaries that make up American corrections. Regardless of the setting, these officers maintain order within the institution and enforce rules and regulations. To keep the facility secure, officers often must search inmates and their living quarters for contraband, settle disputes, enforce discipline, and communicate prisoner requests to higher levels. Officers may be assigned to housing units, perimeter patrols, or inmate work assignments. Correctional officers usually work an eight-hour day, five days per week, on rotating shifts.

Required Qualifications

A correctional officer must be at least 18 to 21 years of age, be a U.S. citizen with no felony convictions, and have at least a high school education or equivalent. To work in a federal prison, a bachelor's degree and three years of experience are required. Most states require qualifying examinations, including personality screenings. Candidates must be in good health and meet fitness, eyesight, and hearing standards. The American Correctional Association sets training guidelines for recruits. Most states have training academies with instruction on legal restrictions, custody procedures, interpersonal relationships, use of firearms, and self-defense. After graduation from the academy, trainees typically receive several weeks or months of training in the job setting under the supervision of an experienced officer.

Earnings and Job Outlook

As states have had to deal with the explosion of the prison population, the number of correctional officers has markedly increased during the past three decades. Although such expansion has slowed in recent years, in part because of budgetary constraints, turnover in the officer corps should provide future openings. With regional variation, the median annual salary for state correctional officers is $39,040.

More Information

See the American Correctional Association website (www.aca.org).

focus on correctional technology

Can Interactive Kiosks Improve Staff Efficiency?

A lot is asked of correctional officers. Among other things, officers count and monitor inmates, they break up fights, and they are expected to regularly tend to inmates' needs. Inmates rely on correctional officers for all sorts of information, such as when visitations will take place. Because prison facilities are not typically very sophisticated when it comes to computer technology, officers who do not know where to look can have trouble helping inmates locate important information. Many prisons around the country are considering a new idea—installing self-service kiosks (free-standing interactive devices that look a lot like an ATM)—to allow inmates to access the kind of information they have traditionally relied on correctional officers for.

The potential benefits of using self-service kiosks are numerous. Perhaps most importantly, however, providing inmates with access to personal information, such as their account balances and visitation schedule, can reduce levels of frustration brought about by the traditional practice of relying on busy correctional officers for information. An added bonus of using self-service kiosks is that correctional officers can better focus on other important tasks, such as monitoring inmates in their cell block.

Of course, the use of kiosk technology in prisons presents many challenges. One problem is that many inmates cannot read and will not be able to use self-service kiosks. Another challenge relates to language use. Many prisons hold inmates who speak different languages, so kiosks will have to be designed to accommodate non-English-speaking prisoners. Another concern is protecting information from inmates who attempt to abuse the system. A variety of safeguards will have to be built into the software used in kiosks. Finally, the machines may be vandalized by inmates. Given this potential, housing the fragile computer equipment in a hard-shell casing is a must.

Critical Thinking

1. Will using self-service kiosks in prisons allow correctional officers to focus more on security?
2. Should inmates have easy access to their personal records?
3. What are some of the potential drawbacks to using self-service kiosks in prisons?
4. How do you think the general public will react to prisons using this type of technology?

Source: Patricia O'Hagan, Edward Hanna, and Roy Sterritt, "Addressing the Corrections Crisis with Software Technology," *Computer* 43 (February 2010): 90–93.

TRAINING   To prepare officers for prison work, most states require cadets to complete a preservice training program. In some states, preservice programs for officers resemble the military's basic training, with a similar emphasis on physical training, discipline, and classwork. During the typical program, recruits receive training in a variety of topics, including report writing, communicable diseases, inmate manipulation, self-defense, inmate classification, and use of force. In states with large Latino populations, preservice training also includes basic Spanish. The length of preservice training varies from state to state.

Training is not limited to preservice programs. Rather, some sort of annual training is required in many state systems. Some training programs are designed to provide low-level supervisors with the knowledge and tools necessary to eventually become successful wardens (see Focus on Correctional Policy, "Effective Leadership Training").

Program Personnel

The contemporary correctional institution is concerned not only with punishing but also with encouraging prisoners to participate in educational, vocational, and treatment programs. Such programs have been a part of corrections since the late 1800s, but the enthusiasm for rehabilitation that swept corrections after World War II created a wider variety of programs, as discussed in Chapter 4. Rehabilitative and educational personnel find it difficult to achieve their goals in institutions whose primary mission is custody.

focus on correctional policy

Effective Leadership Training

The traditional practice of grooming potential leaders in the field of corrections involved promoting employees up the chain of command over a long period of time, say 20 to 30 years. Along the way, eventual leaders performed various jobs and learned firsthand how their facilities operated. While many contemporary wardens and superintendents worked their way up from the rank and file, the old-school approach to preparing employees for high-level leadership positions is no longer sufficient. A lot is expected of today's correctional leaders. They face a greater number of demands and more-complex challenges than did their predecessors.

To help fill the gap, correctional officials now invest in leadership training. Advocates argue that continuing education of this type can help correctional employees become more familiar with important organizational issues and obtain the tools needed to successfully achieve organizational objectives. Unfortunately, cynicism toward training is fairly widespread in the field of corrections. Too often, training sessions are poorly organized, instructors fail to motivate and inspire students, and important information is not communicated.

To develop more-promising leadership training programs that can contribute to long-term change in correctional settings, Rick Ruddell and Lisa Cecil have identified some important steps, including the following:

1. *Use evidence-based training.* When determining which training courses to offer, correctional officials should conduct a needs assessment. Doing so will identify the kind of training that will benefit employees and the organization the most. As well, training courses that draw from existing correctional research should be preferred.

2. *Use training based on measurable learning objectives.* When training programs identify measurable learning objectives, their effectiveness and long-term impact can be evaluated. Investigating whether the training had the desired impact helps correctional professionals determine whether the training was worth the investment.

3. *Involve key agency personnel.* This step helps accomplish two things. First, the presence of existing leaders, such as wardens and superintendents, lets participants know that they have been identified as having leadership potential. Second, the attendance of key personnel reinforces the importance of the courses to participants.

4. *Have an active-learning orientation.* Effective leadership training does not simply rely on lectures but also uses interactive learning techniques that improve cooperation among participants, allowing students to learn from one another and helping participants expand their professional networks.

5. *Make it relevant.* Leadership training should relate specifically to the participants' workplace. In fact, Ruddell and Cecil recommend that participants develop a strategic plan of action during their training experience and put it into action when they go back to their jobs.

It is important to acknowledge that the field of corrections has changed considerably over the past several decades. Prior policies and practices that were once accepted as conventional wisdom, such as the tradition of slowly grooming future wardens and superintendents through a series of promotions and different job assignments, are no longer effective. Today, evidence-based training plays a significant role in developing correctional leaders' knowledge, skill, and ability to effectively meet demands and overcome challenges.

Critical Thinking

1. In your opinion, which of the five steps discussed above is the most important?

2. What other steps might also be included when putting together a leadership training course?

3. In what other areas should future wardens and superintendents receive training?

Source: Adapted from Rick Ruddell and Lisa Cecil, "Ten Steps to Developing Effective Leadership Training," *Corrections Today* 72 (February 2010): 80–83.

Agricultural and Industrial Supervisors

Since the invention of the penitentiary, inmate labor has been used for industry and agriculture. As discussed in Chapter 7, the importance of these functions has varied over time and across regions. In some southern prisons, most of the inmates' time is spent tending crops. In the Northeast, prison farms have disappeared because they are uneconomical and ill-matched to the urban backgrounds of most inmates.

Like other programs, industrial and agricultural production is usually administered outside of the strict custodial hierarchy. But unlike educational or treatment programs, work in a factory or farm requires supervisors. For example, administrators must often mediate disputes over the need for officers in guard towers or housing units and the need for officers in fields or factories.

GOVERNING PRISONS

Traditionally, sociologists have looked at prisons as social systems rather than institutions to be governed. Until fairly recently, our understanding of life inside prison was based on **inmate balance theory**. This theory provides insights on maintaining order and preventing collective violence in prison.[8] According to this view, for the prison system to operate effectively, officials must tolerate minor infractions, relax security measures, and allow inmate leaders to keep order. When officials go too far in asserting their authority by cracking down on inmate privileges, the delicate balance of shared authority is upset, which in turn increases the chances that inmates will become violent.[9]

inmate balance theory
A governance theory which states that for a prison system to operate effectively, officials must tolerate minor infractions, relax security measures, and allow inmate leaders to keep order.

Criminologists have written about the effects of prison conditions on inmates, racial and ethnic divisions, inmate slang and roles, and the informal distribution of authority in prisons. However, as John DiIulio notes, sociological research on prison society does little to help correctional officials manage inmates and staff. In fact, most criminological research about prisons implies that administrators can do little to govern because—despite formal rules and regulations—institutions are run mainly through the informal social networks of the keepers and the kept (see Table 8.2 for one set of formal rules of conduct).[10]

DiIulio and others have developed an alternative explanation of prison disorder, which has been dubbed **administrative control theory**.[11] This perspective states that disorder results from "unstable, divided, or otherwise weak management."[12] Thus, when officials lose control over their institutions, riots and other unruly inmate behaviors become more likely. This administrative breakdown has several effects:

administrative control theory
A governance theory which states that prison disorder results from unstable, divided, or otherwise weak management.

1. Inmates come to believe that their conditions of confinement are not only bad but also unjust.
2. Officials become indifferent to routine security measures and the day-to-day tasks of prison management.
3. Weak management permits gangs and other illicit groups to flourish. These groups, in turn, may help mobilize disturbances.[13]

What distinguishes a well-run prison from a substandard prison? DiIulio argues that the crucial variable is not the ethnic or racial composition of the population, the criminal records of the inmates, the size of the institution, the degree of crowding, or the level of funding. What is important is *governance*: the sound and firm management of inmates and staff.

What quality of life should be maintained in a prison? DiIulio states that a good prison "provides as much order, amenity, and service as possible given the human and financial resources."[14] *Order* is defined as the absence of individual or group misconduct threatening the safety of others—for example, assaults, rapes, and other forms of violence or insult. A basic assumption should be that because the state sends offenders to prison, it is responsible for ensuring their safety there. *Amenity* is anything that enhances the inmates' creature comforts, such as good food, clean bedding, and recreational opportunities. This does not mean that prisons are to function as luxury hotels, but contemporary standards stipulate that correctional facilities should not be harmful to inmates' mental and physical health. Finally, *service* includes programs designed to improve the life prospects of inmates: vocational training, remedial education, and work opportunities. Here, too, we expect inmates to be engaged in activities during

Table 8.2 Rules of General Conduct, Michigan Department of Corrections

1. All residents are expected to obey directions and instructions of members of the staff. If a resident feels he/she has been dealt with unfairly, or that he/she has received improper instructions, he/she should first comply with the order and then follow the established grievance procedures outlined later in this booklet.

2. Any behavior considered a felony or a misdemeanor in this state also is a violation of institutional rules. Such acts may result in disciplinary action and/or loss of earned good time in addition to possible criminal prosecution.

3. Any escape, attempt to escape, walk away, or failure to return from a furlough may result in loss of good time and/or a new sentence through prosecution under the escape statute. At one time or another, most persons in medium or minimum custody have felt restless and uneasy. When this happens, we urge you to see your counselor or the official in charge for guidance and advice. Occasionally, the department has asked that those who have walked away impulsively not be prosecuted when they have turned themselves in immediately after the act, realizing their mistake.

4. Any resident may, if they feel they have no further recourse in the institution, appeal to the Director of Corrections, Deputy Director, the Attorney General, state and federal courts, Michigan Civil Rights Commission, or the Governor in the form of sealed and uncensored mail.

5. Reasonable courtesy, orderly conduct, and good personal hygiene are expected of all residents. Standards for haircuts, beards, and general appearance are listed later in this rule book.

6. Residents cannot hold any group meetings in the yard. Meetings for all legitimate purposes require staff approval; facilities, if available, will be scheduled for this purpose and necessary supervision provided.

7. While residents are permitted to play cards and other games, gambling is not allowed. In card-playing areas there shall be no more than four persons at a table. Visible tokens or other items of value will be sufficient evidence of gambling. Games are prohibited during working hours on institutional assignments.

8. All typewriters, calculators, radios, TVs, electric razors, and other appliances, including musical instruments, must be registered with the institutional officials by make, model, and serial number.

9. Items under Paragraph 8 cannot be traded, sold, or given away without written approval of the Deputy Warden or Superintendent.

10. Residents cannot operate concessions, sell services, rent goods, or act as loan sharks or pawnbrokers.

11. All items of contraband are subject to confiscation.

12. When a resident desires to go from one place to another for a specific and legitimate reason, he/she should obtain a pass from the official to whom [he/she is] responsible, such as the housing unit supervisor, work foreman, teacher, etc.

13. No resident is allowed to go into another resident's cell or room unless specifically authorized.

Source: Michigan Department of Corrections, *Resident Guide Book* (Lansing: Michigan Department of Corrections, n.d.).

incarceration that will make them better people and enhance their ability to lead crime-free lives upon release.

If we accept the idea that well-run prisons are important for inmates, staff, and society, what are some of the problems that correctional administrators must address? There are four factors that make governing prisons different from administering other public institutions: (1) the defects of total power, (2) the limited rewards and punishments, (3) the co-optation of correctional officers, and (4) the strength of inmate leadership. After we review each of these factors, we will consider the administrative systems and leadership styles that can help make prisons safe and humane and serve inmates' needs.

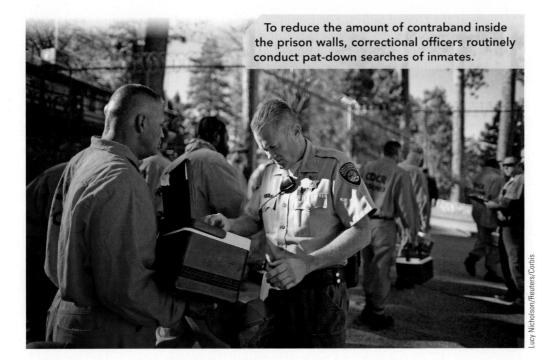

To reduce the amount of contraband inside the prison walls, correctional officers routinely conduct pat-down searches of inmates.

Lucy Nicholson/Reuters/Corbis

The Defects of Total Power

In his classic study of the New Jersey State Prison, Gresham Sykes emphasized that although in formal terms correctional officials have power to induce prisoner compliance, in fact that power is limited and in many ways depends on inmate cooperation.[15] It is from this perspective that the inmate balance theory of management evolved.

Much of the public believes that prisons are run in an authoritarian manner: Correctional officers give orders, and inmates follow them. Strictly enforced rules specify what the captives may and may not do. Staff members have the right to grant rewards and to inflict punishment. In theory, any inmate who does not follow the rules can be placed in solitary confinement. Because the officers have a monopoly on the legal means of enforcing rules and can be backed up by the state police and the National Guard if necessary, many people believe that no question should arise about how the prison is run.

Certainly, we can imagine a prison society made up of hostile and uncooperative inmates ruled by force. Prisoners can be legally isolated from one another, physically coerced until they cooperate, and put under continuous surveillance. Although all these things are possible, the public would probably not tolerate such practices for long because people expect correctional institutions to be run humanely.

Also, prisoners, unlike members of other authoritarian organizations such as the military, do not recognize the legitimacy of their keepers and therefore are not always moved to cooperate. No sense of duty propels prisoners to compliance. This is an important distinction because duty is the backbone of most social organizations. With it, rules are followed—and need not be explained first.

The notion that correctional officers have total power over inmates has many other flaws. As Gresham Sykes points out, "The ability of the officials to physically coerce their captives into the paths of compliance is something of an illusion as far as the day-to-day activities of the prison are concerned and may be of doubtful value in moments of crisis."[16] Forcing people to follow commands is an inefficient way to make them carry out complex tasks; efficiency is further diminished by the ratio of inmates to custody staff and by the potential dangers.[17]

Of course, physical coercion is used to control prisoners. Such tactics may violate criminal statutes and administrative procedures, but they have long occurred in prisons throughout the United States. For example, a study of a Texas prison found that a small but significant percentage of the officers used physical punishment. Force both controlled the prison population and induced cohesion among officers, maintaining a status differential between officers and inmates and helping officers win promotions.[18]

Rewards and Punishments

Correctional officers often rely on rewards and punishments to gain cooperation. To maintain security and order among a large population in a confined space, they impose extensive rules of conduct. Instead of using force to ensure obedience, however, they reward compliance and punish rule violations by granting and denying privileges.

Several policies may be followed to promote control. One is to offer cooperative prisoners rewards such as choice job assignments, residence in the honor unit, and favorable parole reports. Inmates who follow the rules receive good time. Informers may also be rewarded, and administrators may ignore conflict among inmates on the assumption that it keeps prisoners from uniting against authorities.

The system of rewards and punishments has some shortcomings. One is that the punishments for rule breaking do not represent a great departure from the prisoners' usual circumstances. Because inmates are already deprived of many freedoms and valued goods—heterosexual relations, money, choice of clothing, and so on—not being allowed to attend, say, a recreational period does not carry much weight. In addition, according to the inmate code in a particular prison, the defiant convict may gain standing among the other prisoners. Finally, authorized privileges are given to the inmate at the start of the sentence and are taken away only if rules are broken, but few further rewards are authorized for progress or exceptional behavior. However, as an inmate approaches release, opportunities for furloughs, work release, or transfer to a halfway house can serve as incentives to obey rules.

Gaining Cooperation: Exchange Relationships

One way that correctional officers obtain inmate cooperation is by tolerating minor rule infractions in exchange for compliance with major prison rules. The correctional officer plays the key role in the interpersonal relationships among the inmates and serves as the link to the prison bureaucracy. Officers and prisoners are in close association both day and night—in the cell block, workshop, dining hall, recreation area, and so on. Although the formal rules require a social distance between the officers and inmates, their physical proximity makes them aware that each is dependent on the other. To look good to their superiors, the officers need the cooperation of the prisoners, and the inmates count on the officers to relax the rules or occasionally look the other way.

Even though officers are backed by the state and have the formal authority to punish any prisoner who does not follow orders, they often discover that the best course of action is to make "deals" with the inmates. As a result, officers buy compliance or obedience in some areas by tolerating rule breaking elsewhere.

Officers are expected to maintain "surface order." They must ensure that the inmates conform voluntarily to the most important rules, things run smoothly, and no visible trouble and no cause for alarm emerge. Because officers' job performance is judged on their ability to maintain surface order, both officers and prisoners have a tacit understanding and bargain accordingly. The assumptions underlying the accommodative relationships between officers and inmates are as follows:

1. Negotiations are central to prisoner control because correctional officers cannot have total control over the inmates.

2. Once an officer defines a set of informal rules with prisoners, the rules must be respected by all parties.

3. Some rule violations are "normal" and consequently do not merit officers' attention or sanctioning.[19]

DO the Right Thing

Late one night while walking the block, Officer Johnson overheard an inmate quietly talking in a nearby cell. Johnson stopped and listened carefully. "Well, what did your momma say?" the voice said. After a short pause and a muffled laugh, the voice continued, "Just don't give that no mind." Johnson had run into this type of thing before and quickly concluded that the inmate in Cell 390 was using a cell phone. Johnson approached the cell quietly and saw an inmate, Blake Henderson, lying on his bed with a blanket up next to his head. At the sight of Johnson, inmate Henderson pushed the blanket aside, stood up, and approached the cell bars.

After exchanging greetings, Johnson asked, "Do you have a cell phone?"

"Why do you say that?" Henderson responded.

"Because I heard your conversation. I know you weren't talking to your neighbors. They're sleeping. Where's the phone? You can either give it to me, or I'll round up the team and we'll toss your house," Johnson explained. After a little back and forth,

Henderson admitted to having a cell phone and gave it to Johnson. Henderson pleaded, "Please don't give me a ticket for this, man. Can you just say you found it stashed somewhere?"

Officer Johnson has to decide what to do. On the one hand, Henderson is in possession of contraband, and cell phones compromise prison security. Prison policy dictates that he write Henderson up. On the other hand, Henderson is widely considered to be a model inmate who keeps the younger, short-time inmates from wreaking havoc. Johnson benefits from Henderson's ability to control others and doesn't want to jeopardize losing his help in the future.

Critical Thinking

If you were in Johnson's situation, would you give Henderson a misconduct ticket? What problems might result if you decided not to? How else could Officer Johnson get respected inmates to help him maintain control of more-unruly prisoners?

Correctional officers must be careful not to pay too high a price for inmate cooperation (see "Do the Right Thing"). Under pressure to work effectively with prisoners, officers may be blackmailed into doing illegitimate favors in return for cooperation. When this happens, authority is surrendered to the inmates.

Inmate Leadership

In the traditional prison of the big-house era, administrators enlisted the inmate leaders to help maintain order. However, descriptions of the contemporary maximum-security prison raise questions about administrators' ability to run institutions in this way. When the racial, offense, and political characteristics of inmate populations of many prisons began to change in the mid-1960s, the centralized convict leadership structure was replaced by multiple centers of power. As official authority broke down, some institutions became violent, dangerous places.

Prisons seem to function more effectively now than they have in the past. Although prisons are more crowded, riots and reports of violence and escapes have declined.[20] In many prisons the inmate social system may have reorganized, so correctional officers can again work through prisoners who are respected by fellow inmates. Yet some observers contend that when wardens maintain order in this way, they enhance the positions of some prisoners at the expense of others. The leaders profit by receiving illicit privileges and favors, and they increase their influence among inmates by distributing benefits.

Discipline of Prisoners

Maintaining order can be burdensome to prison administrators. In an earlier era, prisoners were kept in line with corporal punishment. Today, withholding privileges, erasing good-time credits, and placing inmates in "the hole" (the adjustment center, or administrative segregation) constitute the range of punishments available to discipline the unruly. The Supreme Court has curbed administrators' discretion in applying these punishments: Procedural fairness must accompany the process by which inmates are sent to solitary confinement and in the method by which good-time credit can be lost because of misconduct.

On entering the prison, the newcomer receives a manual, often running up to a hundred pages, specifying the rules that govern almost all aspects of prison life, from permitted clothing to dining-room conduct and standards of personal hygiene. Prominently listed are types of behavior that can result in disciplinary action: rioting, gambling, sexual activity, possession of currency, failure to obey an order, and so on. Prisoners are warned that some rule infractions also violate the state's criminal law and may be handled by the criminal justice system. However, an institutional committee handles most inmate rule violations. This disciplinary committee may commit an inmate to administrative segregation for the number of days specified for each class of offense or hand down other sanctions. The manuals vary from state to state; some merely list violations and allow disciplinary committees to exercise their discretion when determining the appropriate punishment.

THE DISCIPLINARY PROCESS Custodial officers act like police officers with regard to most prison rules. Minor violations may warrant merely a verbal reprimand or warning, but more-serious violations can earn the prisoner a "ticket": a report forwarded to higher authority for action. Some corrections systems distinguish between major and minor violations. Major tickets go to the disciplinary committee; minor ones receive summary judgment by a hearing officer, whose decision may be appealed to a supervising captain, whose decision may, in turn, be appealed to the committee. In some systems all disciplinary reports go to a hearing officer, who investigates the charges, conducts the hearing, and determines the punishment. The commissioner of corrections can review hearing officers' decisions and reduce punishments but not increase them.

Most prisons have developed rules that specify some elements of due process in disciplinary proceedings. In many institutions a disciplinary committee receives charges, conducts hearings, and determines guilt and punishment. Normally, disciplinary committees comprise three to five members of the correctional staff, including representatives of custody, treatment, and classification, with a senior officer acting as chairperson. Sometimes the committees also include inmates or outside citizens.

Correctional officers conduct cell searches to find and confiscate contraband, such as weapons and drugs.

Lucy Nicholson/Reuters

As part of the procedure, the inmate is read the charge and is allowed to present his or her version of the incident and to present witnesses. In some institutions an inmate advocate may help the prisoner. If the inmate is found guilty, a sanction is imposed. The inmate can usually appeal the decision to the warden and ultimately to the commissioner. Even with these protections, prisoners may still feel powerless and fear further punishment if they challenge the disciplinary decisions of the warden too aggressively.

SANCTIONS Administrative segregation and loss of privileges and good time are the sanctions most often imposed for violating institutional rules. The privileges lost may include visits, mail, access to the commissary, and recreational periods.

The most severe sanction by a disciplinary committee is confinement in administrative segregation (sometimes called "solitary confinement"). Most institutions limit the amount of time that an inmate can spend in segregation and regulate conditions with respect to food, medical attention, and personal safety. Twenty days of continuous segregation is the maximum in many prisons, but inmates can be returned to "the hole" after a short period outside.

Maintaining order among prisoners is a challenge. Officers recognize they must walk a narrow line between being too restrictive and overly permissive. As well, they must recognize that their objective is to encourage cooperation and conformity to the rules. But they must also understand that rewards and punishments are limited and that courts now insist that due process be observed in disciplining and proceeding against violators. This presents a tall order, but with good management practices the objective can be reached.

Leadership: The Crucial Element of Governance

As Edwin H. Sutherland and Donald R. Cressey have observed, any prison is made up of the synchronized actions of hundreds of people, some of whom hate and distrust each other, love each other, fight each other physically and psychologically, think of each other as stupid or mentally disturbed, "manage" and "control" each other, and vie with each other for favors, prestige, power, and money.[21] Still, most prisons do not fall into disarray, although at times certain institutions have approached chaos. Many correctional facilities are well governed. How, then, does management ensure a reasonable quality of life in U.S. prisons?

Management styles vary, even in bureaucracies. In his study of prison management in California, Michigan, and Texas correctional facilities, John DiIulio argues that prisons should be run in a paramilitary fashion, with strict adherence to official rules, regulations, and policies.[22] Others note the value of alternative approaches. For example, Hans Toch argues that prison administrators should involve staff in problem-solving activities.[23] In his study of higher-custody state prisons, Michael Reisig found that flexible and adaptive managerial approaches are most effective at maintaining low levels of prison disorder.[24] Despite the controversy regarding which management style works best, the consensus among practitioners and researchers is that the quality of prison life is mainly a function of management quality.

Prison systems perform well if leaders can cope with the political and other pressures that contribute to administrative uncertainty and instability. In particular, management is successful when prison directors

1. Are in office long enough to learn the job, make plans, and implement them.
2. Project an appealing image to a wide range of people, both inside and outside the organization.
3. Are dedicated and loyal to the department, seeing themselves as engaged in a noble and challenging profession.
4. Are highly hands-on and proactive, paying close attention to details and not waiting for problems to arise. They must know what is going on inside yet also recognize the need for outside support. In short, they are strangers neither in the cell blocks nor in the aisles of the state legislature.[25]

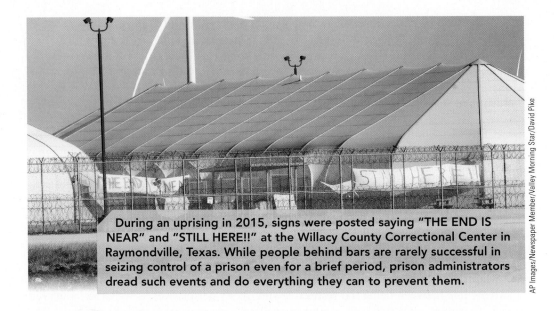

During an uprising in 2015, signs were posted saying "THE END IS NEAR" and "STILL HERE!!" at the Willacy County Correctional Center in Raymondville, Texas. While people behind bars are rarely successful in seizing control of a prison even for a brief period, prison administrators dread such events and do everything they can to prevent them.

AP Images/Newspaper Member/Valley Morning Star/David Pike

From this perspective, making prisons work is a function of administrative leadership and the application of sound management principles. DiIulio's research challenges the traditional assumption of many correctional administrators that "the cons run the joint." Rather, as the success of such legendary administrators as George Beto of Texas demonstrates, prisons can be managed so that inmates can serve their time in a safe, healthy, and productive environment.[26]

VIOLENCE IN PRISON

Prisons offer a perfect recipe for violence. They confine large numbers of men in cramped quarters, some of whom have histories of violent behavior. While incarcerated, these men are not allowed contact with women and live under highly restrictive conditions. Sometimes these conditions, coupled with the inability of administrators to respond to inmate needs, result in violence.

Violence and Inmate Characteristics

For the person entering prison for the first time, anxiety and fear of violence are especially high. Inmates who are victimized are significantly more likely than others to be depressed and experience symptoms associated with posttraumatic stress such as nightmares.[27] Even if a prisoner is not assaulted, the potential for violence permeates the environment of many prisons, adding to the stress and pains of incarceration. Assaults in our correctional institutions raise serious questions for administrators, criminal justice specialists, and the general public. What causes prison violence, and what can be done about it? We consider these questions when we examine the three main categories of prison violence: prisoner–prisoner, prisoner–officer, and officer–prisoner.

Prisoner–Prisoner Violence

Most prison violence occurs between inmates. Hans Toch observed that inmates are "terrorized by other inmates, and spend years in fear of harm. Some inmates request segregation, others lock themselves in, and some are hermits by choice."[28] The Bureau of Justice Statistics reports that the rate of prisoner–prisoner assault in U.S. prisons is 28 attacks per 1,000 inmates.[29] But official statistics likely do not reflect the true amount of prisoner–prisoner violence because many inmates who are assaulted do not make their victimization known to prison officials.

PRISON GANGS   Racial or ethnic gangs (also referred to as "security threat groups") are now linked to acts of violence in most prison systems. Gangs make it difficult for wardens to maintain control. By continuing their street wars inside prison, gangs cause some prisons to be more dangerous than any American neighborhood. Gangs are organized primarily to control an institution's drug, gambling, loan-sharking, prostitution, extortion, and debt-collection rackets. In addition, gangs protect their members from other gangs and instill a sense of macho camaraderie.

Contributing to prison violence is the "blood in, blood out" basis for gang membership: A would-be member must stab a gang's enemy to be admitted; once in, he cannot drop out without endangering his own life. Given the racial and ethnic foundation of gangs, violence between them can easily spill into the general prison population. Some institutions have programs that offer members a way out of gang life. These programs educate members and eventually encourage them to renounce their gang membership.

Prison gangs are often tightly organized and have even arranged the killing of opposition gang leaders housed in other institutions. Research has shown that prisons infested with gangs tend to experience the greatest number of inmate homicides.[30] Administrators say that prison gangs tend to pursue their "business" interests, yet they also contribute greatly to inmate–inmate violence as they discipline members, enforce orders, and retaliate against other gangs.

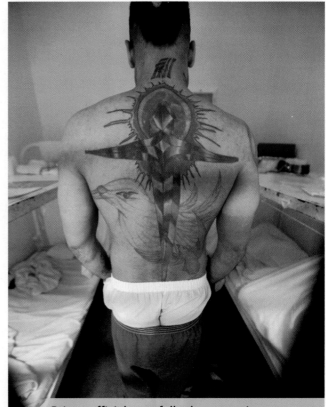

Prison officials carefully document inmate tattoos and use them to identify individuals who are affiliated with gangs or other security-threat groups. The presence of these groups has been linked to prison violence.

AP Images/Reed Saxon

The racial and ethnic basis of gang membership has been well documented in California. Beginning in the late 1960s, a Chicano gang—the Mexican Mafia, whose members had known one another in Los Angeles—took over the rackets in San Quentin. In reaction, other gangs were formed, including a rival Mexican gang, La Nuestra Familia; CRIPS (Common Revolution in Progress); the Texas Syndicate; the Black Guerrilla Family; and the Aryan Brotherhood. Gang conflict in California prisons became so serious in the 1970s that attempts were made to break up the gangs by dividing members among several institutions.

Administrators use a variety of strategies to weaken gang influence and to reduce violence. These strategies include identifying members, segregating housing and work assignments, restricting possession or display of gang symbols, strip searches, mail and telephone monitoring, and no-contact visits.[31] Some correctional departments transfer key gang members to other states in the hope of slowing or stopping a prison gang's activity, while others have set up intelligence units to gather information about gangs, particularly about illegal acts both in and outside of prison.

PROTECTIVE CUSTODY   For many victims of prison violence, protective custody is the only way to escape further abuse. Most prison systems have such a unit, along with units for disciplinary and administrative segregation. Inmates who seek protective custody may have been physically abused, have received sexual threats, have reputations as snitches, or fear assault by someone they crossed on the outside who is now a fellow inmate. Referred to as the "special management inmates," they pose problems for prison administrators, who must provide them with programs and services.

Life is not pleasant for these inmates. Often, their physical conditions, programs, and recreational opportunities are little better than those for inmates who are in administrative segregation because of misbehavior. Usually, they are let out of their cells only

MYTHS in Corrections

Sexual Victimization in State Prisons

THE MYTH: Because state prisons are filled with predatory, violent offenders who are deprived of heterosexual relationships, sexual violence happens with great regularity.

THE REALITY: Using data from the National Inmate Survey, 2011–2012, the Bureau of Justice Statistics reports that 1.7 percent of male prison inmates reported being sexually victimized by another inmate. The prevalence rate for a female prisoner is higher (6.9 percent).

Source: Allen J. Beck, Marcus Berzofsky, Rachel Casper, and Christopher Krebs, *Sexual Victimization in Prisons and Jails Reported by Inmates, 2011–12* (Washington, DC: U.S. Government Printing Office, 2013), 17.

briefly to exercise and shower. Their only stimulation is from books, radio, and television. Inmates who ask to "lock up" have little chance of returning to the general prison population without being viewed as a weakling—a snitch or a punk—to be preyed on. Even when administrators transfer such inmates to another institution, their reputations follow them through the grapevine.

PRISON RAPE Given how regularly violent sexual assaults are portrayed in the media, the public's belief that sexual assault is common in most U.S. prisons is not too surprising. Traditionally, there were no reliable national data on prison sexual violence. On September 4, 2003, the Prison Rape Elimination Act was signed into law. The law calls for the gathering of national statistics on prison rape, the development of guidelines, and the establishment of grants to help states address the problem (see "Myths in Corrections"). The Bureau of Justice Statistics reports that 2.6 percent of former state prisoners were the victims of nonconsensual sexual acts during their most recent period of incarceration. This translates into an estimated 18,700 former prisoners who have experienced nonconsensual sexual victimization. According to the report, 59.7 percent of nonconsensual sexual victimizations involved a weapon or threat of harm, 34.2 percent involved physically restraining the victim, and victims were either harmed or injured in 30 percent of incidents.[32] Other studies have found that victims tend to be the following:

- First-time, nonviolent offenders.
- Those convicted of a crime against a minor.
- Inmates who are physically weak.
- Prisoners who are viewed as effeminate.
- Offenders who are not affiliated with a gang.
- Those who are believed to have "snitched" on other prisoners.[33]

The Bureau of Justice Statistics also reports that most acts of prisoner–prisoner sexual violence involve a single victim (92 percent) and one perpetrator (90 percent). Incidents involving two or more perpetrators make up only 10 percent of known incidents of inmate-on-inmate sexual violence.[34]

Prisoner–Officer Violence

The mass media have focused on riots in which guards are taken hostage, injured, and killed. However, violence against officers typically occurs in specific situations and against certain individuals. Yearly, inmates assault approximately 18,000 prison staff members.[35] Correctional officers do not carry weapons within the institution because a prisoner could seize them. However, prisoners do manage to get lethal weapons and can use the element of surprise to injure an officer. In the course of a workday, an officer may encounter situations that require the use of physical force against an inmate—for instance, breaking up a fight or moving a prisoner to segregation. Because such situations are especially dangerous, officers may enlist others to help minimize the risk of violence. The officer's greatest fear is unexpected attacks. These may take the form of a missile thrown from an upper tier, verbal threats and taunts, or an officer's "accidental" fall down a flight of stairs. The need to remain constantly watchful against personal attacks adds stress and keeps many officers at a distance from the inmates.

Besides physical injury, an attack can compromise an officer's authority. After such an incident, administrators often have no alternative but to transfer the officer to tower duty.

Officer–Prisoner Violence

A fact of life in many institutions is unauthorized physical violence by officers against inmates. Stories abound of guards giving individual prisoners "the treatment" when supervisors are not looking. Many guards view physical force as an everyday, legitimate procedure. In some institutions, authorized "goon squads" comprising physically powerful officers use their muscle to maintain order.

Probably the worst cases of officer–prisoner violence in recent years occurred at the California State Prison at Corcoran. Between 1989 and 1995, 43 inmates were wounded and 7 killed by officers firing assault weapons—the most killings in any prison. Guards even instigated fights between rival gang members. During these "gladiator days," tower guards often shot the gang members after they had been ordered to stop fighting. Each shooting was justified by state-appointed reviewers.[36]

How do we tell when prison officers are using force legitimately and when they are using it to punish individual prisoners? Correctional officers are expected to follow departmental rules in their dealings with prisoners, but supervisors rarely observe staff–prisoner confrontations. Further, prisoner complaints about officer brutality are often not believed until the officer involved gains a reputation for harshness. Still, wardens may feel they must support their officers to retain, in turn, their officers' support. Levels of violence by officers against inmates are undoubtedly lower today than in years past. Nevertheless, officers are expected to enforce prison rules and may use force to uphold discipline and prevent escapes.

Decreasing Prison Violence

According to Lee H. Bowker, five factors contribute to prison violence: inadequate supervision by staff members, architectural design that promotes rather than inhibits victimization, the easy availability of deadly weapons, the housing of violence-prone prisoners near relatively defenseless people, and an overall high level of tension produced by close quarters.[37] The physical size and condition of the prison and the relations between inmates and staff also affect rates of violence.

THE EFFECT OF ARCHITECTURE AND SIZE Prison architectural design is thought to influence the amount of violence in an institution. Many prisons are not only large but also contain areas where inmates can avoid supervision. Much of the emphasis of the new-generation prisons—small housing units, clear sight lines, security corridors linking housing units—is designed to limit these opportunities and thus prevent violence. A recent study compared rates of violence in prisons with different architectural designs (see Chapter 6). The authors of the study found that violence directed toward other inmates and staff did not differ between prisons with the telephone-pole design and the facilities with the campus design. Property- and security-related forms of misconduct were significantly higher in the campus-style prison. The authors conclude that the telephone-pole design seems to deter some types of prisoner misconduct.[38]

The fortress-like prison certainly does not create an atmosphere for normal interpersonal relationships, and the size of the largest institutions can create management problems. The massive scale of the megaprison, which may hold up to 3,000 inmates, provides opportunities for aggressive inmates to hide weapons, dispense private "justice," and engage more or less freely in other illicit activities. Size may also result in some inmates "falling through the cracks," being misclassified and forced to live among more-violent offenders.[39]

The relationship between prison crowding and violence is unclear.[40] Some studies have shown that as personal space shrinks, the number of violent incidents rises. But crowding can be measured in several ways (for example, number of people per area, amount of space per person, amount of unshared space per person), and inmate perceptions of

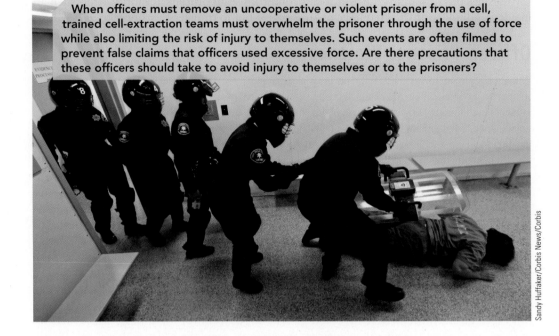

When officers must remove an uncooperative or violent prisoner from a cell, trained cell-extraction teams must overwhelm the prisoner through the use of force while also limiting the risk of injury to themselves. Such events are often filmed to prevent false claims that officers used excessive force. Are there precautions that these officers should take to avoid injury to themselves or to the prisoners?

crowding seem to depend on several factors, such as institutional experiences during incarceration. Clearly, increasing the size of an institution's population strains the limits of dining halls, athletic areas, education and treatment programs, medical care, and so forth. To maintain quality of life, prisons need increased resources to offset such strains. In some institutions the population has more than doubled without increases in violence. Good management seems to be a major factor in keeping conditions from deteriorating.

THE ROLE OF MANAGEMENT The degree to which inmate leaders are allowed to take matters into their own hands can affect the level of violence among inmates. When administrators run a tight ship, security measures prevent sexual attacks in dark corners, the making of "shivs" and "shanks" (knives) in the metal shop, and open conflict among inmate groups. In some states, officials use technology to detect weapons that may be smuggled into the facilities by visitors and those concealed by inmates. A prison must afford each inmate defensible space, and administrators need to ensure that every inmate remains secure, free from physical attack.

Effective prison management may decrease the level of violence by limiting opportunities for attacks. Wardens and correctional officers must therefore recognize the types of people under guard, the role of prison gangs, and the structure of institutions. John DiIulio argues that no group of inmates is "unmanageable [and] no combination of political, social, budgetary, architectural, or other factors makes good management impossible."[41] He points to such varied institutions as the California Men's Colony, New York City's Tombs and Rikers Island, the Federal Bureau of Prisons, and the Texas Department of Corrections. At these institutions, good management practices have resulted in prisons and jails where inmates can "do time" without fearing for their personal safety. Wardens exert leadership and manage their prisons effectively so that problems do not fester and erupt into violent confrontations.

Measures suggested to reduce violence are not always clear-cut or applicable to all situations. The following steps have been proposed:

1. Improve classification so that violence-prone inmates are separated from the general population.

2. For inmates fearful of being victimized, create opportunities to seek assistance from staff.

3. Increase the size, racial diversity, and training of the custody force.

4. Redesign facilities so that all areas can be put under surveillance; there should be no "blind spots." Use smaller institutions.

5. Install grievance mechanisms or an ombudsperson to help resolve interpersonal or institutional problems.

6. Augment the reward system to reduce the pains of imprisonment.

One administrative strategy that has helped bring order to violence-marked institutions is **unit management**. This approach divides a prison into many small, self-contained "institutions" operating in semi-autonomous fashion within the confines of a larger facility. Each of the units houses between 50 and 100 inmates, who remain together as long as release dates allow and who are supervised by a team of correctional officers, counselors, and treatment specialists. The assumption is that by keeping the units small, staff will get to know the inmates better and recognize problems early on, and group cohesion will emerge. Further, because the unit manager has both authority and accountability, policies will presumably be enforced consistently and fairly. The unit-management approach to violence reduction has proved successful in several state and federal institutions.

In sum, prisons must be made safe places. Because the state puts offenders there, it has a responsibility to prevent violence and maintain order. To eliminate violence from prisons, officials may have to limit movement within the institution, contacts with the outside, and the right to choose one's associates. Yet these measures may run counter to the goal of producing men and women who will be responsible citizens when they return to society.

unit management
Tactic for reducing prison violence by dividing facilities into small, self-contained, semi-autonomous "institutions."

Summary

1 Be familiar with the principles used to organize the functioning of prisons.

Prisons are bureaucracies. Accordingly, three organizational principles help explain how they function. Supervision of subordinates follows the principle of unity of command—the idea that employees report to only one superior. Order and directives are issued from the administrative staff and are passed down to lower-ranking staff. This process reflects the different positions of authority among the prison staff, reflecting the chain of command principle. Finally, the span of control principle refers to staff members' ability to supervise only a limited number of subordinates.

2 Be familiar with the different groups of personnel in U.S. prisons.

The institutional managers, consisting of the warden and her or his deputy wardens, are responsible for managing the prison. The warden maintains contact with the world beyond the prison walls (the central office, parole board, legislature), and the deputy wardens oversee a variety of bureaucratic functions (buying supplies, keeping the buildings and grounds, providing food, maintaining records). Officers who make up the custodial force have different ranks (captain, lieutenant, officer). Their performance on the job is judged by how well they manage inmates. Program personnel are responsible for running the educational, vocational, and treatment programs at the prison. Industrial and agricultural activities at the prison are overseen by supervisors. These individuals work outside the custodial hierarchy.

3 Discuss the importance of prison governance.

Prison governance refers to the sound and firm management of inmates and staff. Effective governance is challenging for correctional administrators because the power that officers possess to control inmates is limited, officers have few legitimate rewards to provide inmates for good behavior, and available punishments do not represent much of a departure from the inmates' daily routines. Correctional administrators who successfully govern their institutions do not rely on inmate leadership to control the population, but rather apply sound management principles to prison operations.

4 Explain the different types of prison violence.

The most common type of prison violence involves one inmate attacking another inmate (prisoner–prisoner violence). However, the true extent of this type of violence is unknown because many incidents do not come to the attention of prison officials. In comparison, prisoner–officer violence is less common. Examples of this type of violence include physical assaults, thrown objects, and verbal threats. Officer–prisoner violence is tightly regulated. However, officers are allowed to use necessary levels of physical force in certain situations, such as when attempting to break up a fight between inmates. Instances of inmate abuse by officers sometimes come to the attention of the general public, but such occurrences are undoubtedly less frequent today than in years past.

Key Terms

administrative control theory 203
chain of command 196
coercive power 195
compliance 195
formal organization 195

inmate balance theory 203
line personnel 197
normative power 195
remunerative power 195
span of control 197

staff personnel 197
unit management 215
unity of command 196

For Discussion

1. If you were a prison warden, what sorts of management problems should you expect to face? How would you go about solving them?
2. Would you like to be a correctional officer? What aspects of the job make it attractive? What aspects of the job would you find stressful?
3. How is the idea of total power in the prison setting defective? What steps can be taken to maximize the power of correctional officers?
4. If you were the warden of a maximum-security prison for men, what policies would you adopt to prevent violence in the institution?

Notes

[1] Catie O'Toole, "Auburn Correctional Facility Inmates Attack Officers, Initiate Weeklong Lockdown," *Syracuse.com*, www.syracuse.com/crime/index.ssf/2015/03/auburn_correctional_facility_inmates_attack_officers_initiate_week-long_lockdown.html, March 9, 2015.

[2] Amitai Etzioni, *A Comparative Analysis of Complex Organizations* (New York: Free Press, 1961), 3.

[3] Ibid., pp. 5–7, 27.

[4] Charles Logan, "Criminal Justice Performance Measures for Prisons," in *Performance Measures for the Criminal Justice System* (Washington, DC: U.S. Government Printing Office, 1993), 23.

[5] Ibid., pp. 27–28.

[6] U.S. President's Commission on Law Enforcement and Administration of Justice, *Task Force Report: Corrections* (Washington, DC: U.S. Government Printing Office, 1967), 19–57.

[7] Lucien X. Lombardo, "Alleviating Inmate Stress: Contributions from Correctional Officers," in *The Pains of Imprisonment*, edited by Robert Johnson and Hans Toch (Prospect Heights, IL: Waveland, 1988), 285–97.

[8] Donald Clemmer, *The Prison Community* (Boston: Christopher, 1940); Gresham M. Sykes, *The Society of Captives* (Princeton, NJ: Princeton University Press, 1958).

[9] Bert Useem and Michael D. Reisig, "Collective Action in Prisons: Protests, Disturbances, and Riots," *Criminology* 37 (November 1999): 735–60.

[10] John J. DiIulio, *Governing Prisons* (New York: Free Press, 1987), 13.

[11] Ibid.; Bert Useem and Peter A. Kimball, *States of Siege: U.S. Prison Riots, 1971–1986* (New York: Oxford University Press, 1989).

[12] Useem and Reisig, "Collective Action in Prisons," p. 735.

[13] Ibid., p. 737.

[14] DiIulio, *Governing Prisons*, p. 12.

[15] Sykes, *Society of Captives*, p. 41.

[16] Ibid., p. 49.

[17] James J. Stephan, *Census of State and Federal Correctional Facilities, 2005* (Washington, DC: U.S. Government Printing Office, 2008), 5.

[18] James Marquart, "Prison Guards and the Use of Physical Coercion as a Mechanism of Prisoner Control," *Criminology* 24 (1986): 347–66.

[19] Stan Stojkovic, "Accounts of Prison Work: Corrections Officers' Portrayals of Their Work Worlds," *Perspectives on Social Problems* 2 (1990): 223.

[20] Burt Useem and Ann M. Piehl, "Prison Buildup and Disorder," *Punishment & Society* 8 (2006): 87–115.

[21] Edwin H. Sutherland and Donald R. Cressey, *Criminology* (Philadelphia: Lippincott, 1970), 536.

[22] DiIulio, *Governing Prisons*, p. 237.

[23] Hans Toch, "Trends in Correctional Leadership," *Corrections Compendium* 27 (November 2002): 8–9, 23–25.

[24] Michael D. Reisig, "Rates of Disorder in Higher-Custody State Prisons: A Comparative Analysis of Managerial Practices," *Crime & Delinquency* 44 (April 1998): 229–44.

[25] DiIulio, *Governing Prisons,* p. 242.

[26] John J. DiIulio, *No Escape: The Future of American Corrections* (New York: Basic, 1991), ch. 1.

[27] Andy Hochstetler, Daniel S. Murphy, and Ronald L. Simons, "Damaged Goods: Exploring Predictors of Distress in Prison Inmates," *Crime & Delinquency* 50 (July 2004): 436–57.

[28] Hans Toch, *Peacekeeping: Police, Prisons, and Violence* (Lexington, MA: Lexington, 1976), 47–48.

[29] James J. Stephan and Jennifer C. Karberg, *Census of State and Federal Correctional Facilities, 2000* (Washington, DC: U.S. Government Printing Office, 2003), 10.

[30] Michael D. Reisig, "Administrative Control and Inmate Homicide," *Homicide Studies* 6 (February 2002): 84–103.

[31] Gary Hill, "Gangs Inside Prison Walls Around the World," *Corrections Compendium* 29 (January–February 2004): 26; Chad Trulson, James W. Marquart, and Soraya K. Kawucha, "Gang Suppression and Institutional Control," *Corrections Today* 68 (April 2006): 26–31.

[32] Allen J. Beck and Candace Johnson, *Sexual Victimization Reported by Former State Prisoners, 2008* (Washington, DC: U.S. Government Printing Office, 2012).

[33] Kim English and Peggy Heil, "Prison Rape: What We Know Today," *Corrections Compendium* 30 (September–October 2005): 2.

[34] Allen J. Beck, Paige M. Harrison, and Devon B. Adams, *Sexual Violence Reported by Correctional Authorities, 2006* (Washington, DC: U.S. Government Printing Office, 2007).

[35] Stephan and Karberg, *Census of State and Federal Correctional Facilities, 2000,* p. 10.

[36] Mark Arax and Mark Gladstone, "State Thwarted Brutality Probe in Corcoran Prison, Investigators Say," *Los Angeles Times,* July 5, 1998, p. 1.

[37] Lee H. Bowker, "Victimizers and Victims in American Correctional Institutions," in *Pains of Imprisonment*, edited by Robert Johnson and Hans Toch (Beverly Hills, CA: Sage, 1982), 64.

[38] Robert G. Morris and John Worrall, "Prison Architecture and Inmate Misconduct: A Multilevel Assessment," *Crime & Delinquency* 60 (October 2014): 1083–109.

[39] Anthony E. Bottoms, "Interpersonal Violence and Social Order in Prisons," in *Crime and Justice: An Annual Review of Research*, vol. 26, edited by Michael Tonry and Joan Petersilia (Chicago: University of Chicago Press, 1999), 205–81.

[40] Travis W. Franklin, Cortney A. Franklin, and Travis C. Pratt, "Examining the Empirical Relationship Between Prison Crowding and Inmate Misconduct: A Meta-Analysis of Conflicting Research Results," *Journal of Criminal Justice* 34 (July–August 2006): 401–12.

[41] DiIulio, *No Escape,* p. 12.

9

Special Populations

White fuzz covers his bald head. His sallow skin sags. A wheelchair and cane support his limp legs. This is not the typical image of a prison inmate. But 73-year-old George Sanges is among the burgeoning elderly population behind bars, a group expected to continue to grow as baby boomers age and states implement longer sentences. Sanges, who is serving a 15-year sentence at Men's State Prison in Georgia, has cerebral palsy and takes multiple medications twice a day. His condition has worsened since he

entered prison in 2005 for aggravated assault against his wife of 48 years. Twice while in prison, he was rushed to the hospital for heart problems.

Georgia, with one of the 10 largest prison systems in the country, spends about $8,500 on medical costs for inmates over 65, compared with about an average of $950 for those who are younger. Nationally, inmate medical care costs about $3 billion per year.

Men's State Prison holds the largest number of sickly, elderly inmates in

After reading this chapter you should be able to . . .

1 Understand how the incarceration of elderly prisoners impacts health care costs, correctional programs, and the physical environment of this special population.

2 Identify the complexities involved with the correctional management of inmates who are HIV-infected or who have been diagnosed with AIDS.

3 Analyze how changes in public policy unintentionally have affected the current state of the incarcerated mentally ill.

4 Discuss the implications of long-term sentences for prisoners who must serve them and the responsibility of correctional administrators to offer opportunities for meaningful engagement to this population.

5 Recognize the obligation confronting correctional administrators to meet the needs of incarcerated sexual-minority offenders and understand the emerging case law that is impacting corrections management.

6 Describe the condition of military veterans who are currently involved in the correctional system and the types of specialized programs developed to address their needs.

Andrew Burton/Getty Images News/Getty Images

As a result of longer prison sentences, the proportion of prisoners who are elderly is growing rapidly. The aging prison population poses programming challenges for the correctional system.

Georgia. The medium-security facility, in a quaint rural town, is enclosed by barbed wire just like any other prison. Every inmate here has a medical condition; dementia, hypertension, and diabetes are the most common. Rather than shooting hoops or lifting weights, inmates play card games and checkers. Gang fights are rare, though there are still bickering and catfights from the wheelchair set. Diapers, breathing machines, and hospital beds wrapped in plastic for easy cleanup are visible in almost

(continued from previous page)

every corner of the hostel-style room where prisoners sleep.

Some states allow for the early release of elderly inmates who suffer from serious medical problems. Such early-release policies—referred to as compassionate release, medical clemency, or geriatric release—help to relieve the increasing medical costs caused by the continued incarceration of aging prisoners.

But critics, including victims' advocacy groups, have criticized these policies. They contend that elderly offenders, whether ill or not, are still able to strike again after they are released. Still proponents of early release contend that these actions are reasonable, as this problem is partially caused by stiff sentencing policies such as "three-strikes" and other mandatory minimum sentence laws.[1] ■

THE CHALLENGE OF SPECIAL POPULATIONS IN CORRECTIONS

Over the last several decades, six factors have significantly affected life inside adult prisons: the increased number of elderly inmates, the sizable number of inmates with HIV/AIDS, the thousands of prisoners who are mentally ill, the growing number of long-term prisoners, the complex emerging correctional policies required to address the needs of incarcerated sexual minorities, and the recent recognition of the hardships of incarcerated military veterans. These expanding categories of special populations have very real consequences for correctional staff, correctional management, and inmate society. While correctional staffs have greater familiarity with addressing the needs of aging prisoners and those who are HIV-infected or living with AIDS, the problems of mentally ill inmates and those of sexual-minority inmates are particularly challenging in an age of dwindling fiscal resources and limited understanding of gender variation. In addition, the recent spotlight on military veterans involved in crime and the criminal justice system reveals a new area of public-policy blind spots that must be addressed. This chapter reviews six special populations that affect adult corrections, noting the pressures they present because of their differences from typical correctional populations and because of their growing numbers.

ELDERLY PRISONERS

Although older prisoners still make up a small proportion of the total inmate population, their numbers continue to rise. Analysis of Bureau of Justice Statistics data found that the male prison population over age 55 ballooned 28 percent, from 89,000 in

2007 to 114,700 in 2011. The definition of *elderly* varies by state, with most states defining inmates over 55 as elderly but some placing inmates over 50 in that category.

A 50-year-old is not normally recognized as elderly. However, since 1992 the National Institute of Corrections has recommended that correctional agencies use age 50 to define the older or elderly inmate.[2] But why age 50? This is partially because those who are more likely to be involved in crime and therefore stand a greater chance of incarceration are also likely to be from disadvantaged households and communities. And it is well-known that there is a direct relationship between socioeconomic status and morbidity. In other words, criminals ensnared in the criminal justice system tend to be less healthy than noncriminals. In addition, incarceration itself accelerates health problems because of the very nature of the prison experience. Prisons house a high concentration of persons with poor health conditions in a stress-filled environment. Therefore, a 50-year-old prisoner may present medical problems more often found in older individuals or geriatric patients. **Geriatric offenders** pose a challenge for corrections because they have special needs regarding housing, medical care, programs, and release.

geriatric offenders
Aging or elderly offenders who may require specialized treatment related to the aging process while under correctional supervision.

Housing

Correctional facilities are extremely costly to build and to operate. Maximum use of available space is therefore a priority. This is one reason why specialized housing is less attractive to correctional administrators. So for the majority of correctional facilities, segregated or separate housing for elderly inmates is not provided. Administrators believe that as much as possible, the elderly should remain in the general population but with special accommodations. These accommodations can range from assigning older inmates to a bottom bunk to housing them in a separate wing with grab bars and in-cell showers. Still, whether or not to segregate elderly inmates from the general population is not a settled issue. There are arguments that support separate housing. Noting that elderly inmates could be attractive targets to younger, tougher, and more predatory inmates, removing this potential problem area would be beneficial. Also in support of separate housing are studies indicating that elderly inmates establish social relationships more easily with their own peer group and that they would feel safer in a segregated housing situation.[3] Providing treatment and other programs for older inmates avoids having their needs neglected because of officials' greater focus on dealing with members of the general population, who present a more serious issue for public safety upon release. Moreover, because of mobility issues, elderly inmates are less able to participate in programs and activities designed for the general population and therefore at a disadvantage. However, the central argument against separate housing is the loss of the older inmate as a possible calming influence on a younger, more unpredictable general population.

Some states have specialized facilities for frail inmates and those with physical or mental disabilities.[4] These facilities are used to protect elderly inmates from younger prisoners. Some states, such as Virginia and Pennsylvania, have built geriatric prison facilities that resemble mini-hospitals, equipped with medical devices and staffed with registered nurses. Currently, 18 states have developed separate units for elderly inmates.[5] The Ohio corrections system has six such facilities, the largest of which is the Hocking Correctional Facility. Here, preparing the elderly offender for release includes education on the social and psychological aspects of getting older, training on managing emerging physical limitations, and information on applying for Social Security benefits and other programs for senior citizens.

Medical Care

The results from a national health survey found that chronic diseases such as diabetes, hypertension, and asthma, as well as substance abuse and mental illness, are more prevalent among those incarcerated in U.S. jails and state and federal correctional facilities

One-third of all inmates are over 50 years old. As courts have given longer sentences and parole has been tightened, more and more prisoners can expect to die while incarcerated. Seventy-five prisons now have hospice programs where palliative care is given. In many facilities, inmate volunteers tend dying comrades.

Andrew Burton/Getty Images News/Getty Images

than among their nonincarcerated peers.[6] Elderly inmates are more likely to require medical care for chronic illnesses such as heart disease, stroke, and cancer. The cost of caring for an elderly inmate is much higher than for a younger prisoner. America's aging prisoner population has no doubt contributed to rising health care costs. The health survey also reported that approximately 20 percent of state inmates and more than 65 percent of jail inmates with chronic health problems had not received appropriate medical follow-up since incarceration. Their health problems are certainly compounded by the aging process.

Also added to the health concerns for the elderly inmate is accompanying **brain disease** such as dementia, Alzheimer's, and Parkinson's, and eventually the need for hospice care. Nevertheless, prisons and prison staff are not adequately equipped to respond to these health issues and far less so as the numbers of elderly inmates developing these conditions increase in number. Ironically, while an offender is in prison, his or her life may be prolonged and medical care may be better than if he or she were discharged back to a disadvantaged community. To care for dying patients, 75 hospice programs exist in prisons—up from fewer than 10 a decade ago.

brain disease
An abnormal condition of the brain caused by injury, disease, or aging.

Programs

The arrangement of prison housing has practical concerns that could affect inmate participation in programs and other activities. Correctional authorities strictly arrange the orderly and safe movement of inmates throughout the prison facility. Second to safe movements is the provision of correctional programs. Exercise regimens designed to keep elderly inmates active can contribute to overall health. Other activities, such as work assignments and rehabilitative programs, are tailored to fit the physical and mental abilities of the elderly. However, when elderly prisoners reside in segregated housing areas, their ability to participate in available programs may be compromised, restricted, or impossible if custody personnel are unable to accommodate additional prison movements.

More prisons in the United States are providing specialized programs designed for this population. The Northern Nevada Correctional Center, located in Carson City, Nevada, provides the Senior Structured Living Program, also referred to as "True Grit."[7]

Program participants must be at least 60 years of age. The primary objective of the program is to meet the physical, psychological, and spiritual needs of aging inmates. True Grit offers a variety of daily activities, such as interaction with therapy dogs, arts and crafts, and inmate-run theater productions. The staff has reported favorable outcomes that are especially significant for aging inmates: decreases in the use of psychotropic medications as well as infirmary visits, fewer accounts of depression, and less fear of dying alone. Participation in such programs helps increase feelings of self-worth and helps elderly prisoners think ahead toward their release date and beyond.

Release

Elderly inmates have unique prison experiences that stem from aging and other related developments such as deteriorating health (both mental and physical); as a result, preparing for release should address these issues. Preparation for release of the elderly requires time and special efforts by correctional staff. These efforts may include dealing with multiple governmental and social service agencies to ensure that Social Security and Medicare benefits will be available to the inmates upon release and that medical care will continue. Staff must be proactive to ensure that those who are eligible for release do not stay in prison simply because there is no other place for them to go. Aging in prison challenges the ability to maintain important family relationships and ties to one's community, which are key to release plans.[8] Friends and family are also aging and perhaps dying while the elderly inmate is serving time. Potential support systems may be reluctant to take in an elderly ex-offender who brings more burdens to a financially strapped family.

These losses are particularly exacerbated in a dynamic society that continues to evolve and become less familiar to the long-term offender. This particular aspect of loss and uncertainty is depicted by the character Brooks Hatlen in the popular 1994 film *Shawshank Redemption*. After having served 50 years, Brooks is paroled to a world that is now *alien* to him. He becomes distraught, lonely, and depressed; after determining that he'd rather not live in this world, he hangs himself. **Adapting to change** is critical for these individuals who must be prepared to be self-reliant and to live independently in a community that has changed dramatically. Poor health in the context of a fading support system heightens the difficulty of release. In fact, some studies report that chronically ill elderly inmates are dependent upon the health care provided during incarceration and are reluctant to leave it for the uncertainty that awaits them on the outside.[9]

As people get older, they become less dangerous. But not all elderly prisoners are the same. Some elderly inmates are first-time offenders who committed their crime after age 50. Others are habitual criminals who have been in and out of prison most of their lives. Finally, some received long sentences and aged in prison. Prisoner advocates argue that not all elderly prisoners should remain incarcerated for the rest of their lives. The Project for Older Prisoners (POPS) aims at removing low-risk geriatric inmates from overcrowded prisons. It involves a thorough examination of the risk of recidivism for those under consideration for early or **compassionate release**. If an inmate is determined to be at low risk, the program then locates housing, relevant Social Security information, employment situations, medical assistance, and other social services to aid reentry. All of this information is then presented to the court for consideration.[10] If release is achieved, POPS will continue assisting the offender as he or she transitions and adjusts to the community. The Federal Bureau of Prisons also has compassionate release procedures that may be applied under different circumstances to elderly inmates.[11] For example, inmates age 70 or older who have served a substantial amount of time and are determined not to be a threat to the public may be eligible for a sentence reduction. Or if an elderly inmate at age 65 has a chronic medical condition that restricts his or her ability to function in prison and has served a substantial part of the sentence, he or she may be considered for early release.

Many states have enacted policies that permit the release of elderly inmates who meet the criteria for early or compassionate release. Such policies are also referred to

adapting to change
The ability to adjust or to adapt to new and unfamiliar conditions in one's environment.

compassionate release
An option for the early release of an elderly prisoner who is deemed to be of low risk of recidivism.

focus on correctional policy

Geriatric Release Laws

At the end of 2009, 15 states and the District of Columbia had provisions for geriatric release. However, the jurisdictions rarely use these provisions.

Four factors help explain the difference between the stated intent and the actual impact of geriatric release laws: political considerations and public opinion, narrow eligibility criteria, procedures that discourage inmates from applying for release, and complicated and lengthy referral and review processes.

The Vera Institute of Justice offers recommendations for responding to the disparities between geriatric release policies and practice, including the following:

1. States that look to geriatric release as a cost-saving measure . . . should review the release process to address potential and existing obstacles.

2. More analysis is needed to accurately estimate overall cost savings to taxpayers, not just costs shifted from departments of corrections to other agencies.

3. More-effective monitoring, reporting, and evaluation mechanisms can improve assessments of the policies' impact.

4. Creative strategies allowing older individuals to complete their sentences in the community should be piloted and evaluated.

5. Finally, to protect public safety, states should consider developing relevant risk assessment and needs assessment instruments, as well as reentry programs and supervision plans, for elderly people who are released from prison.[12]

Critical Thinking

Given the apparent reluctance to release elderly inmates because of age or infirmities, how might correctional authorities use risk assessment instruments to determine the likelihood of danger or recidivism with this correctional population?

---

as geriatric release laws. (See "Focus on Correctional Policy: Geriatric Release Laws.") The only alternative to releasing elderly prisoners seems to be an ever-larger population of them living in prison geriatric wards.

However, those states with geriatric release provisions are reluctant to use them. Releasing offenders, even elderly ones, always involves some political risk. Some of

HIV testing is now done on every person sentenced to prison or jail. These Cook County detainees prepare their HIV blood tests for evaluation. People who test positive receive special medical and security care.

Tim Boyle/Getty Images News/Getty Images

the parole conditions prescribed demonstrate this concern. For example, periodic medical exams may be required, but should the offender's physical condition actually improve following release, automatic revocation proceedings could be triggered.[13] Managing elderly prisoners will continue to present real challenges until policy makers address correctional health care demands and costs, provide sufficient staff training and resources, and tackle public safety questions regarding this growing correctional population.

PRISONERS WITH HIV/AIDS

Correctional officials must cope with the problem of HIV—the human immunodeficiency virus that causes **AIDS**—as well as AIDS and related health issues. At year-end 2010, 20,093 state and federal inmates were either infected with HIV or had AIDS. The rate of confirmed AIDS cases in state and federal prisons is 2.5 times the rate in the total U.S. population. The rate of infection among inmates can be explained by prisoners' high-risk behaviors, such as intravenous drug use, needle sharing, and unprotected sex. In 2010, 72 AIDS-related deaths were reported in state and federal prisons.[14] AIDS is the second-leading cause of death in state prisons, behind "natural causes."[15] (See "Focus on Correctional Technology: Testing for HIV.")

Homosexual activity among men is one way that HIV is transmitted in prison populations. Although such behavior is forbidden, many inmates engage in this behavior at one time or another during their sentence. Rates of HIV infection are higher among

AIDS
A medical condition that occurs when the human immunodeficiency virus (HIV) causes a defect in the immune system's ability to function. It increases susceptibility to serious and life-threatening infections, and is transmitted primarily by exposure to contaminated body fluids, especially blood and semen.

focus on correctional technology

Testing for HIV

Although HIV testing services vary among prisons, they usually fall into one of the following categories:

- Compulsory testing—where all inmates are required to have an HIV test;
- Optional testing—where a testing service is offered and inmates can decide whether to have a test; or
- No testing—unless prisoners specifically request to be tested.

A study of Rhode Island prisons affirms the prevention value of routinely screening all inmates for HIV. The Adult Correctional Institutions (ACI) in Rhode Island uses a blood test whose results are returned in about one to two weeks. But the study reported that 43 percent of inmates are released in seven or fewer days.

"So you have almost half of the [newly diagnosed patients] gone within a week. That suggested these individuals likely didn't receive their HIV-positive test results," stated Curt Beckwith, the study's principal investigator. "They don't know they are infected. They may be transmitting the virus unknowingly."

A rapid HIV test . . . delivers reliable results in minutes. It allows prison staff to deliver the results almost immediately and to provide inmates with medical advice and counseling.

Beckwith said a conventional test costs about $10 while a rapid test costs only a couple of dollars more. But a few dollars can add up. . . .

Critical Thinking

Institutional correctional administrators must provide a safe and orderly environment for offenders under their care. For those offenders found to be HIV-positive during incarceration, correctional staff inform them of these test results and provide medical counseling. Do correctional administrators have any obligation to notify offenders who were released before the positive test results were discovered? Why or why not?

Source: Adapted from "Prevention Value of HIV Testing of Inmates Shown," *Providence Journal*, www.cdcnpin.org/scripts/display/NewsDisplay.asp?NewsNbr=55651.

female prisoners (1.9 percent) than male prisoners (1.5 percent).[16] Research shows that childhood sexual abuse is linked to HIV/AIDS risk-taking behavior among female prisoners.[17] Their vulnerability of HIV infection appears to be higher prior to rather than during incarceration.

To deal with HIV/AIDS, prison officials have developed a variety of policies. However, their administration is complicated by a host of legal, political, medical, budgetary, and attitudinal factors as officials decide what actions their institutions should take. Policies concerning separate housing for HIV-infected inmates are controversial. (See "Do the Right Thing.")

While there are those who argue against segregating HIV-infected inmates, still others support it. A report on HIV policy in South Africa and other nations[18] notes that some European and South African correctional authorities see advantages in segregation, including the following: (1) prison violence decreases because other inmates no longer threaten and target HIV-infected inmates, (2) HIV-infected inmates have a compromised immune system and benefit from removal from the general population, (3) additional health care staff and greater access to correctional programs become more and not less available to this population, (4) living accommodations tend to be better—less crowded with more living space—and (5) inmates receive more staff support and specialized care.[19] Still, it appears that segregation policies are falling more by the wayside. (See "Focus on Correctional Practice: Housing HIV-Positive Inmates.")

Correctional officials must also provide a safe working environment for staff. Therapists, academic teachers, vocational instructors, clergy, and social workers are

DO the Right Thing

The policy directive was precise: All inmates will be tested for HIV. All inmates found to be positive will be placed in Wing A, regardless of their physical condition, conviction offense, or time remaining in their sentence.

Testing for the deadly virus began at Elmwood State Prison soon after Warden True's directive was posted. All 753 inmates were tested over a three-week period, and every new prisoner, before entering the institution, had blood drawn at the medical unit for testing.

Six weeks after the directive was posted, the results were known. Most of the inmates breathed a sigh of relief in learning they were not positive. For a few, however, the call to report to the doctor was a prelude to the possibility of a medical death sentence. The news that they had tested positive was traumatic. Most cursed, others burst into tears, and still others sat in stunned silence.

The new policy was leaked to the press. The state chapter of the American Civil Liberties Union and the Howard Association for Prisoners' Rights called for a meeting with Warden True. In a press conference, they protested the "state's invasion of privacy" and

the "discriminatory segregation of gays and drug users, most of the latter being African American and Hispanic." They emphasized that because it would be years before most of the infected would develop a "full" case of AIDS, correctional officials should respond with compassion, not stigmatization.

Warden True told reporters that he was responsible for the health of all inmates and that the policy had been developed to prevent transmission of the disease. He also said that although the HIV inmates would be segregated, they would have access to all facilities available to the general inmate population but at separate times. He denied that he intended to stigmatize the 20 prisoners who had thus far tested positive.

Critical Thinking

1. What do you suppose that Warden True considered in developing this policy?

2. Is the policy likely to cause harm or good?

3. Is it ethical to segregate a segment of the prison population?

periodically exposed to HIV-positive and AIDS-infected inmates. Correctional officers in particular are even more vulnerable than other staff as they are frequently required to break up fights that occur between inmates or to physically handle inmates who are violently resisting being transported from one area of the prison to another—especially for disciplinary reasons. Although there is always the possibility of exposure to blood or other bodily fluids of an infected prisoner, the chances of virus transmission are reportedly low.[20] Nevertheless, as recommended by the National Institute for Occupational Safety and Health (NIOSH), correctional staff should be provided suitable information and training on universal or standard precautions and protocol for postexposure treatment. Correctional administrators are cautious about the control of HIV and other related diseases, and some, but not all, observe restrictive practices. (See "Myths in Corrections.")

MYTHS in Corrections

HIV Testing in Prisons

THE MYTH: Because it is commonly recognized that prisons house significant numbers of HIV-infected persons due to the high-risk behaviors practiced by some offenders, medical testing and treatment for HIV are standard procedure in all U.S. prisons.

THE REALITY: Less than half of prison systems and few jails in the United States routinely provide HIV testing at time of entry. Therefore, it is probable that many inmates who may be infected are not detected in a correctional setting. Each year, approximately 7.5 million inmates are released back into their communities, to their families, and to intimate partners.[21]

focus on correctional practice

Housing HIV-Positive Inmates

Earlier this year [2010], the Mississippi Department of Corrections (MDOC) agreed to end the segregation of prisoners with HIV. The decision by Mississippi's corrections commissioner, Christopher Epps, . . . leaves Alabama and South Carolina as the only states in the nation that segregate prisoners based on their HIV status. Epps made the decision ahead of a forthcoming report by the ACLU and Human Rights Watch analyzing the harmful impact that segregation policies have had in the three states. As Margaret Winter, associate director of the ACLU National Prison Project, stated, "The remaining segregation policies in South Carolina and Alabama are a remnant of the early days of the HIV epidemic and continue to stigmatize prisoners and inflict them and their families with a tremendous amount of needless suffering."

Public and correctional health experts agree that there is no medical basis for segregating HIV-positive prisoners within correctional facilities or for limiting access to jobs, vocational training, and educational programs available to others. Since 1987, however, MDOC has performed mandatory HIV tests on all prisoners entering the state prison system, and it has permanently housed all male prisoners who test positive in a segregated unit

at the Mississippi State Penitentiary, the state's highest-security prison. As a result, prisoners with HIV have been faced with unjustified isolation, exclusion, and marginalization, and low-custody prisoners have been forced unnecessarily to serve their sentences in more-violent, more-expensive prisons.

Epps said he will phase in the new desegregation policy gradually for prisoners currently housed in the HIV unit and will form a committee to make individualized placement decisions for these prisoners. Starting immediately, incoming prisoners will be housed using only criteria set out in the state classification plan such as criminal history, length of sentence, and other factors unrelated to their HIV status.[22]

Critical Thinking

For correctional officers, what are some of the advantages and disadvantages of segregated housing for inmates with HIV/AIDS?

Source: Adapted from Human Rights Watch, "Mississippi Stops Segregating Prisoners with HIV," www.hrw.org/news/2010/03/17/mississippi-stops-segregating-prisoners-hiv, March 17, 2010.

This correctional psychiatric unit in Tacoma, Washington, must be a very lonely place for a person suffering from mental illness. Nationally, more than half of the people who are incarcerated report symptoms of mental illness.

AP Images/Elaine Thompson, File

MENTALLY ILL PRISONERS

After the deinstitutionalization movement of the 1960s, which emphasized the depopulation of large-scale mental hospitals,[23] jails and prisons began to see increasing numbers of the mentally ill within their confines.[24] Ironically, deinstitutionalization was undertaken to remove the mentally ill from the often inhumane and ineffective treatment practices occurring in state hospitals in the United States. Social reformers argued that the mentally ill should be treated in the least restrictive setting so as to further dignity, self-determination, and autonomy.[25] A community setting, one in which the mentally ill had some connection, was preferred. On October 31, 1963, President John F. Kennedy signed into law the **Community Mental Health Act**. The purpose of the law was to fund the construction of community-based mental health centers throughout the country and to better provide mental health services. But the decentralized local structure of community mental health was perhaps ill-equipped to deal with the increasing problem of mental illness.

Community Mental Health Act
A federal initiative to provide funding for community mental health centers and to encourage deinstitutionalization.

The combination of many factors, such as economic downturns, substance abuse, PTSD, strained family relationships, and the problem of homelessness, produced many in need of mental health counseling. Unfortunately, the only existing system able to address these emerging problems was the criminal justice system. Police routinely encounter the mentally ill and have few options other than to arrest and detain them. Here are some of the incidents that police encounter: "a man who had smashed the plate-glass window of a retail store because he saw a dinosaur jumping out at him," and a woman who refused to pay her restaurant bill because she believed that she was the reincarnation of Jesus Christ.[26]

Today, mental illness is more common among the incarcerated, especially those arrested on misdemeanor charges. Recent studies of prison and jail populations find very high rates of mental health problems (see **Figure 9.1**). In fact, 56 percent have symptoms of or a history of mental health problems. These rates are much higher than those found in the general population.

Mental illness is more likely among offenders convicted of violent crimes and less likely among drug offenders. Mental health also differs by race, age, and gender. Inmates who are white, female, and under the age of 25 are more likely to experience mental health problems than are other inmates. Other factors also appear to be related

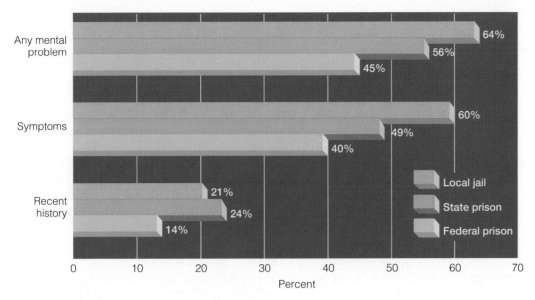

FIGURE 9.1
Percentage of Inmates with Mental Health Problems
A majority of people under correctional authority have a history of mental health problems; for these, problems include visible behavioral symptoms occurring recently.

Source: Bureau of Justice Statistics, *Mental Health Problems of Prison and Jail Inmates* (Washington, DC: U.S. Government Printing Office, September 2006), 1.

to mental health status. For example, prisoners who were sexually abused, homeless during the year prior to incarceration, and/or had a family member who was incarcerated are likely to experience mental health problems in prison.[27]

Mentally ill prisoners pose particular challenges for correctional professionals because they are more likely to be involved in fights than other inmates; about 58 percent of mentally ill state prisoners have been formally charged with rule violations.[28] Prison overcrowding exacerbates the problem of managing mentally ill prisoners. Correctional resources are stretched thin in general when dealing with a population of thousands with a variety of medical, psychological, and social needs. Too often, mental health services are not prioritized when considering other demands that must be met by correctional officials. In addition, the difficulty that prisoners have when adjusting to congested physical environments can worsen the condition of the mentally ill. Recently, the California Department of Corrections and Rehabilitation was ordered by a U.S. district court to correct its mental health delivery system.[29] The commissioned assessment on completed suicides in California's corrections system states that from 1999 through 2012, 437 inmates committed suicide, a number that is significantly higher than that of any other corrections system in the United States. Several explanations are offered in the report to explain why this problem is characterized as a systemic failure, including the following:

1. Failure to refer inmates to higher levels of care when clinically appropriate.
2. Failure to conduct indicated mental health evaluations and/or assessments.
3. Failure to conduct adequate or timely mental health status examinations.
4. Failure to carry out basic clinical procedures such as consultations between mental health and medical providers, conducting Unit Health Record (UHR) reviews following discharges from Department of State Hospitals (DSH), or obtaining necessary clinical records from the UHR.
5. Inadequate completion of serious reportable events (SREs).
6. Inadequate emergency responses.[30]

The availability and type of mental health treatment programs differ from one prison to the next. Approximately 58 percent of state and federal correctional facilities provide psychological or psychiatric counseling to inmates.[31]

Besides the fact that a significant portion of inmates evidence some form of mental illness, it is an additional hurdle for this population to receive an accurate diagnosis followed by access to the appropriate therapies while incarcerated. The lack of consensus on diagnoses of mental illness indicates some of the drawbacks in the general concept that mental illness underlies much criminal behavior. For example, trained psychiatrists disagree on the diagnosis of patients' mental problems as often as half the time. The unreliability of mental illness diagnosis may be one reason that treatments have been so ineffective. Robert Martinson's influential review of treatment programs provides perhaps the starkest conclusion: With few exceptions, rehabilitative efforts had no appreciable effect on recidivism.[32] Martinson was referring to a wide variety of programs, but his conclusion applied particularly to programs designed to improve offenders' emotional or psychological functioning.

The psychological approach is problematic in prison. Most experts would agree that **psychotherapy**, or "treatment of the mind," offers narrow prospects for success even with motivated, voluntary, free patients. Free patients voluntarily enter a financial contract with the therapist for help; either party may terminate the agreement at any time. Because the client is the purchaser, it is easy to see why the therapist keeps the client's interests foremost during the treatment process.

In prison it is not the inmate but society that purchases the therapist's services. The interests of the purchaser assume more importance to the therapist than do those of the offender. This turns the accepted practices of most therapy upside down. The centerpiece is not the offender; instead, it is society's desire that the offender develop a crime-free lifestyle.

Because of the many problems with prison psychotherapy, programs that address inmates' emotional health have become less common in recent years. Today, most prison counselors do not practice psychotherapy with inmates. While 13 percent of today's prisoners receive some sort of counseling, most of this prison treatment tends to focus on concrete problems that prisoners face in adjusting to the prison environment or in dealing with family crises that occur during incarceration. An additional 10 percent of prisoners receive prescription **psychotropic medications**, and only 2 percent receive 24-hour psychiatric care. The practice of dispensing psychotropic medications to mentally ill inmates adds to staff time because the taking of these drugs requires close monitoring and supervision. Staff supervision is necessary to avoid the problems of medication abuse, suicides, or even the stockpiling and trafficking of medications within the inmate population.

Unlike psychotherapy, programs that address prisoners' emotions and thoughts tend to use group therapy, in which offenders come together to discuss mutual problems. Group treatment is considered important because humans are social animals. Most of our behavior occurs in groups, and we learn to define ourselves and to interpret our experiences in groups. This fact is particularly appropriate to criminology because a large proportion of crime is committed by groups or in groups, and much criminal behavior is reinforced by group norms, by manipulation, and by elaborate rationalizations. Therefore, prison treatment groups are often highly confrontational. Group members are asked to "call" the manipulations and rationalizations that others are using to justify their deviant behavior, and they are encouraged to participate wholeheartedly in the process. Theoretically, inmates can then come to understand their own versions of those manipulations and rationalizations.

Most groups in prison use structured approaches in which the group undertakes a series of patterned discussion topics or activities that are targeted not at the offender's emotions but at thought processes. Four of the most common group approaches are reality therapy, confrontation therapy, transactional analysis, and cognitive skill building.

Reality therapy has a simple core tenet: People's problems decline when they behave more responsibly. Things get difficult when people fail to behave in ways

psychotherapy
In generic terms, all forms of "treatment of the mind"; in the prison setting, this treatment is coercive in nature.

psychotropic medications
Drug treatments designed to lessen the severity of symptoms of psychological illness.

reality therapy
Treatment that emphasizes personal responsibility for actions and their consequences.

consistent with life's realities. The therapist's role is to return the client consistently and firmly to the real consequences of his or her behavior, with particular attention to the troubles that follow inappropriate actions. Reality therapy is popular in corrections for three reasons. First, it assumes that the rules society sets for its members are inescapable. Second, its techniques are easy for staff to learn. Third, the method is short-term and thus highly adaptable to prison.

In **confrontation therapy,** a professional group leader encourages group members to confront one another's rationalizations and manipulations, which are common to criminal thoughts and actions. These sessions can become quite vocal, and inmates trying to defend themselves can become quite angry in reaction to aggressive accusations by peers. The therapy aims at pressuring inmates to give up their manipulative rationalizations and to accept responsibility for the harms that their crimes have caused.

Transactional analysis focuses on the roles (ego states) that people play with others. Here the aim is to help people realize that their problems commonly result from approaching the world as an angry Parent or weak Child rather than as a responsible Adult. The therapist's role is largely that of teacher; he or she spends much time explaining the concepts of transactional analysis and showing the client how to use them in analyzing his or her own life. Like reality therapy, transactional analysis is considered well suited to corrections because it is simple, straightforward, and short-term.

Cognitive skill building focuses on changing the thought patterns that accompany criminal behavior. Advocates argue that offenders develop antisocial patterns of reasoning which make them believe that criminal behavior makes sense. To replace these thought patterns, offenders need to learn new skills and techniques for day-to-day living. The group leader uses a variety of procedures to teach these new skills, including role-playing and "psychodramas," that re-create emotionally stressful past occurrences. The aim of the cognitive approach is to teach offenders new ways to think about themselves and their actions.

Some observers question the adequacy of mental health treatment for the incarcerated. For example, Wyoming was found to have a psychiatrist on duty only two days a month at the state penitentiary.[33] What may be more commonly found are the results reported in a recent study by Human Rights Watch, which include the following: Prison actually compounds the problems of the mentally ill, who may have trouble following the everyday discipline of prison life, such as standing in line for a meal. Some exhibit their illness through disruptive behavior (some will simply refuse to follow routine orders). As a result, mentally ill inmates have higher-than-average disciplinary rates,[34] which likely triggers an unproductive cycle of behavior.

Some states are moving to create separate secure facilities to house mentally ill and dangerous offenders. Minnesota recently completed an $8.6-million, 150-bed facility for mentally ill inmates, particularly those serving time for sexual offenses. The objective is to provide mental health services to qualified inmates while maintaining public safety standards.[35]

LONG-TERM PRISONERS

More prisoners serve long sentences in the United States than in any other Western nation. One survey found that nearly 310,000 prisoners are currently serving at least 20-year sentences. Of these inmates, about 10 percent are serving "natural life," which means there is no possibility of parole, a number that has more than tripled since 1992.[36] Each life sentence costs taxpayers an estimated $1 million.[37] But the costs to taxpayers also go up each time the average number of months served in prison increases. Thus, not only do life sentences cost a great deal, but *longer* sentences do as well. A recent Pew report states that offenders released in 2009 had spent 36 percent, or nine months, longer incarcerated than those released in 1990. The costs of those nine months ($23,300 per inmate) multiplied by the thousands cost states approximately $10 billion.[38]

confrontation therapy
A treatment technique, usually done in a group, that vividly brings the offender face-to-face with the crime's consequences for the victim and society.

transactional analysis
Treatment that focuses on patterns of interaction with others, especially patterns that indicate personal problems.

cognitive skill building
A form of behavior therapy that focuses on changing the thinking and reasoning patterns that accompany criminal behavior.

The "get-tough" sentencing practices of the last 30 years have changed the makeup of the lifer population, which now includes more nonviolent offenders.[39] With the changes in sentencing laws that require longer terms for career criminals, those convicted of multiple charges that involve mandatory minimums, those in the drug trade, those involved in violent gang activity, and convicted felons subjected to second and third strikes, long-term inmates are more youthful than those sentenced prior to the "get-tough" era.

Long-term prisoners are not generally seen as control problems by correctional officials. They are charged with disciplinary infractions far less frequently than are short-term inmates. Rather, administrators must face the challenge of making the lives of such prisoners bearable. Experts suggest that administrators follow three main principles when managing long-term inmates: (1) maximize opportunities for the inmates to exercise choice in living conditions, (2) create opportunities for meaningful living, and (3) help the inmates maintain contact with the outside world.[40] Many long-term inmates will eventually be released after spending the best years of their lives behind bars. Will these offenders be able to support themselves when they return to the community? Results from a 1985 survey of correctional administrators on long-term offender issues would suggest that the answer is no.[41] According to this study, from more than 30 years ago, there was only one long-termer prison program active in the United States. It was offered to prisoners in Utah State Prison. Today, Utah State Prison, a maximum-security facility, provides an array of prison programs for prisoners, and none are designated for long-termers only. The following is a list of programs currently offered to Utah State Prison inmates, including long-termers:

- **NIC/Thinking for a Change:** This National Institute of Corrections program is about restructuring, rethinking, and skill building to reduce recidivism. Thinking for a Change curriculum uses . . . a problem-solving program embellished by both cognitive restructuring and social-skills interventions.

- **Thinking Errors:** This course is an in-depth cognitive restructuring class that introduces the concept of thinking errors and motivates personal change. "Commitment to Change" with Stanton E. Samenow, Ph.D., is the course curriculum used.

- **Anger Management Phase I:** Phase I helps offenders recognize problem situations and the types of thoughts and feelings that lead to problematic anger. During this course, offenders will focus on developing the cognitive and behavior skills that enable them to maintain control.

- **Anger Management Phase II—Pulling Punches:** The Phase II curriculum is for "Rage Management." It is designed to reveal how anger has controlled offenders during past trauma and how they can learn healthy conflict resolution.

- **Impact of Crime Phase I and II:** Impact of Crime classes teach offenders to understand how their crimes have affected their victims, to accept responsibility for their criminal behavior, to learn how to associate with positive role models, and to become contributing, law-abiding members of society. The ultimate aim is preventing future victimization.

- **Parenting:** This curriculum is designed to teach offenders the development stages of children in order to promote the essential skills to guide and allow parents to feel comfortable, confident, and competent in raising their children.

- **Parenting from the Inside:** This curriculum provides offenders ideas for communicating and staying connected with their children during their incarceration. Special ideas are organized to accommodate children of all ages.

- **Parenting (Interactive):** This course enables offenders to meet on a regular basis with their children in order to practice positive parenting skills and help promote healthy boundaries.

- **Domestic Violence (Educational):** This is a psycho-educational class designed for women offenders, which teaches them to recognize the patterns and cycles of an abusive relationship.

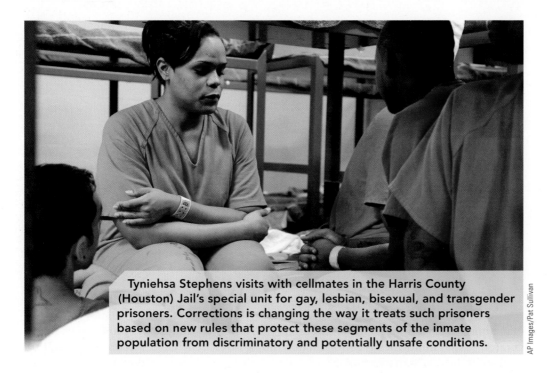

Tyniehsa Stephens visits with cellmates in the Harris County (Houston) Jail's special unit for gay, lesbian, bisexual, and transgender prisoners. Corrections is changing the way it treats such prisoners based on new rules that protect these segments of the inmate population from discriminatory and potentially unsafe conditions.

- **Domestic Violence (Therapy):** Therapy groups and individual therapeutic sessions are provided for women who have been identified as victims of abuse to help them work through their own trauma and cycle of abuse.

- **Financial Literacy:** This course teaches essential financial management skills, which will enable offenders to make informed financial decisions. Students learn about saving, investments, financial planning, setting both long- and short-term goals, and the consequences of poor financial planning.

- **Computer Literacy:** This course provides offenders an opportunity to learn or improve on basic computer skills. The students will learn computer terminology, Windows management, and word processors; they will also be tested on typing skills.[42]

In some maximum-security facilities, long-term prisoners have several options available to them to become involved in correctional programs. Yet some may decline if these programs, with their forward-looking agendas, make adjusting to the realities of a lengthy sentence more difficult psychologically. But for long-termers who desire to be active and invested in programs, these prosocial pursuits could affect their experience in prison and well beyond.

We have examined four special populations of offenders in prisons for adults. Each category has special housing, medical, program, and release needs that set them apart from the general incarcerated population. Each category poses special challenges for correctional administrators and officers. We now focus attention on our fifth group of offenders, who are distinctive because of their unique needs and related implications for correctional management—the special case of sexual-minority inmates.

SEXUAL-MINORITY PRISONERS

According to a 2012 Gallup tracking poll, 3.4 percent of adults in the United States identify themselves as **sexual minorities**: lesbian, gay, bisexual, or **transgendered**—a person who lives as a member of a gender other than that expected based on anatomical sex.[43] (The acronym LGBT is frequently used to refer to these groups.) This finding corresponds

sexual minorities
Groups of people whose sexual orientation or gender identity differs from that of the majority of the population.

transgendered
A person who lives as a member of a gender other than that expected based on anatomical sex.

to other estimates such as those reported by the U.S. Department of Health and Human Services' National Survey of Family Growth. It is unclear how many inmates incarcerated in the United States are sexual minorities; however, a recent survey estimates that this group includes 11 percent of incarcerated males and 28 percent of incarcerated females.[44] It can be speculated that with all of the pressures confronting corrections systems, interest in the identification and classification of sexual minorities has not been a high priority. In addition, comprehensive correctional services for this population have yet to be fully comprehended and made available. Thus, for these reasons and several others, departments of corrections are not inclined to manage this population differently from any other inmate group unless a problem presents itself. Nevertheless, regardless of their actual numbers, this group presents unique problems.

Inmates who are sexual minorities self-identify with one of the following broad classifications of LGBT: lesbian, gay, bisexual, or transgendered—some analysts use the acronym LGBTI to include intersexed individuals. (For our purposes, we limit our attention to that inmate population whose sexual preference is *independent* of the incarceration experience and is not the result of it.)

Sexual Victimization

The abuse and victimization of Roderick Johnson (see Chapter 11) and other incarcerated sexual minorities is unfortunately not a rare occurrence. According to a 2008 Bureau of Justice Statistics survey, 18.5 percent of gay or lesbian inmates were victims of reported sexual abuse in 2007. At one time the rate of sexual assaults against gay men, bisexual men, and transgendered women was as high as 67 percent in six California prisons for men.[45] The abuse of incarcerated transgendered women is considerable, with the Center for Evidence Based Corrections reporting in 2009 a 59-percent sexual-assault victimization rate. These statistics imply the real possibility of the legal liability of correctional authorities for the failure to keep sexual-minority inmates safe. A transgendered female inmate incarcerated in a Florida facility for male offenders sued correctional authorities in 2008 for removing her from protective custody and placing her in general population, where she was subsequently raped by an inmate who was serving time for sexual assault. The basis of her lawsuit is that officials were negligent in failing to protect her and that this nonfeasance violated her civil rights.[46] As a result of increasing awareness of this population and their unique vulnerability to sexual victimization, correctional authorities have an obligation and legal responsibility to take protective measures to minimize these attacks. Failure to do so means litigation, the possible violation of the "cruel and unusual" clause in the Eighth Amendment, and subsequent punitive damages.[47] (See Tables 9.1 and 9.2.)

Besides vulnerability to sexual exploitation, a recent study also shows that transgendered offenders enter prison with a disproportionate amount of substance abuse problems, mental health issues, and past experiences of physical and sexual victimization when compared to other prison populations.[48]

Various state and local corrections systems are developing policies to address the needs of sexual-minority inmates. (See "Focus on Correctional Policy: The District of Columbia's Department of Corrections Gender Classification and Housing Policy.")

A Developing Case Law

The courts have long determined that correctional authorities are responsible for providing medical care to the inmates who are held in their facilities. The obvious reason for this responsibility is that inmates do not have the ability to leave prisons and seek medical treatment on the outside. The state has restricted their movements by virtue of their incarceration. Therefore, not only is the state responsible for *providing* medical services, but if it fails to do so and medical problems worsen, the state will be accountable. One of the most significant findings announced in *Estelle v. Gamble* (1976) is that

Table 9.1 Legal Requirements and Litigation Related to LGBTI Issues

Eighth Amendment to the U.S. Constitution	Excessive bail shall not be required, nor excessive fines imposed, nor cruel and unusual punishment inflicted.
Fourteenth Amendment to the U.S. Constitution	No state shall "deprive any person of life, liberty, or property, without due process of law."
Kosilek v. Spencer, U.S. District Court, District of Massachusetts, September 12, 2012	Defendant shall take forthwith all of the actions reasonably necessary to provide Kosilek sex-reassignment surgery as promptly as possible.
Farmer v. Brennan, 511 U.S. 825, June 6, 1994	A prison official's "deliberate indifference" to a substantial risk of serious harm to an inmate violates the Eighth Amendment. It is the responsibility of prison officials to protect prisoners from each other. (This is the first time that the court addressed prison sexual violence.)
Doe v. Bell, 754 N.Y.S. 2d 846, January 9, 2003	The Supreme Court, New York County, held that the petitioner's gender identity disorder was a disability within the meaning of human rights law. (New York City's Administration for Children's Services failed to make reasonable accommodation for petitioner's disability.)

Source: National Institute of Corrections, "LGBTI Populations: Their Safety, Your Responsibility," http://static.nicic.gov/UserShared/2012-12-31 _pdf_part._guide-lgbti_d11.pdf, November 2012.

failure to provide medical care, even *sufficient* care, may violate the prisoner's Eighth Amendment's protection against cruel and unusual punishment.[49] This legal principle has unique applications for some sexual minorities.

On January 28, 2013, the Fourth U.S. Circuit Court of Appeals determined that a transgendered prisoner can sue correctional authorities for failing to provide a **sex-reassignment surgery**. Ophelia Azriel De'lonta, born Michael Stokes, successfully argued that she suffers from a condition known as **gender identity disorder**.[50] It is commonly described as one feeling trapped inside the wrong body. The unanimous decision of the court stated that for some transgendered persons, therapies involving hormonal treatment and psychological counseling are not sufficient; rather, sex reassignment is the preferred form of treatment. In addition, De'lonta, who is serving a 73-year sentence for bank robbery, has periodically attempted self-castration, which resulted in several hospitalizations.[51]

A similar finding by District Court Judge Mark Wolf occurred in Massachusetts on behalf of transgendered prisoner Michelle Kosilek. In this case, the state is not only ordered to provide sex-reassignment surgery but also to pay Kosilek's legal fees, estimated at $500,000. These court decisions are not without controversy and are not well received by everyone. The following comments made by Massachusetts State Senator Bruce Tarr represent the opinions of critics: "In ruling that the plaintiff is entitled to legal costs in his pursuit of gender reassignment surgery, Judge Wolf is continuing down the wrong path. This second inappropriate decision makes it even more critical for the Department of Correction to file appeals and stand up for the taxpayers of Massachusetts and the integrity of the Eighth Amendment."[52] In 2005 Wisconsin enacted the Inmate Sex Change Prevention Act, which prohibited prison doctors from providing not only sex-reassignment surgery but also hormone therapy for transgendered prisoners. But in 2011 the Seventh Circuit Court of Appeals found the law to be unconstitutional because it violated the Eighth Amendment protection against cruel and unusual punishment.[53]

Until recently, the problems encountered by incarcerated sexual minorities were ignored or responded to with less-than-effective strategies. Within the last several years, however, this situation has dramatically changed. Policies with specific practices

sex-reassignment surgery
Surgical procedures to alter a person's physical appearance so that the person appears more like the opposite gender.

gender identity disorder
The diagnosis used to describe an individual who displays a marked incongruence between experienced or expressed gender and his or her biological gender.

Table 9.2 Selected Characteristics of the Transgender Inmate Population in California's Prison for Men in Comparison to Other Inmate Populations Regarding Violence and Sexual Victimization

Victimization	U.S. Population	CA Population	U.S. Prison Population (Men's Prisons Only)	CA Prison Population (Men's Prisons Only)	Transgender Community	Transgender Inmate Population in CA Men's Prisons
Physical victimization	2.3% (victims of violent crime [including sexual victimization] in a given year)	[no data presented]	11.9% (lifetime physical abuse) 13.4% (lifetime physical abuse)	12.4% (lifetime physical abuse)	37.0% (lifetime physical abuse because of gender) 43.0% (lifetime violent victimization) 51.3% (lifetime physical abuse) 59.5% (lifetime harassment or violence)	61.1% (ever been physically assaulted outside of prison) 85.1% (ever been physically assaulted in lifetime)
Sexual victimization	10.5% (lifetime rape/attempted rape) 17.6% (females only) 3.0% (males only)	[no data presented]	5.7% (lifetime forced sexual contact) 5.8% (lifetime sexual abuse)	5.6% (lifetime forced sexual contact)	13.5% (lifetime sexual assault) 14.0% (lifetime rape or attempted rape) 53.8% (lifetime forced sex) 59.0% (lifetime forced sex or rape)	40.2% (ever had to do sexual things against will outside of prison) 52.7% (ever had to do sexual things would rather not have done outside of prison) 70.7% (ever had to do sexual things against will in lifetime)

Source: Adapted from Lori Sexton, Valerie Jenness, and Jennifer Sumner, *Where the Margins Meet: A Demographic Assessment of Transgender Inmates in Men's Prisons* (University of California, Irvine, 2009), http://ucicorrections.seweb.uci.edu/sites/ucicorrections.seweb.uci.edu/files/A%20Demographic%20Assessment%20of%20Transgender%20Inmates%20in%20Men's%20Prisons.pdf.

focus on correctional policy

The District of Columbia's Department of Corrections Gender Classification and Housing Policy

PURPOSE AND SCOPE. To establish procedures on providing the appropriate treatment of transgender, transsexual, intersex, and gender variant persons who are incarcerated and housed within the District of Columbia Department of Corrections.

POLICY. a. It is DOC policy to provide services in a humane and respectful manner to transgender and intersex inmates while ensuring that they are processed and housed safely and efficiently to the greatest extent possible. For the safety, security and order of the facility, the DOC classifies and houses male and female offenders in separate housing units. DOC shall classify an inmate who has male genitals as a male and one who has female genitals as a female, unless otherwise recommended by the Transgender Committee and approved consistent with this policy.

b. In order to address the special needs of transgender individuals, upon initial intake at Receiving and Discharge (R&D), or at any time that an inmate makes known to DOC staff their transgender or intersex status, staff shall follow the guidelines in this policy in order to determine the inmate's housing based on his or her safety/security needs, housing availability, gender identity and genitalia, if:

1. An inmate indicates that they are transgendered or intersex at anytime during their custody.

2. An inmate's gender identity, appearance, overt expression, or behavior differs from their birth sex or genitalia.

3. A gender designation made by any public entity, government agency or law enforcement agency indicates that the inmate is transgendered. . . .

e. Transgender Committee. Refers to a committee established by the D.C. Department of Corrections comprised of a medical practitioner, a mental health clinician, a correctional supervisor, a Chief Case Manager and a DOC approved volunteer who is a member of the transgender community or an acknowledged expert in transgender affairs. The committee shall determine the transgender inmate's housing assignment after review of all of the inmate records and assessments, and an interview with the inmate during which the inmate's own opinion of his/her vulnerability in the jail population shall be considered.

Housing

a. After completion of the initial intake process, an inmate identified as transgender or intersex shall be afforded the opportunity to request and receive protective custody and be housed in a single cell in the intake housing unit consistent with the gender identified at intake for no more than seventy-two (72) hours . . . until classification and housing needs can be assessed by the Transgender Committee.

In accordance with *PS 4090.3 Classification (Program Review)*, all transgender and intersex inmates will be classified and assigned housing based on their safety/security needs, housing availability, gender identity and genitalia. Intake staff shall assess the transgender and intersex inmates for potential vulnerability in the general population and refer them to the Transgender Committee. . . .

c. The Transgender Committee housing assessment shall address whether the inmate will be housed in the general population or in a protective custody unit of the gender consistent with their gender identity or genitalia. If the Warden's opinion differs from the recommendation of the Transgender Committee, the Warden shall justify the assignment in writing to the Director for final determination. Transgender and intersex inmates have the same right to appeal housing assignments as all inmates consistent with *PS 4090.3 Classification (Program Review)*.

Critical Thinking

The District of Columbia's housing policy for transgendered inmates articulates a detailed process for determining appropriate housing assignments for those entering the corrections system. What limitations may still exist despite this careful effort?

Source: Abridged from District of Columbia Department of Corrections Program Statement, "Gender Classification and Housing," http://doc.dc.gov/sites/default/files/dc/sites/doc/publication/attachments/DOC_PS_4020_3C_Gender_Classificationand_Housing_01112012_wsig.pdf.

---

regarding the intake, assessment, and classification of these inmates now exist where previously they did not. There are more-defined options now that have been developed by correctional administrators to house these inmates in safer environments. Policy makers, practitioners, and academics are also working to identify the needs of this offender population and to introduce correctional programs and resources to address

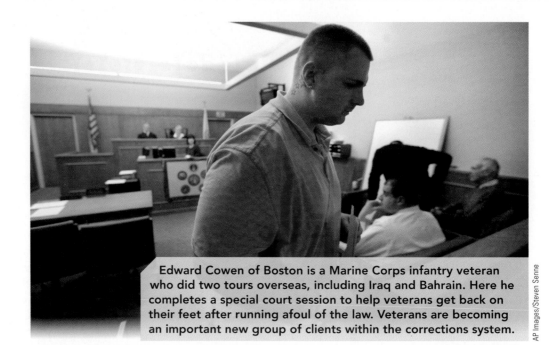

Edward Cowen of Boston is a Marine Corps infantry veteran who did two tours overseas, including Iraq and Bahrain. Here he completes a special court session to help veterans get back on their feet after running afoul of the law. Veterans are becoming an important new group of clients within the corrections system.

their multifaceted problems. Finally, the courts are supportive of the arguments made by transgendered prisoners that departments of corrections must also provide the medical services needed to address gender identity disorder and related conditions, including sex-reassignment surgery.

MILITARY VETERAN PRISONERS

Inmates who have also served in the armed services are not a recent development. In fact, according to the Bureau of Justice Statistics, their numbers in federal and state prisons have actually steadily decreased over the last 30 years.[54] Some veterans who survive combat may struggle with multiple problems once they return stateside: physical injuries, psychological trauma such as posttraumatic stress disorder (PTSD), depression, and drug or alcohol abuse. Prescription drug abuse among military service personnel has also emerged as an area of concern.[55] Recent reports indicate that the Veterans Health Administration has underserved veterans in several critical areas.[56] Some of the persistent problems experienced by veterans may lead to serious antisocial behaviors, suicide, or crimes committed against others. These factors could well offer a plausible explanation for veteran involvement with the criminal justice system. Recent estimates state that approximately 9.4 percent of all prisoners in jails and prisons are veterans.[57]

What We Know About Them

A recent study reported the likelihood of incarceration among various veteran groups.[58] Results indicated that post–9/11 veterans are *less* likely to be incarcerated than veterans from other wars and conflicts. This group made up only 3.9 percent of incarcerated veterans despite being three times more likely to suffer from PTSD. The Bureau of Justice Statistics reports that Vietnam veterans are the largest group among incarcerated veterans in both federal and state prisons.[59] Additional highlights from the report include the following:

- Nearly one in four veterans in state prison were sex offenders, compared to one in ten nonveterans.
- A majority of veterans in state prison (57 percent) were serving time for violent offenses, including over a third who were serving sentences for homicide (15 percent) or rape/sexual assault (23 percent).

- Veterans were more likely than other violent offenders in state prison to have victimized females and minors.

- At the time of arrest, 33 percent of veterans were on probation or parole, while 44 percent of nonveterans had some type of prior criminal justice status.

- At the time of the offense, a quarter of veterans and a third of nonveterans were under the influence of drugs.

- Despite experiencing fewer symptoms of mental health disorders, veterans (30 percent) were more likely than other state prisoners (24 percent) to report a recent history of mental health services.

A Sample of Current Programs

A review of criminal justice programs targeting military veterans shows a growing number of initiatives that have developed in reaction to a pressing need at the local level. Many of these efforts are referred to as **veteran assistance projects**. These are programs that offer important services to the local criminal justice system as well as the veteran. They assist in determining whether the crime was related to the veteran's military service (e.g., brain trauma or PTSD), assess what needs are evident in the veteran's current situation, and assist the veteran in applying for benefits that he or she is eligible to receive from the Veterans Health Administration, such as mental health, substance abuse, or other counseling. Another example is the Veterans Justice Outreach Program in Butler, Pennsylvania, which has also developed a comprehensive program to better serve veterans in the criminal justice system. It offers specific services available to eligible offenders and provides these services in accordance with how the criminal justice system functions (see **Figure 9.2**).[60]

Another program in growing demand is the veterans' court, which first made its appearance in 2008. These are specialized criminal courts that seek to deal more effectively with the complex problems of veterans who are accused of breaking the law. The objective of these courts is to assess the treatment needs of these individuals and to provide program options as conditions of release or in addition to community-based sentences. Veterans' courts can now be found in many states across the country. Finally, some state corrections systems have developed separate housing and special programs for incarcerated veterans. Virginia is piloting a program that houses military veterans in a segregated dormitory-style unit. The Haynesville Correctional Center, which is described as a minimum-security facility, began this program in 2012.[61] Designed to recognize the unique needs of veterans, the program is structured to reflect some aspects of military life. The hope is to provide additional support in preparation for a more successful transition back to civilian life.

Lessons Learned

State, county, and local officials can examine what resources are available to this offender group and address any remaining needs. This was the case in Travis County, Texas. Local law enforcement officials took an interest in determining how veterans in the Travis County criminal justice system were being handled. Their goal was to ensure that veterans were referred to appropriate treatment programs and other services to address recidivism and larger quality-of-life concerns. They were able to document that a sizable number of veterans in the Travis County Jail had substance abuse problems and were repeat offenders. Subsequently, county officials developed a partnership with state and federal agencies to better address the needs of veterans in the criminal justice system, which became the Veterans Intervention Project.

Through the project's survey efforts, the needs of the targeted group were better identified. Approximately one-third of these offenders had been arrested two or more times; 73 percent were arrested on misdemeanor charges and 27 percent on felony charges. Twenty-two percent of the felony charges were for aggravated assault with

veteran assistance projects
Collaborative programs made up of veterans' agencies, community mental health organizations, human services agencies, courts, and other criminal justice organizations. The goal is to link veterans who have encountered the criminal justice system with an array of services that might improve their adjustment in the community.

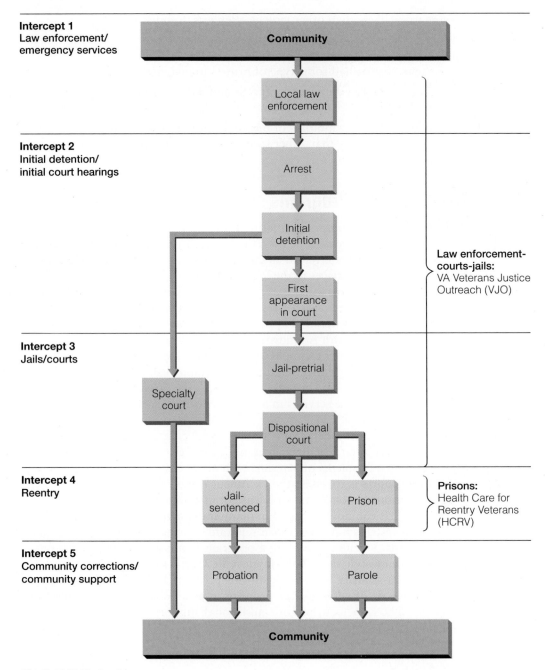

Intercept 1
Law enforcement/
emergency services

Intercept 2
Initial detention/
initial court hearings

Intercept 3
Jails/courts

Intercept 4
Reentry

Intercept 5
Community corrections/
community support

Community

Local law
enforcement

Arrest

Initial
detention

First
appearance
in court

Jail-pretrial

Specialty
court

Dispositional
court

Jail-
sentenced

Prison

Probation

Parole

Community

Law enforcement-
courts-jails:
VA Veterans Justice
Outreach (VJO)

Prisons:
Health Care for
Reentry Veterans
(HCRV)

FIGURE 9.2
Sequential Intercept Model

Source: Brad Schaffer, *Jailed Rural Pennsylvania Veterans in the Criminal Justice System* (Butler, PA: Veterans Justice Outreach Program, 2010), www.ncdsv.org/images/Schaffer_JailedRuralPAVetsInTheCJSystem_9-15 -2010.pdf.

a deadly weapon. Over 85 percent of offenders had received an honorable or general discharge. But the most startling finding was that 65 percent of them had not received *any* VA services.[62] With this evidence the project was able to focus its efforts on making sure that veterans are evaluated at their first arrest and provided with assistance in accessing services that they are eligible to receive.

Just as correctional personnel are challenged to learn about other special populations, they must also learn about the issues that confront incarcerated military veterans. Staff training is essential. One of the more difficult behaviors that correctional officers may need to better understand is PTSD and how it might manifest in a jail or prison setting. The following are some of the recognized indicators of PTSD as listed by the National Institute of Mental Health:

- Tension, agitation, or hypervigilance.
- Sleep disturbance, including dreams and nightmares.
- Flashbacks—intrusive memories and feelings.
- Emotional detachment and social withdrawal—feeling distant from friends and family.
- Mood swings, depression.
- Panic attacks.
- Poor concentration.

Recognizing and responding to these and any other signs of distress in an appropriate manner could avoid worsening a serious problem by writing up violations (tickets) and subjecting these individuals to unnecessary punishments.

Criminal justice professionals must make use of available resources offered by the Veterans Health Administration, crisis-intervention teams administered by the National Alliance on Mental Illness, veteran assistance projects, community corrections, and other organizations that will interact with military veterans who commit crimes. Evidence-based policies and practices of the criminal justice system could go a long way toward responding to a social problem in a more just and effective manner from the point of arrest, during incarceration, and through reentry.

Summary

1 Understand how the incarceration of elderly prisoners impacts health care costs, correctional programs, and the physical environment of this special population.

Inmates over 55 years of age pose a challenge for corrections because they have special needs. For example, elderly inmates have special housing needs. Accommodations may include assigning older inmates to a bottom bunk and to special cells with grab bars. Some states have specialized facilities for frail inmates. Elderly inmates are more likely to require medical care. The cost of caring for an elderly inmate is much higher than that for younger prisoners. Some states are moving to expedite the release of elderly inmates in order to cut costs. Other states are reluctant to do the same based on the belief that being elderly does not negate being dangerous.

2 Identify the complexities involved with the correctional management of inmates who are HIV-infected or who have been diagnosed with AIDS.

The rate of confirmed AIDS cases in state and federal prisons is more than twice that of the U.S. population. To deal with HIV/AIDS, prison officials have developed a variety of policies. However, implementation of these policies is complicated by a host of legal, political, medical, budgetary, and attitudinal factors. Policies concerning separate housing for HIV-infected inmates are controversial. Although the majority of correctional officials no longer segregate infected inmates, correctional managers recognize the reality of risk of exposure not only for uninfected inmates but for correctional staff as well.

3 Analyze how changes in public policy unintentionally have affected the current state of incarcerated mentally ill.

Since the deinstitutionalization movement of the 1960s, which emphasized the depopulation of large-scale mental hospitals, jails and prisons have seen increasing numbers of the mentally ill within their confines. Despite the increasing presence of this offender group, the availability and type of mental health treatment programs differ in sufficiency from one prison to the next. Some state officials have moved toward developing separate secure facilities to provide psychiatric treatment for those mentally ill offenders who are potentially violent and pose a significant risk to the public and others.

4 Discuss the implications of long-term sentences for prisoners who must serve them and the responsibility of correctional administrators to offer opportunities for meaningful engagement to this population.

More prisoners serve long sentences in the United States than in any other Western nation. Each life sentence costs taxpayers an estimated $1 million. But the costs to taxpayers also go up each time the average number of months served in prison increases. A recent Pew report states that offenders released in 2009 spent nine months longer incarcerated than those released in 1990. However, longer sentences are not restricted to violent criminals; get-tough sentencing practices have changed the makeup of the lifer population, which now includes more nonviolent offenders. Long-term prisoners are not generally seen as control problems by correctional officials. The challenge for administrators is to make the lives of such prisoners bearable. Experts suggest that administrators follow three main principles when managing long-term inmates: (1) maximize opportunities for the inmates to exercise choice in living conditions, (2) create opportunities for meaningful living, and (3) help inmates maintain contact with the outside world. In some maximum-security facilities, long-term prisoners have several options available to them to become involved in correctional programs.

5 Recognize the obligation confronting correctional administrators to meet the needs of incarcerated sexual-minority offenders and understand the emerging case law that is impacting corrections management.

Incarcerated sexual minorities, particularly transgendered inmates, are subjected to violent sexual victimization because of a lack of appropriate intake, assessment, and classification procedures for this unique population. Their vulnerability must be minimized by correctional officials, or these officials run the risk of liability. In addition, some transgendered inmates suffer from gender identity disorder, which may require sex-reassignment surgery as the preferred method of treatment. Federal district courts have determined that, in accordance with the Eighth Amendment, correctional authorities must provide and pay for these treatments.

6 Describe the condition of military veterans who are currently involved in the correctional system and the types of specialized programs developed to address their needs.

The numbers of inmates in federal and state prisons who have also served in the armed services have steadily decreased over the last thirty years. However, many of these individuals struggle with multiple problems, including physical injuries, post-traumatic stress disorder (PTSD), depression, and substance abuse. Some of these problems may lead to serious antisocial behaviors, including committing crimes against others. Recent estimates state that approximately 9.4 percent of all prisoners in jails and prisons are veterans. Vietnam veterans are the largest group among incarcerated veterans. Local program initiatives, commonly referred to as veteran assistance projects, have developed primarily in response to the growing unmet needs of returning vets. These projects help eligible vets find available counseling and other benefits. The goal of veterans' courts is to focus attention on the unique problems of veterans involved in the criminal justice system and to provide alternative community-based correctional programs when appropriate. Some state correctional systems administer policies that include segregated housing and treatment programs, with the aim of achieving a successful transition for the veteran to civilian life.

Key Terms

For Discussion

1. The reality of an aging inmate population requires correctional officials to alter the physical plant of some prison facilities to accommodate the needs of this population. Should training manuals for prison staff also be revised accordingly?

2. Although several states have the legislative tools necessary to release elderly inmates to an earlier parole, they often choose not to. Should correctional officials use risk assessment methods to evaluate the potential dangerousness of elderly, fragile, and terminally ill inmates?

3. HIV is spread in several ways, including sexual contact and exposure to contaminated blood via sharing needles. How can prison officials minimize the possibility of these high-risk behaviors?

4. Under what sort of circumstances should prison officials give serious consideration to segregating HIV-infected inmates?

5. With the closing of mental institutions beginning in the 1960s, correctional facilities have seen increased numbers of offenders with mental health problems. Are prisons and jails the best options to respond to the needs of this unique population?

6. Military veterans can and do violate the law. Do you think that society should have a different responsibility regarding how it responds to their criminality? Why or why not?

Notes

1. Stephanie Chen, "Prison Health-Care Costs Rise as Inmates Grow Older and Sicker," *CNN.com*, www.cnn.com/2009/CRIME/11/13/aging.inmates/index.html, November 13, 2009.

2. Joann B. Morton, *An Administrative Overview of the Older Inmate* (Washington, DC: National Institute of Corrections, U.S. Department of Justice, 1992).

3. Israel Issi Doron and Helene Love, "Aging Prisoners: A Brief Report of Key Legal and Policy Dilemmas," *International Journal of Criminology and Sociology* 2 (2013): 322–27.

4. Anthony A. Sterns, Greta Lax, Chad Sed, Patrick Keohane, and Ronni S. Sterns, "The Growing Wave of Older Prisoners: A National Survey of Older Prisoner Health, Mental Health and Programming," *Corrections Today* 70 (August 2008): 70–76.

5. Robert Vann Rikard and Ed Rosenberg, "Aging Inmates: A Convergence of Trends in the American Criminal Justice System," *Journal of Correctional Health Care* 13 (no. 3, 2007): 150–62.

6. Andrew P. Wilper, Steffie Woolhandler, J. Wesley Boyd, Karen E. Lasser, Danny McCormick, David H. Bor, and David U. Himmelstein, "The Health and Health Care of US Prisoners: Results of a Nationwide Survey," *American Journal of Public Health* 99 (no. 4, 2009): 666–72.

7. Mary T. Harrison, "True Grit: An Innovative Program for Elderly Inmates," *Corrections Today* 68 (no. 7, 2006): 46–49.

8. Matthew Davis, "The Reintegration of Elderly Prisoners: An Exploration of Services Provided in England and Wales," *Internet Journal of Criminology*, www.internetjournalofcriminology.com, 2011.

9. Elaine Crawley and Richard Sparks, "Is There Life After Imprisonment? How Elderly Men Talk About Imprisonment and Release," *Criminology & Criminal Justice* 6 (no. 1, 2006): 63–82.

10. Doron and Love, "Aging Prisoners."

11. Federal Bureau of Prisons, *Compassionate Release/Reduction in Sentence: Procedures for Implementation of 18 U.S.C. §§ 3582(c)(1)(A) and 4205(g)*, www.bop.gov/policy/progstat/5050_049.pdf, 2013.

12. Tina Chui, *It's About Time: Aging Prisoners, Increasing Costs, and Geriatric Release* (Vera Institute of Justice, 2010), www.vera.org/download?file=2973/Its-about-time-aging-prisoners-increasing-costs-and-geriatric-release.pdf.

13. Ibid., p. 6.

14. Bureau of Justice Statistics, *HIV in Prisons, 2001–10* (Washington, DC: U.S. Government Printing Office, 2012).

15. Bureau of Justice Statistics, *Suicide and Homicide in State Prisons and Local Jails* (Washington, DC: U.S. Government Printing Office, 2005), 2.

16. Bureau of Justice Statistics, *HIV in Prisons, 2007–08* (Washington, DC: U.S. Government Printing Office, 2009), 1.

17. Janet L. Mullings, James W. Marquart, and Deborah J. Hartley, "Exploring the Effects of Childhood Sexual Abuse and Its Impact on HIV/AIDS Risk-Taking Behavior Among Women Prisoners," *Prison Journal* 83 (December 2003): 442–63.

18. K. C. Goyer, *HIV/AIDS in Prison: Problems, Policies and Potential* (Las Vegas: Institute for Security Studies, Monograph 79, 2003).

19. Ibid., pp. 11–12.

20. Roland C. Merchant, Jacob E. Nettleton, Kenneth H. Mayer, and Bruce M. Becker, "HIV Post-Exposure Prophylaxis Among Police and Corrections Officers," *Occupational Medicine* 58 (no. 7, 2008): 502–05.

21. T. M. Hammett, P. Harmon, and L. M. Maruschak, *1996–1997 Update: HIV/AIDS, STDs, and TB in Correctional Facilities* (Washington, DC: U.S. Department of Justice, National Institute of Justice, 1999).

22. Human Rights Watch, "Mississippi Stops Segregating Prisoners with HIV," www.hrw.org/en/news/2010/. . ./17/mississippi-stops-segregating-prisoners-hiv, March 17, 2010.

23. H. Richard Lamb, "Deinstitutionalization and the Homeless Mentally Ill," *Hospital and Community Psychiatry* 35 (1984): 899–907.

24. Fox Butterfield, "Study Finds Hundreds of Thousands of Inmates Mentally Ill," *New York Times*, www.nytimes.com/2003/10/22/national/22MENT.html, October 22, 2003.

25. E. Fuller Torrey, *Out of the Shadows: Confronting America's Mental Illness Crisis* (New York: Wiley, 1997).

26. E. F. Torrey, J. Stieber, J. Ezekiel, S. M. Wolfe, J. Noble, J. Sharfstein, and L. Flynn, *Criminalizing the Seriously Mentally Ill* (Darby, PA: Diane, 1992).

27. Bureau of Justice Statistics, *Mental Health Problems of Prison and Jail Inmates* (Washington, DC: U.S. Government Printing Office, 2006), 4.

28 Ibid., p. 10.

29 *Ralph Coleman, et al. v. Edmund G. Brown, JR., et al.*, No. Civ. S-90-520 LKK/JFM.

30 Ibid.; Raymond F. Patterson, *Report on Suicides Completed in the California Department of Corrections and Rehabilitation in Calendar Year 2011*, http://solitarywatch.com/wp-content /uploads/2013/04/Coleman-Report-on-Suicides-Completed-in-the -CDCR-in-Calendar-Year-20111.pdf, January 25, 2013.

31 James J. Stephan, *Census of State and Federal Correctional Facilities, 2005* (Washington, DC: Bureau of Justice Statistics, 2008), Appendix Table 19.

32 Robert Martinson, "What Works? Questions and Answers about Prison Reform," *Public Interest* 35 (Spring 1974): 22–54.

33 Butterfield, "Study Finds Hundreds of Thousands."

34 Ibid., p. 10.

35 Mark Fischenich, "15 Patients Slated for 48-Bed Facility—When It Opens," *Mankato Free Press*, http://mankatofreepress.com/local /x657353896/15-patients-slated-for-48-bed-facility-when-it-opens, July 2, 2010.

36 Camille Graham Camp, *The 2002 Corrections Yearbook: Adult Corrections* (Middletown, CT: Criminal Justice Institute, 2003).

37 Marc Mauer, Ryan S. King, and Malcolm C. Young, *The Meaning of "Life": Long Prison Sentences in Context* (Washington, DC: Sentencing Project, 2004), 3.

38 Pew Center on the States, *Time Served: The High Cost, Low Return of Longer Prison Terms* (Washington, DC: Author, 2012), www.pewstates.org/uploadedFiles/PCS_Assets/2012/Pew_Time _Served_report.pdf.

39 Ibid., p. 13.

40 Timothy J. Flanagan, "Adaptation and Adjustment Among Long-Term Prisoners," *Federal Prison Journal* 2 (Spring 1991): 41–51.

41 Cindie A. Unger and Robert A. Buchanan, *Managing Long-Term Inmates. A Guide for Correctional Administrators* (Washington, DC: National Institute of Corrections, U.S. Department of Justice, 1985).

42 Adapted from Utah Department of Corrections, "Life Skills Programs," http://corrections.utah.gov/programs/life_skills _programs.html.

43 UCLA LGBT Resource Center, "LGBTQI Terminology," www.lgbt .ucla.edu/documents/LGBTTerminology.pdf.

44 National Institute of Corrections, "LGBTI: Their Safety, Your Responsibility," Satellite and Internet Broadcast, November 7, 2012.

45 Valerie Jenness et al., *Violence in California Correctional Facilities: An Empirical Examination of Sexual Assault* (Center for Evidence-Based Corrections, University of California Irvine, 2007).

46 Susan Jacobson, "Transgender Former Inmate Sues Over Alleged Jail Rape," *Orlando Sentinel*, http://articles.orlandosentinel .com/2013-03-21/news/os-transgender-jail-inmate-lawsuit-20130321 _1_inmate-transgender-jail-employees, March 21, 2013.

47 *Farmer v. Brennan*, 114 S.Ct. 1970 (1994).

48 Lori Sexton, Valerie Jenness, and Jennifer Sumner, *Where the Margins Meet: A Demographic Assessment of Transgender Inmates in Men's Prisons*, http://ucicorrections.seweb.uci.edu /sites/ucicorrections.seweb.uci.edu/files/A%20Demographic%20 Assessment%20of%20Transgender%20Inmates%20in%20 Men's%20Prisons.pdf, 2009.

49 *Estelle v. Gamble*, 429 U.S. 97 (1976).

50 The *Diagnostic and Statistical Manual of Mental Disorders* replaces the term *gender identity disorder* with *gender dysphoria;* however, the former term is used in this chapter (www.advocate.com/politics/transgender/2012/07/23 /dsm-replaces-gender-identity-disorder-gender-dysphoria).

51 "Ophelia Azriel De'lonta, Transgendered Prisoner, Gets Sex-Change Lawsuit Reinstated," *Huffington Post*, www .huffingtonpost.com/2013/01/29/ophelia-azriel-delonta-sex -change-lawsuit-reinstated_n_2570802.html, January 29, 2013.

52 "Michelle Kosilek, Inmate Born as Robert Kosilek, Eligible for Legal Fees Reimbursement in Addition to Sex Change," *Huffington Post*, www.huffingtonpost.com/2012/09/17/michelle-kosilek -inmate-robert-kosilek-legal-fees-sex-change_n_1890043.html, September 17, 2012.

53 United States Court of Appeals for the Seventh Circuit, Nos. 10-2339 & 10-2466, *Fields v. Smith*, www.aclu.org/files/assets /fields_opinion.pdf.

54 Margaret E. Noonan and Christopher J. Mumola, *Veterans in State and Federal Prison, 2004* (Washington: Bureau of Justice Statistics, 2004).

55 National Institute of Drug Abuse, *Drug Facts: Substance Abuse in the Military*, www.drugabuse.gov/publications/drugfacts/substance -abuse-in-military, 2013.

56 www.va.gov/oig/pubs/VAOIG-14-02603-178.pdf.

57 SAMHSA'S Gains Center, *Responding to the Needs of Justice-Involved Combat Veterans with Service-Related Trauma and Mental Health Conditions*, http://gainscenter.samhsa .gov, 2008.

58 Jack Tsai, Robert A. Rosenheck, Wesley J. Kasprow, and James F. McGuire, "Risk of Incarceration and Other Characteristics of Iraq and Afghanistan Era Veterans in State and Federal Prisons," *Psychiatric Services* 64 (no. 1, 2013): 36–43.

59 Margaret E. Noonan and Christopher J. Mumola, *Veterans in State and Federal Prison, 2004*, www.bjs.gov/content/pub/pdf/vsfp04 .pdf, 2007.

60 Brad Schaffer, *Jailed Rural Pennsylvania Veterans in the Criminal Justice System* (Butler, PA: Veterans Justice Outreach Program, 2010), www.ncdsv.org/images/Schaffer_JailedRuralPAVetsInTheCJSystem _9-15-2010.pdf.

61 Matthew Wolfe, "From PTSD to Prison: Why Veterans Become Criminals," *Daily Beast*, www.thedailybeast.com /articles/2013/07/28/from-ptsd-to-prison-why-veterans-become -criminals.html, July 28, 2013.

62 Veterans Intervention Project, *Report of Veterans Arrested and Booked into the Travis County Jail*, www.justiceforvets.org/sites /default/files/files/Texas%20Veterans%20Justice%20Research .pdf, 2009.

CORRECTIONAL ISSUES

Part Four examines current correctional issues and trends. "Reentry into the Community" (Chapter 10) has lately taken on a special importance because more than 700,000 inmates are now released each year to community supervision. The offender's experience of postrelease life is a major factor influencing recidivism. Legal issues surrounding prisoners' rights and the law with regard to the death penalty are the subjects of Chapter 11. Juveniles offenders have a separate corrections system, and Chapter 12 examines the challenges that juveniles present to corrections. Chapter 13, "The Future of Corrections," brings together certain issues and findings previously discussed. It then directs attention to five dilemmas facing corrections, four current trends, and three challenges for the future of corrections. ■

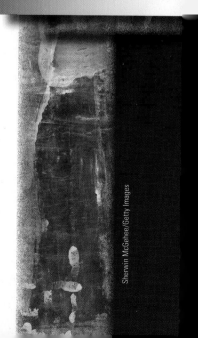

Sherwin McGehee/Getty Images

CHAPTER 10

Reentry into the Community

The background of Robert Francis McDonnell is impressive. He completed his undergraduate work at the University of Notre Dame, served in the U.S. military, and later earned a master's degree from Boston University. He left the service with the rank of lieutenant colonel. After earning a law degree and serving as a prosecutor, McDonnell became Virginia's state attorney general. Shortly thereafter, he was elected to be the seventy-first governor of Virginia, winning the election with nearly 60 percent of the vote. Despite this exemplary record, McDonnell is also the first Virginia governor to go to prison.[1]

McDonnell was found guilty of eleven counts of public corruption and was sentenced by a federal judge to two years in

After reading this chapter you should be able to . . .

1. Understand the nature of parole and how it operates today.

2. Be familiar with the origins of parole.

3. Understand how the release decision is made.

4. Explain the steps taken to ease the offender's reentry into the community.

5. Identify the major problems confronting parolees.

6. Understand why some parolees are viewed as dangerous and how society handles this problem.

Volunteers of America® CHESAPEAKE

Residential Re-Entry Center

Jesse Jackson Jr. checks into a halfway house after being released from federal prison. While serving as a U.S. congressman, he was convicted of violating campaign laws and was sentenced to 30 months in prison. About half of his sentence will be served in the halfway house.

n followed by two years of supervised
se. Once McDonnell is under commu-
supervision, he will likely have at his
osal many resources and the willing

life of McDonnell will no doubt also benefit his reentry experience, the typical
offender embarking on reentry will have
a far different experience from that of the

(continued from previous page)

Ex-prisoners are mostly men with few or no job skills. About one-third of released state inmates have a physical or mental impairment. About two-thirds of all state releasees will return to a few metropolitan areas in their states, where they will live in poor, inner-city neighborhoods. As they leave prison, most offenders receive a new set of clothes, up to $100 in "gate money" (only in some states), instructions as to when and where to report to a parole officer, and a bus ticket home. With the great expansion of incarceration during the past four decades, the number of offenders now returning to the community has increased dramatically. In fact, the number of those on parole has increased every year but one from 2000 to 2013. Parole is essential to the management of correctional populations in the United States. ■

THE ORIGINS OF PAROLE

Parole in the United States evolved during the 1800s following the English, Australian, and Irish practices of conditional pardon, apprenticeship by indenture, transportation of criminals from one country to another, and the issuance of *tickets-of-leave*, a form of conditional release. Such practices generally did not develop as part of a theory of

During the 1800s English prisoners were transported to Australia, Tasmania, and other colonies in the South Pacific. As administrator of the penal colony on Norfolk Island, Tasmania, Captain Alexander Maconochie devised a system of rewards for good conduct, labor, and study. Prisoners meeting his criteria were granted a ticket-of-leave, releasing them to the community. It was out of this practice that parole developed.

punishment or to promote a particular goal of the criminal sanction. Instead, they were all methods of moving criminals out of prison as a response to overcrowding, labor shortages, and the cost of incarceration.

A key figure in developing parole in the nineteenth century was Captain Alexander Maconochie, an administrator of British penal colonies in Tasmania and elsewhere in the South Pacific. A critic of determinate prison terms, Maconochie devised a system of rewards for good conduct and labor. Under his classification procedure, prisoners could pass through stages of increasing responsibility and freedom: (1) strict imprisonment, (2) labor on chain gangs, (3) freedom within a limited area, (4) a ticket-of-leave or parole with conditional pardon, and (5) full restoration of liberty. Like modern correctional practices, this procedure assumed that prisoners should be prepared gradually for release. The roots of the American system of parole can be seen in the transition from imprisonment to conditional release to full freedom.

In Ireland, Sir Walter Crofton built on Maconochie's idea that an offender's progress in prison and a ticket-of-leave were *linked*. Prisoners who graduated through Crofton's three successive levels of treatment were released on parole under a series of conditions. Most significant was the requirement that parolees report monthly to the police. In Dublin a special civilian inspector helped releasees find jobs, visited them periodically, and supervised their activities.

In the United States, parole developed during the prison reform movement of the second half of the nineteenth century. Relying on the ideas of Maconochie and Crofton, American reformers such as Zebulon Brockway, of the Elmira Reformatory in New York, began to experiment with the concept of parole by releasing inmates when their conduct showed that they were ready to return to society. In 1870 the National Prison Association incorporated references to the Irish system into its Declaration of Principles, along with such other reforms as the indeterminate sentence and classification based on a mark system.[2]

As states adopted indeterminate sentencing, parole followed. By 1900, 20 states had parole systems, and by 1925, 46 states did; Mississippi and Virginia finally followed suit in 1942.[3] Beginning in 1910, each federal prison had its own parole board, made up of the warden, the medical officer, and the superintendent of prisons of the Department of Justice. The boards made release suggestions to the attorney general. In 1930 Congress created the U.S. Board of Parole, which replaced the separate boards.[4]

Although used in the United States for over a century, parole remains controversial. When an offender who has committed a particularly notorious crime, such as Mark David Chapman (who murdered famed musician John Lennon), becomes eligible for parole or when someone on parole has again raped, robbed, or murdered, the public is outraged. During the 1970s, both parole and the indeterminate sentence were criticized on the grounds that release was tied to an elusive treatment success, that parole boards were abusing their discretion, and that inmates were being held in "suspended animation" regarding their release. However, remember that although parole may be justified in terms of rehabilitation, deterrence, or protection of society, it has other effects as well. Insofar as it reduces time spent in prison, it affects plea bargaining, the size of prison populations, and the overall ability of the criminal justice system to effectively manage offenders.

RELEASE FROM ONE PART OF THE SYSTEM TO ANOTHER

Reentry is the period of correctional supervision following release from prison. Reentry is ended by an inmate's discharge from parole or return to prison for a new crime or for violating the conditions of release.[5] For most of the twentieth century, the term *parole* referred to both a release mechanism and a method of community supervision. It is still used in this general sense, but with recent changes in sentencing and release policies, the dual usage no longer applies in all states. Now it is necessary to distinguish between a releasing mechanism and supervision. Although releasing mechanisms have changed, most former prisoners must still serve a period under community supervision.

Except for the 7 percent of incarcerated felons who die in prison, all inmates will eventually be released to live in the community. Currently, about 77 percent of felons are released on parole and remain under correctional supervision for a specific period. About 19 percent are released at the expiration of their sentence, having "maxed out," and are free to live in the community without supervision. However, there are about 2,700 sex offenders in 16 states who remain in custody long after their sentence has been completed. They are being held in civil-commitment programs to treat what has been judged to be a mental abnormality.[6]

parole
The conditional release of an inmate from incarceration, under supervision, after part of the prison sentence has been served.

Parole is the conditional release of an offender from incarceration but not from the legal custody of the state. For example, an inmate sentenced to eight years may serve a portion of the sentence in prison and, if awarded parole, will serve the remaining time in the community. Offenders who comply with parole conditions and do not further violate the law receive an absolute discharge from supervision at the end of their sentences. If a parolee breaks a rule, parole may be revoked and the person returned to a correctional facility. Parole, then, rests on three concepts:

1. *Grace or privilege.* The prisoner could be kept incarcerated, but the government extends the privilege of possible release.

2. *Contract of consent.* The government enters into an agreement with the prisoner whereby the prisoner promises to abide by certain conditions in exchange for being released.

3. *Custody.* Even though the offender is released from prison, he or she is still the responsibility of the government because the sentence has not yet expired. Parole is the continuation of correctional supervision into the community.

Only felons are released on parole; adult misdemeanants are usually released directly from local institutions on expiration of their sentences. With the incarcerated population more than quadrupling during the past 40 years, it is not surprising that the number of parolees has also grown, as shown in **Figure 10.1**. Today, more than 853,900 individuals are under parole supervision, a 257-percent increase since 1980.[7] With the massive incarcerations of the past decades, the number on parole is likely to reach one million within the next five years.

Only state and federal (not local) governments implement parole. In many states the parole board (the releasing authority) is part of the department of corrections; in others, it is an autonomous body whose members the governor appoints.

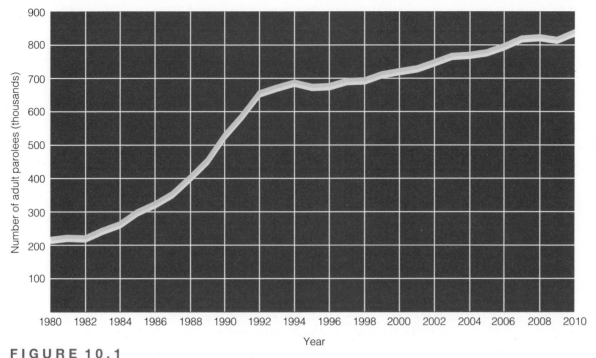

FIGURE 10.1
Numbers of Adults Under Parole Supervision, 1980–2010

As with the incarcerated population, since 1980 the number of offenders on parole has more than tripled.

Source: Ann L. Pastore and Kathleen Maguire, eds., *Sourcebook of Criminal Justice Statistics*, Table 6.1.2009, www.albany.edu/sourcebook/pdf/t612010.pdf, retrieved April 22, 2014.

As you read this chapter, keep in mind that, as with so many other correctional activities, the decision to release is made in the context of complex and competing goals. Traditionally, parole has been justified in terms of rehabilitation. In theory, parole boards evaluate the offender's progress *toward* rehabilitation and readiness to abide by laws. In practice, they consider other factors as well. Even where determinate sentencing or parole guidelines are in effect and limit release decisions, correctional officials can influence release; the decision is not as simple as supporters have claimed.

Many questions bear on the release decision no matter what procedures are followed. Is the offender ready for release? Who will be blamed if the offender commits another crime? Is the prison so crowded that an early release is necessary to open up space? Will the offender's release affect future charging and sentencing decisions?

RELEASE MECHANISMS

From 1920 to 1973, all states and the federal government used indeterminate sentencing, authorized discretionary release by parole boards, and authorized the supervision of prisoners after release. Since the critique of rehabilitation in the 1970s and the move to determinate sentencing and parole guidelines, 16 states and the federal government abolished discretionary release by parole boards. Another 5 states abolished discretionary release for certain offenses.[8] Further, in some of the states that kept discretionary release, parole boards have been reluctant to grant it. But recent trends indicate that this is waning. In Texas, for example, 57 percent of all cases considered for parole release in 1988 were approved; by 1998, that figure dropped to just 20 percent.[9] However, since 2001 the number of paroles have steadily increased, with 31 percent of eligible inmates released on parole in 2011.[10] In 1998 the Georgia Board of Pardons and Paroles instituted a 90-percent rule for offenders convicted of any 1 of 20 crimes. The rule required that these inmates, "regardless of risk or disparity in the sentence,"

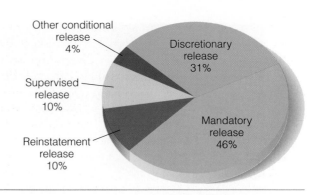

FIGURE 10.2

Methods of Release from State Prison

Entries to parole by type of entry, 2000–2011.

Sources: BJS *Bulletin*, November 2012; Laura M. Maruschak and Erika Parks, *Probation and Parole in the United States, 2011*.

must serve 90 percent of their time before the board will grant release.[11] But a Fulton County Superior Court judge found that the rule was illegally implemented.[12] Following that judicial decision in 2005, the Georgia Board of Pardons and Paroles officially abandoned the 90-percent rule, allowing the board to grant parole earlier for affected inmates.[13] Even California recently passed the Three Strike Reform Act of 2012, which permits eligible inmates to be resentenced to second-strike status. This change not only allows the possibility of parole but also of parole occurring earlier for affected inmates. Greater use of discretionary and mandatory parole release allows correctional authorities to address prison overcrowding as well as the rising costs of incarceration.

There are now six basic mechanisms for release from prison: (1) discretionary release, (2) mandatory release, (3) expiration release, (4) probation release, (5) reinstatement release, and (6) other conditional releases. In addition, some offenders return to the community upon the expiration of their sentence. **Figure 10.2** shows the percentage of felons released by the various mechanisms.

Common Forms of Prison Release: Discretionary Release, Mandatory Release, and Expiration Release

discretionary release
The release of an inmate from prison to conditional supervision at the discretion of the parole board within the boundaries set by the sentence and the penal law.

States retaining indeterminate sentences allow **discretionary release** by the parole board within the boundaries set by the sentence and the penal law. As a conditional release to parole supervision, this approach lets the parole board assess the prisoner's readiness for release within the minimum and maximum terms of the sentence. In reviewing the prisoner's file and asking questions about the prisoner, the parole board focuses on the nature of the offense, the inmate's behavior, and his or her participation in rehabilitative programs. This process necessitates the most involvement by the parole board in the determination of the prisoner's release. By definition, discretionary release indicates that the decision to grant parole is guided by criteria determined by the parole board. Because there are no federal parole standards that constrain state paroling authorities, this form of release places great faith in the ability of independent parole boards to predict the future behavior of offenders.

mandatory release
The required release of an inmate from incarceration to community supervision on the expiration of a certain period, as stipulated by a determinate sentencing law or parole guidelines.

Mandatory release occurs after an inmate has served time equal to the total sentence minus "good time," if any, or to a certain percentage of the total sentence as specified by law. It is primarily used in federal jurisdictions and states with determinate and mandatory sentencing schemes. Mandatory release became more common during the 1970s, as indeterminate sentencing, along with judicial and parole discretion, fell into disfavor. The role of the parole board is largely relegated to an administrative function with emphasis on bookkeeping. Because mandatory parole release is determined by time served and not on the assessment of prisoner rehabilitation, the parole board has limited involvement in the decision to release. Bookkeeping is nevertheless critical as it determines whether the prisoner is legally eligible for release, and it also establishes the anticipated length of parole before the sentence expires. Once these computations have been determined, the prisoner is released conditionally, upon eligibility, to parole supervision for the rest of the sentence.

In addition to discretionary and mandatory release, an increasing percentage of prisoners are given an **expiration release**. These are inmates, usually in mandatory-sentencing states, who are released from any further correctional supervision and cannot be returned to prison for their current offense. Such offenders have served the maximum court sentence, minus good time—they have "maxed out." Such prisoners are released unconditionally.[14] Some prisoners choose this route, forgoing attempts at parole and the restrictions that come with it. Critics are concerned that many offenders who "max out" have spent long terms in prison for serious, violent offenses or have spent extended periods in administrative segregation. They are often hardened, embittered, and likely to return to crime.[15] The number of prisoners preferring to max out has steadily increased. A recent Pew report states that between 1990 and 2012, the number increased from 50,000 to more than 100,000, a growth rate of nearly 120 percent.[16] Of all prisoners released in 2012, the number of those who maxed out and are therefore not under any correctional supervision was one in five. Florida reported the largest number in this category, with 64 percent of all state prisoners maxing out in 2012. Tougher sentencing policies coupled with fewer options for discretionary release have contributed to this developing trend. States with lower numbers of max-out prisoners are ones that have retained discretionary-release procedures.

Several states are proposing statutory changes that would permit the mandatory monitoring and supervision by paroling authorities of prisoners who have maxed out. New Hampshire saw a decrease in its max-out rate after passing legislation in 2010 that requires at least nine months of community supervision before the sentence expires. New Jersey has proposed a graduated period of required monitoring of ex-offenders based on the degree of the committing offense. Those convicted of a fourth-degree offense would be monitored for one year, a third-degree offense would require a two-year period of mandatory monitoring, and so on.[17] Hawaii is proposing a similar bill.

expiration release
The release of an inmate from incarceration without any further correctional supervision; the inmate cannot be returned to prison for any remaining portion of the sentence for the current offense.

Other Forms of Prison Release: Probation Release, Reinstatement Release, and Other Conditional Releases

Probation release occurs when the sentencing judge requires a period of postcustody supervision in the community. Probation release is often tied to shock incarceration, a practice in which first-time offenders are sentenced to a short period in jail ("the shock") and then allowed to reenter the community under supervision. In some jurisdictions this type of sentence is referred to as *shock probation*. Probation release may also be used in split-sentence schemes. Similar to shock incarceration, the split sentence requires the offender to serve a period of incarceration followed by a period of supervision in the community upon release, usually in the guise of probation. A slight difference between shock incarceration or shock probation and split sentences is that the former seeks to *resentence* the offender to probation following the brief period of incarceration. However, the split sentence, with both components of incarceration and probation, is handed down jointly at the time of sentencing.

probation release
The release of an inmate from incarceration to probation supervision, as required by the sentencing judge.

Reinstatement release occurs when offenders are returned to parole after serving a time in prison because of a parole violation. The two reasons for a parole violation are the violation of a condition of parole (a technical violation) or arrest and conviction on a new charge. A technical violation may involve a reinstatement release after a four- or six-month return to prison. However, a new conviction complicates a reinstatement release. Now there are two sentences governing release and parole: the original sentence and the new sentence from the conviction on the offense committed during parole. The offender is again released into the community upon eligibility, with an additional period of supervision from the new offense. In some states where parole revocation is high, such as California, offenders on reinstatement release make up almost 20 percent of those leaving prison.

reinstatement release
The release of offenders to parole supervision following a time in prison for a parole violation.

focus on correctional practice

Computing Parole Eligibility: Discretionary Release

At the time of sentencing, Ben Brooks had been held in jail for six months awaiting trial and disposition of his case. As shown in **Figure 10.3**, he was given a sentence of a minimum of 5 years and a maximum of 10 years for robbery with violence. Brooks did well at the maximum-security prison to which he was sent. He did not get into trouble and was thus able to amass good-time credit at the rate of one day for every four that he spent on good behavior. In addition, he was given meritorious credit of 30 days when he passed his high school diploma equivalency test. After serving three years

and four months of his sentence, he appeared before the board of parole and was granted release into the community.

Critical Thinking

Inmates earning reductions in time served because of good conduct, program participation, and other factors are viewed by some as compromising public safety. Should this concern outweigh the ability of correctional administrators to offer incentives to inmates for prosocial behavior?

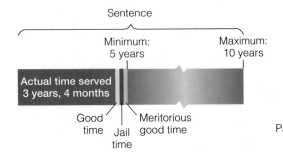

Maximum sentence	3,650	days (10 years)
Minimum sentence	1,825	days (5 years)
"Jail time"	− 180	
	1,645	
Meritorious "good time"	− 30	
	1,615	
"Good time" (1 for 4)	− 404	
Paroled: actual time served	1,211	days (3 years, 4 months)

FIGURE 10.3
Computing Parole Eligibility for Ben Brooks

Various good-time reductions to the minimum sentence are allowed in most corrections systems to determine eligibility for parole. Note how a 5- to 10-year sentence can be reduced to a stay of 3 years, 4 months.

other conditional release
A probationary sentence used in some states to get around the rigidity of mandatory release by placing convicts in various community settings under supervision.

Because of the growth of prison populations, many states have devised ways to get around the rigidity of mandatory release. They place inmates in the community through furlough, home supervision, halfway houses, emergency release, and other programs.[18] These **other conditional releases** also avoid the appearance of the politically sensitive label *discretionary parole*. Nevertheless, they also serve a very important function: They permit the paroling authority to test the readiness of prisoners by placing them in less restrictive environments. This serves the purpose of preparing inmates for their eventual release while simultaneously providing the ability to supervise these individuals, further ensuring public safety.

THE DECISION TO RELEASE

An inmate's eligibility for release to community supervision depends on requirements set by law and the sentence imposed by the court. As noted, in states with determinate sentences or parole guidelines, release is mandatory once the offender has served the required amount of time. In nearly half the states, however, the release decision is

Recent reforms allow victims of the crime to speak to parole boards as they consider parole. Here, Dean Smart, brother of Gregory Smart, speaks to Patrick Randall, who was convicted of Gregory Smart's murder in 1990. Randall was granted parole and will be released after 25 years in prison.

AP Images/Jim Cole

discretionary, and it is designed to allow the parole board to release inmates to supervision in the community when they are deemed "ready" to live as law-abiding citizens.[19]

When parole boards face intense caseload pressures, hearing officers are employed. These career professionals assist board members by preparing reports on individual inmates scheduled for parole consideration, conducting release hearings for eligible inmates, and conducting revocation hearings for inmates who may be returned to custody for parole violation.

Procedure

Eligibility for an appearance before the parole board is a function of the individual sentence, statutory criteria, and the inmate's conduct before incarceration. Often, the offender is eligible for release at the end of the minimum term of the sentence minus good time. In other states, eligibility is at the discretion of the parole board or is calculated at one-third or one-half of the maximum sentence. As an example of the computation of parole eligibility, look at the case of Ben Brooks in "Focus on Correctional Practice."

Release Criteria

What criteria guide the release decision? Most parole boards give inmates a formal statement of the criteria they use to make the decision. These standards normally include at least eight factors:

1. Nature and circumstances of the offense and the inmate's current attitude toward it.
2. Prior criminal record.
3. Attitudes toward family members, victim, and authority in general.
4. Institutional adjustment, along with participation and progress in programs for self-improvement.
5. History of community adjustment.
6. Physical, mental, and emotional health.

7. Insight into causes of past criminal conduct.

8. Adequacy of parole plan.

Although the published criteria may help familiarize inmates with the board's expectations, the actual decision is discretionary and is typically based on various other kinds of information as well as fundamental moral judgments about the severity of the crime, the prisoner's culpability, and the adequacy of the term served as punishment for the crime.

Parole board members do not want public criticism for making controversial decisions. Thus, notorious offenders are unlikely ever to gain parole release even if they behave well in prison. Also, as described in the Focus on Correctional Technology, some states are taking DNA samples from offenders being considered for release to see if they are linked to other crimes.

Although prisoners' participation in rehabilitative programs is technically voluntary, the link between participation and release poses many legal and ethical problems. Prisoners claim that although they are urged to participate in these programs, the corrections system may not have enough places in these programs to serve all of them. Moreover, some kinds of treatment programs, especially for sex offenders, may involve intrusive counseling therapies or medications that have lingering physical effects and a limited likelihood of success. Yet, threatened with denial of parole if they refuse to participate, prisoners may not feel able to decline such treatments. Some of these issues arise in the case of Jim Allen, discussed in "Do the Right Thing."

When release is discretionary, the parole board's power is much like that of the sentencing judge. Detractors emphasize that unlike the judge, the board makes its decisions outside the spotlight of public attention. In addition, they contend that whereas sentencing is done with due process of law, a parole hearing offers few such rights.

focus on correctional technology

DNA and Parole Release

Paroling authorities are concerned with making decisions that reflect public safety needs and the legal rights of inmates. Key to this task is the assessment of risk, which requires answering a number of significant questions: What does the committing offense indicate about the inmate's criminality? What can we learn from the prior history? What does the institutional record suggest about the inmate? Is there evidence of meaningful program participation? Does this individual have supportive ties in the community? Would the release of this inmate create a danger to the public?

These are typical questions that are useful in determining risk. But lately another question has been added: Does the DNA of the inmate link him or her to any unsolved crimes out there? Some may consider this question beyond the scope of paroling authorities, but growing numbers of these officials are referring to this new area. In a *USA Today* survey, 12 state paroling authorities indicated that they do review DNA hits (or would) if such reports are made available to them at the time of a parole hearing.[20]

Apparently, some state law enforcement officials, along with crime victims, are seeking to block the parole release of eligible inmates by providing DNA reports to paroling authorities.

Defense attorneys and civil rights advocates would be concerned about the use of such reports against inmates who routinely appear before parole boards without the benefit of legal counsel. Nevertheless, this is a strategy that is beginning to gain traction. Authorities in Utah, Wisconsin, and Texas have reported denying or deferring parole release decisions because of information provided by DNA reports.

Critical Thinking

1. Should such information be routinely incorporated in parole hearing materials?

2. Should it be the basis of a decision to deny parole?

Supporters of discretionary release maintain that parole boards can rectify sentencing errors. Arguably, legislatures often respond to public pressure by prescribing unreasonably harsh maximum sentences—30, 50, even 100 years. But most penal codes also prescribe minimum sentences that are closer to the actual times served; thus, the parole board can grant release after a "reasonable" period of incarceration. The Bureau of Justice Statistics publishes statistics on the number and nature of cases of parole release. **Table 10.1** shows types of parole release by state.[21]

Table 10.1 Adults Entering Parole, by Type of Entry, 2013 (Federal Parole and Parole by States with 10,000 or More Reported Paroles)

Jurisdiction	Total reported	Discretionary[a]	Mandatory[b]	Reinstatement[c]	Term of supervised release[d]	Other[e]	Unknown or not reported
U.S. total	430,018	183,899	109,768	13,060	85,972	4,782	32,537
Federal	49,212	361	862	69	47,920	0	0
State	380,806	183,538	108,906	12,991	38,052	4,782	32,537
Arizona	11,929	146	117	144	10,576	946	0
California	24,559	..	..	..	..	..	24,559
Georgia	14,565	14,565	0	..	0	0	0
Illinois	28,236	13	26,729	257	N/A	778	459
Kentucky	10,267	6,724	3,543	0	0	0	0
Louisiana	16,058	616	15,105	307	14	16	0
Michigan	10,539	9,174	629	736	N/A	0	0
Missouri	13,863	10,869	834	1,222	N/A	938	0
New York	21,570	5,624	7,036	N/A	8,174	736	0
Pennsylvania[f]	57,654	54,749	0	2,905	0	0	0
Texas	35,076	33,737	509	369	0	461	0

N/A = Not applicable.

*Not known.

[a] Includes offenders entering due to a parole board decision.

[b] Includes offenders whose release from prison was not decided by a parole board, and offenders entering due to determinate sentencing, good-time provisions, and emergency releases.

[c] Includes offenders returned to parole after serving time in a prison due to a parole violation. Depending on the reporting jurisdiction, reinstatement entries may include only parolees who were originally released from prison through a discretionary release, only those originally released through a mandatory release, or a combination of both types. May also include those originally released through a term of supervised release.

[d] Includes offenders sentenced by a judge to a fixed period of incarceration based on a determinate statute immediately followed by a period of supervised release in the community.

[e] Includes parolees who were transferred from another state, placed on supervised release from jail, released to a drug transition program, released from a boot camp operated by the Department of Corrections, and released from prison through a conditional medical or mental health release to parole. Also includes absconders who were returned to parole supervision, on pretrial supervision, under supervision due to a suspended sentence, and others.

[f] Some or all detailed data were estimated for type of sentence.

Source: Adapted from Erinn J. Herberman and Thomas P. Bonczar, *Probation and Parole in the United States, 2013* (Washington, DC: Bureau of Justice Statistics, 2014).

DO the Right Thing

The five members of the parole board questioned Jim Allen, an offender with a long history of sex offenses involving teenage boys. Now approaching age 45 and having met the eligibility requirement for a hearing, Allen respectfully answered the board members.

Toward the end of the hearing, Richard Edwards, a dentist who had recently been appointed to the board, spoke up: "Your institutional record is good, you have a parole plan, a job has been promised, and your sister says she will help you. All of that looks good, but I just can't vote for your parole. You haven't attended the behavior-modification program for sex offenders. I think you're going to repeat your crime. I have a 13-year-old son, and I don't want him or other boys to run the risk of meeting your kind." Allen looked shocked. The other members had seemed ready to grant his release.

"But I'm ready for parole. I won't do that stuff again. I didn't go to that program because electroshock to my private area is not going to help me. I've been here five years of the seven-year max and have stayed out of trouble. The judge didn't say I was to be further punished in prison by therapy."

After Jim Allen left the room, the board discussed his case. "You know, Rich, he has a point. He has been a model prisoner and has served a good portion of his sentence," said Brian Lynch, a long-term board member. "Besides, we don't know if Dr. Hankin's program works."

"I know, but can we really let someone like that out on the streets?" asked Edwards.

Critical Thinking

1. Are the results of the behavior-modification program for sex offenders relevant to the parole board's decision?
2. Is the purpose of the sentence to punish Allen for what he did or for what he might do in the future?
3. Would you vote for his release on parole? Would your vote be the same if his case had received media attention?

Structuring Parole Decisions

In response to criticism that the release decisions of parole boards are somewhat arbitrary, many states have adopted parole guidelines (see "Focus on Correctional Practice"). Release is usually granted to prisoners who have served the amount of time stipulated by the guidelines and who meet the following three criteria:

1. They have substantially observed the rules of the institution in which they have been confined.
2. Their release will not depreciate the seriousness of the offense or promote disrespect for the law.
3. Their release will not jeopardize the public welfare.

The Impact of Release Mechanisms

Parole release mechanisms do more than determine the date at which a particular prisoner will be sent back into the community. Parole release also has an enormous impact on other parts of the criminal justice system, including sentencing, plea bargaining, and the size of prison populations.[22]

One important effect of discretionary release is that the parole board can shorten a sentence imposed by a judge. In some jurisdictions, up to 60 percent of felons sentenced to prison are released to the community after their first appearance before a parole board. Eligibility for discretionary release is ordinarily determined by the minimum term of the sentence minus good time and jail time.

The probability of release well before the sentence expires encourages plea bargaining. Prosecutors can reap the benefits of quick, cooperative plea bargains that look tough in the eyes of the public. Meanwhile, the defendant agrees to plead guilty and accept the sentence because of the high likelihood of early release through parole.

Researchers have raised the question of whether the type of prisoner release affects the likelihood of recidivism. A recent study tested whether mandatory releases saw lower rates of recidivism in comparison to discretionary releases.[23] Mandatory releases are permitted under determinant-sentencing models, whereas discretionary releases are more often applied under indeterminate-sentencing models. The recidivism rates of six states (Maryland, Virginia, New York, North Carolina, Oregon, and Texas) with mixed-sentencing models were examined. Study findings were varied but informative. Discretionary releases saw lower risks of recidivism in New York and North Carolina but not in Maryland and Virginia. In the latter states, mandatory releases were more effective. The remaining two states, Texas and Oregon, saw no significant differences in outcome. Although more research is needed in this area, the study underscored that perhaps the availability and quality of reentry programs have more effect on recidivism than the nature of prisoner release.

Beyond the benefits to prosecutors, discretionary release may aid the overall system because it often mitigates the harshness of the penal code. If the legislature must establish exceptionally strict punishments as a means of conveying a "tough-on-crime" image to frustrated voters, parole can effectively permit sentence adjustments that make the punishment fit the crime. Early release on parole can be granted to an offender who is less deserving of strict punishment, such as someone who voluntarily makes restitution, cooperates with the police, or shows genuine regret.

Discretionary release is also an important tool for reducing prison populations in states with overcrowded prisons and budget deficits. Even states that abolished parole boards, instituted mandatory sentences, and adopted truth-in-sentencing laws in the 1980s are now finding loopholes that allow them to release convicts early.

Women in Alaska's Hiland Mountain Correctional Center are taking a prerelease course on "tips for success" that will help them succeed when they are released back into the community. Correctional facilities used to just let people out, but now they try to prepare them better for their return to the community.

AP Images/Chugiak Eagle River Star/Cinthia Ritchie

focus on correctional practice

Criminal History/Risk Assessment Under the Oregon Guidelines for Adult Offenders

Oregon has developed guidelines to assist the parole board in determining the amount of time to be served prior to release to community supervision. The guidelines are composed of a severity scale that ranks crimes according to their seriousness and a risk assessment score that measures both the offender's criminal history (drug arrests, prior record, age at first conviction, and so on) and risk factors regarded as relevant to successful completion of parole.

Parole board staffs examine the inmate's criminal history/risk assessment score by first adding the points assigned to each factor (**Table 10.2**). By placing that score next to his or her particular offense on the severity scale (**Table 10.3**), the board, the inmate, and correctional officials may calculate the presumptive parole date soon after the offender enters prison. This is the date by which the

inmate can *expect* to be released if there are no disciplinary or other problems during incarceration. The presumptive parole date may be modified. The date of release may be advanced because of good conduct and superior achievement or postponed if there are disciplinary infractions or if a suitable community supervision plan is not developed.

Critical Thinking

Risk assessment tools are meant to minimize discretionary decision making, increase transparency in release decisions, and help with parole release standards. Do you think that these efforts toward more-objective, evidence-based release decisions increase public safety?

Table 10.2 Criminal History/Risk Assessment Under the Oregon Guidelines for Adult Offenders

The amount of time to be served is related to the severity of the offense and to the criminal history/risk assessment of the inmate. The criminal history score is determined by adding the points assigned to each factor in this table.

	Factor	Points	Score
A.	No prior felony convictions as an adult or juvenile:	3	
	One prior felony conviction:	2	
	Two or three prior felony convictions:	1	
	Four or more prior felony convictions:	0	___
B.	No prior felony or misdemeanor incarcerations (that is, executed sentences of 90 days or more) as an adult or juvenile:	2	
	One or two prior incarcerations:	1	
	Three or more prior incarcerations:	0	___
C.	Verified period of three years conviction-free in the community prior to the present commitment:	1	
	Otherwise:	0	
D.	Age at commencement of behavior leading to this incarceration was ___; D.O.B. was ___		
	26 or older and at least one point received in Items A, B, or C:	2	

Table 10.2 (*Continued*)

	Factor	Points	Score
	26 or older and no points received in A, B, or C:	1	
	21 to under 26 and at least one point received in A, B, or C:	1	
	21 to under 26 and no points received in A, B, or C:	0	
	Under 21:	0	___
E.	Present commitment does not include parole, probation, failure to appear, release agreement, escape, or custody violation:	2	
	Present commitment involves probation, release agreement, or failure to appear violation:	1	
	Present commitment involves parole, escape, or custody violation:	0	___
F.	Has no admitted or documented substance abuse problem within a three-year period in the community immediately preceding the commission of the crime conviction:	1	
	Otherwise:	0	
	Total History/Risk Assessment		___

Source: Adapted from State of Oregon, Board of Parole, *ORS* Chapter 144, Rule 255-35-015.

Table 10.3 Number of Months to Be Served Before Release Under the Oregon Guidelines

The presumptive release date is determined by finding the intersection of the criminal history score (see Table 10.2) and the category of the offense. Thus, an offender with an assessment score between 8 and 6, convicted of a category 3 offense, could expect to serve between 10 and 14 months.

Offense Severity	Criminal History/Risk Assessment Score			
	11–9 Excellent	8–6 Good	5–3 Fair	2–0 Poor
Category 1: bigamy, criminal mischief I, dogfighting, incest, possession of stolen vehicle	6	6	6–10	12–18
Category 2: abandonment of a child, bribing a witness, criminal homicide, perjury, possession of controlled substance	6	6–10	10–14	16–24
Category 3: assault III, forgery I, sexual abuse, trafficking in stolen vehicles	6–10	10–14	14–20	22–32
Category 4: aggravated theft, assault II, coercion, criminally negligent homicide, robbery II	10–16	16–22	22–30	32–44
Category 5: burglary I, escape I, manslaughter II, racketeering, rape I	16–24	24–36	40–52	56–72
Category 6: arson I, kidnapping I, rape II, sodomy I	30–40	44–56	60–80	90–130
Category 7: aggravated murder, treason	96–120	120–156	156–192	192–240
Category 8: aggravated murder (stranger–stranger, cruelty to victim, prior murder conviction)	120–168	168–228	228–288	288–life

Source: Adapted from State of Oregon, Board of Parole, *ORS* Chapter 144, Rule 255-75-026 and Rule 255-75-035.

A major criticism of discretionary release is that it has shifted responsibility from a judge, who holds legal procedures uppermost, to an administrative board, where discretion rules. Further, in most states with discretionary release, parole hearings are secret, with only board members, the inmate, and correctional officers present.

Should society place such power in the hands of parole boards? Because there is so little oversight regarding their decision making and few constraints on their decisions, some parole board members will make arbitrary or discriminatory decisions inconsistent with the constitutional system and civil rights. Generally, the U.S. legal system seeks to avoid determining people's fates through such methods.

RELEASE TO THE COMMUNITY

The popular notion is that once offenders have completed their prison terms, they have paid their "debt" and are ready to start life anew. The reality is that the vast majority of released offenders remain subject to correctional authority for some time. The whereabouts of offenders are monitored, and their associations and daily activities are checked. Also constraining the offender's freedom are the difficulties of reentry.

One effect of the explosive growth of the nation's prison population is the huge increase in the number of inmates released to the community after serving their terms. An increasing portion of these "new parolees" are older, were sentenced for drug law violations, have served longer times in prison, and have higher levels of substance abuse and mental illness than those returning in 1990.[24]

The increase in the number of ex-offenders returning to the community has prompted Congress and the states to provide assistance to parolees and help reduce the amount of recidivism among them. The Second Chance Act of 2007 is designed to ensure the successful return of prisoners to the community. The act provides federal grants to states and communities to support reentry initiatives focused on employment, housing, substance abuse and mental health treatment, and children and family services.[25]

focus on correctional practice

Michigan Prisoner ReEntry Initiative

It's a Thursday morning, and 24-year-old Jeffrey Lauderdale is planning his future—one where, he hopes, there are no prison bars. Lauderdale, of Kentwood, Michigan, has been in and out of lockups for drug convictions since age 18. Now, up for his third release from prison, he's enrolled in the four-month Intensive Re-Entry Unit, a program at the Cooper Street Correctional Facility in Jackson. The unit is part of the Michigan Prisoner Re-Entry Initiative, which hopes to reduce the state's high recidivism rate.

With nearly half of Michigan's parolees wanted by authorities or back in prison within two years, the state is trying to better prepare inmates for release to the community. At Cooper Street, inmates learn how to budget their money, interview for jobs, and put together a résumé. They also make plans to get help from community agencies once they've left

prison. In the past, that help has been missing, disorganized, or late, correctional officials say.

On this morning, a four-member "transition team"—a parole officer and three people from social service agencies—is quizzing Lauderdale. The prisoner, who hopes to be released next month, sits on an upholstered chair at a conference table in a prison administrative office. He politely answers questions from the panel talking to him on a large television screen via a video-conference call. He tells them he has restaurant experience and took carpentry classes in prison. "I want to be successful in staying out of prison," Lauderdale, the soon-to-be parolee, said. "I want to do what I need to do." When he was released from prison before, there was little preparation, he said. "I just went home, and that was it."

Source: Adapted from Judy Putnam, "Inmates Get New Help as They Prepare for Freedom," www.mlive.com, October 20, 2005.

Kesler Weaver, a parole officer, works in his office at the State of Alabama Probation and Parole Office in Mobile, Ala.

All states have some form of prison program designed to prepare the offender for release to community supervision. In some states these activities begin as far as two years in advance of the targeted release date; in others they begin only after that date is confirmed. See "Focus on Correctional Practice: Michigan Prisoner ReEntry Initiative."

The best of these programs provide a multiweek, full-time training program for inmates who are within 60 days of release. Inmates are given training in the attitudes needed to get and keep a job, communication skills, family roles, money management, and community and parole resources.

Other programs include transfer of the participating inmates to a housing unit reserved for prereleases. One week of the four-week period is devoted to family re-adjustment training. With the emphasis on reintegration and community supervision, offenders move from one security level to another and from one institution to another as they prepare for release. However, critics argue that only a small percentage of prisoners receive prerelease planning. (See "Myths in Corrections.")

Community Supervision

Parolees are released from prison on condition that they abide by laws and follow rules designed both to aid their readjustment to society and to control their movement. The parolee may be required to abstain from alcohol, keep away from undesirable associates, maintain good work habits, and not leave the community without permission. These requirements, called **conditions of release**, regulate conduct that is not criminal but that is thought to be linked to the possibility of future criminality. All states except Maine have some requirements for postprison supervision, and nearly 80 percent of released prisoners are subject to some form of conditional community supervision upon release.[26]

The restrictions are justified on the grounds that people who have been incarcerated must readjust to the community so that they will not fall back into preconviction habits and associations. Strict enforcement of these rules may create problems for parolees who cannot fulfill all of the demands placed on them. For example, it may be impossible for a parolee to undergo urine monitoring, attend an Alcoholics Anonymous meeting, and work full time while also meeting family obligations.

conditions of release
Restrictions on conduct that parolees must obey as a legally binding requirement of being released.

MYTHS in Corrections

Revolving Doors?

THE MYTH: Two-thirds of these guys will be back in prison within three years.

THE REALITY: It depends upon the state. Almost 60 percent of parolees are returned to prison in California, yet in some other states the percentage of returnees is much lower. For example, in Oregon the recidivism rate is 23 percent.

Source: Pew Center on the States, *State of Recidivism: The Revolving Door of America's Prisons* (Washington, DC: Pew Charitable Trusts, 2011).

In reality, no "clean" start is possible. The status of former convict is nearly as stigmatizing as that of convict, and in many ways more frustrating. Most people look at the parolee askance—an embittering experience for many trying to start over.

When releasees first come out of prison, their personal and material problems are staggering. In most states they are given only clothes, a token amount of money, a copy of the rules governing their release, and the name and address of the parole officer to whom they must report within 24 hours.

With little preparation, offenders move from the highly structured, authoritarian prison life into the complex, temptation-filled free world. Offenders are expected to summon up extraordinary coping abilities, but the lack of adequate resources and other insufficiencies send many parolees back.

Revocation

When people fail on parole, their parole is revoked, and they are returned to prison to continue serving their sentences. Parole can be revoked for two reasons: (1) committing a new crime or (2) violating conditions of parole (a technical violation). Technical violations are controversial because they involve noncriminal conduct, such as failure to report an address change to the parole officer. Less attention is paid to the fact that parole officers more often *manage* problematic adjustments of parolees prior to revocation. In reality, parolee adjustment to community supervision ranges between total compliance and noncompliance. When parolees demonstrate reluctance or resistance toward meeting certain conditions of their parole, the parole officer has a number of tools available to encourage a more positive adjustment. Community-based sanctions are tools applied to reduce the likelihood of revocation. For example, failure to abstain from drug or alcohol could cause a parole officer to require inpatient treatment rather than to continue with an outpatient substance abuse program. Sanctions generally include a more intensive application of a condition, such as intensive parole, or the requirement of a more restrictive one, such as home confinement. A recent study found that when parole officers apply community-based sanctions in an incremental fashion, the likelihood of avoiding recidivism or the length of time prior to recidivism improved.[27] These options may be employed to avoid parole revocation.

In practice, a revocation seldom results from a single rules violation—prisons are far too crowded. To be returned to prison on a technical violation, a parolee usually must show persistent noncompliance or else give the parole officer reason to believe that he or she has returned to crime. Most revocations occur only when the parolee is arrested on a serious charge or cannot be located by the officer.

The U.S. Supreme Court requires a two-stage parole-revocation proceeding. In the first stage the parole board determines whether there is probable cause that a violation has occurred. The parolee then has the right to be notified of charges, be informed of evidence, be heard, present witnesses, and confront the parole board's witnesses. In the second stage the parole board decides if the violation is severe enough to warrant return to prison.

Data on the number of parole revocations are difficult to determine. Taking revocations for new convictions and "technical violations" together, 52 percent of released prisoners are back in prison within three years.[28] In addition, as shown in **Figure 10.4,**

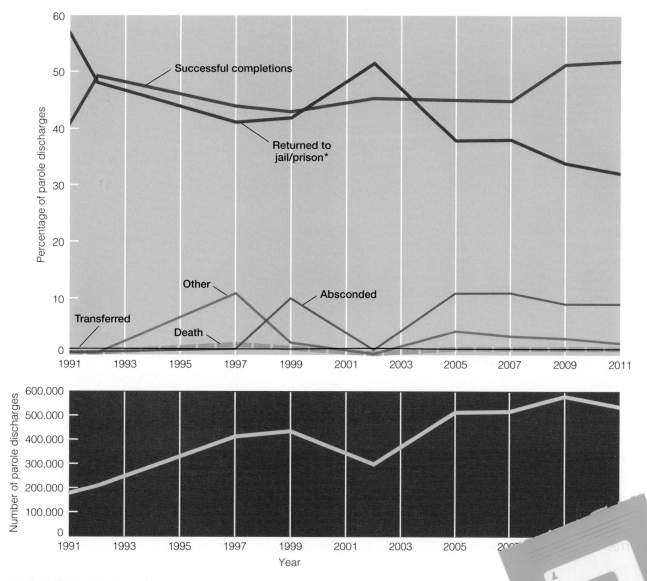

FIGURE 10.4
Trends in State Parole Discharges, 1991–2011

The percentage of parolees who successfully complete their term and are discharged from superv[...] the years. What factors might account for these shifts?

*Includes those returned to prison with a new sentence or for technical parole violations and those returned pend[...] revocation on new charges.

Source: Pew Center on the *States, State of Recidivism: The Revolving Door of America's Prisons* (Washington, DC: Pe[...] [...]ble Trusts, 2011).

the percentage of successful completions as well as the percentage returned to prison shifts over time.

The degree to which these rates reflect technical rules violations varies from state to state (see **Figure 10.5**). These differences have little to do with the way that clients behave and a great deal to do with the way that the system enforces its rules. (See "Focus on Correctional Policy," on revocation in California.) When a parolee is determined to have violated a condition of parole, the parole agency has several options: (1) return the parolee to prison; (2) note the violation, strengthen supervision, and continue parole; and (3) note the violation but take no action at that time.[29] Differences in failure

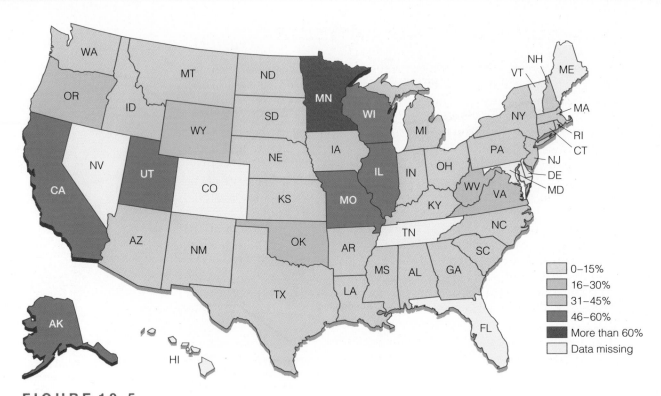

FIGURE 10.5
Percentage of Prison Admissions Who Are Parole Violators

States vary significantly in the percentage of prison admissions who are parole violators. What causes these differences?

Source: Pew Center on the States, Public Safety Performance Project, *State of Recidivism: The Revolving Door of America's Prisons* (Washington, DC: Pew Charitable Trusts, 2011).

rates among the states may reflect agency supervision policies, prison crowding, or political pressures to remove parolees from the community. Nationally, 35 percent of all new prison admissions are violators of parole release; of this group, nearly two-thirds are returned to prison for technical violations.

Too often, parolees fail to abide by their conditions of parole. When that happens, they are returned to face the parole board and may end up back in prison.

AP Images/Damian Dovarganes

AGENTS OF COMMUNITY SUPERVISION

After release, a parolee's main contact with the criminal justice system is through the parole officer, who has the dual responsibility of providing surveillance and assistance. This mission requires parole officers to play two different, some might say incompatible roles: cop and social worker. Whereas parole was originally designed to help offenders make the transition from prison to the community, supervision has shifted ever more toward surveillance, drug testing, monitoring curfews, and collecting restitution. Safety and security have become major issues in parole services.

In their role as cop, parole officers have the powers to restrict many aspects of the parolee's life, to enforce the conditions of release, and to initiate revocation proceedings for violations. Like other bureaucrats in the criminal justice system, officers have extensive discretionary power. The officer's relationship with the offender thus has an authoritative component that can hinder the development of rapport and mutual trust.

Besides policing their charges, parole officers must also act as social workers by helping parolees find jobs, restore family ties, and connect to human service agencies. In this role officers must develop a relationship that fosters trust and confidence, which is not likely to develop if parolees are made constantly aware of the officers' ability to send them back to prison.

How can parole officers reconcile these conflicting roles? One suggestion is to divide the responsibilities so that the officer carries out the supervision and other people perform the casework functions. Alternatively, the officer can be charged solely with casework, and local police can check for violations. States have also experimented with using a team of two officers to handle a caseload jointly. One person is the surveillance officer, and the other is the social worker, providing assistance. However, over time

focus on correctional policy

California: Leading the Nation in the Revocation of Ex-Prisoners

When it comes to supervising parolees, something is going on in California that is vastly different from other states. The numbers are stunning. Less than one-fourth of California's prison releases succeed on parole, a rate lower than any other state but Hawaii. Over two-thirds of those who enter the California prison system are going to prison because they failed during community supervision. Why is it so difficult to make it on parole in California?

The most important difference between California and the rest of the United States is that those who supervise offenders in the community—especially parole officers—are known for their strict enforcement of the rules. Parolees in California are relentlessly tested for drug use, closely monitored for curfews and associations, and strictly required to work and pay their fines, restitution, and other justice fees. The toughness shows in the statistics. Each year California releases 120,000 parolees, and each year 75,000 return to prison for violating their parole on technical grounds. While 70 percent of parolees nationally are returned for new felony

arrests, only 60 percent of California's returnees are cited for that failure.

Some Californians think this is good news. They say that proven risks to the community are being watched much more closely in California than anywhere else in the country. Others say that the high technical failure rate is misleading because California parole officers decide to revoke their parolees on technical grounds when there is a new felony arrest, for this avoids the delays and due process that would occur if the new arrest went to trial.

However, critics of California's approach point out that growing prison populations are expensive, especially in California, where a year in prison costs more than $21,000 per offender. Money tends to be shifted from public education and welfare to pay for the punishments of these offenders, and when so many of them are rules violators, critics wonder if this is a wise investment.

Sources: BJS *Bulletin*, October 2001, p. 11; "California Budget Held Captive by State Prisons," National Public Radio, www.npr.org, June 15, 2009.

careers in Corrections

PAROLE OFFICER

Nature of the Work

Parole officers supervise offenders in the community through personal contact with the offenders and their families. Unlike probation officers, who are generally employed by the county, parole officers are employed by the state.

In most jurisdictions they are armed peace officers with the power of arrest. As an essential ingredient in the reentry process, parole officers help offenders readjust to the community and find housing and employment. They monitor offenders' behavior to ensure that parole requirements are met. If the conditions are not met or the offender commits another crime, the officer may recommend revocation of the parole. Fieldwork may take the officer to high-crime areas, where there is a risk of violence.

Required Qualifications

Qualifications for parole officers vary by state, but a bachelor's degree in social work, criminal justice, or a related field is usually required. Some agencies require previous experience or graduate work. Candidates must be 21 years of age, have no felony convictions, and have no restrictions on their carrying a firearm. Most parole officers receive formal training and typically work as a trainee for up to one year.

Earnings and Job Outlook

The number of parole officers is expected to grow as the number of inmates leaving prison increases during the next decade. Starting salaries vary by region, but the national median salary is $50,378.

More Information

For more information, see the American Probation and Parole Association's website. You can also obtain career information from your state's parole office.

the distinction often becomes vague: Parolees often look to surveillance officers for help and see social work officers as enforcing the conditions of supervision. Despite the conflict, it seems that any person having supervisory contact with the offender must perform both roles. (See "Careers in Corrections.")

The parole officer works in a bureaucratic environment. Like most other human services organizations, parole agencies are short of resources and expertise. Although reformers have long held that parole caseloads should include no more than 36 cases per officer, in reality the caseloads in most urban areas average about 80 parolees per

Peer support is often the best way for people leaving prison to receive the help they need to "make it" in society. This peer-support group, called Free Minds, meets weekly to use group members' poetry, other readings, and frank discussion to inspire the formerly incarcerated to become powerful voices for change in their community.

Jahi Chikwendiu/The Washington Post/Getty Images

officer. This is smaller than the average probation caseload, but the services required by parolees are greater. However, there is no solid empirical evidence that smaller caseloads are more likely to lead to successful outcomes for probationers and parolees.

The caseload affects how often an officer can contact each parolee and how much help can be given. Some states structure low, specialized caseloads for officers who supervise certain types of parolees, but even with specialized caseloads, time available for parolees can be minimal, often less than an hour a month. One reason for the small contact time is that officers must spend time in bureaucratic duties and in the field helping parolees deal with other service agencies—medical, employment, and educational. Parole officers spend as much as 80 percent of their time in nonsupervisory work.

THE OFFENDER'S EXPERIENCE OF POSTRELEASE LIFE

The new releasee faces four harsh realities: the strangeness of reentry, continued correctional supervision, unmet personal needs, and barriers to success. Each must be dealt with separately; each poses a challenge to the newly released offender.

The Strangeness of Reentry

Although release from prison can be euphoric, it can also be a letdown, particularly for parolees who return after two, three, or more years away. The images in their minds of friends and loved ones represent snapshots frozen in time, but in reality everyone has changed (as has the parolee): moved away, taken a new job, grown up, or, perhaps most disturbing, become almost a stranger. Initial attempts to restore old ties can thus be threatening and deeply disappointing.

Moreover, freedom is now an unfamiliar environment. In prison, others make every decision about daily life, so routine decision-making skills are weakened. Returning to the streets after years behind bars is a shock; the most normal, unremarkable events take on overwhelming significance.

In time, the strangeness of the free world can become a source of discomfort and pressure. To deal with this strangeness, ex-offenders are tempted to reach out to the familiar—old friends and old pastimes—and doing so can lead to trouble.

Supervision and Surveillance

One underlying message of supervision is that the ex-offender is not really free. There are rules to be obeyed and authorities to heed. The promise of release, with its aura of freedom, soon dissipates into a hard reality: Ex-prisoners may think they have paid their debt to society, but they cannot yet rejoin their fellow citizens. There is always the chance of running afoul of the authorities and facing return.

Supervision is not a uniformly adverse experience. For many parolees the officer will serve as an important source of help with problems that might otherwise never be overcome. And it seems that supervision may help because research shows that offenders released under supervision experience fewer returns to prison for new crimes than do those who leave without supervision.[30]

The Problem of Unmet Personal Needs

Parolees are aware that they must meet critical needs to make it on the streets. Education, money, and a job tend to top the list. Yet they are not always realistic about how to meet their needs. Participation in vocational and educational programs in prisons has been declining over the past decade, and only a minority of prisoners in need of drug treatment, for example, receive it while incarcerated.[31]

Some parolees face even more serious needs as they reenter the community. Three-quarters report a history of drug or alcohol abuse, up to 100,000 have at least one serious mental disorder requiring psychiatric services, and many—perhaps 10 percent or more—are homeless.[32] In many cases, community supervision addresses these needs, but far too often it does not, with severe consequences.

Barriers to Success

Soon after release, offenders learn that they face restrictions on opportunities beyond the close monitoring of the parole officer. Compounding their adjustment problems are a myriad of impediments to accessing government-assistance programs and employment.

CIVIL DISABILITIES The rights to vote and to hold public office are two civil rights that are generally limited on conviction of a felony. Eighty percent of the states return the right to vote after some period. Seven states return it only after offenders have served their full sentence, but seven bar felons from voting for life.[33] Only through a pardon is full citizenship restored in these last seven states. Many states deny felons other civil rights, such as serving on juries, holding public office, and holding positions of public trust (which include most government jobs).

Nationally, an estimated 5.3 million Americans are barred from voting because of felony convictions. This includes 1.4 million African American men (13 percent of all African American men). In five states that bar ex-offenders from voting, as many as one-fourth of African American men are permanently forbidden to vote.[34]

The more-recent obstructions to reentry have come about through federal legislation in response to the "war on drugs." The Legal Action Center has published a state-by-state analysis of additional hindrances to successful reentry for those convicted of a drug offense.[35] These include access to public assistance and food stamps, living in public housing, having a driver's license, being a foster parent or adopting children, and receiving student loans.

EMPLOYMENT Employers hesitate to hire parolees because they view a conviction as evidence of being untrustworthy. However, the legal barriers to employment are perhaps the most frustrating. Many states deny licenses to hold certain jobs to ex-convicts. Courts have upheld these bans when the work has a connection to the criminal conduct of the offender. An obvious example is the employment of child molesters in day-care centers. Other statutes bar from specified jobs any person who lacks moral character, a trait that many people attribute to convicts.

Making matters worse, such statutes bar some of the jobs that former offenders have been trained to do. For instance, all states restrict former offenders from employment as barbers (even though many prisons provide training programs in barbering), beauticians, and nurses. Indeed, newly released offenders may find themselves legally barred from jobs that they had held before they were incarcerated.

The options for most offenders remain severely limited. The quandary is real: Should offenders tell prospective employers about their criminal records and risk being denied a chance to prove themselves? Or should they lie and risk being fired if their criminal record comes to light?

One solution for many offenders is expungement of their criminal records. In theory, **expungement** means the removal of a conviction from state records. In practice, although offenders whose records have been expunged may legally say they have never been convicted, the records are kept and can be made available on inquiry. Moreover, the legal procedures for expungement are generally both cumbersome and inadequate. Expungement provides little true relief.

The same is true of a **pardon**, an executive act of clemency that effectively excuses the offender from suffering all the consequences of conviction for a criminal act. Pardons serve three main purposes: (1) to remedy a miscarriage of justice, (2) to remove the stigma of a conviction, and (3) to mitigate a penalty. Full pardons are rare but do occur. They are most commonly given to erase the criminal records of first-time offenders, but overall they are given infrequently.

expungement
A legal process that results in the removal of a conviction from official records.

pardon
An action of the executive branch of the state or federal government excusing an offense and absolving the offender from the consequences of the crime.

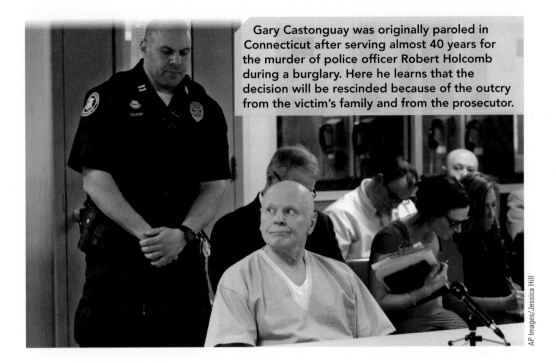

Gary Castonguay was originally paroled in Connecticut after serving almost 40 years for the murder of police officer Robert Holcomb during a burglary. Here he learns that the decision will be rescinded because of the outcry from the victim's family and from the prosecutor.

AP Images/Jessica Hill

Offenders face certain misgivings about reentry: adjustment to a strange environment; the unavoidable need for job training, employment, money, and support; and limitations on opportunities. The stigma of conviction stays with the former felon. The general social condemnation of ex-convicts adds to the pressures of being monitored by a parole officer.

THE PAROLEE AS "DANGEROUS"

Few images are more disturbing than that of a recent parolee arrested for committing a new violent or sexual crime, especially when that crime is against a stranger. The most heinous of these incidents make national news and captivate the nation's attention. Examples include the arrest and conviction of the California parolee Richard Allen Davis for the brutal murder of 12-year-old Polly Klaas, which spurred a national movement toward life sentences for third-time felons, and the rape and murder of 4-year-old Megan Kanka in New Jersey by a paroled sex offender, which led to a series of sex offender notification laws, called "Megan's Law" after the victim.

The fact of repeat violence fuels a public perception that parolees represent an ongoing threat to the public welfare. It also contributes to a belief that the criminal justice system is too lenient, with the result that communities are unsafe. But correctional and paroling authorities do employ more-rigorous methods of supervision to parolees who pose a higher risk to the public. In 1976, Richard Schoenfeld and his accomplices targeted schoolchildren in Chowchilla, California. They hijacked a school bus carrying 26 children plus the driver, transferred the group to a van, and then literally buried the van along with the occupants for several days, while awaiting a response to ransom demands. All of the victims escaped unharmed, but Schoenfeld was convicted, sentenced to life, and served 36 years in prison. In 2012 he was released on parole and is required to wear a GPS ankle monitor as a condition of his parole. Local law enforcement and parole agents will reportedly collaborate in structuring his supervision.

More recently, repeat violent offenders and convicted sex offenders have become the focus of such measures once they are released on parole. Yet for some parole officers, control measures such as notification laws often conflict with their efforts to find housing and employment for sex offenders. In some states the laws prohibit sex offenders from being within 1,500 feet of schools and playgrounds. This can mean that there are no places in a city where an offender can reside or work without violating the law. One result is that sex offenders must congregate in those communities or neighborhoods where the special restrictions do not apply. In view of these and other concerns, there are efforts to identify more-effective means of dealing with dangerous parolees. California recently implemented a program to more closely monitor paroled sex offenders by using GPS technology along with traditional supervisory requirements and various treatment modalities. Initial program evaluation results are promising and include lower recidivism rates and higher degrees of compliance.[36]

Overall, ex-offenders represent a greater risk to community safety than do other citizens. But isolated tragedies can exaggerate the actual danger to the public, especially considering that parolees are such a tiny proportion of the citizens on the streets. A national study estimated that parolees constitute a much greater portion of arrests overall, between 10 and 16 percent.[37] Nonetheless, the increase in ex-prisoners released from incarceration—from 180,000 in 1980 to more than 725,000 today—has not been accompanied by an increase in crime nationally.[38]

THE ELEMENTS OF SUCCESSFUL REENTRY

Prison is such a harsh experience that it would seem unlikely that most who are allowed to leave would eventually return. But the problems just discussed make it easier to see why so many ex-offenders fail. Adjustment to the community is neither simple nor easy. Four factors seem necessary for successful reentry:

1. Get substance abuse under control.
2. Get a job.
3. Develop a support group of family and friends.
4. Get a sense of "who I am."

However, even when offenders get jobs and find support systems, they can face problems that interfere with successful adjustment. Some offenders, when faced with problem situations, lack the skills to cope with them and respond in ways that worsen the problem rather than solve it.[39] Until the ex-offender learns how to deal effectively with the kinds of problems that set up failure, recidivism remains the likely result. Postrelease supervision is thought to be one of the main ways to teach offenders better coping skills. But does it?

The effectiveness of corrections is usually measured by rates of recidivism—the percentage of former offenders who return to criminal behavior after release. However, because the concept of recidivism means different things to different people, the measures of recidivism also represent different things. The rates reported vary from 5 to 50 percent, depending on how one counts three issues: (1) the event (arrest, conviction, and parole revocation), (2) the duration of the period over which the measurement is made, and (3) the seriousness of the behavior. Typically, an analysis of recidivism is based on rearrest or reimprisonment for either another felony conviction or a parole violation for up to three years after release.

A recent report found almost no differences in arrest rates between people who were supervised on parole and those who were not. This study shows that parole boards are able to select good-risk cases for early release, and when the differences in risk were taken into account, even these parolees did not do much better than people released outright from prison. The report concludes that "the public safety impact of supervision is minimal and . . . does not appear to improve recidivism outcomes for violent offenders or property offenders released to mandatory parole [supervision]."[40] On the other hand, some studies have found that mandatory-release cases do *better* than parolees. However, a report from the U.S. Department of Justice indicates that only 33 percent of mandatory releases succeed, compared with 54 percent of parolees.[41]

In short, the effectiveness of parole supervision has earned, at best, mixed reviews. Yet because parolees who remain crime-free for two years often succeed thereafter, correctional administrators continue to revise parole practices in ways that will help offenders make it.

The limited impact of supervision has led scholars to search for new methods to deal with parolees. Some now argue that reentry needs bolstering by the authority of the court system through **reentry courts**. In reentry courts, judges maintain active oversight of parolees they had originally sentenced. A parolee appears before the court on a regular basis so that the judge, together with the parole officer, can assess the ex-inmate's progress. Emphasis is also placed on the involvement of the judge and correctional officials in assessing the prerelease needs of the prisoner and building linkages to family, social services, housing, and employment opportunities.

Some scholars have argued that if all these courts do is increase the amount of pressure on people returning from prison, they will fail as most other such programs have failed. But if they focus on getting parolees involved in their communities and contributing to the welfare of their environments, they will ultimately succeed where traditional methods have not.[42]

reentry courts
Courts that supervise ex-offenders' return to the community and their adjustment to life after incarceration.

WHAT ARE PAROLE'S PROSPECTS?

Many changes have been made in the way that offenders are released from prison, but supervision practices do not reflect these changes. Even states that have altered release laws or policies seem to recognize that offenders need some help or control in the months after release, and research suggests that parole does help them stay crime-free, at least during the early months on the outside. Therefore, most incarcerated offenders will continue to experience postrelease supervision, whether in the form of parole, work release, or some other program.

However, the nature of supervision is likely to change significantly over the next few years. Evidence increasingly suggests that supervision is not appropriate for all offenders but should be oriented toward those who are most likely to fail. The broad discretionary power of the parole officer is disappearing. In its place, a much more restrictive effort is becoming popular, one in which limited special conditions are imposed and stringently enforced. The helping role of the officer—as counselor and referral agent—is being freed from the coercive role, and the help offered is increasingly seen as an opportunity that offenders may choose not to take. Postrelease supervision is likely to be streamlined in years to come as the courts continue to review officers' decisions and their agencies' policies.

What is not likely to change is the situation of the released offender. Poor training and poor education lead to poor job prospects; public distrust of offenders leads to discrimination. Offenders will need to hone their strategies if they are to succeed in the community.

Summary

1 **Understand the nature of parole and how it operates today.**

Parole is the conditional release of an offender from incarceration but not from the legal custody of the state. Parolees must comply with a set of conditions and must not violate the law. If the offender breaks a rule, then parole may be revoked and the person returned to a correctional facility.

2 **Be familiar with the origins of parole.**

Parole in the United States evolved during the nineteenth century, following the English, Australian, and Irish practices. After the passage of an indeterminate sentencing law in 1876, the Elmira Reformatory in New York began to release prisoners on parole. By 1942, all 48 states and the federal government operated parole systems.

3 **Understand how the release decision is made.**

In states with indeterminate sentences, parole boards make discretionary-release decisions by considering the nature of the offense, the inmate's behavior, and participation in rehabilitative programs. In contrast, mandatory release occurs after an inmate has served time equal to the total sentence minus good time, or to a certain percentage of the total sentence as defined by law. A third type of release, probation release, occurs when the sentencing judge requires a period of postcustody supervision in the community. Many states also have other conditional-release mechanisms, such as placing inmates in the community through furlough, home supervision, and halfway houses. Finally, expiration release is used when inmates have "maxed out" their sentence and are released from correctional supervision.

4 Explain the steps taken to ease the offender's reentry into the community.

All states have programs to prepare inmates for release through counseling about the conditions of supervision, as well as searching for employment and a place to live.

5 Identify the major problems confronting parolees.

Release from prison requires adjusting to changes among family members, friends, and the community that have occurred while the parolee has been incarcerated. Parolees must also meet critical needs such as education, money, and a job to make it in the community. Offenders soon learn that they face restrictions on civic participation, access to some government programs, and access to certain types of employment.

6 Understand why some parolees are viewed as dangerous and how society handles this problem.

Certain ex-offenders represent a greater risk to community safety than do other citizens. But isolated tragedies can exaggerate the actual danger to the public, especially considering that parolees are such a tiny proportion of people on the streets.

Key Terms

conditions of release 263
discretionary release 252
expiration release 253
expungement 270

mandatory release 252
other conditional release 254
pardon 270
parole 250

probation release 253
reentry courts 273
reinstatement release 253

For Discussion

1. How does mandatory release affect the corrections system? How will corrections adjust to this harnessing of the discretion of parole boards and judges?
2. What factors should a parole board consider when it evaluates a prisoner for release?
3. Suppose that as a parole board member, you are confronted by a man who has served 6 years of a 10- to 20-year sentence for murder. He has a good institutional record, and you do not believe him to be a threat to community safety. Would you release him to parole supervision at this time? Why or why not?
4. Suppose that you have been asked to decide whether the department of corrections or an independent agency should have authority over release decisions. Where would you place that authority? Why?
5. Given the current public attitude toward criminals, what do you see as the likely future of parole release?
6. Imagine that you have just been released from prison after a five-year term. What are the first things you will do? What problems do you expect to face?
7. Why are some parole officers reluctant to ask that a client's parole be revoked for technical violations? What organizational pressures may be involved?

Notes

1 Matt Zapotosky, Rosalind S. Helderman, and Rachel Weiner, "Robert F. McDonnell Sentenced to Two Years in Prison," *Washington Post*, www.washingtonpost.com/local/virginia-politics/robert-f-mcdonnell-sentenced-to-two-years-in-prison-in-corruption-case/2015/01/06/e51520ca-9049-11e4-ba53-a477d66580ed_story.html, January 6, 2015.

2 Harry Elmer Barnes and Negley K. Teeters, *New Horizons in Criminology* (Englewood Cliffs, NJ: Prentice-Hall, 1944), 550, 553.

3 Lawrence M. Friedman, *Crime and Punishment in American History* (New York: Basic, 1993), 304.

4 Peter B. Hoffman, "History of the Federal Parole System: Part I (1910–1972)," *Federal Probation* 61 (September 1997): 23.

5 Alfred Blumstein and Allen J. Beck, "Reentry as a Transient State Between Liberty and Recommitment," in *Prisoner Reentry and Crime in America*, edited by Jeremy Travis and Christy Visher (New York: Cambridge University Press, 2005), 3.

6 *New York Times*, March 13, 2007, p. A18.

7 Laura M. Maruschak and Erika Parks, *Probation and Parole in the United States, 2011—Statistical Tables* (Washington, DC: Bureau of Justice Statistics, 2012).

8 Joan Petersilia, *When Prisoners Come Home: Parole and Prisoner Reentry* (New York: Oxford University Press, 2003), 65.

9 Tony Fabelo, *Biennial Report to the 76th Texas Legislature* (Austin, TX: Criminal Justice Policy Council, 1999).

10 Cindy Horswell, "Texas Says Rise in Paroles Give State Bragging Rights," *Houston Chronicle*, www.chron.com/news/houston-texas/article/Texas-parole-system-cited-as-a-national-model-3788468.php, April 18, 2013.

11 James Austin, "Prisoner Reentry: Current Trends, Practices, and Issues," *Crime & Delinquency* 47 (July 2001): 327.

12 *Griffin, et al. v. Nix, et al.*, Civil Action No. 2004-CV-92152 (Superior Court of Fulton County, Georgia, 2007).

13 Althea Francois, "90% Policy Ends, Thousands Await Parole Board's Decisions," *Fairness for Prisoner's Families*, www.fairness4families.org/Newsletters/May%20June.pdf, May/June 2005.

14 BJS *Bulletin*, November 2006, p. 8.

15 Katharine Bradley and R. B. Michael Oliver, "The Role of Parole," in *Policy Brief* (Boston: Community Resources for Justice, 2001); Petersilia, *When Prisoners Come Home*, p. 60.

16 Pew Charitable Trusts Report, *Max Out: The Rise in Prison Inmates Released Without Supervision*, www.pewtrusts.org/~/media/Assets/2014/06/04/MaxOut_Report.pdf, 2014.

17 Assembly No. 241, State of New Jersey, Assemblyman Jon Bramnick.

18 Pamela L. Griset, "The Politics and Economics of Increased Correctional Discretion Over Time Served: A New York Case Study," *Justice Quarterly* 12 (June 1995): 307; Bureau of Justice Statistics, *Correctional Populations in the United States, 1997* (Washington, DC: U.S. Government Printing Office, 2000), 95–104.

19 Susette Talarico, "The Dilemmas of Parole Decision Making," in *Criminal Justice: Law and Politics*, 5th ed., edited by George F. Cole (Pacific Grove, CA: Brooks/Cole, 1988), 442–51.

20 Kevin Johnson and Richard Willing, "New DNA Links Used to Deny Parole," *USA Today*, www.usatoday.com/news/nation/2008-02 07-paroledna_N.htm?loc=interstitialskip, February 8, 2008.

21 Erinn J. Herberman and Thomas P. Bonczar, *Probation and Parole in the United States, 2013* (Bureau of Justice Statistics, U.S. Department of Justice, 2013), www.bjs.gov/content/pub/pdf/ppus13.pdf.

22 Samuel Walker, *Taming the System: The Control of Discretion in Criminal Justice, 1950–1990* (New York: Oxford University Press, 1993), 141.

23 Yan Zhang, Lening Zhang, and Michael S. Vaughn, "Indeterminate and Determinate Sentencing Models: A State-Specific Analysis of Their Effects on Recidivism," *Crime & Delinquency* 60 (2014, no. 5): 693–715.

24 Austin, "Prisoner Reentry," pp. 322–23.

25 Open Society Policy Center, "The Second Chance Act of 2005 (HR 1707)," www.opensocietypolicycenter.org/resources/publications.php, March 29, 2007.

26 Petersilia, *When Prisoners Come Home*.

27 Benjamin Steiner, Matthew D. Makarios, Lawrence F. Travis III, and Benjamin Meade, "Examining the Effects of Community-Based Sanctions on Offender Recidivism," *Justice Quarterly* 29 (2012, no. 2): 229–57.

28 BJS *Special Report*, June 2002, p. 1.

29 Jeremy Travis and Sarah Lawrence, *Beyond the Prison Gates: The State of Parole in America* (Washington, DC: Urban Institute, 2002), 21.

30 Diana Sepejak, "Reoffending Rates for Parolees and Nonparolees: A Five Year Comparison," *Forum on Correctional Research* 10 (no. 2, May 1998): 15–18; BJS *Bulletin*, October 2001.

31 Joan Petersilia, "Prisoner Reentry: Public Safety and Reintegration Challenges," *Prison Journal* 81 (no. 3, September 2001): 360–75.

32 Jeremy Travis, Amy L. Solomon, and Michelle Waul, *From Prison to Home: The Dimensions and Consequences of Prisoner Reentry* (Washington, DC: Urban Institute, 2001).

33 *New York Times*, March 28, 2004, p. 19.

34 Ryan S. King, *Expanding the Vote: State Felony Disenfranchisement Reform, 1997–2008* (Washington, DC: Sentencing Project, 2008), 2.

35 Legal Action Center, *After Prison: Roadblocks to Reentry* (New York: Author, 2004).

36 Stephen V. Gies, Randy Gainey, Marcia I. Cohen, Eoin Healy, Dan Duplantier, Martha Yeide, Alan Bekelman, Amanda Bobnis, and Michael Hopps, *Monitoring High-Risk Sex Offenders with GPS Technology: An Evaluation of the California Supervision Program, Final Report* (Washington, DC: National Institute of Justice, 2012).

37 Richard Rosenfeld, Joel Wallman, and Robert Fornango, "The Contribution of Ex-Prisoners to Crime Rates," in *Prisoner Reentry and Crime in America*, edited by Jeremy Travis and Christy Visher (New York: Cambridge University Press, 2006), 80–104.

38 James P. Lynch and William J. Sabol, *Prisoner Reentry in Perspective* [*Crime Policy Report*, vol. 3] (Washington, DC: Urban Institute, 2001), 7.

39 Edward Zamble and Vernon Quinsey, *The Criminal Recidivism Process* (Cambridge, England: Cambridge University Press, 1997).

40 Amy L. Solomon, Vera Kachnowski, and Avinash Bhati, *Does Parole Matter? Analyzing the Impact of Postprison Supervision on Rearrest Outcomes* (Washington, DC: Urban Institute, 2005), 15.

41 Timothy A. Hughes, Doris J. Wilson, and Allen J. Beck, "Trends in State Parole, 1990–2000," BJS *Bulletin*, October 2001, p. 1.

42 Shadd Maruna and Thomas LeBel, "Welcome Home? Examining the 'Reentry Court' Concept from a Strengths-Based Perspective," *Western Criminology Review* 4 (no. 2, 2003), http://wcr.sonoma.edu/v4n2/marunalebel.html.

CHAPTER 11

Legal Issues and the Death Penalty

In April 2002, **Roderick Johnson** filed a suit in the federal district court in Wichita Falls, Texas, against prison officials who permitted this gay African American to be repeatedly raped and sold as a sexual slave over an 18-month period. His attorney argued that Johnson's rights under the Eighth and Fourteenth amendments to violated by the Texas Department of Criminal Justice.[1] In September 2004 the United States Court of Appeals for the Fifth District in New Orleans ruled that Johnson's civil rights suit should go to trial. The ruling, the first to acknowledge the equal protection rights of homosexuals abused in prison, said that the evidence in the case

After reading this chapter you should be able to . . .

1 Discuss the foundations that support the legal rights of prisoners.

2 Describe the role of the U.S. Supreme Court in interpreting correctional law.

3 Understand the constitutional rights of prisoners.

4 List and describe alternatives to litigation.

5 Discuss the case law concerning the application of the death penalty.

Roderick Johnson sued the Texas prison system for failing to protect him from rape while he was incarcerated. He was victimized repeatedly over an 18-month period.

Back in January 2000, Johnson, a 33-year-old Navy veteran, reentered the Texas prison system for bouncing a $300 check while on parole for breaking and entering. He was sent to Huntsville Prison for processing and classification. There he told intake workers that he was gay and a target for sexual victimization. Johnson was given safekeeping (protective custody) status when he was transferred to the Allred Unit in Wichita Falls.

At his first classification review at Allred, Johnson told the board that he had been placed in safekeeping in Huntsville and had

(continued from previous page)

been told that he would remain in that status at Allred. The complaint alleged that a member of the board said, "We don't protect punks on this farm." Johnson was placed in the general population, where he was raped almost at once.

Within a month, predatory inmates were calling Johnson "Coco," thereby designating him as available for sexual exploitation. In the suit, Johnson said that the Gangster Gang claimed "ownership" and that he was raped by gang member Andrew Hernandez. When Johnson reported the rape and asked for medical care, it was denied. Hernandez continued to sexually abuse Johnson, made him clean the rapist's cell, and forced him, on the threat of death, to have sex with his friends. In December, Hernandez stole Johnson's radio and commissary goods. Johnson reported the theft to correctional officials, who "laughed and insinuated that he should go get his property by himself." When he asked Hernandez to return the property, he was assaulted and spent nine days in the medical center. Johnson learned that Marty Smith, a Bloods gang member, had "bought" his services from the Gangster Disciples. Johnson then filed the first of several life-endangerment claims with the director of classification, explaining that other inmates were sexually attacking him, and asked for safekeeping. The federal suit claimed that these requests were ignored.

In February 2001, Johnson again came before the classification board to request safekeeping status. One member told him, "You need to get down there and fight, or get you a man." There's no reason, another member said, "why Black punks can't fight and survive in a general population if they don't want to f—."

It was not until Johnson contacted the American Civil Liberties Union, which sent a letter to the executive director of the Texas Department of Criminal Justice, that he was placed in secure housing. Two weeks later, the ACLU helped Johnson file the multiclaim lawsuit.

For many Americans, the idea that a prisoner can sue correctional officials over constitutional rights seems absurd. They believe that criminals do not have the same rights as free citizens. Until the 1960s, the courts agreed. This belief was well stated by a Virginia judge in *Ruffin v. Commonwealth* (1871): "The prisoner has, as a consequence of his crime, not only forfeited his liberty, but all his personal rights except which the law in its humanity accords to him. He is for the time being the slave of the state."[3]

But since the late 1960s, federal and state courts have become increasingly involved in correctional matters other than routine petitions. Although much of correctional law involves claims by inmates that their rights have been violated, judges have also insisted that the due process rights of probationers and parolees be upheld. In some jurisdictions the courts have declared entire corrections systems to be operating in ways that violate the Constitution.

In this chapter we examine the legal foundations on which correctional law is based, analyze the constitutional rights of offenders, and explore the complex issue of the death penalty. ■

THE FOUNDATIONS OF CORRECTIONAL LAW

Four foundations support the legal rights of individuals under correctional supervision: (1) constitutions, (2) statutes, (3) case law, and (4) regulations. Most correctional litigation has involved rights claimed under the U.S. Constitution. State constitutions generally parallel the U.S. Constitution but sometimes confer other rights. Legislatures are, of course, free to grant additional rights to offenders and to authorize correctional departments to adopt regulations that recognize those rights.

Constitutions

Constitutions contain basic principles and procedural safeguards, and they describe the institutions of government (legislature, judiciary, and executive), the powers of government, and the rights of individuals. Constitutional rights are basic protections held by individuals against improper limitations of their freedom. For example, the first 10 amendments to the United States Constitution, together known as the Bill of Rights, provide protection against government actions that would violate basic rights and liberties. Several have a direct bearing on corrections because they uphold freedom of religion, association, and speech; limit unreasonable searches and seizures; require due process; and prohibit cruel and unusual punishment.

During the early 1960s the U.S. Supreme Court decided to require state governments to respect most of the rights listed in the Bill of Rights. Before that time, the Bill of Rights protected citizens only against actions of the federal government. As a result of Supreme Court decisions, the power of all government officials is limited by the U.S. Constitution and by their own state constitution.

When convicted of a crime, an individual does not lose all his or her constitutional rights. However, some rights may be limited when they are outweighed by legitimate government interests and when the restriction is related to those interests. The courts have recognized three specific interests as justifying some restrictions on the rights of prisoners: (1) the maintenance of institutional order, (2) the maintenance of institutional security, and (3) the rehabilitation of inmates. Thus, on a case-by-case basis, the

constitution
Fundamental law contained in a state or federal document that provides a design of government and lists basic rights for individuals.

The Supreme Court of the United States has the final word on questions concerning interpretations of the Constitution. During the 1970s the Court ended the hands-off policy and greatly extended the rights of prisoners.

Eric Nathan/Alamy

courts must ask the following: Are proposed restrictions reasonably related to preserve these interests? Later in this chapter we discuss specific amendments to the U.S. Constitution and decisions of the U.S. Supreme Court as they relate to prisoners' rights.

Statutes

Statutes are laws passed by legislatures at all levels of government. Within the powers granted, the U.S. Congress is responsible for statutes dealing with problems concerning the entire country. Thus, laws passed by Congress define federal crimes and punishments, allocate funds for criminal justice agencies of the national government, and authorize programs in pursuit of criminal justice policies.

Each state legislature enacts laws that govern the acts of its governments (state and local) and individuals within their borders, and appropriates funds for state agencies such as corrections. The penal codes of the national and state governments contain statutes defining criminal behavior.

Statutes are written in more-specific terms than are constitutions. Nonetheless, courts must often interpret the meaning of terms and rule on the legislature's intention. For example, in 1998 the U.S. Supreme Court was asked to rule whether the Americans with Disabilities Act of 1990 applied to state prisoners. The case, brought by a Pennsylvania offender, was opposed by most states. In a unanimous decision, the Court said that "the statute's language unmistakably includes state prisons and prisoners within its coverage."[4]

Prisoners may sue officials who fail to fulfill their statutory duties and obligations. If such claims are upheld, inmates may be entitled to collect monetary damages from the responsible officials and/or to receive a court ruling ordering that a practice be stopped.

statute
Law created by the people's elected representatives in legislatures.

case law
Legal rules produced by judges' decisions.

precedent
Legal rules created in judges' decisions that serve to guide the decisions of other judges in subsequent similar cases.

Case Law

Court decisions, often called **case law**, are a third foundation of correctional law. The United States operates under a common-law system in which judges create law or modify existing law when they rule in specific cases. In deciding the cases presented to them, U.S. judges are guided by constitutional provisions, statutes, and decisions in other cases. These prior rulings, also known as **precedent**, establish legal principles used in making decisions on similar cases. When such a case arises, the judge looks to the principles arising from earlier rulings and applies them to the case being decided. The judge's ability to adjust legal principles when new kinds of situations arise makes the common law, or case law, flexible when responding to changes in society.

As we have noted, constitutions often have phrases that lack clear, definite meanings. An example is the Eighth Amendment's phrase *cruel and unusual punishment*, which judges have had to interpret in various cases. In *Ford v. Wainwright* (1986), the U.S. Supreme Court was asked to consider whether it was cruel and unusual punishment to execute an offender who became mentally ill while incarcerated. In his opinion for the Court, Justice Thurgood Marshall concluded that the Eighth Amendment prohibits the state from executing a prisoner who is insane. He said that in common law, executing an insane person has little retributive value, has no deterrence value, and simply offends humanity.[5] He also said that Florida's procedures for determining a prisoner's sanity were inadequate.

With this decision, *Ford v. Wainwright* became a precedent (and part of case law) that judges are to use when the execution of a mentally ill death-row inmate is challenged. The decision also alerts states that they should not have sanity-determination procedures similar to those of Florida.

Regulations

Regulations are rules made by federal, state, and local administrative agencies. The legislature, president, or governor gives agencies the power to make detailed regulations governing specific policy in areas such as health, safety, and the environment.

A department of corrections may create regulations regarding the personal items that prisoners may have in their cells, when prisoners may have visitors, how searches are to be carried out, the ways that disciplinary procedures will be conducted, and so forth. Often, these regulations are challenged in court. For example, weekend visiting hours in some prisons are regulated so that half of the inmates are eligible for a visit on Saturday and the other half on Sunday. This is justified because of the great numbers of people who swamp the visiting area on weekends. However, a challenge to the regulation might be mounted by those who for religious reasons cannot travel on the designated day.

Regulations are a form of law that guides the behavior of correctional officials. They are often the basis of legal actions filed by prisoners and correctional employees, who may claim that the regulations violate constitutional protections or statutes or that officials are not following the regulations.

regulations
Legal rules, usually set by an agency of the executive branch, designed to implement in detail the policies of that agency.

CORRECTIONAL LAW AND THE U.S. SUPREME COURT

For most of U.S. history, the Bill of Rights was interpreted as protecting individuals only from acts of the federal government. This meant that the Bill of Rights had little influence over criminal justice, because the vast majority of cases are in state courts and state corrections systems.

The Fourteenth Amendment, ratified in 1868, bars states from violating the right to due process and the right to equal protection of the law. But not until the 1920s did the U.S. Supreme Court begin to name specific rights that were protected by the Fourteenth Amendment from infringement by states. Only during the 1960s did the Court begin to require that state officials abide by the specific provisions of the Bill of Rights.

Prior to the 1960s, the courts maintained a **hands-off policy** with respect to corrections. The hands-off period refers to the historical time frame (from the earliest beginnings of correctional practices in the United States until the 1960s) in which courts would not respond to inmate claims. In general, courts saw correctional officials as the best arbiters of inmate queries and complaints. Although in some states judges applied their states' constitutions to correct abuses in jails and prisons, most judges followed the belief of the Virginia judge in *Ruffin v. Commonwealth* (1871) that prisoners did not have rights. Judges also argued that the separation of powers among the three branches of government prevented them from interfering in the operations of any executive agency. Judges supposed that because they were not penologists, their intervention in the internal administration of prisons could disrupt discipline.

hands-off policy
A judicial policy of noninterference concerning the internal administration of prisons.

The End of the Hands-Off Policy

The U.S. Supreme Court decision in *Cooper v. Pate* (1964) signaled the end of the hands-off policy.[6] The Court said that because of the Civil Rights Act of 1871 (referred to here as Section 1983), state prisoners were *persons* whose rights are protected by the Constitution. The act allows suits against state officials to be heard in the federal courts. Because of *Cooper v. Pate,* the federal courts now recognize that prisoners may sue state officials over such things as brutality by guards, inadequate nutrition and medical care, theft of personal property, and the denial of basic rights.

By allowing prisoners' grievances to be heard, the federal courts destroyed the custodian's absolute power and the prisoners' isolation from the larger society. Such litigation heightened prisoners' consciousness and politicized them.

Although Section 1983 is the most commonly used legal action to challenge prison and jail conditions, inmates may also seek relief by filing a **habeas corpus** petition. This is an ancient legal writ (judicial order) in which prisoners (or pretrial detainees) ask the courts to examine the legality of their imprisonment and ask for release from illegal confinement.

habeas corpus
A writ (judicial order) asking a person holding another person to produce the prisoner and to give reasons to justify continued confinement.

Prisoner-inspired litigation skyrocketed after *Cooper v. Pate.* The number of suits brought by state prisoners in federal courts alone rose from 218 in 1966 to a high of 41,952 in 1996.[7] Additional cases, of course, were filed in state courts. This onslaught of prisoner litigation drew criticism from correctional officials who said they spent precious time and resources responding to the suits.

In recent years the Supreme Court has issued several decisions limiting opportunities for prisoners to file habeas corpus petitions. In 1995 Congress passed the Prison Litigation Reform Act (PLRA), which makes filing lawsuits more difficult for prisoners. The law establishes a twofold threshold that prisoners must meet to establish eligibility to file a lawsuit, standards that did not exist prior to the enactment of the PLRA. First, a prisoner must satisfy the "exhaustion" criteria. This requires that the prisoner must first complete the prison's established grievance procedure, including the appeals process. For each claim the prisoner makes and for each correctional personnel (respondent) involved in the matter, a proper grievance must be filed. If the institution has a clear grievance process that is responsive to prisoner complaints, this criterion should be manageable. But a poorly articulated procedure could be elusive to prisoners. Second, once exhaustion has been accomplished, the prisoner must be certain that he or she has not previously filed three lawsuits that were dismissed as frivolous. The PLRA contains a "three-strikes" provision, which states that once a prisoner has filed three lawsuits that have been dismissed as being without merit, the filing fees for a subsequent lawsuit must be fully paid beforehand. The exception to this provision is if the prisoner can show that he or she is in imminent physical danger. Finally, should the court find in favor of the prisoner, the settlement reached will be one that is as narrowly drawn as possible without infringing upon the compelling interests of the prison officials to maintain a safe and orderly institution. An additional law that limits inmate lawsuits is the anti-terrorism act that was enacted in 1996. Its primary restraining action gives inmates just one year from the time of conviction to file a federal habeas petition. These laws seek to control the occurrence of prisoner lawsuits that lack validity but expend costly courtroom time, often at taxpayer expense.

Access to the Courts

Supreme Court decisions that eased prisoner access to the courts contributed to the increase in filings. Until the 1970s, many states limited communication between prisoners and their attorneys, prohibited jailhouse lawyers, and did not provide prison law libraries. These limitations were imposed on the grounds of institutional security, but prisoners needed access to the courts to ensure that officials followed the law.

The leading case on access to courts is *Johnson v. Avery* (1969).[8] Johnson, a Tennessee inmate, was disciplined for violating a regulation prohibiting one inmate from assisting another with legal matters. The Supreme Court ruled that prisoners are entitled to receive legal assistance from other prisoners unless alternative resources are provided to help prepare necessary legal documents. However, the Court said that the prison could impose reasonable regulations on "jailhouse lawyers" in keeping with the need for order and security.

focus on correctional technology

Electronic Law Libraries

As a result of *Bounds v. Smith,* correctional facilities are required to provide adequate law library resources to inmates. Typically, law library resources include law books, typewriters, copying machines, and assistance from "jailhouse lawyers." Today, electronic law libraries are available to correctional facilities throughout the country. An example is the Touch Sonic Technologies (TST) Law Library System.

This particular system uses a kiosk and a system of monitoring that claims to securely deliver a fully compliant electronic law library to the inmate population. It has a shatterproof touch screen that allows inmates access to legal data and research materials as mandated by law. Also, the TST kiosks operate on an isolated, secure, closed-loop system to prevent any Internet access.

Critical Thinking

Do you see any problems with giving inmates access to a system such as this one? Why or why not?

Source: Adapted from www.touchsonic.com/index.html.

In a second case, *Bounds v. Smith* (1977), the Supreme Court extended the principle of prisoner access by addressing the question of law libraries. The Court ruled that "the fundamental constitutional right of access to the courts requires prison authorities to assist inmates in the preparation and filing of meaningful legal papers by providing prisoners with adequate law libraries or adequate legal assistance from persons trained in the law."[9] Today, technological advancements provide additional tools that make law materials more readily available to correctional facilities and inmates (see "Focus on Correctional Technology: Electronic Law Libraries").

The Prisoners' Rights Movement

As an outgrowth of the civil rights movement, organizations such as the NAACP's Legal Defense and Education Fund and the American Civil Liberties Union became concerned

The first prisoners' rights decisions by the U.S. Supreme Court concerned the most egregious violations of constitutional rights, such as conditions at the Cummins Farm Unit of the Arkansas State Prison, as depicted in the film *Brubaker.*

20th Century Fox Film Corp./Everett Collection

These Muslim inmates are exercising one of the most precious rights of a person who is confined—the freedom to practice one's religion. Religious groups play an important role in prison programming.

about prisoners' rights. In the climate of the times, legal protections for inmates were placed high on the political agenda of many groups. It was no longer unheard-of for prisoners to sue wardens or commissioners of corrections.

The first successful prisoners' rights cases involved the most-excessive prison abuses: brutality and inhumane physical conditions. In 1967, for example, the U.S. Supreme Court invalidated a Florida inmate's confession of rioting after he had been thrown naked into a "barren cage," filthy with human excrement, and kept there for 35 days.[10] The notorious Cummins Farm Unit of the Arkansas State Prison was declared in violation of the Eighth Amendment by a federal district court in 1971. In that case the judge, noting that Arkansas relied on trusties (inmates who serve as "guards") for security and housed inmates in barracks, ruled that leaving the inmates open to "frequent assaults, murder, rape, and homosexual conduct" was unconstitutional.[11]

By the end of the 1970s, federal judges had imposed changes on prisons and jails in nearly every state. In addition, important decisions were made requiring due process in probation and parole. By 1990, most of the worst abuses had been corrected, and judges stopped expanding the number and nature of prisoners' rights.

Over the past four decades, prisoners have pursued rights guaranteed in the U.S. Constitution by filing Section 1983 petitions in the federal courts. They have asserted that civil rights found in the Bill of Rights have been violated. We now examine the case law that has evolved as the Supreme Court has considered these inmate claims.

CONSTITUTIONAL RIGHTS OF PRISONERS

The rights applicable to inmates are summarized in a handful of phrases in four of the amendments to the U.S. Constitution. Three of these—the First, Fourth, and Eighth amendments—are part of the Bill of Rights. The fourth, the Fourteenth Amendment, became effective in 1868. In this section we discuss rights provided under each of them.

Realize that constitutional rights are not always guaranteed, meaning rights may be limited. For example, just as the U.S. Supreme Court stated in 1919[12] that a person cannot yell fire in a crowded theater and expect First Amendment protection, so may the rights of prisoners be similarly constrained. Yelling fire in a crowded theater would compromise public safety. In a similar fashion, correctional administrators are very concerned with running a safe and orderly institution. But how do correctional administrators fulfill this responsibility and still observe the constitutional rights of prisoners? Prison regulations are constructed to achieve an orderly institution. When prisoners' constitutional rights are limited by such regulations, courts may determine if the regulations are necessary. The Supreme Court did not fully address these tensions until 1987 in *Turner v. Safely*. Before the *Turner* decision, lower courts developed a number of tests to resolve these cases.

The First Amendment

Amendment I: *Congress shall make no law respecting an establishment of religion, or prohibiting the free exercise thereof; or abridging the freedom of speech, or of the press; or the right of the people peaceably to assemble, and to petition the government for a redress of grievances.*

Some lower courts have held rules in conflict with First Amendment protections to be unconstitutional unless they were the **least restrictive method** of dealing with an institutional problem. For example, a court struck down the punishment of inmates for writing inflammatory political tracts, because officials could merely have confiscated the material.[13] Other courts have stated that a right may be limited if it interferes with a **compelling state interest**, such as the goal of maintaining security. A rule prohibiting receiving nude photographs of wives and girlfriends was found unconstitutional. The court ruled that the right to receive such photographs was protected; however, because other inmates might be aroused by the sight of them, a rule against their display would have been proper as a security measure.[14] Limitations on receiving certain publications have been upheld on the grounds that such publications present a **clear and present danger** "to the security of a prison, or to the rehabilitation of prisoners."[15]

With courts using different methods to distinguish constitutional from unconstitutional policies, the Supreme Court needed to set standards. Guidance for the lower courts was first spelled out in *Turner v. Safley* (1987), in which the Court upheld a Missouri ban on correspondence among inmates in different correctional institutions. Justice O'Connor, writing for a 5–4 majority, said that such a regulation was valid only if it was "reasonably related to legitimate penological interests."[16] She specified the four elements of the **rational basis test:**

1. There must be a rational connection between the regulation and the legitimate interest put forward to justify it.

2. There must be alternative means of exercising the rights that remain open to prison inmates.

3. There must be a minimal impact of the regulation on correctional officers and other inmates.

4. There must be no less-restrictive alternative available.

This test is the current standard for the analysis of not only prisoners' First Amendment claims but other constitutional claims as well.

Since the 1940s, the Supreme Court has maintained that the First Amendment holds a special position in the Bill of Rights because it guarantees those freedoms essential in a democracy. Because of the preferred position of this amendment, it is not surprising that some of the early prisoners' rights cases concerned rights protected by it: access to reading materials, noncensorship of mail, and freedom of religious practice. Table 11.1 shows some of the most significant cases decided under this amendment.

SPEECH Since the 1970s, courts have extended the rights of freedom of speech and expression to prisoners and have required correctional administrators to show why restrictions on these rights must be imposed. For example, in 1974 the Supreme Court ruled that censorship of mail was permissible only when officials could demonstrate a compelling government interest in maintaining security.[17] The result has been a marked increase in communications between inmates and the outside world. However, in *Turner v. Safley* the Court allowed Missouri to ban correspondence between inmates at other prisons as a means of combating gang violence and the communication of escape plans.[18]

least restrictive methods
Means of ensuring a legitimate state interest (such as security) that impose fewer limits to prisoners' rights than do alternative means of securing that end.

compelling state interest
An interest of the state that must take precedence over rights guaranteed by the First Amendment.

clear and present danger
Any threat to security or to the safety of individuals that is so obvious and compelling that the need to counter it overrides the guarantees of the First Amendment.

rational basis test
Requires that a regulation provide a reasonable, rational method of advancing a legitimate institutional goal.

Table 11.1 Selected Interpretations of the First Amendment as Applied to Prisoners

The Supreme Court has made numerous decisions affecting prisoners' rights to freedom of speech and expression and freedom of religion.

Case	Decision
Procunier v. Martinez (1974)	Censorship of mail is permitted only to the extent necessary to maintain prison security.
Turner v. Safley (1987)	Inmates do not have a right to receive mail from one another, and this mail can be banned if "reasonably related to legitimate penological interests."
Beard v. Banks (2006)	Prison policies that deny magazines, newspapers, and photographs to the most incorrigible inmates in the prison system in an effort to promote security and rule compliance are constitutional.
Fulwood v. Clemmer (1962)	The Muslim faith must be recognized as a religion, and officials may not restrict members from holding services.
Gittlemacker v. Prasse (1970)	The state must give inmates the opportunity to practice their religion but is not required to provide a member of the clergy.
Cruz v. Beto (1972)	Prisoners who adhere to other than conventional beliefs may not be denied the opportunity to practice their religion.
Kahane v. Carlson (1975)	An Orthodox Jewish inmate has the right to a diet consistent with his religious beliefs unless the government can show cause why it cannot be provided.
Theriault v. Carlson (1977)	The First Amendment does not protect so-called religions that are obvious shams, that tend to mock established institutions, and whose members lack religious sincerity.
O'Lone v. Estate of Shabazz (1987)	The rights of Muslim prisoners are not violated when work makes it impossible for them to attend religious services if no alternative exists.

RELIGION The First Amendment prevents Congress from making laws respecting the establishment of religion or prohibiting its free exercise. Cases concerning the free exercise of religion have caused the judiciary some problems, especially when the practice in question may interfere with prison routine and the maintenance of order.

The growth of the Black Muslim religion in prisons set the stage for suits demanding that this group be granted the same privileges as other faiths (special diets, access to clergy and religious publications, and opportunities for group worship). Attorneys for the Muslims succeeded in winning several important cases that helped to establish for prisoners the First Amendment right to free exercise of religion. These decisions also helped Native Americans, Orthodox Jews, and other prisoners to practice their religions. Even unconventional and what some might consider peculiar religious beliefs can be practiced by prisoners. The Court's 2005 decision in *Cutter et al. v. Wilkinson* provided that Ohio prisoners who were followers of Asatru, Christian Identity (both reflecting elements of white separatism), Wicca, or Satanism could observe their faith within the prescribed limits. However, what continues to remain unresolved is the question of what constitutes a legitimate religion. Correctional officials will grapple with this important issue as social and cultural traditions continue to evolve.

Court decisions have upheld prisoners' rights to be served meals consistent with religious dietary laws, to correspond with religious leaders, to possess religious literature, to wear a beard if their belief requires it, and to assemble for services (see "Do the Right Thing").

DO the Right Thing

The warden of the Pleasantville Correctional Facility has received a petition signed by five inmates requesting the use of the prison library on Thursday evenings for religious instruction and services. The inmates profess to be followers of the Wicca religion, a neopagan, nature-based philosophy that includes rituals using magic and eight seasonal-based festivals. In a written response the warden pointed out that the facility had a chaplain and a chapel to serve the spiritual needs of the population. Further, the warden noted that the library was used by the book discussion group on Thursday evenings. The warden also questioned whether Wicca was a recognized religion. The inmates responded that Wicca

was a religion with an international membership. They said that they could not practice their religion with a Christian chaplain and a chapel with Christian symbols and that Thursday was the traditional time for their meetings. They also said that the U.S. Supreme Court had ruled that correctional officials had to make arrangements for members of religious minorities to freely exercise their faith.

Critical Thinking

Suppose that you are the state's attorney general. Provide a legal opinion that will guide the warden's decision.

The Fourth Amendment

Amendment IV: *The right of the people to be secure in their persons, houses, papers, and effects, against unreasonable searches and seizures, shall not be violated, and no warrants shall issue but upon probable cause, supported by oath or affirmation, and particularly describing the place to be searched, and the persons or things to be seized.*

The Fourth Amendment prohibits unreasonable searches and seizures. However, on entering a correctional institution, prisoners surrender most of their rights to privacy. The amendment prohibits only "unreasonable" searches and seizures. Thus, regulations viewed as reasonable to maintain security and order in an institution may be justified.

Table 11.2 outlines some of the Supreme Court's Fourth Amendment opinions. They reveal the fine balance between the right to privacy and institutional needs.

Two principal types of searches occur in prisons: searches of cells and searches of persons. In *Hudson v. Palmer* (1984), the Supreme Court made clear that the Fourth Amendment does not apply within the confines of the prison cell. However, the Court noted that this does not necessarily mean that prisoners have no protections against the

Table 11.2 Selected Interpretations of the Fourth Amendment as Applied to Prisoners

The Supreme Court has often considered the question of unreasonable searches and seizures.

Case	Decision
Lanza v. New York (1962)	Conversations recorded in a jail visitor's room are not protected by the Fourth Amendment.
U.S. v. Hitchcock (1972)	A warrantless search of a cell is not unreasonable, and documentary evidence found there is not subject to suppression in court. It is not reasonable to expect a prison cell to be accorded the same level of privacy as a home or an automobile.
Bell v. Wolfish (1979)	Strip searches, including searches of body cavities after contact visits, may be carried out when the need for such searches outweighs the personal rights invaded.
Hudson v. Palmer (1984)	Officials may search cells without a warrant and seize materials found there.

harmful consequences of some searches. For example, if the inmate's property is damaged or destroyed, the prisoner may file a lawsuit against the correctional officers.[19]

Searches of the person may be conducted at different levels of intrusiveness: metal detectors, pat-down searches of clothed inmates, visual "strip" (nude) searches, and body cavity searches. Correctional administrators must craft regulations to demonstrate clearly that the level of intrusiveness is related to a legitimate institutional need and not conducted with the intent to humiliate or degrade.[20]

The most-intrusive personal searches involve body cavity examinations. These may require a visual or digital examination of the inmate's body openings, an X-ray, or the forced taking of a laxative if it is believed that contraband has been hidden in the body. For example, inmates in Bureau of Prisons facilities, including those in pretrial detention, are required to expose their body cavities for visual inspection following every contact visit with a person from outside the institution. In *Bell v. Wolfish* (1979), judges argued that this requirement violated the Fourth Amendment. In a 5–4 decision, however, the Court said that "balancing the significant and legitimate security interests of the institution against the privacy interests of the inmates, we conclude that they can [conduct the searches]."[21]

However, to justify a digital examination to probe the anus or vagina, the courts have ruled that there must be reasonable suspicion based on factual circumstances to justify such procedures. For example, if an officer observes an inmate receiving a small packet from a visitor and it is not found after pat-down and strip searches, a body cavity search may be justified.[22]

With the employment of both male and female correctional officers in all institutions, lawsuits have been brought to stop opposite-sex officers from viewing and searching inmates' bodies. Some courts have ruled that staff members of one sex may not supervise inmates of the opposite sex during bathing, use of the toilet, or strip searches.[23] Here, the inconvenience of ensuring that the officer is of the same sex as the inmate does not justify the intrusion. Yet the courts have upheld the authority of female guards to pat down male prisoners, excluding the genital area.[24] Complicating this issue is the claim that equal opportunity laws are violated if male or female officers are not allowed to carry out the same job responsibilities, including opposite-sex searches.

In general, the courts have favored the security and safety interests of prison officials when dealing with search and seizure issues. Only the most intrusive physical searches have come under scrutiny and must be justified on the grounds that officers expected to find contraband.

The Eighth Amendment

> **Amendment VIII:** *Excessive bail shall not be required, nor excessive fines imposed, nor cruel and unusual punishments inflicted.*

The Constitution's prohibition of cruel and unusual punishments has been tied to prisoners' need for decent treatment and minimal health standards. The courts have applied three principal tests under the Eighth Amendment to determine whether conditions are unconstitutional: (1) whether the punishment shocks the general conscience of a civilized society, (2) whether the punishment is unnecessarily cruel, and (3) whether the punishment goes beyond legitimate penal aims. Table 11.3 summarizes some of the major Eighth Amendment cases.

totality of conditions
The aggregate of circumstances in a correctional facility that, when considered as a whole, may violate the protections guaranteed by the Eighth Amendment.

Federal courts have ruled that although some aspects of prison life may be acceptable, the combination of various factors—the **totality of conditions**—may determine that living conditions in the institution constitute cruel and unusual punishment. When courts have found brutality, unsanitary facilities, overcrowding, and inadequate food, judges have used the Eighth Amendment to order sweeping changes and even, in some cases, to take over the administration of entire prisons or corrections systems.

Several dramatic cases demonstrate this point. In Georgia, for example, prison conditions were shown to be so bad that judges demanded change throughout the state.[25]

Table 11.3 Selected Interpretations of the Eighth Amendment as Applied to Prisoners

The Supreme Court is called on to determine whether correctional actions constitute cruel and unusual punishment.

Case	Decision
Ruiz v. Estelle (1975)	Conditions of confinement in the Texas prison system are unconstitutional.
Estelle v. Gamble (1976)	Deliberate indifference to serious medical needs of prisoners constitutes the unnecessary and wanton infliction of pain, and thus violates the Eighth Amendment.
Rhodes v. Chapman (1981)	Double-celling and crowding do not necessarily constitute cruel and unusual punishment. It must be shown that the conditions involve "wanton and unnecessary infliction of pain" and are "grossly disproportionate" to the severity of the crime warranting imprisonment.
Whitley v. Albers (1986)	An innocent prisoner mistakenly shot in the leg during a disturbance does not suffer cruel and unusual punishment if the action was taken in good faith to maintain discipline rather than for the mere purpose of causing harm.
Wilson v. Seiter (1991)	Prisoners must not only prove that prison conditions are objectively cruel and unusual but also show that they exist because of the deliberate indifference of officials.
Overton v. Bazetta (2003)	Regulations suspending visiting privileges for two years for those prisoners who have "flunked" two drug tests do not constitute cruel and unusual punishment. The regulations relate to legitimate penological interests.

In *Ruiz v. Estelle* (1980), described more fully in "Focus on Correctional Policy," the court ordered the Texas prison system to address unconstitutional conditions. Judicial supervision of the system continued for a decade.[26]

However, the Supreme Court has indicated that unless extreme conditions are found, courts must defer to correctional officials and legislators. Yet the federal courts have intervened in states where institutional conditions or specific aspects of their operation violate the Eighth Amendment.

The determination of cruel and unusual took an unexpected turn in a recent controversial decision handed down by a federal judge. The state of Massachusetts was ordered by U.S. District Court Chief Judge Mark L. Wolf to provide an unusual medical procedure for convicted murderer Robert Kosilek. Kosilek, a transsexual, was diagnosed as suffering from a gender identity disorder and thus required sex-reassignment surgery.[27] The court determined that the state's refusal to provide the surgery was a violation of the Eight Amendment's cruel and unusual punishment clause. Far more common than demands to consider sex-reassignment surgery is the issue of proper health care for pregnant prisoners. The following disturbing incident was not that uncommon in the past.

While held in the Kern County Jail (Bakersfield, California) in May 1987, Louwanna Yeager went into labor. Despite needing medical personnel, none were available to monitor her advancing labor. A few hours later, she gave birth on a mat that was placed on the floor just outside of the clinic in the jail.[28]

This incident and other similar ones resulted in a series of class-action lawsuits that affected the policies of jails and prisons regarding the treatment of pregnant prisoners and those in active labor. Nevertheless, there are no national standards in place to ensure similar treatment in state and local correctional facilities across the country.

Ms. Yeager was not shackled during her ordeal. However, the shackling of female prisoners during labor and delivery has been a common practice in the United States.

focus on correctional policy

The Impact of *Ruiz v. Estelle*

In December 1980, William W. Justice, federal judge for the Eastern District of Texas, issued a sweeping decree against the Texas Department of Corrections. He ordered prison officials to address a host of unconstitutional conditions, including overcrowding, unnecessary use of force by personnel, inadequate numbers of guards, poor health care practices, and a building-tender system that allowed some inmates to control other inmates.

Eastham is a large, maximum-security institution housing recidivists over the age of 25 who have been in prison three or more times. It is tightly managed and has served as the depository for troublemakers from other Texas prisons. To help with these hard-core criminals, the staff used to rely on a select group of inmates known as building tenders (BTs). By co-opting the BTs with special privileges, officials could use them and their assistants, the turnkeys, to handle the rank-and-file inmates.

In May 1982, Texas signed a consent decree, agreeing to dismantle the building-tender system by January 1983. BTs were reassigned to ordinary prison jobs; stripped of their power, status, and duties; and moved to separate cell blocks for their protection. At the same time, Eastham received 141 new officers, almost doubling the guard force, to help pick up the slack. These reforms were substantial and fundamentally altered the guard and inmate societies.

Major changes took place within the prison community related to interpersonal relations between the guards and inmates, the organization of inmate society, and the guard subculture and work role.

Guards and Inmates

Formerly, ordinary inmates had been subject to an all-encompassing, totalitarian system in which they were "dictated to, exploited, and kept in submission." But with the new relationship between the keepers and the kept, inmates challenged the authority of correctional officers and were more confrontational and hostile. In response, the guards cited inmates for more infractions of the rules. The changes in the relationship between guards and inmates resulted from many factors, including that there were more guards, the restrictions on the guards meant that physical reprisals were not feared, the guards no longer had the BTs to act as intermediaries, and the social distance between guards and prisoners had diminished. The last factor is important because one result of the civil rights movement is that prisoners are no longer viewed as "nonpersons." Inmates now had rights and could invoke due process rules to challenge decisions of guards and other officials. As a result, guards had to "negotiate, compromise, or overlook many difficulties with inmates within the everyday control system."

Reorganization Within the Inmate Society

The purging of the BT–turnkey system created a power vacuum characterized by uncertainty. One outcome was a rise in the amount of inmate–inmate violence. Whereas in the past the BTs had helped to settle disputes among inmates, during the postreform period these conflicts more often led to violence in which weapons were used. Violent self-help became a social necessity. As personal violence escalated, so did inmate gang activities. Gang members knew that they had to have the assistance of others if they were threatened, assaulted, or robbed. For nongang prisoners, heightened levels of personal insecurity meant that they had to rely on themselves and avoid contact with inmates known for their toughness.

Guard Subculture and Work Role

The court-imposed reforms upset the foundations of the guard subculture and work role. The guards' world of work was no longer well ordered, predictable, or rewarding. Among rank-and-file guards, fear of the inmates increased. After removal of the BTs, guards were assigned to cell-block duty for the first time; this placed them in close contact with inmates. The fact that most of the guards were new to prison work meant that they were hesitant to enforce order. Many officers believed that because they could not physically punish inmates and their supervisors did not back them up, it was better not to enforce the rules at all. They thought that their authority had been undermined and that the new disciplinary process was frustrating. Many preferred simply to look the other way.

The court-ordered reforms brought Eastham's operations more in line with constitutional requirements of fairness and due process but disrupted an ongoing social system. Before the *Ruiz* decision, the prison had been run on the basis of paternalism, coercion, dominance, and fear. During the transition to a new bureaucratic–legal order, levels of violence and personal insecurity increased. Authority was eroded, combative relations between inmates and officers materialized, and inmate gangs developed to provide security and autonomy for members.

Judicial supervision of the Texas prison system as a result of this case lasted for a decade and ended on March 31, 1990.

Critical Thinking

What are some of the problems that you, as a warden, would face in dealing with conditions such as those found by the court to be unconstitutional?

Source: Adapted from James W. Marquart and Ben M. Crouch, "Judicial Reform and Prisoner Control: The Impact of *Ruiz v. Estelle* on a Texas Penitentiary," *Law and Society Review* 19 (1985): 557–86. See also *Ruiz v. Estelle*, 503 F.Supp. 1265 (S.D. Tex. 1980).

Shackling involves placing restraints such as handcuffs and/or ankle shackles on prisoners—including during childbirth. This controversial practice falls under the purview of the Eighth Amendment's clause of cruel and unusual punishment. But this standard is complicated by the primary objective of correctional officials to maintain a safe, secure, and orderly correctional facility. For medical care to implicate the Eighth Amendment, it must be shown that prison officials' conduct (or lack thereof) was an affront to standards of care and thus created an unnecessary and substantial risk of harm to the prisoner. This is similar to a reckless-disregard posture: an awareness of the potential for harmful results. Consider the account of Melissa Hall, who was pregnant during her incarceration for possession of a controlled dangerous substance in 2006:

> As I was close to delivering my baby, I was in a lot of pain, and I was screaming for the nurse. . . . The sheriff didn't give me any sympathy or any privacy. He left the handcuff shackled to the bed and the leg iron shackled to the stirrup while I was delivering my baby.[29]

Like Ms. Yeager, Ms. Hall was eventually part of a class-action suit, which in this case resulted in a $4.1-million settlement for being subjected to this practice. Currently, some federal courts have interpreted shackling as unconstitutional during childbirth, and several states have passed laws that prohibit shackling during active labor, delivery, and recovery. In May 2014 Massachusetts became the twenty-first state to pass an anti-shackling law.[30] Restraints cannot be used on pregnant prisoners past the first trimester. California has gone a step further and has prohibiting shackling throughout the entire time of pregnancy. The state's anti-shackling bill was signed into law by Governor Brown in 2012.

A different area of concern to correctional officials is court orders requiring an end to prison crowding. For example, the courts have stated that cells must afford each inmate at least 60 square feet of floor space. However, in *Rhodes v. Chapman* (1981), the U.S. Supreme Court upheld double-bunking (two inmates in a cell designed for one person) in Ohio as not constituting a condition of cruel and unusual punishment. To prove a violation of the Eighth Amendment, the Court noted, it must be shown that the punishment either "inflicts unnecessary or wanton pain [or is] grossly disproportionate to the severity of the crime warranting punishment." Unless the conditions in the Ohio prison were "deplorable" or "sordid," the Court declared, the courts should defer to correctional authorities.[31]

The Fourteenth Amendment

> **Amendment XIV:** *All persons born or naturalized in the United States, and subject to the jurisdiction thereof, are citizens of the United States and of the state wherein they reside. No state shall make or enforce any law which shall abridge the privileges or immunities of citizens of the United States; nor shall any state deprive any person of life, liberty, or property without due process of law, nor deny to any person within its jurisdiction the equal protection of the laws.*

One word and two clauses of the Fourteenth Amendment are relevant to the question of prisoners' rights. The relevant word is *state*. Recall that by the 1970s the Supreme Court had ruled that through the Fourteenth Amendment, the Bill of Rights restricts state governments.

The first important clause concerns procedural due process. **Procedural due process** requires that all individuals be treated fairly and justly by government officials and that decisions be made according to procedures prescribed by law. Prisoners sometimes file claims based on the due process clause when they believe that state statutes or administrative procedures have not been followed regarding, for example, parole release, transfers to other prisons, transfers to administrative segregation, and disciplinary hearings.

The second important clause is the **equal protection** clause. Claims that prisoners have been denied equal protection of the law concern issues of racial, gender, and/or religious discrimination.

procedural due process
The constitutional guarantee that no agent or instrumentality of government will use any procedures other than those prescribed by law to arrest, prosecute, try, or punish any person.

equal protection
The constitutional guarantee that the law will be applied equally to all people, without regard for such individual characteristics as gender, race, and religion.

People who are incarcerated should know their rights. The administrators who run their prisons have to explain prison policy and to make sure that the rights of the confined are respected.

Jesse Dearing/The Boston Globe/Getty Images

DUE PROCESS IN PRISON DISCIPLINE Administrators have the power to discipline inmates who break institutional rules. Until the 1970s, disciplinary procedures could be exercised without challenge because the prisoner was legally in the hands of the state. In addition, formal rules of prison conduct either did not exist or were vague. For example, disrespect toward a correctional officer was an infraction, but the characteristics of "disrespect" were not defined. The word of the correctional officer was accepted, and the inmate had little opportunity to challenge the charges.

In a series of decisions in the 1970s, the Supreme Court began to insist that procedural due process be part of the most sensitive of institutional decisions: those by which inmates are sent to solitary confinement and the methods by which good-time credit can be taken away because of misconduct.

The 1974 case of *Wolff v. McDonnell* extended certain due process rights.[32] The Supreme Court specified that when a prisoner faces serious disciplinary action that may result in segregation or the withdrawal of good time, the state must follow certain minimal procedures that conform to the guarantee of due process. These included the rights to receive written notice of the charges, to present witnesses, to have an impartial hearing, and to receive a written statement concerning the outcome of the hearing.

However, the Court also recognized the special conditions of incarceration. It further stated that prisoners do not have the right to cross-examine witnesses and that the evidence presented by the offender shall not be unduly hazardous to institutional safety or correctional goals.

As a result of the Supreme Court's decisions, some of which are outlined in **Table 11.4**, disciplinary proceedings have most elements of due process. Usually, a disciplinary committee receives charges, conducts hearings, and decides guilt and punishment. Such committees usually include administrative personnel, but sometimes they also include inmates or citizens from the outside. The New York corrections system has adopted detailed procedures that clearly meet the *Wolff* standards (see "Focus on Correctional Practice").

EQUAL PROTECTION In 1968 the Supreme Court firmly established that racial discrimination may not be official policy within prison walls.[33] Segregation can be justified only as a temporary expedient during periods when violence between races is imminent. Equal protection claims have also been upheld in relation to religious freedoms and access to reading materials of interest to racial minorities.

Table 11.4 Selected Interpretations of the Fourteenth Amendment as Applied to Prisoners

The Supreme Court has ruled concerning procedural due process and equal protection.

Case	Decision
Wolff v. McDonnell (1974)	The basic elements of procedural due process must be present when decisions are made concerning the disciplining of an inmate.
Baxter v. Palmigiano (1976)	Although due process must be accorded, an inmate has no right to counsel in a disciplinary hearing.
Vitek v. Jones (1980)	The involuntary transfer of a prisoner to a mental hospital requires a hearing and other minimal elements of due process, such as notice and the availability of counsel.
Sandin v. Conner (1995)	Prison regulations do not violate due process unless they place atypical and significant hardships on a prisoner.

The most recent cases concerning equal protection deal with issues concerning female offenders. Although the U.S. Supreme Court has yet to rule, state and lower federal courts have considered several relevant cases. In *Pargo v. Elliott* (1995), Iowa female inmates argued that their equal protection rights were violated because programs and

focus on correctional practice

New York State's Disciplinary Due Process (Summarized)

You Have a Right to:

1. *Written notice of the charge.* The CDC Form 115 Rule Violation Report must include the specific charge; the date, time, and place of the alleged violation; and a statement of the evidence relied upon. You must be given the form within 15 days after prison staff discover information leading to the charge.

2. *Assignment of an investigative employee (IE)* who will investigate the facts when the issues are complex and require further investigation.

3. *Assignment of a staff assistant (SA)* if you need to have a confidential relationship with the person who is helping you, if you are illiterate or non-English speaking, or if you need assistance to understand the charges or the disciplinary process.

4. *Effective communications.* If you have a disability, you will be assigned a staff assistant, a qualified interpreter or a reader, or other accommodations such as large-print materials or sound-amplification devices.

5. *Request witnesses both friendly and hostile* to be interviewed by the IE and to attend the hearing. This request may be disallowed only for specific reasons such as endangerment of the witness. A witness may be made available via telephone.

6. *Present documentary evidence* in defense or mitigation of the charge.

7. *A hearing within 30 days* after you receive written notice.

8. *An impartial decision maker.* The hearing officer may not be someone who reported, observed, classified, or investigated the alleged violation or assisted you in preparing for the hearing.

9. *Be present at the hearing.*

10. *The standard for the determination of guilt at the hearing shall be the preponderance of the evidence.*

11. *A complete copy of CDC Form 115* containing the disposition, findings, and specific evidence shall be provided within 5 working days after it has been reviewed by the Chief Disciplinary Officer.

12. *Appeals* go through the CDC administrative appeals process.

Critical Thinking

Do you think that these rights granted to New York inmates are sufficient? Why or why not?

Source: Adapted from www.prisonlaw.com/pdfs/Discipline.pdf.

services were not at the same level as those provided male inmates. The court ruled that because of differences and needs, identical treatment is not required for men and women. It concluded that there was no evidence of "invidious discrimination."[34] In the next few years the U.S. Supreme Court is likely to consider equal protection for female prisoners.

A Change in Judicial Direction

The early years of the prisoners' rights movement brought noteworthy victories. But it was not until 1974, in *Wolff v. McDonnell,* that the Court "provided the kind of clarion statement that could serve as a rallying call for prisoners' rights advocates." In that case Justice Byron White, speaking for the Court, wrote the following:

> *Lawful imprisonment necessarily makes unavailable many rights and privileges of the ordinary citizen, a retraction justified by the considerations underlying our penal system. . . . But though his rights may be diminished by the needs and exigencies of the institutional environment, a prisoner is not wholly stripped of constitutional protections when he is imprisoned for crime.*[35]

This language, and that contained in the Court's decisions in several subsequent cases, gave prisoners' rights advocates the feeling that the Supreme Court was backing their efforts.

During the past 30 years, however, the Supreme Court has been less supportive of the expansion of prisoners' rights, and a few decisions reflect a retreat. In *Bell v. Wolfish* (1979), the Justices took pains to say that prison administrators should be given wide-ranging deference in the adoption and execution of policies.[36] The concept of deliberate indifference surfaced in *Daniels v. Williams* (1986). Here the Court said that an inmate could sue for damages only if officials had violated rights through deliberate actions.[37] This reasoning was extended in the 1991 case of *Wilson v. Seiter,* where the Court ruled that a prisoner's conditions of confinement are not unconstitutional unless it can be shown that administrators had acted with "deliberate indifference" to basic human needs.[38]

Many scholars believe that the deliberate-indifference requirement indicates a shift from the use of objective criteria (proof that the inmate suffered conditions protected by the Eighth Amendment) to subjective criteria (the state of mind of correctional officials, namely, deliberate indifference) in determining whether prison conditions are unconstitutional.

In 1996 Congress passed the Prison Litigation Reform Act, as described earlier, which makes it more difficult for prisoners to file civil rights lawsuits and for judges to make decisions affecting prison operations. For example, the act requires that inmates exhaust the prison's grievance procedure before filing a lawsuit and to pay filing fees ($150 "up front"). Since the act became law, the number of Section 1983 lawsuits filed in federal courts has dropped dramatically, even though the number of state prisoners has continued to rise (see **Figure 11.1**).

The lower federal courts and many state courts continue to support judicial intervention to uphold civil rights, but the Supreme Court and Congress seem less sympathetic toward prisoners' claims. A return to a strict hands-off policy seems highly unlikely, but greater deference is being given to prison administrators. Many scholars believe that the era of institutional reform has ended.

Although in recent years the Supreme Court has reduced its support for the expansion of prisoners' rights, some general changes in American corrections have occurred since the late 1970s. The most obvious changes are improvements in institutional conditions and administrative practices. Overcrowding remains a major problem, but many conditions have greatly improved, and the more brutalizing elements of prison life have diminished.[39]

Real changes have occurred over time. The prisoners' rights movement has clearly influenced correctional officials. The threat of lawsuits and public exposure has placed many in the correctional bureaucracy on guard. One can argue whether or not such changes will ultimately prove useful. On the one hand, this wariness may have merely further bureaucratized corrections, requiring staff to prepare extensive and

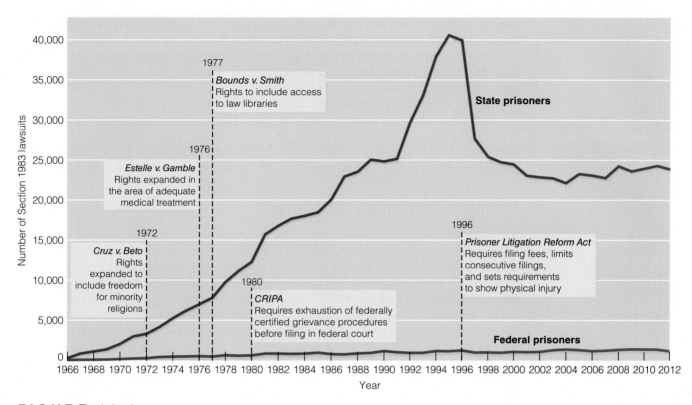

FIGURE 11.1

Section 1983 lawsuits

The number of Section 1983 lawsuits brought by state prisoners has dropped dramatically since the passage of the Prison Litigation Reform Act of 1996.

Sources: Bureau of Justice Statistics, *Sourcebook of Criminal Justice Statistics, 1977* (Washington, DC: U.S. Government Printing Office, 1978), Table 5.28; Ann L. Pastore and Kathleen Maguire, eds., *Sourcebook of Criminal Justice Statistics*, Table 5.65.2012, www.albany.edu /sourcebook/, February 18, 2014.

time-consuming documentation of their actions to protect themselves from lawsuits. On the other hand, judicial intervention has forced corrections to rethink existing procedures and organizational structures. As part of the wider changes in the "new corrections," new administrators, increased funding, reformulated policies, and improved management procedures have, at least in part, been influenced by the prisoners' rights movement. The actual impact of extending constitutional rights to prisoners has not yet been measured, but evidence suggests that court decisions have had a broad effect.

ALTERNATIVES TO LITIGATION

Although many prisoners do have legitimate legal claims, correctional specialists, judges, and even lawyers are questioning the suitability of lawsuits as the only means to resolve them. Some legal scholars argue that litigation is a cumbersome, costly, and often ineffective way to handle such claims. Annually, more than 23,000 state prisoners petition the federal courts to halt certain correctional practices or to seek monetary awards for damages. The courts deem many of these suits frivolous and dismiss them for failure to state legitimate claims. Among the remainder, only a few are decided in ways that affect anyone but the litigant.

Still another problem is that although most Section 1983 suits that prisoners file are dismissed, the remaining cases force correctional officials to expend time and resources in litigation, to face the possibility of being sued personally, and to risk the erosion of their leadership. Correctional administrators have charged that much prisoner litigation is designed merely to "hassle" them.[40]

From the prisoner's perspective, litigation may be neither effective nor satisfying. Most prisoners face three problems: (1) they generally lack legal representation, (2) constitutional standards are difficult to meet, and (3) even if a suit succeeds, changes in policies or financial compensation may take a long time.

Four alternatives to litigation appear in the corrections systems of various states: (1) inmate-grievance procedures, (2) use of an ombudsman, (3) mediation, and (4) legal assistance. All are designed to solve problems before the inmate feels compelled to file suit, but mediation and legal assistance can also be invoked after a suit has been initiated.

Inmate-Grievance Procedures

Although informal procedures for hearing inmates' complaints have existed for many years, only since the mid-1970s have formal grievance mechanisms been widely used. All states and the Federal Bureau of Prisons now have grievance procedures.

Most corrections systems use a three-step inmate-grievance process. A staff member or committee in each institution usually receives complaints, investigates them, and makes decisions. If the inmate is dissatisfied with the outcome, he or she may appeal the case to the warden and ultimately to the commissioner of corrections. Reports indicate that some grievances are more easily resolved than others. For example, many inmates complain that they are not receiving proper medical treatment, but because medical personnel can usually document the treatment provided, such complaints normally subside. The many complaints of lost personal property are another matter. Most involve items deposited at the reception center at the time of arrival but not transferred with the prisoner to another institution. Staff members often cannot account for missing property, and the process for receiving compensation for property lost or damaged can be complicated. Probably the most difficult situation to resolve is alleged brutality by a guard. Such a complaint virtually always comes down to the inmate's word against the officer's, because staff members rarely testify against other officers.

The inmate-grievance procedure can help defuse tensions in correctional facilities. It also serves as a management tool. By attentive monitoring of the complaint process, a warden can discern patterns of inmate discontent that may warrant actions to prevent the development of deeper problems.

The Ombudsman

ombudsman
A public official who investigates complaints against government officials and recommends corrective measures.

Ombudsman programs are the second most common dispute-resolution mechanism in corrections. An **ombudsman** is a public official with full authority to investigate citizens' complaints against government officials.

Ombudsman programs succeed if inmates have quick and easy access to the office. When inmates respect their ombudsman, his or her advice on the merits of grievances may help to reduce the number of frivolous claims; when ombudsmen see merit in claims, they can try to convince authorities that it would be in their interest to resolve the matters out of court.

Mediation

mediation
Intervention in a dispute by a third party to whom the parties in conflict submit their differences for resolution and whose decision (in the correctional setting) is binding on both parties.

Mediation is a consensual and voluntary process in which a neutral third party assists disputants in reconciling their differences. The informality of the process stands in contrast to the complex, cumbersome procedures of the courtroom. It also offers a special advantage to prisoners, most of whom would not have counsel were they to take their cases to court. Mediation is particularly effective when the essence of a complaint is not a conflict of abstract principles but a problem requiring an administrative solution. However, it has not lived up to its potential in the correctional arena because in many cases neither party seems willing to be bound by the decision.

Legal Assistance

Since the early 1970s, several legal-assistance mechanisms have been developed in correctional institutions, including staff attorneys to assist inmates with their legal problems, inmate ("jailhouse") lawyers, and law school clinics.

Providing legal assistance may seem counterproductive if the goal of correctional administrators is to avoid litigation, but lawyers do more than simply help prisoners file suits. They also advise on the legal merits of complaints and thus can discourage frivolous suits. Further, counsel can help determine the underlying issues of a complaint and therefore frame questions in terms that people with legal training will understand.

THE DEATH PENALTY

The death penalty is a sentence unlike all others. It requires that the state terminate the life of the convicted as a form of punishment. The stakes can't be higher: Should the ultimate error occur (the execution of an innocent), there is no going back. Therefore, multiple constitutional, statutory, and regulatory laws govern the administration of the death penalty. In addition, there have been complex and unexpected issues that arise from the application of capital punishment that were eventually dealt with by the U.S. Supreme Court. For example, in 1947 the Court determined that if a prisoner does not die during the state's attempt to execute him or her, a second attempt does not implicate double jeopardy, nor does it constitute cruel and unusual punishment.[41] While some may view this decision as somewhat insensitive (the prisoner, Willie

Lethal injection is thought to be the most humane way of carrying out the death penalty. Because of cases during which the procedure was "botched," some claim that the method is cruel and unusual punishment in violation of the Eighth Amendment.

AP Images/Amber Hunt

Francis, was successfully electrocuted a year later), the Court has since made decisions on death penalty cases that may be viewed as more socially just. For example, on March 1, 2005, the Court decided that individuals who were under the age of 18 at the time of their crimes could no longer be executed.[42]

These two cases are clear examples of how U.S. Supreme Court decisions concerning the death penalty have evolved over the last several decades. The following section discusses a selected number of important Supreme Court decisions regarding the death penalty, including issues regarding who is eligible for capital punishment and how it should be administered.

Key U.S. Supreme Court Decisions

In *Furman v. Georgia* (1972) the U.S. Supreme Court ruled that while the death penalty was constitutional, the way it was used constituted cruel and unusual punishment. The Justices were concerned about the ambiguity of the wording in some state statutes and the lack of consistency in the use of the death sentence. The Court invalidated the death penalty laws in 39 states and the District of Columbia.[43] Shortly after the *Furman* decision, 35 states enacted new death penalty laws that provided more-careful decision making and the use of more-modern methods of execution, such as lethal injection. (See "Myths in Corrections.") The new laws were tested before the Supreme Court in 1976, in the case of *Gregg v. Georgia*.[44] The Court upheld those laws that required the sentencing judge or jury to take into account specific aggravating and mitigating factors in deciding which convicted murders should be executed. Under the *Gregg* decision, states must have "bifurcated" hearings to determine guilt and the proper sentence. In other words, one proceeding is used to determine whether the offender is guilty. A second proceeding then takes place at a later date to determine whether the guilty person is to be sentenced to death. **Figure 11.2** shows the number of executions by state.

One of the more significant challenges since *Gregg* has charged that racial discrimination is a factor in the application of capital cases. Since 1976, 35 percent of defendants on death row have been black,[45] a number disproportionate to the 12.9 percent of blacks in the general population.[46] Warren McCleskey, a black male, was convicted of murder in Georgia and sentenced to death. He appealed his conviction and also argued that the state of Georgia administered the death penalty in a racially discriminatory manner that violated the Eighth and Fourteenth amendments. McCleskey relied on the results of the Baldus study—a statistical analysis of 2,000 Georgia murder cases—which concluded among other things that "prosecutors sought the death penalty in 71 percent of the cases involving black defendants and white victims; 32 percent of the cases involving white defendants and white victims; 15 percent of the cases involving black defendants and black victims; and 19 percent of the cases involving white defendants and black victims."[47] Despite these troubling statistics, in *McCleskey v. Kemp* (1987) the Court determined by a slim 5–4 vote that McCleskey had failed to show that racial discrimination occurred during his capital case. Moreover, Justices said that the Baldus study would be better handled in the state legislature than in the courts. For many, this decision also signaled that it would be more difficult to successfully challenge the constitutionality of criminal proceedings based on claims of racial discrimination. McCleskey was eventually executed in September 1991.

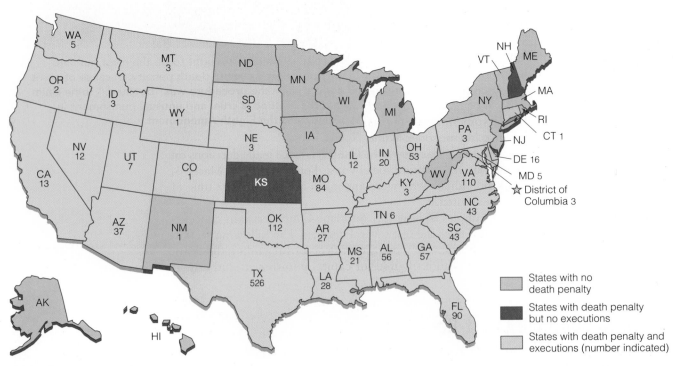

FIGURE 11.2
Executions by State, 1976–2014

Just over 65 percent of executions have been carried out in five southern states—Texas, Virginia, Oklahoma, Florida, and Missouri—yet the highest homicide rates are found in Louisiana, Mississippi, New Mexico, Nevada, and Maryland. What might explain the lack of correspondence between homicides and executions?

Source: Death Penalty Information Center.

In June 2002 the Court broke new ground. First, in *Atkins v. Virginia* (2002) the Justices ruled that execution of the mentally retarded was unconstitutional.[48] Writing for the majority, Justice John Paul Stevens noted that the number of states prohibiting executions of the mentally retarded had grown from 2 in 1989 to 18 in 2002. At trial, these defendants have problems remembering details, locating witnesses, and testifying credibly on their own behalf.

Second, in *Ring v. Arizona* (2002) the Court ruled that juries, rather than judges, must make the crucial decision on whether a convicted murderer should receive the death penalty.[49] The *Ring* decision overturned the law of five states, where judges alone decided whether aggravating circumstances warranted capital punishment. The decision also called into question the practices of four other states, where judges decided life imprisonment or death after hearing the jury's recommendation.

As mentioned earlier, in 2005 the U.S. Supreme Court reduced the scope of the death penalty even further. In *Roper v. Simmons* a majority of the Justices decided that offenders cannot be sentenced to death for a crime they committed before they reached the age of 18.[50] Prior to that decision, the United States was among only a half-dozen countries in the entire world with laws that permitted death sentences for juveniles. Because the Court was divided on the issue, some observers wonder if future changes in the Court's composition may lead to a reversal of this decision.

MYTHS in Corrections

Only Twenty-First-Century Methods of Execution Are Used Throughout the United States

THE MYTH: Prisoners are no longer executed by hanging or by firing squad.

THE REALITY: On June 18, 2010, Utah executed convicted murderer Ronnie Lee Gardner by firing squad. A five-man team took part in the execution by shooting the hooded and seated Gardner. Under Utah law, death row inmates convicted before 2004 may choose either lethal injection or firing squad as their means of execution. All subsequent convictions require lethal injection only. Oklahoma is the only other state that permits execution by firing squad should electrocution or lethal injection be held unconstitutional.

Source: www.nytimes.com/2010/06/17/us/17death.html, June 17, 2010.

Continuing Legal Issues

The case law since *Furman* indicates that capital punishment is legal as long as it is imposed fairly. However, opponents continue to raise several issues in litigation. Now that the mentally retarded and juvenile offenders have been excluded from eligibility for the death penalty, some people argue that the mentally ill should also be excluded. Other legal issues include the effectiveness of counsel, the use of death-qualified juries, capital punishment for crimes other than murder, the lengthy period that condemned offenders spend on death row awaiting execution, and the use of lethal injection.

EXECUTION OF THE MENTALLY ILL A criminal defendant who is incapable of understanding the difference between right and wrong may be found to be legally insane. Such individuals are not held criminally responsible for their actions. Alvin Ford, who was convicted of murder in Florida and sentenced to death, *became* insane while awaiting his execution. In *Ford v. Wainwright* (1985) the question before the Supreme Court was whether executing an individual who was sane at the time of the crime but later became insane violated constitutional protections against cruel and unusual punishment. The Court decided here in the affirmative: An insane person cannot be executed. The Eighth Amendment prohibits the execution of a prisoner who is insane at the time of the scheduled execution.

EFFECTIVENESS OF COUNSEL In *Strickland v. Washington* (1984) the Supreme Court ruled that defendants in capital cases have the right to representation that meets an "objective standard of reasonableness."[51] As noted by Justice Sandra Day O'Connor, the appellant must show "that there is a reasonable probability that, but for counsel's unprofessional errors, the result of the proceeding would have been different."[52]

Scott Panetti, on death row in Texas, understands that the state intends to kill him for the murder of his in-laws. However, he says that the state, in league with Satan, wants to kill him to prevent him from preaching the Gospel. That delusion has been documented. In 2007 the U.S. Supreme Court ordered that his case be sent back to the federal district court to determine whether Panetti has no "rational understanding" of the connection between the act and the execution. In March 2008 the lower court ruled that Panetti, although suffering from schizophrenia, was competent to be executed. As of June 2010, no date had been set.

MICHAEL STRAVATO/The New York Times/Redux Pictures

In recent years the public has learned of cases where the defense attorney's competency has been put in doubt. In March 2000 a federal judge in Texas ordered the release of Calvin Burdine after 16 years on death row.[53] At his 1984 trial, Burdine's counsel slept through long portions of the proceedings. As the judge said, "Sleeping counsel is no counsel at all." The right to effective counsel was reaffirmed by the Supreme Court in 2003, when it overturned the death sentence of Kevin Wiggins. The seven-member majority declared that Wiggins's inexperienced lawyer had failed to provide adequate representation by neglecting to introduce mitigating evidence at sentencing regarding the horrendous abuse that Wiggins had endured throughout his childhood.

DEATH-QUALIFIED JURIES Should people who are opposed to the death penalty be excused from juries in capital cases? In *Witherspoon v. Illinois* (1968) the Supreme Court held that potential jurors who have objections to the death penalty, or whose religious convictions oppose its use, cannot be automatically excluded from jury service in capital cases. However, it upheld the practice of removing, during voir dire (part of jury selection), those people whose opposition is so strong as to "prevent or substantially impair the performance of their duties."[54]

In *Uttecht v. Brown* (2007) the Supreme Court appears to have enhanced the state's ability to remove potential jurors with doubts about the death penalty. In a 5–4 decision the Court upheld a trial court judge who excused from the jury a person who had merely expressed doubts about the death penalty, not strict opposition to it.[55]

Mark Costanzo points to research indicating that death qualification has several effects. First, those who are selected for jury service are more prone to convict. A second, subtler impact is that jurors answering questions about their willingness to vote for a death sentence often conclude that both defense counsel and prosecutors anticipate a conviction and a death sentence.[56]

EXECUTION FOR CHILD RAPE Because of the heinous nature of the crime, several states have laws permitting use of the death penalty for adults who rape children but do not murder them. In *Kennedy v. Louisiana* (2008) the U.S. Supreme Court, in a 5–4 decision, held that a capital sentence where the crime did not involve murder was in violation of the Eighth and Fourteenth amendments.[57] The majority cited their decision in *Coker v. Georgia* (1977), which ruled that the use of the death penalty for the rape of an adult was unconstitutional.[58] But observers note that the narrow division of the Justices in *Kennedy* could be reversed with future changes in the court's composition.

APPEALS Many argue that the appellate process in capital cases takes too long, traumatizes victims' families, and burdens states with millions in extra costs for defense counsel and for housing convicted killers. Others point out that an appellate process that carefully examines each case is necessary because during the 1990s, 26 percent of state death sentences were overturned on appeal.

In *McCleskey v. Zant* (1991) the Court sharply curtailed the ability of offenders to file multiple challenges to the constitutionality of their sentence. The Court ruled that, except in exceptional circumstances, the lower federal courts must dismiss a prisoner's second and subsequent habeas corpus petitions.[59] Further restrictions were placed on appeals in 1993, in the case of *Herrera v. Collins*. Leonel Herrera was sentenced to death for the 1982 murder of two police officers. Ten years later, Herrera's nephew asserted in an affidavit that before his father, Raul, died in 1984, he had confessed to the crime. Three other people asserted that Raul Herrera was the murderer. Texas law provides only thirty days for filing a motion for a new trial based on newly discovered evidence. The Supreme Court rejected Leonel Herrera's argument that his case should be reopened. Chief Justice Rehnquist, speaking for the majority, said that only in "truly persuasive" cases should a hearing be held.[60] Herrera was executed in 1993.

LETHAL INJECTIONS—ARE THEY PAINLESS? The primary method of execution in the United States is lethal injection. Today, 35 of the 36 states that have the death penalty use this method of execution. The motivation for adopting this method was to effect a more humane and painless execution. It essentially involves the administration of a combination of drugs that leads to the death of the condemned prisoner. Although states have different operating procedures surrounding execution, administering the prescribed drugs attempts to accomplish three medical responses: sedation, which leads to unconsciousness; paralysis of the diaphragm, which causes cessation of breathing; and finally cardiac arrest. Ideally, the prisoner is unconscious when death occurs. However, recent unsettling developments during executions have called this assumption into question. In 2011 Arizona and Georgia carried out executions that caused the prisoners to remain open-eyed, conscious, and aware despite the sedative. Experts observed that these individuals likely suffered excruciating pain as paralysis set in but were unable to express their discomfort. Two more recent executions produced the same troubling result. Both Ohio and Oklahoma use Midazolam as the sedative. But reports indicated that both men moved violently, attempted to speak, and appeared to consciously struggle to breathe, gasping for several minutes after receiving Midazolam. Both men died, but the manner of their deaths called for the review of protocols. As a result of a petition brought by Oklahoma prisoners, the U.S. Supreme Court announced in January 2015 that it would hear arguments in April on the constitutionality of the drug protocols used by Oklahoma and other states.[61]

There are strong feelings about the death penalty on both sides of the question. Today, the use of the death penalty appears to be waning, in part because of declining public support.

Katherine Taylor/Epa/Landov

Who Is on Death Row?

Death row inmates tend to be poorly educated men from low-income backgrounds. Further, the number of minority group members on death row is far out of proportion to their numbers in the general population (see **Figure 11.3**). The criminal history of these death row inmates shows that 65.4 percent have a prior felony conviction, 8.4 percent have a prior homicide conviction, 26 percent were on probation or parole, and 3.6 percent were in prison at the time of the capital offense.[62]

Public Opinion and the Death Penalty

How does the public feel about the death penalty? Public support for capital punishment has shifted over the 80 years of polling on the topic by the Gallup organization. The highest level of support for the death penalty was recorded in 1994, when 80 percent of Americans said they supported it. Since then, however, support has dropped; by October 2008, it was 64 percent.[63] Public opinion research shows that when the public is given an alternative to the death penalty, such as life in prison with no chance of parole, the percentage of Americans who favor the death penalty drops.

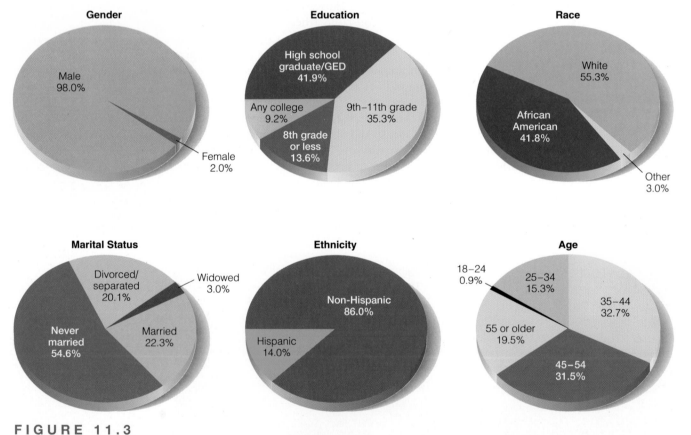

FIGURE 11.3
Characteristics of Death Row Inmates
Like other prisoners, death row inmates tend to be younger, less-educated men. Minority group members are also disproportionately represented on death row.

Source: Bureau of Justice Statistics, Tracy L. Snell, July 2013, *Capital Punishment, 2011—Statistical Tables.*

Summary

1 **Discuss the foundations that support the legal rights of prisoners.**

The foundations that support the legal rights of prisoners are found in constitutions, statutes, case law, and regulations. Constitutions describe the institutions of government and list the basic rights of individuals. Statutes are laws created by elected representatives at all levels of government. Case law refers to judges' decisions in specific cases that create new law or modify existing law. Regulations are rules developed by government agencies intended to guide officials' decisions.

2 **Describe the role of the U.S. Supreme Court in interpreting correctional law.**

In the mid-1960s, the Court abandoned the "hands-off policy" and recognized that prisoners could sue state officials for violating their constitutional rights. This led to the prisoners' rights movement, resulting in more legal protections for inmates in correctional facilities and offenders on probation and parole.

3 **Understand the constitutional rights of prisoners.**

The constitutional rights of prisoners are found mainly in the First, Fourth, Eighth, and Fourteenth amendments to the Constitution. The First Amendment protects freedom of speech and expression, as well as the establishment and free exercise of religion. The Fourth Amendment protects inmates from "unreasonable" searches and seizures. The Eighth Amendment protects inmates from cruel and unusual punishments. The Fourteenth Amendment provides inmates due process in prison discipline and protection against racial discrimination.

4 **List and describe alternatives to litigation.**

Inmate-grievance mechanisms are designed to help defuse tensions in correctional facilities. Prison ombudsman programs use a public official to investigate inmates' complaints and recommend corrective measures. Mediation is a consensual and voluntary process in which a third party assists disputants in resolving differences. Legal-assistance mechanisms are available to inmates to help them with legal matters.

5 **Discuss the case law concerning the application of the death penalty.**

In *Furman v. Georgia* (1972) the U.S. Supreme Court ruled that the way the death penalty was used constituted cruel and unusual punishment. The Justices were concerned about the ambiguity of the wording in some state statutes and the lack of consistency in the use of the death sentence. The decision invalidated the death penalty laws. Shortly after the *Furman* decision, 35 states enacted new death penalty laws that provided more-careful decision making, following Georgia's lead (*Gregg v. Georgia*). Under the *Gregg* decision, states must have "bifurcated" hearings to determine guilt and the proper sentence. The Court decided in *Ford v. Wainwright* (1986) that an insane person cannot be executed, based on the Eighth Amendment protection against cruel and unusual punishment. Despite statistical evidence that suggested the possibility of racially discriminatory practices in the application of capital cases in Georgia, the Court determined in *McCleskey v. Kemp* (1987) that such evidence must be present in a particular case to have merit. In 2002 the Court prohibited the execution of the mentally retarded (*Atkins v. Virginia*). Finally, in 2005 the Court discontinued the execution of those who committed their crimes when younger than 18 years of age (*Roper v. Simmons*).

Key Terms

case law 280
clear and present danger 285
compelling state interest 285
constitution 279
equal protection 290
habeas corpus 282

hands-off policy 281
least restrictive methods 285
mediation 296
ombudsman 296
precedent 280
procedural due process 290

rational basis test 285
regulations 281
statute 280
totality of conditions 288

For Discussion

1. After the courts abandoned the hands-off policy, what problems did correctional administrators encounter?
2. What difficulties might you, as a correctional officer, foresee in attempting to run your unit of the institution while at the same time upholding the legal rights of the prisoners?
3. Suppose that you are a prison warden. What if a group of prisoners calling themselves the "Sons of the Purple Flower" and claiming to be a religious organization requested a special diet and permission to chant when the moon is full as part of their First Amendment rights? How would you determine whether you must grant these requests?
4. What can a correctional employee do to reduce the potential for lawsuits contesting conditions of confinement?

Notes

1 Fox Butterfield, "Mistreatment of Prisoners Is Called Routine in U.S.," *New York Times,* May 8, 2004, p. A14.

2 Adam Liptak, "Ex-Inmate's Suit Offers View into Sexual Slavery in Prisons," *New York Times,* October 16, 2004, p. 1.

3 *Ruffin v. Commonwealth,* 62 Va. 290 (1871).

4 *Pennsylvania Department of Corrections et al. v. Yeskey,* 524 U.S. 206 (1998).

5 *Ford v. Wainwright,* 477 U.S. 399 (1986).

6 *Cooper v. Pate,* 378 U.S. 546 (1964).

7 Bureau of Justice Statistics, *Sourcebook of Criminal Justice Statistics, 2003* (Washington, DC: U.S. Government Printing Office), Table 5.65.2005.

8 *Johnson v. Avery,* 393 U.S. 413 (1969).

9 *Bounds v. Smith,* 430 U.S. 817 (1977).

10 *Brooks v. Florida,* 389 U.S. 413 (1967).

11 *Holt v. Sarver,* 442 F.2d 308 (8th Cir. 1971).

12 *Schenck v. United States,* 249 U.S. 47 (1919).

13 *Brown v. Wainwright,* 419 F.2d 1308 (5th Cir. 1969).

14 *Pepperling v. Crist,* 678 F.2d 787 (9th Cir. 1982). However, the U.S. Court of Appeals for the Seventh Circuit, in *Trapnell v. Riggsbuy,* 622 F.2d 290 (7th Cir. 1980), found absolute prohibition a "narrowly drawn and carefully limited response to a valid security problem."

15 *Sostre v. Otis,* 330 F.Supp. 941 (S.D.N.Y. 1971).

16 *Turner v. Safley,* 482 U.S. 78 (1987).

17 *Procunier v. Martinez,* 416 U.S. 396 (1974).

18 *Turner v. Safley,* 482 U.S. 78 (1987).

19 *Hudson v. Palmer,* 468 U.S. 517 (1984).

20 *Smith v. Fairman,* 678 F.2d 52 (7th Cir. 1982).

21 *Bell v. Wolfish,* 441 U.S. 520 (1979).

22 *United States v. Oakley,* 731 F.Supp. 1363 (S.D. Ind. 1990).

23 *Lee v. Downs,* 641 F.2d 1117 (4th Cir. 1981).

24 *Smith v. Fairman,* 678 F.2d 52 (7th Cir. 1982).

25 Bradley S. Chilton, *Prisons Under the Gavel: The Federal Court Takeover of Georgia Prisons* (Columbus: Ohio State University Press, 1991).

26 *Ruiz v. Estelle,* 503 F.Supp. 1265 (S.D. Tex. 1980).

27 Milton J. Valencia, "Judge Orders Mass. to Pay for Inmate's Sex-Change Surgery," *BostonGlobe.com,* www.bostonglobe.com/metro /2012/09/04/federal-judge-rules-state-must-provide-sex-reassignment -surgery-for-michelle-kosilek-who-was-convicted-murdering-his-wife -man/DktBaXITvlnbz1CKJZ56hJ/story.html, September 4, 2012.

28 Kelly Parker, "Pregnant Women Inmates: Evaluating Their Rights and Identifying Opportunities for Improvements in Their Treatment," *Journal of Law and Health* 19 (no. 2, 2004–2005): 259–95.

29 Evan Feinauer, Aaron Lee, and Jullia Park, *The Shackling of Incarcerated Pregnant Women: A Human Rights Violation Committed Regularly in the United States,* https://ihrclinic.uchicago.edu/sites /ihrclinic.uchicago.edu/files/uploads/Report%20-%20Shackling %20of%20Pregnant%20Prisoners%20in%20the%20US.pdf.

30 Heather Schultz, "An Anti-Shackling Wake-Up Call," www .americanprogress.org/issues/women/news/2014/05/22/90306 /an-anti-shackling-wake-up-call, May 22, 2014.

31 *Rhodes v. Chapman,* 452 U.S. 337 (1981).

32 *Wolff v. McDonnell,* 418 U.S. 539 (1974).

33 *Lee v. Washington,* 390 U.S. 333 (1968).

34 *Pargo v. Elliott,* 49 F.3d 1355 (1995).

35 *Wolff v. McDonnell,* 418 U.S. 539 (1974).

36 *Bell v. Wolfish,* 441 U.S. 520 (1979).

37 *Daniels v. Williams,* 474 U.S. 327 (1986).

38 *Wilson v. Seiter,* 111 S.Ct. 2321 (1991).

39 James B. Jacobs, "Judicial Impact on Prison Reform," in *Punishment and Social Control,* edited by Thomas G. Blomberg and Stanley Cohen (New York: Aldine DeGruyter, 1995), 63–76.

40 Jeffrey H. Maahs and Rolando V. del Carmen, "Curtailing Frivolous Section 1983 Inmate Litigation: Laws, Practices, and Proposals," *Federal Probation* 59 (December 1995): 53–61.

41 *Louisiana Ex Rel. Francis v. Resweber,* 329 U.S. 459 (1947).

42 *Roper v. Simmons,* 543 U.S. 551 (2005), 112 S.W. 3d 397, affirmed.

43 *Furman v. Georgia,* 408 U.S. 238 (1972).

44 *Gregg v. Georgia,* 428 U.S. 153 (1976).

45 "National Statistics on the Death Penalty and Race," Death Penalty Information Center, www.deathpenaltyinfo.org/race-death -row-inmates-executed-1976.

46 "The Black Population 2000," U.S. Census Bureau, www.census .gov/prod/2001pubs/c2kbr01-5.pdf.

47 *McCleskey v. Kemp,* 481 U.S. 279 (1987).

48 *Atkins v. Virginia,* 122 S.Ct. 2242 (2002).

49 *Ring v. Arizona,* 122 S.Ct. 2428 (2002).

50 *Roper v. Simmons,* 125 S.Ct. 1183 (2005).

51 *Strickland v. Washington,* 466 U.S. 668 (1984).

52 Ibid.

53 *New York Times,* March 2, 2000, p. A19.

54 *Witherspoon v. Illinois,* 392 U.S. 510 (1968).

55 *Uttecht v. Brown,* No. 06-413 (June 4, 2007).

56 Mark Costanzo, *Just Revenge* (New York: St. Martin's, 1997), 24–25.

57 *Kennedy v. Louisiana,* No. 07-343 (2008).

58 *Coker v. Georgia,* 453 U.S. 584 (1977).

59 *McCleskey v. Zant,* 111 S.Ct. 1454 (1991).

60 *Herrera v. Collins,* 506 U.S. 390 (1993).

61 Robert Barnes and Mark Berman, "Supreme Court Will Review Lethal Injection Drug Protocol Used in Executions," *Washington Post,* www.washingtonpost.com/politics/courts_law/supreme -court-will-review-lethal-injection-drug-protocol-used-in-executions /2015/01/23/10841c10-a347-11e4-9f89-561284a573f8_story.html, January 24, 2015.

62 Tracy L. Snell, *Capital Punishment, 2007—Statistical Tables* (Washington, DC: Bureau of Justice Statistics, 2008), www.ojp .usdoj.gov/bjs/pub/html/cp/2007/tables/cp07st08.htm.

63 See www.gallup.com/poll/1606/Death-Penalty.aspx, December 8, 2008.

12

Corrections for Juveniles

Adolpho Davis was 14 when he and a couple of fellow gang members killed two members of a rival gang during a drug heist.[1] Because he was sentenced to life without parole, he assumed that he would die of old age in prison. But 22 years into his sentence, he was given new hope when the U.S. Supreme Court ruled in its 2012 landmark case *Miller v. Alabama* that life-without-parole sentences for juveniles are unconstitutional if imposed without special consideration for the "hallmark features of youth—among them, immaturity, impetuosity, and the failure to appreciate risks and consequences." The Court said there must be "individualized sentencing" of juveniles convicted of serious crimes.[2]

After reading this chapter you should be able to . . .

1. Describe the nature and extent of youth crime today.

2. Analyze the history of the development of juvenile corrections in the United States.

3. Describe the new "evidence-based" movement in juvenile corrections and explain how it has affected juvenile justice.

4. List the ways that juvenile offenders are sanctioned.

5. Critically assess the future of juvenile corrections.

Alyssa Schukar/The New York Times/Redux

Adolfo Davis, who has spent the last 24 years in prison serving a mandatory sentence of life without parole for a crime he committed as a child, was granted a new sentencing hearing in Chicago, to comply with a Supreme Court decision about life-without-parole sentences for juveniles.

On April 13, 2015, Davis went back before Judge Angela Petrone, whose job it was to reconsider the original sentence. Prosecutors argued that Davis was, at 14, already a hardened criminal who deserved to be locked up forever. His defense attorney countered that Davis had been punished enough, having been locked up for more than half of his life. The two sides disagreed on whether he had become rehabilitated in the 24 years since the crime.

For his part, Davis just said, "I'm praying you find it in your heart to give me a second chance."[3]

(continued from previous page)

Davis is one of an estimated 2,100 people currently serving life sentences without parole, sentenced for crimes committed as juveniles.[4] The Supreme Court did not apply the *Miller* decision retroactively, but left that to the states. In the years that have followed, 10 states have decided that *Miller* was retroactive and started resentencing the people who were sentenced to life without parole when they were youths. Five states said *Miller* was not retroactive and left their convicts to serve out their sentences.

This kind of inconsistency regarding a principle of constitutional rights is a problem. So the Supreme Court has announced that it will decide once and for all whether all cases where people were sentenced as youths to life without parole should be sent back for resentencing. Reformers applaud this move by the Supreme Court because they believe that people serving life sentences imposed when they were children are often completely rehabilitated and deserve to be released from prison.[5]

But the new legal option is far from automatic. Davis found this out when, on May 4, 2015, three weeks after his resentencing hearing, the judge reimposed the sentence of life without parole. "This sentence is necessary to deter others. It is necessary to protect the public from harm. The defendant's acts showed an aggression and callous disregard for human life far beyond his tender age of 14," the judge said. Davis quietly wept, then returned to prison, bereft of hope.

In this chapter we explore the juvenile corrections system, constructed to handle the half-million juveniles whose conduct is serious enough for corrections to be involved. This is but a fraction of the 875,000 juveniles who were arrested in 2013[6] and the 600,000 who went to court—the vast majority of the "usual" cases involving juvenile misconduct and crime.[7]

Although separate from adult corrections, the juvenile system is linked to it at many points. What sets the juvenile corrections system apart are differences in philosophy, procedures, and programmatic emphasis. The philosophy of juvenile corrections places a higher premium on rehabilitation and prevention, as opposed to punishment, than does its adult counterpart. Less dominated by firm due process rules, the procedures of juvenile corrections support a degree of informality and discretionary decision making. This informality is in part intended to enable program administrators to develop innovative strategies that promise to keep juvenile offenders from returning to crime as adults. ■

THE PROBLEM OF YOUTH CRIME

It disturbs us to think of a child as "dangerous" or "sinister," but the daily news forces us to consider the unpleasant truth that some young people commit serious crimes. In the most recent year for which data are available, 614 youths under age 18 were arrested for homicide, 2,089 for forcible rape, and a troubling 25,016 for aggravated assault.[8] Some of these cases became local or national news stories. The incidents remind us that some juveniles are capable of deeply distressing behavior. Because these cases alarm and frighten us, the need for greater confidence in the juvenile justice system has become a major issue for correctional professionals and policy makers.

Even so, extremely serious juvenile crime incidents are rare. In a nation with 74 million people 18 years of age or younger, 875,000 arrests of juveniles took place in 2013 (the most recent year for juvenile court statistics), only 43,651 of which (about 5 percent) were for violent crimes. After rising between 1988 and 1994, the juvenile violent crime rate has dropped by more than 50 percent; it is now the lowest it has been since at least 1980. Property crime has decreased by more than half since the peak in 1991, with a 12 percent decline in the last year alone.[9] Yet when Americans are asked to identify the two or three most serious problems facing children, they often cite drugs and crime.

Most of us are particularly unsettled by juvenile crime for reasons beyond the numbers. Young people represent the future. We expect them to be busy growing up—learning how to become productive citizens and developing skills for a satisfying life. We do not expect them to be committing crimes that damage the quality of community life.

Because they are starting criminal behavior so young, we worry about the future—how long before a young person's criminal career fades? How much damage will be left in its wake? (See "Do the Right Thing.")

DO the Right Thing

Carlton Franklin makes a strange-looking defendant in a juvenile court. Described as "wrinkled" and "soft around the middle," Franklin is 52 years old, but when he was 15 years old, he committed a horrific crime: He cold-bloodedly bludgeoned, raped, and then stabbed to death Lena Triano, a 47-year-old legal secretary who lived alone in a nearby town. He got away with the crime for nearly 40 years, but he was caught when a cold-case investigator, Vinnie Byron, got a DNA match from evidence that remained from the original investigation.

In the intervening years, Franklin had not been a model citizen, having served 17 years in prison because of serious criminal activity at the age of 20. But for the 14 years since his release, he had worked a steady job and lived without an arrest, making a living as a truck driver.

Under the law applicable in 1976, his sentence must promote "wholesome mental and physical development."

Critical Thinking

1. What should the judge consider in imposing a disposition? (Remember, he is being handled as a juvenile under juvenile law, and not as an adult.)

2. How important are Franklin's previous criminal offenses, followed by the lengthy period of community adjustment? Does it matter that he is now, apparently, "rehabilitated"?

3. If you were the judge, what would you do? Why?

Source: Kate Zernike, "Man, 52, Is Convicted as a Juvenile in a 1976 Murder, Creating a Legal Tangle," *New York Times*, www.nytimes.com/2012/12/22/nyregion/a-52-year-old-man-is-convicted-in-juvenile-court-of-a-36-year-old-murder.html, December 21, 2012.

JUVENILE CORRECTIONS IN THE UNITED STATES

Table 12.1 outlines five periods of American juvenile justice. Each period was characterized by changes that reflected the social, intellectual, and political currents of the time. During the past 200 years, population shifts from rural to urban areas, immigration, developments in the social sciences, political reform movements, and the continuing problem of youth crime have all influenced the treatment of juveniles in the United States.

parens patriae
The court standing in and acting as the "parent" of the child.

The first juvenile court was established by a legislative act in Cook County (Chicago), Illinois, in 1899. Based on **parens patriae**, the new juvenile court took the role of guardian, the substitute parent of the child. Decisions about a juvenile's fate were linked less to guilt or innocence and more to the "best interests" of the child.

Table 12.1 Juvenile Justice Developments in the United States

Period	Major Developments	Causes and Influences	Juvenile Justice System
Puritan 1646–1824	Massachusetts Stubborn Child Law (1646)	• Puritan view of child as evil • Economically marginal agrarian society	Law provides • Symbolic standard of maturity • Support for family as economic unit
Refuge 1824–1899	Institutionalization of deviants; House of Refuge in New York established (1825) for delinquent and dependent children	• Enlightenment • Immigration and industrialization	Child seen as helpless, in need of state intervention
Juvenile Court 1899–1960	Establishment of separate legal system for juveniles; Illinois Juvenile Court Act (1899)	• Reformism and rehabilitative ideology • Increased immigration and urbanization, large-scale industrialization	Juvenile court institutionalized legal irresponsibility of child
Juvenile Rights 1960–1980	Increased "legalization" of juvenile law; *Gault* decision (1967); Juvenile Justice and Delinquency Prevention Act (1974) calls for deinstitutionalization of status offenders	• Criticism of juvenile justice system on humane grounds • Civil rights movement by disadvantaged groups	Movement to define and protect rights as well as to provide services to children
Crime Control 1980–2005	Concern for victims, punishment for serious offenders, transfer of serious offenders to adult court, protection of children from physical and sexual abuse	• More-conservative public attitudes and policies • Focus on serious crimes by repeat offenders	System more formal, restrictive, punitive; increased percentage of police referrals to court; incarcerated youths stay longer periods
Evidence-Based 2005–present	Emphasis on evaluating programs and policies and doing "what works"	Focus on programs and reducing system costs	Reduced use of confinement and focus on prevention

Sources: Adapted from Barry Krisberg, Ira M. Schwartz, Paul Litsky, and James Austin, "The Watershed of Juvenile Justice Reform," *Crime and Delinquency* 32 (January 1986): 5–38; U.S. Department of Justice, *A Preliminary National Assessment of Status Offenders and the Juvenile Justice System* (Washington, DC: U.S. Government Printing Office, 1980), 29.

The main tenets of the juvenile court can be summarized as informality, individualization, and intervention.

Informality was intended to move juvenile corrections away from the formality and due process requirements of the adult courtroom. Instead of rules of evidence and cross-examination, judges would run the sessions as conversations in which interested people such as parents, teachers, and social workers could comment on the case. Individualization was based on the idea that each child ought to be treated as a unique person with unique circumstances. Intervention was the method of the juvenile court. The final aim of all juvenile processing was "adjustment"—to help the child develop a law-abiding lifestyle. Thus, the court was not to punish children but to identify and solve the problems that led them astray and to provide treatment that would avert a life of crime.

To implement this approach, the juvenile court developed its own language, procedures, and rules. In place of standard adult processing practices, the juvenile system established a new version to achieve its new aims. Table 12.2 compares the terminology of the adult and juvenile systems.

There was widespread enthusiasm for the new juvenile court model. Following the Chicago example, every state revised its penal code and established a separate juvenile court within a few years. The age of jurisdiction often varied—some states took juveniles as old as 18 or 19, whereas others required anyone over age 16 to be handled as an adult. The courts were given jurisdiction over delinquent, neglected, and dependent children. A **delinquent** child is one who has committed an act that if committed by an adult would be criminal. A **neglected** child is one who is not receiving proper care because of some action or inaction of his or her parents. This includes not being sent to school, not receiving medical care, being abandoned, or not receiving some other care necessary for the child's well-being. A **dependent** child either has no parent or guardian or, because of the physical or mental disability of a parent or guardian, is not receiving proper care.

Even though there were high hopes for the juvenile court, the lack of due process protections for juveniles soon came under significant criticism. It was thought that all

delinquent
A child who has committed an act that if committed by an adult would be criminal.

neglected
A child who is not receiving proper care because of some action or inaction of his or her parents.

dependent
A child who has no parent or guardian or whose parents are unable to give proper care.

Passage of the Juvenile Court Act by Illinois in 1899 established the first separate court for delinquent, dependent, and neglected children. Judge Julian W. Mack presided over Chicago's juvenile court, which became a model for the nation.

© CORBIS

Table 12.2 Comparison of Terminology in the Adult and Juvenile Justice Systems

Function	Adult System	Juvenile System
Taken into custody	Arrested	Detained (police contact)
Legal basis for holding	Charged	Referred to court
Formal charges	Indicted	Held on petition
Person charged	Defendant	Respondent
Determination of guilt	Trial	Hearing
Outcome of court case	Verdict	Finding
Term for "guilty"	Convicted	Adjudicated (as responsible)
Sanction	Sentence	Disposition
Custodial sentence	Incarcerated	Placed or committed
Incarceration facility	Prison	Training school
Release supervision	Parole	Aftercare

too often the informality of the juvenile court led to outcomes that were not in the child's best interest. Soon enough, the Supreme Court began to require the extension of important constitutional rights to youths charged with crimes, reducing the discretion so important to the juvenile court movement (see **Table 12.3**).

Policy makers around the country are today rethinking the juvenile court in light of a new policy ethic: evidence. Both legislators and juvenile justice administrators are asking themselves, "What do we know about reducing juvenile crime, and how can we design the juvenile justice system to take better advantage of that knowledge?"

At age 17, Meagan Grunwald, was with her boyfriend when he fatally shot a Utah deputy and fled in a pickup truck. Meagan drove the getaway car to try to escape. Because she is a minor, she is ineligible for the death penalty.

AP Images/The Salt Lake Tribune/Al Hartmann, Pool

Table 12.3 Major Decisions by the U.S. Supreme Court Regarding the Rights of Juveniles

Since the mid-1960s, the Supreme Court has gradually expanded the rights of juveniles but has continued to recognize that the logic of a separate system for juvenile offenders justifies differences from some adult rights.

Case	Significance for Juvenile Offenders
Kent v. United States (1966)	"Essentials of due process" are required by juvenile offenders.
In Re Gault (1967)	The "essentials" of due process required by *Kent*—notice, hearing, counsel, cross-examination—are specified.
In Re Winship (1970)	A standard of "beyond a doubt" is required for delinquency matters.
McKeiver v. Pennsylvania (1971)	Jury trials are not required for juvenile court hearings.
Breed v. Jones (1975)	Waiver to adult court following adjudication in juvenile court violates the constitutional guarantee against double jeopardy.
Smith v. Daily Mail Publishing Co. (1979)	The press may report certain aspects of juvenile court cases and matters.
Eddings v. Oklahoma (1982)	The age of a defendant must be considered as a mitigating factor in capital crimes.
Schall v. Martin (1984)	Preventive pretrial definition is allowed for juvenile defendants who are found "dangerous."
Stanford v. Kentucky (1989)	Minimum age for capital punishment is 16.
Roper v. Simmons (2005)	To impose the death penalty on someone for a crime committed before the age of 18 violates the Eighth Amendment prohibition of "cruel and unusual punishments."
Graham v. Florida (2010)	Extends *Roper v. Simmons* to prohibit life-without-parole sentences for juveniles who do not commit homicide.
Miller v. Alabama (2012)	The Eighth Amendment forbids a sentencing scheme that mandates life in prison without possibility of parole for juvenile homicide offenders.

This conclusion has led to the emergence of a new generation of community-based strategies to reduce juvenile crime before the justice system is invoked (see "Focus on Correctional Practice: Evidence in Juvenile Justice Programs"). Rather than a heightened policy of crime control that emphasizes surveillance, arrest, and incarceration, this new era tends to look to a host of studies that have provided added clarity to our understanding of what works and what does not. They suggest three principles:

1. **Limited use of detention and incarceration.** It has become clear that putting youths in correctional facilities often exacerbates the problems that lead to criminality while too infrequently preparing the youths for adjustment to society after release. Instead, current policy emphasizes diverting as many youths as possible from juvenile justice, especially confinement, instead using a variety of community-based options, including civil citations instead of arrests.[10] As confirmation of this new thinking, the number of juveniles incarcerated in the United States fell by over 40 percent between 1995 and 2010.[11] In five states (Connecticut, Tennessee, Louisiana, Minnesota, and Arizona), juvenile incarceration rates have been cut by more than half.[12] According to the FBI, arrest rates for juveniles are dropping significantly (see **Table 12.4**).

focus on correctional practice

Evidence in Juvenile Justice Programs

Recent reports have tried to summarize what we know about juvenile justice, with a special emphasis on juvenile correctional programs. They base much of what we know on **meta-analyses** of more than 600 studies, published and unpublished. Systematic reviews support certain strategies as most likely to be effective:

1. *Interventions with a "therapeutic" philosophy.* Programs that attempt to change youthful offenders by working on their behavioral problems and thinking patterns reduce recidivism rates by as much as 25 percent. Programs that attempt to build job and classroom skills reduce recidivism rates by 10 percent or more. In contrast, programs that try to change behavior through imposing discipline or emphasizing punitive deterrence actually *increase* recidivism rates by nearly 10 percent.

2. *Working with high-risk youths.* Programs that target services to high-risk youths are more likely to be effective than programs designed to work with moderate- or low-risk youths, and this is especially true when youths have a history of violence.

Programs that provide intensive services for first-time delinquents often result in *higher* failure rates than if those services had not been provided.

3. *Program quality.* Programs that provide a broader array of services, provide greater intensity of services, and are implemented more completely have a greater chance of being effective. Programs that are badly managed or have weak administrators are more likely not to work.

The implication of this work is that programs for juveniles can be purposefully designed to be effective. They can also be designed in such ways as to make failure much more likely. In order to help policy makers develop more-effective programs, sociologist Mark Lipsey has designed a program-assessment system that can be used to build programs that reflect the evidence about what we know is effective.

Sources: Mark W. Lipsey, James C. Howell, Marion R. Kelly, Gabrielle Chapman, and Darin Carver, *Improving the Effectiveness of Juvenile Justice Programs: A New Perspective on Evidence-Based Practice* (Washington, DC: Center for Juvenile Justice Reform, 2010); Mark W. Lipsey, "The Primary Factors That Characterize Effective Interventions with Juvenile Offenders: A Meta-Analytic Overview," *Victims and Offenders* 4 (2009): 124–47.

meta-analysis
The statistical analysis of a large number of studies to find a pattern of effects.

Table 12.4 Juvenile Arrests, 2004–2013

Arrests of juveniles have declined by about a third in the last three years.

Year	Number of Arrests (in Thousands)
2004	1,579
2005	1,528
2006	1,626
2007	1,650
2008	1,623
2009	1,515
2010	1,288
2011	1,129
2012	1,020
2013	875

Source: Federal Bureau of Investigation, *Crime in the United States, 2004–2013*, Table 38, www.fbi.gov /about-us/cjis/ucr/ucr-publications.

2. **A focus on prevention in the community.** Juvenile justice interventions with youths convicted of serious crimes are often seen as coming too late. If the crimes could have been prevented, everyone would benefit—the victim, the youth, and the society at large. Several studies have shown that earlier interventions into **at-risk youths'** lives lead to better outcomes in terms of juvenile delinquency and save money. Indeed, studies have shown that when the juvenile court gets involved in a youth's life, the chances of that youth staying out of the adult system diminish.[13] As a result, the newest programs for juveniles try to focus on at-risk youths early in their lives and provide noncorrectional support and services devoted to diverting them from serious crime in later years.

3. **Designing programs based on proven strategies.** Today, policy makers have access to hundreds of studies of juvenile justice programs and their outcomes. It is possible to rethink current juvenile justice analysis in light of a growing foundation of evidence about what works and what does not. Juvenile justice activists have partnered with leading reformers in legislatures and in the justice system to strip juvenile justice of old programs that have not worked and replace them with empirically proven strategies.

at-risk youths
Young people who are of an earlier age than most serious delinquents—as young as five or six—but who have characteristics showing that they are more likely than others at their age to end up as juvenile delinquents in their teen years.

SANCTIONING JUVENILE OFFENDERS

Originally, separating juvenile justice from adult justice was intended to enable justice workers to give the highest priority to preventing crime by rehabilitating delinquents. Juvenile correctional agencies provide a range of services from diversion to probation, detention, and aftercare. Although rehabilitation does indeed figure prominently in their practices, that ethic is quite fragile in reality.

Overview of the Juvenile Justice System

Juvenile corrections suffers from the same type of fragmentation as its adult counterpart does, with agencies sometimes operated under the courts, sometimes under the executive branch; sometimes housed with the institutional function, sometimes separated from it; sometimes run by counties, sometimes run by the state. Such fragmentation makes generalizing about juvenile corrections policies difficult. Nearly any policy arrangement that a person can imagine exists somewhere, and what is true of one jurisdiction may not be true of the next.

In 2013 just over 875,000 juveniles (persons under age 18) were arrested, representing 12 percent of all arrests made by the police.[14] As **Figure 12.1** shows, juveniles were involved in a much smaller proportion of violent crime arrests than property crime arrests.

Less than a third of juvenile arrests were for murder, sexual assault, aggravated assault, robbery, burglary, larceny-theft, arson, and motor vehicle theft. Of juvenile arrestees, 74 percent were male, and 27 percent were age 15 or younger. People of color made up 16 percent of the juvenile population but were arrested out of proportion to their numbers. Especially troubling is the fact that, of those arrested for violent offenses, more than half were African American.[15]

A juvenile arrest clears proportionately fewer crimes than does an adult arrest. This is true because juveniles tend to commit crimes in groups and are more likely to be arrested for their crimes, thus clearing fewer crimes with more arrests.[16]

The arrest numbers are troubling, as 25,000 juveniles were arrested for aggravated assault, a serious, violent personal crime. Further, arrest rates are increasing faster for girls than for boys. Yet we must take these numbers in their proper context. In all, about one-tenth of one percent of all Americans age 10–17 were arrested for a violent offense in 2013. Violent crime among young people is alarming, but it is not common. And the juvenile portion of all crime is dropping, as well.[17] Since 2000, juvenile

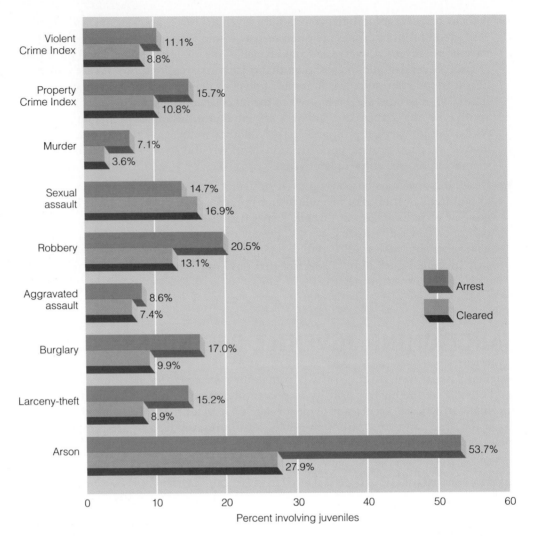

FIGURE 12.1

Of All Arrests, Percentage That Are of Juveniles and Percentage of Crimes* Cleared by Arrests of Juveniles

Juveniles were involved in a much smaller proportion of violent crime arrests than property arrests.

*A crime that is reported to the police and is considered "solved" by virtue of at least one arrest. One arrest can clear many crimes if the offender has committed many; alternatively, if a group commits a crime, which is common for juveniles, only one crime is cleared through several arrests.

Source: Federal Bureau of Investigation, *Crime in the United States, 2013,* Tables 28 and 38.

arrests for violence have declined 20 percent, while adult arrests have increased by 25 percent.[18]

In fact, serious juvenile offenders (those who commit felonies) are not all violent, nor are they chronic. Violent offenders commit felonies that threaten physical harm. Chronic offenders offend in repetitive patterns. **Figure 12.2** shows the overlap of these types of juvenile offenders—some juveniles engage in all three patterns, but most are one type of offender only. Violent offenders commit the fewest crimes.

These differences mean that the offense alone is not enough to predict whether or not the offender is someone whom society should fear. Among juveniles, the rate of false positives (incorrect predictions of dangerousness) is quite high. Studies show that instead of relying on the offense alone to identify the highest-risk juvenile offenders, we

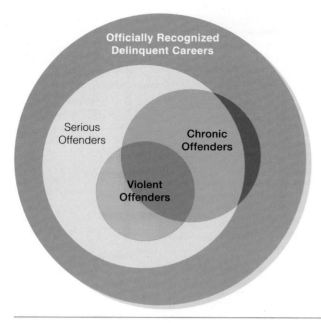

FIGURE 12.2

The Overlap of Violent, Serious, and Chronic Juvenile Offenders

Juvenile offenders who most concern us have important differences in their patterns of offense.

Source: Office of Juvenile Justice and Delinquency Prevention, *Juvenile Offenders and Victims: 1997 Update on Violence* (Washington, DC: U.S. Government Printing Office, 1997), 25.

should be concerned about other factors in each juvenile's history. Among them are the following:

- Persistent behavioral problems during the elementary school years.
- Onset of delinquency, aggression, or drug use between the ages of 6 and 11.
- Antisocial parents.
- Antisocial peers, poor school performance, impulsivity, and weak social ties between the ages of 12 and 14.
- Membership in delinquent gangs (see "Myths in Corrections).
- Drug dealing.

Disposition of Juvenile Offenders

MYTHS in Corrections

Juvenile Gangs

THE MYTH: Most gang members are committed to violence because they like their violent lifestyle and are not scared of being hurt.

THE REALITY: Many gang members use violence out of fear—that they will not be protected by their peers or respected by them if they are not quick to use guns. But this lifestyle is very stressful, and many gang members are eager for the violence to stop.

Source: David Kennedy, *Don't Shoot! One Man, A Street Fellowship, and the End of Violence in Inner-City America* (New York: Bloomsbury, 2012).

About 1.5 million juvenile offenders were referred to juvenile court in 2009, the most recent year for which we have statistics.[19] The first decision made in a juvenile court is whether or not to file a petition of juvenile jurisdiction. If the petition is granted, there is a hearing on the merits of the charges, with the intention of making the juvenile a ward of the court if the charges are sustained. Cases that are not petitioned involve informal dispositions in which the juvenile consents to whichever outcome is determined by the court.

As **Figure 12.3** shows, nearly half of the referrals to juvenile court do not result in a petition. Of these cases, 41 percent have their charges dismissed, and another 22 percent are assigned to an informal probation. On rare occasions, nonpetitioned juveniles receive placements, typically in mental health facilities; more commonly, some alternative sanction results. The petition decision is largely invisible, but it has major implications for the juvenile justice system. Recent studies have shown that black youths who are arrested by the police are one-fourth more likely to be petitioned to the juvenile court than are white youths.[20]

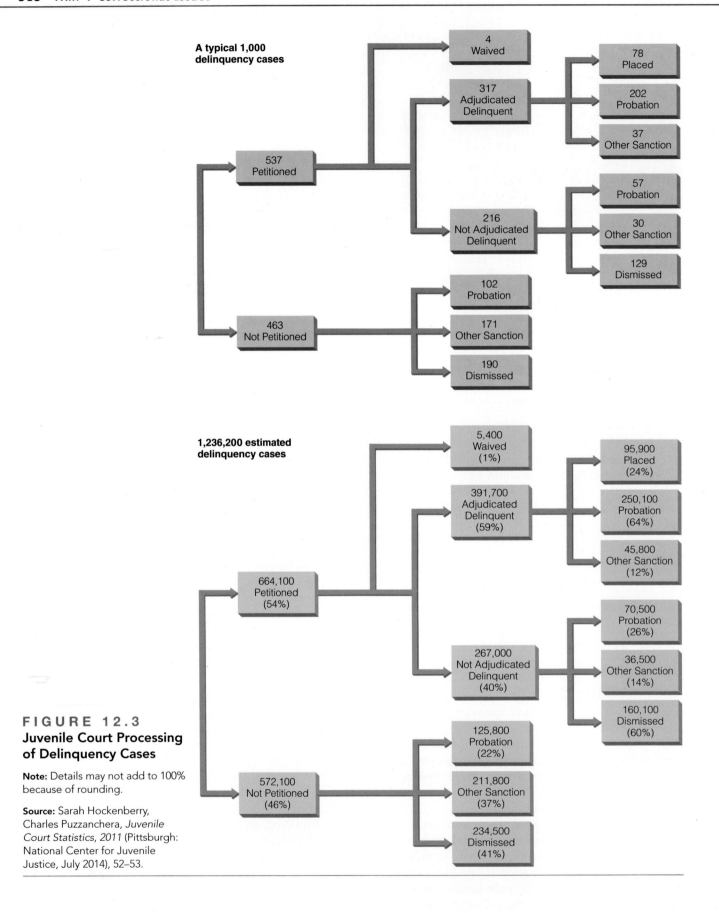

A typical 1,000 delinquency cases

537 Petitioned

4 Waived

317 Adjudicated Delinquent
- 78 Placed
- 202 Probation
- 37 Other Sanction

216 Not Adjudicated Delinquent
- 57 Probation
- 30 Other Sanction
- 129 Dismissed

463 Not Petitioned
- 102 Probation
- 171 Other Sanction
- 190 Dismissed

1,236,200 estimated delinquency cases

664,100 Petitioned (54%)

5,400 Waived (1%)

391,700 Adjudicated Delinquent (59%)
- 95,900 Placed (24%)
- 250,100 Probation (64%)
- 45,800 Other Sanction (12%)

267,000 Not Adjudicated Delinquent (40%)
- 70,500 Probation (26%)
- 36,500 Other Sanction (14%)
- 160,100 Dismissed (60%)

572,100 Not Petitioned (46%)
- 125,800 Probation (22%)
- 211,800 Other Sanction (37%)
- 234,500 Dismissed (41%)

FIGURE 12.3
Juvenile Court Processing of Delinquency Cases

Note: Details may not add to 100% because of rounding.

Source: Sarah Hockenberry, Charles Puzzanchera, *Juvenile Court Statistics, 2011* (Pittsburgh: National Center for Juvenile Justice, July 2014), 52–53.

When a petition is filed, the court must consider whether it will take jurisdiction in the case. In about 1 percent of cases, jurisdiction is waived to adult court. In the usual case the juvenile must decide whether or not to contest the charges—if so, an adjudication hearing follows, in which the accuracy of the charges is considered. Almost half of the time, the charges are sufficiently minor, the facts are in so little dispute, or the likely disposition is sufficiently acceptable that the juvenile waives this hearing, and the court proceeds directly to disposition of the charges. Without an adjudication hearing, charges are usually dismissed. It is also common for the juvenile to accept a probation term or some other moderate penalty.

The juvenile usually contests the charges in the petition if they are serious or the disposition is potentially severe. However, this strategy succeeds in getting the charges dismissed only 5 percent of the time. Further, even though the usual disposition is a term of probation, almost one-third of adjudicated offenders get placed in a reform school, training school, or some other institution for juveniles.

This review of the juvenile justice process shows some reasons why the process has faced criticism in recent years. Among adult felons, for example, 77 percent of those convicted of violent crimes, as well as 67 percent of those convicted of property offenses, receive sentences involving terms of confinement.[21] This compares with confinement for only 26 percent of juveniles adjudicated for offenses against persons, and 24 percent for property offenses.[22]

WAIVER Those who are uneasy with the juvenile justice system often favor an increased use of waiver to adult court. Waiver (also referred to as "transfer to adult court") is an option available when the court believes that the circumstances of the case, such as the seriousness of the charges or the poor prospects of rehabilitation, call for the young person to be handled under adult court procedures and laws (see "Myths in Corrections"). Waiver has long engendered controversy. In the late 1980s a surge in state legislation to broaden the waiver statutes increased the number of crime categories that are automatically waived to adult court—especially for serious crimes such as murder and sexual assault (see **Figure 12.4**).

The public debate about waiver has been part of a significant drop in its use. The overall proportion of waived delinquency cases was just over 4 percent in the early 1990s but had dropped to less than 2 percent by 2010. Today, the number of cases granted waiver is about what it was in the mid-1980s, before the states engaged in waiver age and crime reform.[23]

Some question how waiver decisions are made, because more than half of the juveniles who are transferred to adult court are drug, property, or public order offenders, not violent offenders. Waiver opponents question the effectiveness of such results. Some experts have observed that juveniles who are waived may end up serving less actual time in confinement than those not waived on the same type of offense. One major study of juvenile waiver in New York and New Jersey concluded that the use of waiver there did not accomplish the goals of the waiver system—it did not materially increase the severity of the penalty that juveniles received and often resulted in illogical treatment of the young offenders.[24] Studies have suggested that many juveniles are waived for low-level offenses[25] and that dealing with juveniles in adult court leads to higher recidivism rates, suggesting that adult punishments may actually exacerbate crimes

MYTHS in Corrections

The Age of Delinquency

THE MYTH: Young people who are over the age of 18 should be handled in adult court because adult court will better prevent criminality.

THE REALITY: Young offenders between 18 and 24 who are processed by adult courts are more likely to recidivate than similar youths who end up avoiding adult court. Most people who engage in delinquency stop their criminality in their twenties. But when youths under the age of 24 are handled in adult court, they do not do as well as those who are diverted from the court system. This suggests that interventions that focus on services rather than punishment for this age group may be called for.

Source: David P. Farrington, Rolf Loeber, and James C. Howell, "Young Adult Offenders: The Need for More Effective Legislative Options and Justice Processing," *Criminology & Public Policy* 11 (no. 4, 2012): 729–50.

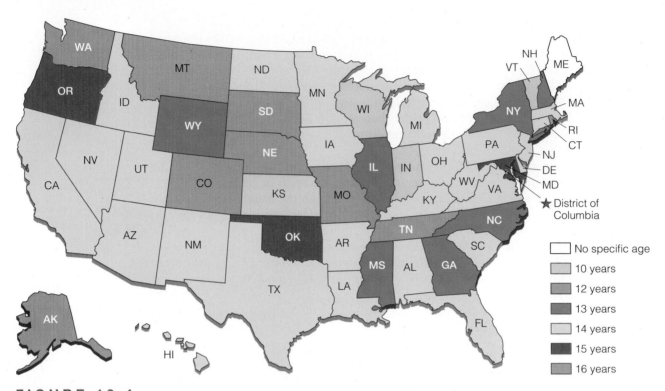

FIGURE 12.4
The Youngest Ages at Which Juveniles May Be Transferred to Adult Criminal Court

Source: Melissa Sickmund and Charles Puzzanchera, *Juvenile Offenders and Victims*, 2014 (Pittsburgh, PA: National Center for Juvenile Justice) December 2014, p. 101.

rather than deter them.[26] Finally, African Americans are vastly overrepresented among those cases waived to criminal court.[27] Concerns about the fairness of waiver laws and practices have grown, and in recent years at least 21 states have made changes that restrict the practice of juvenile waiver.[28]

Because the number of juveniles waived to adult court is so small, the number of juveniles serving time in adult facilities is also small. Recent data suggest that less than 2 percent of the adult prison population is under the age of 20[29] and that around 6,000 juveniles were held in local jails (two-thirds serving sentences from adult courts)—less than 1 percent of the jail population.[30] The young offender in adult facilities is a management problem because of special needs, not because of large numbers.

DIVERSION The conceptual opposite of waiver is diversion. Although waiver attempts to avoid the lenient treatment of the juvenile justice system, diversion seeks to avoid the burdensome consequences of formal processing. This informal adjustment to a case can occur at any stage of the juvenile justice process, but it is most often chosen prior to filing formal charges in a petition to the court.

Diversion can take two forms. The most direct form is simply to stop processing the case, in the expectation that the main objectives of the justice process have been achieved—the juvenile has realized the wrongness of the conduct and has shown a convincing willingness to refrain from it in the future. Florida has had a great deal of success just handing out "citations," which officially notify the youth of misconduct but do not require a court hearing.[31] This form of diversion is seldom final—if the young person returns to court on a new referral, the old charges may be considered again with the new one.

In the second form, juveniles are diverted to specific programs. This option may be selected when the court determines that the young person's delinquency is a result of certain problems in the child's life that may best be addressed by a program designed to help the juvenile. These diversion programs often deal with developmental issues such

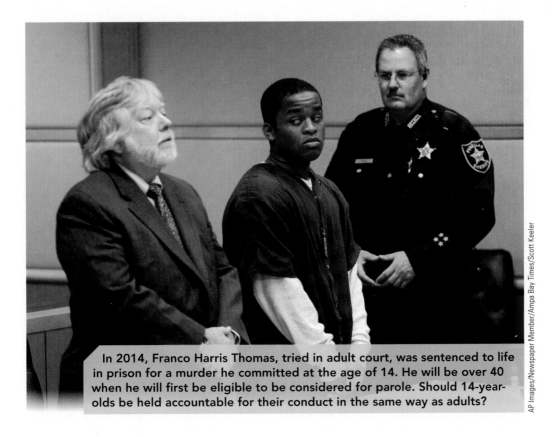

In 2014, Franco Harris Thomas, tried in adult court, was sentenced to life in prison for a murder he committed at the age of 14. He will be over 40 when he will first be eligible to be considered for parole. Should 14-year-olds be held accountable for their conduct in the same way as adults?

as the child's social skills or response to frustration in school performance. Diversion to mental health treatment for emotionally disturbed youths is also commonly preferred to formal processing.

The logic of diversion is based on the developmental pattern of delinquency. It is thought that most juveniles drift into delinquent behavior gradually, as a part of growing up. As their misconduct becomes more serious, they "signal" a need for help to get off the pathway to delinquency. The diversion strategy tries to provide that help as early as possible. For example, misbehaviors such as stubbornness, resistance to authority, and interpersonal aggressiveness, when exhibited in preadolescence, indicate a risk of later delinquency. That is why diversion programs that help disruptive children learn to cope and those that retain children in school are considered important aspects of delinquency prevention that do not require formal juvenile processing. Whatever the logic and wisdom of diversion, it used to be the most frequent strategy for addressing complaints against juveniles. However, its popularity has diminished over the years, and pre-court diversion is now used in only one-fifth of the cases brought to the attention of the police.[32]

CORRECTIONAL PROGRAMS FOR JUVENILE OFFENDERS The impact of juvenile treatment programs differs from programs for adults in two ways. First, juvenile programs show somewhat greater success than do adult programs. Second, the benefits of juvenile correctional programming considerably surpass those of their adult counterparts.

The research on the effectiveness of juvenile correctional programs identifies a handful of particularly promising strategies. Most of these programs are early intervention programs, designed to identify children at high risk of delinquency and provide a concentration of services to help them change their destinies. For youngsters age 11–18, for example, limited basic social skills and poor school performance are two important predictors of delinquency. Programs that increase social interpersonal competence—usually through cognitively oriented skill-development strategies—and that decrease school failure tend to reduce delinquency. For girls, programs that improve family discipline and problem solving also prevent delinquency. In short, evidence increasingly suggests that the systematic support of all aspects of family life for families in which at-risk youths are being raised reduces delinquency and antisocial behavior over the long run and saves money as well, and the earlier such programs are used in the child's life, the better.[33]

Although evidence for the value of early intervention for at-risk youths has been strong for quite a few years, political support has been slower to develop. Until recently, a public that has been willing to invest billions in bricks and mortar for more prison cells tended to see intervention programs as "soft" social welfare. Today, that seems to be changing. In many jurisdictions around the country, new political energy has been developing for expanded intervention programs, which may be charting a new future for juvenile justice.

DETENTION   Approximately 21 percent of juvenile arrestees are detained—256,800 cases in 2011.[34] Most juvenile detention is brief—the median stay is just over two weeks—until an initial appearance before a juvenile court judge (or judicial referee, who represents the court in detention hearings).[35] After a petition decision is made, most juveniles are released to their families. But about one out of five, found to endanger others or be at risk of flight, is kept in detention for days or weeks until an adjudication hearing can be scheduled.

Federal law requires that juveniles housed in adult jails be segregated from adult prisoners and be taken before a magistrate for an initial appearance within 24 hours of arrival in the facility. As minors under special protection of the court, these juveniles also have legal rights to education and basic services, yet most juveniles receive little special programming.

Such programming clearly should be a priority. Many juveniles in detention have special needs that make treatment appropriate. Juvenile delinquents disproportionately suffer from learning disabilities that make them lag in school performance, so time in detention only makes matters worse after release. Still other juveniles are members of gangs, which places them at risk of assault by other members detained in the same facilities. Studies show that detention experiences significantly worsen later subsequent behavior and increase the chance of continued delinquency.[36] Moreover, gang members seem to benefit less from juvenile treatment programs.[37] In general, detention centers for juveniles are places where great strides could be made in preventing delinquency by dealing with youths in crisis, but far too little is being done.

ADJUDICATION   When the juvenile court receives a case, the facts of the case are heard, and the court determines if the facts justify the determination that the youth did commit the alleged offense and therefore is "delinquent." Nationally, in 2011, 391,700 cases brought to the court were adjudicated delinquent.[38] After an adjudication of delinquency, the court imposes a **disposition**, called a **placement**. The typical placements available to the court are probation, intermediate sanctions, community programs, and out-of-home placement: confinement.

JUVENILE PROBATION   The most common disposition after a youth is adjudicated delinquent is placement on probation. Fully 64 percent of the time, the youth is placed on probation and released to the custody of a parent or guardian—250,100 cases in 2011.[39] Although probation has been the most common disposition for many years, the number of probation placements nationally has declined by 35 percent since a peak in 1997, corresponding to a similar drop in the number of cases found delinquent.[40] Often, the judge orders the delinquent to undergo some form of education or counseling. The delinquent may also have to pay a fine or make restitution while on probation.

The differences between adult probation and juvenile probation are subtle and stem from the differences between adult and juvenile offenders, described earlier. Juvenile probation officers often try to develop personal relationships with their clients, a move discouraged for adult probation officers. To achieve this bond, juvenile probation officers often engage in recreation with their clients or accompany them to social activities. Through this bond, officers seek the youngster's trust, which they hope will form the basis for long-lasting behavioral change. Sometimes officers will mix the child on probation with other young people who are not under court supervision to further

disposition
The judicial decision of how to handle a case when there has been a finding of delinquency, analogous to the sentence for an adult convicted of a crime.

placement
The removal of a youth from parental authority and the assignment of that authority to another agency, such as probation or a youth facility.

careers in Corrections

JUVENILE PROBATION OFFICER

Nature of the Work

Juvenile probation officers are responsible for the supervision and guidance of youths under age 18 who have been referred to them by the court, police, or social service agencies. Through the development of close ties with offenders' families, school authorities, and health agencies, probation officers help juvenile offenders meet their educational and treatment needs. These officers also monitor their behavior to ensure that court-ordered requirements are met. Caseload size varies by agency, by the needs of the offenders, and by the risks that they pose. Caseloads for juveniles tend to be lower than those for adult probationers. Officers may be on call 24 hours per day to supervise and assist offenders.

Required Qualifications

Background qualifications for juvenile probation officers vary by state, but a bachelor's degree in social work, criminal justice, or a related field from a four-year college or university is usually required. Some agencies require previous experience with youths or graduate work. Candidates must be 21 years of age and have no felony convictions. Most juvenile probation officers receive both formal and on-the-job training.

Earnings and Job Outlook

The number of probation officers for juveniles is expected to grow about as fast as other occupations during the next decade. Probation officers handling a juvenile caseload report a high level of personal satisfaction in their work. Juvenile probation officers earn just over $48,000 per year.

More Information

Visit the website of the American Probation and Parole Association. Career information can also be obtained from your state, juvenile court, or probation office.

Source: Bureau of Labor Statistics, www.bls.gov/ooh/community-and-social -service/probation-officers-and-correctional-treatment-specialists.htm.

his or her reintegration into more socially acceptable peer relationships. Often, adult mentors are called in to give children effective role models; mentoring programs reduce antisocial activities and school misbehavior by as much as one-third.

In carrying out supervision, the probation officer must work closely with community social service agencies that are involved with the juvenile and the family. Probation officers spend time in the schools, talk to teachers and guidance counselors, and learn about programs for troubled youths, such as recreational programs and youth counseling programs. Probation officers also establish close contact with family service agencies, welfare providers, and programs that support young mothers and provide substitutes for missing fathers. In some respects the probation officer serves as a linchpin for the array of community services that might help a young person stay out of trouble. "Careers in Corrections" offers a closer view of the work of a juvenile probation officer.

Although the ideals of rehabilitation and reintegration matter in all community supervision, they receive special emphasis among juvenile probation workers. However, it is important to recognize that juvenile probation is changing. A sense of unease about how juvenile probation handles serious offending among youths has led to a new interest in the techniques and practices of adult supervision: surveillance and control.

WORKING IN THE SCHOOLS Most juveniles spend a significant portion of their day in school; up to age 16, they are required by law to be in school. Recent studies have criticized schools for "zero-tolerance" approaches to classroom discipline.[41] Rapid expulsion of students who misbehave (or get involved in the juvenile court) leads many of these youths to drop out of school, a precursor of a life of crime. The propensity of school to reject youths who are struggling with behavioral problems has been called the **school-to-prison pipeline** because so many of these youths who fail in school end up in prison. Juvenile justice agencies—probation in particular—typically develop school-based programs to increase overall effectiveness with youths under supervision of the juvenile court.

School-based programs try to address this problem. They typically have three objectives: keep potential truants in school, reduce school violence, and improve the academic performance of at-risk youths.

school-to-prison pipeline
The fact that many youths who fail in school end up in prison.

Effective programs have been developed for each of these objectives. Successful school-safety programs focus on reducing bullying behavior and eliminating weapons and drugs on school grounds.[42] School dropout programs create networks of services within the community; this concentration of efforts seeks to increase an at-risk youth's academic self-confidence and personal commitment to staying in school, while reducing problem behaviors.[43] With so many juveniles processed by the juvenile justice system later returning to public schools, there is a need to find effective programs for these identified, at-risk youths.

INTERMEDIATE SANCTIONS FOR JUVENILES

The complaint that few sanctioning options exist between traditional probation and custodial dispositions is perhaps even more true in juvenile justice than in criminal justice. Only about 15 percent of delinquents receive an intermediate sanction. One reason for slowness in developing juvenile intermediate sanctions is that traditional juvenile corrections already resembles intermediate sanctions. Adult probation involves intensive supervision as an intermediate sanction, but adult intensive supervision probation (ISP) caseloads are often about the same size as many traditional juvenile caseloads—in the twenties or thirties. The adult system develops electronic monitored home detention; the juvenile system routinely uses curfews that restrict youths to home except during school hours. Community service and restitution have been standard juvenile court dispositions for many years.

Some juvenile probation agencies have begun to develop supervision approaches that are far more intensive than adult ISPs. A juvenile ISP officer may carry 15 cases or fewer and may well see each client almost every day—more than once a day if necessary. Police–probation partnerships intensify juvenile intensive supervision even further, because the police add surveillance to the probation services. Juvenile corrections systems have also developed work-based community service, restitution centers where young people work to pay victims back, and after-school assignments that minimize free time. Under intermediate sanctioning approaches, juveniles may be required to complete programs to increase their awareness of the impact of crimes on victims, and they may be sent to summer camps that require community service in the form of cleaning parks and other public places.

One of the most widespread new intermediate sanctions for juvenile offenders is the boot camp, described in Chapter 4. As noted there, the results have not been promising, with most studies showing that boot camp graduates do no better than do youths placed in other programs and that sometimes they do worse. This has led to the development of specialized aftercare caseloads of boot camp graduates to try to reduce their failure rate.

In Lucas County, Ohio, the juvenile court has regular hearings bringing together the Department of Youth Services, the courts, schools, social workers, probation officers, and mental health providers to work to safely divert juveniles from detention. The money they save creates more community-based treatment alternatives and allows youths to live at home and go to school.

Melanie Stetson Freeman/Christian Science Monitor/Getty Images

JUVENILE COMMUNITY CORRECTIONS   Despite the lukewarm evaluations of juvenile community corrections, interest has continued in this approach, for two main reasons. First, most people realize that removing a young person from the community is an extreme solution, reserved for extreme cases. Disrupting community and family relationships can interfere with long-term prospects for successful adjustment by damaging these already fragile supports. Second, and just as compelling, for most youths the institutional stay will be short—six months to a year in custody is common. Eventually, the youth returns to the community, and the real work of successfully adjusting to community life occurs there. Advocates of community corrections ask, "Why wait?"

Community corrections offers additional advantages for juveniles. The cost of custody in a juvenile training school is usually at least double that for an adult in prison, which means there is more money to work with in creating incentives to keep offenders out of trouble and in designing and implementing effective alternatives in the community. Moreover, public opinion toward youthful offenders is not as harsh as that toward adult offenders, so it is easier to obtain public support for juvenile community corrections.[44] Finally, because youth incarceration numbers are smaller than the adult numbers, it is easier to show success in saving money by diverting offenders to local programs.

A program in Ohio, gaining national acclaim, seeks to return funds to communities that retain juvenile offenders rather than sending them to state-run schools. RECLAIM Ohio—Reasoned and Equitable Community and Local Alternatives to Incarceration of Minors—provides a significant payback to county leaders who can show that juveniles who might have been sent to training schools paid for by state taxes are instead being kept in local, innovative programs designed especially for local needs. The program has proved popular because it appeals to conservative ideals of cost-effective public policy and local control, while appealing to liberal beliefs in rehabilitation of juvenile offenders.[45]

JUVENILE INCARCERATION   Of those juveniles adjudicated delinquent, 24 percent are placed in public and private facilities—in 2011, 97,900 youths.[46] The national incarceration rate (including detention) per 100,000 juveniles age 10–18 is 224.[47] Nationally, 69 percent of incarcerated juveniles are held in public facilities, with the remainder in private facilities, and 57,190 offenders under age 21 are held in 2,547 facilities.[48] But juvenile placements have been dropping nationally, with an overall drop of 31 percent since 1985.[49] **Figure 12.5** displays the types of juvenile custodial facilities.

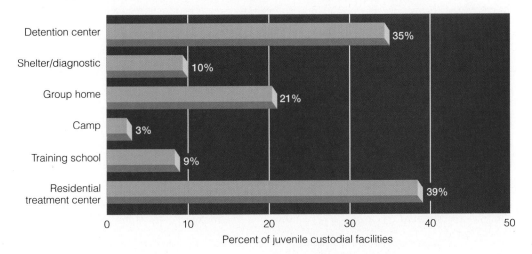

FIGURE 12.5
Types of Juvenile Custodial Facility
Most juvenile facilities are low security, but almost two of five juvenile facilities are for detention or long-term placement.

Source: Sarah Hockenberry, Melissa Sickmund, and Anthony Sladky, *Juvenile Residential Facility Census, 2012: Selected Findings*, Washington, DC: Office of Juvenile Justice and Delinquency Prevention. March, 2015, p. 3.

Policy makers are concerned about the overrepresentation of incarcerated African American juveniles. The Juvenile Justice and Delinquency Prevention Act of 1988 requires states to determine whether the proportion of minorities in confinement exceeds their proportion in the population. If such overrepresentation is found, states must demonstrate efforts to reduce it. *Disparity* means that the probability of receiving a particular outcome (for example, being detained in a short-term facility rather than not being detained) differs among different groups. If more African Americans are detained than others, this, in turn, may lead to more of them being adjudicated in juvenile court and may lead to a larger proportion being placed in residential facilities. **Table 12.5** shows the rate of African American overrepresentation (as a proportion of the population) at each major decision point of the juvenile corrections system. The disproportionate confinement of minority juveniles often stems from disparity in the early stages of case processing.

Institutions for juvenile offenders include foster homes, residential centers, reform schools, and training schools. In recent years more juveniles are also being sent to adult prisons. These institutions vary in the degree of security and the amount of programming available. We now describe them in order of least to greatest amount of custody supervision.

Foster homes and residential centers typically take small numbers of delinquents. These locations are not considered punitive—judges use foster homes and residential centers when the juvenile's family cannot provide an adequate setting for the child's development. Foster homes are often run by a married couple, and the juveniles live in them, sometimes as cohabitants with the adults' biological children. The court pays the

Table 12.5 Overrepresentation of African Americans in the Juvenile Corrections System

African American youths are almost twice as likely to be arrested as white youths. At subsequent stages the overrepresentation, while still a problem, is less pronounced.

Type of Ratio[a]	Rates per 100 Youths		
	White	African American	Overrepresentation of African Americans
Juvenile arrests to population[b]	6.1	11.5	1.9
Cases referred to juvenile arrests	68.9	75.6	1.1
Cases detained to cases referred	18.4	25.1	1.4
Cases petitioned to cases referred	54.9	64.7	1.2
Cases waived to cases petitioned	0.7	0.8	1.1
Cases adjudicated to cases petitioned	70.6	58.5	0.8
Placements to cases adjudicated	21.5	26.5	1.2

[a] For example, 6.1 white youths were arrested per 100 youths in the general population, 68.9 white youths out of 100 white youths who were arrested were also referred, and so forth.

[b] Population age 10–17 equals 25,994,400 (white) and 5,431,300 (African American).

Source: Howard N. Snyder and Melissa Sickmund, *Juvenile Offenders and Victims: 2006 National Report* (Pittsburgh: National Center for Juvenile Justice, 2006), 189. See also Joshua Rovner, *Disproportionate Minority Contact in the Juvenile Justice System* (Washington, DC: Sentencing Project, 2014).

careers in Corrections

JUVENILE GROUP HOME COUNSELOR

Nature of the Work

Juvenile group home counselors are responsible for supervising and guiding youths under age 18 who have been placed in a group home by a juvenile court. Counselors spend their days with youths who reside in the home, provide one-on-one counseling, and implement treatment programs dealing with the special problems of youths. Typically, they work with 8–12 youths at a time in a residential setting.

Required Qualifications

Background qualifications for juvenile group home counselors vary by state, but a bachelor's degree in social work, criminal justice, or a related field from a four-year college or university is usually required. Some agencies require previous experience with youths or graduate work. Candidates must be at least 21 years old and have no felony convictions. Most juvenile group home counselors receive both formal and on-the-job training.

Earnings and Job Outlook

The number of juvenile group home counselors is expected to be stable during the next decade. Juvenile group home counselors report a high level of personal satisfaction in their work. They earn about $40,000 per year, with entry-level salaries under $25,000 in many regions.

More Information

Visit the website of the American Probation and Parole Association. Career information can also be obtained from your state, juvenile court, or probation office.

couple a per diem for each foster child, usually not enough to cover all the expenses involved, and the adults in the home provide supervision in cooperation with probation officers. Foster children attend the local school system and operate under whatever restrictions the foster parents and probation officer deem suitable—curfews, associations, leisure activities, and the like. Residential centers operate much like foster homes, with residents attending local schools and living under certain restrictions. The main difference is that residential centers are run by professional staff, not adult volunteers. It may also be the case that a small amount of residential treatment programming occurs in residential centers, usually as group counseling sessions. See "Careers in Corrections" for more on being a juvenile group home counselor.

Compared with group homes, reform schools and training schools offer far less freedom to the child placed within them. They do not hesitate to impose a strict regime, and they regard one of their functions as punishment. As seen in **Figure 12.6**, the delinquents assigned to these facilities have committed serious offenses.

These 24-hour facilities severely limit residents' freedom. School is on campus, and the residents work to maintain the facilities. In almost every way, reform schools and training schools are the equivalent of adult prisons, developed for adolescents under custody. As such, they have some of the same problems that plague adult prisons and jails: violence, sexual assault, staff–resident conflict, and disciplinary control problems

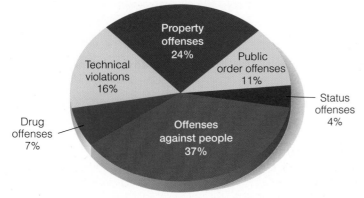

FIGURE 12.6
Juvenile Delinquents in Public Custodial Facilities: Types of Offenses

Some youths in confinement are there for violent crimes, but the majority are confined for other, less serious offenses.

Source: Melissa Sickmund and Charles Puzzanchera, *Juvenile Offenders and Victims, 2014*. Pittsburgh: National Center for Juvenile Justice December 2014, p. 188

(see "Do the Right Thing"). Because the residents are younger and somewhat more volatile than adults, behavioral control is often an everyday issue, and fights and aggression are common situations.

aftercare
Services provided to juveniles after they have been removed from their home and put under some form of custodial care.

JUVENILE AFTERCARE The term **aftercare** refers to services provided to juveniles after they have been *placed*—that is, removed from their home and put under some form of custodial care. Aftercare operates in a way similar to adult parole. It receives juveniles who have been under some form of custody—typically the state's training school, but sometimes a foster home or residential placement—and provides supervision and support during the period of readjustment to community life. The importance of aftercare rests on the fact that youths face significant obstacles of adjustment after they have been away from their homes, which makes their chances of failure quite high.

Aftercare workers know that youths who have been returned from confinement face significant adjustment problems and require substantial attention and support. First of all, a youth who has been placed in a custodial setting by the court has either engaged in some form of serious criminal behavior or has shown a pattern of persistent disobedience of less serious laws and/or of court-ordered rules of behavior. In either case, there is a potential for trouble. The serious offender has committed a frightening crime and faces a fearful community, a family who may not welcome his or her return, and a school system that doubts the juvenile's readiness to behave. The persistent delinquent has been a source of trouble to family, neighbors, school officials, and others and will not be received with open arms. The aftercare worker negotiates the return to the community by helping the juvenile understand the community's apprehension, while showing the community evidence that the juvenile deserves a second chance.

The aftercare worker must also closely follow the juvenile's adjustment, even while serving as advocate. The risk of recidivism is high enough that the community feels a stake in the aftercare scrutiny. All involved in the aftercare system recognize that a careful balance is needed between support and control because these juveniles include the

DO the Right Thing

Trayvon, age 16, was hustling home from after-school practice because he had promised his mom he would babysit his four younger siblings. He was delayed in getting home because his bike had been taken from him by a group of teens a few days earlier. So when his cousin suggested they steal someone else's bike to get home faster, it kind of made sense. They stopped a stranger, Trayvon pointed a gun at him, and they took the bike. The next day, he was arrested for armed robbery.

At pretrial detention the probation officer learned a few things about Trayvon: The gun was a BB gun, he had a strong family life, he had never been arrested before, and on the standardized risk assessment, he scored out as "low risk." He has admitted the delinquent act and says that he has learned his lesson and won't do it again.

The prosecutor says, "This was an armed robbery. Once Trayvon pulled out the gun, anything could have happened. It doesn't matter that it was a BB gun; there could have been a progression of violence

that resulted in someone really getting hurt. He needs to learn a lesson, and the community's values need to be upheld. He needs to do some time."

The juvenile probation officer says, "He is low risk. This was a classic act of pure impulse, not a life-threatening deed. If you put him behind bars, he will only get worse."

Critical Thinking

1. What is the role of risk assessment in a situation such as this?
2. How does risk assessment balance with the need to maintain community standards and uphold the law?
3. What should be your goal in dealing with Trayvon?
4. How would you know that you succeeded in accomplishing your goal?

Source: Stacy Teicher Khadaroo, "How Communities Are Keeping Kids Out of Crime," *Christian Science Monitor*, February 15, 2015.

most-serious cases in the juvenile justice system. Much is to be gained. When an after-care worker can successfully negotiate a juvenile through the first months of return to the community, a lifetime of crime can be avoided.

THE FUTURE OF JUVENILE JUSTICE

High-profile gang criminality and the recent spate of school shootings have ended the anonymity of juvenile correctional work (see "Focus on Correctional Policy: The Prevalence of Gangs"). Public policy makers are turning their attention to the juvenile justice system. This meant that in the 1990s, many of the themes of reform in adult corrections since the 1970s were replayed in the juvenile justice arena. This led to public calls for get-tough measures that took the form of pressure to increase waiver of serious juveniles to adult courts, with their longer, harsher punishments. We should not have been surprised to see these familiar echoes of changes in the adult system arising in respect to juveniles, as the public spotlight has landed there.

However, reform efforts for juveniles seem today to be turning away from the pattern exhibited by the adult process. Some of this reflects facts about youths who commit crimes. No matter how the media portray extreme cases, the everyday juvenile offender remains unsophisticated and susceptible to change under appropriate programs. Most juvenile crime is still minor misbehavior, not at all like the highly charged cases of serious violence that dominate the news. To paint all juvenile offenders with a broad, adult criminal brush would not only be inaccurate but also unwise.

Some of this also reflects a growing respect for evidence about effective policy for young people who commit crimes. While it is clear that the relative anonymity once enjoyed by the juvenile justice system is now past, it is also clear that the new attention being paid to juvenile justice policy will not result in a simple replay of the stricter adult system. Some of this has to do with widespread dissatisfaction with the adult model, but just as important has been a new respect for evidence that suggests a different strategy will work out better.

focus on correctional policy

The Prevalence of Gangs

Every year, the National Gang Center does a survey of 3,500 U.S. law enforcement jurisdictions to determine the nature and extent of youth gangs. The most recent survey estimated that there were 28,100 gangs with 731,000 members actively operating in the United States.

Just over one-third of all U.S. cities had active gang activity taking place in them—a figure that is down from 15 years ago (when the first survey was done) but has been fairly stable in recent years. As might be expected, gang activity is more concentrated in larger cities, where four-fifths report active gang presence. By contrast, only one-sixth of the rural police departments report gang activity. The extent to which gangs are an urban problem is highlighted by the fact that 96 percent of all gang-related homicides occur in densely populated cities and their immediate suburbs.

Although much gang violence is drug related, the center has concluded from studies of gangs that "most youth gangs lack the necessary organizational structure and capacity to effectively manage drug distribution operations; however, [an individual's] drug use and drug sales have been shown to increase after joining a gang, and then decrease after a period of incarceration." Two other factors that influence the level of gang violence are intergang conflict over "turf" and young men returning from prison who—quite often—provoke violence when they reconnect with their old gang relationships.

Source: Arlen Egley, Jr., and James C. Howell, *Highlights of the 2009 National Youth Gang Survey* (Washington, DC: Office of Juvenile Justice and Delinquency Prevention, 2011).

Summary

① Describe the nature and extent of youth crime today.

In the most recent year for which data are available (2013), 614 youths under age 18 were arrested for homicide, 2,089 for forcible rape, and a troubling 25,016 for aggravated assault. Even so, extremely serious juvenile crime incidents are rare. In a nation with 74 million people 18 years of age or younger, 875,000 arrests of juveniles took place, only 43,651 of which (about 5 percent) were for violent crimes. After rising between 1988 and 1994, the juvenile violent crime rate has dropped by almost 50 percent; it is now the lowest it has been since at least 1980. Property crime has decreased by about half since the peak in 1991.

② Analyze the history of the development of juvenile corrections in the United States.

The first juvenile court was established by a legislative act in Cook County (Chicago), Illinois, in 1899. Based on *parens patriae,* the new juvenile court took on the role of guardian, the substitute parent of the child. Decisions about a juvenile's fate were linked less to guilt or innocence and more to the "best interests" of the child. The main tenets of the juvenile court can be summarized as informality, individualization, and intervention.

③ Describe the new "evidence-based" movement in juvenile corrections, and explain how it has affected juvenile justice.

Policy makers around the country are today rethinking the juvenile court in light of a new policy ethic: evidence. Both legislators and juvenile justice administrators are asking themselves, "What do we know about reducing juvenile crime, and how can we design the juvenile justice system to take better advantage of that knowledge?" This has led to the emergence of a new generation of community-based strategies to reduce juvenile crime before the justice system is invoked. Rather than a heightened policy of crime control that emphasizes surveillance, arrest, and incarceration, this new era tends to look to a host of studies that have provided added clarity to our understanding of what works and what does not.

④ List the ways that juvenile offenders are sanctioned.

The main sanctions are juvenile probation, intermediate sanctions for juveniles, juvenile community corrections, juvenile incarceration, and juvenile aftercare.

⑤ Critically assess the future of juvenile corrections.

Reform efforts for juveniles seem today to be turning away from the pattern exhibited by the adult process. Most juvenile crime is still minor misbehavior, not at all like the highly charged cases of serious violence that dominate the news. To paint all juvenile offenders with a broad, adult criminal brush would not only be inaccurate but also unwise.

Key Terms

aftercare 328
at-risk youths 315
delinquent 311
dependent 311

disposition 322
meta-analysis 314
neglected 311
parens patriae 310

placement 322
school-to-prison pipeline 323

For Discussion

1. Why is juvenile crime so alarming to the public, even though it has been declining for several years?
2. What does the history of juvenile justice in America tell us about correctional reform movements?
3. What kinds of juvenile crime should the most severe sanctions be used for, and why?

4. How has the history of juvenile justice reform compared to adult correctional reform? What does this tell us about juvenile justice as compared to adult justice?
5. What will the future juvenile justice system look like? What forces will shape the development of juvenile justice?

Notes

1 Erik Eckholm, "A Murderer at 14, Then a Lifer, Now a Man Pondering a Future," *New York Times*, April 11, 2015, pp. 1, 11–12.

2 *Miller v. Alabama*, 577 U.S. __ (2012).

3 Annie Sweeney, "I'm Just Praying for a Second Chance, Convict Says at Resentencing," *Chicago Tribune*, April 14, 2015.

4 Gary Gately, *Supreme Court to Weigh Retroactivity of Mandatory JLWOPI* (Philadelphia: Juvenile Justice Information Exchange, Juvenile Law Center, 2015).

5 See the Campaign for the Fair Sentencing of Youth: http://fairsentencingofyouth.org/what-is-jlwop.

6 Uniform Crime Reports, 2013, www.fbi.gov/about-us/cjis/ucr/crime-in-the-u.s/2011/crime-in-the-u.s.-2013/tables/table-38.

7 M. Sickmund, A. Sladky, and W. Kang, "Easy Access to Juvenile Court Statistics: 1985–2012," www.ojjdp.gov/ojstatbb/ezajcs.

8 Uniform Crime Reports, 2013.

9 Ibid., p. 9.

10 Theda Roberts, *Florida's Statewide Civil Citation: Part of the Community, Part of the Solution*, (Tallahassee: Florida Department of Juvenile Justice, 2015).

11 Amanda Paulsona, "Why Juvenile Incarceration Reached Its Lowest Point in 38 Years," *Christian Science Monitor*, www.csmonitor.com/USA/Justice/2013/0227/Why-juvenile-incarceration-reached-its-lowest-rate-in-38-years, February 27, 2013.

12 Justice Policy Institute, *Measuring Reform: Focus on Juvenile Incarceration* (Washington, DC: Author, 2013).

13 Uberto Gatti, Richard E. Tremblay, and Frank Vitaro, "Iatrogenic Effect of Juvenile Justice," *Child Psychology and Psychiatry* 50 (no. 8, 2009): 991–98.

14 Federal Bureau of Investigation, *Crime in the United States, 2013*, Table 38.

15 Ibid., tables 38, 42, and 43b.

16 Charles Puzzanchera and Benjamin Adams, "Juvenile Arrests 2009," OJJDP *Bulletin*, December 2011.

17 Ibid.

18 Comparing FBI, *Crime in the United States, 2000*, table 32, to FBI, *Crime in the United States, 2013*, table 38.

19 Charles Puzzanchera, Benjamin Adams, and Sarah Hockenberry, *Juvenile Court Statistics 2009* (Pittsburgh: National Center for Juvenile Justice, 2012), 45.

20 George E. Higgins, Melissa L. Ricketts, James D. Griffith, and Stephanie A. Jirard, "Race and Juvenile Incarceration: A Propensity Score Matching Examination," *American Journal of Criminal Justice* (March 2012).

21 Sean Rosenmerkel, Matthew Durose, and Donald Farole, Jr., *Felony Sentences in State Courts, 2006—Statistical Tables* (Washington, DC: Bureau of Justice Statistics, 2009), 4.

22 Sarah Hockenberry and Charles Puzzanchera, *Juvenile Court Statistics, 2011* (Pittsburgh: National Center for Juvenile Justice, 2014), 54.

23 Melissa Sickmund and Charles Puzzanchera, eds., *Juvenile Offenders and Victims: 2014* (Pittsburgh: National Center for Juvenile Justice, 2014).

24 Aaron Kupchik, *Judging Juveniles: Prosecuting Adolescents in Adult and Juvenile Courts* (New York: NYU Press, 2006). See also Joe M. Brown and John R. Sorenson, "Race, Ethnicity, Gender and Waiver to Adult Court," *Journal of Ethnicity in Criminal Justice* 11 (no. 3, 2013): 282–95.

25 Campaign for Youth Justice, *The Consequences Aren't Minor: The Impact of Trying Youth as Adults and Strategies for Reform* (Washington, DC: Campaign for Youth Justice, 2007).

26 Task Force on Community Preventive Services, "Effects on Violence of Laws and Policies Facilitating the Transfer of Juveniles from the Juvenile Justice System to the Adult Justice System: A Systematic Review," *American Journal of Preventive Medicine* 32 (no. 4, April 2007): 7–28.

27 Sickmund and Puzzanchera, *Juvenile Offenders and Victims: 2014*, p. 174.

28 Neelum Arya, *State Trends: Legislative Changes from 2005 to 2010: Removing Youth from the Adult Criminal Justice System* (full report) (Washington, DC: Campaign for Youth Justice, 2011).

29 E. Anne Carson and William J. Sabol, *Prisoners in 2011* (Washington, DC: Bureau of Justice Statistics, 2012), 7.

30 Todd D. Minton, *Jail Inmates at Midyear 2011—Statistical Tables* (Washington, DC: Bureau of Justice Statistics, 2012): 6.

31 Roberts, *Florida's Statewide Civil Citation*.

32 Sickmund and Puzzanchera, *Juvenile Offenders and Victims: 2014*, p. 152.

33 David P. Farrington and Brandon C. Welsh, *Saving Children from a Life of Crime* (New York: Oxford University Press, 2007).

34 Hockenberry and Puzzanchera, *Juvenile Court Statistics, 2011*, p. 38.

35 Sickmund and Puzzanchera, *Juvenile Offenders and Victims: 2014*, p. 215.

36 Gatti, Tremblay, and Vitaro, "Iatrogenic Effect of Juvenile Justice," pp. 991–98.

37 Paul Boxer, Joanna Kubik, Michael Ostermann, and Bonita Veysey, "Gang Involvement Moderates the Effectiveness of Evidence-Based Intervention for Justice-Involved Youth," *Children and Youth Services Review*, March 10, 2015.

38 Hockenberry and Puzzanchera, *Juvenile Court Statistics, 2011*, p. 42.

39 Ibid., p. 52.

40 Ibid., p 49.

41 Jacob Kang-Brown, Jennifer Trone, Jennifer Fratello, and Tarika Daftary-Kapur, *A Generation Later: What We've Learned About Zero Tolerance in Schools* (New York: Vera Institute of Justice, 2013).

42 Sandra Jo Wilson and Mark W. Lipsey, *The Effectiveness of School-Based Violence Prevention Programs for Reducing Disruptive and Aggressive Behavior*, report to the National Institute of Justice (Washington, DC: Center for Evaluation Research and Methodology, Institute for Public Policy Studies, Vanderbilt University, 2005).

43 John Paul Wright, Pamela M. McMahon, Claire Daley, and J. Phil Haney, "Getting the Law Involved: A Quasi-Experiment in Early Intervention Involving Collaboration Between Schools and the District Attorney's Office," *Criminology & Public Policy* 11 (no. 2, 2012): 227–50.

44 Daniel S. Nagin, Alex R. Piquero, Elizabeth S. Scott, and Laurence Steinberg, "Public Preference for Rehabilitation Versus Incarceration for Juvenile Offenders: Evidence from a Contingent Valuation Survey," *Criminology & Public Policy* 5 (no. 4, 2006): 627–52.

45 Christopher T. Lowenkamp and Edward J. Latessa, *Evaluation of Ohio's RECLAIM-Funded Programs, Community Corrections Facilities, and DYS Facilities*, report to the Ohio Department of Youth Services (Cincinnati, University of Cincinnati, 2005).

46 Hockenberry and Puzzanchera, *Juvenile Court Statistics, 2011*, p. 52.

47 Andrea J. Sedlak and Carol Bruce, *Youth's Characteristics and Backgrounds: Findings from the Survey of Youth in Residential Placement* (Washington, DC: Office of Juvenile Justice and Delinquency Prevention, 2010).

48 Sarah Hockenberry, Melissa Sickmund, and Anthony Sladky, *Juvenile Residential Facility Census, 2012: Selected Findings* (Washington, DC: Office of Juvenile Justice and Delinquency Prevention, 2015), 3.

49 Hockenberry and Puzzanchera, *Juvenile Court Statistics, 2011*, p. 44.

CHAPTER

13

The Future of Corrections

As we pause to think about the future of corrections, we might begin by asking what the American corrections system is best known for across the world.

There was a time when the American corrections system was viewed as the most progressive in the world. When the modern prison was invented after the Revolution, it was envied worldwide. When the nation's penologists met in Cincinnati in 1870, they affirmed a mission of rehabilitation that became a model for corrections systems around the globe. At the turn of that century, modern probation was invented here, and this innovation has also has been copied worldwide. For most of the nineteenth and twentieth centuries, the U.S. corrections system was at the forefront of thinking

After reading this chapter you should be able to . . .

1 Understand how the philosophy of the U.S. corrections system has changed over the years and what this has meant for the corrections system.

2 Know the major dilemmas facing the corrections system and how they might be resolved.

3 Identify four substantial forces that face corrections and describe their importance.

4 Understand what "good leadership" means in the context of the current U.S. corrections system and know what it will take for these leaders to more widely implement "what works" in corrections.

5 Describe the aspirations for the U.S. corrections system and how those aspirations might be achieved.

Kevork Djansezian/Getty Images News/Getty Images

The American correctional system has grown continually for almost 40 years. Today it is at least six times larger than it was a generation ago. What has the growth of corrections meant for America? How has it affected our political and cultural life?

...ut the best ways to deal with people ...break the law, and U.S. methods were ...ly celebrated and emulated.

...oday, the U.S. corrections system is ...onger the progressive beacon for the ...d's systems of punishment. If a panel

the U.S. system of corrections, it is likely that they would not point to progressive programs or leading innovations in thought. Instead, they would say that what sets the U.S. corrections system apart from those elsewhere in the world is that it is

(continued from previous page)

Since the mid-1970s, by every measure, the American corrections system has grown by unprecedented amounts. Between 1973 and 2010, the imprisonment rate increased from under 100 people per 100,000 to almost 500 per 100,000. Including probation, parole, and jails, the number of people under correctional control has also skyrocketed in that same time, from under a million to more than 7 million.

This growth has disproportionately affected minority group members. For example, over one in three African American men in their twenties has come under correctional control—more black men are behind bars than attending colleges and universities. Some observers estimated that in Los Angeles, about one in three African American youths is arrested each year, though far fewer are prosecuted. It is not hard to see why many residents in these communities believe that the criminal justice system is designed to oppress them and that the corrections system is intended to remove men from their neighborhoods.

It is also hard to believe that over the past 40 years we have deliberately created the corrections system we most want. To the contrary, most of those in charge of today's corrections system would argue that what we are doing is self-destructive and that an overhaul of the corrections system is long overdue.

As we suggest in Chapter 1, we can think of the last 40 years of unprecedented growth in corrections as a kind of grand "social experiment," and it is time to figure out what we have learned from this experiment. For example, the population of drug offenders in U.S. prisons has increased by over 700 percent since 1980, more than five times the rate of increase of other offenders; this was largely the result of the "drug wars" of the 1980s and 1990s. Two decades later, almost nobody would say that we have "won" those wars.[1] Now what?

There are signs that things are changing. Starting around 2000, the rate of growth in the U.S. corrections system, high throughout the 1990s, began to decelerate. By 2010, the prison system stabilized, and the populations in all parts of the corrections system—prison, probation, and parole—have actually declined for the past four years.

Perhaps the biggest change is in public opinion. The recent announcement of the formation of a prison reform coalition that aligns leading advocacy groups on the political left and the right is a powerful indicator that thought-leaders in the public now agree that the corrections system has to get smaller—especially the prison system.[2] It seems that policy makers in the United States are beginning to reconsider the last 40 years of correctional policy. Is the U.S. corrections system turning a new page? Has the "experiment" ended and a new era started?

In this, our closing chapter, we step back to look at the big picture of corrections. What can we make of the corrections system we have described in this book? Where is it headed, and what issues does it face? What is its future? We explore these questions with a critical eye because even though nobody can foresee the future in perfect focus, the way we ask ourselves about the future tells us a great deal about how we feel about the present. We begin with a discussion of five dilemmas that corrections faces—indeed, has always faced throughout history. We describe four important forces that will shape corrections in the future. We then consider three key, pressing challenges that anyone interested in corrections must undertake. ■

FIVE DILEMMAS FACING CORRECTIONS

A *dilemma* is a situation that forces one to choose between unsatisfactory alternatives. Corrections faces many dilemmas—any worker in the field will attest to this fact. We have selected five dilemmas as particularly important because they are what we consider "orienting" dilemmas for corrections. That is, not only must each corrections system confront them as it moves further into the twenty-first century, but the way it confronts them will profoundly affect the resolution of most other issues—from daily problems in offender management to larger considerations.

Indeed, today's difficulties and tomorrow's potential solutions are quite bound up in how these five dilemmas were faced in the past. Unlike much of the material in this book, our description of the dilemmas is not an objective restatement of facts and studies; rather, it is a subjective interpretation of many facts, studies, and observations. We return to the systems perspective as we identify five core concerns: mission, methods, structure, personnel, and costs.

Mission

Corrections lacks a clear mission. One reason for this is that it has so many different clients—offenders, the general public, other government agencies—each of which has different expectations of corrections. In simple terms we recognize that offenders want fairness, leniency, and assistance; the public wants protection from and punishment of criminals; government agencies want cooperation and coordination. Obviously, these expectations often come into conflict. Thus, one goal of corrections must be to disentangle the expectations and establish a set of priorities for handling them.

At the same time, none of these competing expectations can be ignored. How do courts respond when corrections fails to provide rehabilitative services to offenders? How does the public respond to instances of brutal recidivism? How do government agencies manage balky correctional officials?

One common solution in corrections is to attempt to meet all expectations: provide the services that are requested, take actions to protect citizens when public safety becomes an issue, cooperate with agencies when asked to do so. The advantage of this approach is that corrections can avoid the strains that accompany goal conflict, such as making hard choices about priorities. Of course, this supposed advantage can never be fully realized. The conflicts between serving clients and protecting the community, or between coordinating government practices and providing assistance or protection, are real. When corrections tries to meet all these competing expectations equally, correctional workers must resolve the conflicts informally. Corrections must confront the problems created by ambiguity of mission. Doing so requires that choices be made. In the early 1960s, most people agreed that the primary mission of corrections was the rehabilitation of offenders, but the devaluation of treatment and the movement toward harsh, mandatory sentences left a void in this area. Some observers have suggested that corrections must take on the role of offender management; others have argued that the role of corrections is risk control; still others have suggested punishment as its mission. Today, an increasing interest in community justice and a desire to minimize prison populations have worked their way into many correctional mission statements.

Whatever the choice, correctional leaders must articulate their philosophy of corrections and establish a clearer policy to guide its implementation. Both staff members and people outside the system must be aware of what corrections does and what they can expect from its efforts.

Methods

Obviously, if the correctional mission is unclear, the best correctional strategies and techniques will be ambiguous as well. When goals are in conflict, staff members have difficulty choosing among competing methods to perform their work: surveillance or

Advances in information technology now are being adapted for applications to corrections. Here, Orleans Parish Sheriff Marlin Gusman shows how a control station in a housing pod of the new Orleans Parish jail works.

Michael Democker/The Times-Picayune/Landov

service, custody or treatment. But this is not the only problem with correctional methods; much more significantly, correctional techniques often do not seem to work.

Technical uncertainty has implications for corrections; chronic uncertainty has other consequences as well. A debilitating lack of confidence results when apparently promising strategies, upon evaluation, turn out to lack merit. The list of failed correctional methods includes reduced caseloads, offender counseling, family counseling, group treatment, restitution, and offender classification. All these and many more methods have been promoted as the answer to a given pressing problem. Each time another correctional strategy proves ineffective, the failure feeds an already pervasive feeling among workers that corrections is incapable of performing its basic functions well.

This is one reason why the short-term history of corrections seems dominated by fads. As each "innovative" technique or program is implemented, corrections is confronted by the method's limited ability to immediately solve the technical problems it was intended to solve, so it is replaced by something newer still.

The consequences of these frequent changes in approach are largely negative. No firm, central technical process is allowed to develop and mature. Because corrections works with people, its central technologies should involve interpersonal communication and influence; however, the parade of new programs subtly shifts the emphasis from process to procedures. The dynamic work of corrections is stalled by the static and routinized activities that ebb and flow with each new program. Bureaucratic approaches to offender management come to dominate the technical approach to the job. Workers become cynical about changes and about the potential of the work itself. And who can blame them? The most experienced correctional workers have seen many highly praised programs come and go, having failed to produce the expected results.

Another issue associated with correctional methods is fairness: Offenders should be punished equally in accordance with the seriousness of their offenses. This seems to be a straightforward assignment. Yet the fact is that the most stringent correctional methods are applied in practice almost exclusively to the poor and predominantly to minorities. One is left with the feeling that merely to be "equal" in our application of state power under these circumstances is not really to be fair in the broadest sense of the term. Genuine fairness must enhance the lives and the life potential of those we bring under correctional control. But if the history of corrections has taught us anything, it is that we often injure the people we try to help. We know little about how to assist offenders effectively, but it is certainly not enough just to punish them equally. The dilemma of methods is complex. Can we overcome the tradition of faddism in corrections without becoming stodgily bureaucratic in method? Can we improve the life chances of correctional clients without injuring them further despite good intentions? (See "Focus on Correctional Practice.")

Structure

Corrections is simply not in a position to influence its own fate significantly. Much of this inability has to do with its structure—internal and external. Internally, corrections is a process divided against itself. Jails, prisons, probation, and parole all struggle with one another; the practices of each become contingencies for the others. Externally, corrections represents the culmination of the criminal justice process, and it has little formal capacity to control the demand for its services. Thus, correctional leaders face two structural dilemmas.

First, their colleagues are often the ones who put the most immediate obstacles in the way of their attempts to manage their operations effectively. Second, the corrections system depends on significant factors outside of its control. The practical consequences of the structural dilemma are sometimes quite startling.

In many jurisdictions, for example, large amounts of money have been spent renovating old jails or building new ones because the existing facilities are substandard, overcrowded, or both. Too often, the new version is soon just as overcrowded as the old one was, or else it is deemed legally substandard. The fault rests with the inability

focus on correctional practice

Reducing Recidivism for People Reentering Society

Since the turn of the century, we have been in the "era of reentry." President Clinton's administration coined the term *reentry* to apply to people who were returning to the community from prison. A national awareness developed that annually as many as 700,000 such people return. Recognizing that the entire nation shares a stake in how well returning prisoners do, President George H. W. Bush made improvements in reentry a policy priority. His Second Chance Act funded significant progress in support services for people leaving prison, and he made effective reentry an issue important to political conservatives. President Obama's Justice Department has continued this emphasis. This kind of national leadership has helped create an era in which more attention is paid to the problems of reentry than ever before. Led by nationally prominent experts and federal guidance, state and local governments mounted reentry projects designed to improve services for people leaving prison.

Many of these initiatives were subjected to some form of evaluation, and the early results were not promising. One of the key examples was Project Greenlight, a comprehensive service strategy for people leaving New York's correctional facilities. A rigorous study found no evidence that people exposed to the services did better in almost any way, from getting a job to staying out of trouble with the law. In fact, they did worse.[3] A national study of 15 sites that implemented comprehensive services as a part of the Serious and Violent Offender Reentry Initiative concluded that even though the program improved services for people leaving prison, it did not affect their rates of rearrest.[4] A review of programs for people in reentry found that while some programs show good effects, most programs fail to incorporate what is learned from successes and failures in evaluation studies.[5]

These studies show how hard it is to affect rearrest rates through service delivery. Nobody believes that we should eliminate services for people who are returning from prison. To do so would be folly. But we are forced to confront the difficult conclusion that we simply do not yet know how to organize services in ways that will guarantee making a difference.

Critical Thinking

What are some of the problems that you see in developing programs to reduce recidivism?

---

of corrections to coordinate architectural planning with the programmatic needs of such nonjail agencies as the courts and probation. What initially seemed to be a problem of how much space is available really reflects a problem of how available space is used, which, in turn, is influenced by people other than jail administrators. The courts (through sentencing and pretrial release), law enforcement (through arrest), and probation/parole (through revocation) all use jail space for their own purposes. The lack of agencies to lessen the effects of population growth on corrections can eliminate the benefits of opening a new prison. This is only one of the deficiencies that repeatedly occur in correctional planning.

Formally, the problem of structure in corrections is one of interdependence and coordination. The ability of corrections to function effectively depends in some ways on external processes that it must respond to, influence, or at least understand. To do so, its own processes must be better coordinated with those of the external agencies that produce the dependence—and the dissension.

The problem is that there is really no easy way to coordinate these processes. Separation of powers is both a constitutional and a traditional bulwark of our government. Each agency is protective of its own power and reluctant to reduce it by coordination or planning. Thus, when a new jail is being designed, the approval of the municipal engineering bureau is seen as a hurdle to be cleared rather than a potential resource to be tapped. Each time an interagency control is put into place, it becomes an obstacle rather than a coordinating mechanism.

Most correctional administrators find that their greatest frustrations lie in getting other agencies to avoid actions that severely constrain their ability to function. A recent trend has been the formation of "partnerships" meant to improve coordination, either high-level commissions composed of heads of correctional, justice system, judicial, and executive-branch agencies, or task forces of line-level personnel. This is a promising step, but a small one.

Personnel

Because corrections is a people-processing operation, its personnel are its main resource. The two essential goals in regard to staff are (1) attracting the right kinds of people to work in corrections and (2) motivating them to remain once they are employed. Corrections traditionally has not done well in either area.

The initial recruitment problem frequently stems from the low starting salaries. Although salaries vary widely from place to place, correctional employees often earn less than workers in comparable positions elsewhere. For example, correctional officers frequently begin at wages lower than those of local law enforcement officers. Likewise, the starting salaries of probation and parole officers, who are normally required to have a college degree, often are not competitive with those offered to social workers and teachers.

For this reason, correctional positions may be regarded as a good entry to the work world. A person new to the job market can obtain stable employment for a year or two while seeking alternative employment. The most-qualified individuals find it relatively easy to move on to other occupations; less-qualified people often stay longer, some for their entire careers. Further, people who have exemplary "experience" qualifications—those who have previous criminal records but have turned their lives around—are too often barred from employment in the corrections system (see "Do the Right Thing"). In fact, a case can be made that those who have successfully navigated reentry after incarceration make exactly the right kinds of staff to help others "make it."[6]

Further, as a result of collective bargaining, most correctional employees receive equal pay raises regardless of performance. Inevitably, a system of equality becomes a disincentive to employees whose work efforts surpass those of others. Too frequently,

DO the Right Thing

You are the director of a small, nonprofit agency that provides services to people who are in reentry from prison. You employ some people with previous criminal records because you have found that they can be very effective with the kinds of clients your agency has. Before you hire people with a record, however, you check their background very carefully, and you keep careful track of their work, especially in the early months of their career.

One of your employees, Hidalgo Vegas, has been especially successful for the last three years. He has a 10-year-old felony conviction for drug sales, and during that period of his life, when he used drugs regularly, he had several misdemeanor arrests and convictions, mostly for low-level misdemeanors—never involving

violence. But yesterday Vegas came into your office to tell you he has been arrested in a domestic dispute, and the charge is assault. He says he and his wife were fighting, and things got out of control. Your investigation indicates that he shoved her around a bit but did not hit her. The prosecutor says that the victim will not press charges. But his counseling job in your agency often requires him to work with people who have domestic violence in their background, both as victims and as offenders.

Critical Thinking

What do you do? Do you fire him? Let him keep working? Take a different action?

significant personnel decisions such as promotions, raises, and increased responsibilities are completely out of the hands of correctional administrators.

In times of fiscal abundance, salary is not as great a problem, but decades of salary crunches in government employment, combined with a constricted job market, can embitter many correctional employees. The organizational culture of many correctional operations is dominated by animosity toward management and cynicism toward the job. Too often, correctional employees feel unappreciated, manipulated, and alienated. Under these conditions, it is exceedingly difficult for a corrections system to perform its "peoplework" function effectively because its most valuable resource—the staff—is demoralized.

On the surface, the solution to the personnel problem seems simple: Measure the performance of staff, reward those who are productive, and get rid of those who are not. Unfortunately, this approach does not work in government employment (and may not work well in the private sector, either). For one thing, correctional performance is exceedingly difficult to assess. Although the general yardsticks of recidivism, institutional security, and so forth provide useful measures of correctional performance, they are inadequate indicators of an individual's performance. Who can say that a parolee's failure was the parole officer's fault? Indeed, a case can be made that it represents an officer's successful surveillance.

Secondary performance measures, such as contacts with clients, paperwork, and training, are therefore often substituted for primary measures of job success. These secondary measures tend to be fairer because they fall within the staff's control. But for a secondary measure of performance to be useful, it must be clearly related to organizational success. In this respect, most secondary measures in corrections are inadequate. In another vein, government employment is often sought because of its purported job security; altering the personnel picture to overcome lethargy is likely to cause extreme strain among the staff.

The correctional leader's choices in the personnel area, unhappily, involve no short-term solutions. The answer, if there is one, lies in long-term staff development. A sound staff is built by innovative selection and promotion methods; professional growth on the job is encouraged by education and training incentives. "Human resource" management approaches are taken to involve staff in the operations of the organization. However, turnover at the top of the correctional hierarchy may be so great that the administrator who tries to address personnel issues may not be around to reap the rewards of his or her efforts.

MYTHS in Corrections

Recidivism

THE MYTH: Once a person commits a crime, he or she will always pose a higher risk to the community than people who have never committed a crime.

THE REALITY: After the passage of sufficient time, people who have a criminal conviction have no more risk of a new arrest than those who have never been arrested. For people convicted of robbery, the time period needed is about eight years; for people convicted of burglary, the span is about four years.

Source: Alfred Blumstein and Kiminori Nakamura, "Redemption in the Presence of Widespread Criminal Background Checks," *Criminology* 47 (no. 2, 2009): 327–59.

Costs

One of the most notable aspects of corrections is that it is expensive. The cost of building a prison is more than $100,000 per cell, excluding financing. Each personnel position represents expenditures equal to twice his or her annual salary when fringe benefits, retirement costs, and office supplies are taken into consideration. The processing of an offender through the corrections system is usually at least $25,000 in direct costs and nearly half that much again in indirect costs (such as defaulted debts, welfare to families, and lost wages and taxes). The decision to punish an offender is a decision to allocate precious public resources, often irretrievably (see "Myths in Corrections"). Correctional administrators understand all this now more than ever. Wisely allocating correctional resources poses a huge challenge.

Attracting, motivating, and retaining outstanding personnel are key to an effective corrections system. What is the future for these new officers?

Institutional crowding, combined with fiscal restraint, has produced an unprecedented concern about correctional costs. The public is beginning to question the advisability of correctional growth. One might say that the public is exhibiting a form of political schizophrenia: The desire to punish criminals is not backed up by a willingness to pay for the punishment.

The ambivalence about punishment and funding has left correctional leaders in a bind. The arguments for expansion of large, secure facilities must be weighed against equally strong arguments for increased emphasis on community-based corrections. These arguments are in some ways easy to understand. Crime continues to be a matter of great public concern, and prisons may never have been as crowded as they are today.

Most correctional officials recognize that focusing on prisons is a regressive rather than a progressive approach. Many of our existing secure facilities are decrepit and need to be replaced, but the evidence is quite strong that (1) prison construction does not alleviate crowding and (2) the incapacitation strategy for crime control is both imperfect and highly prone to error. Officials also know that once a prison is built, it represents a continuing management focus for as long as it is used—in contrast to field services, which are much more responsive to change and innovation.

There are indications that the nation is on the verge of a change. One of America's worst economic recessions started in 2008, and it has resulted in a substantial reduction in tax revenues for state government. Virtually every state has been forced to try to find ways to reduce spending, and one of the areas receiving the closest scrutiny is correctional budgets—especially for prisons. After a generation of ever-growing costs of corrections, state legislators are looking for equally effective but less expensive ways to deal with people who are convicted of serious crimes. This is one of the reasons that the Council of State Government's "Justice Reinvestment" initiative has been so popular—it reduces correctional costs in ways that promote public safety. Studies show that programmatic investments in poor communities can result in lower crime rates.[7] Moreover, some states have had significant success reducing their prison populations without increasing crime,[8] and as these experiences become more widely known, policy makers will look for ways to match these results.

To this puzzle must be added the recent trend toward privatization of corrections. Only time will tell if this trend will become a lasting force; meanwhile, privatization is a potential threat to administrators' ability to manage the system. Most privatization plans call for skimming off the best of the worst—the nonserious offenders who can be efficiently processed. Thus, the government-run part of the corrections system faces the possibility of having to manage only the most costly, most intractable offenders on a reduced budget.

FOUR TRENDS IN THE CORRECTIONS SYSTEM

The future is produced by the way that present forces play out over time. But foretelling the future is not easy. It is possible to know the major forces buffeting corrections, but it is not so easy to know exactly how those forces will change the system. In 1972, when most experts were talking about how the prison system had failed and how community corrections was the future, who would have thought that we were about to embark on a 38-year period of growing prison populations? In the early 1990s, looking back at a decade of rising crime, who would have thought that we were about to experience an even longer period of dropping crime rates?

And looking forward a mere decade ago, after more than a quarter-century of steady correctional growth, who would have predicted that we would be experiencing a multiyear drop in all forms of corrections? Who would have foreseen a consensus across the political spectrum that we have too many people behind bars?

So if we want to foresee the future of corrections, we must begin with two facts. The forces that will produce the future of corrections lie right in front of us. Yet we do not know, with certainty, how those forces will play out to produce the future.

With that caveat in mind, we identify four forces that are at work today and that will create the corrections of the future. We will describe the forces themselves because we are confident that they will prove to be very important. In our thinking about how these forces will affect corrections over coming years, we will be more tentative.

Evidence-Based Practice

In recent years a premium has been placed on "evidence" that derives from studies of correctional policy. Of course, different kinds of studies produce different kinds of "evidence." For example, if a person wants to know about prison culture, the best way is to spend time in a prison watching how people interact and documenting it. If a person wants to know what people think about a correctional policy problem, the best way is to find out is a survey.

Typically, however, when a person thinks about "evidence" regarding corrections, the image is an answer to the question "What works?" We want to know which correctional programs have the greatest effect on reducing recidivism rates so that we can make successful approaches widely available. The desire to increase the evidence base for correctional practice has grown to the point that it is now referred to in shorthand: EBP (evidence-based practice). The scientific method for determining "what works" is to conduct an evaluation, and the best kind of evaluation is called a **random field trial**. Borrowed from the field of medicine, the random field trial creates an experiment in which some people are given the treatment and an identical group is not, so whatever the difference in how the two groups turn out—recidivism rates, for example—it is believed that the difference is caused by the treatment.[9]

EBP has come to stand for a strategy of correctional development. In this strategy the professional field becomes increasingly cognizant of new studies of correctional effectiveness, and increasingly, over time, the field will be using proven programs that reduce recidivism. It is an appealing image of an ever-smarter, ever-more-effective corrections system, learning continually from the results of its programs, jettisoning failures and embracing successes.

There is reason to think that evidence-based corrections will fundamentally improve the effectiveness of correctional practice. EBP is one of those rare ideas getting wide acceptance from many different correctional constituents: conservatives and

random field trial
Evaluating the effectiveness of a program by randomly assigning some people to the program and others to no program, and seeing which group does better.

Techno-corrections—the interaction of decision-making systems and machines—is becoming ever more important for professionals in corrections work. Will machinery ever really replace the human element in corrections?

liberals, old-timers and new-generation leaders, practitioners and researchers. As new studies come in, the hunger for an increasingly strong evidentiary base for correctional practice grows.

But there are also doubters.[10] Critics point out that the transitory political problems with which correctional leaders grapple are often far more important influences on correctional programs than are scientific studies, no matter how well done. By the same token, random field trials are expensive, and most such experiments yield unclear results. Ironically, EBP is an inherently conservative strategy, and therefore it does not easily avail itself of new ideas that, while unproven, may promise extraordinary benefits.

Techno-Corrections

Just as the role of technology is expanding in every aspect of the contemporary world, technology will grow in importance in the field of corrections. Indeed, it is already happening. We can easily visualize the importance of technology for the corrections system of the future by a brief look at its impact over just the last few years.

A good example of this is provided by electronic monitoring (EM). When they first came on the market a quarter-century ago, EM devices seemed like some sort of space-age gimmick, alien to most correctional professionals. The promise of electronic monitoring was simple: know the whereabouts of people under community supervision at times when they are not reporting to their probation or parole officer. But many—perhaps most—community correctional leaders were dubious. Some thought the idea silly because simply knowing where a person was at any given time said almost nothing about what the person was *doing*. If the idea is to change behavior, critics said, then how does a monitor contribute to that aim?

There were also significant technical problems. Some EM systems were beset with technical failures; some places had trouble implementing the managerial controls necessary to make EM work. For example, what probation officer wants to get up in the middle

focus on correctional technology

New Risk Assessment Methods

Risk assessment methods have high rates of failure. Many people who are predicted to do well in the community do not, sometimes with severe costs to victims. Many people who are thought to be bad risks turn out to do well, with the implication that they were kept in prison too long because of the erroneous prediction. Trying to reduce error rates in predictions has been very difficult. Recently, however, statistician and criminologist Richard A. Berk has applied a new way of analyzing data, referred to as "ensemble methods for data analysis," to assess the risk of probationers and parolees. This method, now in its experimental phases, seems to have much higher prediction accuracy rates than most traditional risk assessments. It identifies nearly all the potentially violent incidents in a test sample, with very low rates of false identifications of high risk. The method is now being tested,

and much more work needs to be done. But the implication is very clear: As criminologist Lawrence Sherman has said, "Probation can be used as the best sentence to prevent murder."[11]

Critical Thinking

What faith do you think a judge might have in making sentencing decisions based upon a risk assessment device?

Sources: Nancy Ritter, "Predicting Recidivism Risk: New Tool in Philadelphia Shows Great Promise," *NIJ Journal* 271 (February 2013), www.nij.gov/nij /journals/271/predicting-recidivism.htm; Richard A. Berk, Brian Kriegler, and Jong-Ho Baek, "Forecasting Dangerous Inmate Misconduct: An Application of Ensemble Statistical Procedures," *Journal of Quantitative Criminology* 22 (no. 2, 2006): 131–45.

---

techno-corrections
Achieving correctional goals through the use of new technologies.

of the night to check on an AWOL probationer? The early studies were not very promising. EM systems seemed not to save money and not to reduce rates of supervision failure.

But the appeal of technology is strong. This is the essence of **techno-corrections**. The idea that the community correctional agency could have a constant awareness of where its clients were at any given time was too attractive to die easily. Imaginative administrators experimented with targeted use of the device: on high-risk clients or those who might otherwise go to prison. A new generation of community correctional workers felt more comfortable with the importance of technology. And studies began to find that EM could enhance the effectiveness of corrections. Eventually, EM systems became common, and judges have gotten used to them as an option in sentencing decisions in most jurisdictions.

Perhaps this is the life story of many correctional technologies: appealing imagery, problematic initial implementation, revision and improvement, and then customary practice. (See "Focus on Correctional Technology.") If this scenario is true, then today's technologies will be tomorrow's basic strategies.

As we have demonstrated throughout the book, there are many new ideas in the application of technology to corrections. Most of these have to do with ways of increasing the surveillance capacity of the corrections system: drug testing, eye-recognition systems, spatial monitoring systems, and computer-aided decision making. Institutions try to prevent possible disturbances with cameras placed in important locations. There is no question that the surveillance and control functions of corrections will be increasingly influenced by developments in technology.

But there have also been important technical developments in the human aspects of correctional work. Risk assessment systems are nearly ubiquitous, and ways of improving them are constantly being tested. Mapping technologies have made it easier to identify where services need to be located so that clients in reentry can access them more easily.[12] Treatment regimes are being developed and standardized as strategies for supervision. Proven ways of communicating and motivating people, called **motivational interviewing**, are now being widely used for people who are on probation or parole.[13] One of the questions will be whether the human technologies will stay strong in the face of the strong appeal of the control technologies.

motivational interviewing
A systematic method of interacting with clients that increases their willingness to change their behavior.

The Mount McGregor Correctional Facility in Wilton, NY, formerly operated as a medium-security prison, housing several hundred people. In 2014, it closed. As correctional populations begin to decline, states will be able to close some of their more inefficient prisons. What should the savings be used for?

AP Images/Newspaper Member /Daily Gazette/Patrick Dodson

Falling Crime Rates

There can be no question that falling crime rates are one of the most important external dynamics affecting the corrections system. Equally, the drop in crime may have substantial implications for corrections. After all, a person does not go very far into the corrections system unless there has been a conviction for a crime.

The problem is that the way that changes in crime rates affect the corrections system is not very straightforward. Earlier in this book, we made the point that today's crime rates are similar to crime rates in the 1970s but that the corrections system handles about five times more people now than it did then. During the first decade of the 2000s, many states' corrections systems grew even though crime rates were falling. Just because the crime rate falls does not mean that the corrections system will shrink. See "Focus on Correctional Policy: The Size of the Prison Population."

But there are implications that the drop in crime will affect corrections in some way or another. For one thing, as crime rates drop, the general public begins to feel less alarmed by crime, and the public opinion that has been such an important part of the "get-tough" movement may begin to erode. When we put together a national fiscal crisis that has crippled states' ability to fund public services such as schools and hospitals with a decline in public alarm about crime, we get a new policy opportunity in which reductions in correctional populations—and, as a consequence, expenditures—seem possible.

But just as many people did not foresee the sustained drop in crime we have experienced for a decade or so, we cannot estimate how long this decline will last. Obviously, if crime rates continue to drop or even stabilize, the pressure on the corrections system to accommodate growing numbers of people who are convicted of crimes will gradually abate. Some people see this as an enormous opportunity for innovation and improvement in correctional strategies. When crime was a pressing public issue, the corrections system always seemed to be playing catch-up, trying to deal with groups of offenders under ever-changing rules; for instance, laws affecting repeat offenders, sex offenders, drunk drivers, and others have been in almost constant flux for a quarter of a century. But with crime rates leveling off, those pressures may decline, creating a window of opportunity for correctional reform on its own terms rather than in reaction to legislative initiatives.

If crime rates increase, all bets are off.

focus on correctional policy

The Size of the Prison Population

There is a great deal of policy interest these days in saving money on prisons. Because it is impossible to save much money on the *running* of a prison—costs of meals and recreation are a small portion of the overall cost of confinement—the desire to save prison dollars translates into a desire to close prisons. But how is that to be done?

There is, of course, the obvious point about scale. If the goal is to close a prison, then diverting a few people from prison cannot achieve it. Prisons house hundreds of people, and hundreds need to be diverted before a prison becomes empty. This is why a small initiative designed as an alternative to incarceration is not enough—especially if many of the people who are placed in the alternative end up in prison anyway when they fail to abide by the program's rules. Experience shows that opening a few new programs almost never results in the ability to close a prison.

What is the answer? At one level, the answer is very simple. Recently, two criminologists coined the phrase "The Iron Law of Prison Populations"[14] to refer to a very simple idea: The size of a prison population is determined by (1) the number of people who are sent to prison and (2) how long they stay. The implication is clear: To reduce the size of a prison population enough to allow the closing of a prison, the flow into prison and the stay there must be changed.

From a policy perspective, the flow into prison comes from two routes. Judges sentence people to prison, and people on probation or parole are revoked and sent to prison. In states such as California, where about half of prison intake comes from probation and parole revocations, reducing the rate of community supervision failure—especially by reducing technical revocation—can have a substantial impact on the prison population. Other states, such as Florida, have low rates of technical revocation. For these states, any policy designed to reduce the flow into prison will have to address judicial sentences in the first place, increasing the use of probation for people convicted of felonies.

Length of stay is an entirely different issue. Nationally, prison length of stay has nearly tripled in the last 30 years. If prison sentences were to revert back to the level used in 1980, length of stay would be cut almost in half by that alone.[15]

This analysis suggests that the solution to large prison populations is not more prison programs. It is sentencing reform. The policy problem is not only one of numbers. It has an important political dimension, too. Not only do policy makers need to find a way to stem the flow into prison and the unnecessarily long stays there, but they also need to find the political ability to get the public to support them. No politician wants to be branded as "soft on crime." So how does a responsible public leader reduce the prison system and stay in office?

The political pressure to be "tough" is ending. In 2011 a group of some of the nation's most-conservative elected officials, calling themselves the Smart on Crime Coalition, published a two-volume set of recommendations for Congress to enact in order to reform the criminal justice system. It was devoid of "get-tough" rhetoric and instead emphasized the need to provide correctional programs that cut recidivism, reduce the size of the prison population, and deal with drug crime in ways that do not explode the prison population.[16] In many of our so-called "red" states, where conservative politics is very strong, local elected officials are not only calling for ways to reduce the number of prisoners; they are also implementing legal and programmatic ways that lead to fewer people behind bars.

Critical Thinking

As a state legislator, what factors might influence you to support programs designed to reduce the flow of offenders to prison? Would you support sentencing reform?

Professionalization

The number of correctional employees has grown dramatically at the same time that the correctional population has grown. Correctional employees also make up a far larger professional employee pool than ever before.

The signs of this new professionalization are widespread. In the last 40 years, a new national academic discipline of "criminal justice" has grown from a fledgling major with a weak reputation to a nationally respected field of study. New journals have been developed that present the best research available on crime, justice, and corrections.

Professional associations such as the American Probation and Parole Association and the American Corrections Association now offer professional certification programs for people who will become probation or parole officers, and the National Institute of Corrections also offers training.

The emergence of a profession has had two important consequences for corrections. The first consequence is that the field is "smarter," so performance meets a higher standard. With a large number of people with advanced degrees in their areas of specialty, and with a host of employees who have special certification in areas such as substance abuse treatment and mental health, the standard of work for the field has improved. This bodes well for the future, as new methods and new knowledge provide a stronger foundation of training and abilities for those who do the work of the field.

But the creation of a strong professional core for the field has also added a new dynamic to it. Correctional employees are no longer content to merely follow the leadership of the administration of their agencies. With professional skills and knowledge of their own, new correctional professionals expect to have a say in the strategies undertaken by corrections systems and the programmatic priorities that correctional policy makers set. They have become a distinct voice in the milieu of correctional action, advocating policy and arguing for action in a way that reflects professional interests, not just narrow personnel matters. It is this aspect of professionalization that will pose some of the more interesting dynamics as the field moves forward in the coming years. Will the profession be a force for new and exciting ideas, or will it resist change? Will the new correctional professional adapt to the new techno-correctional changes of the field, or will there be conflict? Whatever answer to these questions the future holds, it is clear that the advance of professionalism in corrections has been one of the most important forces in the field today.

THREE CHALLENGES FOR THE FUTURE OF CORRECTIONS

The growth in the penal system has been, as we mentioned, something like a grand social experiment. If we had conducted a deliberate experiment, we would also expect to see clear "results." But in the case of nearly 40 years of correctional growth, the results are not compelling. The crime rate today is about what it was in 1973, the year that prison populations first began to grow. Indeed, during most of those years crime has been much higher than it is today, so some claim that the crime rates would have been even higher had we not expanded the corrections system. But to have *seven times* the number of people under correctional supervision yet still have the same crime rate suggests at a minimum that the correctional expansion has not been an efficient crime-prevention method. Moreover, because state correctional budgets have more than doubled in the past decade while allocations for education, transportation, and the like have declined, the fiscal consequences of a bigger corrections system have been important.

If we could go back to the early 1970s and begin again to build a corrections system with an eye toward the year 2010, would we envision the costly, cumbersome behemoth we have today? Most people would say no.

But what are we to do? Of course, we cannot re-create history. But we can examine today's corrections system in light of what we want it to become. Here are three challenges for re-creating corrections with an eye to the future.

Challenge 1: Reinvigorate a New Correctional Leadership

The field of corrections will get nowhere without effective leadership. It is from its leaders that corrections will get the vision for a new future; it is from its leaders that corrections will find the capacity to embark on the difficult road of change.

Great leaders are not so easy to come by. There have been many studies of leadership, and they suggest an important idea about "fit"—how the skills of a leader need to be the right ones for the problems being confronted. The idea of "fit" means that different situations call for different kinds of leaders because the skills needed for solving one kind of problem are not the same as the skills needed for dealing with a completely different set of issues. For example, historians tell us that Winston Churchill's tenacity and tirelessness were perfect for England during wartime, but his lack of interest in give-and-take did not work well after peace was restored. When a leader's skills fit the situation, effective leadership follows. Some people argue that those who have previously been under correctional authority—incarcerated or under community supervision—and have gone on to succeed may do so because they have some of the knowledge and perspective that *fits* the needs of today's most effective leaders.[17]

So what are the characteristics of the situation that corrections now faces? The key consideration facing a new generation of leaders in the corrections system is how to redirect an enormous enterprise in need of a new vision. There are numerous pressures—political, economic, and social—that have created the corrections system in its current form. The pressures will have to be balanced effectively, even while a new idea of the correctional agenda is put forward.

At the same time, correctional leadership will never be *solely* about a vision for the future. The problem of leadership is subtle. Good leaders have strong vision for their work, but they also have an on-the-ground ability to motivate people working in the system to do their best. Although education and experience are known to be important qualities in effective leadership, we also know, from history, that good leaders come from all walks of life and from every kind of background. The challenge facing corrections is how to attract the best leaders to the field.

Challenge 2: Refocus Our Investments in What Works

As a hallmark of the evidence-based movement in corrections, studies of program effectiveness have grown dramatically. Where once we would be lucky if we had barely even a study or two to decide a course of action, we now have literally hundreds of quality studies to inform our work in corrections. High-quality studies are now common enough in criminology that there is a new academic society devoted to promoting them and understanding them: the Campbell Collaboration on Criminology, with its new *Journal of Experimental Criminology*.

The many new studies have enabled researchers to go from studying correctional programs to studying *studies* of programs, looking for patterns and consistencies in findings. Called "systematic reviews," these studies help to show what kinds of programs are powerful and what kinds are not promising. For example, it is from systematic reviews that we have come to accept that boot camps do not work while restorative justice programs often do.

So while we know a great deal about "what works," we know much less about how to get these programs into practice. Programs that have been proven ineffective have surprising staying power, while programs that have a proven track record are sometimes difficult to mount. Programs that work often involve providing the kind of support for people who have broken the law that the general public is disinclined to approve of. Programs that fail often have appealing aspects, like "scaring kids straight," and therefore engender unwarranted support.

Criminologists David Farrington and Brandon Welsh argue for a national strategy to combat crime that focuses not just on people who have been convicted of crimes, but begins with children. They say we need the following:

- *Early prevention* measures implemented in the early years of a child's life from (or sometimes prior to) birth through early adolescence, with a focus on children and youths before they engage in delinquency in the first place.

■ *Risk-focused, evidence-based programs* that identify the key risk factors for offending and implement proven—by systematic study—prevention methods designed to counteract them.

■ A *national council on early prevention,* modeled after successful nationwide approaches used in Europe and seeking to support the early crime-prevention strategy.

■ *Local-level prevention* that collaborates with other government departments, develops local problem-solving partnerships, and involves citizens.

■ *Communities That Care,* a strategy of comprehensive, locally driven approaches that use promising individual, family, school, and community programs.[18]

There is no shortage of crime-prevention or crime-control strategies that work. In a recent issue of *Criminology & Public Policy,*[19] 30 leading criminologists were invited to write short essays describing policies that, in their opinion, had been studied sufficiently so that a case could be made for their widespread adoption. These were not "new" ideas but established ones that had been thoroughly studied and whose results confirmed warranted wider acceptance—ranging from the elimination of past felony screening for employment to earned release from parole supervision. The fact that 30 such essays could be written testifies to our ample knowledge base for effective crime policy. The fact that they *needed* to be written is testimony to how far our policies now stray from what we already know makes sense. The challenge we face is bringing our practice more into line with our knowledge. This is not just a challenge of knowledge—it is also a challenge of leadership.

Challenge 3: Reclaim the Moral and Ethical High Road

There is something disturbing about the new American punitiveness. All of us would agree that people who break the law should be punished, so the mere fact of punishment is not disturbing. Plainly, however, the U.S. corrections system is far more punitive today than it has been for a long time, maybe forever. Comparing the 1970s to today, people who are convicted of crimes are twice as likely to go to prison, and those who go to prison serve sentences that are more than twice as long. And people who are placed on probation or parole face a larger set of requirements that mean they are more likely to fail and be sent to prison. But even *that* is not what is disturbing, because people can reasonably disagree about whether U.S. prison sentences are too likely or too long, or the supervision methods too stringent.

What is disturbing about the U.S. corrections system is the way it has become so much more *harsh* than the systems of other free societies. Here are some of the things that can be found somewhere in the U.S. system:

■ chain gangs wearing black striped shirts and cleaning roads

■ men in jail made to wear pink underwear

■ signs in yards and on cars saying the person has been convicted of a crime

■ children serving time in adult prisons

■ eviction of people from their homes because of convictions for drug crimes

■ refusals of college loans because of convictions for drug crimes

There are other worrisome aspects of the U.S. corrections system. Health care in some prison systems is appallingly bad, especially for the mentally ill. In California, for example, the shockingly deficient health care provided to people who are behind bars was a major basis for a recent federal appellate court ruling that ordered the state to reduce institutional crowding by releasing at least 40,000 people from prison.[20] Routinely, correctional programs emphasize being tough and providing close surveillance over providing support and promoting change. A nationwide set of laws demonizes sex offenders irrationally and contributes to fear and retributive actions that are counterproductive to correctional aims and democratic values. The growth of surveillance alone is cause for concern.

The social costs of the growth of the penal system have been borne most substantially by minority communities that already struggle with poverty and other forms of disadvantage. Among these social costs are broken families, deteriorated health, teenage births, weakened labor markets, juvenile delinquency, and even more crime. As a nation committed to basic ideals of social justice, these consequences of a burgeoning corrections system have to concern us.

The corrections system we have built does not highlight what is best about the American heritage: optimism, entrepreneurial spirit, and a belief in the possibilities that arise when people are allowed to pursue their dreams. There are good reasons why so many of the Western democracies around the world look elsewhere for new horizons in correctional practice.

The next generation of correctional leaders can aim the sights of the American corrections system toward higher aspirations. Part of this can be accomplished by molding a smarter corrections system: emphasizing the kinds of strategies that good studies tell us will bear fruit and turning away from approaches that do not. But part of this will just as surely be about basic values. The challenge facing us all is how to articulate those values in a compelling way—how to clarify what corrections is all about in language and imagery that makes us, once again, a beacon of freedom and justice for all the world to see.

CHANGING CORRECTIONS: A FINAL VIEW

Throughout this book we have portrayed corrections as a system buffeted by its environment, changing yet unchanging. External pressures arise to move correctional leadership in one direction, only to be replaced by counterpressures. One state abolishes parole release; another reinstates early-release mechanisms. One prison reduces its treatment programs; another adds professional counseling staff. The image is one of an unplanned, reactive management style rather than a planned, proactive attempt to lead corrections down a path of gradual improvement.

Although this image is largely accurate, it too is changing, partly because corrections continues to develop. Several forces contribute to this change—predominantly, professional associations and government agencies.

Perhaps the greatest influence is exercised by the National Institute of Corrections (NIC), a division of the Federal Bureau of Prisons in the Department of Justice. The NIC has served as (1) a national clearinghouse of information about correctional practices, (2) a source of technical assistance to local and state correctional agencies that wish to upgrade their practices, and (3) a training operation, both basic and advanced, open to any correctional employee. The NIC has become to corrections what the FBI is to law enforcement: a strong force for professional standards, policy and procedural improvement, and general development of the field.

Similarly, the American Correctional Association (ACA) has become an active lobbyist for the field. A quarter-century ago, it promulgated a set of national standards for correctional practices in jails, prisons, and field services. Correctional agencies that meet these standards may be accredited, much as universities are accredited by outside agencies. Although the ACA has faced its share of criticism, its work indicates the kind of ground-level upgrading going on in corrections today.

The American Probation and Parole Association (APPA) serves a function similar to that of the ACA but is focused on field services. It has only recently begun a highly visible national campaign to organize the profession and to develop an improved professional consciousness of the importance of field services in probation and parole.

As important as these forces for change are, a new force for steady correctional growth and development is likely to outstrip them all. That force is represented by the person who is reading this book: you, the student of corrections. For most of its history, the field has been the domain of amateurs—part-time reformers who were moved by a zeal to help prisoners—and local workers who took the jobs because nothing else was available. In recent years, corrections has become a field of study for people interested in long-term professional careers, perhaps people like you. This is a dramatic change because it represents a group of potential correctional employees who can sustain the field's growth and development (see "Myths in Corrections"). This, more than any other influence, may be a stabilizing force for corrections in the years to come.

MYTHS in Corrections

The Winds of Change

THE MYTH: The corrections system is too buffeted by political and social forces to be able to change.

THE REALITY: The corrections system changes when people with new vision devote themselves to improving it.

Source: Three hundred years of history and the present realities described in this book.

Summary

1 **Understand how the philosophy of the U.S. corrections system has changed over the years and what this has meant for the corrections system.**

There was a time when the U.S. corrections system was the most progressive in the world. For most of the nineteenth and twentieth centuries, the U.S. corrections system was at the forefront of thinking about the best ways to deal with people who break the law, and U.S. methods were widely celebrated and emulated. Instead, what sets the U.S. corrections system apart from those elsewhere in the world today is that it is so *big*. Since the mid-1970s, by every measure, the American corrections system has grown by unprecedented amounts. Including probation, parole, and jails, the number of people under correctional control has also more than quadrupled in that same time, from under a million to more than 7 million. Starting around 2000, the rate of growth in the U.S. corrections system, high throughout the 1990s, began to decelerate. By 2010, the prison system stabilized, and the populations of all parts of the corrections system—prison, probation, and parole—have actually declined in recent years.

2 **Know the major dilemmas facing the corrections system and how they might be resolved.**

Corrections faces five core dilemmas: (1) Mission—corrections lacks a clear mission, and it operates in an environment of competing expectations that cannot be ignored. Correctional leaders must articulate their philosophy of corrections and establish a clearer policy to guide its implementation. (2) Methods—when goals are in conflict, staff members have difficulty choosing among competing methods to perform their work: surveillance or service, custody or treatment. We must overcome the tradition of faddism in corrections and embrace the methods that improve the life chances of correctional clients. (3) Structure—correctional leaders' colleagues are often the ones who put the most immediate obstacles in their way, and the corrections system depends on significant factors outside of its control. Through the formation of "partnerships," the impact of structural problems can be reduced. (4) Personnel—two essential goals are attracting the right kinds of people to work in corrections and motivating them to remain once they are employed. A sound staff is built by innovative selection and promotion methods; professional growth on the job is encouraged by education and training incentives. (5) Costs—corrections is expensive. The public desire to punish criminals is not backed up by a willingness to pay for the punishment. Making the costs of correctional policies clear is an essential step in making them effective.

3 **Identify four substantial forces that face corrections and describe their importance.**

Four important forces now shaping corrections are (1) evidence-based practice, which seeks to base correctional programs on solid evidence about "what works"; (2) techno-corrections, which alters the strategies of the corrections system by using new technologies such as electronic monitoring; (3) falling crime rates, which open the door for a reduction in the number of people processed by the corrections system; and (4) professionalization, which has resulted in an improvement in the skill sets of those who work in the field.

4 **Understand what "good leadership" means in the context of the current U.S. corrections system and know what it will take for these leaders to more widely implement "what works" in corrections.**

There have been many studies of leadership, and they suggest an important idea about "fit"—how the skills of a leader need to be the right ones for the dilemmas being confronted. Good leaders have strong vision for their work, but they also have an on-the-ground ability to motivate people working in the system to do their best. While education and experience are known to be important qualities in effective leadership, we also know, from history, that good leaders come from all walks of life and from every kind of background. The challenge facing corrections is how to attract the best leaders to the field.

5 **Describe the aspirations for the U.S. corrections system and how those aspirations might be achieved.**

There are three challenges for re-creating corrections with an eye to the future. Challenge 1: Reinvigorate a new correctional leadership. It is from its leaders that corrections will get the vision for a new future; it is from its leaders that corrections will find the capacity to embark on the difficult road of change. Challenge 2: Refocus our investments in what works. While we know a great deal about "what works," we know much less about how to get these programs into practice. Challenge 3: Reclaim the moral and ethical high road. The corrections system we have built does not highlight what is best about the American heritage: optimism, entrepreneurial spirit, and a belief in the possibilities that arise when people are allowed to pursue their dreams. The challenge facing us all is how to articulate those values in a compelling way—how to clarify what corrections is all about in language and imagery that make us, once again, a beacon of freedom and justice for all the world to see.

Key Terms

motivational interviewing 346   random field trial 344   techno-corrections 346

For Discussion

1. Why has the corrections system in the United States grown so much? What are the pros and cons of this growth?
2. What are the alternative philosophies to the punitive philosophy currently in vogue in the U.S.

corrections system? Are these alternatives feasible? Preferable?
3. Do you see yourself in a correctional career? What might you do to improve the corrections system?

Notes

[1] For an example, see Gary S. Becker and Kevin M. Murphy, "Have We Lost the War on Drugs?" *Wall Street Journal*, January 4, 2013, p. 15.

[2] Carl Hulse, "Unlikely Cause Unites the Left and the Right: Justice Reform," *New York Times*, February 18, 2015.

[3] James A. Wilson, "Habilation or Harm: Project Greenlight and the Potential Consequences of Correctional Programming," *NIJ Journal* 257 (2007).

[4] Pamela K. Lattimore, Danielle M. Steffey, and Christy A. Visher, *Prisoner Reentry Experiences of Adult Males: Characteristics,* *Service Receipt, and Outcomes of Participants in the SVORI Multisite Evaluation* (Research Triangle Park, NC: RTI International, 2009).

[5] Cheryl Lero Jonson and Francis T. Cullen, "Prisoner Reentry Programs," in *Crime and Justice: A Review of Research,* edited by Michael Tonry, vol. 44 (Chicago: University of Chicago Press, 2015).

[6] F. McNeill, S. Farrall, C. Lightowler, and S. Maruna, "Reexamining Evidence-Based Practice in Community Corrections: Beyond a

'Confined View' of What Works," *Justice Research and Policy* 14 (2012): 35–60.

[7] David M. Ramey and Emily A. Shrider, "New Parochialism, Sources of Community Investment, and Street Crime," *Criminology & Public Policy* 13 (no. 2, 2012): 193–216.

[8] The Sentencing Project, *Fewer Prisoners, Less Crime: A Tale of Three States* (Washington, DC: Author, 2014).

[9] David Weisburd, "Justifying the Use of Non-Experimental Methods and Disqualifying the Use of Randomized Controlled Trials: Challenging Folklore in Evaluation Research in Crime and Justice," *Journal of Experimental Criminology* 6 (2010): 209–27.

[10] See Todd R. Clear, "Policy and Evidence: The Challenge to the American Society of Criminology: 2009 Presidential Address," *Criminology* 48 (2010): 1–18.

[11] Lawrence Sherman III, "Use Probation to Prevent Murder," *Criminology & Public Policy* 6 (no. 4, 2007): 843–49.

[12] J. Mellow, M. D. Schlager, and J. M. Caplan, "Using GIS to Evaluate Post-Release Prisoner Services in Newark, New Jersey," *Journal of Criminal Justice* 36 (no. 5, 2008).

[13] W. L. Marshall and L. E. Marshall, "Psychological Treatment of Sex Offenders: Recent Innovations," *Psychiatric Clinics of North America* 37 (no. 2, 2014): 163–71.

[14] Todd R. Clear and James Austin, "Reducing Mass Incarceration: Implications of the Iron Law of Prison Populations," *Harvard Review of Law and Policy* 3 (no. 1, 2010): 308–24.

[15] James F. Austin, "Reducing America's Correctional Populations: A Strategic Plan," *Justice Research and Policy* 12 (no. 3, 2010).

[16] Smart on Crime Coalition, *Smart on Crime: Recommendations for the Administration and Congress* (Washington, DC: Constitution Project, 2011).

[17] Lindsay Freeman, "Transforming the Formerly Incarcerated into CEOs," *Huffington Post*, www.huffingtonpost.com/lindsay-freeman/transforming-the-formerly-incarcerated-into-ceos_b_7012642.html.

[18] David P. Farrington and Brandon C. Welsh, *Saving Children from a Life of Crime: Early Risk Factors and Effective Interventions* (New York: Oxford University Press, 2007).

[19] *Criminology & Public Policy* 6 (no. 4, 2007).

[20] *Coleman et al. v. Schwarzenegger*, U.S. District Court for California, No. C01-1351 TEH, www.ca9.uscourts.gov/datastore/general/2009/08/04/Opinion%20&%20Order%, February 10, 2009.

GLOSSARY

absconders People who fail to appear for a court date and have no legitimate reason for doing so.

adapting to change The ability to adjust or to adapt to new and unfamiliar conditions in one's environment.

administrative control theory A governance theory which states that prison disorder results from unstable, divided, or otherwise weak management.

aftercare Services provided to juveniles after they have been removed from their home and put under some form of custodial care.

AIDS A medical condition that occurs when the human immunodeficiency virus (HIV) causes a defect in the immune system's ability to function. It increases susceptibility to serious and life-threatening infections, and is transmitted primarily by exposure to contaminated body fluids, especially blood and semen.

Antabuse A drug that, when combined with alcohol, causes violent nausea; it is used to control a person's drinking.

at-risk youths Young people who are of an earlier age than most serious delinquents—as young as five or six—but who have characteristics showing that they are more likely than others at their age to end up as juvenile delinquents in their teen years.

authority The ability to influence a person's actions in a desired direction without resorting to force.

bail An amount of money, specified by a judge, to be posted as a condition for pretrial release to ensure the appearance of the accused in court.

blameworthiness The amount of blame that the offender deserves for the crime.

bondsman An independent businessperson who provides bail money for a fee, usually 5–10 percent of the total.

boot camp A physically rigorous, disciplined, and demanding regimen emphasizing conditioning, education, and job training that is designed for young offenders.

brain disease An abnormal condition of the brain caused by injury, disease, or aging.

campus style An architectural design by which the functional units of a prison are individually housed in a complex of buildings surrounded by a fence.

case law Legal rules produced by judges' decisions.

chain of command A series of organizational positions in order of authority, with each person receiving orders from the one immediately above and issuing orders to the one immediately below.

classification A process by which prisoners are assigned to different types of custody and treatment.

clear and present danger Any threat to security or to the safety of individuals that is so obvious and compelling that the need to counter it overrides the guarantees of the First Amendment.

client-specific planning Process by which private investigative firms contract with convicted offenders to conduct comprehensive background checks and suggest to judges creative sentencing options as alternatives to incarceration.

coercive power The ability to obtain compliance by the application or threat of physical force.

cognitive skill building A form of behavior therapy that focuses on changing the thinking and reasoning patterns that accompany criminal behavior.

community corrections A model of corrections based on the assumption that reintegrating the offender into the community should be the goal of the criminal justice system.

Community Mental Health Act A federal initiative to provide funding for community mental health centers and to encourage deinstitutionalization.

community service Compensation for injury to society by the performance of service in the community.

compassionate release An option for the early release of an elderly prisoner who is deemed to be of low risk of recidivism.

compelling state interest An interest of the state that must take precedence over rights guaranteed by the First Amendment.

compliance Obedience to an order or request.

conditions of release Restrictions on conduct that parolees must obey as a legally binding requirement of being released.

confrontation therapy A treatment technique, usually done in a group, that vividly brings the offender face-to-face with the crime's consequences for the victim and society.

congregate system A penitentiary system developed in Auburn, New York, in which inmates were held in isolation at night but worked with other prisoners during the day under a rule of silence.

constitution Fundamental law contained in a state or federal document that provides a design of government and lists basic rights for individuals.

construction strategy A strategy of building new facilities to meet the demand for prison space.

continuum of sanctions A range of correctional management strategies based on the degree of intrusiveness and control over the offender, along which an offender is moved based on his or her response to correctional programs.

corrections The variety of programs, services, facilities, and organizations responsible for the management of individuals who have been accused or convicted of criminal offenses.

courtyard style An architectural design by which the functional units of a prison are housed in separate buildings constructed on four sides of an open square.

crime control model A model of corrections based on the assumption that criminal behavior can be controlled by increased use of incarceration and other forms of strict supervision.

custodial model A model of correctional institutions that emphasizes security, discipline, and order.

day fine A criminal penalty based on the amount of income that an offender earns in a day's work.

day reporting center Facility where offenders such as pretrial releasees and probation violators attend daylong intervention and treatment sessions.

delinquent A child who has committed an act that if committed by an adult would be criminal.

dependent A child who has no parent or guardian or whose parents are unable to give proper care.

determinate sentence A fixed period of incarceration imposed by a court; determinate sentences are associated with the concept of retribution.

direct supervision A method of correctional supervision in which staff members have direct physical interaction with inmates throughout the day.

discretionary release The release of an inmate from prison to conditional supervision at the discretion of the parole board within the boundaries set by the sentence and the penal law.

disposition The judicial decision of how to handle a case when there has been a finding of delinquency, analogous to the sentence for an adult convicted of a crime.

drug court A specialized way of handling drug-involved offenders in which the court takes a more active role in the probationer's progress while the probationer is under supervision.

electronic monitoring Community supervision technique, ordinarily combined with home confinement, that uses electronic devices to maintain surveillance on offenders.

Enlightenment (Age of Reason) The 1700s in Europe, when concepts of liberalism, rationality, equality, and individualism dominated social and political thinking.

equal protection The constitutional guarantee that the law will be applied equally to all people, without regard for such individual characteristics as gender, race, and religion.

evidence-based corrections A movement to ensure that correctional programs and policies are based on research evidence about "what works."

evidence-based practice Using correctional methods that have been shown to be effective by well-designed research studies.

expiration release The release of an inmate from incarceration without any further correctional supervision; the inmate cannot be returned to prison for any remaining portion of the sentence for the current offense.

expungement A legal process that results in the removal of a conviction from official records.

federalism A system of government in which power and responsibilities are divided between a national government and state governments.

fee system A system by which jail operations are funded by a set amount paid per day for each prisoner held.

forfeiture Government seizure of property and other assets derived from or used in criminal activity.

formal organization A structure established for influencing behavior to achieve particular ends.

gender identity disorder An individual who displays a marked incongruence between his or her experienced or expressed gender and his or her biological gender.

general deterrence Punishment of criminals that is intended to be an example to the general public and to discourage crime by others.

geriatric offenders Aging or elderly offenders who may require specialized treatment related to the aging process while under correctional supervision.

good time A reduction of an inmate's prison sentence, at the discretion of the prison administrator, for good behavior or for participation in vocational, educational, and treatment programs.

habeas corpus A writ (judicial order) asking a person holding another person to produce the prisoner and to give reasons to justify continued confinement.

hands-off policy A judicial policy of noninterference concerning the internal administration of prisons.

hepatitis C A disease of the liver that reduces the effectiveness of the body's system of removing toxins.

home confinement Sentence whereby offenders serve terms of incarceration in their own homes.

incapacitation Depriving an offender of the ability to commit crimes, usually by detaining the offender in prison.

indeterminate sentence A period of incarceration with minimum and maximum terms stipulated so that parole eligibility depends on the time necessary for treatment; indeterminate sentences are closely associated with the concept of rehabilitation.

inmate balance theory A governance theory which states that for a prison system to operate effectively, officials must tolerate minor infractions, relax security measures, and allow inmate leaders to keep order.

inmate code A set of rules of conduct that reflect the values and norms of the prison social system and help define for inmates the image of the model prisoner.

intensive supervision probation (ISP) Probation granted with conditions of strict reporting to a probation officer with a limited caseload.

intermediate sanctions A variety of punishments that are more restrictive than traditional probation but less severe and costly than incarceration.

jail A facility authorized to hold pretrial detainees and sentenced misdemeanants for periods longer than 48 hours. Most jails are administered by county governments; sometimes they are part of the state government.

judicial reprieve A practice under English common law whereby a judge could suspend the imposition or execution of a sentence on condition of good behavior on the part of the offender.

justice reinvestment A movement in which money saved by reducing prison populations is used to build up crime-prevention programs in the community.

lease system A system under which inmates were leased to contractors who provided prisoners with food and clothing in exchange for their labor.

least restrictive methods Means of ensuring a legitimate state interest (such as security) that impose fewer limits to prisoners' rights than do alternative means of securing that end.

lex talionis Law of retaliation; the principle that punishment should correspond in degree and kind to the offense ("an eye for an eye, a tooth for a tooth").

line personnel Employees who are directly concerned with furthering the institution's goals—workers in direct contact with clients.

lockup A facility authorized to hold people before court appearance for up to 48 hours. Most lockups (also called drunk tanks or holding tanks) are administered by local police agencies.

mandatory release The required release of an inmate from incarceration to community supervision on the expiration of a certain period, as stipulated by a determinate sentencing law or parole guidelines.

mandatory sentence A sentence stipulating that some minimum period of incarceration must be served by people convicted of selected crimes, regardless of background or circumstances.

mark system A system in which offenders are assessed a certain number of points at the time of sentencing, based on the severity of their crime. Prisoners could reduce their term and gain release by earning marks through labor, good behavior, and educational achievement.

maximum-security prison A prison designed and organized to minimize the possibility of escapes and violence; to that end, it imposes strict limitations on the freedom of inmates and visitors.

mediation Intervention in a dispute by a third party to whom the parties in conflict submit their differences for resolution and whose decision (in the correctional setting) is binding on both parties.

medical model A model of corrections based on the assumption that criminal behavior is caused by social, psychological, or biological deficiencies that require treatment.

medium-security prison A prison designed and organized to prevent escapes and violence, but in which restrictions on inmates and visitors are less rigid than in maximum-security facilities.

meta-analysis The statistical analysis of a large number of studies to find a pattern of effects.

methadone A drug that reduces the craving for heroin; it is used to spare addicts from painful withdrawal symptoms.

minimum-security prison A prison designed and organized to permit inmates and visitors as much freedom as is consistent with the concept of incarceration.

motivational interviewing A method for increasing the effectiveness of correctional treatment, in which workers interact with clients in ways that promote the clients' stake in the change process.

neglected A child who is not receiving proper care because of some action or inaction of his or her parents.

new-generation jail A facility with a podular architectural design and management policies that emphasize interaction of inmates and staff and provision of services.

normative power The ability to obtain compliance by manipulating symbolic rewards.

null strategy The strategy of doing nothing to relieve crowding in prisons, under the assumption that the problem is temporary and will disappear in time.

ombudsman A public official who investigates complaints against government officials and recommends corrective measures.

other conditional release A probationary sentence used in some states to get around the rigidity of mandatory release by placing convicts in various community settings under supervision.

pardon An action of the executive branch of the state or federal government excusing an offense and absolving the offender from the consequences of the crime.

parens patriae The court standing in and acting as the "parent" of the child.

parole (1) The conditional release of an inmate from incarceration, under supervision, after part of the prison sentence has been served. (2) A system of supervision of those who have been released from confinement, sometimes including the option of early release from confinement before the expiration of the sentence.

penitentiary An institution intended to isolate prisoners from society and from one another so that they could reflect on their past misdeeds, repent, and thus undergo reformation.

performance-based supervision An approach to probation that establishes goals for supervision and evaluates the effectiveness of meeting those goals.

placement The removal of a youth from parental authority and the assignment of that authority to another agency, such as probation or a youth facility.

podular unit Self-contained living areas, for 12–25 inmates, composed of individual cells for privacy and open areas for social interaction. New-generation jails are made up of two or more pods.

positivist school An approach to criminology and other social sciences based on the assumption that human behavior is a product of social, economic, biological, and psychological factors and that the scientific method can be applied to ascertain the causes of individual behavior.

power The ability to force a person to do something that he or she does not want to do.

precedent Legal rules created in judges' decisions that serve to guide the decisions of other judges in subsequent similar cases.

presentence investigation (PSI) An investigation and summary report of a convicted offender's background, which helps the judge decide on an appropriate sentence. Also known as a presentence report.

presentence report A report prepared by a probation officer, who investigates a convicted offender's background to help the judge select an appropriate sentence.

presumptive sentence A sentence for which the legislature or a commission sets a minimum and maximum range of months or years. Judges are to fix the length of the sentence within that range, allowing for special circumstances.

pretrial diversion An alternative to adjudication in which the defendant agrees to conditions set by the prosecutor (for example, counseling or drug rehabilitation) in exchange for withdrawal of charges.

preventive detention Detention of an accused person in jail, to protect the community from crimes that the accused is considered likely to commit if set free pending trial.

principle of interchangeability The idea that different forms of intermediate sanctions can be calibrated to make them equivalent as punishments despite their differences in approach.

prison An institution for the incarceration of people convicted of serious crimes, usually felonies.

prison programs Any formal, structured activity that takes prisoners out of their cells and lets them perform personal tasks.

prisonization The process by which a new inmate absorbs the customs of prison society and learns to adapt to the environment.

private prison The operation of a prison by a private company under contract with a local, state, or the federal government, often as a for-profit business.

probation (1) A sentence allowing the offender to serve the sanctions imposed by the court while living in the community under supervision. (2) An agency that supervises the community adjustment of people who are convicted of crimes but are not sentenced to confinement in prison or jail.

probation center Residential facility where persistent probation violators are sent for short periods of time.

probation release The release of an inmate from incarceration to probation supervision, as required by the sentencing judge.

procedural due process The constitutional guarantee that no agent or instrumentality of government will use any procedures other than those prescribed by law to arrest, prosecute, try, or punish any person.

psychotherapy In generic terms, all forms of "treatment of the mind"; in the prison setting, this treatment is coercive in nature.

psychotropic medications Drug treatments designed to lessen the severity of symptoms of psychological illness.

punitive conditions Constraints imposed on some probationers to increase the restrictiveness or painfulness of probation, including fines, community service, and restitution.

radial design An architectural plan by which a prison is constructed in the form of a wheel, with "spokes" radiating from a central core.

random field trial Evaluating the effectiveness of a program by randomly assigning some people to the program and others to no program, and seeing which group does better.

rational basis test Requires that a regulation provide a reasonable, rational method of advancing a legitimate institutional goal.

reality therapy Treatment that emphasizes personal responsibility for actions and their consequences.

recidivism The return of a former correctional client to criminal behavior, as measured by new arrests or other problems with the law.

recognizance A formally recorded obligation to perform some act (such as keep the peace, pay a debt, or appear in court when called) entered by a judge to permit an offender to live in the community, often after posting a sum of money as surety, which would be forfeited by nonappearance.

reentry courts Courts that supervise ex-offenders' return to the community and their adjustment to life after incarceration.

reformatory An institution for young offenders that emphasized training, a mark system of classification, indeterminate sentences, and parole.

regional jail Facility operated under a joint agreement between two or more government units, with a jail board drawn from representatives of the participating jurisdictions, and having varying authority over policy, budget, operations, and personnel.

regulations Legal rules, usually set by an agency of the executive branch, designed to implement in detail the policies of that agency.

rehabilitation The goal of restoring the convicted offender to a constructive place in society through vocational training, educational services, and/or therapy.

rehabilitation model A model of correctional institutions that emphasizes the provision of treatment programs designed to reform the offender.

reinstatement release The release of offenders to parole supervision following a time in prison for a parole violation.

reintegration model (1) A model of correctional institutions that emphasizes maintenance of the offender's ties to family and the community as a method of reform, in recognition of the fact that the offender will be returning to the community. (2) The belief that crime is caused by poverty, inequality, and lack of opportunity; dealing with crime requires that the effect of these problems be reduced.

release on recognizance (ROR) Pretrial release because the judge believes that the defendant's ties in the community are sufficient to guarantee the defendant's appearance in court.

remunerative power The ability to obtain compliance in exchange for material resources.

restitution Compensation for financial, physical, or emotional loss caused by an offender, in the form of either payment of money to the victim or to a public fund for crime victims, as stipulated by the court.

restitution center Facility where probationers who fall behind in restitution are sent to make payments on their debt.

restoration Punishment designed to repair the damage done to the victim and community by an offender's criminal act.

retribution Punishment inflicted on a person who has infringed the rights of others and so deserves to be penalized. The severity of the sanction should fit the seriousness of the crime.

school-to-prison pipeline The fact that many youths who fail in school end up in prison.

selective incapacitation Making the best use of expensive and limited prison space by targeting for incarceration those offenders whose incapacity will do the most to reduce crime in society.

sentencing disparity Divergence in the length and types of sentences imposed for the same crime or for crimes of comparable seriousness when no reasonable justification can be discerned.

sentencing guidelines An instrument developed for judges indicating the usual sanctions given previously to particular offenses.

separate confinement A penitentiary system developed in Pennsylvania in which each inmate was held in isolation from other inmates, with all activities, including craft work, carried on in the cells.

sex-reassignment surgery Surgical procedures to alter a person's physical appearance so that the person appears more like the opposite gender.

sexual minorities Groups of people whose sexual orientation or gender identity differs from that of the majority of the population.

shock incarceration A short period of incarceration (the "shock"), followed by a sentence reduction.

shock probation A sentence in which the offender is released after a short incarceration and resentenced to probation.

social control Actions and practices, of individuals and institutions, designed to induce conformity with the norms and rules of society.

span of control A management principle holding that a supervisor can effectively oversee only a limited number of subordinates.

specific deterrence Punishment inflicted on criminals to discourage them from committing future crimes.

staff personnel Employees who provide services in support of line personnel (for example, accountants and training officers).

standard conditions Constraints imposed on all probationers, including reporting to the probation office, reporting any change of address, remaining employed, and not leaving the jurisdiction without permission.

statute Law created by the people's elected representatives in legislatures.

system A complex whole consisting of interdependent parts whose operations are directed toward common goals and are influenced by the environment in which they function.

technical violation The probationer's failure to abide by the rules and conditions of probation (specified by the judge), resulting in revocation of probation.

techno-corrections Achieving correctional goals through the use of new technologies.

telephone-pole design A prison architectural plan calling for a long central corridor crossed at regular intervals by structures containing the prisoners' functional areas.

totality of conditions The aggregate of circumstances in a correctional facility that, when considered as a whole, may violate the protections guaranteed by the Eighth Amendment.

transactional analysis Treatment that focuses on patterns of interaction with others, especially patterns that indicate personal problems.

transgendered A person who lives as a member of a gender other than that expected based on anatomical sex.

treatment conditions Constraints imposed on some probationers to force them to deal with a significant problem or need, such as substance abuse.

unit management Tactic for reducing prison violence by dividing facilities into small, self-contained, semi-autonomous "institutions."

unity of command A management principle holding that a subordinate should report to only one supervisor.

urinalysis A technique used to determine whether someone is using drugs.

utilitarianism The doctrine that the aim of all action should be the greatest possible balance of pleasure over pain, hence the belief that a punishment inflicted on an offender must achieve enough good to outweigh the pain inflicted.

veteran assistance projects Collaborative programs made up of veterans' agencies, community mental health organizations, human services agencies, courts, and other criminal justice organizations. The goal is to link veterans who have encountered the criminal justice system with an array of services that might improve their adjustment in the community.

victim impact statement Description in a PSI of the costs of the crime for the victim, including emotional and financial losses.

wrongful conviction A conviction that occurs when an innocent person is found guilty by either plea or verdict.

INDEX

Boldface numbers in this index refer to the page on which the term is defined.